89

St. Louis Community College

Forest Park
Florissant Valley
Meramec

Instructional Resources
St. Louis, Missouri

Islands in a Far Sea

Islands in a Far Sea

Nature and Man in Hawaii

John L. Culliney

SIERRA CLUB BOOKS   SAN FRANCISCO

Library of Congress Cataloging-in-Publication Data

Culliney, John L., 1942–
    Islands in a far sea.

    Bibliography: p. 393
    Includes index.
    1. Natural history—Hawaii.   2. Man—Influence on
nature—Hawaii.   I. Title.
QH198.H3C85   1988   509.969   88-42551
ISBN 0-87156-735-0

Production by Eileen Max
Jacket design by Bonnie Smetts
Book design by Abigail Johnston
Illustrations by Aileen Matsuyama-Feldman

Printed in the United States of America
10 9 8 7 6 5 4 3 2 1

To Barbara
who loves Hawaii-nei

Contents

Preface   ix

Acknowledgments   xiii

PART ONE   ISLAND EVOLUTION: A HAWAIIAN PRIMER   1

     1 Out of the Earth   3

     2 From the Forces of Life   27

     3 Arrival and Adaptations   39

PART TWO   THE SURROUNDING SEA   57

     4 Blue Abyss and Twilight Slopes   59

     5 A Place for Whales   75

     6 The Coral Rim   87

     7 Decline of a Lagoon   109

     8 The Seal and the Turtle   118

     9 Seabirds High and Low   134

PART THREE   SHORES OF MANY MOODS   153

     10 Lonely Rocks and Atolls   155

     11 Coasts of Change   170

PART FOUR   GREEN CRAGS AND CANYONS   191

     12 Rain Forests in Transition   193

     13 Fresh Waters   215

     14 Dying Songs: Hawaii's Forest Birds   237

     15 Insects and Snails: Evolutionary Tales   262

PART FIVE   VOLCANOES IN THE SKY   281

    16 Cloudlands and Drylands   283
    17 Alpine Fire and Ice   302

PART SIX   THE FATE OF THE LIVING LAND   311

    18 Hawaii Before Man   313
    19 Aina and Ahupuaa   321
    20 The Remaking of Eden   333
    21 The Wave of the Future   352

    Notes   369
    Supplementary Sources for Illustrations   393
    Index   395

Preface

The Hawaiian Archipelago is the most isolated major group of islands in the world. Thousands of miles separate them from the nearest continents and other high islands of the Pacific. The archipelago has existed for many tens of millions of years, although individual islands are known to last only a fraction of that time. Over the eons, in a benign, ocean-tempered climate, these islands were slowly colonized by life. The colonizers then evolved into uniquely Hawaiian species, often many of them from a single ancestral type, showing the wonderful plasticity of protoplasm, adapting to the great variety of island habitats. At last, a new breed of colonizer, the human species, reached these far shores, and life was never the same again.

What has happened to Hawaii? In distant views the islands seem to maintain their charms amid burgeoning development. Visitors are still enchanted by the deep blue ocean breaking in foam over aquamarine reefs, by the stunning cliffed shorelines, the dramatic, rain-dissected uplands, and the giant volcanoes. Such panoramic vistas must look virtually the same today as they did to the Polynesian discoverers.

Closer up, man-made environmental change is rampant. Its history began with the Polynesians whose immense agricultural energies transformed the Hawaiian lowlands. Under Western influence, the forces of change intensified and diversified. These forces have led to measurable and often gross degradation of island environments in many places.

Much of the change has been subtle. It is the loss of an essence of Hawaii that lies close to the ground and within the local waters. This is the living psyche of the islands—the plants and animals that are truly Hawaiian—a fabric of nature that enfolded itself over this part of the earth and no other. The diminishment of native wildlife has been more acute in Hawaii than anywhere else in the United States.

The statistics are dismal. During the tenure of man in the islands nearly 70 percent of non-migrant Hawaiian birds have become extinct. Of the native plants, conservative estimates suggest hundreds of species have become extinct since human contact, and some 50 percent of the survivors are now candidates for the federal endangered species list.

Combining statistics for plants and birds, ecologists have recently calculated that about one third of the entire United States' roster of endangered species (including formally declared candidates for listing) are
Hawaiian species. The natural devastation of the islands extends to less
conspicuous creatures as well. Perhaps 50 percent of the native insects
have disappeared forever. An entire genus of land snails comprising
nearly 40 species is officially listed as endangered; many of those species
are believed extinct. The bell is clearly tolling for Hawaiian nature.

Such devastating losses can be numbing, and there is a danger of
despair and indifference concerning Hawaiian nature. Indeed, such
sentiments have led to numerous efforts to replace the living landscapes
of the islands. Today, promoters of purely theatrical attractions in
Hawaii pose as environmentalists and suggest that the fate of native
species is immaterial as long as there is still some greenery on the hills
and a few live birds, of whatever provenance, to animate the backdrop
of the latest giant resort. Better still, say some of these gurus of glitter,
bring in some really exotic live stuff—flamingos, monkeys, and zebras.
Tourists and residents alike no longer know or care what is truly
Hawaiian.

Happily, there are signs that this depressing prognostication is off
the mark. More and more interest and concern about the real Hawaii
is surfacing. It can be seen in new programs of nature study and ap-
preciation in the schools and in the growing interest of visitors in the
wonderful native wildlife that still thrives in remote regions, especially
in Hawaii's national parks. The concern is evident in new initiatives,
public and private, to preserve remaining areas of high natural value.
The interest in Hawaiian natural history is manifest in the rising popularity of illustrated guides to birds, plants, and marine life of the islands;
also in growing membership and activism of Hawaii's conservation
organizations. Such public enthusiasm is leading to awakening concern
of the part of government, especially at state and local levels, where
it has lagged for many years.

There is a renewed realization that Hawaiian nature constitutes an
ecological and evolutionary phenomenon of world-class importance.
Charles Darwin seems to have been the first to recognize this when he
offered a 50 pound stipend to any naturalist who would undertake
systematic collections in the islands. Today, Hawaii is recognized as
America's Galápagos. These two island groups have been contrasted by
ornithologist Roger Tory Peterson as, respectively, "benign and harsh
Edens" in recognition of their very different climates and their roles
as evolutionary cradles in the development of new and fascinating
species. Of the two Edens, Hawaii is by far the more spectacular in its
biological productions. Botanists, ornithologists, entomologists, ecologists, and other scientists from all over the world find in Hawaii an

unparalleled natural laboratory in which to study how life has evolved and adapted on our planet.

Islands are often microcosms of the larger world, but are less complex in ways that range from their geological structure to their biological dynamism to their economic development by man. This relative simplicity aids understanding of the course of evolution on islands and of the changes in island ecosystems wrought by human activities. Moreover, perhaps owing to their simplicity, islands seem to have a special vulnerability. The pace of environmental degradation and destruction of species in Hawaii has been one of the fastest in the world. Having a clear picture of the course of environmental change in these islands can help us comprehend what is happening to the natural heritage of the planet as a whole.

This book is about the intersection of natural and human history in the islands. Within the limitations of a single volume, it attempts to provide an overview of the nature of the Hawaiian Islands from the nearshore sea to the mountaintops and also to document the major trends of human impact on one of the earth's great natural treasures. The themes are evolution, ecology, environmental history, and conservation. The book takes the part of Hawaiian nature. While there is no question that a balance must be struck between development and wilderness and that human security and fulfillment require some domestication of the natural world, it is clear that in Hawaii there has been a vast overkill. The historical perspective is especially crucial to an understanding of the state of nature in Hawaii today. However, the book does not purport to comprehensively cover the many current environmental issues, conservation battles, and management proposals that are ongoing in Hawaii. Those are many and varied and would make a book in themselves.

In scientific discussions, readers will encounter occasional passages of speculation. If such passages elicit a raising of eyebrows by scientific specialists, I can only plead that some speculation may be permissible in the roiling caldera of discovery that characterizes sciences such as ecology, paleontology, and marine biology in Hawaii today. Within constraints of scientific realism, speculation can provoke productive research. It is also fun, and, in informal, unguarded moments, is practiced by many specialists.

To readers in Hawaii and elsewhere who are helping to restore proper usage of the Hawaiian language, I wish to apologize for retaining conservative spellings of Hawaiian words. Over the last few years a new orthography has been emerging. The aim is to guide correct pronunciation, which is the key to usage in this originally unwritten language. Hence recent Hawaiian dictionaries employ the okina (glottal stop) and macron (emphasis mark) in the spelling of words. However, linguists are not yet in full agreement regarding the changes. Because of that uncertainty, together with time constraints on finishing the manuscript, editing and printing difficulties enough with terms in English, Latin, and Hawaiian, and, finally, a projected mainland readership largely unfamiliar with the cultural renaissance in the islands, I have opted to keep the simpler form of written Hawaiian, first transcribed in the 1820s and still in wide use. When in doubt about Hawaiian pronunciation, it is best to sound all the vowels—as in Halemaumau (Ha-lay-ma-oo-ma-oo), a major volcanic crater on the Big Island. To more closely approach the correct sound of the language, read this book with a new Hawaiian dictionary by your side and look up the names of places and landforms and wildlife as you come to them.

The purest spelling and pronunication of a species' name cannot help keep it from extinction or conjure it back from that ultimate death of a living form. By any names, the remaining Hawaiian plants, animals, and ecosystems are worth saving, and that can only happen if people who live in the islands, together with visitors, know and care about the true nature of Hawaii. To that end this book is dedicated.

John L. Culliney
Waimanalo, Oahu
May, 1988

Acknowledgments

Many people influenced the evolution of this book. For encouragement and enlightenment and often for sharing personal discoveries in Hawaiian nature, I am indebted to Jak Ayres, Ed Crockett, Tom Culliney, Otto and Isa Degener, John Flanigan, Varis Grundmanis, Charles Lamoreux, Fred Maas, Bruce Miller, Frank Perron, Sanford Siegal, Art Thorstad, and Keith Zeilinger.

The draft manuscript benefited greatly from the ruminations of a diverse community of experts who read sections appropriate to their interests. Russ Apple, George Balazs, Paul Banko, Robert Borofsky, John Engbring, John Ford, Wayne Gagné, William Gilmartin, Richard Grigg, Tim Holland, William Kramer, Virginia Macdonald, John Maciolek, and Storrs Olson all provided substantive comments and corrections, and I am very grateful to them. Of course, I am responsible for any errors remaining in the book.

Special thanks to Paul Ehrlich and Sherwin Carlquist for their interest and helpful commentary on the book in general.

Various staff members of key libraries and other institutions, including the Hamilton Library of the University of Hawaii, Bernice P. Bishop Museum, Hawaii State Archives, National Park Service, and U.S. Fish and Wildlife Service contributed invaluable assistance. The Pacific Collection of Hawaii Loa College was especially useful in historical research. James DiGiambattista and Colin Umebayashi, in particular, facilitated the assembling of needed resources.

The original illustrations by Aileen Feldman reflect her exceptional cooperation, creativity, and commitment to accuracy.

My editors at Sierra Club Books, Diana Landau and Jim Cohee, and their independent colleague Suzanne Lipsett, were especially dynamic factors in the genome of this project. One or another of them provided guidance in the shaping of the book from its embryonic stages to its final expression.

My wife Barbara and our children, Susan and Aaron, were extraordinarily helpful in many and often subtle ways. They were my nurturing island, supporting my need for isolation while writing, sustaining the generations of revision, and gracefully welcoming the final emergence of the manuscript. To them a most heartfelt Aloha!

As this book was going to press, the conservation community in Hawaii suffered a great loss in the untimely death of Wayne Gagné, Pacific entomologist and educator at the Bishop Museum in Honolulu. Dr. Gagné's knowledge of Hawaiian natural history was unsurpassed in its depth and breadth. His professional writings, public lectures, and direct comments on the manuscript informed several chapters of *Islands in a Far Sea*. He will be greatly missed as a scientist, but perhaps most of all as a tireless advocate of endemism in these islands.

PART ONE

Island Evolution: A Hawaiian Primer

1

Out of the Earth

Deep in the earth beneath the central Pacific Ocean, a monumental birthing has been proceeding for tens of millions of years. An immense, hot geological womb has spawned one of the planet's mightiest mountain ranges. Along a northwest to southeast axis, its back breaking the surface in a chain of islands like the humps of some unfathomable sea serpent, the Hawaiian mountain range stretches for more than 1,500 miles. Its birth has been so protracted that the islands to the northwest have worn down to mere vestiges of their former selves. Here the humps of the beast resemble irregular scales, virtually flat at the ocean's surface and tiny against its immensity. Their edges are coral reefs and shoals; in aerial view, they are tinted iridescent green and frothy white, and they present a sharp contrast with the surrounding deep blue.

Beyond these last of the Hawaiian Islands, with the unfamiliar names Kure and Midway, the beast lies hidden, but its length is doubled. A chain of giant seamounts marks the continuation of the great mountain range, which makes a tremendous bend to the north. On modern charts of the ocean floor, this is designated the Hawaii-Emperor Bend, for the big submerged peaks of former islands are named after emperors famous in Japanese history. This Emperor Seamount Chain reaches due north almost to the Aleutians.

Today, construction of this immense mountain range continues at its southeastern end, most visibly on the island of Hawaii, the "Big Island." Unlike vulcanism in many other places, Hawaiian eruptions have been generally quiet and easeful. On the Big Island, geoscientists can often approach intense volcanic activity literally at arm's length. Their work is based primarily at the Hawaii Volcano Observatory of the U.S. Geological Survey, located at the summit of the world's most continually active volcano, named Kilauea by the ancient Hawaiians for its occasional spectacular, high-shooting, eruptive plumes. Here, scientific understanding of volcanoes and the islands they build has advanced greatly in recent years. This geological knowledge has been ably compiled and integrated by Macdonald, Abbott, and Peterson in the text *Volcanoes in the Sea*,[1] which was a major source in the writing of this chapter.

Vulcanologists have a ready explanation for the characteristic restraint of the eruptions that have built the Hawaiian Islands and their ancient sunken predecessors as well as other archipelagoes, many of them in

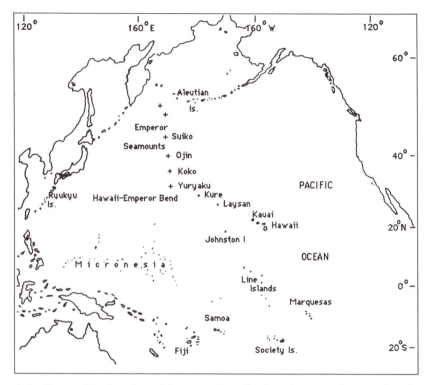

1.1 Geographical setting of the Hawaiian Islands and major submerged peaks of the Emperor Seamount Chain.

the Pacific Ocean. The liquid rock, or magma, that has produced these mountains is extremely hot compared to that which forms many other volcanic masses, and its high temperature—up to 1,200° C (2,200° F) as it reaches the surface—makes it very fluid.

In the throat and subsidiary passages of a Hawaiian volcano, the magma flows like water—or perhaps a very heavy syrup would be a better analogy. At a lower temperature, the magma would begin to congeal and crystallize here and there, producing blockages that temporarily resisted the essentially irresistible forces building up below. Such blockages, often combined with large volumes of pressurized steam formed by the heating of groundwater within the volcano, produce the devastating behavior of a cooler and more dangerous breed: a Mount St. Helens or a Krakatau.

The very hot Hawaiian magma comes from a place in the earth that geologists have yet fully to fathom. Believed to reside tens to hundreds of miles down, completely remote from any possibility of sampling or direct observation, and glimpsed only emphemerally by virtue of the muffling of certain seismic waves of earthquakes and human-made explosions that rumble through this part of the earth, a great lake of melted rock exists under unimaginable pressure. This so-called Hawaiian hot spot is still a partly theoretical construct. Its ultimate source, which may somehow focus upwelling plumes of heat, could lie as deep as 2,000 miles into the dense rind of the planet. The true nature and history of the hot spot are likely to remain enigmatic for some time.

Properly speaking, the huge molten body from which all these islands have been ejaculated lies in the region of the mantle, the thickest of the earth's concentric shells. This places it well below the thin crustal plates that form the shifting, shuffling floors of the oceans. Geologists believe that the hot spot has remained almost stationary while the wide Pacific Plate that carries the seafloor has moved very slowly toward the north and later the northwest. Almost continuously (as time is measured on the geologist's clock) for at least some 70 million years, rivers of liquid rock have rushed out of the hot spot for many miles along hot, tortuous channels toward the sea—upward toward a tumultuous, freezing release. From time to time in the crust above the mantle new channels would open, while old ones, carried farther and farther away, would finally cease to flow. At some point roughly 30 to 40 million years ago, something caused the direction of plate movement in the North Pacific to change from almost due north to northwest, and this change, which could have taken place gradually over millions of years, is recorded in the Hawaii-Emperor Bend.

The sites where especially massive sea mountains and islands were to appear may have featured unusual weaknesses in the crustal rocks slightly below the seafloor, and huge gouts of magma would have intruded into such places. Probing with seismic sounding equipment beneath several of the older of the main Hawaiian Islands, geologists have found returning echoes from large masses of extremely dense rock believed to be frozen magma. One such giant plug of stone lies beneath eastern Oahu, its upper surface now centered approximately a mile directly under Kawainui Marsh near the town of Kailua. Another big, dense mass underlies the Waianae Range to the west, remnant of the older of the two giant volcanoes that formed Oahu. Thus, beneath the older islands these great basal magma masses are solid and immobilized, but closer to the hot spot they represent downstream lakes in the strange, upside-down drainage system of the earth's crust and upper mantle.

The hot spot itself, enormously larger than the magma lakes beneath individual volcanic massifs, lies deep beneath the highest ground of the archipelago, the region of its most familiar islands. The hot spot is centered, just now, approximately under the southeastern part of the youngest and largest island, Hawaii itself. The shortest, most direct, and most voluminous magma conduits, therefore, probably connect to Kilauea and Mauna Loa, southeasternmost and youngest of the five

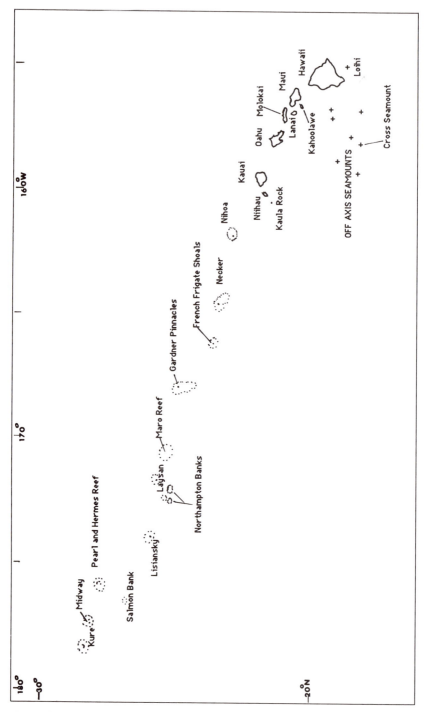

1.2 The Hawaiian Archipelago, including major neighboring seamounts and submerged shoals.

volcanic domes that form the so-called Big Island. This prediction is confirmed by the fact that these two mountains are almost certainly the most active observable volcanoes on earth. A less well-known contender for the overall title of most active is very near. The summit of Mount Loihi, about thirty miles off the southern coast of Hawaii, now lies only some 3,000 feet beneath the sea surface.[2] It has been building for some time, since its southerly base begins on the deep seafloor about 15,000 feet down. Recently, scientists have sampled and photographed fields of very fresh looking volcanic rock on and near its summit. Close above the hot spot and with free-running magma channels, Loihi will probably form the next Hawaiian island.

EVOLUTION OF AN ISLAND

The life expectancy of a Hawaiian volcano that begins its existence well connected to the hot spot is roughly between 5 and 10 million years. More precisely, this is the approximate period that volcanic rock, the tip of an immense sea mountain, remains above the surface of the ocean. The time prior to an island's emergence at sea level is much more difficult for geologists to gauge, but may be no more than a million years.

In the beginning, for hundreds of millennia, molten rock pours in absolute silence from vents in the deep ocean floor. The tremendous pressure of the overlying water prevents any flashing of water to steam. The lava—for this is the proper term once the fluid magma has issued from the solid earth—freezes quickly in large lumps and twisted strands. The most characteristic forms are irregular mounds up to the size of a compact car but averaging considerably smaller. They frequently look like understuffed and hard-used pillows, and the fanciful name pillow lava has found its way into the worldwide geological literature.

For a very long time, the pillow lavas and their ropy matrix accumulate as the volcano builds toward the surface in the form of a huge lava dome. Eventually, at the threshold of sunlight and warmth, and as if gathering and focusing its energy for a leap into a new phase of existence, the uppermost region of the mountain begins to explode—mildly at first, then more and more violently, with successive eruptions at shallower depths. This explosive phase intensifies as water pressure steadily diminishes with the mountaintop's approach to the sea surface. The sudden boiling of water into steam becomes inevitable, and it happens on a massive scale when countless tons of incandescent rock are injected at high velocity into the porous, water-filled upper layers of the volcano.

Every time it erupts, the emerging mountain announces itself with a roar accompanied by billows and geysers of superheated steam. Then, still closer to the sea surface, it throws stupendous columns of pulverized rock—volcanic ash and cinders—high into the air. Hundreds, perhaps thousands of times, the top of the mountain is blown apart. Enormous piles of exploded fragments build up to the surface and slightly higher, hold for a few days, months, years, and then are battered down and washed away like a child's sandy ramparts on a beach. For a very long time, the nearly continuous, slow-rolling violence of the sea is a match for the short, fierce outbursts of the volcano. However, behind its frontal assault, the volcano has a second strategy that slowly gains ground through consolidation of small amounts of hard lava under each successive cap of exploded fragments. Foot by foot, meter by meter, the mountain lays down a solid, wave-resistant shield that finally pushes through the sea surface and remains.

The mountain, now known to geologists as a subaerial shield volcano, is an island, and new lava flows* begin to raise its stature rapidly. Prior to its emergence, the mountain is called a submarine shield. This term comes from the shape of this kind of volcano, which, due to its very fluid lava, is a gently sloping dome reminiscent in outline of the shields of ancient warriors—Greeks or Romans, not Hawaiians. The shield reference becomes more apt as the new island rises from the sea and the sloping lavas afford it protection from pounding waves. The eruptions continue and slowly and steadily the ocean retreats from a steaming, prograding shoreline as the mountain gains bulk and height at a growth rate that can produce an alpine climate high above tropical shores in less than a million years.

No Hawaiian volcano is currently in this early shield-forming stage, although in another thousand centuries or so seamount Loihi may present a young shield to Pacific skies. If it hurries, it may even grow enough to weld itself to Mauna Loa and become a giant southerly extension of the Big Island. Geologists believe that the early subaerial stage features very frequent, if not nearly continuous, eruptions, with lakes and ponds of magma ever present not far below the summit. But the imagined situation of a radially symmetrical dome growing primarily via summit eruptions may be an oversimplification. If it ever exists, it is not destined to persist for very long.

A rapidly growing volcano represents an enormous mass piling up over a small part of the earth's surface, and, as anyone can imagine, something must compensate for the increasing weight. One compensation occurs in the earth's crust beneath the volcano. The crust is slowly deformed and warped downward into the less rigid mantle. This con-

---

*There are two major forms of lava: *pahoehoe* is very hot and fluid. It may freeze as such in sinuous, pooled, or smoothly mounded patterns, or it may change as it cools to *aa*, a mass of irregular, incandescent boulders, or clinkers, that finally freeze in a chaotic jumble.

forms with a cardinal principle in geology called isostasy: the buoyant adjustment of large crustal masses with respect to their vertical position—the level at which they "float"—in the mantle. Isostasy resembles Archimedes' Law writ huge, but with complications due to the not-quite-fluid nature of the mantle, and also the fact that the uneven heating of rock masses that are close to melting significantly alters their density, causing them to sink or rise in relation to their surroundings.

Another kind of compensation, perhaps partly an extension of the first, takes place in the structure of the volcano itself. The dome of brittle, loosely layered rock begins to crack under its own weight. The cracks, or rifts, extend in meandering but definite lines from the massive center of the mountain outward through the flanks. The main rifts, two or three in number, roughly bisect or trisect the shield and even continue along its submarine slopes.

Inevitably, along these rift zones, which extend thousands of feet down into the structure of the mountain, the cracks and stress-relieving fissures in the rock are penetrated by magma. In old, cold, and eroded volcanoes, the ancient rifts are traceable along linear concentrations of dikes—irregular, upward-trending slabs and sinuous obelisks of hard, dense rock formed when the crack-filling magma froze slowly before it reached the surface. Because dike material is more resistant to erosion than most of the surrounding fast-frozen lavas, it persists in stark ridges, buttresses, and pinnacles, forming some of the more dramatic scenery in the older islands.

Once a rift zone in a growing volcano has developed good connections to the major magma sources beneath the volcano's central region, eruptions, although they may continue with force and frequency at the summit, also begin to occur out along the rift zone. These flank eruptions, which may happen miles away from and far below the summit, mark a coming of age of the shield volcano. They often radically alter the mountain's shape, elongating it on the trend of one rift or another. Pele, the matron goddess of Hawaiian (and other Polynesian) volcanoes, stretches her fiery limbs outward from the summit. In so doing she enlarges her central abode at the mountaintop and forms the ultimate general shape of the island that will persist far into the future.

At the summit of a typical Hawaiian volcano, the presence of a wide, step-sided depression, often hundreds of feet deep, known as a caldera is a sign of vigorous maturity. Both Kilauea and Mauna Loa on the Big Island are currently in this stage of development. Many other Hawaiian volcanoes are believed to have passed through it, although not all may have formed calderas. To keep terminology as precise as possible, it should be noted that the word *crater* may refer to any steep-walled, roughly circular pit in the ground ranging from a few feet to perhaps a mile across. A caldera is generally much larger, much less regular in

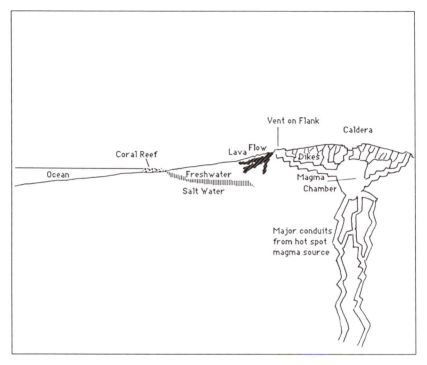

1.3   Profile of a Hawaiian shield volcano.

shape, and more complex in origin, and always occurs at the summit of a volcano. Craters may appear virtually anywhere on a volcanic island, but are most common along rift zones. They also form within calderas. To Pele, in her rambling, many-tiered stone mansion, craters are rooms among which she moves redecorating here and there, sometimes at a frenetic hourly pace, sometimes at leisure over the millennia.

A caldera is formed mainly by subsidence, an actual caving in of the top of the mountain. At first, only a sizable crater (or sometimes a few of them) marks the summit area of the growing shield. Setting the stage for caldera formation is a process the geologists call stoping: the melting of rock directly beneath the summit by a terrific and mounting concentration of heat in that region. The melted or semimelted material merges in huge drips and gobs with the magma just below and, even as the volcano grows, this process keeps pace, permitting only a thin shell of truly solid rock to remain covering the top of the mountain. As flank eruptions commence along the rift zones, huge volumes of magma are drawn away from the main central reservoir, and the summit's thin shell periodically caves in from lack of support. This subsidence, which begins across perhaps two or three miles of the summit, produces the caldera.

As flank and summit eruptions continue—sometimes one or the other, sometimes both simultaneously—the caldera becomes larger and its structure more complicated. Huge craters may form around active vents in the floor of the much larger caldera, and the collapsing terrain may approach and capture craters that formerly stood well beyond the caldera's edge. Over long intervals, the caldera may fill and overflow, and then reform. From time to time, intense activity within the mountain will result in a continuous circulation of molten rock between the caldera and its underlying reservoir. Then the caldera, or one of its large craters, becomes an unearthly lake, seething, slow-swirling, steaming; red and black in cooler areas, yellow and white-hot elsewhere, casting a hellish glow skyward to reflect beneath low clouds. This was the scene in Kilauea Caldera's Halemaumau Crater from about 1823 to 1924—to be sure, only a moment in the life of the mountain.

Since 1924, summit eruptions on Kilauea have been less frequent than flank eruptions; the lava lake has reappeared sporadically in Halemaumau Crater but has never lasted long. The most spectacular manifestations of Pele's talents have been lava fountains—up to 1,800 feet high in 1959 and nearly that in 1983. These are awesome plumes of finely shredded yellow- and red-hot rock that freezes as it falls like dense sleet.

Flank eruptions are often less spectacular than those at the summit, but they are literally earthshaking and earthmaking events for miles along the rift zones. Even before any surface manifestations occur, geologists and local residents become aware that an eruption is imminent. The scientists use seismographs to record the underground movement of magma out along the rifts as continuous, low-level earthquakes termed harmonic tremor, a kind of drumming in the surface of the mountain. On the rift, people without instruments can often feel it through their feet. A ranger at Hawaii Volcanoes National Park says it feels like a heavy train speeding along just underground. Another, more lyrical, calls it a pulsing birth convulsion in the earth, and one imagines huge liquid slags surging in immense heat and pressure through a dark tunnel toward a distant vent and a monstrous spawning of a new generation of earth's substance.

Flank eruptions on Kilauea's East Rift Zone have occurred as far away from the summit as twenty-five miles. Such eruptions in 1955 and 1960 cremated and buried much of the town of Kapoho, and the 1960 flow entered the sea, extending a new peninsula on the Big Island's southeastern coastline a half mile into the Pacific.

From giant Mauna Loa, numerous historic lava flows have traversed dozens of miles, sometimes reaching the sea from high on the southwest rift. From the northeast rift, several flows in the last two centuries, including one in 1984, have approached the city of Hilo, which lies on ground barely centuries old. Future redecorating of this area by Pele is inevitable. Demonstrations of the power of mature, active volcanoes are common on Mauna Loa, whose eruptive spectacles typically dwarf those of Kilauea. For a short period during the former's 1950 eruption, geologists reported continuous fountaining that extended for twelve miles along the southwest rift; it was a curtain of fire (the term is used in the scientific literature on volcanoes), evoking the awe that inspires a poet's voice.

Awe is not uncommon among scientists, park rangers, and residents of the region. Hawaiians in particular feel a reverence for the living land beneath their feet and homes. From their ancestors came much poetry and even accurate scientific conclusions couched in poetry about the volcanoes in their lives. Much of this, originally held in memory for oral recitation, has not been preserved—an excruciating loss (judging from what remains) to those who value richly expressed perceptions of the human condition in an epic natural setting.

The early Hawaiians knew that Pele had long ago made her home on Kauai and then wandered down the chain, settling for a time on the other islands until she reached her present abodes in Kilauea and Mauna Loa.[3] Occasionally, she would leave the Big Island for short visits to former haunts such as Haleakala. Pele continues to haunt the minds of the faithful. Wherever the mid-1980s lava flows from Kilauea's East Rift reached residential areas near the town of Kalapana, offerings of appeasement—flower leis, foods, and beverages, including expensive brands of hard liquor—were left along the cooling banks and fronts, which resembled hellish glaciers, crusty and black. Beginning in late 1986, the goddess, unmollified, sent some of her incandescent streams all the way to the sea in this region near the coastal headquarters of Hawaii Volcanoes National Park. Along the way these flows ignited and buried dozens of homes.

As an oceanic volcano comes of age, the caldera achieves its largest dimensions, up to ten or twelve miles across; eventually it fills with lava for a final time. Eruptions become less frequent, and erosion and subsidence are already taking a substantial toll on the substance and stature of the mountain. In a few cases volcanic activity virtually ceases at this stage. But it is probable that in a majority eruptive life is further extended into a vigorous old age.

Remember that the fires of its youth slowly diminish as an island volcano drifts away from the hot spot. With time the underlying magma lake cools and changes in chemical composition as certain minerals begin to crystallize out of the thickening fluid rock. Eruptions of this more viscous magma become more explosive. Now the lava that issues forth more closely resembles continental types. For example, compositions of andesite, the igneous-mineral namesake of the South American Andes Range (and also found in other continental mountains), are fairly common in late-stage Hawaiian lavas such as those capping the Big Island's Mauna Kea. Because late-stage lavas are cooler and thicker, they do not flow as far as material from youthful eruptions. The mountain builds up a steeper profile above the caldera. Before it is over, this last stage of major activity may pile up thousands of feet of rock covering many tens of square miles over the earlier shield.

For a long time, the period between eruptions has been lengthening; at last it is measured irregularly in centuries. Finally, the mountain-building forces within the central volcanic mass are frozen and stilled, and a long period of quiet, as long as 1 or 2 million years, descends over the island. Eruptions have all but ceased, but the quiet is deceptive. From place to place—along exposed coasts, in deepening stream valleys, below talus-strewn fault scarps—it is not truly quiet at all. Year by year, century by century, storm after storm, earthquake after earthquake, the island is diminishing. Its bulk is wasting away as rock and soil are carried by the megaton in storm-gorged torrents down to the all-swallowing sea.

Reduction in an island's stature also comes from wholesale sinking. The isostatic imperative is at least part of the story, but a second, recently proposed mechanism may also be operating. This involves an initial up-ward bulging of the earth's crust that results from melting and expansion over the tremendous concentration of heat in the vicinity of the hot spot. At first, islands ride high on the crest of this so-called asthenospheric bump, or swell. The oceanic crust, with its linear stip-pling of islands, then gradually subsides through contraction of its rocky underpinnings as the tectonic plate is rafted away from the hot spot into progressively cooler regions.[4]

Such a history of gradual erosion and submergence seems common to most, if not all, the older Hawaiian volcanoes. However, on some islands sudden and massive earth movements may have augmented the effects of normal erosion. Evidence comes from the island of Lanai in the form of coastal debris, including coral chunks and volcanic beach gravel, deposited along southerly parts of the island at elevations up to about 1,300 feet. The classic explanation was that the level of the sea had risen that high, held for a time during which reefs and beaches formed, then receded again.[5] Alternatively, could Lanai, in middle post-eruptive age, have been somehow thrust upward, leaving old coastal deposits so high above the sea? These explanations are virtually impossi-ble to reconcile with modern geological understanding, which accords with gradual island sinking and relatively minor rises in sea level dur-ing the lifetime of Lanai. Although still in the realm of speculation, a theory has developed that a huge chunk of Lanai's southern undersea flank broke away all at once and slid into the deep sea. The resulting tidal wave could have been 1,300 feet high on the near side of Lanai and might have tossed shoreline debris to that elevation.[6] Such a catastrophic ripple would have spread, diminishing somewhat as it reached neighboring islands. Further evidence of its impact may appear in a peculiar hiatus of soil and surface strata at roughly the 800-foot level on the nearby island of Kahoolawe, a suggestion that "the sea was once that high and washed away the loose soil."[7] But instead of the classical sustained rise in sea level, one giant lick at the island by the ocean may be the explanation.

Sea level has fluctuated in the past due to great gradual tectonic shifts in the ocean's crust and withdrawals of water from and deposits to the sea during the earth's glacial and interglacial epochs. But during the existence of the Hawaiian Islands, the world's oceans are thought not to have risen more than about 250 feet higher nor fallen more than 350 feet lower than present sea level. Numerous traces of apparent old shorelines and reefs are evident around the main islands within these elevational limits.

Long, long after epochs of shifting sea level, of islands sinking isostatically and riding down the asthenospheric swell, after fringing coral reefs have grown on lost shorelines and bouts of erosion have sculpted the igneous domes into jagged tropical mountains above the sea, the volcanoes reawaken. Infrequently, sometimes with quiet intervals of 10,000 years or more, eruptions have broken out on nearly all the older high islands of the Hawaiian Chain and have persisted into fairly recent geological time.

These so-called posterosional eruptions, however, have contributed little bulk material to any given island, although deep former valleys have been partly filled with new lava and coastal configurations altered here and there. In the oldest islands affected, Kauai and Oahu, this latest activity has been conspicuously located on parts of the islands closest to the hot spot—that is, the eastern and southeastern sectors. The old volcanic conduits, stretched and riven by crustal shifts, apparently find new outlets to the surface in such regions, for the patterns of posterosional eruptions, at least on Kauai and Oahu, do not coincide with the rift zones of the ancient shields. What brings about this long-delayed activity? So far, an answer has proved elusive. Could there be an infrequent oscillation in the amount of energy generated in or around the hot spot—perhaps an extraordinary surge of heat that melts some of the congealed magma close beneath the older islands, bringing on a brief, fiery episode of new landscaping?

Old oceanic volcanoes die slowly in one of two ways: decapitation or simple drowning. Decapitation seems to occur if a protecting sea-level reef does not form or fails to be maintained during late erosional phases of an island's history (see chapter 6). Then the sea begins to pound the volcanic coast, undercutting it and continuously causing cave-ins from above. Storm waves and *tsunamis,* seismic sea waves, periodically sweep away the rock debris at the base of the cliff, which becomes progressively higher as the island is eaten back at sea level. Geologists speculate that in such situations, ocean waves eventually cut across an island several miles wide. Thus, fairly small extinct shields and late erosional remnants of once-large islands are thought to be candidates for this sort of demise.

Alternatively, the quiet drowning and sea burial of a volcanic island occurs if a coral reef is well maintained essentially throughout the old age of the shield remnant. The continued slow subsidence of the island's mass by isostatic adjustment and/or descent of the cooling crustal swell brings about a final sinking of the much-eroded and sediment-covered igneous mountain, as the corals and coralline algae grow from a fringe on the old island's flanks up, around, and over it.

A high island's drowning, then, gives birth to an atoll, a kind of living shroud. In a very approximate way, this shroud preserves the outline of the old volcanic mountain, albeit smaller, since a fringing reef usually takes form only after erosion and subsidence have made substantial gains. There are several Hawaiian atolls at the northwestern end of the chain. Some of them may have persisted longer than the volcanic island that originally gave them shape.

This theory of atoll formation—as the growth of coralline caps from fringing reefs to cover old, slowly submerging volcanic pedestals that themselves once stood as high islands—was formulated by Charles Darwin in 1842.[8] Confirmation of the idea came more than a century later with drilling tests through the reef caps of several Pacific atolls. Midway, near the end of the present Hawaiian Chain, was one of the test sites.[9] In the two holes bored on Midway, the drill penetrated ancient reef limestone for hundreds of feet, then hit volcanic clays and finally solid basalt. The overlying reef deposits revealed samples of corals and algae that could only have grown at the sea surface. And the nature of the volcanic materials indicated that they were once above sea level. Dating of the samples placed the existence of a high volcanic island at Midway some 20 to 25 million years ago.

HAWAIIAN LANDFORMS: A PASSAGE AMONG THE ISLANDS

Geology deals with time almost as glibly as do computer science and nuclear physics. In the abstract, 20 million or even 20,000 years are about as incomprehensible as a picosecond. Yet nearly everywhere on earth we are surrounded by natural clockworks in a vast array of forms, from the microscopic to the immense and from the very subtle to the highly obvious. From our earliest sentient generations, the stony markers of elapsed time have been sources of wonder, and in them, shaped by nature in layer over layer, has been found the richly detailed history of the earth. Perhaps nowhere are such markers with their stark graphics more revealing at first glance than in the Hawaiian Islands. The concluding pages of this chapter constitute a short tour of the islands today, a guide to readily seen results of geological processes earlier discussed, and a view of landscapes steeped in time.

The Big Island, Hawaii, is huge and amply covered with raw, recent rock that slopes nearly everywhere in long, gentle lines toward the sea. Such contours on the face of the land are those of youth. From every side Mauna Loa looks from a distance like a huge rounded hill, almost organic in its smoothness. To the Hawaiians in the southwest district of Kau, where the view of the mountain is often cloud-free, it resembled a woman's breast. A better structural analogy is an onion, or the tip of one. Rising nearly 14,000 feet above the ocean, Mauna Loa, along with two earlier shields that it apparently buried, is seen in vertical section to consist of thousands of nearly uniform layers of frozen crusty stone averaging ten to fifteen feet thick. Even the onion model is not quite right, because the layers are not really formed as continuous sheets but in the coalescence of countless, fairly narrow dribbles running downhill from the summit and rift zones. Individual eruptions and lava flows are finite events in a human lifetime and fit easily into our sense of time, but each one is like a spoonful of concrete in some inconceivably immense building project. On the human scale, time has been lavished in the construction of Mauna Loa, but its incredible mass is thought to have been raised in less than a million years.[10]

Since both Mauna Loa and Kilauea have been discussed earlier in the narrative on shield building, this elementary geology tour will pass on to other points of interest. Additionally, the highlights of both of those youngest of Hawaii's mountains are eminently on display and expertly interpreted at Hawaii Volcanoes National Park; anyone interested in exploring and understanding the total Hawaiian environment should make an extended visit there.

The three other giant volcanoes of the Big Island are definitely past the prime of eruptional life. Of them, only Hualalai, the 8,000-foot dome behind Kailua-Kona, has erupted in historic time. In 1800 and 1801 it sent lava coursing for miles down to the Kona coast. The 1801 flow spread in a broad fan more than three miles wide along the coast; the modern Kona airport has been built on the southern edge of this fan. Taking the highway north from the airport, you first cross the broad apron of the 1801 flow; then, after several miles of slightly less raw-looking terrain, the road intersects two narrower lobes of the 1800 flow. A short distance farther on is yet another extremely fresh-looking lava field. This flow also reached the sea, but it came in 1859 from high on

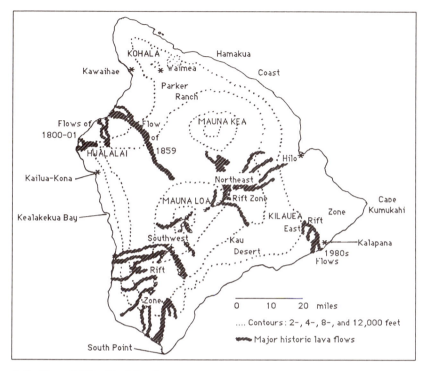

1.4   Hawaii (the Big Island).

Mauna Loa, and it marks the boundary between the lavas of Hualalai and those of Mauna Loa. These dated lava flows are recognizable because they are the most hellish heaps of slag in the region. A desert climate here and ground that will hold no moisture have prevented the growth of any significant vegetation. Even lichens are inconspicuous after time that begins to be measured in centuries.

There are no eruptions on record for Mauna Kea and Kohala Volcano, to the east and north, but on both mountains big cinder cones and lava fields that are not much older than human occupation of this island indicate that the volcanoes are only napping. Mauna Kea, slightly over-topping Mauna Loa as the island's highest peak at 13,796 feet, had a glacier or two at the climax of the last ice age. One of them descended from snowfields near the summit to about the 11,000-foot level and left its telltale piles of broken stones in classic moraines when it finally melted about 15,000 years ago.[11]

Other prominent time markers on the Big Island include seacliffs up to 1,400 feet high and several huge riverine valleys. These features typify the northeast Kohala coast. The terrain here stands in sharp contrast to the low coastal scarps and minor stream gorges cut into the much

younger Mauna Kea lavas to the east. On a clear day the erosional differences between the two shields are readily seen by air travelers on
the usual route between Honolulu and Hilo.

Northwest from Kohala, across a forty-mile-wide ocean channel,
looms the immense shield dome of Haleakala, the eastern bulwark of
the island of Maui. Incised deep into the mountain's summit, the famous
Haleakala "Crater," where the demigod Maui snared the sun and secured
more daylight for humanity, is not actually a volcanic crater or caldera.
It is the product of a million years of snow and ice and torrential rains,
of stream erosion that scooped out giant valleys—one from the north
(Keanae Valley) and one from the south (Kaupo Valley)—whose deep
amphitheater heads eventually came to lie next to one another, separated
by an ever-narrowing rock wall that bisected the crater-to-be. When
the wall wore down to a stubby ridge, the twin hollows in the mountain's summit area merged into one—now a stunning wilderness of rare
plants and vast silences. Fairly recent eruptions have covered the old
valley floors with great cinder cones of red and yellow and charcoal
hues amid an occasional black veneer of lava and soft volcanic ash.
Although the present summit of the huge Haleakala shield is on the west
crater rim just above 10,000 feet, geologists believe the mountain originally stood some 3,000 feet higher and may have resembled Mauna Kea,
which is often visible above the clouds on the southeastern horizon.

Haleakala is frequently spoken of as an extinct volcano, but *dormant*
is the proper adjective. Remember that the hot spot lies so deep relative
to the horizontal spread of the islands that the angular displacement
of Maui, owing to its northwestward drift, is really very slight. At least
some of the fissures and channels that feed the perhaps now slushy
magma lake beneath Haleakala are still well connected, for Haleakala
has erupted in historic time.

The date has been fixed in round terms at 1790 and is known thanks
to some historical sleuthing by geologist B. L. Oostdam.[12] On the southwest flank of Haleakala, lore and legend have long since recorded an
eruption witnessed by named ancestors of local families. All such accounts place the date of the eruption in the late eighteenth century.
Oostdam's inspiration was to examine charts of the Maui coastline made
by cartographers accompanying two early explorers: La Pérouse in 1786
and Vancouver in 1793. Vancouver's map clearly shows, in the right
spot, a prominent peninsula nearly two miles wide. Known today as
Cape Kinau, this coastal feature is nowhere to be seen on the earlier
La Pérouse chart. Both maps faithfully depict other major details along
this coast, so it is highly unlikely that La Pérouse merely overlooked
Cape Kinau. Today one reaches this area at the end of a rough, dusty
road that heads south from the village of Makena. Suddenly, at Cape
Kinau, lava fields appear that resemble the starker regions of the Big

Island. The jagged black landscape is virtually barren; it looks as if it could be only months old instead of nearly two centuries.

The second of Maui's two volcanoes is much smaller and at least hundreds of thousands of years older than Haleakala. Called simply West Maui, it shows its age in its deep dissection by streams. From near the present summit at 5,788 feet to near sea level, fantastic pinnacled ridges and impossibly steep, narrow green gorges are this mountain's wrinkles of age. On leeward slopes, however, where rain comes less frequently, there are places where the gentle inclined contours of the old shield still cover many square miles.

On West Maui, near the leeward village of Oluwalu, which lies south of Lahaina, is evidence of a raised shoreline. It is now about 250 feet above sea level and thought to represent the highest incursion of the sea in Hawaii due to a global ice-melting episode during the Pleistocene epoch.[13] The site of the purported old coastline abuts the south side of a small cinder cone just over one mile north of Olowalu. It is not a fossil reef, but may be a former beach or flat of coral sand intermingled with lava stones. After the ocean had subsided from this high level, the coralline sediments slowly set like concrete around and within the stony bed, forming a conglomerate. This site faces Lanai, and one wonders if the stranded coralline deposits here were really part of an ancient shoreline or were left after the run-up of a colossal wave.

Maui's smaller neighbor islands, Kahoolawe and Lanai, were formed by single independent shield volcanoes. Kahoolawe, which straddles the offshore extension of Haleakala's southwest rift, is the smaller and is a virtual desert island in the rain shadow of its gigantic neighbor. Twice as high and less of a desert than Kahoolawe, Lanai is also in a partial rain shadow behind West Maui and Molokai. Large parts of the island's western and northern slopes are the old, gentle shield contours. However, giant cliffs up to 1,000 feet high have formed on the southwest coast. Very high southerly coastal cliffs are atypical in Hawaii, where the greatest sustained wave action comes from a northerly direction. On its windward side, however, Lanai has been protected for a long time by its near island neighbors, and its north and east coasts have broad fringing coral reefs extending from low sandy shores.

Nearby Molokai was formed by a coalescence of shields. All told, there are four, although only two are readily recognizable. The names of the two main shields are simply taken from the compass. West Molokai, the older, is a long, low shield originally called Mauna Loa by the Hawaiians for its resemblance in shape, not size, to the massive long mountain of the Big Island. Unspectacular erosion features dominate the physiognomy of West Molokai, ranging from modest seacliffs on the north coast to extensive beaches and sand dunes on the south and west. Old hardened sand dune deposits from the glacial period are found near

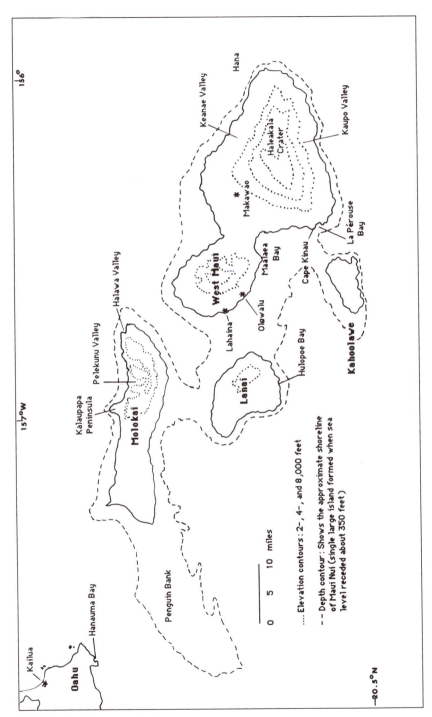

Kailua

Oahu

Hanauma Bay

Penguin Bank

Molokai

Kalaupapa Peninsula

Pelekunu Valley

Halawa Valley

West Maui

Lahaina

Olowalu

Lanai

Hulopoe Bay

Maalaea Bay

Cape Kinau

Kahoolawe

La Pérouse Bay

Kaupo Valley

Haleakala Crater

Makawao

Keanae Valley

Hana

157°W

156°

20.5°N

0 5 10 miles

... Elevation contours: 2-, 4-, and 8,000 feet

-- Depth contour: Shows the approximate shoreline of Maui Nui (single large island formed when sea level receded about 350 feet)

1.5 Maui, Molokai, Lanai, Kahoolawe (offshore contour shows approximate land area of Maui-nui during the last glacial epoch of lowered sea level).

the central north coast and in a few other places, and in them are scattered fossil bones of highly unusual extinct birds (see chapter 18).

East Molokai is a much higher and more deeply eroded mountain mass with gentle leeward slopes and an incredibly truncated northern exposure. Rearing up to 3,600 feet on this coast are the highest seacliffs in the world. Three big stream canyons along with lesser valleys and gorges, all of them lush with jungle on this well-watered coast, pierce the twelve-mile line of precipices.

It has been suggested that the East Molokai cliffs formed along a fault line, that the northern part of the original shield dropped with time and innumerable earthquakes down below the ocean's surface. Indeed, twenty miles offshore in very deep water, a major fault appears to be associated with the Molokai Fracture Zone, a great rent in the Pacific crust extending toward North America. There seems to be no shoreward connection, however. Relatively small faults are known in the East Molokai Shield, but they do not show the trend in earth movement that would have formed the present north coast. To most geologists who have studied the region, the tremendous cliffs appear to have been formed by the sea, with its ceaseless waves undercutting a slowly submerging shoreline.[14]

Just north of the great cliffs, a few small rocky nubs project from the sea. Mokapu Island is such a sea stack, a hard remnant of the former shield left standing offshore when the softer material around it wore away. Such erosional relics are strong evidence against faulting as the primary cliff-forming mechanism on East Molokai.

Although a coral reef has not formed on Molokai's northern coast, at least not in its recent geological history, a contrasting situation prevails on the island's south side, where the widest fringing reef in Hawaii is found. This is a quiet, drowsy shore of broad shallow mud and sand flats, grading gradually out to clear shallows and eventually an actively growing coral reef.

Between East and West Molokai, clinging to the north coast and projecting a short distance into the ocean, is a miniature shield. Having erupted long after the principal volcanoes, this is Kalaupapa Peninsula, site of the world-famous leper settlement; it will probably disappear long before the rest of the island. In our time, its conspicuous geological landmarks include a large pit crater containing a brackish pond; a giant collapsed lava tube extends for a mile or more north of the crater.

Curving far out to the west into the ocean channel toward Oahu is an elongated part of Molokai that is now slightly submerged. It is a peninsula terminating in Penguin Bank, a shallow seamount platform measuring approximately eight by twelve miles. This whole broad extension of Molokai became dry land during the last ice age, easily doubling the size of Molokai proper. Barely 100 feet deep at its shallowest levels to-

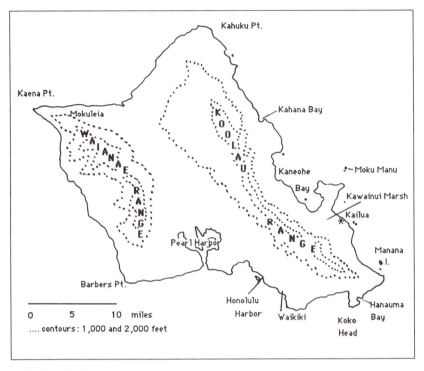

1.6 Island of Oahu.

day, Penguin Bank is sometimes discernible as a lightening of the deep
blue of the concealing ocean. In season, its crest is often marked by
a number of humpback whales. To geologists, the bank appears to be
the stub of another modest shield that may have been decapitated by
the sea.

Oahu is another volcanic pair. The Waianae Shield on the west is
older than its eastern neighbor, the Koolau Volcano. Both have eroded
into magnificent, rugged mountain ranges, but from a few seacoast van-
tages and especially in the central region of the island, where lavas of
the two shields flowed together, you can trace by eye the long, easy
slopes of their youth. The leeward Waianae Mountains reach just over
4,000 feet in elevation, a thousand feet higher than the Koolau, but are
drier owing to the substantial interruption by the latter of the moisture-
bearing northeast trade winds. Huge valleys, partly filled by sediments
and late volcanic eruptions, mark the Waianae coast along the southwest
side of the island.

Numerous deposits of shallow-water marine fossils, ancient coral
reefs, and sand dunes occur on Oahu. All of them currently above sea
level are found no higher than about 250 feet, the putative maximum

elevation reached by the sea during a former interglacial ice-melting episode. Below present sea level, however, Oahu provides abundant evidence of former shorelines and reefs, some now deeply submerged. In samples taken from the drilling of wells in Waianae valleys and near Pearl Harbor, geologists have found ancient stream sediments as well as reef limestones and shallow marine fossils much farther below present sea level than can be explained by glacial control. In some cases, ancient coral reefs extend to nearly 800 feet, and former lowland stream beds are now buried 1,200 feet below sea level.[15] Clearly, Oahu has sunk far down into the sea.

Visitors to Oahu usually see more of the Koolau Range than the Waianae. The southern end of the Koolau forms the backdrop to Honolulu. The shield was and is extraordinary for its elongation. Originally probably shaped like a loaf of French bread, the Koolau Volcano built largely along a northwest-trending rift. Erosion by water, primarily on the northeastern, heavy-weather side of the long shield, has cut back well beyond the original high spine of the volcano. The ancient summit, believed to have been about 6,000 feet high, thus lay east of the crest of the present range. The towns of Kaneohe and Kailua are located within the old caldera boundary, as are the stark pinnacles of Olomana Mountain near Waimanalo; those peaks are clusters of erosion-resistant dikes that formed near the caldera's southern rim.

The Koolau Range is famous for its windward *pali*, a ragged line of cliffs up to 2,000 feet high, tracing much of the long axis of the eroded shield. The *pali* was formed primarily from the headwalls of numerous parallel valleys cut from the northeast deep into the Koolau shield. Eroding at virtually the same rate, the valleys extended through the original summit region back into the descending leeward slopes. Miles of high cliffs resulted in recent geological time when the sidewalls of a number of adjacent valleys wore away. In some places you can still see the last traces of the old sidewalls. They appear as giant buttresses projecting from the cliffs toward the sea.

One of the striking features of Hawaiian cliffs is their fluted appearance; they look like accordions of stone. The natural groove-and-spur architecture has resulted from the action of hundreds of parallel waterfalls that form with every rain. The cliffs are literally hung with waterfalls after a storm, and from a distance the scale is deceiving. Get close to the cliffs (one of the easiest places is on the trans-Koolau Likelike Highway) and what looked like mere threads of falling water from a mile away turn out to be roaring cataracts six to ten feet thick.

A truly astounding amount of solid earth has been removed in less than 2 million years from the eastern side of the Koolau Volcano. Many geologists believe that typical, gradual erosion by water and wind coupled with normal earthquake activity and subsidence of the island is enough to account for this massive wastage of the original mountain. Others suggest catastrophic crumpling and slumping of the Koolau flank. They point to huge irregular masses that appear in sonar scans 6,000 to 12,000 feet down on Oahu's eastern submarine slope. A similar genesis has been proposed for the stupendous cliffs of East Molokai. Landslide debris from both Oahu and Molokai could have converged to produce the present pattern of chaotic topography far down on the seafloor fronting both islands.[16]

Although Oahu has been inching away from the hot spot for a long time, it may not yet have reached its final volcanic repose. Oahu's youngest terrain lies in Manoa Valley, beneath the University of Hawaii and surrounding residential areas, and also along the southeast coast, where it is embodied in a chain of craters and cones including Koko Head, Hanauma Bay, Koko Crater, and Manana Island, just off Sea Life Park in Waimanalo. These features formed quickly and probably not more than about 20,000 years ago as small embellishments on the flank of the already existing (for at least 2 million years) Koolau Volcano.[17] Some of the brief flows of magma came up under the shallow seafloor and obliterated a several-mile stretch of ancient coral reef that had hugged the earlier southeastern contours of the island. Violent steam explosions wherever magma contacted sea water fragmented everything solid in the vicinity, and a new expanded coastline was formed as debris ranging from dust to congealing boulders fell in huge piles around the centers of eruption. Today you can see white pieces of the old reef embedded in the now-cemented volcanic ash all along this coastline and all the way to the top of thousand-foot-high Koko Crater.

These youngest volcanic landforms on Oahu are now eroding rapidly. This coast is typically dry, but infrequent flash floods have torn deep gashes down the sides of the cones. With its deceptively slow rhythm and more or less contained violence, the sea also flicks and jabs away at these ashstone formations and loose conglomerate bluffs, which were born in colossal firefalls. Yet it may not be entirely over on Oahu. To a Hawaiian volcano, 20,000 years may be just a good night's rest.

The island of Kauai was formed by a single enormous shield, now greatly submerged and eroded and redecorated in many places by later-erupted material. Kauai had a giant summit caldera, some ten to twelve miles across; as the volcano entered old age the caldera filled with lava like a many-layered pudding. The large, relatively flat summit area that remains today is made of the ancient horizontal lava beds once located deep inside the caldera.

Great valleys have been incised in the Kauai shield. One of them, Waimea Canyon, which can be explored from Kokee State Park, is eroding far back into the former caldera region. Other valleys are extending from the north and south; eventually the summit plateau may

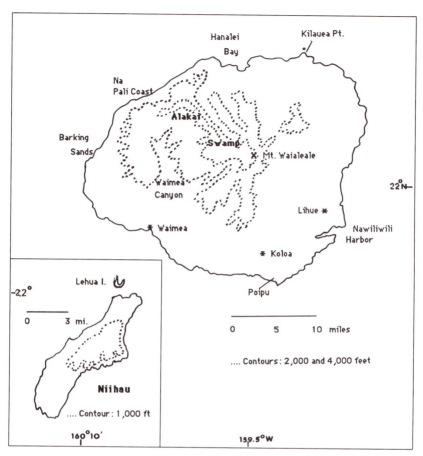

1.7 Islands of Kauai and Niihau.

be completely cut through and carved up into dozens of sharp peaks and ridges.

Kauai's majestic Na Pali Coast is a line of tremendous seacliffs penetrated by numerous stream valleys. Some of the valleys are hanging— that is, they have not been cut down to sea level but end on a cliff with streams plunging in waterfalls to the sea. Such sights are also common on the windward cliffed coasts of Molokai and the Big Island.

Posterosional eruptions have been extensive on Kauai; they have occurred primarily on the eastern half of the island. Here, after a quietus that may have lasted 1.5 million years, innumerable lava flows deposited igneous beds up to 2,100 feet thick in a few deep valleys.[18] Cinder cones that must be roughly contemporaneous with better known counterparts on Oahu dot the landscape of eastern Kauai. The presence of these piles of loosely cemented fragments suggests the probability that even Kauai has not yet become cold and dead.

Southwest of Kauai, and clearly visible from Polihale State Park on the west coast, is the seventh largest of the Hawaiian Islands, Niihau. It is a very old piece of a once-substantial shield. Seacliffs up to 1,200 feet high extend along its northeastern coast. The western and southern sides of the island feature a broad coastal plain with western seacliffs now stranded far inland. The central plateau reaches only marginally above 1,200 feet and is dissected by valleys several hundred feet deep, opening to the west.

It appears that much of the old shield was eroded by the sea on both the east and west, but the slope of the lava beds indicates that the original volcanic summit stood over what is now deep water a mile or two east of the present high-cliffed coast. A hugely disproportionate amount of the shield seems to have been removed from the east. Some geologists believe that vertical faulting has been responsible for the disappearance of this great portion of the eastern shield. This means that seaward of the fault a good half of the volcano sheared away and gradually dropped into the depths.

Quite recently, geologically speaking, a tiny cone of volcanic cinders called Lehua Island has been thrown up above the Pacific on Niihau's northern shelf. It is already eroding away and will be gone long before its big ancient neighbor.

Niihau and Kauai were both built along a major southwest trending rift on a giant undersea ridge projecting off the main axis of the Hawaiian Chain. This same alignment extends beyond Niihau to tiny Kaula Island (usually called Kaula Rock). Kaula is the remnant of another consolidated cinder cone, similar to Lehua off Niihau and Diamond Head on Oahu. Kaula probably represents the last gasp of yet another independent shield volcano that once formed a sizable island within sight of Niihau. Apparently, this early shield was decapitated by the ocean and is now a relatively flat-topped platform about eight miles long by four wide. Kaula, at the eastern edge of this slightly submerged table mountain, may well disappear in a few thousand years.

Just south of the main Hawaiian Islands, a number of large seamounts rise from the deep ocean floor to within 1,000 feet or so of the surface. Recent surveys by oceanographers have indicated that at least some of these huge submarine landforms, such as Cross Seamount, were once islands, but they were apparently not formed over the Hawaiian hot spot. Rather, samples obtained from these "off-axis" seamounts—they are not aligned with the axis of the Hawaiian Chain—indicate that they formed perhaps 70 million years ago at the then Pacific spreading center well south and east of Hawaii. Carried on the Pacific Plate, they have arrived near Hawaii in our time and are now companion travelers with the main islands.[19] Perhaps such seamounts occasionally rode right across the hot spot and were radically altered or buried under a nominal Hawaiian island. Still others might have come close enough to be uplifted on the asthenospheric swell, although none seems to have been at the sea surface in recent geological time.

Beyond the region of Kauai and Niihau and extending to the northwest is the remainder of the Hawaiian Chain—volcanic stubs, submerged shoals atop truncated shields, and true atolls that punctuate an ocean reach of approximately 1,200 miles. Some of these islands combine various features. For example, the large, shallow platform of French Frigate Shoals has a sea-level reef with sandy islets around part of its perimeter, and it thus forms a partial atoll. But a few miles away, rising from the same shallow platform, are two massive chunks of basalt; the bigger one is 120 feet high and 500 feet long. These are seastacks of an ancient shield, all that remains of a former high Hawaiian island. Lost in the immense Pacific, known best to a million generations of big turtles and oceanic birds and countless underwater creatures, this chain of lonely rocks and shoals constitutes some of the most obvious, though little seen, markers in the long tenure of Hawaii.

2

From the Forces of Life

The geological forces that raise and shape islands reveal only the cruder range of nature's creative powers. Less demonstrative but more profound are transformations effected in the living stuff of the earth, and nowhere can this evolutionary alchemy be seen and understood better than in the Hawaiian Islands. Their various habitats are crucibles in which life reacts and interacts on a range of levels from the purely chemical, or molecular—in the realm of microorganisms and plants—to the complex social behavior of higher animals such as insects and birds. Over and over again, living mixtures become unstable, and out of such ecological volatility species, the primary reagents of living nature, are inevitably created and transformed.

Since long before Darwin, the concept of species has provoked controversy. Modern biologists, however, in considering most forms of life, agree on a definition of *species* that involves successful reproduction. For example, nearly everyone knows, if only passively, that coconut palms do not interbreed with any of the various kinds of pine trees. Also widely understood is the fact that among palm trees themselves there are many separate entities—date palms, fan palms, royal palms, and so on—which do not naturally hybridize with coconut palms, nor indeed with each other. However, the individuals of the entity we recognize as coconut palms throughout the world's lowland tropics, despite regional variations in height, foliage, nut size, and the like, *do* interbreed successfully, and botanists call all of them by one scientific name, *Cocos nucifera,* the nut bearer. The second name in the couplet designates the species.*

Species are islands of heredity, said to be reproductively isolated from each other. Such isolation resulting in separate lines of heredity is often clear-cut: different species simply do not mate together. Or, in the case of plants and some aquatic animals whose reproductive congress depends on environmental aids such as wind, water currents, or the services of other organisms, such as insect pollinators, fertilization fails to take place, owing to some incompatibility. Even if the mating of two divergent life forms does yield healthy hybrid offspring, isolation may still be a fait accompli, as in the classic hybridization between horse and donkey. Sterile mules are the first and only generation of offspring from this dysfunctional marriage. Evolutionary biologists summarize the reproductive barrier among species in a way that leaves no loopholes: grandchildren can only be produced by matings within a true species.

Since heredity specifies the detailed makeup of organisms, species are also islands of form. Sometimes they are as easy to distinguish as apple trees and orange trees or cats and dogs; however, dogs, wolves, and coyotes are not always easy to tell apart and sometimes successfully interbreed. Such borderline cases raise controversies over the criteria that are used to classify species. With less familiar creatures, determining species is an arcane art reliably practiced by people only after years of field and laboratory observation.

Most of the time, scientists concerned with these matters rely on discreteness of form—shapes and structures of body parts of various kinds. From the nooks and crannies of a coral reef, an expert collects an assemblage of worms ranging from the plain to the outlandishly in-

*In the Linnaean classification scheme used in modern biology, the first name in the couplet is the generic name, or genus. Genus is never as definitive as the reproductively isolated species, but designates a broader range of related life forms. Progressively more distant relatedness is expressed in higher classifications: family, order, class, phylum, and kingdom. Often there are intervening ranks: superfamily, suborder, etc. Below the level of species, there are often recognized subspecies, or races. Hence, scientific names are sometimes a trinomial. *Pterodroma phaeopygia sandwichensis* is the Hawaiian race of the dark-rumped petrel, a rare seabird.

tricate and ornate, and after returning to the laboratory sorts them into species. At first the going is easy. Little heaps of worms with similar characteristics, obviously separate clans, are built up on the sorting table. But toward the end, the separations become very difficult. The sorter uses a microscope to pin down fine-scale, consistent differences that set closely related species apart. With a variety of complex organisms, the differences between males and females or juveniles and adults of the same species can be highly confusing. This is especially true of birds and fishes, for example. But once the important features of the anatomical landscape are well mapped, it becomes clear that despite sex-specific and age-specific differences in bodily form, the variation between species nearly always represents a discrete boundary, not an overlapping of the variation within a species.

Underlying these truths and the nature of species is the dense microscopic terrain of genetics. Heredity ultimately depends on a chemical, DNA, contained in the tiny bodies called chromosomes found in all living cells. The chromosomes and the DNA are copied and transmitted from generation to generation of life by germ cells, or sex cells (most often the familiar sperm and egg).

DNA, which can make exact copies of itself, contains a genetic code, or program, that directs the machinery of living cells to make proteins. Chemical-assembly instructions, called genes, which specify the synthesis of hundreds to thousands of different proteins, are contained in the DNA of each species. The proteins are diverse manufactured goods needed for a smooth-running organic economy. Many proteins (the enzymes) are highly specialized tools analogous to those on an auto assembly line, each with one small but important function in the construction of organic parts. Others have a role in keeping the machinery running, controlling the flow of energy to various systems. Still other proteins are building materials themselves. They form strong but flexible girders and glassy substances; they are matrix and mortar for articulated frameworks beyond the dreams of modern architects; they are durable and decorative claddings and coatings of the living structures. In a real sense, all living things might say, "We are our proteins."

The story of how DNA directs the hereditary process and the assembly of proteins can be found in any good college-level biology text. The fine details are not needed for a basic understanding of the relationship of genes to the process of evolution and its manifestations in Hawaii. We do need to appreciate, however, that while the genetic code within a species varies slightly from individual to individual, it is qualitatively discreet and distinctive when compared to that of another species. In the emergent scientific view, the DNA that shapes the proteins that shape organisms has rifted and drifted widely in time and now underlies a vast living archipelago.

If DNA were to remain unchanged generation after generation, then life would remain in stasis: no variations in the proteins of a species would appear; no evolution could take place. But DNA does undergo alterations. The long, segmental, threadlike molecules are fairly easily broken by high-energy radiation, including the ubiquitous and inescapable cosmic rays, and also by contact with smaller molecules of various reactive chemicals called mutagens. No matter where a break in the DNA occurs, or even if a linear section is obliterated, the DNA molecule is able to repair itself. The severed ends quickly bond together, reestablishing the continuous thread. But now a change in the molecule's precise order of segments, called nucleotides, may have occurred. Changes can involve not only lost nucleotides, but also potential reversals in their original order, and even the insertion of new, spare nucleotides into the DNA thread at the point of breakage. Gross changes even involve whole chromosomes. All of the changes in DNA are called mutations; they represent new genes that dictate changes in the proteins of the organisms that carry them.

Significant changes in proteins may result in something new expressed in the organism, or something lacking that had been expressed by the original protein. In the first case, a new trait may be hidden—for example, sickle-cell hemoglobin in humans or, perhaps more obvious, a change in the texture of a shell, scales, feathers, or hair. Most of the changes that result directly from mutations, however, are changes in the structure of enzymes, proteins that act as catalysts in the myriad chemical reactions that build a given organism and keep it functioning. An altered enzyme translates into altered chemical products—for example, a chemicle responsible for color vision in a bird species, or one affecting moisture retention in the leaves of a plant or the cuticle of an insect.

The role of mutation in evolution, then, is that of a random surprise. Within the context of an organism's environment and life habits, mutations may be beneficial or deleterious. A mutation is like a mistake in a computer program; its result, or expression, in an organism resembles a mistake in a printed text. A key word or sentence left out may yield nonsense, and the text may have to be scrapped. But omission of a word of lesser importance, such as *the,* or perhaps the printing of *the* as *then,* may not constitute a fatal flaw in the text. Still, if the text itself is in competition with a more polished version, editorial selection may bring about its demise. Yet again, a word may be inadvertently added or substituted that improves the meaning or clarity—this would be a favorable mutation.

This region of knowledge was nearly entirely shrouded in Charles Darwin's day. He recognized that each species embodies within its population of many individuals certain ranges of variation—in form, physiology, behavior, and the like—and that from these ranges of variation inheritable traits possessed by one or a few individuals could be selected by agricultural and pet breeders to yield a whole new population of "improved" plants or animals. Basically the same kind of selection, Darwin reasoned, was exerted by nature; this natural selection resulted in a population that over the generations would be honed and improved with respect to its adaptation to the local environment.

Thus, mutation (unknown to Darwin as the source of the variation he observed in individual organisms) is the feedstock of natural selection. And the overall effect of that process is twofold. First, it provides a continuous weeding out of organisms with deficiencies that make them less hardy or less competitive than others of their species. Sometimes the so-called selection pressure against a mutation is intense. For example, predators will be strongly attracted by white wing color in a moth living on dark terrain such as a recent lava flow. The gene responsible will probably have a short tenure in the local population. Always the superior, best adapted individuals (here the darker individuals of the species) tend to leave more offspring, which themselves tend to have inherited the "right stuff." The second effect of natural selection is to creatively fine tune a species' adaptations to its environment and way of life. For example, the sharp eyesight of hawks and other raptorial birds has been honed over countless generations of gradual selection. With genes and their environmental settings in almost continual flux, the biota of any given region is continuously in a state of self-creation, of testing fitness against new surroundings.

Basic modes of reproduction have a major effect on the pace and lavishness of evolutionary production. To the vast array of organisms with sexual reproduction—combining in offspring a doubled complement of DNA from the germ cells of two parents—belongs the great evolutionary potential of testing a new mutation with numerous combinations of existing genes. In the continuous, generation-by-generation shuffling of gene combinations, natural selection may favor a mutation in some combinations but not in others. Such shuffling, or recombination, which produces new "editions" of the organism every generation, is not possible in the simpler asexual form of reproduction, whereby a single parent produces exact copies of itself analogous to photocopies of a text.

Sex confers another advantage in light of the fact that many genes occur as so-called dominant-recessive pairs. The dominant member, or allele, of a pair masks the recessive allele when the two come together—one from the male parent, one from the female—in the new generation. That is, the result, or expression, of the recessive does not appear in the organism; the dominant allele does the work, so to speak, of expressing the gene. Only when both parents contribute recessives for a particular gene does the recessive character actually appear in an off-spring, and only then can a recessive trait be tested by natural selection.

An organism harboring dominant and recessive alleles of a given gene is said to be a carrier of the recessive. Since natural selection cannot test a masked recessive in a carrier individual, such an allele has the chance to remain in the wings of the "ecological theater" for a long time.[1] If, at its first appearance, a new recessive mutation is not quite right for a part in a species' evolutionary drama, it may come into its own later, after a climate shift or some other change in the environment or after an organism is displaced to a new environment such as an oceanic island. Thus, in a whole breeding population of sexual organisms the double complement of DNA can build a hidden reserve, a hedge of the species' bets against future environmental change, a set of options for many ecological contingencies.

SPECIES AND ISLANDS

In a philosophical sense, DNA is immortal stuff. Biologists have a way of thinking about genes as having lives of their own, as merely being housed in animate shells that carry them through paired shufflings at frequent intervals. Genes are seen as flowing through space and time, generation after generation, while here and there mutations are added and other genes disappear with the deaths of the last unfortunate individuals to carry them. In spatial terms, genes are thought of as forming gene pools, fluid genetic islands, the largest of which have geographic boundaries coinciding with those of the species as a whole.

While the distribution of a species may extend hundreds of miles in different directions, or even span a continent or more, there are almost always disjunctions—large-scale examples are mountains, deserts, rivers, lakes, and oceans. Smaller, less dramatic disjunctions are legion. It is the distribution pattern of a species (as a gene pool) with respect to such disjunctions that sets the stage for evolution.

In evolutionary theory, the genes of any given species are mixed, mingled, and shared most effectively and homogeneously through matings within small, local breeding populations called demes. For example, all the tree crickets of the species X in a patch of forest bordered by the treeless terrain of recent lava flows would constitute a deme. Deme members can readily share genes throughout the small local population. With random mating, a favorable mutation might be able to spread through the deme in just a few generations. That is, gene flow is virtually unhindered and complete shuffling is likely to occur.

Beyond the lava fields are other forested areas with crickets of the same species. Once in a while a wayward cricket will cross the open ground to reach a neighboring deme. Gene flow between populations that are partially isolated from each other takes time, but it may occur. Mutations have the potential to spread through all of the slightly disjunct local populations of a species, but at a given time, if investigators could probe and examine deeply and minutely enough, they would find slight differences among demes in the DNA and proteins and their varied living expressions.

While demes of fairly sedentary species may be small in area and their boundary barriers modest (e.g., a small stream), there are a few organisms for which it may be that no physical barriers to gene flow exist on today's earth: some of the petrels and related shearwaters and albatrosses of the globe-circling southern ocean, for example. Sperm whales and certain large pelagic fishes may likewise roam the seas virtually without restriction, mingling genes within the entire global range of their respective species.

For most species, however, the irregular subdivision of the entire gene pool into the semi-isolated pockets called demes appears to prevail. Biologists think of each deme with its own slightly variant gene pool as having the potential to become a new species. Here is a population already a step removed from the species norm and poised for greater change if gene flow from other demes should become further restricted or cease for a time. A wide stretch of ocean certainly provides nearly absolute isolation for populations of many terrestrial plants and animals, and remote oceanic islands are therefore settings for demes that are almost certain to evolve into new species.

When a small part of a species' gene pool is suddenly isolated on a remote oceanic island, a new species is in the making provided the immigrant organism, called a founder (perhaps just a single seed or a female animal carrying fertilized eggs or embryos), manages to survive and establish a breeding population. This is literally a deme apart. With gene flow interdicted, new mutations that occur in the island population cannot spread back to the rest of species, and vice versa. Natural selection and qualitatively new environmental conditions on the island can result in rapid evolutionary change. It is probable that, as a result of accumulating genetic differences and responses to natural selection, within a few thousand generations the island population will look, function, and behave differently from its ancestral species. It will be, in fact, a different species, and even if physical contact between the two populations could be reestablished, interbreeding would not, or would not be able to, occur. The original, purely physical isolation would have been followed by reproductive isolation, which is the acid test of speciation.

It is an axiom of evolutionary biology that a gene pool divided for a long enough time will never flow together again. The time required to generate a new species (or two if the ancestor's identity also changes)

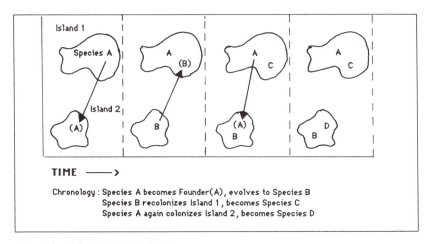

2.1 Island hopping speciation.

varies for different organisms but must be related to numbers of off-spring and frequency of generations. Environmental factors related to climate may also be important; in general it is likely that rates of evolu-tion are greater in the tropics than elsewhere. For most plants and animals the time needed for speciation probably lies in the range of a few thousand to a few hundred thousand years, although it is possible that Hawaiian moths of the genus *Hedylepta* have speciated in as little as a few hundred years.[2]

Once a new species has become established on an island within an archipelago such as the Hawaiian Chain, further events of speciation become probable, almost inevitable in many kinds of organisms. Acci-dental interisland transfers of plants, small forest birds, insects, spiders, land snails, and the like may occur only very infrequently. Thus, new demes, established by island hopping at long intervals, commonly evolve to reproductive isolation. When a group of high islands is scattered across thousands of square miles of ocean, an astonishing multiplier ef-fect seems to take place with respect to the generation of new species. This was first deduced by the British ornithologist David Lack in studies of Darwin's finches of the Galápagos Islands,[3] but in recent decades Hawaii's flora and fauna have emerged as epitomes of the phenomenon.

The mechanism of interisland species generation works as depicted in figure 2.1. Even in the simplest case of two islands, each newly evolved species has the chance of recolonizing the island from which its founder came, thus evolving into yet a third species. Within a million years after its arrival in the archipelago, an ancestral plant or animal may have split into a number of distinct species distributed rather haphazardly among the islands. Darwin's finches are the most famous example, but Hawaii holds even more striking ones—birds, insects, plants, and others.

Intrinsic reproductive isolation that defines the point at which former segments of a single breeding population have diverged into discrete species has been found to occur in many fascinating guises. In one of the simplest cases, different sets of accumulated mutations may have altered the shapes of the reproductive organs of the two populations; so upon reestablishment of geographical contact, as when in figure 2.1 species *B* recolonizes island 1, attempted matings between *A* and *B* are frustrated. Or a kind of natural contraception may prevail in which the chemicals that allow sperm to precisely recognize and penetrate the eggs of its species have differentiated in *A* and *B,* rendering their cross-matings infertile.

Visual, olfactory, or auditory cues for mating may have changed beyond the precise recognition of one population for the other. After thousands of generations apart, mating calls and critical sexual rituals or postures may have changed. Variation in the intricate courtship behavior of Hawaiian fruit flies (family Drosophilidae) has been confirmed as a major factor in the evolution of hundreds of species in the archipelago.[4] Adaptation to habitat may play a role here as well. Over the millennia, an evolving species in a remote locale may become wedded to very different environmental conditions than the ancestral population from which it came. Even if *A* and *B* once again came to occupy the same island, they simply might not frequent or tolerate each other's turf and would thus remain reproductively isolated.

Such premating isolating factors may not always appear or may not develop enough to completely inhibit cross-matings between *A* and *B,* and hybrids might result from such matings. If the hybrids are healthy and fertile, the two incipient species could merge back into one, although the resulting species might exhibit a different norm of appearance and physiology than at the time the population was split.

However, where the period of physical isolation has been long, the chances are that mutations have altered the chromosomes of the populations in ways that have rendered them incapable of pairing precisely, a vitally important process in the formation of normal, healthy germ cells. In a hybrid, this incompatibility between the complements of chromosomes received from the male and female parents translates into sterility. Matings of *A* with *B* will produce no grandchildren, and the two therefore qualify as different species. Other, more subtle incompatibilities can result from differences in the protein products of the genes. These differences may prove antagonistic in a hybrid, making it weaker and less capable of survival or reproduction than pure strains from matings of *A* with *A* and *B* with *B.* Of course, strong and vigorous hybrids are also possible, but the extent of prior separation

and genetic change during isolation of the ancestral stocks is all important in determining whether hybrids will be reproductive (and evolutionary) dead ends.

If hybrids are even slightly less fit for life and reproduction than the
offspring of matings *A-A* and *B-B,* then the two new incipient species
will tend to diverge more strongly; in a genetic sense they will put more
distance between themselves, and this can happen rapidly in a few
generations. Here, nature appears to conspire on the side of discriminating individuals. In the event of hybrid unfitness, the very tendencies
toward sloppy sexual recognition, imprecise expression of physical and
chemical characters, and behavior important in sexual signaling will tend
to die out, leaving the most distinctive cues for recognition to become
genetically fixed in each new species population.

Natural selection at this critical time in the origin of species also favors
any new mutations in *A* and *B* that will keep them separated—that is,
anything that will keep them from the "mistake" of interbreeding and
producing defective offspring or no offspring at all. Thus, a relatively
rapid differentiation that evolutionists call character displacement often
seems to ensue after reestablishment of geographical contact between
two divergent populations that have crossed genetic boundaries to
become incipient species.[5] Some ecologists have proposed that character
displacement is also driven by the hypothetical imperative that the two
new species must avoid competition for the same set of basic resources
such as food, nesting habitat, and so on in order for both to survive.
Thus, for two sibling species to succeed on the same island, they must
become somewhat differently specialized vis-à-vis available ecological
resources, and such specialization should be favored by natural selection. As a result, it is likely that new species pairs, as they confront one
another in competition for mates and resources on a single island, may
diverge in appearance, behavior, and the like more within a few critical
generations of early encounters than in a million years thereafter.

There is no need to invoke mysticism to account for the observable
processes of evolutionary change. The emergence and inevitability of
these processes trace back to basic laws of chemistry and physics. Their
outcomes with regard to specific life forms depends on chance and
history. Life is in continual flux, always on the move, voluntarily or
not. No island is so remote that founders will fail to reach it. Mutations
are always occurring. Evolution proceeds now slowly, now rapidly. The
most unexpected forms lie masked and dormant within every organism
—chihuahuas and corgis drawn out of the wolf by human selection in
an instant of geological time; Hawaiian silverswords *(Argyroxiphium)*
and peculiar trees and shrubs *(Dubautia, Wilkesia)* drawn by nature
at a more leisurely pace from small, spreading tarweeds (family Com-
positae) that reached Hawaii perhaps some time in the Pliocene epoch.

Once a type of animal or plant has colonized a remote island and managed to build up a breeding population, there seems to follow in many cases what might be called a greatly expanded evolutionary opportunity, a chance for a given gene pool to exploit radically new resources and habitats. This chance tends to be available on islands because habitats and ecological niches (the term *niches* encompasses the total of a given species' environmental needs and preoccupations) are not often occupied by many other kinds of organisms. More importantly, they are usually not tenanted by what ecologists term a superior competitor—for example, an animal whose ideally shaped mouth parts, efficient digestive system, or aggressive habits would allow it to monopolize a given type of food overwhelmingly—or, in the case of a plant with a toxic root secretion and rapid growth, to dominate a given habitat. When such competitors are absent or few, newcomers have an evolutionary entrée to adapt to a variety of habitats that would probably be closed to them in continental terrain, which is typically crowded with species that are efficient users of the available niches.

Imagine an oceanic island where a newly established population of seed-eating birds acquires a mutation affecting the shape of the beak. Suppose that this mutation slims and lengthens the beak slightly. Birds with such a beak can catch insects, though clumsily, in nooks and crannies, and some avidly pursue this nutritious new food resource. In such a population, further mutations honing the beak into a probing, quick-snapping implement would probably be favored by natural selection. Gradually, by means of accumulated mutations, the birds would become better insect catchers. Note that inept early stages in such a transition would not be likely to survive in a tightly competitive continental ecosystem where quick, efficient insect eaters already abound and dominate the field. The survival of clumsy intermediates between two or more adaptive peaks has long posed a problem for evolutionary biology. Oceanic islands, with their forgiving environments of few or no competitors, would foster evolutionary experimentation on the scale of geological time, and as nurturing and proving grounds may have significantly contributed to shaping life's rich diversity through the eons.

One possible evolutionary pathway followed by the endemic forest birds of Hawaii called honeycreepers (see chapter 14) proceeded from seed eating to insect eating and also branched in the direction of yet a third niche, nectar feeding. The most striking and highly specialized of these birds acquired long, delicate, and beautifully curving bills suited for insertion into long-throated flowers. Even so, the long-billed species continued to probe bark and other likely places for insects.

This process, whereby a single founder evolves into a varied suite of related species in a setting of diverse ecological opportunities, is called adaptive radiation. The creative power of natural selection is seen here

2.2 Adaptive radiation: variation in three species of Hawaiian honeycreepers. All evolved from a single founder.

at its best, bringing forth new forms of life from "hopeful mutant" material and fitting them with new adaptations into relatively uncontested landscapes. At the same time, adaptive radiation is a dramatic exhibition of life's talent for multiplicity of self-expression. The Hawaiian Archipelago is a museum of nature's virtuosity with a fresh canvas.

Adaptive radiations probably occur more frequently in insular settings than in continental ones, although the latter may host evolutionary experimentation on a much more prolonged and grander scale—for example, the radiation of the dinosaurs, which was followed by that of the mammals. But in considering the wondrous life forms that arise on islands such as those in the Hawaiian Chain, it is intriguing to ask this question: Does the unique life of remote island always end there, dying out somewhere in midocean? Or do some of these laboratories of evolution make more lasting contributions in the history of life?

Oceanic islands seem to have been commonplace for hundreds of millions of years. During the Mesozoic era, before the Emperor Seamount Chain existed, many islands are believed to have drifted via plate tectonics from the south and west and welded themselves to the Pacific rim of North America, where they have been recognized as a complex jigsaw assembly of exotic "terranes."[6] While individual islands of the Hawaiian type may wear away and submerge in a few millions of years, whole archipelagos extend the evolutionary life-spans of their biotas to tens of millions of years or more.

Imagine that like some outlandish ark (or chain of them) an island approaches a continental coast. Even as it nears a destination it may not ever reach (if an ocean trench lies next to the continent), for perhaps a million years there will disembark wholly unique plants and animals—silverswords of other times and places, brand-new insects and exquisite birds, many an ancient family redistributed across the earth after an epic sea change. Perhaps some of these reverse founders will establish a beachhead on new ground.

It is possible that subtle traces of such evolutionary round trips can be found—tiny pulses of biotic enrichment in the form of odd animals and plants that appear suddenly in continental fossil beds. As ocean basins closed at certain times in the past and many islands were swept up against large land masses, a wide variety of new, island-generated life forms might have been "suddenly" stranded in mainland ecosystems. Whether the future Hawaiian Islands, perhaps some fifty million years from now, will participate in this sort of biogeographical pangenesis is the stuff of amusing speculation, but it brings with it a question concerning human stewardship and responsibility for life on earth.

3

Arrival and Adaptation

Many biologists now consider the Hawaiian Islands to be the world's finest natural laboratory for the study of evolution. Insights gained here may be of more than academic interest as humans force a widening adaptive crisis on the earth as a whole. This chapter relates how life came to Hawaii's shallow surrounding seas, its fresh waters, and its mountains. It is a story that begins with the chance arrival and isolation of demes and moves on to examine problems of survival and long-term biotic accommodation in often unique insular surroundings.

The first arrivals, even before a volcano breaks the sea surface, are marine. But even these organisms do not reach a remote island easily. Marine life in shallow water is not identical with that in the deeper parts of the ocean. Most of the creatures of the sunlit upper submarine flanks of an oceanic island are restricted to a crudely doughnut-shaped volume of the sea in which the island itself occupies the hole. In this sense they are like the fauna and flora of a high mountain rising out of a desert. They cannot migrate down and across the vast hostile terrain below to reach the blue-green heights of another mountain. For shallow-water tropical marine life the barriers to such a migration are darkness, the very cold water and high pressure in the depths, and a scarcity of food.

Of course, fishes and some other kinds of shoal dwellers are capable of fairly rapid swimming across intervening deep water from island to island, and a few kinds do this routinely, but most do not. Like small, nonmigrating forest birds, they typically stay very close to the reassuring bulk of their mountainside. Other familiar forms of the shallows—crabs, shrimps, lobsters, snails, clams, worms, starfishes, corals, sponges, seaweeds, and so on—appear even less able to migrate and colonize remote shallows and reefs. But there is a time in their lives, an inconspicuous childhood, when most of these creatures, including many of the small reef fishes, roam widely in the open sea. They go out from an island's flanks as clouds of larvae on drifting voyages of up to thousands of miles.

At this stage they are members of the plankton, feeble swimmers that go where the ocean currents carry them. Food becomes quite scarce in the clear blue "desert" of the outer ocean, and away from the roiling, teeming shallows, the development of larvae seems to slow down or become arrested. Patiently drifting for weeks or months, some of these minute creatures become teleplanic, or long-distance larvae,[1] which can cross entire ocean basins. Often, their lives appear to be virtually suspended until they reenter shoal waters—those of a continental shelf or the shallows near an island.

Upon such reentry, the larvae typically react to specific environmental cues that may promise later success in the adult phase of their species—perhaps a dissolved chemical that signifies an abundance of the adult's food, or perhaps simply an aggregation of the adults themselves (an assurance of eventual reproductive opportunity). The larval reaction is often immediate settlement onto the seafloor followed by rapid development. At this time, many invertebrates undergo a metamorphosis; in a few minutes to a few hours, a radically different shape of creature emerges from the larval guise of the species to grow toward adulthood.

Thus, in the sea the main larval function is dispersal, the colonization of new frontiers for the species and the maintenance of gene flow to its far-flung outposts. Despite the many seaways traveled by oceanic larvae, however, geographical isolation of demes clearly occurs. Barriers to gene flow are common; some, such as latitudinal temperature belts, are subtle; others, such as the Central American Isthmus, which closed genetic communication between Pacific and Caribbean reefs a few million years ago, are rock solid. Nevertheless, the sea must be far less cordoned off with respect to the wide wanderings of its many forms of life than is the land. Perhaps merely by colonizing the land (including fresh waters), life stepped up the pace of its evolution.

Arrival by flotsam is the second major means of colonization by shallow-water marine life. Every year, drifting objects ranging from a few floating trees to countless smaller items—twigs, seeds, and buoyant seaweeds—wash ashore in the Hawaiian Islands. Nearly always they carry populations of cnidarians, crabs, barnacles, mollusks, seaweeds, and so on. Sometimes, too, hiding beneath the floating mass will be one or more kinds of fish. Many of these creatures are habitual drifters, hangers-on and hitchhikers clinging to floating debris. Most, including the fishes, are species of the clear, open sea and cannot survive in the more turbid, sediment-laden waters near shore. Once in a while, however, a true shoreline species may become attached to a floating object, thereby, after a passage of weeks or months, gaining the chance to become a founder. Even a small breeding population may arrive in this manner, and it would conceivably be more successful in establishing a new deme than tiny larvae arriving scattered and alone.

Very large logs and drifting mats of land vegetation, carried to sea by hurricanes or flood-swollen rivers, can transport terrestrial organisms in addition to marine life, but for every raft that carries a potential terrestrial founder such as an insect to a remote archipelago such as Hawaii, thousands of marine colonists must reach the same shores.

Hawaiian shallow-water marine life derives overwhelmingly from the south and west. Hawaii is the far northeastern outpost of the fauna and flora that constitute the Indo-Pacific marine biogeographic province. Scattered on countless island reefs and along continental coasts, extending halfway around the tropical earth to the Indian Ocean coast of Africa, is a biota—marine algae, invertebrate animals, and fishes—exhibiting a high degree of interrelatedness. In some cases individual species extend across the entire range with many demes, most of them encompassed by island reefs. A diver in the Red Sea would have no trouble recognizing *Zanclus cornutus* as the same fish whose striking yellow and black patterning, pursed snout, and sickle-shaped dorsal fin can be seen nearly everywhere along Hawaii's reefs and in comparable clear, shallow tropical waters nearly everywhere in between. This fish, called the Moorish idol, surely exhibits minor racial differences from place to place, but it seems that *Z. cornutus* has maintained its gene flow from archipelago to archipelago and along continental reefs across this vast expanse of the oceanic tropics. The same appears true of a wide range of other reef species—for example, many kinds of cone shells, tritons, helmets, and pen shells among the mollusks, plus coral shrimps and tropical lobsters, sea urchins, sea cucumbers, brittle stars, corals, and a variety of worms.

Yet it is by no means true of all. Some organisms even as larvae are feeble migrants, and it presumably requires freakish events, perhaps rare shifts in regional current patterns, for them to become founders in unexpected places. Thus, in the shallow-water biota of a remote place such as Hawaii, the proportion of endemism, a term referring to organisms that have evolved in and are unique to a given location, is high. Numerous endemic marine species are found off Hawaiian shores; some may classify in higher categories, genus and family, indicating a very long residence in the islands. Yet another measure of Hawaii's isolation is a fairly low diversity or richness of the marine biota as a whole, especially in comparison with the life of the teeming reefs to the south and west. Hawaii simply has been a difficult place for many marine organisms to reach. Hit-or-miss island-hopping dispersal has progressively filtered out would-be colonizers.

Southwest of the Hawaiian Chain is a galaxy of atolls that shares most of Hawaii's marine species but also harbors many kinds of Indo-Pacific organisms that do not reach Hawaii. The closest stepping-stone is Johnston Atoll, about 500 miles from the Hawaiian reefs of French Frigate Shoals. Farther to the south are the Line Islands, straddling the equator, and even farther to the southwest are outliers of the Marshall Islands. Basing their judgments on the number of shared life forms, biogeographers believe that major pathways of marine migrants have come through these deep tropical archipelagos.[2] At least some of their reef dwellers that do not appear in Hawaii may be inhibited by the latter islands' relatively cooler waters.

More recently, it has been suggested that numerous species of Hawaiian shallow-water fishes originally came from the subtropical Ryukyu Islands south of Japan. This idea is based on strong similarities in the nearshore fish faunas of Hawaii and the Ryukyus and the speculation that larvae of fishes from this part of the western Pacific could have reached Hawaii by drifting in great eastward-looping currents, or gyrals, that spin off a mainstream called the Kuroshio, or Japan current—the Pacific counterpart to the Gulf Stream of the Atlantic.[3]

Little of Hawaii's marine life has ties to the east. Here, the nearest shallow-water inhabitants are in kelp forests and other bottom communities on the narrow continental shelf of western North America, well over 2,000 miles away. Although ocean currents from this region do eventually flow toward Hawaii, the regional marine life is adapted to fairly cold water and is unlikely to survive a very long passage into a much warmer realm. The nearest tropical-shoal water is much farther away, as the coast of Central America trends far to the southeast. The currents from this region are not favorable for transporting larvae or flotsam to Hawaii. It is a measure of this oceanic isolation between Hawaii and the Americas that extremely few species of shallow-water fishes and invertebrates have been found that seem to have colonized the islands from the east.

Recent scientific reviewers have taken stock of the uniqueness of both fishes and invertebrates that inhabit the coastal waters of Hawaii. Only a few of the major groups of marine animals, for example triggerfishes and sea urchins, do not seem to contain any endemic Hawaiian species. The overall levels of species endemism noted are 30 percent for fishes and 32 percent for invertebrates.[4]

While endemism is certainly conspicuous in Hawaiian marine life, it is outstanding in freshwater and land organisms of the archipelago. This is to be expected, because in every direction, the transoceanic barrier to dispersal of such creatures is formidable. Of Hawaiian native angiosperms (flowering plants), comprising some 1,400 species, more than 96 percent are endemic (the rest are indigenous, meaning that they also occur naturally in other places in the Pacific region). Native ferns, the second most conspicuous group, comprise about 170 species, with around 65 percent endemism. Mosses and liverworts resemble ferns in those statistics, while lichens have a somewhat lower proportion of endemism. Hawaiian angiosperms and ferns, the best-studied groups, have the largest fraction of their ancestry in Southeast Asia and the In-donesian region, and, like shallow-water marine life, progenitors prob-ably spread in saltatory fashion across reaches of the western and cen-tral tropical Pacific that have long been studded with islands. However, up to 20 percent of Hawaiian flowering plants and approximately 12 percent of the ferns clearly evolved from founders that must have crossed the vast, unbroken eastern ocean from the Americas.[5]

By what means did the founding terrestrial vegetation reach the Hawaiian Islands? Of course, very small seeds or spores enable a plant to propagate on the wind. A variety of ferns, with their tiny spores, certainly must have arrived in the islands by this means. But modern research suggests that birds are responsible for introducing the ancestors of up to three-quarters of Hawaiian inland and upland plants. The founders were seeds that were adapted as long-distance air cargo, adher-ing to birds' feathers, encased in dried mud on the feet, or else capable of surviving a passage of several days through the avian digestive tract. Such adaptations can still be found in some Hawaiian plant seeds or fruits, but there is a clear trend for them to be lost with ongoing evolu-tion in an insular setting.[6] These hitchhiking traits of seeds or fruits—including small size, a sticky texture or barbed projections for attaching to feathers, or resistance to grinding in the crop and to corrosive digestive fluids—are found to be far more prevalent in the crowded, competitive milieu of continental ecosystems.

The most consistent vectors for long-distance seed transport in the Pacific have been oceanic birds and shorebirds. Oceanic wanderers such as the frigate birds and tropic birds may visit many widely separated island groups in a lifetime. Shorebirds are even more likely seed carriers. In the present geological epoch, more than two dozen species are winter visitors to the Hawaiian Chain; many are regular yearly migrants from North America and East Asia.

The terms *oceanic bird* and *shorebird* often belie these creatures' habits. Some of the former nest miles inland and up to thousands of feet above sea level on mountainous tropical islands. Nesting sites include places where the birds cannot avoid contact with seed-bearing vegetation. On cliff ledges and windswept ridgetops, adult birds sometimes have to push through the concealing brush to reach their nests; other species prefer to nest directly in the canopies of a wide variety of trees and shrubs.

Many of the so-called shorebirds have probably had ample opportunity to carry seeds from both coastal and inland continental habitats. For example, the killdeer *(Charadrius vociferus),* though not a regular visitor to Hawaii, may well have flown here in the past from much of western North America as far south as Mexico. The wandering tattler *(Heteroscelus incanus),* a yearly winter migrant to Hawaii and many other Pacific islands, breeds in the mountains of western Canada. Some of the tattlers, along with other migrants, fly on to other destinations—as far south as Samoa and Tonga—from which they may carry seeds of Indo-Pacific plants back to Hawaii on their return trips.

Also important as conveyors of seeds, it seems, were ducks and geese. More than twenty species of ducks and several of geese presently come to Hawaii, mainly in the winter, from both sides of the North Pacific. Some of these powerful fliers, such as the pintail *(Anas acuta),* which in America breeds as far south as Arizona, are regular Hawaiian migrants. Like early Polynesians, undaunted by immense oceanic distances, many of these birds have been able to navigate to Hawaii and back to their points of origin; they too carried living baggage, and their migrating tradition, or instinct, has persisted through a vast span of time.

Except for the native shoreline vegetation, the arrival of viable seeds in ocean flotsam seems to have been relatively unimportant in Hawaii's vegetational history. According to biogeographer Sherwin Carlquist, less than one-fifth of the total founding flora of Hawaii arrived as ocean drift, and this proportion was dominated by shoreline-adapted plants.[7] Few founders that were already adapted as inland or upland vegetation could have come by sea. Relatively few kinds of seeds can survive more than

3.1 Golden Plover, *Pluvialis fulva* (*kolea*), in non-breeding plumage. This bird migrates annually in large numbers to the main Hawaiian Islands.

a matter of days in tropical sea water, let alone the weeks or months it would take to reach Hawaii from any direction. The best adapted for ocean drifting are produced by seaside plants—typically, fairly large, buoyant seeds or thick, woody fruits. Still, some of the most likely ones—mangroves, for example—and *Barringtonia,* the ubiquitous beach tree of the South and Indo-Pacific, with its big, woody-fibrous, plumb-bob fruits, apparently never made it to Hawaii on their own.

The Hawaiian shoreline, however, may still have been the most important proving ground for new vegetation arriving in the islands, for this is where most of the migratory birds arrive. They would have continuously sown the coastal zone with all manner of seeds carried from distant lands. Thus, the shore areas must have acted as filters for many more kinds of plants than could have drifted to Hawaii, and in sporadic episodes of favorable climate perhaps as unlikely nurseries for a generation or two of plants whose continued survival required much different inland habitats. Then, once in a while, local birds or gale winds might have provided the final necessary seed transport for successful colonization.

Then, too, for periods of thousands of years, when glaciers piled high on northern continents, sea level fell slowly and remained as much as 350 feet below present levels around the islands. Original shore-adapted vegetation would eventually have found itself situated in an inland environment once former beaches and coastal dunes, marshes and mud flats were stranded miles from a Pleistocene shore. Some of the original coastal plants might have begun to evolve into something different during the slow transformation of their habitat.

Birds are also implicated in the transport of various smaller animals to Hawaii. Small insects, some spiders, and even small land snails have been found hitchiking on migratory birds. Like most of their kind, the native Hawaiian land snails are capable of closing the aperture of the shell with a moistureproof plug of mucus. They can remain thus sealed up, unharmed by dry environmental conditions. As the mucus secretion dries, it also acts as a glue and holds the snail firmly to virtually any solid surface, including a bird's feather or foot. The moisture-loving snails last out dry spells in this manner for days, weeks, or longer.

Land snails might conceivably have rafted to Hawaii. However, sea water is lethal to them and would prevent formation of their mucus plugs. Hence, it is unlikely that they would have survived on wave-washed flotsam. As outlandish as it seems, the avian assist is the only likely way that these ill-equipped travelers could have reached Hawaii, as well as other islands all over the Pacific, where their evolutionary diversification is famous.

Again, the shore zone and coastal marshlands are likely sites for snail arrivals after direct transfer on wintering shorebirds and ducks. Oceanic birds, too—having recently frequented other high islands, such as the Samoas, where lush rain forest is common right down to sea level— might have brought snails to Hawaii.

Flying insects and birds are the most capable terrestrial colonizers of oceanic islands. They came to Hawaii from virtually all points of the compass. However, both natural selection and sheer chance imposed by the long ocean crossing have filtered out many kinds of potential colonists. Hawaii's insect and land bird fauna, like its vegetation, developed conspicuous gaps. But once flying founders established themselves in the islands, some evolved into unique flightless species.

The original flightless arthropods that reached Hawaii probably came in a variety of ways: small ones in the wind, others with birds, some perhaps on ocean drift. Spiders are well known for ballooning as tiny hatchlings. They spin a long silk thread out into the wind and are wafted away to points unknown. Very small airborne creatures—insects and spiders—along with disseminules such as spores, seeds, and microbes form a partial analog of the ocean's plankton. While the aerial drifters seem not to constitute a functional community with established food chains, they perform the dispersal role, pioneering new ground for their species. In the case of transport of young animals, however, frequent introductions such as those effected by migratory birds would have to occur in fairly concentrated spots to assure the establishment of a breeding population.

Except for aquatic insects, which originally flew to Hawaii, the conspicuous inhabitants of the islands' fresh waters have evolved from marine ancestors. They include several kinds of fishes, crustaceans, and mollusks. In bodily form they have not diverged greatly from existing marine relatives, and their lives remain intimately tied to the ocean. Their eggs and larvae must reach sea water in order to develop. This early developmental period in the plankton provides for these creatures roughly the same opportunities for dispersal as it does for reef dwellers, and the marine larvae of stream animals easily reach neighbor islands of the archipelago. Given time, they may find streams to colonize in distant archipelagoes. Leaving the sea, they gradually move upstream as small juveniles. While native Hawaiian freshwater life consists of relatively few species, most of them are endemic to the archipelago.

Thus, beginning tens of millions of years ago, the ancestors of today's marine, terrestrial, and freshwater organisms began to arrive along unknowable Hawaiian reefs and shores. The terrestrial and freshwater fossil record of the earlier islands is nonexistent, and that of deeply buried and submerged ancient reefs too expensive and difficult to pursue,* so we will not have the chance to examine the remains of those early ancestors of Hawaii's biota. Inferences have been made regarding the relatedness of current Hawaiian plants and animals to those of Pacific Rim continents, and clues might be sought in Cenozoic fossil deposits of mainland areas, but most such evidence will remain speculative. Then, too, it is likely that a large number of Hawaiian organisms, including many as unusual and striking as any now known, lived, evolved, and disappeared long before they could be perceived by any human eye. All we can know for sure about those early times is that islands rose sterile from the sea and with time presented a wealth of new habitats to a variety of potential colonists on and over the horizon.

THE GREENING OF ISLANDS

The filling of islands with life is a subject that has long fascinated ecologists and biogeographers. The classic Theory of Island Biogeography[8] suggests that colonization will come to equilibrium with extinc-

---

*Fossils recovered by scientific drilling, such as at Midway Atoll (see chapter 1), are primarily microfossils; identifiable remains of larger organisms are rare in such samples.

tion on any island. The balance between the two opposing forces would take longer to establish—and of course biotic diversity can be greater—on larger islands than on smaller ones, owing to a wider range of habitats (or, more technically, ecological niches) on the former. Implicit in the theory is the idea that competition for limited resources such as food leads to a rising rate of extinction as the island becomes more crowded with life.

This theory has been widely but crudely tested in field studies of various suites of organisms such as birds and insects. In some cases involving small islands close to continental sources of colonization, observations seem to fit the theory, but recent analyses have called it into question.[9] Application of the theory to large, remote islands such as those in the main Hawaiian Archipelago seems especially controversial. One attempt to fit the theory to Hawaii's native birds rested on the known avifauna of the islands up to the mid-1970s.[10] This calculation was destroyed by recent finds of Hawaiian bird fossils that nearly triple the number of coexisting species in the islands before the arrival of humans.[11] In general, the Theory of Island Biogeography misses the mark in its interpretation of biotic history in Hawaii. Nature seems never to have filled the many habitats of Hawaii with enough competing life forms to force a rising extinction rate. In fact, the opposite phenomenon has ensued. Habitats have been so open and uncontested in Hawaii, and colonization from remote places so slow, that adaptive radiation has accounted for most of the filling of habitats in the islands.

As a volcanic island grows out of the ocean, it brings with it the most basic kind of terrestrial habitat: rock. Of course, from the first some of this rock is finely pulverized into volcanic ash and sand, but most is solid though porous, rugose in the near view yet smoothly contoured overall, utterly bare and swept by the elements. Within the first few tens of thousands of years of a remote island's existence, it is undoubtedly a hostile place for most potential arrivals. Only hardy plants capable of withstanding environmental extremes of ultraviolet radiation, pelting rain, scouring dust, baking heat, severe drought, and, eventually at higher elevations, freezing nights are successful at establishing populations. Such founders might come from other seashores or possibly coastal deserts.

As soon as plant populations have become established, they themselves begin to create habitats, altering the surface of the island beneath them and nearby. The growth of the pioneering plants contributes food, shade, moisture retention, temperature amelioration, and soil and wetland development.

In a broad sense, habitat development on an island through ages of geological time includes two major components: a geomorphological component shaped by physical factors including climate, and the com-

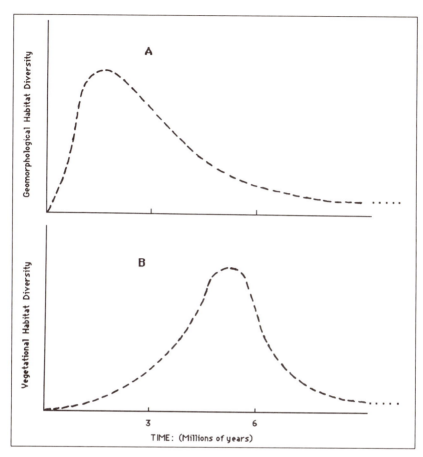

3.2 Speculative scenarios of habitat development on an oceanic island. Graph A represents physiographic habitat formed by geological and climatological forces. Graph B indicates biologically-formed habitat (primarily generated by vegetation).

ponent contributed by vegetation, which provides more and more diverse conditions with the burgeoning of plant life. Figure 3.2 broadly summarizes the rise and fall of these components of the inventory of habitats on a remote oceanic island. As the graphs suggest, the range of complex vegetational habitats must develop slowly (for it depends on rates of plant colonization and evolution) as compared to that engendered by the purely geophysical molding of the island's topography. Figure 3.3 represents the addition of the graphs in figure 3.2. It suggests the composite trend in overall habitat development on an isolated tropical island as it evolves from a young shield volcano to an atoll.

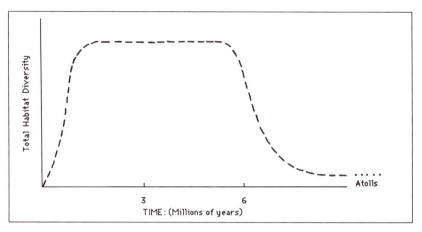

3.3 Model of the rise and fall of composite, or total habitat diversity on an oceanic island.

From the point labeled zero on figure 3.3, when the volcano first appears above sea level, the curve of habitat diversity, or the general availability of ecological niches, rises steeply. In perhaps a million years or so, a plateau is reached. In the plateau phase, a combination of nonliving and living forces produces a rich variety of habitats resulting in a golden age for colonization and adaptation by terrestrial life. Thus, the volcanic island is sculpted by water and wind and begins to be tendered by vegetation to a long maturity that features a wealth of living spaces.

At the start of the plateau period, an island of the Hawaiian type rears thousands of feet with an area covering hundreds of square miles. Its eruptive activity is becoming infrequent, but truncated conical hills stud the terrain along rift zones at various elevations. Erosion now bites deeply into the shield's flanks, creating ridge-and-valley topography, widening watersheds, and perhaps coastal estuaries and protected embayments. There are altitudinal temperature belts and at all elevations relatively wet and dry regions that are governed by the island's orientation to the moisture-bearing winds. Climate and elevation in turn control the varied chemical and physical qualities of soil and its abundance from place to place. In addition, here and there highly specific habitats—coastal dunes, small and large cave networks, plunge pools beneath waterfalls, and many others—lie open to appropriate colonizing life forms. From its beginning as a low dome of steaming lava with a sea-level climate, the island has become a very diverse place.

During all this time, the greening of the island gradually accelerates. The creation of new habitats by vegetation is an inexorable process and ultimately becomes a major factor in the island's ecology. Early in the plateau period, however, the island's niches for life are mainly in the form of geomorphological habitats, and, except for the seashore, where a few species of cosmopolitan maritime land plants and animals may prosper throughout the island's existence, it is obvious that initially the island must be a proving ground for plants.

During the million years or so after the cessation of frequent vulcanism, erosion and subsidence combine to lower a high island by thousands of feet, and the higher mountain climates are progressively lost. In Hawaii, running water erodes the land most strongly on northeastern exposures between about 2,000 and 6,000 feet, where trade wind clouds loose most of their precipitation. Rapidly at first, and then perhaps slowing somewhat, an island diminishes to a vestige of its former stature.

It is likely, however, that the loss of habitats of cooler climates, high ridges and valleys, alpine heath, upper montane forests, and so on is roughly compensated by new kinds of vegetation evolving and adapting on rugged, wet windward terrain as well as drier leeward slopes and coastal plains. All of this growing complexity in the plant communities means that long after the island has lost much of its height and area, it is still rich in habitats. They are qualitatively different and more confined than before but offer emergent adaptive opportunities for many kinds of organisms, especially an increasing array of animal life.

The swift decline in habitat diversity probably starts when erosion lowers the spine of the island below about 2,000 feet. Perennial streams would begin to dry up then. Over the millennia, lush windward valleys would parch. Extinctions would increase sharply. Moisture-loving plants and those animals whose food chains depended on such vegetation would begin to disappear. Drought-tolerant organisms would inherit the windward region. With increasing competition, there would be some continued evolution and adaptation and perhaps even a few new successful coastal colonists, but overall a great ecological winnowing would be in progress.

The end of the high island is in sight—a final small ridge of desert rock that minutely wrinkles the vast enfolding sea and sky. Close up, one can see that it is crowded with seabirds, its former identity revealed by a few hardy shrubs and grasses, some lichens, a few insects and spiders, and perhaps a lonely species of finch. Although the sea will eventually close over the last visible volcanic rock, the corals and coralline algae that once formed fringing reefs around the high island may have roughly preserved its earlier outline. As an atoll, such an island is destined to last for many more millions of years. Typically exhibiting a few small sandy islets on its rim, it retains a small number of coastal habitats and narrow ecological niches. There comes an end, however, even to the renewable ramparts of atolls. Carried by their crustal foundations, they move into cooler waters, slowing the rate of coral con-

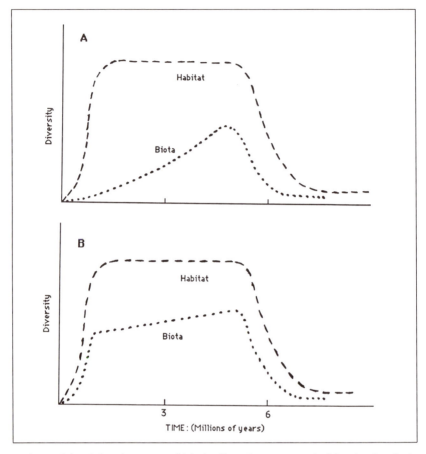

3.4 Models of development of biotic diversity on oceanic islands. Graph A: single remote island; graph B: an island in an archipelago. (The composite habitat graph—figure 3.3—is superimposed in each case.)

struction. Subsidence and perhaps a rise in sea level from the melting of faraway glaciers bring the island to its end.

In the long span of time from the emergence of a shield volcano to the demise of an atoll, how would an island's geological passages, its rise and decline in available habitats and niches, affect its colonization and the evolution of its life? Figure 3.4 suggests what would happen in two cases. Graph A represents the trend in biotic diversity on a single isolated island. Graph B depicts the same trend for an island that is part of an archipelago containing islands of different ages, currently the case in Hawaii. In each graph, the composite habitat curve from figure 3.3 is superimposed on the curve representing overall biotic diversity.

Islands that stand alone and remote during their entire geological existence seem less common than ones that occur in chains or clusters. Perhaps the case in figure 3.4 has never occurred in Hawaii. Still, a comparison of the two situations may be revealing of how life populates oceanic islands.

On a remote, single island, the expectation is that biotic diversity will increase very gradually. All of the colonizing organisms must come from far away. Their chances of establishment on the island are extremely low at first, but they improve somewhat during the plateau period of high habitat diversity. For a long time, most potential animal founders must perish. If they are plant eaters, their type of food may well be unavailable. If they are predators with any specialized taste or requirement, their prey is probably not here. Even for those that do become established, the rate of evolution may be slow.

Graph B summarizes a strikingly different natural history on an island that is part of an archipelago. One or more neighboring islands are probably in the plateau range of habitat diversity and have developed relatively high biotic diversity. The expectation is that a new island will be colonized fairly rapidly by founders from those neighbor islands. Such founders traverse only tens, rather than hundreds or thousands, of miles of ocean. Often, such islands are visible from one another to the image-forming eyes of birds and insects. Thus, the biota of the neighbor islands "tracks" the developing habitat of the new island and colonizes it fairly soon after its formation in geological time. The buildup of vegetation in this situation also provides many ecological opportunities for animals at early stages of the island's existence.

An initial peak in graph B results when most of the preestablished biota has reached the new island. To be sure, a few kinds of plants and some animals—for example, flightless species—will be missing. On the other hand, evolution will probably have produced some new forms on the young volcanic terrain.

As the island matures, continued evolution, especially by the island-hopping speciation mechanism, along with the continued gradual influx of remote founders, increase biotic diversity at a steady pace and to a higher level than on the lone island (graph A). Note that remote arrivals now have a larger target, the archipelago. If successful as founders on any island, they have the chance to spread later to neighbor islands.

In graph B, a second peak of biotic diversity is reached late in the plateau period of habitat diversity. From this point the curve follows the downward trend shown in the single-island situation, and for the same reason: the drastic loss of habitat in the late erosional stages of the island.

The chance of the survival and establishment of any immigrant organism depends on a complex array of factors within both the organ-

ism and the island environment. Ecologists who are computer-minded
attempt to reduce island environments, with their range and diversity
of habitats, into computer programs, or models. In this context, islands
can be thought of as complex repositories of information. Whenever
potential founders arrive they must, in a metaphysical sense, query their
new surroundings. The life programs coded in their genes must be com-
patible with the environmental program of the island—or at least with
one of its habitat subroutines. When the island is silent or communicates
nonsense, they die.

Thus, despite the fact that islands of the Hawaiian type condense a
near-continental diversity of habitat or general niches, there are no
guarantees for individual arriving organisms. Those with special requirements may not find a specific resource for survival; some may arrive at the wrong period in the island's existence—bark beetles at a time
when no thick-barked trees have become established—or an essential
resource may be patchy in its distribution. Consider a gravid female fruit
fly straggling in from lowland Central America. Assume that at the time
the island does contain plants with pulpy fruits suitable for sustaining
the fly's life cycle. However, the potential founder arrives in an arid
canyon separated from the nearest oviposition site (the fruit trees) by
a 10,000-foot ridge with opposing prevailing winds and a subalpine
climate. Maybe the female will make a fifty-mile flight around the coast
before its short life is over. Maybe the fruit will be in season when it
arrives. Maybe not.

Arriving plant seeds must reach fallow ground and they must grow
to reproduce. How many pioneering sprouts that germinated on a
Hawaiian Island were destroyed too soon—withered by the onset of
a dry season, carried away in a flood, buried in an avalanche, eaten by
hungry beetles that themselves were precarious survivors?

In the jargon of the ecologist, the colonizers most likely to succeed,
particularly early in an island's existence, are generalists (with regard
to nutritional resources and environmental tolerances) rather than
specialists with highly specific food requirements and an inability to
survive outside a narrowly defined ecological niche. Later, however,
generalists may evolve into or give rise to specialists on the island.

With the right kinds of ecological data, one might roughly estimate
the probability that a given type of organism will become established
by natural means on a remote oceanic island. These would be the factors entering the calculation:

A. the founder's chance of arrival during the existence of the is-
    land (for example, 1 in 10,000)
B. the fractional period of the island's existence with suitable
    habitat for the organism in question (for example, one third)

C. the organism's chance of establishing a breeding population after reaching the island (for example, 1 in 1,000)

Overall probability of colonization: $A \times B \times C =$ in this example: $1/10,000 \times 1/3 \times 1/1,000 =$ one chance in 30 million

As crude as it is, this formula suggests that arrivals of many types of potential founders on a remote island are a lot more frequent than one might expect. Even if term A were 1, representing the certainty of a founder's arrival, terms B and C still mitigate against the establishment of a population. For each successful take on the island, many of the same species may have made the first improbable oceanic leap and failed, and many more species may have cast dice on those far shores and never come up as winners.

The simple calculation above implies nothing about the likelihood of tenure of a successful founding organism. Gradually, in the few-million-year life-span of a high island, such an organism may evolve into daughter species and perhaps genera, though rarely a new family. Such a course of evolution would probably be enhanced in an archipelago. However, island species may also become extinct, possibly even during a period of abundant habitat and resources. Consider the following scenario.

A founder female of a large, nectar-feeding species of fly arrives and establishes a population on an island. Within a hundred thousand years, several new species have evolved from the founder. Their host plants have become more abundant than before. Owing to a complete lack of predation, no significant defensive programs have been keyed into their DNA, and they have gradually lost any ancestral protective mechanisms. With their habitat seemingly secure, the flies fill the well-watered valleys with their humming. They are big and slow-moving, the most conspicuous insects on the island.

The end of the big nectar-fly dynasty comes quickly after dragonflies become established. Within a century or two, the droning in the valleys falls silent as the newcomers, flying carnivores that catch their prey on the wing, zero in on the last of the big, bumbling targets. The dragonflies themselves may now face a crisis; even before they extinguish the nectar flies their populations will be declining and, unless other suitable prey exists, they too will become extinct after only an instant (geologically speaking) of island residence. Note that dragonflies have other vital requirements. Their eggs and nymphs, or larvae, develop in fresh water; the nymphs themselves are predators, which means the appropriate small aquatic prey must be available. Animals such as dragonflies, with their complex resource requirements, may not be successful colonizers of remote islands until the buildup of considerable biotic diversity.

This vignette is imaginary, but may well have had parallels in Hawaii's vanished past. It suggests the precariousness of life in natural island ecosystems and dramatizes the kind of low-level turmoil that probably characterized the ecology of the Hawaiian Archipelago: sporadic biological interactions punctuated now and then by an eruption, *tsunami,* and the long passages of sea level between ice ages. This was the way it was before the coming of human beings.

When human founders reached the islands, irreversible impacts on delicate ecosystems and an acceleration of environmental change became inevitable. The human species is the unexcelled predator of all time. *Homo sapiens* remakes whole landscapes, disturbing and destroying natural communities with powers that rival those of volcanoes and are more persistent. Our species itself introduces new organisms of many kinds, and while not all such importations disturb the natural balances of islands, some—including goats and cattle, mosquitoes and ants, *Lantana* and *Passiflora*—have had devastating effects. And humans introduce new species, intentionally and unintentionally, at a rate thousands of times faster than nature.

The new era in the environmental history of Hawaii began in a familiar vein. Against great odds, the human founders reached the islands; they were generalists and pioneers arriving on a frontier of great potential opportunity. However, this founding species differed qualitatively from all the rest. It would shape island habitats and biota far more than they would shape it, and it found the conquest of the Hawaiian wilderness to be easy. Changes in island ecosystems were gradual at first but later increased in magnitude and, according to recent archaeological revelations, became massive and widespread centuries before Captain Cook when the Polynesians launched an era of agricultural expansion in the Hawaiian lowlands. Thus, the nature of Hawaii was far from pristine when the Europeans and Americans began to influence the islands. However, they intensified and profoundly diversified the environmental assault, and have nearly completed the despoilation of one of the rarest and most improbable living assemblages on the earth.

The chapters that follow are about major Hawaiian habitats and their biota and what has happened to them during the tenure of human beings in the islands. Most of the native organisms are now rare and endangered; many are already extinct. Entire native habitats have virtually disappeared or are degraded to the point of oblivion. Hawaii's natural environments and biota had such chancy and precarious beginnings and those now in existence are so rare and improbable that on both scientific and aesthetic grounds they deserve unqualified protection. The islands are a microcosm. The nature we save now in Hawaii may well be proportionate to what is left on earth a century from now.

PART TWO

The Surrounding Sea

4

Blue Abyss and Twilight Slopes

A clear view of the Hawaiian Islands from the air or from the sea well offshore rarely fails to attract interest. These large mountains rearing from a remote expanse of ocean have excited human travelers since the first Hawaiians entered local waters some 1,500 years ago. Yet until very recently, a wholly different Hawaii not far from the familiar cloud-wreathed summits, sharp relief, pastoral slopes, and sunny beaches has remained unperceived and all but unknown. Nevertheless, this part of Hawaii, extending far beneath the sea, is immensely greater in extent than the terrain that meets the eye. And both the hidden Hawaii and the visible are connected by subtle threads, the lives of sea creatures that migrate offshore and back to the islands, and also the schemes of people probing a new wilderness ever more deeply.

The underwater slopes and ridges of the Hawaiian Range are rarely as steep and dramatic as the rain- and wind-eroded splendor of the islands above the sea. Even on drowned terrain, the sudden drops and cliffs created by long-ago surface waves and vertical faulting appear less stark; hard edges and angles have been softened through eons of falling sediment. Perhaps some of the submarine canyons, carved and occasionally scoured by undersea avalanches that attain high speeds and great erosive power as they descend toward the deep-sea plains, create topography that approaches the spectacular scenery above sea level.

Views of these features come largely from sonic depth-recording equipment used in surveys by surface ships, although in recent years submersibles have carried marine scientists down over a few square kilometers of these dusky lands. Lately, such visitors have included modern prospectors seeking peculiar deposits of rare metals and beds of precious corals that live far below their reef-building relatives.

Another view, practically infinitesimal but powerfully evocative, is achieved by a scuba diver in such places as South Kona off the Big Island. Shelving reefs are absent along most of this coast, and right from the shoreline the seafloor descends steadily toward the abyss. Free as a fish, hovering in vast blue space, one can follow the slope of the mountain down to 150, 175, 200 feet below the ocean's surface. The ceiling of fractured sunlight seems very remote; the water is like congealed air; the terrain below drops away into twilight and then perpetual night, and one can conjure an explorer's image of the inverted Himalaya that lies so near and extends so far.

Off some of the older shores of the Hawaiian Islands, modest shelves often a mile or two in width have been built, partly from reef-forming processes in the past, partly by ocean wave action that cuts into island flanks and distributes the loose rock and sediment as terraces on an island's undersea margin. Such a shelf extends from Oahu's western coast. In most places it is a composite of two or three terraces descending in wide, irregular steps to the edge of the deep island slope, which begins at depths roughly between 350 and 650 feet well offshore. Between each set of terraces is a low escarpment, or cliff. Large and small canyons can be traced across the terraces; they cut through the escarpments, carrying rivers of sand toward the deep sea. Some of these canyons are obvious continuations of valleys on shore. Once, the now-drowned lands offshore ran with rushing streams and finally lowland rivers draining the nearby mountains that were then much higher above the sea. Flanking the major canyons are rocky ridges projecting seaward. These too are traceable to the land, where they form the stark, basaltic headlands separating the spectacular valleys incised into the Waianae Shield.

The sandy terraces themselves resemble strips of desert, as compared to both the fringing coral reefs that hug the island shoreline and the rocky zones of the offshore escarpments. Yet certain forms of marine life can be abundant in the sand. Among them are heart urchins, *Brissus,* which generally remain just out of sight as they plow through the shallow layers of the sand. These are often the most common large invertebrates in the open terrace habitat. Large bivalve mollusks, *Pinna muricata,* also aggregate here. The wrinkled tips of their shells protrude slightly above the surface of the sand and look like giant distorted keyholes in the seafloor. At depths near 200 feet dense Hawaiian *Pinna* beds, in which the clams' shells appear to be touching, have been found extending unbroken for nearly a mile.[1]

At greater depths, large shrimp, *Heterocarpus,* constitute a fishery resource on some sandy terraces. Marginally commercial quantities of the shrimp were first discovered in the mid-1970s on the submerged plains of Penguin Bank between Oahu and Molokai. Modest shrimp populations probably occur in similar habitats around most of the islands. Their depth range extends to more than 2,500 feet.[2]

Few fishes make their home on the lone and nearly level sands. One denizen that is also seen closer to shore in sand channels of the coral reefs is the razor fish,* *Hemipteronotus pavonius,* called *laenihi,* meaning "narrow forehead," by the Hawaiians. When threatened, this small fish dives straight into the sand, fluidizing it with rapid vibrations of its body. In this way it can actually swim laterally within the sand for at least several yards and emerge well away from a mystified pursuer.

---

*Razor fishes belong to the wrasse family, Labridae.

4.1 Razor fish, *Hemipteronotus pavonius (laenihi).* From Jordan and Evermann (1905) Bull. U.S. Fish Commission for 1903.

One of the characteristic predators on the open sands offshore is the big stingray, *Dasyatis hawaiiensis.* It probably consumes primarily clams, heart urchins, and crabs that it finds in this habitat. Huge specimens of this long-tailed, flattened fish, which weighs more than 200 pounds, have been taken on the terraces off Oahu. The beautiful spotted eagle ray, *Aetobatus narinari,* is also fairly common over the outer shelves, and is frequently seen as well by divers and snorkelers closer to shore. Almost always in graceful "flight," its elegant form is far more conspicuous than the drab, bottom-hugging dasyatid.

The rocky escarpments between terraces at different depths display the most spectacular arrays of marine life, which may rival those of most of the coral reefs inshore. Many of the fishes in the rocky zones of the terraces are the same as those that frequent the nearshore reefs. One of the commonest in both areas is the butterflyfish, *Chaetodon miliaris.* Explorations by submersible of the shelf area off western Oahu revealed dense aggregations of this species and sometimes others over fixed locations along the crests of escarpments. Irregular swirling towers of hundreds to thousands of fish were seen above small (less than 150-foot-wide) patches of slightly raised bottom. These kaleidoscopic formations extended high off the bottom through some 40 to 130 vertical feet. These butterflyfishes are unusual in being plankton feeders (most are bottom browsers) and unusual aggregations of plankton might explain such fish swarms on the outer Oahu shelf.[3] Possibly their location is related to rising plumes of fresh water from aquifers (although none has yet been confirmed here). Tiny ocean plankton animals might be slowed or stunned—a known effect of fresh water on such organisms—along the edges of such discharges.

Typically, at the bottoms of escarpments are banks of boulders and fractured rocky ground with a great diversity of Hawaiian fishes and invertebrates living among the caves and interstices. Prowling the twilight taluses are the major predators of the region: big deepwater snappers (family Lutjanidae) known locally as *opakapaka, ehu,* and *onaga.* * Usually red to pale pink in color, these slow-growing, big-eyed fishes drift like ghosts over the gloomy terrain. They are avidly sought by trap and handline fishermen down to perhaps 1,000 feet on the island slopes. Their firm, sweet meat brings up to ten dollars per pound right at the dock for the fresh, intact fish, which can exceed fifty pounds (rather, they used to come that big, for native snapper populations are dwindling rapidly in the main islands).

THE FLUID FRONTIER

Over and beyond the terraces and island slopes, the open sea off Hawaii is a complex ecosystem divided into layers, some quite well defined and some with boundaries that merge almost imperceptibly. The layers are characterized variously according to distributions of such factors as light, temperature, nutrients, and sediments, and the pattern can be highly intricate. Layers relating to different properties may overlap and, from place to place and time to time, these layers of the sea wax and wane in thickness and may even disappear altogether. This stratified yet fluid world has its greatest stability in the tropical region. Here, the major layers have the clearest functional relationships to the forces that sustain and govern life on earth.

Rarely extending down from the surface more than 200 feet is the sunlit skin of the sea, the layer of abundant solar energy called the euphotic zone. From its typically tossing, windswept surface to its base, this zone has a simple functional definition. Its often shifting lower boundary occurs where diminishing sunlight is just sufficient for photosynthesis to generate the energy needed by plant cells for their own maintenance. At this boundary, no surplus, or stored, energy is produced, and below it the cells of green plants cannot hold their own. This photosynthetic boundary is one of the most significant in the ocean, for from the euphotic cellar down to the bottom of the sea virtually all permanent residents depend on the often meager surpluses that trickle down from life in the sunshine. In the deep ocean, the chemical energy originally made from sunlight may in turn nourish several kinds of bodies. Each consumption results in new flesh, but with each, owing to inexorable ther-

---

* *Opakapaka* (Pristipomoides filamentosus); *ehu* (Etelis carbunculus); *onaga* (Etelis coruscans).

modynamic laws, there is less produced to nourish the next consumer, and in vertical miles of dark water this trickle nearly vanishes.

The euphotic zone roughly coincides with the less clearly defined epipelagic layer, the realm of surface ocean currents such as the wide, shallow flow that passes among the Hawaiian Islands from east to west. Epipelagic life is relatively conspicuous and abundant, and some of its food chains serve humankind with important species—anchovies, herrings, tunas.

The last-named fishes constitute a major fishery in Hawaii, as several of the world's dozen-plus species of tuna commonly roam the offshore waters of the archipelago. In this family of fishes, scientists have discovered dynamic and superlative adaptations. The tunas are nature's most highly perfected swimming machines; the larger species are the fastest animals in the sea, capable of short bursts of speed at ten to twenty times body length per second.*[4] The inner muscular system of tunas is served by an intricate circulatory arrangement that keeps the core of the body significantly warmer than the surrounding water over a wide range of environmental temperature.[5] Thus, all tunas are now considered "warm-blooded," and some may approach the thermoregulatory efficiency that characterizes birds and mammals. With this adaptation, a tuna can cruise over an immense range of ocean and descend a thousand feet or more, traversing warm water and cold, with no change in its sustained swimming power. The wide-wandering tunas are capable of precise, ocean-spanning feats of navigation, and ichthyologists in Hawaii have recently discovered what appears to be an organic compass in these fishes' heads. The fishes may sense and use the earth's magnetic field with a precision as fine as that of any human mariner using a compass.[6]

Also recently developed in Hawaii is the capability to track individual tunas in the open sea.[7] The signals from fantastically miniaturized transmitters attached to the big fish have been followed by shipboard researchers night and day. Encoded in the telemetered signals is information on depth and temperature. One of the findings is that skipjack, or *aku (Katsuwonis pelamis)* and yellow fin tuna, or *ahi (Thunnus albacares),* occupy fairly fixed stations around islands and over remote shoals such as Penguin Banks. Lately, these species have been found homing to large buoys moored off the islands. From these bases, the fish roam at night, seemingly at random, for miles, but they return to their stations precisely at dawn. Along with a detailed and calibrated mental map of their home region, the fish have a fine sense of time. When an individual's nocturnal travels have taken it farther afield than usual, it hurries to get home by daybreak.

---

*For a six-to-eight-foot-long fish, this translates into fifty to a hundred miles per hour.

Under the blue epipelagic world, turbulent with energy from the wind and alive with the eddies of active creatures, lies a great transition zone, the mesopelagic layer, quieting midwaters of the sea. Light in this zone, while not strong enough for photosynthesis, is still sufficient for vision on the part of increasingly large-eyed creatures down through deepening twilight for another thousand feet or more.

Between the epipelagic and mesopelagic layers of the tropics there occurs a fairly sharp drop in temperature, the thermocline. Beginning barely deeper than about 350 feet in the vicinity of the Hawaiian Islands, the water chills steadily from a relatively balmly temperature in the low twenties (degrees Celsius—about 70° Fahrenheit), down through the next thousand feet or so to less than 10° C (50° F). Below this zone of major change, the temperature continues to decline very gradually to just a little above freezing in constant blackness two to three miles below. This tropical thermocline is a permanent one, distinct from the much shallower seasonal thermocline that forms in summer at higher latitudes. The tropical thermocline reaches its deepest level in latitudes south of Hawaii where solar energy is at its most intense and the ocean is generally most tranquil.

In the epipelagic and mesopelagic layers near the islands, a chemical and biological enrichment is found that does not occur elsewhere in the bland open sea far from land. The islands represent elevated concentrations of nutrients, natural fertilizers containing nitrogen, phosphorus, and so on, that stimulate the growth of single-celled planktonic plants— the green fodder for marine food chains. Brought into the sea by river runoff, storm waves, and tidal surges, much of the eroded island soil and humus, as well as debris from coastal flats and reefs, quickly begins to settle close to shore. Some of it, however, reaches channels that carry it across terraces and down the island's flanks. Some of this detritus forms flocculent layers buoyed on the cool, dense strata of the thermocline; heavier material is eventually carried far down to the abyssal seafloor via major submarine canyons. Certain lightweight organic debris may have the most far-reaching influence. Slowly decomposing through the agency of natural marine bacteria, this subtle compost drifts away from a high island as a "nutrient shadow," a wide plume of enrichment extending perhaps 100 miles or more downstream—from the Hawaiian Islands, generally westward—along prevailing surface currents. Besides stimulating plant-cell growth and ultimately epipelagic fisheries, such plumes may also provide faint directional cues that might be followed by sea turtles or shoalwater fishes toward an island beyond the horizon.

Surprisingly, a majority of the species known as reef fishes spend the early part of their lives out in the open sea, many miles from the islands. They are the common inshore fishes of Hawaii, the ones a snorkeler sees everywhere in coastal bays and around the reefs. They belong to major families—wrasses, goatfishes, butterflyfishes, surgeonfishes—and many minor ones such as filefishes and parrotfishes.

Most of these fishes have their main breeding period in winter or early spring (sometimes a second, minor peak of spawning occurs in summer or fall). Their free-drifting eggs* and larvae disappear almost immediately from the shallow coastal waters. At least in some areas, such as Kaneohe Bay off windward Oahu, some species (for example, parrotfishes) make seaward spawning runs to broadcast their eggs beyond the outermost coral reef and over the descending offshore terraces. Many species seem to time the release of their spawn to coincide with strong tidal flushing of inshore waters.[8]

Weeks to months later, the next generation of these fishes appears near the surface as young-of-the-year members of the nekton (open-sea swimmers, as opposed to plankton, which, except when they exhibit vertical locomotion, are passive drifters). The reef fish babies, now an inch or two long, begin to make their way back to island shoal waters from somewhere offshore. Occasionally, favorable conditions for breeding and early survival result in an astronomical number of such fingerlings belonging to one species or another. As they return in spring and summer, the hordes of babies produced by such species as the filefish *(Pervagor spilosoma)* constitute a major feeding resource for skipjack tuna, or *aku (Katsuwonis pelamis)*. In 1984–1985, however, the tuna clearly did not make much of a dent in the filefish crop. The little speckled, orange-tailed creatures washed in on the beaches of Kauai and Oahu by the millions after they apparently overgrazed their nearshore food supply and starved. Similarly spectacular mass mortalities of this species have been noted in the past. The ancient Hawaiians reportedly believed that the phenomenon foretold the death of a high noble or king.[9]

Baby goatfishes, too, are often so abundant offshore that they form a major feeding resource for oceanic birds.[10] The return of the goatfishes as four-to-six-inch juveniles called *oama* has always been celebrated by Hawaiians, as these little creatures, whose barbels and long faces give them a fanciful resemblance to their terrestrial namesake, are both delicious to humans and an irresistible bait for larger fishes.

Highly intriguing to marine scientists is the hidden phase in the lives of the inshore fishes. Where do the planktonic larvae go after the drifting eggs hatch outside the reefs? How is it that the larvae are not lost—carried by prevailing surface currents so far away that return to the islands would be unlikely, even after they had grown to become capable swimmers? What explains the reappearance of the reef fishes, having

---

*A minority of Hawaiian reef fishes including, for exmaple, gobies and some damsels, produce eggs that cluster on the bottom. Hence, their young tend to remain in the shallows.

grown from larvae to juveniles, weeks later and only a few tens of miles offshore, and even to windward (upcurrent) of the islands? One recent theory is that the eggs and larvae of inshore fishes may be swept into huge rotating eddies that form off the Hawaiian Archipelago, mainly to the west, or leeward of the islands. Eddies are not always present but apparently form several times per year at irregular intervals as looping spin-offs from the main east-to-west North Equatorial Current after it anastomoses in the channels threading among the islands. Eddies as large as 50 miles in diameter are now known to form behind (west of) the Big Island.[11]

This theory, developed primarily by biological oceanographer Philip Lobel, depends on eddies remaining close to shore long enough for some critical number of larvae from a major spawning to graduate from the plankton—that is, to become competently swimming nekton. This could take on the order of eight to ten weeks. Depending on an eddy's size, the developing larvae might ride several times around their revolving nursery before jumping off at the closest point to shore and returning to the island. So far, evidence for the eddy-retention theory is scant. Lobel and colleagues sampled a large eddy off the Kona Coast in the summer of 1984 (the off-season for fish reproduction). Few fish larvae were found, and the eddy remained stationary for only six weeks before moving southward toward the open Pacific.

No doubt some of the reef fish larvae do become trapped in offshore eddies, and perhaps this mechanism helps return some to their insular habitat. It is just as reasonable to envision the eddies transporting clouds of shoal-water plankton away from their home islands. Like a huge, whirling spaceship in the sea packed with potentially colonizing life forms, an eddy might very infrequently reach another distant archipelago.

Another possible mechanism to help explain the nearshore disappearance of the young of common reef fishes and their later reappearance well offshore is a phenomenon called winter cascading. First described in Bermuda,[12] cascading starts with the cooling of shallow surface water surrounding an island. Although this phenomenon hasn't been demonstrated in Hawaii, it would be most likely to happen on calm, clear winter nights between November and March when sea-level air temperatures from radiational cooling and flows of cool air from the mountains reach an un-Hawaiian 10° to 15° C (about 50° to 60° F). In some years, episodes of such cooling can persist almost unabated for two to three weeks at a time, although durations of a few days to a week are more common. The cooled water of bays and reefs becomes denser than the warm epipelagic waters just offshore, and near the edge of the reefs the shore water begins to sink. The term *cascading* suggests the slow-motion mass flow of cool, relatively dense water down over the submerged terraces and slopes. Shallow submarine canyons may carry much of this water, and it continues to sink through the mixed epipelagic layer—possibly into the thermocline—until it reaches a zone of equal density. Then, given sustained flow or repeated, pulsed flow, the cascade might spread slowly outward, floating atop the colder, denser layers of the deep sea.

The question, so far just a speculation, is whether newly hatched fish larvae might be entrained in sinking layers of shore water and carried down through the mixed layer. Eggs and larvae of most of the fishes in question have always been thought to remain at the surface, but then why do they disappear almost immediately and so nearly completely from the shallows? Offshore eddies alone seem too capricious to account for such a vanishing.

Perhaps the cascading mechanism provides a boost for the larvae, carrying them beyond the range of the tides, which move water back and forth around the islands but do not extend their influence very far off the shores and reefs. Fish hatchlings may follow their food supply down a few hundred feet or so where the nutritious pelagic dust (called particulate organic matter) tends to concentrate. Submersible surveys off western Oahu located this thin gruel, perhaps a manna for fish larvae, as a turbid layer floating on the thermocline.[13] Much of it may come down from the shallows via cascading.

Whether or not larvae are swept up in an ocean eddy, they must develop for weeks in a mosaic of plankton patches scattered well offshore around the islands. Then they seem to materialize out of the depths in immense numbers and begin to make their way back toward the distant reefs. At this time, they could be dispersed and shuffled among island demes of their particular species. Whatever mechanism conserves them around the archipelago at large, it could be a fine example of ecological circuitry composed of linkages that couple the fates of reef dwellers with those of fishes and birds of the blue epipelagic out to where a high island is only a smudge on the horizon.

Below the euphotic epipelagic zone is a true inner space. As habitat it dominates the planet; its drifting biological community may be nearly ubiquitous in the world ocean. Many of the creatures here expand their range at night. They rise toward the surface, some migrating vertically hundreds of feet into rich feeding territory near or on the surface. Then, like miniature graveyard monsters, beautifully adapted nightmare constructs from biology's underworld, they sink into the depths at the first glimmer of dawn.

Well represented off Hawaii, the midwater (mesopelagic) fishes are a wonderful study in adaptive demonology. The enlarged heads, dagger-like dentition, and distensible bellies of some of the predators are all helpful in securing a meal, which may range from very small to far larger than the normal (fasting) dimensions of the feeder. No meal in this world, where meals are so scarce, is to be missed.

In the deep, as light from above fades, small sparks and motes of light begin to flash and dance in the fluid dusk. This is bioluminescence, light produced by life. Patterns appear and change shape as their bearers shift position like agile nocturnal craft lit from within. Rows of light like tiny portholes, odd polygonal stipplings, flashing semaphores, single flares at the tips of long, ceaselessly moving tendrils or barbels—all serve various urgent necessities of animal life such as attracting food, finding a mate, or deceiving a hunter in the drifting darkness.

The vast majority of mesopelagic life forms are small. Even the toothy predators—dragonfish, viperfish, and similar types—are diminutive horrors, most of which could hide in a swimsuit pocket. Somewhat larger forms include the two-foot-long shark *Isistius brasiliensis,* which waits in ambush in the mesopelagic gloom. Slender and delicate, quite innocuous looking for a shark, *Isistius* nevertheless attacks prey far larger than itself. These prey are chiefly deep-diving porpoises and fishes such as tunas and billfishes.[14] The habits of this shark have earned it the name cookie-cutter shark, a reference to the action of its jaws, which when distended form an almost circular cutting tool to gouge out hemispherical scoops of flesh from its victims. The little shark must be quick to bite and quicker to flee. In Hawaiian waters it leaves its signature in the form of cratered scars on the flanks of even such powerful creatures as the spinner dolphin, *Stenella longirostris.*

Magnificent exceptions to the rule that small size is favored in the mesopelagic zone are embodied in such creatures as the giant squids. They must loom like immense ghostly spaceships in this world without borders. Squids are well known to inhabit mesopelagic waters, but surprising discoveries are occasionally made as well. In 1976, a new form of shark, *Megachasma pelagios,* was brought to light after becoming entangled in U.S. Navy equipment about 600 feet below the surface some 25 miles northeast of Oahu.[15] Dubbed megamouth long before its formal scientific naming, the bulky fish was fourteen feet long and weighed 1,653 pounds. Several interesting features suggested its way of life in the twilight zone. It had an enlarged head and an enormous mouth with a thick, bulbous tongue. The teeth were very short, and useless for attacking large prey. Muscles and fins were soft and flabby, and the skeleton weakly calcified, both of which features indicated that megamouth was a sluggish swimmer. The low-density skeleton may help the shark achieve near-weightlessness. A curious silvery, pore-studded oral lining provoked speculation that megamouth had a mouthful of bioluminescence. Advanced tissue decomposition, however, prevented confirmation of this idea.

Biologists who have studied this beast envision it as a perennial drifter in the near-night layer of the sea. Open-mouthed, the shark may reveal in its oral cavity a constellation of tiny lights. They would shine within a black hole in the surrounding watery darkness and provide a fatal attraction for small deepwater, shrimplike creatures. These small crustaceans (heaps of them were found in megamouth's stomach) tend to travel in small, dense schools; they may seek smaller luminescent prey, and they might be lured practically inside the stealthy giant's mouth. A sudden expansion, perhaps aided by a pistonlike retraction of the tongue, and the little school of shrimp would be slurped in and swallowed.

This scenario is speculative, and humans may never be able to observe a megamouth in the act of feeding. But the creatures may not be rare. In 1984, a second individual of *Megachasma* was found in deep water off California.

DISTURBING THE DEEP

In the great twilight deep along the Hawaiian Chain, natural history and human history have intersected only very recently. During the latter half of the twentieth century, human exploitation of various marine resources and the disturbance of the environment beyond Hawaii's reefs have begun to loom large. Three categories of civilization's impact on this heretofore pristine Hawaiian wilderness bear watching: fishing, dredging for precious corals and rare metallic ores, and submarine waste disposal.

Of the major marine fisheries in Hawaii—those sustaining reef and shore fishing, offshore pelagic fishing (primarily for tunas), and offshore bottom fishing—the last and seemingly least accessible is probably the most vulnerable to depletion and disturbance. This bottom fishery and its sustaining environs are well worth conserving, for its handful of marketable species, notably snappers and shrimp, rank with the most valuable in the Pacific region. Their vulnerability lies partly in the small expanse of their habitat, no more than tiny plateaus on offshore banks and thin strips contoured around the islands. Because of the high resolution of modern depth-sounding gear, fishermen can easily identify topography known to concentrate the target species—for example, the sharp dropoffs with bouldery taluses at their bases, which constitute the preferred habitat for snappers such as *opakapaka*. The better equipment clearly shows fish schools and even big solitary individuals above the bottom.

Other, more subtle factors may be killing off desirable native bottom fishes in the offshore region. For once, pollution cannot be blamed. One thing that *is* being blamed, and cursed heartily by the deep trap-and-line fishermen, is an introduced species, itself a snapper, called the *taape*. This fish, *Lutjanus kasmira,* also called the blue-lined snapper or yellow Tahitian perch, was introduced to Hawaii in the late 1950s and early 1960s by the Hawaii Division of Fish and Game. On several

occasions, releases of hundreds of *taape* were made off Kaneohe and
Hawaii Kai on Oahu.[16] The Hawaiian range of this species now extends
from the Big Island to French Frigate Shoals.[17] And as the native Hawaiian snappers are overfished, they are being replaced by *taape,* which
apparently grow faster initially than the natives and, in the ecologist's
phrase, may be better competitors. Although *taape* never grow larger
than about twelve to fifteen inches, they are fierce little predators and
may even eat the young of the larger, more valuable species. Some
fishermen call the *taape* a marine mongoose, in reference to the terrestrial depredations of that voracious little introduced mammal. Catches
on the offshore grounds around Oahu are becoming dominated by this
small, yellow species, which brings little more than fifty cents per pound
at market. Even if fishing for the big native snappers ceases entirely,
the big snappers may never recover their former abundance as long as
the *taape* occupy their territory.

A few other kinds of bottom fishes, widespread species with major
populations extending deeper than the snappers mentioned above, could
be important for future Hawaiian fisheries. Two of these species—armor-
head *(Pseudopentaceros wheeleri)* and alfonsin *(Beryx splendens)*—are
already being taken in fairly large numbers by foreign trawlers fishing
at the end of the Hawaiian Ridge northwest of Kure Atoll and on the
Emperor Seamounts. Alfonsin seems to range in abundance as far south
as the main Hawaiian Islands. However, even there this species apparently prefers offshore seamounts, where it lives near bottom at depths
of several hundred meters.[18]

Precious corals constitute another kind of living resource that occurs in patches on bare, rocky bottom well below the coral reefs that
fringe the Hawaiian Islands. The adjective *precious* stems from two at-
tributes of these corals. They are generally rare, and they are highly
valuable when cut into segments, polished, and manufactured into handsome items of jewelry. Their rarity in large, exploitable populations
appears to be controlled by their habitat requirement—bare, rocky exposures on the island slopes where sediment cannot smother their extremely slow-growing tree- or bushlike forms.

Known chiefly by their colors—black, red, and gold—the precious
corals are colonial animals that are distantly related to the more typical
corals of the shallow reefs but possess much harder, denser skeletons
and lack the symbiotic algae found in the reef builders. In Hawaii, the
largest populations of precious corals grow in depths of between about
150 and 2,000 feet. Black coral of the genus *Antipathes* occupy chiefly
the upper part of this range, while Hawaiian red *(Corallium)* and gold
coral *(Gerardia)* thrive in the deeper zones. Another distinct species
of *Corallium* occurs much deeper on the flanks of the Emperor Seamounts northwest of Midway Island. Very large beds of this species were

4.2   Black Coral, Genus *Antipathes,* with deepwater snapper.

discovered at depths of between 3,300 and 5,000 feet in the late 1970s. Uncontrolled exploitation of these major finds resulted in temporarily glutted markets worldwide for red coral.

Richard Grigg, a coral specialist at the University of Hawaii, has summarized the major aspects of the ecology and resource management of Hawaiian precious corals.[19] Most importantly, in relation to management objectives, Grigg presents evidence that reproductive potential and recruitment, or establishment, of young are generally low for these corals, and that they are extremely slow growing compared with shallow-water reef corals. Normally, these factors are offset by longevity; a mature tree of black coral that reaches slightly over three feet in height can be seventy-five years old. But such a life history indicates that these strange animals, which grow in leafless bonsai thickets that never cast a shadow, can be easily depleted. Commercially more like a mined resource than a fishery, precious corals are primarily obtained by dredging from the surface. Grigg's estimate, based on life-history factors, is that if depletion is to be avoided only a small fraction (less than 3.5 percent in one black coral species) of any particular population can be harvested annually. Uncontrolled, indiscriminate dredging wipes out decades of slow growth in these fragile forests.

While the twilight terraces and slopes have not yet been greatly disturbed in Hawaii, nor indeed oceanwide, this habitat is fairly rare and nearly as vulnerable as the coral reefs in the zone above. The slow growth and maturation of species such as deepwater snappers and precious corals make for more rapid depletion of even dominant deep-bottom organisms than is likely for their counterparts on the warm, sunlit reefs.

Besides fishing and coral harvesting, the human activities off Hawaiian shores that may adversely affect the deeper living marine life are under-sea mining and perhaps large-scale waste disposal. The mining could involve two kinds of resources from two submarine regions: sand from the island terraces for use in construction ashore and, in deeper zones, the metallic ore deposits called cobalt-rich ferromanganese crusts. Large-scale mining of the sand beds just off the islands could have debilitating effects on marine life. The most damaging impacts might ensue if mining were to occur close to one of the scarps, or rocky drop-offs, where spectacular concentrations of fishes and other animals have been found. These creatures of the clear, deepening offshore zone may not tolerate greatly increased sedimentation and other forms of acute environmental disturbance.

The ferromanganese crusts are thin, crumbly layers of minerals that have been precipitated over the eons on the undersea island slopes and, farther offshore, on the upper slopes of seamounts. These deposits, which are best developed on sediment-free bottom at depths mainly between about 2,500 and 6,500 feet, are generally similar in their metallic content to the better-known ferromanganese nodules of the much deeper and more remote ocean basins. Like the nodules, Hawaiian crusts are rich in iron and manganese and contain small amounts of cobalt, nickel, copper, and other metallic elements. The crusts differ from nodules in containing more cobalt and less nickel. Even though the combined concentrations of cobalt and nickel in both nodules and crusts are rarely more than about 2 percent of the dry weight of the mined ore, those two metals, which are vital for the manufacture of high-strength steel alloys, account for most of the industrial interest in mining the undersea ferromanganese deposits.[20]

Strip mining the crusts will be expensive, but the idea is becoming more attractive as terrestrial sources of cobalt and nickel are depleted. Furthermore, the United States possesses no reserves of these metals on land, and imports might be subject to future political difficulties or cartel action among major suppliers such as Zaire and New Caledonia. Regarding Hawaiian crusts there is the political nicety that, unlike the nodule beds, over which international disputes have frothed since the mid-1970s, the crust deposits are within the exclusive economic zone, or EEZ (the 200-mile limit of national sovereignty over marine resources) of the United States.

Some recent assessments make it appear that mining around the islands is not imminent. In 1985, the position of the U.S. Interior Department's Office of Strategic and International Minerals was that the Hawaiian reserves—"millions of tons of cobalt/nickel and manganese-rich crusts"—would not be needed until the twenty-first century.[21] However, the state of Hawaii is pressing for rapid development of undersea strip mining off its shores. Reams of technical information have been gathered from oceanographic surveys off the islands. A prototype mining machine the size of a grain harvester is under development. Towed along the bottom behind a surface ore-carrying ship, it will crush and grind the thin, metal-rich crust and then suck the gritty rubble all the way to the surface in a huge hydraulic vacuum cleaner.[22]

Fortunately, in a draft environmental impact statement issued in January 1987,[23] federal and state authorities ruled out mining on the undersea flanks of the islands themselves. Instead, a number of seamounts, well offshore but within the EEZ, will be the focus of the initial mining operations. However, even here, careful procedure is warranted to avoid unnecessary damage to other potential future resources. One of the probable mining sites is Cross Seamount, about 100 miles south of Oahu. This seamount, which lies off the axis of the main Hawaiian Island Chain, was probably once a substantial island with remote origins in the eastern Pacific (see chapter 1). Now its summit lies about 1,000 feet below the surface. Recent initial surveys by University of Hawaii oceanographers revealed a small population of precious corals on the summit and confirmed that the commercial species of fish known as alfonsin inhabits the upper flanks of the mountain.

Beside the simple obliteration of living bottom communities in the path of the mining apparatus, a more widespread potential environmental problem associated with mining crusts on the island slopes, as well as sand on the terraces closer to the islands, would seem to be that clouds of disturbed sediment might be carried into areas inhabited by valuable species and their food chains. Remember that these offshore creatures live in and are presumably adapted to some of the clearest of ocean water. The fact that the two proposed mining zones—for sand and crusts—bracket levels of potential fisheries for shrimp, precious corals, and perhaps alfonsin should signal a special caution at the inception of such strip mining on this delicate frontier.

If international economics and Law of the Sea treaties develop favorably, nodule mining could precede mining for the Hawaiian crusts. Technology to dredge the former was perfected by the mid-1970s, and the undersea ores could be shipped to Hawaii for processing. The Big Island, which lies nearer the huge Pacific nodule fields than any other feasible processing site, has long been touted for this purpose by the state's government. Disposal of millions of tons of waste, or tailings, whether from nodules or crusts, will present an immense environmental problem. The waste, probably representing well over 90 percent of the original mass of ore, will be sodden with acids and other noxious chemicals from the metal-extraction treatments. Owing to the problems of treating such waste on land (see chapter 21), especially in a tourist destination, there may be a strong temptation to dump it in the sea. One imagines clouds of toxic slurries spreading over hundreds to thousands of square miles, perhaps making once-clear waters off Hawaii the marine equivalent of skies dirtied by large coal-fired power plants in the southwestern United States.

Some proposals have suggested alternatives to simply dumping megatons of poisoned mud willy-nilly into the blue abyss: injecting the tailings below the thermocline in one designated region or emplacing them very close to the bottom in deep water. One well-publicized suggestion was that ferromanganese processing wastes be dumped specifically in the Puna Submarine Canyon, an undersea extension of the Kilauea Southeast Rift Zone that descends east of the Big Island into very deep water.[24] Even here, however, some precautions are in order. Roughly 50 miles long and 20 miles wide, the Puna Canyon region remains unexplored except for some depth profiles by surface ships and a few tiny patches of bottom that have been viewed from a submersible. The possibility exists, according to University of Hawaii geologists, that this region harbors hydrogeothermal springs, especially along the volcanically active south rim of the canyon. Such undersea hot springs, first discovered near the Galápagos Islands and now known from several other places scattered along the great East Pacific Rift, are inhabited by marine life new to science in wholly unique ecosystems that are energized not by the sun, but by the heat of the earth's interior. A dumpsite in Puna Canyon could bury or smother a Hawaiian version of these truly astonishing and wonderfully rare deep-sea oases.

As new opportunities for exploitation and new uses for a pristine environment bring human activity increasingly into the deep ocean off Hawaii, it is to be hoped that nature there will fare better than it did on the islands themselves. Hawaii's offshore realm is so huge and clean, it is hard to believe it would ever be spoiled or drastically altered. But the North American prairie was once another kind of wild, limitless sea. Now its soils are widely stripped and poisoned, its surface and groundwaters are becoming contaminated with wastes, and much of its native life is endangered or extinct. These changes may parallel future developments in the sea off the Hawaiian islands. Might the snappers, the precious corals, perhaps even the tunas, like species on bygone frontiers, succumb to the technological hunt and to a slow, progressive alteration of their environment?

5

A Place for Whales

Among the few cetaceans that are relatively common or occur predictably in Hawaiian waters, the best known are a dolphin called the spinner *(Stenella longirostris)* and the celebrated humpback whale *(Megaptera novangliae)*. These represent, respectively, the two major groups of their kind: the odontocetes, or toothed whales, and the mysticetes, or baleen whales, named for the tough, fibrous substance that forms the filter-feeding plates in the mouth. Despite strong scientific interest in the natural history of whales, these animals remain imperfectly understood and may hold dazzling biological secrets yet to be fathomed.

S. longirostris, specifically named for its long delicate snout, is a year-round resident, while *Megaptera* is a regular migrant from the far North Pacific, visiting Hawaii in winter and spring. The two never seem to interact in any significant way. Each must have a long history in Hawaii, but the two lead very different lives.

Spinner dolphins occur in all warm oceans; tropical Atlantic forms have a shorter snout than their Indo-Pacific cousins.[1] The common name comes from this animal's habit of leaping clear of the water, whirling like a dervish in the air, and falling back sideways with a splash. Sometimes several animals leap and spin repeatedly for several minutes. Such a display seems a wildly exuberant celebration of energy, a cetacean gymnastic event. But this is oceanarium prose. Some biologists think this activity helps the animal dislodge skin parasites, mainly blood-sucking crustaceans that resemble lice. Others believe the noise of the splash conveys some signal to the pod. Whatever the function of this dramatic behavior, it makes spinners excellent communicators to humans of the ethic for maritime wilderness preservation. In Hawaii the dolphins' performance is often as accessible as it is compelling. The show is at its best against a pristine coastal backdrop with the audience seated ten feet away in an ocean kayak.

Spinners are highly gregarious. In Hawaii they are primarily coastal animals, island lovers forming subpopulations of up to several dozen individuals.* Typically, discrete populations occupy selected bays and coves. Such a group spends most of its day resting in its home bay; at

---

*Much larger populations of *S. longirostris* are also found in remote, midocean areas far from land. This species, along with others, often accompanies pelagic tuna schools. There is some speculation that Hawaiian coastal spinners are a separate race (see note 1).

5.1 Hawaiian spinner dolphins (*Stenella longirostris*).

night, as a loosely coordinated pod, it moves several miles out to sea to feed over deep water. Feeding dives may reach the upper mesopelagic zone. Here, spinners are apparently sometimes plagued by the insidious cookie-cutter shark, *Isistius brasiliensis,* which scoops out a chunk of flesh and disappears into the mesopelagic gloom before even a dolphin can react.[2]

As mammals, dolphins are fairly familiar to us in their general physiology and pattern of reproduction, nurture, and care of young. Much of our knowledge of the biology and behavior of spinners has been discovered by noted cetologist Kenneth Norris and his students at the University of California at Santa Cruz. Often in affiliation with the oceanarium at Sea Life Park on Oahu, Norris studied spinner dolphins in captivity and in the wild. His most successful observations of a wild population were accomplished at the Big Island's Kealakekua Bay. There, by watching from the overhanging cliffs, snorkeling in the bay's clear waters, and even following the spinners out to sea in a jerry-built submarine, Norris and his co-workers pioneered in the sociobiology of wild dolphins. These studies of Hawaiian spinners are published in scientific journals to be found in any university library.[3] Norris's popularly written summary, *The Porpoise Watcher,*[4] is an excellent starting point for anyone interested in dolphin biology and society.

Another popular book containing much information on spinners is Karen Pryor's *Lads Before the Wind;*[5] the title was taken from a paean to porpoises in Herman Melville's *Moby Dick.* Pryor was an innovative dolphin trainer at Sea Life Park. Her book emphasizes observations of captive dolphins of several species. She also worked with Norris at Kealakekua Bay, and *Lads Before the Wind* contains some unforgettable passages—one describes snorkeling through a wild pod of apparently sleeping spinners, slowly rising and sinking in cool, dappling sunlight.

The late Gregory Bateson, a behaviorist who conducted research on dolphins at Sea Life Park, once characterized spinners as resembling cats in their aloof, coquettish ways with their trainers. Other species, which develop an eager familiarity with humans, Bateson likened to dogs.[6]

Around the Hawaiian Islands there is currently little conspicuous threat to spinners and other dolphins. Of course, these mammals are fully protected by law. The same protection does not forestall poaching on sea turtles, but direct exploitation of dolphins seems to be a thing of the past. An instance of Hawaiians catching dolphins for food was recorded in 1840 by Titian Peale, a naturalist with the U.S. Exploring Expedition: "Sixty of these animals were driven ashore by natives at Hilo Bay, Island of Hawaii, at one time. They were considered a dainty food and yielded a valuable stock of oil."[7] The species involved in this incident was probably the melon-headed whale (also called the Hawaiian dolphin), classified by Peale as *Phocaena (Delphinus) pectoralis* and now renamed *Peponocephala electra*.[8]

Today, curiosity about dolphins by a large segment of the boating public is a subtle but perhaps serious threat to the animals. Well-intentioned harassment may displace dolphins from favorite resting bays. If these daytime habitats are ecologically important, possibly as nurseries for young and refugia from large pelagic sharks, their forced abandonment, even sporadically, may reduce coastal dolphin numbers. Spinner dolphin pods that include young animals seem to be shy and move away from aggressive human intrusion such as splashy swimmers and noisy boats.

In the Northwestern Hawaiian Islands (NWHI), the human presence is now negligible except on Midway and Kure Atoll. Yet dolphins may be more severely threatened in the NWHI if the oceanic drift-net fishery for squid (see chapter 8) continues and expands north of the islands. Already, in Alaskan waters, the same kind of net used in the salmon fishery has caused the deaths of thousands of Dall's porpoises *(Phocoenoides dalli)*.[9]

Dolphins are dynamic and enigmatic, close to human sensibilities in their playfulness and purported intelligence. However, when it comes to sheer fascination with more than a tinge of awe, the marine mammal to watch is one that has become a symbol of Hawaii. The humpback whale evokes the extravagant grandeur of the islands themselves.

Humpbacks inhabit all oceans, even the fringes of the Arctic. Worldwide, they have been classically divided into a number of more or less discreet populations, or "stocks." For example, there may be two or three stocks in the North Pacific and perhaps two in the North Atlantic. Similar subdivisions are found in the Southern Hemisphere. Each population is thought to migrate and breed largely as a unit. The pattern of migrations is poleward in summer for feeding and fattening, and equatorward in winter for breeding. Humpbacks do not appear to cross the equator; thus, northern and southern populations may be especially well segregated.

Much of the basic anatomical knowledge of humpbacks comes from Australian studies; the data were supplied by large catches of humpbacks in recent decades. Most of the information on behavior and natural history of humpbacks has come from recent American studies. Since about 1976, Hawaii has been a headquarters for the scientific observation of living humpback whales, free if not undisturbed in an ocean setting of eminent accessibility and island-girt beauty. The general account of the lives of humpbacks that follows has been gleaned from a number of recent sources.[10]

Humpbacks are medium-large whales. The largest of these animals reach a length of approximately fifty feet and a weight of thirty-five to forty tons. Humpbacks appear capable of living for fifty years or so. Both males and females reach sexual maturity at lengths of thirty-six to thirty-eight feet, when they are four or five years old. Females seem to average slightly larger than males at this age.

After a gestation period of eleven to twelve months, females calve and nurse, and often seem to mate as well, at wintering sites in the tropics or subtropics. Research in Hawaii indicates that at least some females come into estrus shortly after giving birth, and mating can occur at virtually any time during the period in which the female is nursing her calf. But this may vary regionally, or conception may fail to occur on an annual basis. Anatomical studies of Southern Hemisphere humpbacks indicate that many females are on a biennial cycle, with a resting year after each birth. Nursing lasts at least several months after the approximately twelve-foot-long calf is born. Toward the end of this time, calves begin to feed on small nekton but may also continue to nurse for a year or more. Yearlings frequently remain in close association with their mothers.

During much of the period spent on the wintering grounds (approximately between January and April in Hawaii), the female and her calf will be accompanied by what is called an escort whale. Invariably a male, the escort appears to defend the female and calf. In Australian waters, one escort was seen warding off killer whales, *Orcinus orca,* with smashing blows delivered by its flukes.[11] Much more often, escorts seem to ward off other male humpbacks. Hawaii researchers frequently find old scars and fresh scrapes and bruises on males, and particularly escorts; these wounds apparently derive from battles in which escorts struggle against rivals for the favored position near the female. Slashing strokes of the animals' massive tails and powerful butts of the head seem to account for most of the injuries. Escorts also appear to warn away or intimidate other adult whales by blowing masses of air bubbles in their paths. Presumably the escort acquires the first, or perhaps an exclusive, mating opportunity with a receptive female. However, a given escort is sometimes replaced by another individual after one of the bruising, battering skirmishes.

Another general behavioral trend noted in recent years is that females and calves will spend more time in very shallow water closer to shore than adult whales in general. Sometimes this movement inshore looks like an actual retreat from a roisterous battle of potential suitors. In such cases, the victorious male resumes the escort role and follows the female and calf, but typically remains slightly farther offshore and waits, perhaps in a protective vantage point.

Singing, for which humpback whales have become famous (numerous commercial recordings are currently available), is now thought to be an exclusively male activity. Cows have never been identified as singers. Some of the males positively identified as singers were clearly escorts, and with strong indications that mating is the goal of escort behavior, it seems possible that the striking and beautiful songs of these whales are love songs. Another possibility, less sentimental, is that they are war cries or threats directed at rival males. There is no evidence that whale-song involves language in an intellectual sense. It is surely not some kind of oral epic of the species—one of the more fanciful speculations of a decade ago. Current perceptions of the humpbacks' singing bring this behavior into the mainstream of scientific interpretation of similar displays by other animals—for example, birds and amphibians. Although whalesong may include far more detail than the tiny snatches of vocalizations by other species, the biological forces behind the songs are probably the same.

Many Hawaiian humpbacks may migrate from summering grounds near the central Aleutian Islands. However, in recent years known individuals among the Hawaiian migrants (identified from photographs of conspicuous natural markings) have been seen in the summer off Southeast Alaska. There they mingle with a putative eastern Pacific stock, which typically migrates to waters off Mexico. The positive identification of an individual humpback near Mexico's Socorro Island just two years after it was recorded in Hawaii further confirms overlap in North Pacific migrating populations.[12]

Furthermore, cetologists no longer view Hawaii as a simple fixed destination for the humpbacks. The whales apparently come in a slowly "passing parade." That is the phrase of Roger Payne, who pioneered in the study of humpback behavior in Bermuda and Hawaii. He was commenting on a study of Darling, Gibson, and Silber, which indicates that individual whales stay in Hawaii eleven weeks at most and not for the whole winter-spring season.[13] This realization has led to a happy reassessment of the size of the Hawaiian migratory population—from 200–500 in the late 1970s, when the group was viewed as static, to around 900 or more.[14]

Thus, we never see all the whales at one time around the islands. Where goes the parade when it leaves Hawaii, and what are the actual migration routes to and from the North Pacific? No one yet knows. Humpback whales or their evolutionary antecedents may well have migrated to Hawaii for millions of years. Calves may have been born in the shelter of northwestern high islands now laid low. Of course, there is no fossil record of whales in Hawaii to tell us of their tenure in the islands.

WHALES AND HUMANS IN HAWAII

University of Hawaii behaviorist Louis Herman takes the extreme alternative view that migratory humpbacks have appeared in Hawaiian waters only very recently.[15] On the basis of negative evidence—a lack of published information on Hawaiian humpbacks before the 1840s and an apparent lack of interaction with whales by prehistoric Hawaiians—Herman suggests that humpbacks only began to migrate to Hawaii around the mid-nineteenth century.

It may not be surprising that the ancient Hawaiians would have largely ignored whales. The Hawaiians were a practical people, and natural phenomena reflected in their culture were primarily those with which they had practical relationships. Whales would have been merely around— on a predictable seasonal schedule, but scattered in the ocean. They were useless as landmarks (unlike capes, peaks, and cinder cones, about which legends arose concerning memorable nearby events). Left alone, whales were not dangerous (unlike sharks, which did provide epic tales and efforts of appeasement). To the Hawaiians, large whales, which they called *kohola* (accent on the last syllable) may have seemed too difficult to tackle for food. More to the point, whales were probably never needed for food in Hawaii. Nevertheless, the Hawaiians took an interest in some whales. A prized possession among the *alii* (nobility) was the *palaoa*—in its paramount form, a sperm whale's tooth (lesser odontocete teeth were also valued and especially coveted by women of rank).[16] Before European contact, these teeth were apparently obtained from rare beached carcasses.

Herman's review (see note 15) of the scant aboriginal whale lore in the Pacific provides no real evidence that Polynesians anywhere hunted whales before being taught by Europeans and Americans. One or two

5.2 Nineteenth-century whaling in Hawaii.

cultural legends of whales come from the South Pacific, but despite Herman's regret that "there has been very little anthropological effort devoted to the topic of whales in Oceania," nothing in the prehistoric cultures there regarding an interest in whales leaps out to be noticed.

It seems as valid to assume that humpback whales were ignored in ancient times as to imagine that the old Hawaiians would have been overawed or would have reacted to them aesthetically or scientifically as we do today. A lack of lore and artistic representation of whales does not really imply their absence, as Herman suggests. It simply seems unlikely that *Megaptera* might have discovered Hawaiian wintering grounds only a century and a half ago when *Monachus* (the monk seal) must have found the islands, and from farther away, millions of years ago (see chapter 8).

Commercial whaling in the Pacific began in the early nineteenth century and increased rapidly, later explosively, in intensity and volume. By 1820, when a rich concentration of sperm whales was discovered off Japan, Hawaii began to be a home away from home for the foreign fleet. The fishery rapidly expanded. In April 1822, the touring English missionaries Tyerman and Bennett counted nineteen and twenty-four ships in port, respectively, at Kealakekua Bay and Honolulu.[17] Most of them were whaleships, with a few sandalwood traders. Ships from New England rapidly came to dominate the entire North Pacific, but more than a half-dozen European countries and the Hawaiian Kingdom itself were also represented by whaling vessels that rested and provisioned at Hawaiian ports during the classic era of Pacific whaling, which was to last until the 1870s.

The whaling captains early began to favor Lahaina, Maui, but a majority eventually gravitated to Honolulu as that village, with its reef-protected harbor, became the political and economic center of the islands. Lesser ports included Hilo and Kealakekua Bay on Hawaii and Koloa on Kauai. From the 1830s to the 1860s, the whaling business dominated Hawaii's economy. It involved provisioning and repairs to dozens and then hundreds of ships each year. It provided for transshipment of oil and whalebone (baleen) to the United States; after 1855, much of this went via the railroad across the Isthmus of Panama. Sundry services to captains and crews supported institutions as variable as bethels and banks, brothels and bars. Occasional bad years plagued the fishery, and in Hawaii businessmen worried about whether leviathan would endure. Several of his species in the northern seas nearly did not. During this hectic half-century, the widening chase spread west to the Marianas and Japan and then north to the Arctic Ocean. By the 1860s, whaling had even begun to shift to the southern ocean, creating boomlets in ports such as Russell, New Zealand. Then, for a time, the killing tapered off everywhere as whale oil prices fell in response to competition from a new and superior substitute, kerosene, produced abundantly after 1860 from cheap Pennsylvania petroleum.

During those decades of classic whaling, the islands were at the hub of the hunt. Through Hawaiian ports may well have passed the rendered essences of a majority of the right, bowhead, Pacific gray, and humpback whales that lived in the North Pacific and adjoining Arctic seas during the nineteenth century. Those were the easiest whales to catch. Of them, only the now cherished gray whale *(Eschrichtius robustus)* population of the eastern Pacific has recovered to what may be a healthy demographic status. Sperm whales, too, were drastically decimated beginning in the nineteenth century. In fact, they were more avidly sought than any other species, but their scattered populations were much larger and their wanderings wider and less predictable than those of the others. They were better survivors and even today are the most numerous of large whales.

The economic and sociological impacts in Hawaii of the classic whaling era are fairly well documented from about the 1840s on. However, a minor mystery has always existed regarding the fate of migratory humpbacks in Hawaiian waters during the nineteenth century. What was the pattern of their exploitation in Hawaii? Whales and whalers congregated in the islands during the same months of the year, and humpbacks could be caught in their nearshore calving areas with little effort and expense. During the midcentury decades, early Hawaiian news sources *(The Friend, The Polynesian, The Pacific Commercial Advertiser)* do indicate that opportunistic whaling was practiced locally. On Maui, shore-based whaling operations were noted beginning in the late 1840s. They were presumably established to attempt catching humpbacks, the only species that would consistently attract attention so close to the islands. But one company made news by taking a sperm whale.[18]

Founded in 1843, *The Friend* in particular specialized in maritime news. Reports of whale abundance and catch statistics of whaleships in remote Pacific locations appeared in the "Memoranda" section of every regular monthly issue. From the 1840s to the 1870s, *The Friend* contains only a handful of reports of humpbacks in local waters. Three of those reports appeared in 1855 and may indicate a resurgence of the Hawaiian humpback population around that time:

> January 1855 (communicated by S.E.B., a Lahaina correspondent): Two mates of whaleships have bought boats and whaling tackle and will engage in humpback whaling at Kalepolepo Bay on Maui. "I have often seen humpbacks in the channels around us and am sure they would have many chances for a fish" (vol. 4 [New Series], no. 1:2).

> April 1855: The whaling post at Kalepolepo, Maui, announced the capture of three humpbacks. "Well done, boys, this is making a better season of it than most of the ships" (vol. 4, no. 4:28).

> April 1855: The whaleship *Lark* took a humpback off Kawaihae, Hawaii. It yielded 45 barrels of oil which sold for about $1,400. at Honolulu. "More whales were seen, but the rugged weather prevented their capture" (vol. 4, no. 4:29).

These reports imply that the humpbacks were valuable, usually easy to catch, and probably widely distributed in Hawaiian waters. And if the local whales made a brief comeback in the 1850s, exploitation was rapid. In 1856, Lahaina business interests placed an ad in *The Polynesian* (16 February 1856: p. 162) designed to lure whaleship captains away from Honolulu ("they can amuse their leisure hours in taking whales in our harbor, thereby adding to their wealth").

In the winter of 1859, shore whaling stations on Maui were still successful. Kills by three of them were reported in the 10 March 1859 issue of *The Polynesian* (page 186). For every whale taken, however, others may have escaped wounded and later died. Whaling was especially easy in the islands because a harpooner could attach to a slow-moving calf and save his killing lances for the mother when she invariably came to the aid of her stricken infant.[19]

During the 1860s, humpbacks again seem to have become scarce in Hawaiian waters. *The Friend* contains perhaps the last echoes of the classic whaling era in Hawaii.

> April 1869: "Letter from Hilo" described the taking of a large whale close to shore by a Captain Fisher and his crew, which afforded local residents the opportunity to witness the "interesting and somewhat perilous operation of the capture of the whale" (vol. 19, no. 4:25).

Then, after two years with no mention of Hawaiian humpbacks,

> February 1871: A brief account of a humpback whale that drifted ashore at Koolau (Oahu). Apparently this whale had been wounded earlier by a whaleship. "The natives got a good store of oil" (vol. 21, no. 2:10).

The partially documented history of exploitation of Hawaiian humpbacks during the midnineteenth century suggests that the wintering populations were very low for some time before the late 1840s, then increased, were vigorously hunted, and shrank again. It seems likely that this cycle had begun some thirty years earlier, when the first whale hunters came to Hawaii and rapidly increased in numbers. The timing would seem about right: decimation, or commercial extinction, in the 1820s followed by slow recovery during the 1830s and 1840s. But that earlier cycle of exploitation, if it occurred, received no public notice. Here is a project for a maritime historian with access to whaleship logs and the correspondence of pioneering Yankee captains in the Pacific. Was there indeed a first intense phase of Hawaiian whaling before newspapers were published and catch statistics recorded in the islands?

By 1870, whaling was in decline all over the Pacific. Freed for a time from intense hunting pressure, the Hawaiian humpback population again may have begun to increase late in the nineteenth century. However, shore-based whaling persisted as a cottage industry long after the big overwintering fleets were just a memory. In his memoirs, the Hawaii entrepreneur Chun-Kun Ai described his family's token whaling business on the Big Island's Kona Coast in the 1890s.[20] He mentions that whales were commonly seen there, as they are now, within a mile or two of the shore.

Not long afterwards, in the early twentieth century, the hunting began again in earnest, although Hawaii no longer played any significant role in the business. With new technology and industrial power, species such as the humpback, which had been depleted in the Northern Hemisphere, were now progessively driven toward extinction everywhere in the world ocean. Whalebone was passé in ladies' fashions, but the animals' oil was in greater demand than before for lubricants, soaps, and cosmetics, and the meat now began to be processed, most of it ground up for animal feeds.

In the North Pacific, the last major whaling effort directed at humpbacks was by Russians in 1962 and 1963.[21] They took nearly 3,500 animals, drastically reducing the western Pacific stock, whose whales winter south of Japan. It is possible that this kill included some central Pacific (Hawaiian) migrants as well.

Since about 1970, whales have received widespread public attention. Movies and television have made cetaceans' spectacular forms, behavior, and vocalizations familiar to millions. Threats to the very existence of these animals and the idea that they might possess a high level of intelligence made for pressing and poignant arguments for their preservation. At a time when environmental awareness and sensitivity were making great upward leaps, whales were adopted as powerful symbols and standard bearers for those bent on protecting the oceans and the rest of the planet.

Humpbacks became especially well recognized in the early 1970s after Roger Payne of the New York Zoological Society began recording their eerie underwater voices off Bermuda. In the company of other researchers, Payne later shifted his humpback studies to Hawaiian waters, where during winter and spring off West Maui these whales are more concentrated and accessible than anywhere else in the world. In 1976, when research interest was mounting and the popularity of whales booming, the state of Hawaii declared the humpback its official state marine mammal, and in 1977 Maui County, encompassing the islands of Maui, Molokai, Lanai, and Kahoolawe, dedicated the waters off West Maui as a county whale reserve. These designations were of dubious benefit to the whales, however. They included no protective measures, but merely served to advertise the whales' presence.

The humpbacks were quickly exploited by the Hawaii tourist industry. If the typically calm, lee waters off West Maui were ideal for wintering whales, they were also perfect for boatloads of camera-clicking whale lovers. Indeed, the whales were loved, and they received raves for their performances. To new fleets of whale chasers and entrepreneurs in Lahaina, the whales were once again an economic resource.

For a time, concern for both whales and tourists focused on the fast hydrofoil ferries then plying the waters among the islands. The riskiest area for a collision between the giant, high-tech speedboats that cruised at sixty knots and the slow-moving humpbacks was near West Maui. By the end of the 1970s, however, Sea Flite, the hydrofoil company, had ceased operating in Hawaiian waters. No collisions had been recorded. The Maui volunteers, who with their spotter scopes and portable radios had watched and warned Sea Flite captains of whales in their cruise paths, came down from the nearshore hills.

Professional protection of whales in the United States waters is the responsibility of the National Marine Fisheries Service (NMFS), an agency of the Department of Commerce. Since 1972, with the passage of the Marine Mammal Protection Act, federal law has prohibited the "hunting, pursuit, and harassment" of marine mammals. Hunting is easily defined and fairly easily interpreted in the field, but recognizing and proving infractions involving pursuit and harassment are more difficult. In such cases, enforcement follows guidelines established by the NMFS after consultation with experts on the different species concerned. Regarding pursuit and harassment of humpback whales in Hawaii, present guidelines make it unlawful to come between a female and a calf or to approach within 100 yards of any humpback. Aircraft must maintain a vertical distance of more than 1,000 feet in a 300-yard radius surrounding any whale.

To look out over the wide waters among the islands is to realize that comprehensive surveillance of human encounters with whales is out of the question. Incredibly, the NMFS employs only two regular enforcement agents in Hawaii, although they get intermittent assistance from California-based colleagues. Even more surprisingly, these agents are charged not only with protecting whales, but also with enforcing compliance with a wide variety of other laws, regulations, and guidelines governing ocean fisheries. And as if this isn't enough, their territory of responsibility extends across the Pacific through the remaining U.S. territories in Micronesia to American Samoa and the Marianas Islands. A third agent stationed on Guam assists in the western part of the region.

Of recent concern is the possible harassment of whales by research scientists. While the general public must not approach whales closer than 100 yards, whale researchers can obtain special federal permits to come within touching distance. More critical screening of permit applications has begun to limit and coordinate research, especially to prevent duplication of work by different scientists.

All of these concerns for the well-being of the whales figured in a lengthy and laborious effort to establish a federal sanctuary for humpback whales in Hawaii. The effort began in 1977 and ended abortively in 1984. Along the way, the proposals, issue papers, environmental impact statements, public hearings, state legislative resolutions, lobbying, and news coverage featured predictable antagonists—environmentalists and scientists, including such notables as Kenneth Norris and Roger Payne, who promoted the sanctuary, versus a coalition of fishermen, charter-boat companies, and other maritime commercial interest groups who opposed it. On another level, far from real concerns about whales or multiple use of coastal waters, the main issue was "Who's in charge, the federal government or the state of Hawaii?"

The proposed Hawaii Humpback Whale National Marine Sanctuary[22] would have been unique in its focus on a single species as the resource protected. But the sanctuary proposal was swimming feebly amid turbulent controversy in the summer of 1984 when Hawaii Governor Ariyoshi, using a loophole in earlier agreements, declared he would withdraw state waters from inclusion in the project. Thus, like so many of the long-harried creatures it was intended to protect, the whale sanctuary movement received its mortal wound, rolled over, and died. A few months later, the whales returned to Hawaiian waters singing a song that, as expected, was a little different from that of the previous year. One wonders if it included a little rueful laughter during that season of 1984–1985.

Hawaii is still a place for whales. The public is increasingly sensitive about harassment, and Gene Witham, a senior official in the NMFS enforcement branch in Honolulu, reports that most of his agency's actions concerning humpbacks originate with whale sympathizers who call to report apparent violators. It is to be hoped that such voluntary public trusteeship will take the place of the defunct formal sanctuary.

The annual return of the whales to Hawaii has become a famous phenomenon, another natural wonder in a cluster of islands that is blessed with many of them. But still the whales cannot be taken for granted, a truth that was succinctly summed up by Professor Ian McTaggert Cowan, an eminent Canadian cetologist and one of the Hawaii whale sanctuary planners:

> Though it seems to some who live adjacent to the winter concentration area in Hawaii that the species is abundant, looked at against the world scene it is a rare and badly depleted species. . . . Given low birth rate, an unknown mortality rate from birth to sexual maturity, and an unknown rate of loss of adults, the Hawaiian stock can be seen as pitifully small and vulnerable.[23]

6

The Coral Rim

Coral reefs are among the earth's most impressive monuments to the power and persistence of life. Precipitated from clear, warm seawater, these constructions can gradually grow to a thickness of thousands of feet. Some of them, finally, are raised by tectonic forces into high continental mountains. Even after tens to hundreds of millions of years, such stranded fossil reefs often reveal the intricate signatures of their tiny primitive artisans. Beside their works, the mightiest and most durable human artifacts are evanescent.

Most tropical reefs house tremendously complex ecosystems with many hundreds of different life forms contributing to a welter of geobiological processes. But the permanence and preeminence of the main type of tropical reef habitat are due not to corals alone, but to the combined life forces of those simple animals and simple kinds of plants called algae.

Modern research has confirmed that the algae are at least as important in reef formation and maintenance as the corals.[1] Two categories of algae are involved. One type exists as single cells that invade the soft tissues of larval corals even before they begin the rapid growth and colonial development that produces a massive skeleton of limestone. These single-celled plant invaders are called zooxanthellae.

Although they actively penetrate and then grow and divide within the tissue-thin flesh of corals, zooxanthellae are the antithesis of a parasite. The symbiotic relationship they establish with a coral is known as mutualism, a partnership between two dissimilar organisms in which both partners benefit. Covered by translucent membranes, the algae bask in a protective living greenhouse, a milieu that supplies ample carbon dioxide and high-nitrogen fertilizer (both coral waste products) for plant-cell growth. The coral benefits largely from the fact that the presence of the algae changes its internal chemistry in a way that allows it to grow much faster than it could alone. Absorption of carbon dioxide during photosynthesis by zooxanthellae reduces the acidity in the coral's tissues, making it possible for the coral to deposit limestone (calcium carbonate) in its skeleton at a rapid rate.

Zooxanthellae must possess some simple power of selectivity, for not all types of corals become hosts to them. The so-called hermatypic corals that harbor zooxanthellae are reef builders; other corals, which lack this symbiotic companionship, tend to be far less massive in stature and grow much more slowly. In Hawaii, according to recent estimates, some forty hermatypic species are distributed among sixteen genera. However, only three species in two of those genera, *Porites* and *Pocillopora,* account for more than 90 percent of the acreage of Hawaiian reefs covered by living corals.[2]

The role of the hermatypic corals is to establish the reef's framework, a chockablock arrangement of living and growing boulders, stony plates, and multitined candelabralike forms. These grow most vigorously within a few feet of the surface. Down the outer reef slope, over a vertical range of several tens of feet, growth of these framework corals diminishes rapidly. The reason is that fading light limits the photosynthesis of the zooxanthellae, and this in turn curtails the rapid deposition of the coral's calcium carbonate, the stony stuff of the reef.

The second major role in reef construction is that of sediment production; again, this material is primarily calcium carbonate, the most common skeletal substance of marine life in general. Under a microscope, the sediment grains are often recognizable as bits and pieces of once-living creatures of the reef: shelled protozoans, sponges, sea urchins and starfish, snails and clams, and many others. And in terms of sheer tonnage, the sediment outweighs and outbulks the framework corals. Like drifting snow, this sand and mud fills the irregular gaps, cracks, and voids among the coherent coral "heads." Thus, the living canopy of the reef manages to stay only a little above a rising floor consisting of the reef's past sweepings and midden debris.

However, on most coral reefs, certain types of algae are the greatest producers of sediment, sometimes contributing more than half the total mass of the reef itself. Unlike the tiny cryptic zooxanthellae, albeit often scarcely less strange, they are many-celled forms. Most of these brittle plants—for example, species in the genera *Porolithon* and *Lithothamnion*—collectively called calcareous, or coralline, algae, are pink or reddish in color. They are allied to a major group of algae, the phylum Rhodophyta. As vegetation, these calcareous red algae assume outlandish dimensions. Some grow as thin pink layers over rocky surfaces in shallow water; others form rugose stony balls that look like small coral heads. They precipitate limestone out of calcium and carbon dioxide in sea water faster than any coral. Some of the ball-like and encrusting forms have a role in framework formation, particularly on the shallow crest of the reef, but most are relatively fragile. A few of the sediment producers on the reef are green algae (Chlorophyta)—for example, species of the genus *Halimeda,* which are common throughout the world's tropics. They resemble miniature sprigs of prickly-pear cactus, but are rigidly constructed with tiny limestone plates underlying a green veneer of living cells.

Beyond framework and sediment production, one other major role of organisms is vital to reef formation. The reef dwellers involved live primarily on or in the sediments that fill the framework interstices. Their tubes, organic cements, filamentous projections, and meshworks—a variety of organic anchoring devices—help to bind the loose stuff together. Sediment binding seems especially important near the outer edge of a reef or along channels abutting on deep water. Such organisms, through adaptations for their individual survival, help to hold the upper reef sediments in place against the winnowing action of currents and surge, and the erosive power of storms.

Finally, well below the thin living surface of the reef, a process of physical compaction and chemical cementation fuses the entire mass of sediment and chunks of framework into a hard composite limestone.

All three of the classic reef types—fringing, barrier, and atoll—are represented in the Hawaiian Archipelago, although only one clear-cut barrier reef exists. It lies off Oahu's Kaneohe Bay.[3] Fringing reefs, coralline terraces built out from shore on a high island's submarine flank, are the type seen by most visitors to the islands. Here and there on the shallow shelf, or reef flat, which ranges from a few inches to a few feet deep, framework corals grow almost to the surface until they are killed back by tidal exposure or freshwater damage from major storms. Typically, the active sustained reef growth is along the seaward edge. There, in a strikingly narrow band, the largely monotonous reef flat gives way to a diverse, flourishing, bouldery maze of framework corals. Coralline algae appear less sensitive to fresh water and exposure. They often dominate the reef's rocky surfaces near outlets of freshwater streams.

Around the main Hawaiian Islands, the coral rim, with its colorful fishes and other organisms, is irregular and discontinuous. Hawaii's reefs vary from mere strips a few tens of yards wide to immense shoals reaching more than a mile offshore. The widest are those off the south coast of Molokai, and here, they also form one of the longest continuous Hawaiian reef formations—about thirty miles long—broken only by a few offshore extensions of stream channels, some of which have been widened and deepened to serve as small harbors.

Elsewhere around the main islands the prevailing pattern of reef development has been patchy. Although wide fringing reefs occur along some coasts of Kauai, Oahu, and Lanai, they are interrupted wherever rocky points and ridges thrust out to sea. In fact, the control of reef formation by island topography is striking. If they are present at all, reefs occur exceedingly sparsely and are barely developed off coastlines that rise steeply from the sea. Thus, Maui's reefs are limited in occurrence, and the Big Island, except off the gently sloping North Kona Coast, is largely bereft of coral reefs.

There may be a variety of reasons why reefs generally fail to form off steep shores despite abundant settlement of individual coral larvae and coralline algae. On rainy coasts such as occur north of Hilo on the Big Island, steep terrain offers no catchment such as floodplains or estuarine marshes to retard floodwaters. Muddy torrents pour freely down the valleys and into the sea, flooding the nearshore zone. Both fresh water and smothering silt damage or kill coral. Off such coasts, fresh water also emerges under pressure from seafloor aquifers. This phenomenon was well known to the prehistoric Hawaiians and described by early foreign explorers such as the astute Hilo missionary Titus Coan. He noted the roiling disturbance at the sea surface caused by masses of upwelling, buoyant fresh water from hidden underwater springs.[4] Today, scuba divers discover them as large rooms or house-sized volumes of cold water rising from cracks in the seafloor. On the outside, fish play skittishly along the blurry borders formed by the mixing of fresh water with salt; inside the cold, transparent space, one finds gray rocks devoid of obvious life.

Where seacliffs have formed, storm waves toss rock debris around the nearshore bottom. Reef development is probably impossible in such a chaotic, bowling-alley milieu. In zones of active vertical faulting, coral reefs may be carried down to killing depths in a series of earthquakes. This seems to be what happened to coral reefs that grew perhaps less than 10,000 years ago along the northwestern coast of the Big Island. Those defunct reefs now lie between about 3,000 and 5,000 feet deep on the Kohala Submarine Terrace.[5]

Of the living reefs of Hawaii, many of the best developed are in the Northwestern Hawaiian Islands (NWHI), the part of the chain beyond Kauai and Niihau. Here, in such places as French Frigate Shoals (FFS) and the smaller atolls of Midway and Kure, are textbook coral reefs: ramparts of living rock that break deep ocean swells and protect sprawling, blue-green shoals behind. Yet on some of the shallow plateaus here, notably those surmounted by the volcanic remnants of Nihoa, Necker, and Gardner Pinnacles, reefs have not developed in recent times even though framework corals grow on the bottom for many miles around the volcanic stubs. The failure of reefs to form in these places has never been satisfactorily explained.

In the main islands, as noted, the best reef development is off flat or gently rising older coasts. Even in such places, the typical fringing reefs are broken by drainage channels that trace to nearby coastal streams and rivers. The channels are probably maintained by a reef-killing combination of freshwater runoff, siltation, and erosive power of storm drainage. On the whole, the high-island reefs may be more vulnerable to damage by storms and perhaps *tsunamis* than the reefs of the NWHI.

LIFE ON THE REEFS

The life of Hawaiian reefs and coastal shallows, even though not as varied as that of other tropical marine beauty spots, notably in the western tropical Pacific and Caribbean, comprises a wonderful panoply of sea creatures. There is not room in this chapter, nor indeed in a whole book of this length, to adequately describe even the conspicuous Hawaiian marine life that one could encounter in an underwater excursion from the shoreline out to the modest depths that limit the growth of hermatypic corals. The summary of nearshore marine life that follows can be supplemented with publications of the Bernice P. Bishop Museum, University of Hawaii, and others. Field guides to Hawaiian reef and shore life are available in local bookstores and scuba shops. The references cited in the following sections are only a few islets in the vast archipelago of marine biological literature concerning Hawaii and the tropical Pacific.

Reef and Shore Algae

The simple multicellular plants of the benthic, or bottom, nearshore environment, come in three basic colors: red, green, and brown.[6] These form the basis for the major algal subdivisions. Already noted are the calcareous forms of red and green algae that are primary sediment contributors to the reef mass, but there are many other kinds with little or no calcium carbonate mineralization. They exhibit a variety of growth forms ranging from encrusting, lichenlike plants to miniature tree shapes up to a few inches high. Among the largest Hawaiian benthic algae are some of the browns, notably the diffusely branching *Dictyopteris,* whose soft shrubbery grows to be perhaps a foot high from shallow flats and bay bottoms. Superficially resembling *Dictyopteris* but more robust and rigidly textured are species of Hawaiian *Sargassum,* bottom-dwelling plants related to the famous floating types of this seaweed, namesakes of the Sargasso Sea. On many Hawaiian reef flats, the rat's foot algae, *Turbinaria,* is a common sight to snorkelers. Only three or four inches high, its short, thick, rubbery branches terminate in fringed swellings that, with a stretch of the imagination, resemble little clawed feet. Also ubiquitous in Hawaiian shallows are species of *Padina,* whose rippled, fanlike fronds are often lightly calcified. These tropical brown algae are distantly related to the much larger rockweeds and kelps of cooler continental waters.

Like the brown algae, greens are usually true to their color. Among the most common are species of *Ulva,* the sea lettuce, a genus that is quickly recognized by beachcombers the world over. Dense growths of *Ulva* in Hawaii often signify proximity to excess plant nutrients, as for example in the vicinity of sewage outfalls and near the mouths of streams that drain overfertilized residential subdivisions. Other greens are common here and there on Hawaiian reef flats and along rocky volcanic shorelines: dark green *Codium,* with its stubby, fingerlike growth; delicate *Caulerpa,* with its fronds like tiny ferns or miniature clusters of grapes; and *Cladophora* in grasslike tufts.

Superficially, red algae are often the most difficult to recognize. They can exhibit many colors other than the typical red or pink, and most species in Hawaii are quite small, huddling within an inch or two of a rocky bottom. One of the larger rhodophytes is *Ahnfeltia,* grassy-looking algae found in the intertidal zone. Often yellowish in color, it sometimes produces extensive mats on the rocks. *Ahnfeltia's* habitat is the high intertidal. Many more kinds of red algae commonly dominate the lowest rocky intertidal zone on coasts with moderate to strong surf. Here, the biological community is often characterized as an algal turf. Where it is best developed, dozens of species of algae form a dense carpet of many colors on the rocks and in pools and sluice channels. It is a rich feeding ground for many kinds of small marine animals that graze over and within this stubbly forest an inch or two high. The algal turf extends offshore on shelving rocks, but is generally most diverse at the very base of the intertidal zone. Perhaps this is because fewer kinds and numbers of grazing animals are able to hold their place amid the churning wash of the surf than in quieter conditions a short way offshore.

Major Invertebrates

Except for the conspicuous corals themselves, most invertebrates—animals without backbones, which include the overwhelming majority of forms in the animal kingdom—are often overlooked by explorers of Hawaiian reefs. However, they are present in great abundance and diversity.[7] While their scientific classification is based on numerous technical points of anatomy, we can group them in ways that cut across traditional zoological relationships and relate to their activities and functions in nearshore waters and on the reefs.

First, a majority of these animals begin life as drifting eggs and larvae. Their fate is not as well studied as that of nearshore fish larvae (see chapter 4). Although some are carried offshore by currents and may or may not return to the island of their origin, many seem to remain in coastal waters, where they must balance the advantages of richer feeding and faster growth against a greater abundance of predators. Once they have metamorphosed and assumed their adult form, these creatures begin to take up lifestyles by which they might be categorized, though not always exclusively, as clingers, creepers, burrowers, leapers, or swimmers.

Sponges and Other Clingers. Hawaiian sponges tend to be fairly small. None of the large vases and other giant forms of these simplest of multicellular animals that are so conspicuous on reefs of the Caribbean are found in Hawaii. Here, the most common sponge habitat is underneath rocks, where sometimes a natural display of sponges will resemble a sloppy artist's palette of vivid color patches—reds, oranges, yellows, blues.

To the untutored eye, tunicates often resemble sponges. This is especially true of the often brightly colored colonial forms of these strange, rubbery-textured animals whose bodies are enclosed in a thick, flexible protective sheath, the tunic. But the internal anatomy of tunicates, with its highly integrated systems of tissues and organs, is vastly more complex than that of sponges. This is true as well of the solitary tunicates, often called sea squirts, which do not form colonies under one tunic, but still may occur in clusters on rocks, pier pilings, and other hard surfaces in the shallows of the reef. Tunicate larvae, known as invertebrate tadpoles, are anatomically more sophisticated than adult tunicates. These microscopic swimmers, before they settle to the bottom and metamorphose, possess several basic features of fishes and other vertebrates. Some of the best evolutionary speculation has it that vertebrates arose from invertebrates through a stage similar to these transitional tadpoles. Thus, of the invertebrates of the reef, the lowly tunicates clinging to the rocks could be our closest kin.

Coral Relatives. These include hydroids along with anemones, zoanthids, and certain other flowerlike animals that possess specialized stinging cells, called nematocysts, for defense and catching prey. Many of them in Hawaii are small and inconspicuous clingers on rocks and shells. Hydroids are generally delicately constructed as compared to the usually robust anemones and zoanthids.

Hydroids have an alter ego, the swimming medusa, or jellyfish. One form begets the other in an alternation of generations. Most Hawaiian jellyfishes are small, even microscopic, and rarely noticed by a swimmer. The Portuguese Man-of-War *(Physalia)*, which blows in from the blue epipelagic to litter many Hawaiian beaches during windy weather, is a peculiar relative of hydroids and jellyfishes. Instead of having a fleshy, pulsating bell for swimming, the Man-of-War possesses a gas-filled, sail-like float.

The anemones and zoanthids are more closely related to corals than hydroids. They have no jellyfish stage. Generally familiar to snorkelers and tidepool explorers, they are still often overlooked when they assume a puckered posture, hiding their circlets of identifying tentacles. While most anemones cling to rocks, a few have adapted to live on sand, where they anchor themselves in a tube that extends some distance into the bottom. A quite different way of life is seen in *Calliactis polypus*, common in Hawaii which hitchhikes on shells occupied by hermit crabs. Zoanthids *(Zoanthus* and *Palythoa)* often look like clusters of small and uniform-sized anemones with short, stubby tentacles. However, they are colonial creatures that form rubbery mats in shallow water, often intertidally. When the tentacles of a patch of zoanthids are expanded, the surface of the colony commonly appears greenish owing to the presence of symbiotic algae in the surface tissues of the animals. Some of the Hawaiian zoanthids possess potent toxins. On Maui, the old Hawaiians named one of these species *limu make o Hana,* meaning the deadly seaweed of Hana. They reportedly smeared spear tips with extracts of this zoanthid. Hawaiian lore asserts that even a slight wound from the poisoned spear could kill a man.

Sea Urchins and Their Kin. Other clinging invertebrates of Hawaii's reefs and rocky coasts include the sea urchins, which are adept at maintaining a fierce grip on the substratum amid strong surges of water. One that clings in the wildest surf on exposed coasts is *Colobocentrotus*

6.1 Common reef invertebrates. Near top: nudibranchs on the coral *Porites lobata*. Middle region: antler coral, *Pocillopora eydouxi;* the slate-pencil urchin, *Heterocentrotus mammilatus;* and starfish, *Linckia multiflora* on an encrusting coral (genus *Montipora*). Near bottom: the 7–11 crab, *Carpilius maculatus;* burrowing urchin (genus *Echinometra*); and tentacles of spaghetti worm (*Loimia medusa*).

atratus. This armor-plated, dome-shaped little urchin is never seen in zones of quiet water. The more typical urchins, with their pincushion defenses, live away from the worst of the surf, or else in places where they can shelter in crevices and holes, often of their own making.

Clingers can also be creepers. Urchins creep on their hundreds of little tube feet, and some even burrow into the softer varieties of rocky bottom. They forage in a small local area, then consistently return to a preferred clinging spot, and there gradually rotate and rasp their way deeper, forming a protective pocket in the rock. Along some Hawaiian coastlines, intertidal and shallow-water urchins of the genus *Echinometra,* turn coralline and volcanic terrain alike into a semblance of stony Swiss cheese. Sea urchins in general may be important agents of reef-habitat renewal over a wide range of depth. Because they feed by scraping rocky surfaces, they create newly cleared space for the settlement and growth of new generations of algae and clinging invertebrates, including corals. Their role on the reef resembles that of fire under natural conditions on land. Too many or too few urchins, however, can destroy the balance that maintains a healthy underwater landscape.

Numerous other echinoderms, such relatives of sea urchins as starfishes and sea cucumbers, are locally common on Hawaiian reef lands and nearshore bottoms. Among the more conspicuous are the sea stars *Linckia* and *Acanthaster.* The former features five long arms (in uninjured specimens) and a clean, smooth texture. The largest are more than a foot in diameter and are often a brilliant blue. *Acanthaster* is a beast of another color, shape, and texture. This is the infamous crown-of-thorns starfish. Its many arms (ten to eighteen are common) are short and thick and extend from a wide central disk. The upper surface is covered with stout, sharp, and moderately toxic spines. Draped on the reef, larger specimens, which reach eighteen inches in diameter, resemble exotic, red-and-green and very bristly circular doormats. It is fortunate that these creatures are not abundant in Hawaii, for they are insatiable coral eaters. The cushion star, *Culcita,* is another coral eater, but less voracious. Its greatly inflated form all but hides its five arms. Its colors are stunning: red to purple laced with delicate white or yellow tracery. Another group, the so-called brittle stars, are a class apart from the sea stars mentioned above. Brittle stars are much more lively and move with rapid, thrashing movements of their long, snaky arms. For all that, however, they roam only at night. During the day, almost any rock turned on a Hawaiian reef flat will reveal one or more brittle stars of the genus *Ophiocoma.* An average specimen spans two or three inches in diameter. They may well be the most abundant reef animals of their size range in Hawaii.

The sea cucumbers round out the echinoderm creepers on the reef. Sluggish, thick, dun-colored forms in the genera *Holothuria* and *Actin-*

opyga can be found nearly everywhere in the shallows. The more active and brightly patterned soft-bodied *Ophiodesoma* is often taken for a large worm. These "slinkies," as they are sometimes called, frequent calm, protected bays. These animals are sediment swallowers, digesting what they can from their haphazard diet.

The remaining major groups of reef invertebrates include many kinds of worms, mollusks, and crustaceans. The majority of them are far less conspicuous than the animals discussed so far. Of Hawaii's host of marine worms, most are burrowers and seldom seen. Some are important as sediment binders on the reef; they form dense clusters of tubes that act like snow fences to prevent shifting of the loose bottom sediment. Other worms, however, are clingers. One such is the feather duster *(Sabellastarte),* which, with its body surrounded by a sediment-formed tube and protectively ensconced in the interstices of dead coral, pokes a large, conical fan of tentacles out into the water to feed. Its nourishment comes from tiny drifting organic particles caught by the fan and funneled to the waiting mouth. Another tentacle feeder is the spaghetti worm, *Loimia.* Its long, white tentacles, poking from under a rock, catch food particles on their surfaces; they look like a large cluster of fishing lines constantly being reeled in and out. One of the more unusual burrowing worms is *Spirobranchus,* the Christmas tree worm. Its small (about one-half-inch diameter) spiraling array of feeding tentacles projects from its burrow in a living coral colony. This is one of few organisms able to make a home on the growing surface of a coral.

The mollusks are best known as shelled creatures—snails and clams—but also comprise squids and octopuses, among other less familiar animals. Not all snails have shells, and some of those exceptions are among the most colorful of Hawaiian reef life, the nudibranchs.[8] The epitome among them must be the Spanish dancer *(Hexabranchus),* which grows up to ten inches long (four to six inches is more typical). This lovely gliding creature, scarlet with flecks of cream color or yellow, is a wonderful find for a snorkeler. If it is gently lifted off the bottom and released in open water it will perform its flamenco-style dance, flapping and gyrating until it again settles to ground. Such instinctual antics, along with the brilliant colors of many nudibranchs, are thought to advertise to potential predators that these creatures are distasteful or poisonous. Sometimes large flatworms are mistaken for nudibranchs on Hawaiian reefs. They too feature brilliant, day-glo colors, but they lack the clustered external gills of the nudibranchs and overall are much more simply constructed animals.

Many of Hawaii's shelled snails are famous for their beauty. Some, such as augers *(Terebra, Hastula),* miters *(Mitra),* and many of the cone shells *(Conus)* hide it by burrowing in sand; others cover it up with a coating of rough protein that often incorporates a felt of algae. The sensuous cowries *(Cypraea)* partially conceal it through the thin veil of their mantle tissue, but when touched they retract the veil and reveal smooth, lovely curves and stunning nacreous patterns.

Most of the snails are creepers, but some are inveterate clingers. Hawaiian limpets, called *opihi (Cellana),* are famous for adhering (excuse the pun) to this lifestyle. In the zone of most powerful surf, they share coastal rocks with the little purple *Colobocentrotus* urchins. Adaptive evolution has given both animals a shallow, conical shape, the best design to shed the ferocious energy of the breakers.

Many of the bivalves are burrowers in sediments and thus not usually observed by explorers on the reef. A few, such as the date mussels *(Lithophaga),* are borers into limestone and, like the rock-burrowing sea urchins, can be locally important in eroding the substratum. Yet other bivalves, such as *Pinctada,* whose species are known as pearl oysters, are clingers and slow creepers. These flat, plate-shaped bivalves fasten to rocks by means of a short cluster of tough anchoring threads called a byssus. Occasionally they cast off their mooring lines and move to another spot by creeping with a wormlike foot. Long ago, a few places in Hawaii were famous for concentrations of pearl oysters, but they are uncommon today. Found under rocks in shallow water, the much smaller hatchet oysters *(Isognomon)* are sometimes confused with true pearl oysters. The large clinging bivalve commonly called the jewel box *(Chama iostoma)* is found attached by its own cement to underwater boulders often as deep as sixty feet. Jewel boxes are so well disguised, however, that they look like mere knobs on the rocks. The vast majority of bivalves, including the ones named above, are filter feeders, merely straining tiny particles out of the water and consuming the edible ones.

The most transcendent of the mollusks are the squids and octopuses. True squids are uncommon around Hawaiian reefs. The primary haunts of these masterful swimmers lie seaward in pelagic inner space. However, the octopus, which is called a squid by local fishermen, is mainly a night-active bottom creature. Two species of octopus are still locally common on some Hawaiian reefs, where they stalk and seize prey such as crabs and cowries. Sometimes they become swimmers, using powerful jets of water to propel themselves away from danger.

Crustaceans constitute the last major group of reef invertebrates. They are members of the great phylum of arthropods (joint-legged animals). Their familiar relatives, the insects, dominate many habitats on land, and the crustaceans have been similarly successful in occupying the sea. Many kinds are found in coral reef environments. They range from barnacles (inconspicuous in Hawaii) to tiny, flitting copepods to familiar and not so familiar crabs, hermit crabs, shrimps, tropical lobsters, and others.

Many of the copepods are benthic creepers or burrowers, somewhat more robust than the delicate swimming types usually depicted in elementary textbooks, films, and the *National Geographic*. A few of the crabs are good swimmers, fast as an average fish. Their last pair of legs has become a set of flattened, articulated paddles, capable of high-speed swimming strokes; such crabs appear to turn on a dime without slowing down. Various species of the mantis shrimps make their home in lairs and burrows on the reef. Some of these creatures, also called stomatopods, reach twelve inches in length. Distantly related to the common run of shrimp (decapods), the stomatopods are spectacular predators. One group, the spearers, transfix soft-bodied prey such as fish with lightning fencing lunges of barbed, rapierlike anterior appendages. A second group, the smashers, use rock-hard "knuckles" on the same appendages to crack open shelled prey such as clams and crabs. Reportedly, big smashers can strike with the force of a small-caliber bullet.[9] The large tropical lobsters—that is, the spiny variety, *Panulirus,* and the less familiar, flattened slipper lobsters, *Scyllarides*—have been badly depleted off settled Hawaiian shores. These days in Honolulu, restaurant populations of lobster tails mainly imported from Australia and Mexico are larger than those on local reefs. Also found in Hawaii in modest numbers is a small clawed lobster that, except for a being strangely covered with bristles, resembles the famous New England crustacean.

Major Reef Fishes

While the corals and algae of Hawaiian reefs are generally drab and the invertebrates, with a few exceptions, are inconspicuous, fishes create wonderful displays of color and motion in the nearshore waters of the islands.[10] Several major families of reef fishes—butterflyfishes, surgeonfishes, wrasses, and damsels—are known for their flamboyant species. However, others, such as blennies, gobies, and scorpion fishes, are often cryptically colored, or camouflaged. Yet others can be brightly hued or distinctly patterned, as are squirrelfishes, cardinalfishes, and many moray eels, but spend the day in hidden places and emerge after dark. The scientific view of fishes on the reef now extends far beyond mere classification. Fishes are more than just decorative browsers or predators on the scene, but play more subtle ecological roles. For example, species that forage away from the reef and return to shelter are importers of vital nutrients.[11] They provide extra fertilizing nutrients for the growth of reef algae, perhaps even the zooxanthellae in their hermatypic hosts. Many such invisible threads of dependence form a vital and subtle web of interactions in the reef's living, growing fabric of many colors, patterns, and textures.

Butterflyfishes (Family Chaetodontidae). These are the little classic gems of the reef. They flit over the corals and sand channels picking off tiny prey and other organic material as they browse on exposed surfaces. Typically ovate in shape and averaging three to six inches in length, they are divided into numerous species; most are easily recognizable by their bright colors and bold patterns. They are often solitary though are sometimes found in pairs and rarely in groups. Some feature false eyespots near the tail or dorsal fin, and a cryptic stripe or splotch may conceal the real eye to confuse a lunging predator. Butterflyfishes are closely related to angelfishes (classified by some in a separate family, Pomacanthidae). The brilliantly striped *Pomacanthus imperator,* the imperial angelfish, up to fiften inches long, is the largest of this group on Hawaiian reefs. This species must be a rare immigrant in the islands. It has only been reported once.

Surgeonfishes (Family Acanthuridae). Although overall not as vividly colored as the butterflyfishes, some surgeons, also known as tangs, are nevertheless brightly splotched or boldly striped. The most common surgeon on Hawaiian reefs is the convict tang, or *manini (Acanthurus sandvicensis)*. The name "convict" comes from its pattern of vertical black bars on otherwise pale gray skin. *Manini* means small, or of little significance. This fish, often seen in large schools grazing on the algal turf over rocky bottom, rarely exceeds about six inches in length. Another small surgeon, common on leeward reefs, is the lovely, all-yellow *Zebrasoma flavescens*. The largest tangs in Hawaii reach about two feet in length, among them the peculiar unicorn fishes, or horned *kala*. Two such species in the genus *Naso* develop blunt, bony projections on their foreheads.

Wrasses (Family Labridae). This is a large, colorful, and diverse group varying greatly in size from the little three-inch cleaner wrasse *(Labroides phthirophagus),* to species that in Hawaii reach more than two feet long. The cleaner wrasse, of course, is well known to tropical snorkelers as the proprietor of a cleaning station—a grooming parlor that attracts many larger species on the reef. *Labroides* removes skin parasites from its customers and even picks their teeth for them; the gleanings provide its nourishment. Many other less specialized but often colorful wrasses live in the nearshore waters of the islands. In most cases juveniles are strikingly different in colors and patterns from adults of the same species, and past ichthyologists have sometimes named two species where only one exists. Extreme sexual dimorphism is common in wrasses too; this trait is also found in parrotfishes, and in both it correlates with routine sex changes of individuals of these fish families. Wrasses are day-active predators. They virtually disappear at night, and it is thought that most species bury themselves in patches of sandy bottom. The little cleaner wrasses, however, spend the night like the parrotfishes, on a rocky

6.2   Common Hawaiian reef fishes. Near top: parrotfish, *Scarus perspicillatus* and a pair of unicorn tang, *Naso unicornis.* Mid-level (left to right): *manini,* or convict tang, *Acanthurus triostegus;* moorish idol, *Zanclus cornutus;* and racoon butterflyfish, *Chaetodon lunula.* Bottom: triggerfish, *Rhinecanthus rectangulus* (*humuhumunukunukuapuaa*) and damsels, *Dascyllus albisella.*

surface, but wrapped in a quilt of mucus that they secrete around themselves.

Parrotfishes (family Scaridae), called *uhu* in Hawaiian, are closely related to wrasses but on Hawaiian reefs are often much larger. They are major predators of reef-building corals. They possess a hard, bony beak used to scrape the thin layer of organic tissue from living coral surfaces. Some of the tropical puffers (family Tetraodontidae, with several species in Hawaii) feed in the same manner. Large populations of these coral feeders can cause significant local damage to reefs. The white scrapes left by fish bite on corals can take weeks to heal and can become infected by pathogenic microbes, especially in zones of chronic pollution.

Damselfishes (Family Pomacentridae). Damsels are active little fishes, some colorful or boldly patterned, others quite drab. A few are solitary and pugnaciously defend a small patch of territory on the reef or in a tidepool. Others school around a single, large coral head and dive as one into its protective crevices when danger looms. The sergeant major, *Abudefduf abdominalis,* is unusual for a damsel. A relatively large member of its family, up to eight inches long, it forms large schools in open water along the edges of reefs in relatively protected waters. Its vertical black-barred pattern somewhat resembles that of the *manini* tang, but novice snorkelers can distinguish *A. abdominalis* by its overall yellowish cast and its plankton-feeding habits.

This marvelous potpourri of fishes makes Hawaiian reefs into a dream landscape alive with gliding, flitting, darting creatures of dazzling color. Along the bottom, less conspicuous than the types noted above, are many others. Lizardfishes wait in ambush for unwary small fry. Moray eels of several species lurk in crevices. Big-eyed squirrelfishes and cardinalfishes huddle in rocky caves by day. Most of them have bright red pigmentation, and in some unfished spots—for several of these species are delectable quarry for spearfishermen—the dark recesses of a coral cavern may be so packed with hovering fishes that it flashes red in the beam of a diver's light. Hawkfishes act more like kingfishers. Perched on a coral snag over-looking a small sand channel, one will swoop down on small prey—fish or invertebrate—and then return to its waiting station. Goatfishes roam sandy bottom, sensing small prey with their chin barbels. Young are sometimes seen in large schools; older individuals are solitary or associate in pairs. Clownish, solitary triggerfishes, including the common *Rhinecanthus rectangulus*—the famous *humuhumunukunukuapuaa* of Hawaiian songs and legends—roam the outer surface of the reef. Most of the venomous scorpionfishes *(nohu)* blend into mottled scruffy terrain where they ambush their prey, but one Hawaiian species, *Taenianotus triacanthus,* with its bright, variable color and pattern, resembles a frond of seaweed and behaves accordingly. It sways gently back and forth in one spot to deceive both potential prey and predators. The gaudy lion-fish, or turkeyfish *(Pterois sphex)*, is an exhibitionist among scorpaenids. In the face of a threat these small fish, which reach only a few inches in length in Hawaii, flaunt their venomous hypodermic weaponry.

Overall, the reef life of Hawaii is remarkably similar from one end of the archipelago to the other. Nevertheless, over this span, which would reach halfway across the continental United States, one finds some nota-ble regional differences. One of the most obvious is that the reefs of the NWHI play host to the Hawaiian seal, *Monachus schauinslandi.* They are almost never seen around the main islands. Large Hawaiian green turtles, *Chelonia mydas,* do roam the entire chain, but are much more abundant in the NWHI, as are sharks. The latter, especially the gray reef shark *(Carcharinus amblyrynchos)*, the Galápagos shark *(C. galapagensis)*, and the tiger shark *(Galeocerdo cuvieri)* are major predators on the reefs of the NWHI.[12] In the main islands, sharks are rarely seen on the reefs or in coastal bays and shallows except during breeding periods.

Interesting patterns have been found recently in studies of reef fish distributions over the whole span of the Hawaiian Archipelago.[13] Al-though many species occur throughout the island chain, there are strong differences in species abundance, or dominance, at either end of the chain. For some reason, dominant species in the northwest at Kure and Midway Atolls, such as the saddle wrasse *(Thalassoma duperrey)*, are still found to be fairly common all the way through the main islands. By contrast, a number of the most abundant species around the main islands—for example, the butterflyfish *(Chaetodon multicinctus)*—become more scarce as one island-hops to the northwest, and a few virtually disappear beyond FFS. Another notable phenomenon is that certain fish species found in very shallow water at Kure and Midway occur in progressively deeper water around islands to the southeast. Distributions of some reef invertebrates along the Hawaiian Chain also show considerable variation, but research has yet to reveal major trends.

The NWHI reefs harbor some unexpected rarities—for example, the hermatypic coral genus *Acropora.*[14] This is a major reef builder farther west and south in the Pacific. It ought to be at home in the mild, tropical waters of the southeastern Hawaiian Islands; indeed, along with other western Pacific corals, *Acropora* species once enriched reefs now fos-silized in such places as Nanakuli, Kahuku, and Waimanalo on Oahu. Then, during the Pleistocene epoch, they vanished, and Hawaiian reefs became poorer in species. Perhaps extreme fluctuations in climate and sea level somehow triggered extinctions. Now, the only records of liv-ing *Acropora* outside the NWHI are from a couple of pinpoint locations on the reefs of Kauai. But surprisingly, significant beds of three *Acropora* species flourish at FFS, located near the middle of the Hawaiian

Chain. Here, too, accompanying the anomalous corals are other kinds of Indo-Pacific reef dwellers—for example, *Chaetodon trifasciatus* and *C. citrinellus,* two butterflyfishes rarely seen anywhere else in Hawaii.[15] The reefs of FFS thus have a striking uniqueness and may be the main Hawaiian port of entry for reef life from the equatorial Pacific whose larvae may come via Johnston Atoll, the closest jumping-off point to the south. University of Hawaii marine biologist Rick Grigg elaborates this view and speculates that *Acropora* is just beginning to reestablish itself on the reefs of Hawaii after its Pleistocene disappearance.[16]

There are so many individual adaptive and evolutionary stories among the life forms of coral reefs that a marine ecologist would need an extended life-span to study more than a few of them. At the other end of the spectrum of reef study, scientists seek to understand these incredibly complex living edifices as working systems. In a sense the reefs are magnificent, sprawling, natural mechanisms. They process energy and grow with a measurable metabolism; in a broad sense they respond to stimuli and adjust or adapt slowly; they have immense life-spans and their metapopulations of framework corals, sediment producers, and binders, in the manner of roots and canopies of trees, wax and wane in vigor over the eons as they meet with favorable or unfavorable conditions for growth. Some scientists think of the entire coral reef system as a kind of superorganism.

Across the tremendous span of the Hawaiian Archipelago, the growth, or production, of coral reefs changes dramatically. Off the island of Hawaii at the southeastern, tropical end of the chain, corals and reefs, where they can establish themselves, grow rapidly. Growth declines steadily toward the northwest until, at temperate Kure Atoll, it can barely keep pace with the physical and biological forces that erode and destroy the structure of the reef. Declining coral growth correlates with higher latitude, and hence with cooler water temperature and a lessening annual intensity of sunlight.[17] At Kure, the Hawaiian Chain includes the northernmost coral atoll in the world at the physical limits of its existence.

THE FATE OF THE REEFS

Human exploitation of Hawaii's coral reefs began with the arrival of the first Polynesians from the South Pacific sometime before 500 A.D. These people would have been wholly familiar with the reef environment, would have recognized most of Hawaii's reef life, and would have been skilled in a wide range of reef-gleaning and fishing techniques. A modern fisherman can imagine with some awe the abundant and easy harvest that spread before those first humans to explore Hawaiian reefs.

The aboriginal Hawaiians' depletion of the reef fishes and other marine edibles is impossible to quantify. Indirect evidence leads to the suspicion that some species may have become scarce during the last centuries before the arrival of Captain Cook. Such evidence includes a system of traditional Hawaiian fish and game laws that came under the general heading of chiefly or royal *kapu* (or *taboo,* in the vernacular of early western Pacific seafarers). The term meant "forbidden," and could be used to reserve anything a chief wanted for himself. This was clearly the case, for example, in *kapus* placed on sea turtles and certain delectable reef fishes such as *moi (Polydactylus sexfilis).*[18] But in addition, the *kapu* system may have been applied in cases involving the perceived good of society. In this context, *kapus* that were apparently widespread and that regulated fishing for certain species in their breeding seasons, which the Hawaiians well knew, could have functioned as conservation laws.[19] Hawaiian society was feudal, and a hierarchy of chiefs controlled territory, including reefs, that ranged from small parcels to whole islands. Thus, a *kapu* could apply locally or on a very large scale.

The existence of conservation-style *kapus* suggests that the Hawaiians were responding to the threat of depletion. By the time of Western contact, very large Hawaiian population centers had formed, and overfishing in those regions could have been severe. Of course, other human-created problems in the Hawaiian era, such as marine siltation after the clearing of coastal forests, may also have damaged the reefs and killed or displaced important fishery species (see chapter 19).

In the decades after Captain Cook, human influences on the coral reefs must have lessened in all but a few places owing to the drastic diminishment of the Hawaiian population from disease and demoralization. Overall, the islands lost at least five-sixths of their population during this time,[20] and, coincidentally or not, extremely abundant fish populations were noted in the islands—for example, in the 1830s.[21]

Only reefs near historical coastal centers such as Honolulu and Lahaina would have seen continued exploitation at a high level. But in the nineteenth century, as such places evolved from Polynesian to Western settlements, coral reefs came to be perceived in new ways—for example, as impediments to large ships entering certain harbors and as a handy source of building material.

By midnineteenth century, Honolulu was said to possess some of the best coral buildings in the world.[22] The geologist James Dwight Dana, who visited in 1841, pointed out that old limestone, or reef rock,* not live framework coral, was used for building blocks.[23] In the heyday of coral construction in Honolulu, quarrying at low tide on the reefs front-

---

*Perhaps left from a former high stand of sea level.

ing the town was simple and labor intensive, as described by an observer in 1853: "From these reefs the materials that compose the best and most public buildings in the town are procured, simply by hewing them out with axes while in a wet state."[24] Extensive walls were also made of coral rock; one noted on Oahu in 1832 was "several miles in extent."[25] Several decades of stripping reef material near Honolulu may have had an early impact in terms of siltation. Some of the coralline construction from this period is still visible—for example, at the Mission Houses compound in downtown Honolulu.

Industrial-scale modification of Hawaiian reefs wasn't long in coming. One of the first big projects was described by a Honolulu newspaper in January 1859 as an eighteen-month dredging operation to create new coastal land west of Honolulu. The work was being done by convicts using steam-driven heavy equipment.[26] Another such project was located at the other end of the chain at Midway Island. In 1859, that island had been claimed for the United States by its discoverer, a Captain Brooks, even though he was sailing under the Hawaiian flag at the time. In 1867, it was formally declared a U.S. possession and four years later was briefly occupied by the Pacific Mail and Steamship Company, whose executives convinced the U.S. Congress to put up $50,000 for blasting and dredging a ship channel through the south reef into the lagoon. The chief motivation for the steamship company, which planned to establish a coaling station for its steamers between San Francisco and China, was to avoid the high taxes imposed at Hawaiian controlled ports.

The Midway project in 1871 was a colossal failure.[27] The money ran out after a few months, and the proposed channel, which was to have been 600 feet long by 200 feet wide by 24 feet deep, was nowhere near completion. One wonders, however, at the extent of the environmental damage wrought by the dynamite blasts and gangs of laborers on the pristine Midway reef and ashore on Sand and Eastern Islets, the atoll's only two significant patches of land. Then, ill luck followed poor planning and performance. After giving up on Midway in October 1871, the company evacuated the last of its workers and equipment on the steamship *Saginaw,* and just before dawn, only hours after departure, the vessel inexplicably ran straight onto the Kure Atoll reef, fifty-six miles west of Midway. The ship was a total wreck but all ninety-three men aboard reached shore safely. A few later died attempting to reach Kauai in a small boat. The rest subsisted largely on monk seal and albatross for more than two months before being rescued.

Since the nineteenth century, massive dredging has altered and damaged reefs in numerous places in Hawaii. During World War II, a ship channel 12,000 feet long, 200 feet wide, and 20 feet deep was blasted through the reefs of French Frigate Shoals from the south and a seaplane landing area measuring 8,000 feet by 1,000 feet was cleared there.[28] Similar projects were undertaken in Kaneohe Bay on Oahu (see chapter 7).

Early fisheries that developed under European and American economic priorities were sometimes different from those of traditional Hawaii, but the effect of intensive exploitation was probably often the same. One of the first historical commercial fisheries was for pearls from the bivalve *Pinctada,* which in the early nineteenth century was said to be numerous in the South Oahu embayment named Pearl River (later Pearl Harbor). Nearly every Westerner's journal describing Oahu between about 1790 and 1820 mentions the pearls.[29] They were said by some to be of inferior quality but were acknowledged as property of the king, Kamehameha I, who reportedly traded them to ship captains. Pearls and pearl oysters seem to have vanished from Pearl Harbor not long after this early peak of notoriety, and they have not returned. *Pinctada*'s former presence suggests Pearl Harbor was far less of a muddy estuary in the early postcontact period than it became later, after the felling of its watershed forests, which were rich in sandalwood trees[30] (chapter 12). Pearl oysters prefer hard, open bottom under clear, calm sea water. Quite possibly, changes in the land above Pearl Harbor brought devastating flash floods that destroyed its original character as a marine lagoon. Incidentally, Pearl Harbor was not used by early shipping, because its entrance was blocked by dangerous shallow reefs.

Much, much later, a century after the pearl era on Oahu, modest populations of pearl oysters were discovered in the NWHI. In 1928, the market was for the shell, whose pearly lining was processed into buttons. Almost immediately, the shellfish were overexploited and became commercially extinct.[31]

Overfishing on the reefs and siltation and pollution from domestic and agricultural wastes have all gradually accelerated to become immensely greater than any such effects engendered by the organic subsistence culture of the old Hawaiians. Unlike the destruction of Hawaiian land ecosystems, human-caused damage to the reefs seems primarily a modern phenomenon. So far, few if any marine species have become extinct since humans have inhabited the islands, but some, such as the monk seal, are endangered and others are close to that status. It seems that in terms of environmental degradation the reefs are perhaps a century behind the mountain forests and several centuries behind the old coastal forests of Hawaii (see chapters 11 and 12). Thus, the environmental history of Hawaii's coral rim is still in a formative period. Now, distressing trends are evident, especially around Oahu, most of whose reefs have suffered severe damage. Owing to the intensity of modern disturbance, the reefs may be destroyed much faster than the old Hawaiian forests. Current threats to the life of Hawaiian reefs that bear watching in the 1990s include the following:

Massive dredging and shoreline construction. A new industrial city is under development near Barbers Point, Oahu, west of Pearl Harbor. The richest of Oahu's remaining coral reefs lie off this site. Elsewhere around the main islands, including Lanai and Molokai, an unprecedented burst of coastal resort development is currently underway. Most of this new construction, which inevitably alters the nearshore marine environment, is on remote leeward shores, away from the prevailing trade winds. These zones feature the best developed reefs in the islands with the calmest, clearest water in Hawaii and species such as the lovely lemon tang *(Zebrasoma flavescens),* which is almost never found off turbulent windward shores.

A proliferation of net fishing. Monofilament gill nets are used with little regulation in Hawaii. Some of them extend a mile or more, acting as deadly fences that kill fishes indiscriminately all across a reef or coastal bay. Sometimes nets or large fragments of them are lost, and the subsequent, wholly wasteful "ghost fishing" continues indefinitely, for the synthetic meshes do not decompose. Many fishery conservationists feel that the immense proliferation of gill net fishing in the last decade or so is responsible for the demonstrable decline in many Hawaiian reef fishes, especially on Oahu.

Illegal fishing methods. These include dynamite fishing and "juicing," or the use of chlorine bleach. The former was developed in the late nineteenth century and outlawed even then, but it persisted in remote locations. The Robinson family banned it on Niihau around 1890,[32] and Max Schlemmer, the antiecologist of the NWHI (see chapters 9 and 10) was restrained from dynamiting fish at Laysan Island shortly after 1900.[33] Bleach can be as deadly as dynamite. Released or squirted into crevices or caverns in the reef, it permeates and spreads over a wide area and kills everything. Life is slow to reestablish itself in the poisoned area, and ecological balance may take years to restore.

Shell collecting. Many of Hawaii's shells are beautiful, and some are valuable. A clean, unscratched specimen of the small rare cowrie *Cypraea ostergaardi* fetches several hundred dollars. Shell collecting is almost a mania with many scuba divers who roam across the reefs with steel pry bars, overturning and smashing up coral heads to find the lovely molluskan prizes hidden within. Whole dive clubs go shell hunting and leave visible swaths of destruction across the shallow seafloor. With the proliferation of resorts in formerly remote locations, the last relatively undisturbed Hawaiian reefs will be subject to this kind of activity.

Aquarium fish collecting. This activity has developed into a major commercial fishery in Hawaii only recently, but the business is still growing. It focuses on small species and especially on young specimens of many colorful reef fishes. Markets are chiefly in North America and

Europe; with high-tech aplomb, the live fish are shipped air express to continental pet dealers.

The intensity and kinds of harvest from the reefs today would astonish the old Hawaiians. One imagines that many conservation *kapus* would have gone into effect some time ago around Oahu, where even certain edible reef algae *(limu)* have been virtually wiped out by commercial gatherers selling to specialty markets for Polynesian and Oriental gourmet foods. While fisheries for a few kinds of reef organisms, such as lobsters, are nominally regulated with closed seasons, size limits, and the like, little effort and a minimum of funding are devoted to enforcement. A handful of tiny marine conservation plots have been established by the state of Hawaii. They are rarely patrolled; poaching is common. Except in the NWHI, where strong federal conservation laws prevail and isolation itself protects, the life of Hawaiian reefs and nearshore waters is under siege.

7

Decline of a Lagoon

Eastern Oahu fronts on the sea with extensive fringing reefs. These extend almost continuously from the island's northern tip at Kahuku Point southeastward past Kaaawa, a straight-line distance of sixteen miles. This is the windward side of the island, and from the perspective of an *iwa* (frigate bird) high in the northeast trades, the white breakers on the shallow coral rim trace a much longer meandering line, broken only where major stream valleys intersect the coast.

At Kaaawa, however, the simple coralline shelf is interrupted dramatically. A wide marine lagoon extends far into the land beneath dramatic heights toward the main Koolau range. This is Kaneohe Bay, a unique Hawaiian lagoon of approximately twenty square miles of calm water. It is protected across a wide sea entrance by a three-mile-long barrier reef, the only one in the main Hawaiian Islands. To a latter-day explorer afloat on the bay, this is a coastal setting that despite creeping urbanization and a nearby military base is still steeped in beauty. Sadly, the same can no longer be said of much of the environment below the surface of the bay, which once included some of the richest and loveliest of Hawaiian reef lands.

Kaneohe Bay had its origins in the last ice age as a coalescence of stream valleys cut into a wide windward coastal plain. In those millennia of far-away, ice-covered continents, the sea had receded from the island. Its edge was well to the east and some 300 feet lower than its present position. Freshwater runoff reached this late Pleistocene shoreline mainly via river channels off either end of the present bay. Long, low bluffs, possibly capped by sand dunes, spanned the wide front of this region between the two main river channels. Behind this frontal barrier, the rivers carved channels and sloughs in the present basin areas of the bay and left behind smaller bluffs and promontories that stood well above the valley floors. Then, with the melting of the great continental glaciers beginning about 15,000 years ago, the sea rose, and on Oahu it progressively drowned the Kaneohe region's river channels and valley floors and finally began to creep over the basin promontories behind the central rise.

Perhaps 8,000 years ago, the sea rose above the last of the land barrier fronting the bay, and from then on conditions over the area would have been predominantly marine. Within a few centuries, framework corals must have built substantial foundations on the front ridge and on many of the drowned promontories in the basin. Upward growth of the reef with the incremental transgression of the Holocene sea accounts for the present coralline barrier across the mouth of the bay. The same process has produced tiny islets, expanses of intertidal sandbars, and the many small patch reefs that stud the basin area like miniature, barely submerged atolls. Modern studies of coral reef growth[1] suggest that existing Kaneohe Bay reefs are no more than thirty to fifty feet thick and developed in the last 6,000 to 8,000 years.

Beneath a splendor of blue-green mountains, the bay held a variety of littoral habitats and sustained a wealth of aquatic life quite different from that of the shorelines and reefs of the outer coast. The lower streams were estuaries, grading from fresh water to marine as they reached the bay. Low-lying shore areas near the mouths of major streams were wetlands, some covering hundreds of acres. Such marshes were probably wide and open (since there were no native mangrove trees) and raucous with vanished Hawaiian birds and flocks of seasonal migrants. On the steep hills flanking parts of the bay, native Hawaiian forests composed of trees and other plants now utterly erased from this region (and nearly everywhere else in the Hawaiian lowlands) helped to retard runoff and slow erosion. Along miles of bay shore, a fringing reef developed, a qualitatively different reef than occurs along the open coast. At its surface and edge, the bay's fringing reef has a smoother and trimmer appearance than its oceanfront counterpart. Bay reefs also lack the large surge channels and so-called buttressed architecture that develop in reefs that stand against the open sea. Framework structures and the corals themselves are more fragile. One species of finger coral, *Porites compressa*, overwhelmingly dominate the bay's reefs; the even more delicate lace coral, *Pocillopora damicornis*, which is nearly impossible to find on shallow oceanfront reefs, is commonly seen by snorkelers in the bay. Instead of pounding breakers, the main coral-destroying forces here are fresh water and smothering silt. Both have been in the ascendancy since humans began to rend the local ecological fabric, which featured important woven connections between the bay and the land. Especially critical was mass human wastage of the lowland marshes and forests that once soaked up the fierce windward rains like massive green sponges.

When the first Hawaiians arrived, these clear waters and quiet shores must have been a maritime Eden. During the Hawaiian era, environmental change, especially the clearing of lowland forests, had major impacts on the coastal zone (see chapter 11), and probably degraded or destroyed a number of land ecosystems around Kaneohe Bay. However, it is clear that much of the bay itself remained essentially pristine and highly productive. Perhaps having lost some ground, the bay settled into a new ecological equilibrium that accommodated Hawaiian activities. Much later, just after Captain Cook but before the tragic epidemics of white people's diseases, conservative estimates of the Hawaiian population around Kaneohe Bay ranged between ten and twenty thousand people, making this region a major population center on Oahu.[2] Primary settlements were situated in several major watersheds between Kaneohe proper and Kualoa Point at the bay's northern end. The people subsisted on a few agricultural staples dominated by taro. Their protein came largely from Kaneohe Bay.

The treasured fish of the region was the mullet *(Mugil cephalus)*, called *ama-ama* or *anae* in Hawaiian. These plump, densely schooling, blunt-headed fish reach about eighteen to twenty inches in length. Their young, small silvery fry, are found in shallow pools on rocky shores, where they can be netted by the hundreds. Observing such concentrated young mullet with their vacuum-cleaner style of feeding (they eat algae and bits of organic detritus strained from the water and bottom sediments) probably gave the Hawaiians the idea of artificially cultivating them in stone-walled fish ponds. By the time of European contact, Kaneohe Bay had perhaps the greatest concentration of such aquaculture in the islands.[3] Along the fringing reefs of the bay, at least thirty fish ponds still existed in the midnineteenth century. Remains of only twelve can be identified today.[4] Some of them were nearly a mile wide; reportedly their operation was sophisticated. For example, excessive evaporation and rising salinity in the shallow ponds was coun-

7.1 Hawaiian stone-walled fishpond, Kaneohe Bay. State Archive Photo. Inset: mullet, *Mugil cephalus (anae,* or *ama ama*). From Jordan and Evermann.

tered by opening sluice gates that connected to an adjoining freshwater stream. Besides mullet, the Hawaiians stocked juveniles of other species, especially milkfish, or *awa (Chanos chanos)* in the ponds.

Although pond construction and operation as well as intensive glean- ing by thousands of Hawaiians must have caused considerable environ- mental change on the fringing reefs of Kaneohe Bay, the essentially organic Hawaiian culture probably did not greatly impair the produc- tive marine ecosystem of the bay at large. Even peak populations in the region probably did not exceed the bay's capacity to support them. In- tensive mullet and milkfish cultivation, although it reduced diversity along the coastal flats, actually may have lessened fishery impacts else- where in the bay. Because these two species are nearly exclusively her- bivorous, their flesh is produced with the lowest possible expenditure of energy available in the bay for the growth of fish. Thus, the Hawaiians were fostering an ecologically efficient protein resource; in modern jargon, they were eating low on the ocean's food chain.

Hawaiian lore as well as early historical records indicate that bay reef lands and basins were rich in species that indicated diverse food chains. Besides mullet and milkfish, the fish called *nehu, Stolephorus purpureus* (an anchovy); *aholehole, Kuhlia sandvicensis* (an endemic sea perch that ranges into freshwater streams); and *ulua* (large jacks, family Carangidae) receive special mention along with octopus as traditionally abundant seafood items in Kaneohe Bay.

Today, these fisheries are sadly depleted. Of *nehu*, only small, scattered remnants of reportedly once immense living shoals remain. These little fishes have long been the preferred chum and baitfish for the local fresh tuna industry. Kaneohe Bay and Pearl Harbor are the only locations on Oahu (and the best in the state) for large populations of *nehu*. In both places its numbers have declined so greatly that efforts are being made to find substitute baits. However, none seems to attract tuna quite as well, and *nehu* are still avidly sought by fishermen. The problem is that the very tight schooling behavior of this surface-dwelling species makes it fairly easy to locate and a cinch to catch, even when its overall population is very low. Hence, commercial extinction will come perilously close to the real thing.

The stream-running sea perch called *aholehole*, a small, silvery predator reaching about a foot in length, is a common reef dweller as an adult; juveniles prefer brackish to fresh water. One of the major watershed valleys, Waiahole, near the north end of the bay, was named in prehistoric times for this fish.

At least one species of large jack, known to the Hawaiians as *ulua*, was formerly abundant in the bay. Some of these swift, powerful predators attain a length of five feet and weigh more than 100 pounds. Typically fishes of clear ocean waters along the outer reefs, certain jacks occasionally congregate inshore, even in the mouths of tropical estuaries. Here they flirt with the tides, perhaps seeking aggregations of prey— *nehu* or *aholehole*. In the late nineteenth century, big jacks, probably either *Caranx ignobilis* or *Gnathodon speciosus*, could still be found in the Waikalua River at Kaneohe. They came far enough into this estuary at the south end of the bay to enter drainage channels of the rice fields that covered the area at that time, and in that improbable habitat field hands caught the big fish.[5] Today, while juvenile jacks, known as *papio*, occur sporadically in the bay, adult *ulua* have become scarce nearly everywhere around Oahu.

Octopus, called *hee*, were once found in great abundance on the reefs of Kaneohe Bay. Nevertheless, Hawaiian chiefs declared lengthy annual *kapu* restrictions on the octopus fishery, a sign that this resource was carefully managed. Often the eccentric mollusks were forbidden game for four to six months. As the end of the ban approached, specially appointed scouts would tour the reef flats of a district to assess the prospects for the coming octopus harvest. They focused in particular on areas, such as around Kapapa Island and Kualoa in Kaneohe Bay, that were renowned for concentrated populations of octopus. In those places, the bottom was covered with these animals' burrows in such density that it was likened to ground rooted up by pigs. Everywhere in the clear shallows, the animals' bulky heads were visible, looking like clumps of dark earth.[6]

Despite the Hawaiians' exploitation of the bay and their ecological remaking of its shores and watersheds, this picture of the bay as a marine Eden in productive equilibrium with its harvesters persisted into the historic period. Then, beginning around the midnineteenth century, came a renewed onslaught on the bay and its supporting environs that continues today. No new equilibrium is in sight.

First there was a new round of wholesale land clearing around the bay—the beginning of agribusiness Hawaiian style. From the 1850s to the 1920s, a succession of intensive cattle ranching, sugar cane cultivation, and pineapple planting spread far and wide over the lands bordering the bay. From 1880 to the 1920s, commercial rice production was intensively pursued in the well-watered valley bottoms of the region. This latter enterprise all but submerged the pitiful remnants of taro farming here that formerly sustained whole valleys of Hawaiians. The new waves of deforestation, grazing, and ploughing brought unprecedented erosion—gross tonnages of silt injected directly from bald hillsides into the bay.

Then came the water withdrawals. Beginning in 1916, a series of irrigation tunnels was bored into and through the Koolau mountain wall to the arid slopes overlooking central Oahu. These water projects were as ambitious as the one fictionalized in Michener's novel *Hawaii*; one of the tunnels was four miles long. The water from rainy windward valleys, among them major watersheds feeding Kaneohe Bay, triggered an immense burst of agriculture on the lee side of the Koolau Range, but the diversions drastically curtailed the normal freshwater flow to the bay, especially in its northern reaches. Because the irrigation systems were built to overflow into the valley at high water, however, they did nothing to relieve the inundations of mud from torrential rains.

Nevertheless, early twentieth century was a time when some parts of the bay were still clear and clean, with healthy coral reefs and a host of colorful fishes still apparent. And for the first time, the bay's environmental wonders were publicly acknowledged. The southern region near Kaneohe became known for its "coral gardens." Around 1911, the Coral Gardens Hotel was built here on the shore of the bay. This resort's featured attraction was a glassbottom-boat tour of the nearby reefs. A brochure printed in 1919 described the underwater scenery:

> Only those who have seen the Gardens can appreciate the marvelous beauty of their marine growth and the variety of undersea life they hold. Looking through the glass bottom boat, one sees a natural aquarium of vast extent, set in an undersea forest of strange trees and crags, valleys and hills.[7]

These enthusiastic remarks were written by then territorial governor C. J. McCarthy. They may constitute the first promotion of an underwater tourist attraction in Hawaii.

The original Coral Gardens resort and its tours persisted until shortly before World War II. Then, more than a decade of massive dredging and removal of whole reefs for primarily military purposes obliterated the coral gardens in the calm, sheltered southern bay. Much of the dredged reef mass here, at least 15 million cubic yards,[8] went into landfill and runway construction at the base now known as Kaneohe Marine Corps Air Station on Mokapu Peninsula. Many of the south bay's pedestal reefs, which had loomed pale and lovely just below the water's surface, were blasted apart to clear landing zones for seaplanes.

Dredging kills marine life over a much wider area than the actual wholesale removal of reef mass itself and in a variety of ways. Fine-grained sediments by the ton are churned up and spread along the paths of tidal currents in smothering clouds. This is especially true during the removal of soft sediments to deepen ship channels. Dredging for that purpose has occurred all over the bay, most intensively during the 1940s and 1950s. Aerial photographs of Kaneohe Bay during dredging episodes in the 1940s show milky, silt-laden water covering several square miles at a time.[9] Dredging also releases noxious and toxic chemicals, such as spilled petroleum products, that have been buried in the sediments, and it raises and stirs into the water fertilizing nutrients for marine plant growth. The result is widespread poisoning of many organisms and the rapid growth of a few hardy kinds of phytoplankton and bottom algae, which can be just as smothering to delicate coral tissues as silt. In addition, increased turbidity in the water drastically dims the light needed for normal growth by the reef builders. Since the 1950s, continued dredging and a host of other activities associated with urban development and military operations have largely prevented regrowth and reestablishment of the ruined reefs in the south bay, and degradation has crept northward.

Another debilitating environmental disease in the bay resulted from the buildup of sewage effluent through the mid-1970s. Piped from the sprawling military complex on the Mokapu Peninsula and from the largest civilian centers in windward Oahu, this immense load of plant nutrients and toxins was rapidly turning the southern bay into a cesspool. The exchange of these waters with cleaner waters to the north and seaward was slow. Marine scientists measure such exchange of water in a semi-isolated basin as a *flushing rate*, an especially apt phrase in the case of southern Kaneohe Bay. Stimulation of algal growth was one of the worst effects of the sewage pollution in the bay. Plankton blooms clouded the water nearly continuously, and on the bottom a proliferation of *Dictyospheria cavernosa*, the so-called green bubble algae, reached alarming dimensions. Its growth form, a quilted, rubbery green mat, spread over nearly every kind of exposed hard surface, including living corals, which promptly died. By the 1970s any surviving remnants of the old coral gardens in southern Kaneohe Bay were merely limestone banks beneath carpets of *Dictyospheria* often inches thick. To find healthy, living reefs, one had to go well into the northern half of the bay, and even there the green bubble algae was spreading.[10]

Removal of the sewage outfall in 1977 and its relocation to the open ocean beyond the fringing reef off Kailua helped to stabilize the bay's environmental health, but at this writing the bay's condition can only be listed as guarded, and continued intensive care is needed merely to treat the symptoms of further decline in its vital ecosystems. A full recovery is highly unlikely.

Using medical metaphors for the bay's condition requires some clarification. The bay is not about to die in the sense that an organism does. Life can be found in places that are far more polluted than Kaneohe Bay; a few kinds of the hardiest life forms thrive in the filthiest of the world's harbors. Nevertheless, the kinds of living organisms present are greatly diminished in such places.

At present the bay can be said to be aging rapidly and unnaturally. Sediment buildup is a measure of age in a coastal basin such as Kaneohe Bay. Given a static sea level, all such bodies of water eventually fill, becoming mud flats and finally marshes. But human erosion-promoting activities can accelerate this process tremendously. By any reasonable estimate, Kaneohe Bay has aged more in the last century than perhaps in the previous thousand years, roughly the tenure of the Hawaiians in the area.

During World War II, national need in wartime prevailed over any expressed concern for environmental conservation in Kaneohe Bay. Today, however, despite volumes of paper protection for the bay's environment, a vast and expanding carelessness manifests itself in numerous ways—as a petroleum sheen that can sometimes be traced all across the southern bay to the Marine Corps Air Station and, to a lesser extent, to private marinas and yacht anchorages; as inadequately controlled siltation from construction on the bay's hilly shores; as agricultural and domestic pesticide runoff dangerously uncontrolled by the state of Hawaii. These environmental impacts and insults continue to sap the bay's vitality and diminish the dappled vistas that once delighted visitors to the Coral Gardens.

Perhaps one human influence in the bay with a positive effect was the introduction of mangrove trees, but this seems to have happened by accident. Mangroves, those tropical saltwater shoreline trees whose seeds float and sprout as they drift, are not native to Hawaii. The first import seems to have been the Florida species *Rhizophora mangle*, which was planted on the South Molokai shoreline about 1902. By the

1920s, young specimens were found growing in several places around Kaneohe Bay, and the speculation of the time was that the green, pencil-like floating seeds (or seedlings) had drifted some sixty minutes down-wind from Molokai, where the only mature trees then existed.[11] Other species of mangroves were later introduced from the Philippines, and one of them, *Bruguiera sexangula*, is also now established in Kaneohe Bay. These trees sprout tangles of buttressing prop roots that trap silt and stabilize muddy shores. They also contribute greatly to certain near-shore food chains. But that contribution is in the form of masses of decomposing leaves, and mangroves can grow like woody weeds over shallow reef flats. The presumed beneficial role of mangroves in Kaneohe Bay has not yet been proven.

Many other plants and animals have been introduced in and around the bay. Underwater, one of the most conspicuous plants is the large, fleshy red algae, *Eucheuma*, several species of which were introduced from the Philippines in the mid-1970s. As escapees from experimental cultivation at the University of Hawaii's Institute of Marine Biology at Coconut Island, *Eucheuma* can now be found all over the bay.[12] They are especially abundant in the southern portion, where these alien plants festoon the reefs around Coconut Island.

Animal invaders of Kaneohe Bay include a variety of invertebrates and fishes. The earliest of them to be purposefully introduced was prob-ably the Chesapeake oyster, *Crassostrea virginica*. It was initially seeded into Pearl Harbor in 1866 and was flourishing in Kaneohe Bay by 1890.[13] To what extent such foreign organisms have changed the bay's ecology is simply not known. Adjustments in biotic communities after species invasions often take decades or longer, and in the shallow marine en-vironment changes due to interactions between aliens and natives may be masked by effects of dredging, pollution, and the like.

There are still a few places in the bay, well to the north, away from the worst of the chronic oil spills, urbanization, and epicenters of species invasions, where one can glimpse fragments of former underwater splendors—stretches of reef crowded with finger corals, lacelike forms, and tiered clusters of stony plates up to several feet in diameter. The landscape is alive with color; coral hues range from soft beige and brown to bright yellow and electric blue. A kaleidoscopic display of life swims, crawls, glides, and hops about the living rockery. Striking invertebrates such as tropical lobsters and octopus are not yet uncommon in a few scattered retreats. Tribes of painted fishes—butterflies, wrasses, parrots, tangs, the silvery *aholehole*, clownish Moorish idols, and elegant lyre-tailed *kala*—revel over these last aboriginal reefs in Oahu's lagoon.

Once again there is a glassbottom-boat tour in the bay. Now it em-barks from Heeia, well north of Kaneohe proper, and it seeks the re-maining beauty spots. But sometimes weather or scheduling delays prevent the long trip to the best remaining reefs, and tourists have to settle for the average underwater attractions of the bay. The view is obscured by drifting detritus and plankton blooms. Amid dimly seen yellow and brown coral heads with a *Dictyospheria* fringe, a few fishes—species labeled mudfish and poopfish by bay area residents—turn and weave, their colors dulled by the cloudy water. The populations of some of these hardy types such as the sergeant major are high, but this merely indicates that a polluted bay is an analog of a garbage dump, where rats and mice, seagulls and starlings, may abound but from which other wildlife has retreated.

In a more environmentally sensitive time and society than plantation-era Oahu, Kaneohe Bay might have become a national park. Many other countries in the world would probably have accorded it such status. The uniqueness and spectacle of its topography and life forms would have argued well for its protection. Today, the bay's fate should prompt the citizens of Hawaii and the United States to safeguard what remains of the bay's natural heritage and warn against further avoidable destruction of the remaining unique habitats in the Hawaiian Islands.

8

The Seal and the Turtle

Northwest of Kauai in the leeward Hawaiian Chain, an ecologist could compile an impressive list of unique plants and animals from the land and surrounding reefs. Many of these species are threatened or endangered, but two creatures here are special symbols of the rarity and fragility of their tiny, gemlike Hawaiian ecosystems lost in the immensity of the central Pacific. The Hawaiian monk seal, *Monachus schauinslandi*, and the Hawaiian race of the green sea turtle, *Chelonia mydas*, would receive high priority on any conservationist's protect-at-all-costs list for Hawaii. These two animals draw together concerns for both the reefs and the shores of the Northwestern Hawaiian Islands, and they surely have an ancient standing in the archipelago.

Both the Hawaiian seal and the green turtle come from ancestors that can be traced far back in geological time. Marine mammalogists and paleontologists have recently uncovered evidence that *M. schauinslandi* (named for a late nineteenth-century German naturalist who collected the first Hawaiian seal specimens for scientific study) is the most primitive of living pinnipeds. A number of skeletal features link the Hawaiian seal to ancient monk seals of the temperate North Atlantic and Mediterranean areas—their evolutionary cradle in mid-Miocene time. The scientific story,[1] pieced together from burgeoning fossil evidence, much of it studied only since the 1970s, suggests that monk seals (subfamily Monachinae) came very early to Hawaii via the Caribbean region. The time was roughly 15 million years ago, long before the tectonic upheaval of lower Central America closed the wide tropical seaway between the Atlantic and the Pacific. Perhaps from off some proto-Mexican coast, the founder(s) of the Hawaiian seal species departed on a one-way, one-time-successful migration westward. Such an extraordinary transoceanic leap is termed *waif dispersal* by modern biogeographers although the event has little significance unless the waif establishes a breeding population and becomes a *founder*. Still, for a coastal seal lost for weeks in the vastness between the Americas and Hawaii, *waif dispersal* seems especially evocative.

By 8 or 10 million years ago, monk seals were beginning to evolve rapidly, as fossils discovered in such places as the Chesapeake Bay region reveal. From such major centers of dispersal, monk seals crossed the equator, penetrated high southern latitudes, and, after a major adaptive radiation, became the dominant Antarctic pinnipeds of today. All of these known forms, however, whether fossil or living, diverged significantly from their ancient ancestors.

Not so the isolated Hawaiian population. It still features unfused tibia and fibula bones in its hind flippers, a condition seen in the earliest fossil seals. Also, in a variety of ways the Hawaiian seal exhibits the least amount of change in the structure of the bony capsule and enclosed organs of the inner ear. Major evolutionary structural modifications in the ears of most seals are believed related to the developments of deeper diving capabilities and a directional sense in underwater hearing. The lack of change of these features, among others, in the Hawaiian seal indicates the species' evolutionary stasis. Even features of its soft anatomy, which are not traceable to fossils, appear primitive. For example, in *M. schauinslandi*, the fine structure of the posterior vena cava, the largest vein returning blood to the heart, is less similar to that of any living seal than to that of fissiped carnivores,* which once shared a common ancestor with seals.

Of the northern monk seals, only isolated populations of three species, including the Hawaiian seal, survived into the age of scientific biogeography. The Mediterranean monk seal, *Monachus monachus*,

*Modern placental land carnivores such as dogs, cats, and bears.

whose extinct cousins once ranged a huge inland sea all the way to the Caspian Basin, is extremely rare today. It still frequents a few small islands off the Northwest African coast. Jacques Cousteau, in his book *The Silent World*, provided a lively description of some small seal colonies in that region.[2]

The Caribbean species, *Monachus tropicalis*, is almost certainly extinct. No reliable reports of it have surfaced in several decades. In the nineteenth century, this mammal was hunted mercilessly for its oil, and commercial extinction resulted throughout its range in the western Caribbean. After that, its final fate was only a matter of time, as casual hunting and human disturbance spread to all of its vulnerable island haunts. The last Florida sighting of a monk seal was near Key West in 1922.[3] In the early 1950s, reliable reports of seals on small cays at Seranilla Bank off Yucatan represent the last, sad glimpse of this species. In 1973, the marine mammalogist Karl Kenyon made a 4,000-mile aerial survey at altitudes under 200 feet that covered all of the remote cays and reefs within the known former range of the Caribbean seal. No seal was seen, but at every promising site was evidence of chronic human presence—fishing vessels or shacks on the beach.[4]

Caribbean seals are no longer available for live observation, and Mediterranean monk seals are barely surviving, but anatomical studies of old museum specimens indicate that significant evolutionary development occurred in both species. They are later models than their Hawaiian cousin, which thus appears to be a true primitive. It is the last of an ancient stock, a sleek, warm-blooded swimmer of clear coralline shoals, denizen of lonely atolls, an associate of sharks, albatrosses, and giant turtles.

If the seal reached Hawaii 15 million years ago, the turtle may well have preceded it. Sea turtles are classic antediluvians, and *Chelonia mydas* may hail from true Tethyan times, when a second major seaway in the Mediterranean region would have allowed a turtle to swim all the way around the earth in warm salt water.

Recent studies of chromosomes from forty-eight species of turtles representing nine families, when correlated with tenure of those families in the fossil record, indicate that no major changes have occurred in the chromosomes of chelonians (sea turtles) for some 200 million years.[5] While the morphological evolution of chromosomes does not coincide precisely with overall morphological change in the animal, there is probably a strong correlation. The very conservative family Cheloniidae includes the loggerhead, Ridley, and hawksbill species as well as the green turtle, but chromosomal change in the entire clade of cryptodiran (retractable-necked) turtles seems to have been so slight, at least since the Cretaceous period, that the green turtle, *C. mydas*, as a species may well claim enormous antiquity. Simply put, turtles have evolved ex-

8.1   Hawaiian monk seal and green sea turtle.

tremely slowly, and they appear to have slowed down even more in the last 100 million years or so.

Beneath its stolid, sluggish mien, the green turtle behaves in marvelously subtle ways that may have startling evolutionary implications. A study of a population in the Atlantic that swims from Brazilian coastal waters to breed at Ascension Island, halfway to Africa, has revealed an exquisitely honed instinct—and spawned a hypothesis regarding a kind of living-fossil behavior that may have originated some 90 million years ago.[6] At that time, in the opening Atlantic between Africa and South America, the first in a long series of midocean volcanic islands might have been visible on the horizon from either continental shore, and, the hypothesis suggests, it was used by the turtles as a largely predator-free nesting site. Eon after eon, adopting progressively subtler clues, the turtles navigated to the same spot as the ocean widened and new nesting islands arose on the Mid-Atlantic Ridge, replacing older ones carried outward and drowned on the spreading seafloor. A chain of seamounts reaching toward Brazil from today's Ascension Island attests to the likelihood of this geological history. If the biological history regarding *C. mydas* is also true, we have stumbled onto something utterly transcendent: that an instinct outlasts islands and is as durable as the oceanic crust over which it drives the turtle to self-renewal.

Embodied in sea turtles is more than a suggestion of near-perfect adaptation to an essentially timeless environment and mode of life. These creatures have long been suspended in a deep evolutionary equilibrium that biologists call strong normalizing natural selection. A similar stability seems to have accrued to the Hawaiian monk seal once it became isolated on these mid-Pacific "shoals of time."

Perhaps nowhere else in the world are a marine mammal and reptile so much in each other's company. While the seal and the turtle are not ecological competitors (except occasionally for space on a beach) or in any obvious way mutual benefactors, this zoological odd couple can be found sharing virtually all the islets and reef habitats from French Frigate Shoals to Kure Atoll. Toward the southeast they become scarcer; the seal is especially rare around the main islands.

On the beaches the turtle and the seal meet haphazardly; one or both may have come ashore for breeding—in respective modes that are poles apart on the vertebrate reproductive spectrum—but both come ashore at other times for what appear to be rest and recuperation, and quite likely escape from large sharks. There may be physiological benefits too, especially for the turtles. For example, the rate of digestion, the healing of wounds, and other functions should be enhanced by such basking behavior here, where the surrounding waters are relatively cool for tropical animals. Quite strikingly, male green turtles are often found basking here; elsewhere in the world they almost never come ashore.

The breeding biology of the green turtle has been well studied. Most of the details are contained in Archie Carr's classic book *So Excellent a Fishe.*[7] The following brief summary is based largely on that source as well as a thorough recent review by National Marine Fisheries Service scientist George Balazs of biological data pertaining to the green turtle in Hawaii.[8]

Copulation occurs in the water, usually near the shore. However, females do not need to mate before each nesting. Reportedly, they can store viable sperm for months or even years. At times they appear to come ashore to escape males, whose sexual ardor is legendary, leading them on occasion to attempt to mount snorkelers and even chunks of driftwood having a vaguely tortugan shape.

Females with eggs to lay nearly always come ashore at night and, with their hind flippers, dig a nesting pit well above the high-tide mark. The eggs are deposited into the pit, which widens toward the bottom like a flask about two feet deep. On the average, a female leaves about 100 eggs. Each is the shape and approximate size of a raquet ball, but with a pliable, leathery shell. The nesting pit is filled with sand by the female before she returns to the ocean. Females may lay several times during the season, which, at French Frigate Shoals where 90 percent of Hawaiian green turtles breed, lasts from May to September. A new nest is dug for each batch of eggs.

All the eggs in the nest seem to develop at nearly the same rate. Temperatures within the nest have been monitored at Caribbean sites and found to be amazingly stable, usually between 28° and 29° C (approximately 82° and 84° F), for the sand is a good insulator. Recent research strongly indicates that the sex of turtles, which have no X and Y chromosomes, is determined by small differences in temperature in the nest.[9] In studies of *C. mydas*, cool nests slightly below about 28° C (82° F) produced almost no females; nests warmer than 29.5° C (about 85° F) produced nearly all females. In a normal, well-insulated nest, metabolic heating within the pile of eggs probably controls gender, and substantial numbers of both sexes result—females from the warmer interior of the pile and males from around the periphery. It appears that the middle trimester of the roughly sixty-day incubation period is the most critical time for sex determination, which probably depends on induction of alternate enzymes or biochemical pathways at the slightly different temperatures. Disturbance to nests, including well-meaning attempts to protect or relocate eggs by conservationists, a common practice in the 1970s, may drastically alter normal sex ratios by changing the delicate thermal balance within the nest.

Most of the baby turtles emerge from the eggs nearly in unison. Early hatchlings wait for others for perhaps a few hours or a day; then, at some signal that may involve a threshold of mass activity, all begin a vigorous scratching and treading and packing of sand beneath their small feet. The ceiling of the nest falls and the floor rises as the hatchlings literally stomp their way en masse to the surface. Later hatchlings are left behind at the bottom of the nest and are doomed. They are powerless to dig their way out singly or as a small group. They often constitute 5 percent or so of the total hatch in nests at French Frigate Shoals, according to sea turtle specialist George Balazs.

Emergence on the sand surface is also a concerted action, and the turtle babies show a fine sense of timing. If necessary they wait just under the surface. Nearly always, the escape from the nest occurs at night; the sand suddenly comes alive with small turtles, and they are all out and scratchily waddling toward the water within five minutes. This may serve to temporarily overwhelm the capacities of any predators waiting in their path. At FFS, hatchlings are occasionally caught and eaten on the beach by large ghost crabs *(Ocypode ceratopthalmus)*, but such predation on land here is minimal by comparison to that during both egg-laying and nest escape by sea turtles on continental beaches. In the Caribbean region, for example, opossums, raccoons, peccaries, coyotes, and night herons as well as crabs are known to take a toll. Night herons,

Nycticorax nycticorax, occur only in the main Hawaiian Islands, and other potential turtle predators there include feral cats and dogs, rats, and the Indian mongoose *(Herpestes auropunctatus)*. The mongoose is on record as having killed hatchlings from a green turtle nest at Sea Life Park on Oahu. Green turtles used to breed on the main islands; records exist for Kauai, Oahu, and Lanai. George Balazs has found that a nesting colony existed at Polihua Beach on Lanai into the twentieth century, and with protection it might be reestablished there. The breeding of green turtles was wiped out in the main islands mainly by human predation and habitat disturbance.

Once in the water, the baby turtles face a host of new enemies. At FFS, these include fishes such as jacks and small sharks and, less commonly, barracuda, large wrasses, and perhaps octopus. Most of these species are quickly left behind, however, as the hatchlings move offshore. They swim singlemindedly away from the lagoon, across the reef, and into deep, blue water. And there they disappear.

When they return to coastal waters a few years later, they are 15 to 18 inches long and have outgrown most predatory threats except from large sharks. From this time on they are known to feed primarily on bottom algae and sea grasses, generally at depths less than about thirty feet and sometimes less than ten feet.

But where do they spend those first years at sea? This is one of the great remaining mysteries in marine natural history. The mystery is common to all sea turtles in all oceans they inhabit. Solving it may prove more difficult than locating the haunts of the chambered nautilus or the midocean breeding grounds of freshwater eels *(Anguilla)*, both of which are becoming fairly well known.

In the tropical Atlantic, young green turtles, along with other species such as the hawksbill, have been found in and around patches of the floating *Sargassum* weed, which is common in that region and offers a rich feeding resource for young turtles. However, the pelagic *Sargassum* habitat does not occur in Hawaiian waters. In 1986, Archie Carr speculated that baby turtles may be more generally associated with pelagic drift lines marking oceanic fronts, or convergences.[10] These are boundary zones in the sea between different currents and water masses. Floating materials such as driftwood are often concentrated in such zones and carry clinging coats of marine organisms—algae, hydroids, barnacles, etc.—that would provide nutritious browse for young turtles.

Only a few tens of thousands of hatchlings are in Hawaiian waters per year, most from FFS. Perhaps they merely disperse into a million or so square miles of ocean around the archipelago (figure 8-1). Even if they were to concentrate in local convergences, or fronts, they would be hard to find due to the shifting nature of those watery weather patterns. George Balazs has appealed to commercial and sports fishermen to watch

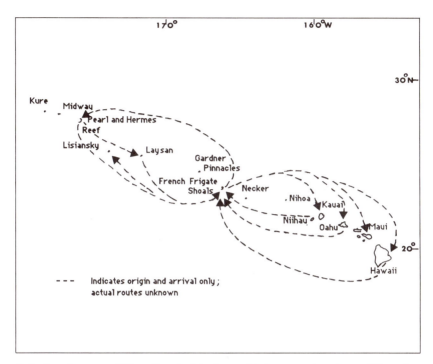

8.2 Local waters of Hawaiian Archipelago with known migrations of Hawaiian green sea turtles. Based on G. Balazs. 1980. Synopsis of biological data on the green turtle in the Hawaiian Islands. NOAA Tech. Memorandum (NMFS-SWFC-7). U.S. Dept of Commerce.

for baby turtle remains in the guts of tunas, billfishes, wahoo, and other open-sea predators. None has ever turned up. Maybe the problem is just a statistical one, and time will tell where the young turtles go.

When the young turtles return to the shallows, many of them come in to the southeastern islands. At times, young turtles in the fifteen- to twenty-inch-long range concentrate at scattered places in the main islands. It is possible to see half a dozen or more on a single dive off southeastern Oahu, but overall many miles of Hawaiian reefs have no turtles.

The turtles seem to grow more wary of boats and divers with age. Big ones are generally solitary around the main islands. You can occasionally find them napping, or so it seems, in sheltered canyons or caverns in the reef. Since *C. mydas* (along with other sea turtles) is fully protected under the U.S. Endangered Species Act, it is a federal and state of Hawaii crime to harm or molest it in any way. Uninitiated snorkelers and divers should also be aware that the flipper can be on the other foot. A big turtle confronted in a hole in the reef may barrel right through you to escape.

The endangered status of the Hawaiian green turtle is heightened by the species' dependence on breeding sites at French Frigate Shoals. Tagged migrating turtles from all over the archipelago converge on this premier nesting atoll. Serious, sustained environmental disturbance at FFS could easily wipe out virtually the entire Hawaiian turtle population. Even a single major event such as an oil spill fouling the beaches in the hatching season (July to November) or a festooning of the reef with miles-long nylon drift nets, lost from North Pacific fisheries, could take a huge toll.

A mystery to biologists is that while several other islands northwest of FFS seem well suited for turtle breeding, they are at present little used, except for basking. Kure and Midway, to be sure, have an established human presence, and this presumably keeps most breeding turtles and seals away. However, former large turtle-breeding colonies at Pearl and Hermes Reef and Laysan Island have declined drastically. These islands, along with Lisiansky, have been free of chronic human disturbance for decades, and no one knows why the turtles are not breeding abundantly on their beaches.

Hawaiian seals come ashore in the same places and for the same general purposes as the turtles. Research and observations on the seals are fairly limited. A comprehensive bibliography on *M. schauinslandi*, which comprises scientific and historical references through 1979, has been compiled.[11] However, many of the ecology and life-history details of this species have been learned only in the 1980s. William Gilmartin and J. R. Henderson, biologists with the Southwest Fisheries Center of the U.S. National Marine Fisheries Service in Honolulu, and their co-workers have been largely responsible for recent advancements in our understanding of the life of the Hawaiian seal.

As in the case of the green turtle, FFS is currently the main breeding ground for the seals, and low-level breeding also occurs on several other islands in the Northwest Hawaiian Chain. Pupping takes place on shore, mainly between March and May, although births have been recorded in every month of the year. Typically, the sex ratio in the newborn population is one to one. On the average, mother seals nurse their single pups for five to six weeks. During this time the mothers remain on shore, do not feed, and lose much weight, while their pups grow rapidly on a rich milk diet from an approximate birth weight of 35 to as much as 200 pounds at weaning. Pupping occurs from the beach proper to the grass and shrub zone, slightly inland. Nursing of pups occurs in these areas and also, during hot weather, in the water near the beach. During periods of rain and high wind, much of the seal population on shore seeks the meager shelter of the scrub vegetation behind the beachcrest.

Quite suddenly, after about 40 days of lactation, the mother seal abandons her pup on shore and leaves for extended foraging on the outer reefs. From this time on, pups must fend for themselves, which means they must learn to catch fish and other prey entirely on their own. Occasionally, a pup will encounter another lactating female and continue to nurse for a time. However, most begin to swim in the shallows and gradually acquire adult foraging skills. Judging from early appearances, they are slow and clumsy predators for weeks or months. They lose a large amount of weight and often become noticeably emaciated—hence, the value of the initial period of nonstop nursing that builds extensive fat reserves. Yearling seals range between 100 and 200 pounds in weight and are about 4 feet long.

Known foods of the Hawaiian seal include fishes, especially conger eels, surgeonfishes, and wrasses, and also invertebrates, notably octopus and spiny lobsters. All of this prey is caught on or near the bottom. Hawaiian seals are fair to middling divers. While most recorded dives have ranged between 30 and 130 feet deep, repeated dives of two young seals have been recorded beyond the reef edge to at least the 500–600-foot range. This was the limit that could be recorded by the instruments attached to the seals in the experiment.[12]

Typically, the seals' lives seem to alternate between periods of basking on the beach and periods of feeding. The latter sometimes involves several days spent far out on the shoals and remote reefs of their home islands. A few seals do make the long, open-sea crossings to neighboring islands in the chain. A peculiar greenish fur color of such animals is due to a coating of algae that accumulates after what may be weeks at sea. Rarely, seals have been found with attached gooseneck barnacles *(Lepas)*, those classic indicators of a long sea passage that are commonly seen on beached logs and other flotsam.

Seals are popularly perceived to be innately gentle creatures, carefree inhabitants of a benign environment, and vulnerable victims of human exploitation and habitat disturbance. Recent studies of Hawaiian monk seals show that, aside from the seals' vulnerability to man, this perception is a myth. In fact, known threats to monk seal survival include a startling sexual brutality within the species itself. Like green turtles, seals mate in fairly shallow water near the islands, and like the turtles, females may be mobbed by a gang of males. In fact, at some of the breeding islands, adult male seals greatly outnumber adult females—up to three to one at Laysan and four to one at Kure Atoll. Whenever males in a group, sometimes more than twenty, pursue a female, they may kill her. For years, females were observed to have extensive scars on their backs or were seen with massive open back wounds that are now known to be caused by the bites of males during episodes of copulation or attempted copulation. The following is typical of several recent close observations of Hawaiian seals by researchers:

13 May 1982: "A mass mating involving one female and approximately 27 males was observed from the vessel *Feresa*. . . . Observers on the *Feresa* radioed the field camp on Laysan that the seal sustained numerous tearing back wounds and that large tiger sharks were circling underneath. Although the seal was roughly within 0.4 km. of shore when the *Feresa* departed the scene, she was never seen on Laysan."[13]

Reports of similar events have now come as well from Lisianski and Kure. One attack by twelve males on a lone female continued for three hours, and this female too disappeared after numerous sharks gathered at the scene. Sharks are common in the Northwestern Hawaiian Islands (NWHI), even very close to shore, and must often finish off such injured and exhausted females.

Male seals attack females of any age, beginning with newly weaned pups. Juvenile males are sometimes attacked as well. William Gilmartin points out that once the sex ratio shifts in favor of males, a vicious positive feedback can take hold and lead to the collapse of a breeding colony. Without helpful human intervention, this may be the imminent situation at Kure Atoll, where pupping has declined sixfold since the mid-1960s—from an estimated thirty births per year to five or fewer in the mid-1980s. Other seal islands, notably Lisiansky, have been losing population as well.

The fierce behavior described above seems to be another facet of the Hawaiian seals' primitive nature. Most other pinniped species exhibit a more highly evolved pattern of sexual and social behavior. Mass rape is prevented by dominant males, which accumulate harems and defend them against other males.

Aside from sexual self-destruction, the monk seals encounter serious natural threats concealed in their seemingly idyllic environment. In the spring of 1978, at least fifty seals were discovered to have died on Laysan Island.[14] The suspected cause was ciguatera poisoning. This condition, which also afflicts humans in scattered areas of the oceanic tropics, is caused by certain dinoflagellates, single-celled algae akin to the toxic red-tide organisms of cooler coastal regions of the world. The nervous system is poisoned, and both seals and humans can die of asphyxiation from paralysis of the breathing mechanism induced by the ciguatera toxin. The toxin accumulates in the food chains of coral reef ecosystems. Certain fishes, including several in the seal's diet, are known to concentrate it. In Hawaii, ciguatera is relatively uncommon, and concentrations of toxin tend to be low. Typically, the condition is undetectable for months or years at any given Hawaiian island and then shows up without warning.

Hawaiian seals also suffer from a variety of parasites.[15] Most of these have not been well studied but must have intermediate hosts in various reef animals in the seal's food chain. The worst of them seem to be nematodes (roundworms), which cause bleeding wounds in the digestive tract and sometimes appear to have been the immediate cause of death when seals have been found moribund or dead on the beach.

Of course, both seals and turtles are killed by sharks. Large sharks are much more common in the NWHI than around the main islands. Three species, *Carcharinus amblyrynchos, C. galapagensis,* and *Galeocerdo cuvieri,* account for nearly all shark sightings around the reefs and sometimes to within a few feet of NWHI beaches. Of these, tiger sharks (the last-named species above) are the most dangerous predators to both seals and turtles. Neither animal ever outgrows the appetite and jaws of a large tiger shark.

HUMAN IMPACT

Most scientists who have studied the seal and the turtle populations in the NWHI consider the human threat the worst one. Like most other Hawaiian marine environmental impacts, this threat has become serious only since contact was made with the West. To be sure, the prehistoric Hawaiians did hunt sea turtles; they nearly always reserved them as food for the chiefs. No doubt turtle catchers interfered with much of the potential breeding of *C. mydas* on beaches of the main islands and caught some of the wandering turtles down from the NWHI, but they would not have affected nesting success on FFS and the rest of the leeward chain. Whether seals ever inhabited the coastal waters of the main islands in any numbers is uncertain though unlikely. Traces of seal bone are extremely rare in Hawaiian archaeological sites. Hawaiian cultural references to seals are nil. Historical observations of seals around the main islands are scant. Today, despite dense coastal boating traffic and widely distributed surfers, paddlers, and divers, months may go by between reports of seal sightings. Only around Kauai, which lies closest to the main NWHI populations, are sightings made with any regularity—typically a seal or two at a time.

It is possible to trace large fluctuations in seal and turtle populations since the early nineteenth century. In 1825, the pioneering Pacific whaler Morrell provided the first detailed observations of most of the NWHI.[16] He reported large numbers of turtles at virtually every island except FFS, which was not visited. Morrell thought he saw elephant seals on the islands, but he seems to have gone ashore rarely, and these animals were undoubtedly monk seals. In 1856, Captain John Paty, a respected navigator in the service of the Hawaiian kingdom, surveyed the known Northwest Chain.[17] He too appears to have missed FFS, but visited Laysan, Lisiansky, and Pearl and Hermes Reef and reported those islands' beaches to have "abounded" with seals, turtles, and birds. At Lisiansky, unconcerned with human visitors, they formed a living environmental-historical diorama amid casks and spars of an 1844 shipwreck. Even on rockbound Nihoa, Paty saw about a dozen seals sharing the single tiny beach.

By midnineteenth century, the NWHI were becoming known for their biological resources, which could be garnered by means of accurate navigation and careful seamanship. A fear years before Captain Paty's survey, Albert Osbun, a widely traveled American physician, visited Pearl and Hermes Reef on a voyage from Samoa to San Francisco. Osbun's diary in August 1850 records that the ship was after turtles. His ship's captain apparently aimed to market most of them in California. Although August is the middle of the turtle breeding season, for some reason only one turtle was seen and captured in the water. None was found on shore (perhaps an earlier ship had just cleaned them out). As consolation, Osbun notes, the shore party

> killed 10 or 12 seal and brought aboard their livers and hearts from which we made several excellent meals. I consider them equal to Beef liver. No other part is considered eatable and they were of course left upon the beach. A heavy sacrifice of life for so little meat.[18]

One applauds that twinge of conservation (or waste-not) sentiment at the end. However, Osbun was an educated man, not a rough-and-ready mariner. His intimation that seal organ meats were esteemed fare by seafarers of the time makes it fortunate for the seals that, in Osbun's words, "the islands here are very seldom visited, the navigation being extremely dangerous." One wonders if any of these seamen ever developed symptoms of ciguatera from consuming monk seal liver, the primary toxin-concentrating organ in the body. Such consumption might have become self-correcting.

As the nineteenth century waned, both seals and turtles became scarcer. This was probably related to a growing human presence—wrecks and wreckers—in the NWHI. Expeditions for birds' eggs and feathers, the development of fisheries, and the establishment of camps and settlements for other commercial, and eventually military, activities also brought mounting ecological disruption of the low Hawaiian Archipelago (see chapter 10).

By 1912, three years after nominal partial protection was conferred on the NWHI by Theodore Roosevelt's designation of them as a federal bird refuge, the seals and probably the turtles had diminished to record low numbers. For several months in the winter and spring of 1912–1913, an expedition from the American Museum of Natural History searched for seals. One of the scientists, A. M. Bailey, described the sites visited:[19]

At French Frigate Shoals they found a rude shelter; " . . . four pegs with tattered canvas . . . the numerous bleaching turtle bones told plainly the main source of food." No seals were seen.

On Laysan, during a three-month stay (and this was where they expected, from previous reports, to find the largest seal colony), they found and killed (for science) one large male seal on the beach. No others were seen, even in the surrounding waters.

At Lisiansky they found one adult pair and killed the female, but the male escaped.

At Midway, there were no seals, but the expedition was told by Cable Company representatives then stationed on the island that seals "occasionally wandered ashore."

From Midway the expedition doubled back to Pearl and Hermes Reef, where, on the largest islet, they found about sixty seals with a few more in the water and on other islets. About twenty females were observed to have pups. The expedition of 1912–1913 never went to Kure Atoll, which was then uninhabited by humans and probably harbored some seals. Only some fifty-five miles from Midway, Kure would have been the likely source of the occasional stragglers noted by the Midway cable-station staff.

Hawaiian seals were very close to extinction in the early twentieth century, probably closer than at any time before or since in the historical period. From their extremely contracted state at Pearl and Hermes Reef and perhaps Kure Atoll, seal populations expanded until the late 1950s, when their numbers throughout the NWHI probably peaked at somewhat more than 2,000 animals.[20] Is this number representative of Captain Paty's "seals abounding" of a century before? Today we seem to be in another period of population collapse. Overall, seal numbers are down to 1,325 (estimated in summer 1983; see note 20), with breeding colonies severely depressed everywhere except at FFS, where half the total population now resides and half the total births now occur.

At present, conservationists' concern is high over the fate of both the seal and the turtle. Because the latter habitually wanders to the main islands, and because of the traditional turtle fishery in Hawaii, the endangered *C. mydas* is still killed surreptitiously and butchered in the name of subsistence. However, while truly needy people certainly deserve consideration in a poaching case, typical "subsistence" in contemporary Hawaii involves the illegal catch being smuggled in a late-model pickup truck back to a comfortable suburban home where turtle steaks may be cooked over charcoal but could just as well be done in the microwave.

The greatest conservation efforts are now focused on providing secure habitat for the seal and turtle in the NWHI. Here, both animals ashore for breeding are disturbed by close encounters with humans. A female seal will leave her pup to chase a human intruder. In extreme cases, such distraction might lead to abandonment of young. During recent years this problem, once reportedly severe on islands such as Kure, Midway, and FFS, has been alleviated by a growing sensitivity on the part of the U.S. Navy and Coast Guard as well as civilian contractors and researchers.

On the other hand, if hearsay reports are believed, monk seal interactions with fishermen are not as encouraging. On NWHI bottom-fishing grounds, seals are blamed for stealing bait off hooks and sometimes removing a catch itself. Rumor has it that fishermen shoot at seals and, at closer quarters, try to run them over or hit them with two-by-fours. According to William Gilmartin, the full extent of this problem is unknown.

By far the worst artificial threat in the NWHI today is the oceanic proliferation of nylon netting and other plastic debris, much of it from the fishing industry. Rescuing entangled seals and turtles has become almost routine for researchers visiting the NWHI, as has finding dead animals ashore and at sea wrapped and trapped in netting that takes years to degrade in the natural environment. Not only monk seals and green turtles, but rare hawksbill turtles *(Eretmochelys imbricata)* and rarer leatherbacks *(Dermochelys coriacea)*, the world's largest and most fully pelagic sea turtle, are being killed regularly in this way.[21] The enormous, free-drifting nets used in modern open-sea fisheries extend as far as ten miles and hang down twenty feet from chains of surface floats. They have been used for many years by Japanese salmon fishermen in the far North Pacific, where they inadvertently catch and kill hundreds of thousands of seabirds annually. Now they are being used to catch squid near the NWHI, among other places, and not only by Japanese vessels but by Koreans and Taiwanese as well. Here there is the imminent threat of regional extinction of the ponderous leatherbacks, whose feeding grounds north of the NWHI (approximately 35° to 43° N and 175° to 179° W) first became apparent in 1979. It may be a hopeful sign that in Japan conservation-based reaction to the killing of seabirds led to a ban on using these nets west of longitude 170° E by boats operating north of 20° N—that is, the nets are prohibited within Japan's regional waters (see note 21).

Also, sea turtles commonly consume plastics, and sometimes this proves fatal.[22] In December 1984, George Balazs autopsied a small hawksbill, probably one to two years old, that had apparently died from intestinal blockage. This turtle was extremely emaciated; it had virtually no fat and appeared to have absorbed some of its shell cartilage—a sign of starvation. Its small intestine, about a foot below the stomach, was grossly distended by two boluses of debris, each approximately three inches in diameter, that included dozens of chips and shards of tough, hard plastic. These were densely interwoven with fibrous polypropylene strands frayed from variously colored rope. Other categories of junk included strips of thin, cellophanelike plastic, a golf tee, and a few volcanic pebbles. One wonders if the pebbles were swallowed in some last-ditch instinctive effort to physically purge the digestive tract.

Such plastic debris is found floating nearly everywhere around the main islands. Often it is concentrated at oceanic fronts—the hypothetical turtle nurseries. Closer to shore, where older turtles feed, it forms long lines, shaped by the tidal currents. How many other turtles succumb to the sort of fatal constipation observed in the hawksbill? A young green turtle was also examined that day. Like the hawksbill, it had plastic chips and strips in its gut along with frayed filaments from synthetic cord or rope, but in Balazs' opinion there was no actual blockage, and the cause of its death was unclear.

A variety of wildlife-management efforts are now underway to safeguard the existing seal and turtle populations in Hawaii.[23] Perhaps the most effective will be the declaration of the NWHI and their shoal waters out to a specified depth beyond the outer reef crests as critical and protected habitat. This would greatly enhance the protected status of the two animals as endangered species. Deeming this habitat critical would mandate careful consideration of potential impacts and might preclude any inshore fishing as well as a proposed onshore fishing base at FFS that the state of Hawaii has been planning for many years.

Other specific measures, some already started, include monitoring nesting and pupping sites and possibly rescuing the hundreds of hatchling turtles that fail to escape their nests. Shark fishing has been proposed to remove some of the large predators of both seals and turtles, but some biologists think this might enhance the survival of small sharks and other lagoon predators that take hatchling turtles. Another project is to fence shallow-water seal nurseries to keep out sharks and adult male seals. And a pilot effort is underway to identify and remove the most sexually aggressive male seals. In late 1984, nine males from Laysan Island, known offenders in mass rape episodes, were captured and taken to Johnston Atoll 600 miles to the southeast. At this writing, one of the males remains at Johnston; the rest have disappeared.

Although few see them in the wild, the seal and the turtle are two of the more striking and symbolic life forms of Hawaii's unique biota. They are ancient treasures and living fossils. They and their wild reefs and shoals are worth preserving. Society often places a high value on ancient things, both living and nonliving. Antiques hold threads from the remote past and are somehow comforting to have around in a world of rapid change. Like New Zealand's *tuatara* and the lesser primates of Madagascar, the green turtle and the Hawaiian seal are venerable relics. They embody the hope that we too may yet survive for a significant time on our island, Earth.

9

Seabirds High and Low

The Hawaiian Archipelago hosts a spectacle of seabirds. They are diverse in size and form, ranging from storm petrels like long-winged robins to giant albatrosses, and from ethereal, snow-white terns to big angular boobies. Some of them are habitual ocean wanderers that come to the islands only in the breeding season. Others are primarily archipelagic in occurrence and are found in predictable places, onshore and offshore all year round. Some species range throughout the island chain; others are more restricted.

Recent studies by the U.S. Fish and Wildlife Service have established that twenty-two species (see Table 9.1), forming a total population of nearly 6 million seabirds, breed in the Hawaiian Chain.[1] Of these, four species occur nearly exclusively in the main islands from Kauai and Niihau southeast to Hawaii. The remaining eighteen species have their major populations in the Northwestern Hawaiian Islands from Kaula Rock to Kure Atoll, and the overall importance of that part of the chain is evident from the fact that the NWHI harbor more than 90 percent of all Hawaiian seabirds.

Somewhat paradoxically, few people are aware of Hawaii's seabirds. Most tourists and even a majority of residents probably never notice them. Along settled coasts and around harbors and marinas their absence is conspicuous. No raucous gulls wheel in the air or convene in disputatious flocks on wharfs or jetties. Pelicans and cormorants, too, are missed in such places. Only rarely do these kinds of birds stray to Hawaii from continental coasts, where they are dominant elements of the avifauna. Although western gulls, *Larus occidentalis,* were deliberately introduced into the Hilo area early in the twentieth century, they failed to produce a breeding colony.[2] The absence of such continental birds may be due to a scarcity of proper wild habitat; large expanses of intertidal sand or mud flats, the natural feeding grounds for gulls, are uncommon owing to Hawaii's two-foot tidal range. Nowadays, however, gulls might be more successful in Hawaii. They have learned to forage in garbage dumps, a habit that sustains enormous populations of gulls in North America, Europe, New Zealand, and elsewhere. But because gulls encroach on nesting grounds of smaller species such as terns, it is probably just as well that they have not caught on in Hawaii.

Hawaiian seabirds, then, have less conspicuous habits than the types familiar to most people. They prefer more remote feeding and breeding sites. Yet it is still possible, with perseverence, to observe a majority

TABLE 9.1: BREEDING HAWAIIAN SEABIRDS

Species	*Important Concentrations*
Laysan Albatross: *Diomedea immutabilis*	NWHI, especially FFS to Kure; rare on Kauai
Black-footed albatross: *D. nigripes*	NWHI, especially FFS to Kure
Wedge-tailed shearwater: *Puffinus pacificus*	Archipelago-wide
Newell's or Townsend's shearwater: *P. puffinus newelli*	Kauai; rare on other main islands
Christmas shearwater: *P. nativitatis*	Chiefly NWHI, especially Laysan
Dark-rumped petrel: *P. phaeopygia sandwichensis*	Main islands; rare
Bulwer's petrel: *Bulweria bulwerii*	Chiefly NWHI, especially Nihoa
Bonin petrel: *Pterodroma hypoleuca*	NWHI, especially Laysan and Lisiansky
Sooty storm petrel: *Oceanodroma tristrami*	Nihoa, Laysan, Pearl and Hermes Reef
Harcourt's storm petrel: *O. castro*	Main islands; rare
Great frigatebird: *Fregata minor*	NWHI; windward Oahu; Kauai
Masked booby: *Sula dactylatra*	Chiefly NWHI
Brown booby: *S. leucogaster*	NWHI; Moku Manu (off Oahu)
Red-footed booby: *S. sula*	NWHI; Kauai; Oahu
White-tailed tropicbird: *Phaeton lepturus*	Main islands
Red-tailed tropicbird: *P. rubricauda*	Chiefly NWHI; uncommon on Kauai
Sooty tern: *Sterna fuscata*	Oahu (offshore islets) to Kure
Gray-backed tern: *S. lunata*	NWHI, Moku Manu
White tern: *Gygis alba*	Oahu to Kure
Brown noddy: *Anous stolidus*	Archipelago-wide
Black noddy: *A. minutus*	Archipelgo-wide
Blue-gray noddy: *Procelsterna cerulea*	Nihoa and Necker

of these species in the main Hawaiian Islands without venturing out to sea. Many can be seen from vantage points on the coasts, and some, perhaps surprisingly, are observable in the mountains.

In the classic ornithological classification, these Hawaiian seabirds are divided into seven families representing three orders:

O.PROCELLARIIFORMES
  F. Dromedeidae
    (albatrosses)
  F. Procellariidae
    (shearwaters
    and petrels)
  F. Hydrobatidae
    (storm petrels)

O. PELECANIFORMES
  F. Phaethontidae
    (tropicbirds)
  F. Sulidae
    (boobies)
  F. Fregatidae
    (frigatebirds)

O. CHARADRIFORMES
  F. Laridae
    (terns and
    noddies)

However, a sweeping revision of bird phylogeny is emerging based on molecular research, largely by U.S. ornithologists Charles Sibley and Jon Alquist, whose studies represent a modern revolution in ornithology. Using a technique called DNA-DNA hybridization, they have examined the closeness of relationships of hundreds of species of birds, especially passerines (perching birds, or songbirds), but also a variety of other orders.[3] Work on seabirds indicates that frigatebirds actually belong in the Procellariiformes and tropicbirds in an order by themselves. The latter now appear to have been the first of the existing types of oceanic birds, having evolved perhaps some 40 million years ago.[4]

Procellariiform species include the largest and some of the smallest seabirds—the albatrosses seem monsters beside the dainty storm petrels—and all roam widely between breeding periods. After fledging, juvenile albatrosses do not return to land until they are sexually mature several years later. The procellariiforms include two Hawaiian breeders that are among the world's rarest seabirds: the dark-rumped petrel *(Pterodroma phaeopygia sandvichensis)* and Newell's race of the Manx shearwater *(Puffinus puffinus newelli)*.

The big, fork-tailed frigatebirds (in Hawaii the breeding species is *Fregata minor)* look piratical. Actions confirm the image when one of these blackguards encounters a smaller seabird with a fish. The swift aerial attack and capture of its victim's prize earned this bird its nickname from early European sailors. They called it the man-of-war bird.

The pelecaniform birds, which, with the acceptance of Sibley's and Alquist's taxonomic revisions, will have only the boobies as Hawaiian representatives, are all relatively large (up to the size of geese). Boobies bear mostly hidden resemblances to pelicans, lacking the latter's huge bill and pouch structure. Ponderous fliers when the weather is calm, they come into their element when the trade winds turn brisk and gusty, raising ruffled seas. The powerful birds skim the wave troughs and suddenly catapult up over the crests like expert windsurfers. They closely resemble gannets, which represent the family Sulidae in colder waters from middle to high latitudes. Some species of boobies have vividly pigmented feet and/or head markings, from which common names are derived (red-footed booby, masked booby, and so on).

Tropicbirds are elegant, snow-white fliers with long tail feathers, or streamers. The two species that breed in Hawaii are known by the color of the streamers and have distributions that are very nearly discrete. The white-tailed tropicbird *(Phaeton lepturus)* breeds on the mountainous main islands. Only one nest of this species has been found in recent years in the NWHI, on Midway. The red-tailed tropicbird *(Phaeton rubricauda)* breeds almost exclusively in the NWHI.

The terns and noddies are fairly small birds. The different species that breed in Hawaii have very diverse habits. The sooty tern *(Sterna*

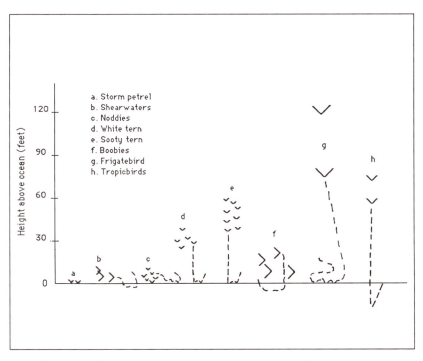

9.1   Flying and foraging maneuvers typical of various Hawaiian seabirds.

fuscata) is Hawaii's most abundant seabird. It accounts for nearly 50 percent of all breeders in the NWHI,[5] and large colonies also exist on offshore islets around the main islands.

All the seabirds are well adapted for pelagic life, and some features are shared by all—for example, the physiological ability to excrete ingested salt rapidly and efficiently, maintaining total blood salts well below the concentration of sea water. To do this, the birds depend not on highly efficient kidneys as marine mammals do, but on special organs, the so-called nasal salt glands. A pair of these small structures is located near the top of the head, just above the eyes. Twin ducts from the gland open at the upper base of the beak. A brine solution several times the strength of sea water drips from the ducts,[6] and the droplets are shed by a sideways flick of the bird's head. Thus, these birds never require fresh water, and many thrive on a diet of salty invertebrate prey such as squids and crustaceans.

All of the oceanic birds are epipelagic predators. However, recent research indicates that various species tend to specialize on certain classes of prey.[7] Fishes predominate in the diets of most species. Flying fish (family Exocetidae) are an extremely important food resource for most larger species of Hawaiian seabirds. Smaller birds such as terns and noddies, though they feed well offshore, depend significantly on juveniles of inshore fishes such as goatfishes (family Mullidae). Squids are eaten by at least eighteen species of Hawaiian seabirds and constitute a major staple for many. Well over half of the prey consumed by the Laysan albatross consists of squid. Storm petrels may catch the widest variety of prey. Feeding at the very surface of the sea, they take their food from the neuston, or uppermost marine community. Here, they may even consume such unusual items as *Halobates,* a small, blue water strider, the world's only open-sea insect. At times this bug becomes extremely abundant off the Hawaiian Islands.

A diversity of the fish-eating birds is well known to congregate over schools of minnow-sized prey. Often, these same small fry are being chased from below by tunas, jacks, or other large fish. Birds in such feeding flocks accumulate rapidly, sometimes by the thousands, as scattered individuals are attracted from several surrounding square miles toward the milling, excited aerial throng.

Feeding flocks are often of mixed species. Many of these birds have been closely observed in flight and in maneuvers above and in the water, and stereotypic feeding patterns have been noted in a number of species. Some merely land on the water and seize prey from a sitting position on the surface. This is typical of albatrosses. Gliding close to the water and momentarily dipping the head to seize prey at the surface is practiced by several species, commonly the frigatebirds, which frequently are merely retrieving the booty, dropped under duress, of another bird. Frigatebirds, moreover, maintain searching stations in the air higher than most other species. The most dramatic feeders are the birds that plunge on their prey from high in the air. Terns are famous for this, but the boobies and especially the tropicbirds are the champion high divers in Hawaiian waters. The latter drop stright down from heights of up to fifty feet and pursue fish as deep as ten feet or more in clear, blue water. A few kinds of shearwaters also dive below the surface in pursuit of prey, but they barely submerge. Storm petrels and noddies typically dabble and flutter across the surface, rarely wetting more than their feet as, robinlike, they pluck tiny fish and invertebrates from the very skin of the sea. Figure 9.1 summarizes some of these feeding patterns, from which an observer at sea can make at least tentative identifications of various birds, even in a mixed flock.[8]

Seabirds that breed on oceanic islands far from continental shores depend on land to varying degrees but in this aspect of their ecology they seem to fall into two general groups. One consists of species that come to the islands only in the nesting season, mainly between spring and fall. Juvenile birds, and adults of this group when they are not breeding, roam over the remote tropical ocean. They even sleep on the water and perhaps nap in the wind. These species often show broadly defined annual patterns of movement over immense distances. This most pelagic group of birds cuts across taxonomic relationships and includes terns, tropicbirds, and numerous petrels, shearwaters, and albatrosses.

The second group among the remote-island breeders is composed of species that have entirely pelagic feeding habits but are usually not wide wanderers. They tend to remain within fifty miles, often closer, of their home island and return daily, or at least frequently, to roost. Boobies and noddies dominate this group in warm oceanic regions. Many frigatebirds, too, remain close to home islands, but occasional individuals are seen soaring above seas a thousand miles or more from the nearest land.

A majority of oceanic birds lay only one egg. Exceptions occur among the boobies and noddies, where a clutch of two eggs is typical of some species. Several types of Hawaiian seabirds nest in sheltered situations such as recessed ledges, sea caves, and sea-cut arches. Some shearwaters and petrels carry this habit to its most extreme. They excavate deep burrows in soft soil and beneath tussocks of grass and shrubs. Burrows tend to be reused year after year, enlarged and renewed after accidental collapse. Whole hillsides or parts of offshore islets with suitable terrain may be riddled with tunnels, such that a person cannot walk anywhere without breaking through.

Perhaps the most unexpected breeding habits among Hawaiian seabirds involve species that nest miles inland and thousands of feet high on volcanic ridges and slopes. At the highest elevations—between 7,200 and 9,600 feet, on the rim of Maui's Haleakala Crater—are found the extraordinary, fifteen-foot-long burrows of the *uau,* Hawaii's dark-rumped petrel.[9] Breeding colonies of this bird may persist up to 10,000 feet on Mauna Kea and Mauna Loa, but even at such extreme heights, the population has been decimated, chiefly, it is thought, by the introduced mongoose, but also by rats and cats. Both the state of Hawaii and the federal government list the *uau* as an endangered species.

Newell's shearwater *(ao),* probably a race of the widely distributed Manx shearwater, is another rare mountain breeder listed as threatened. Nesting sites at elevations between about 1,500 and 3,000 feet have been confirmed on Kauai since the late 1960s,[10] although this species, like the dark-rumped petrel, probably once bred on most or all of the high islands of the archipelago. With a body about the size of a quail and a nearly three-foot wingspan (about the same as that of the dark-rumped petrel) the *ao* is highly secretive, returning to its remote rookeries after dark and scrambling down through dense vegetation to underlying nesting burrows. Before the birds locate their individual nests, they fly over the slopes calling incessantly in loud nasal tones that have been likened to "a combination of jackass braying and crow calling."[11]

9.2 Hawaiian seabirds. In the air: frigatebird (top left); Laysan albatross (top right); wedge tailed shearwater (lower left); and red-tailed tropicbird (center). On the ground: wedge tailed shearwater in burrow; red footed booby atop *Scaevola* bush; and sooty tern with chick (see Table 9.1 for scientific names).

A number of hopeful reports in recent years concern the possible return of Hawaii's rarest seabirds to former breeding grounds—the *uau* to Lanai and to Mauna Loa on the Big Island[12] and the *ao* to the Hamakua slopes and Kohala Mountains on Hawaii and the Koolau Pali on Oahu.[13] The evidence has come from road-dead birds, unmistakable nocturnal calling, and sightings of birds at night attracted to lights. Actual nesting sites, however, are hard to confirm in the extremely difficult terrain favored by these birds.

Nests of some species—for example, red-footed boobies and frigate-birds—are typically built a few feet off the ground atop bushes such as *Scaevola (naupaka)*. Still other boobies build nests on the ground, as do several of the terns and noddies. Open terrain is often dominated by sooty terns, which in early summer form teeming rookeries such as the one on Manana Island (Rabbit Island), a mile off the coast of southeastern Oahu (opposite Sea Life Park). Several birds nest on ledges. The white-capped noddy *(Anous minutus)*, also known as the black noddy, is an example. One place it is common is along the northern coast of Molokai, nesting on the seacliffs sometimes only just above the wash of the waves. This same species also frequents the larger, partly flooded sea caves and stone arches along this spectacular coast, where, if disturbed by human intruders, the small, dusky birds flutter and scatter amid unearthly, electric-blue half-lights that glint from the dark, transparent water.

The most eclectic nesting habits among seabirds in Hawaii must belong to the lovely white tern *(Gygis alba)*, also known as the fairy tern in other parts of the Pacific. This species never constructs a real nest. It lays a single egg almost whimsically in the crotch of a tree or on a block of coral on a remote beach, on a cliff ledge, or in a drain gutter of a building near the sea. White terns nest with equal abandon from the parks and open spaces of downtown Honolulu to the loneliest islets of the NWHI.

White-tailed tropicbirds sail across high, rugged landscapes to mountain nesting sites from Kilauea Crater and vicinity on Hawaii to Kauai's Waimea Canyon and Na Pali Cliffs. Against some of the tortured terrain of Hawaii Volcanoes National Park, their wraithlike flight evokes scenes from Dante. Typically silent and alone on the wind, they seem creatures of pure air and cloud. Nowhere in Hawaii do these birds appear very common, nor do they concentrate there in breeding colonies. Hawaiian populations are sparser than those at some other Pacific locations—for example, the northern slopes of Tutuila Island in American Samoa, where dozens may be seen at a glance, soaring over the dark green canopy of rain forest. In the South Pacific, the white-tailed phaeton frequently nests in big jungle trees, but in Hawaii it lays its egg most often high up on steep, barren ledges.

The red-tailed tropicbird nests high and low almost exclusively in the NWHI. It breeds on all of the islands from Nihoa to Kure Atoll and on the volcanic remnants Lehua and Kaula near Niihau. Formerly, this species also bred, probably widely, in the main islands. Its near disappearance there seems related to a combination of factors, including predation by rats, mongooses, and humans, and perhaps a susceptibility to the introduced avian pox virus.[14] Preferred nesting sites are in sheltered locations: on low islands typically beneath vegetation, and on high islands often under overhanging ledges.

The secretive breeding habits of the small storm petrels tend to keep them out of the public eye, and some species continue to elude even professional ornithologists. The Hawaiian race of Harcourt's storm petrel *(Oceanodroma castro cryptoleuca)* is an example. This eight- to nine-inch-long species, also known from such remote Atlantic islands as the Azores and St. Helena, is thought to breed on Kauai and probably Hawaii, but its nest and eggs have never been found. Only occasional immature birds are seen on those islands.[15]

In some species, the parents abandon the chicks well before they are able to fly. For example, the young of wedge-tailed shearwaters *(Puffinus pacificus)* remain in or near the nesting burrow for two or three weeks after the parents leave, around late October or early November. During the ensuing month, many of these young birds wash in on Oahu's Waimanalo Beach, having failed to fly on their first attempt from the large wedge-tail rookery on Manana Island, just offshore. They are frequently exhausted and occasionally injured, but even the active ones seem unable to take off in sustained flight from the water. A beached bird rescued one November and later safely released revealed clues as to how this species makes the momentous transition from burrow dweller to soarer on the Pacific winds. This fledgling would lie quietly in a cardboard box during the day, but at night its behavior was driven by a powerful climbing instinct. Even in a residential living room it would climb, hop, flutter, and claw its way upward—from the floor to the seat to the back of a chair, to drapes, all the way to the ceiling. It made no cries, only the small sounds of its striving. From this, one can imagine Manana Island on November nights, alive and rustling with birds scrambling upward to reach the highest accessible ridge or peak. Then the fledglings launch out into the dark rush of the trade wind. Perhaps they are naturally attracted to bright stars, an adaptation that could help keep them in the air that first night of learning to fly. Nowadays, wedge-tails and other related species appear fatally attracted to bright artificial lights around coastal centers and along highways. Many become grounded and die in such places.

HUMAN PURSUIT AND PERSECUTION

Before the arrival of human beings in Hawaii, seabird populations in general were probably larger throughout the islands. Breeding grounds in the main islands would have been virtually unlimited, and the populations of some species may have been truly immense, controlled primarily by the availability of food. Nevertheless, native predators would have taken some toll. A Hawaiian eagle (now extinct) and perhaps other raptors may have preyed selectively on seabirds (see chapter 18). Then, as now, frigatebirds and the native Hawaiian night heron (a race of the North American black-crowned species, *Nycticorax nycticorax)* would have fed on chicks of small seabirds. The existing native owl *(pueo),* *Asio flammeus,* is an occasional predator on terns.[16] Two or three species of extinct owls might also have taken seabirds. Another easily overlooked predator is the flat-bodied, fast-scuttling *aama* crab *(Grapsus tenuicrustatus),* which is extremely common on rocky Hawaiian shorelines. These crabs climb to seabird rookeries up to perhaps 25 feet above sea level and, with their small but powerful claws, seize newly hatched terns or other small chicks, and kill and partially consume them. Even less conspicuous is a major predator on adult seabirds, the tiger shark *(Galeocerdo cuvieri).* No swimming bird is safe from this denizen of offshore waters. In Hawaii, tigers are known to reach eighteen feet in length and to have a bite that would make a whole albatross seem a tidbit. In a recent study throughout the NWHI, marine biologists have found more seabirds in the guts of tiger sharks than any other prey, which included turtles, lobsters, cephalopods (squids and octopus), and fish.[17]

Of course, human impacts on Hawaii's seabirds and their habitats have been enormous. In general however, the destruction has been less comprehensive than that directed against the native terrestrial birds and their fragile ecological settings. Still, when the Polynesians arrived, Hawaiian seabirds were faced with their first mammalian predators—domestic dogs, pigs, and the Pacific rat, *Rattus exulans* (the rat came as a stowaway or perhaps a pet) as well as human beings themselves. Polynesians ate a variety of seabirds, although they seem to have shunned eggs. Certain species, notably terns and petrels, were esteemed over others.[18] Some Hawaiian lore indicates that chicks were generally more favored as food than adult seabirds. In Hawaii, the dark-rumped petrel, *uau,* was especially sought after, and, at least in fairly recent times, was reserved for chiefs.[19] These birds were netted in the evening along mountain ridges as they returned from the sea to their rookeries. Sometimes smoky fires were lit in the paths of incoming flocks; the birds would become disoriented and disabled in the smoke and could then be caught by hand.[20]

An old Hawaiian story recorded in midnineteenth century by a French visitor named de Remy suggests that dark-rumped petrels were not easy to obtain even in earlier times.[21] In the story, a chief Hua wanted some *uau* to eat and sent two servants off to catch them. Reluctant to go into the mountains for these birds, the servants made the much easier trek to the seacoast, procured some of the abundant wedge-tailed shearwaters *(uau-kani)* nesting there and returned with them to their master. Chief Hua, a procellariiform gourmet, was not fooled when he tasted the inferior birds. The fate of the two servants was left to the hearer's imagination.

Excessive hunting of these birds by Hawaiians, as well as intensified predation by introduced mammals since European contact, probably accounts for this petrel's present rarity and restricted nesting at extremely high elevations. Ornithological surveys in the past have indicated that this bird's former nesting range was between 1,500 and 5,000 feet.[22] On Kauai, a large colony of *uau* reportedly persisted until midnineteenth century on the slopes of Kilohana Crater (about 1,100 feet in elevation) just inland from Lihue, the present island capital.[23] The ensuing burst of agricultural development in this region, with a simultaneous expansion of the dog, cat, and rat populations, doomed the Kilohana breeding colony.

Now extirpated on Kauai, and pushed thousands of feet higher than former preferred elevations on Maui and Hawaii, these birds may be close to absolute physiological limits in terms of adult energetics and the gas-exchange requirements of eggs.[24] Thus stressed, they would seem to be endangered beyond the mere numerical definition, for they are hanging on only at the very edge of their habitable breeding range.

The early Hawaiians hunted birds not only as food, but also for their feathers. Capes or cloaks, ceremonial helmets, leis, and other regalia were made largely from the feathers of small, brightly colored passerine birds, but according to Brigham, perhaps the foremost authority on the subject, at least three species of seabirds were also sought for their plumage.[25] The long tail feathers of both of Hawaii's tropicbirds were used in making *kahilis,* large, cylindrical feather clusters attached to long poles. *Kahilis* were carried by special bearers in processions and on occasions of state. They were symbols of rank of participating chiefs. *P. rubricauda* was valued more by the Hawaiian feather hunters than the white-tailed species. As late as 1879, however, Sanford Dole, the famous missionary scion, statesman, and revolutionary and an avid amateur ornithologist, reported that the red-tailed tropicbird was still common on Kauai and Niihau, and that "the natives climb the almost inaccessible cliffs to get the rose-colored tail feathers which they pull from the birds on their nests."[26] In the 1890s, Brigham indicated that this species could be found abundantly only on Nihoa and Necker Islands in the NWHI. He himself plucked tail feathers from a sitting bird, "who did not seem to greatly resent the outrage."[27] However, many of these birds did not get off so lightly. Brigham also records that the satiny white body plumage was used for capes, and other sources indicate that tropicbirds were eaten by Hawaiians.[28]

Frigatebirds were also traditionally hunted for their plumage. Their long, black, glossy feathers were used for both *kahilis* and cloaks. The latter were sometimes exquisitely trimmed with a border of small red and yellow feathers from forest birds.[29]

With the Euro-American development of the islands, seabird populations began to diminish under new onslaughts. Besides the major introduced predators of earlier times, a number of others appeared. The worst of them seems to be the small Indian mongoose *Herpestes auropunctatus,* released on numerous sugar plantations in the 1880s in the hope that it would control rodents. Other introduced predators include the barn owl, *Tyto alba,* brought to Hawaii from California in 1958, and the common myna, *Acridotheres tristis,* imported from India in 1865. The barn owl has been seen to kill wedge-tailed and Newell's shearwaters, Bulwer's petrel, brown noddies, and two species of terns.[30] The omnivorous myna is on record as preying on eggs of wedge-tailed shearwaters on Kauai; nests attacked were in shallow burrows that allowed the eggs to be seen from outside. Mynas on Midway Atoll were seen attacking noddies and white terns on their nests. Eggs and chicks were thrown out and then apparently eaten by mynas on the ground.[31]

Introduced diseases have ravaged Hawaii's native birds, although seabirds have been generally less affected than others. Still, the diseases are spreading. One of the worst is avian pox. Caused by a mosquito-borne virus, avian pox has long been a scourge of passerine birds in the islands (see chapter 14). However, as mentioned, red-tailed tropicbirds seem especially susceptible to avian pox, which may have been a factor in this species' retreat from the main islands. Now avian pox has spread to Midway Atoll, where introduced canaries and mynas are believed to serve as carriers of the virus transmitted to seabirds by the introduced mosquito *Culex quinquefasciatus.* An alarming rate of pox infection has also been found recently in Midway's population of Laysan albatross.[32]

As the ravages of predators and disease intensified after European contact, direct human impacts on seabirds also increased and went farther afield. A new era of feather hunting opened toward the end of the nineteenth century; this time it was driven by the dictates of affluent society worldwide, which favored bird plumage in fashionable attire, particularly ladies' hats. The exploitation in Hawaii was focused in the NWHI, and, in contrast to the cottage craft of the early Hawaiians, its style became expeditionary and industrial.

Few Hawaiians were involved in feather collecting at this time. One exception became a tragicomic incident in 1885, when Princess (later Queen) Liliuokalani and a large party of Honolulu's elite, about 200 gentleman and ladies, sailed to Nihoa for feathers and an adventurous outing. The gentlemen did some exploring and scientific observing on the side. While ashore, the expeditionaries accidentally started a brush fire that swept across the island. No one was injured, but much of Nihoa's then very dry vegetation was destroyed.[33]

Subsequent feather hunting in the islands was no Victorian picnic, but a grim market hunt carried on primarily by Japanese. Japan was a major supplier to the world millinery trade, which, from about 1870 to 1920, was an insatiable devourer of birds with unusual or attractive plumage. By the early twentieth century, reaction to the slaughter had brought legal protection of many so-called plume species—for example, in the southeastern United States.[34] Such restrictions in the supply coincided with the rather late extension of exploitation to the seabirds of the NWHI.

Massive kills are well documented for Laysan, Lisiansky, and Midway, but probably occurred all along the leeward chain. On Midway in 1902, a scientific expedition found thousands of recently slaughtered birds with wings and tails removed.[35] In 1904, a U.S. military patrol arrived at Lisiansky to find a Japanese crew of about seventy-five packing up. Estimates of their kill on the island (also later reported as occurring in 1905) approached 300,000 birds. The wings and skins, dried and packed in bales, were reported as having a value of $20,000; the snow-white tern, *Gygis alba,* had been a special target of the Lisiansky hunters, but only the drab noddies were considered worthless and spared.[36] The Lisiansky hunters were not prosecuted, for no law specifically protected the birds. It took five more years of increasing public outrage over the NWHI bird kills to get official action. At last, in 1909, President Theodore Roosevelt by executive order established the Hawaiian Islands Bird Reservation. It included all of the NWHI except Midway Atoll, which was and still is under U.S Naval jurisdiction. Later, the name was changed to the Hawaiian Islands National Wildlife Refuge.

The most notorious bird massacre was on Laysan.[37] In 1904, a bumptious entrepreneur named Max Schlemmer applied to the Hawaiian Land Commission for a ninety-nine-year lease to the islands of Laysan, Lisiansky, and French Frigate Shoals. Schlemmer was then the NWHI agent for the Pacific Guano and Fertilizer Company, which, after more than a decade of mining on Laysan, had largely depleted the phosphate resource and was suspending operations on the island. Although the company still held the property lease to Laysan and other islands, it sold its mining equipment and resource rights to Schlemmer.

Although he did continue to exploit the diminishing guano reserves for several more years, the "King of Laysan Island," as Schlemmer came to be called, conceived of a variety of other commercial schemes (see chapter 10) on his tiny calcined kingdom. Among these, he proposed an annual harvest of feathers and skins that included thousands of sea-birds—up to 5,000 per season of some species such as Laysan albatrosses and sooty terns. Schlemmer's list even included the unique endemic land birds of the island.[38] For example, his suggested bag limit for the flightless Laysan rail *(Porzanula palmeri;* see chapter 10) was 1,000 per season.

Mining guano and waiting for his lease proposal to rise through multiple bureaucratic layers in Honolulu, Schlemmer apparently finally decided that his agent's commission from the mining company gave him discretionary control over all exploitable resources in his purview. In December 1908, he concluded a deal in Tokyo, selling to Japanese interests for fifteen years all rights to "Phosphate, Guano, and products of whatever nature in and from the islands of Laysan and Lisianski."[39] Max Schlemmer's own lease (for fifteen years) to Laysan and Lisiansky came through in February 1909, but it specifically forbade the killing or capturing of birds, and it came just five days after Roosevelt's establishment of the Hawaiian Islands Bird Reservation.

A year later, Schlemmer was suspected of aiding and abetting Japanese bird-killing crews on Laysan and Lisiansky. He was tried twice on charges of poaching on a federal reservation and importing illegal aliens, but was acquitted even though authorities had discovered in his little settlement on Laysan approximately two and a quarter tons of feathers and more than 300,000 birds' wings. Estimates of the value of the grisly harvest ranged from $96,000 to about $130,000. This time, albatross wings were the item of choice; the two Hawaiian-breeding albatross species accounted for a majority of the hundreds of thousands of birds killed between April 1909 and January 1910. The Japanese poachers were rounded up and brought to Honolulu, but charges against them were dismissed, and they were deported. The only benefit from this sad slaughter accrued to flies and carrion beetles. According to eye witnesses, those insects teemed in astronomical proportions around the countless bird carcasses littering the low, insular landscapes.

Feather trading was only part of Max Schlemmer's otherwise legal but utterly devastating career in the NWHI (see chapter 10). One of his innovations was to collect (mostly albatross) eggs, tons of them at a time. He sold the bulk of them for the manufacture of photographic emulsion.[40] Reportedly, he even made trips to Johnston Island, hundreds of miles to the south, to collect cargoes of "gooney eggs and guano."[41]

After 1910, when all the commercial-grade guano had been strip mined, Laysan was steadily stripped of its vegetation by introduced rabbits, which also crowded out burrowing seabirds. Lisiansky suffered a similar plague of rabbits. The naturalist W. A. Bryan, who visited Laysan

9.3 Laysan Island impact. Albatross, *Diomedea immutabilis,* amid egg collecting operations in early twentieth century. State Archive Photo.

in 1902 and again in 1911, estimated at least a tenfold reduction in the seabird population during that interval.[42] The island further declined to a sandy wasteland populated primarily by starving rabbits. Only after 1923, when the last of the rabbits died, did Laysan and its seabird populations begin a slow recovery.

Later twentieth-century impacts on seabirds were generally less concentrated and more varied. Many of them were related to military activities in the islands. U.S Navy and Coast Guard bases at French Frigate Shoals, Midway, and Kure Atoll brought habitat destruction and inevitable hazards to the birds, which were killed on runways and in collisions with buildings and antenna wires. Deliberate "bird control" was sometimes deemed necessary. The navy "managed" the albatross population on Midway, and the coast guard thinned out sooty terns on FFS. Elsewhere, military actions ranged from such harassment as firing big guns over island rookeries to send up the birds (a sport of bored ships' crews since cannons were first carried to sea) to modern saturation bombing and shelling of specified target islands.

Foremost among the targets have been Kaula, southwest of Niihau, and Kahoolawe, seventh largest of the Hawaiian Chain. Both islands are (or were) major seabird nurseries. On Kahoolawe, dangerous unexploded ordnance litters much of the island. A few procellariiforms still raise young in their flimsy bunkers amid the blasted, cratered terrain of modern warfare. Although the military establishment in Hawaii professes concern over ecological and wildlife issues, unofficial callousness is sometimes evident even away from the target islands, as for example in several mass shootings in 1979 of nesting red-footed boobies at a nominally protected rookery near a U.S. Marine Corps rifle range on Oahu.[43]

Recently, a number of marine ecologists and seabird specialists have studied major environmental factors that affect Hawaiian seabird populations. Predation is still an extremely serious threat. In the NWHI, introduced rats have been a severe scourge on Midway and Kure Atolls. Midway's rats arrived with the U.S. Navy during World War II. On Kure, Polynesian rats *(R. exulans)* were observed as early as 1870 and probably came from a shipwreck. Modern scientific observers report that although these rats are largely herbivorous, sporadic population explosions of rats have coincided with extensive predation on at least ten species of Kure's seabirds. Between 1964 and 1968, rats are believed to have caused complete breeding failure of Bonin petrels *(Pterodroma hypoleuca)* on the island, and in 1968 they destroyed all eggs and young in the sooty tern colony. Along with those species, grey-backed terns *(Sterna lunata),* red-tailed tropicbirds, and the Laysan albatross were especially hard hit. Amazingly, groups of rats on Kure seem to have learned to cooperate in attacking large birds, including albatrosses. The rats leap on a bird's back and slowly kill it by gnawing into its back muscles, then partially consume the carcass. A poisoning program begun on Kure in the late 1960s is helping to control the rats.[44]

On the main islands, predation at nesting sites is a longstanding impact. It is especially critical with regard to the rare procellariiforms that breed in remote mountain areas. Yet even some well-known rookeries are perennially plundered by dogs and cats where protection is as simple as building and maintaining a good fence. On Kauai, at two accessible coastal sites, including panoramic Kilauea Point, Laysan albatrosses have attempted to breed nearly every year since the late 1970s. However, chicks as well as adults have been consistently killed by dogs, and albatross eggs even removed by humans.[45] The Kilauea site, a few acres with a lighthouse and stunning cliffside vistas, was formerly a coast guard station and is now protected as a tiny federal wildlife refuge. However, many of the seabirds that attempt to breed there, including the albatross and red-tailed tropicbird, do so outside the refuge's pitifully small fenced area on land that is slated for residential development. There is some hope of extending the federal refuge to include more of the prime rookery terrain. So far, however, the state of Hawaii, though it could expedite the effort, seems little interested in protecting its most spectacular seabirds, which, at no cost, are attempting to reintroduce themselves to the main islands. With better protection, Kilauea Point would make a unique visitor attraction in the manner of Tairoa Head on New Zealand's South Island. There, a reestablished colony of the royal albatross is beginning to flourish along with well-managed tours to view and photograph the fabled birds.

Mongoose control would also help to assure the tenure of some seabird populations in the main islands. Out in the NWHI, efforts to control the spread of avian diseases and their vectors, especially mosquitoes, are also needed. Exotic carriers of avian pox should be removed from Midway and prevented from establishing populations on any other of the Northwestern Hawaiian Islands.

Future large-scale developments in mid-Pacific fisheries could endanger Hawaiian seabirds. The expanding pelagic squid fishery north of the Hawaiian Chain is a distinct threat. The enormously long drift nets used for squid are deadly traps for birds, just as they are for sea turtles (see chapter 8). Lost nets and net fragments, by the yard and by the mile, have begun to festoon the reefs and beaches of the NWHI and entrap wildlife there. In Alaska, kills of hundreds of thousands of seabirds trapped in virtually identical nets used by the salmon fishery are on record.[46] In Hawaii, snarls of fishing line, plastics, wire, and other entangling trash discarded from passing vessels add to the potentially lethal litter. This is a worldwide problem of growing magnitude.[47]

Seabirds and humans are competitors on the sea, and overfishing by man may have direct effects on seabird populations. Of course, many of the species selected by birds are not those consumed by people. Yet both extract energy from pelagic food chains. In Hawaiian waters, humans and birds do compete directly for several fishes—for example, *akule (Selar crumenopthalmus),* a small mackerel; also goatfishes (family Mullidae); and the baitfish, or *nehu (Stolephorus).* Likewise, an expanding squid fishery close to the NWHI would take food from the mouths of all eighteen species of seabirds that breed on those islands. Currently, NWHI birds consume an estimated 490 million pounds of squid annually,[48] a far greater amount than for any other single category of prey.

A majority of Hawaii's seabirds catch their prey within the uppermost foot or two of the sea, and it is now thought that the common relationship between feeding flocks of seabirds and schools of large predatory fish is not merely opportunism on the part of the birds. Many of these birds probably depend on big fish to drive their common prey to the very surface of the sea. Concern has arisen among biologists and environmentalists in Hawaii that extreme exploitation of regional tuna stocks could diminish food availability for seabirds. The tuna connection is a vital ecological cooperation, another example of the seamless weaving of evolution across biospheric borders.

Seabirds are high in the marine food chain and tend to concentrate trace substances from the sea. In continental areas with a history of industrial and agricultural pollution, they harbor large and damaging body burdens of such contaminants as DDE and PCBs (compounds related to DDT and other chlorinated hydrocarbon pesticides) and toxic metals such as mercury and cadmium. In the mid-1980s, however, Hawaii's ocean ecosystems are still relatively untainted with these biocidal products of modern industrial society. While it has been found that levels of the classic pollutants—petroleum, pesticides, and heavy metals—are indeed elevated in a few harbors, pollution diminishes rapidly offshore. And so far, Hawaiian seabirds carry only traces of the toxins found abundantly in their continental counterparts. For example, wedge-tailed shearwater eggs from Oahu contained the highest organochlorine concentration in recent Hawaiian samples (up to 1.5 ppm DDE).[49] By contrast, in eggs of California brown pelicans during the 1970s, average DDE/DDT levels were well over 100 ppm, having declined from nearly 1,000 ppm in 1969 during the era of disastrous reproductive failures in pelican rookeries on California's Channel Islands.[50] Metal contamination of Hawaiian seabirds is also well below that of most North American species, and while oil spills severely threaten seabirds, so far Hawaii has avoided large-scale problems in that category. However, a proposed fishing port in the NWHI would bring the danger of toxic-fuel oil spills to one or more islands and their wildlife.

For seabirds in both the main islands and the NWHI, the most critical immediate issue is to protect breeding habitats. Whether land predators or oil spills decimate the rookeries, the result is the same. In the broad sweep of time and the Pacific, Hawaii will be diminished. Stewart Fefer and colleagues at the U.S. Fish and Wildlife Service, in their recent comprehensive study of seabirds of the NWHI, call the overall breeding colony there one of the most important in the world.[51] Indeed, these small islands, which resonate to the wingbeats and voices of birds, host one of the earth's most impressive concentrations of wildlife. Because of their isolation, they can remain largely unaffected by the ongoing loss of wildlife and the retreat of wildness worldwide. The birds of the ocean are wonderful symbols of freedom and the vast potential of life, symbols that are bound to be treasured in future decades and by future human generations.

PART THREE

Shores of Many Moods

10

Lonely Rocks and Atolls

Most accounts of the nature of the Northwestern Hawaiian Islands consider only present appearances. The seabirds are extolled; the green sea turtle and the Hawaiian seal are given special mention. To be sure, the origin of these islands from big shield volcanoes is alluded to, but the terrestrial ecosystems of the NWHI seem to fade to insignificance beside those of the sprawling, young mountainous islands to the southeast. And yet it should be remembered that only yesterday in the geological history of Hawaii, when the sea level was lower by hundreds of feet, the northwestern islands were much larger. Some of them covered hundreds of square miles. And there were more of them. Most of the submerged banks and shoals that lie scattered among today's vestigial islands presented dry land to Pleistocene Pacific skies.

Among the largest, comparable in planar area to Kauai or Oahu, were Necker Island Shoal, the shallow platform that supports Maro Reef (a place where there is no dry land today), and an unnamed twenty-by-fifty-mile bank that at present supports Gardner Pinnacles near its northern edge. Others—such as French Frigate Shoals; Neva Shoal, which surrounds Lisiansky Island; and Pearl and Hermes Reef—were nearly the present size of Lanai but lacked its volcanic profile. They were islands of low relief on limestone soil. With a cool, wet glacial-epoch climate, as cold fronts probably pushed into subtropical latitudes with greater vigor than today, they may have featured lakes and bogs and sluggish streams among ranges of sand hills. The interior terrain probably looked like that of Martha's Vineyard or central Florida, except where the incongruous basalt spires of Gardner Pinnacles, La Pérouse Rock, Necker, and Nihoa reared high above the plains.

In combined area, the Northwest Chain, prior to 10,000 years ago, rivaled today's main Hawaiian Islands. In terrestrial flora and fauna, the emerged atolls and shoals must have been richer than today, and their reef life, compressed into fairly narrow marginal contours, may have been poorer. One wonders about the status of seabirds then and especially that of the green turtle and Hawaiian seal. What would have been the ecological effect of the tremendously augmented shoreline area in the NWHI versus the loss in shallow foraging habitat for those animals?

For a million years or so while the world's great ice sheets ebbed and flowed on faraway continents, the NWHI went through several long cycles of submergence and emergence. One thing seems certain: the tiny

155

northwestern islands of today, which encompass about five square miles and less than one-tenth of one percent of the land area of the archipelago, should not be considered typical. Recent analyses of long-term sea-level fluctuation indicate that the NWHI may have been in an expanded state for more than 100,000 years before, very recently, being submerged by the worldwide melting of glaciers.[1] Humans missed seeing them as a major landform in the Hawaiian Islands only by a few millenia.

At present, there are ten Northwestern Hawaiian Islands (see map, chapter 1). Kaula Rock, a curving, eroded remnant of a volcanic tuff cone that dots an eight-mile-wide shoal southwest of Niihau, is often considered part of the group, but Maro Reef, a huge shoal of coral and sand awash at low tide in many places but with no dry land, is excluded.

The NWHI range in age from Midway and neighboring Kure, which have been islands of one sort or another (with perhaps occasional interludes of total submergence) for more than 25 million years, to Nihoa, located about 150 miles northwest of Kauai. Nihoa's rocks, which form the largest volcanic remnant in the NWHI, have been dated at approximately 7.5 million years old.[2]

In size, the present islands range from Laysan, with about 1.5 square miles, or nearly 1,000 acres (including a small saltwater lake in its center), to Gardner Pinnacles, something more than three acres of steep, crumbling volcanic rock covered with bird dung. Nihoa is the highest of the group, reaching just over 900 feet above the sea.

The climate of the Northwest Chain is oceanic subtropical. There is none of the topographically controlled variation seen in the larger Hawaiian Islands. Much of the twenty-five to forty inches of annual rainfall occurs in the cooler winter months. Winter brings bouts of stormy weather with winds that reach gale strength. Summers tend to be breezy but warm with only occasional rain showers. Hurricanes are rare but potentially devastating to the ecology of these low islands. Tidal waves (more properly, *tsunamis*) constitute another rare but inevitable environmental force here. However, without the funnel-shaped embayments and coastal valleys that magnify the local effect of a *tsunami,* such a wave would take the form of a powerful, low surge or rapid rise in sea level rather than a steep breaking wave. A very low island might be entirely swept over but retain most of its salt-resistant plant life intact. Storm waves, with their great turbulence, are apt to be more destructive. For example, in December 1969, huge storm seas washed completely over eight-foot-high Tern Island at FFS, removing much of the island's vegetation and severely damaging the U.S. Coast Guard navigation station there. Several people and three dogs were rescued from the roof of one of the damaged buildings.[3]

10.1 View from Nihoa Island. In the foreground: Nihoa fan (*loulu*) palm, *Pritch-ardia remota*; also the rare, spreading legume shrub, *Sesbania tomentosa (ohai)*.

Terrestrial biotic diversity in the NWHI ranges from its nadir at Gardner Pinnacles—which has a single species of flowering plant, the widespread succulent, *Portulaca lutea,* and five species of insects—to the relative species richness of Nihoa. The latter island has at least several dozen native land plants and animals. A majority of the latter are insects. Nihoa's living diversity, however, may have been second to that of Laysan Island before the latter's devastation by human activities beginning in the late nineteenth century.

Today, the native vegetation of the NWHI is very similar to that of the less disturbed shorelines of the main islands. Along the beaches, many of the typical coastal shrubs and herbs are the same from Hawaii Island to Kure Atoll. The beach *naupaka (Scaevola sericea); alena (Boerhavia);* the *nohu,* or puncture vine *(Tribulus);* a couple of morning

glories *(Ipomoea);* and several native grasses and sedges are nearly ubiquitous. On Necker and Nihoa, the graceful *ohai (Sesbania tomentosa)*
maintains a precarious existence. This is probably the rarest of several
native *Sesbania* shrubs (the genus is also represented by species on
Molokai and Hawaii). The only other habitat of *S. tomentosa* is on
westernmost Oahu, where it is nearly extinct (see chapter 11).

Nihoa Island boasts the last stand of native trees in the NWHI. The
Nihoa trees belong to a species of small fan palm, *Pritchardia remota;*
congeners grow on the main islands, primarily in areas of greater rainfall. Fan palms up to fifteen feet tall also grew on Laysan Island into
the 1890s. They were certainly native trees and identified as the genus
Pritchardia, but were destroyed before a specific classification could
be confirmed.[4] A shrubby Laysan sandalwood, *Santalum cuneatum,**
also now extinct, has been regarded as an endemic variety, or subspecics,
known as *laysanicum.*[5]

A few other plants of the NWHI are classified as endemic in that portion of the archipelago. An example is in the genus *Nama,* a matlike
plant with small, pale blue flowers. According to the botanist Sherwin
Carlquist, slight consistent differences seem to separate a variety from
Laysan from one found in the main Hawaiian Islands. Nihoa's flora includes several endemic varieties and species—for example, *Solanum
nelsoni,* a rare nightshade also found on the tiny islets of Pearl and
Hermes Reef.[6]

A greater proportion of endemicity is found in the land animals of the
Northwest Chain. For example, six of the seven native species (among
five genera) of land snails on Nihoa are endemic to the island. The
families Endodontidae and Achatinellidae, both represented by thriving populations on Nihoa, were once enormously diverse and abundant
on the main Hawaiian Islands (see chapter 15), but have suffered massive
extinction there in the last century. The endodontids, regarded by some
experts as having primitive features, have been virtually eradicated
throughout the Pacific. Perhaps the two species in two genera that survive on Nihoa can be regarded as living fossils. They appear to be the
last of some 200 species of this family native to Hawaii.[7]

Native land snails have been found on all the NWHI except FFS and
Gardner Pinnacles. These unique mollusk populations are all that is left
of an evolutionary phenomenon: an extraordinarily rich Hawaiian lowland snail fauna that is now mostly a scattering of dry and dusty shells.

Also on Nihoa Island is a giant endemic cricket in the genus *Thaumatogryllus.* It is related to much smaller species of tree crickets on the
main islands. Wayne Gagné, a senior entomologist at Honolulu's Bishop
Museum, suggests that if giant forms of such crickets ever existed on

---

*Now called *S. ellipticum.*

the larger Hawaiian Islands, they would have been highly susceptible to predation by rats introduced by the early Polynesians, and so could have died out well before Western contact. Other arthropods, such as weevils, mites, and spiders, have speciated, or at least diverged into distinct races on various islands of the NWHI.

The most celebrated of the land fauna of the NWHI are endemic birds. Nihoa and Laysan, the two largest islands in the group, possibly along with Lisiansky, had the only native land birds by the time Western observers arrived and took time to record such things. On Nihoa there are two species; one is an old-world warbler (family Sylviidae), *Acrocephalus familiaris kingi*. Small, secretive, and cryptically colored, this species keeps to dense, brushy cover on the island and was discovered only in 1923. It was nicknamed the millerbird for its predation on moths called millers, which are abundant flying insects on Nihoa. The second bird is the Nihoa finch *(Telospyza cantans ultima)*. It is a Hawaiian honeycreeper (family Drepanididae*) and was long thought to have been isolated from its remarkable relatives in the main islands whose adaptive radiation has exhibited such spectacular flourishes. Recently discovered fossils, however, indicate that birds identical in skeletal anatomy to the Nihoa finch were common in the lowlands of Oahu and others of the high islands until Polynesian times.[8] Westerners discovered the Nihoa finch in 1917. It was given the scientific name *ultima* when it was presumed that no more Hawaiian birds remained to be found. Then, in 1923, the Nihoa millerbird turned up, and even this turned out not to be the ultimate (see chapter 14).

On Laysan, until early in the twentieth century, was found an astonishing suite of native, nonoceanic birds. They had all been discovered well before the Nihoa birds. One was a flightless rail, *Porzanula palmeri*. Early descriptions along with a few paintings, photographs, and museum specimens reveal it to have been about six inches long and concealingly patterned with light and dark brown streaks. The eye, however, was bright red. Newly hatched chicks were jet black with yellow bills. A short tail and rounded, stubby wings made the Laysan rail resemble related birds known historically from numerous oceanic islands, including Hawaii and perhaps Maui and Molokai (and now known too as recent fossils distributed even more widely). The family Rallidae on oceanic islands seems to have a powerful evolutionary predeliction to flightlessness (see chapter 18).

Eyewitness accounts of the Laysan rail endow the species with a quirky charm and make its loss a poignant one for any lover of birds. It was an exceedingly fast runner, said to snatch flies out of the air. Reportedly, five-day-old chicks were as swift as adults; their little black

---

*Or the subfamily Drepanidinae in the finch family, Fringillidae (see chapter 14).

10.2   The extinct flightless Laysan rail. From W. Rothschild. 1893–1900. *The Avifauna of Laysan and the Neighboring Islands.* R.H. Porter, London.

bodies appeared to roll at high speed over the ground.[9] The birds were omnivorous, feeding on carrion and small seabird eggs as well as insects and vegetation. A naturalist in 1891 described how the Laysan rail dealt with eggs that were too hard to crack by normal pecking. It jumped high over the egg in order to magnify the force of its beak on impact, and repeated the performance until the shell was broken.[10]

Laysan's avifauna also included two honeycreepers, of which one—a pretty red and black form *(Himatione sanguinea freethii,* a race of the species called *apapane* in the high islands)—became extinct in 1923. Earlier visitors to the island marveled at its tameness; when captured, one reportedly continued to sing as it was held in an ornithologist's hand. The other is the Laysan finch *(Telospyza cantans cantans).* Distinct from the Nihoa finch at the subspecies level, it still thrives under strict protection of its home island's habitat. Although by the 1920s drastically reduced, its breeding population once again numbers a few thousand, making for an average of several birds per acre on Laysan.

Like the rail, *T. cantans* on both Laysan and Nihoa was noted as omnivorous and an egg eater. With its stout beak, the finch can break open eggs fairly easily. Early observers on Laysan noted that a rail sometimes waited until a finch had broken open a seabird's egg, and then chased the finch away and ate the contents.[11]

There was also a Laysan millerbird *(Acrocephalus familiaris familiaris),* again deemed a racial variant of the same species as on Nihoa, and similar in appearance and habits. The Laysan millerbird was extinct by the 1920s. And finally there is a duck, *Anas laysanensis,* clearly related to the *koloa (A. wyvilliana)* of the main islands but considered a distinct species. In the early nineteenth century, resident ducks were reported on Lisiansky Island as well as Laysan, but later visitors to Lisiansky did not mention them, and a scientific survey of that island in 1891 confirmed their disappearance.[12]

Laysan ducks do much of their foraging at night. They subsist largely on insects—grubs and caterpillars gleaned from vegetation and the maggots of flies and beetles in the carcasses of seabirds. Along the shore of Laysan's saline lake, they consume salt-pan flies *(Neoscatella),* and on the seashore they sometimes forage for marine life in shallow pools.[13]

In recent years this duck's population on Laysan has fluctuated from a few dozen to a few hundred breeding pairs. Fortunately, successful captive breeding programs have been established at a number of zoos and aviaries in Hawaii and abroad. The Laysan duck probably evolved in the sprawling marshes of the Pleistocene NWHI. Since that time, nature and man have drastically restricted its horizons and prospects for survival, making it one of the world's rarest ducks.

MULTIPLE USE AND ABUSE

The Hawaiians of Captain Cook's day apparently knew little about the Northwest Chain. Kaula Rock and another island, the phantom Ka Moku Papapa, said to lie a day's paddle southwest of Kaula, were mentioned to Cook's party by some of the first Hawaiians they encountered. These two places were touted as rich in seabirds and turtles, gourmet foods for *alii,* the Hawaiian nobility. Captain Cook himself charted Kaula on his departure from Niihau in February 1778, but Ka Moku Papapa, which means "the flat island," has never turned up in the area designated. Other legends mention Nihoa, but the Hawaiian name for Necker apparently was lost. Both had early Hawaiian settlements that seem to have been short-lived. By the time of Cook's arrival, islands to the west of Kauai were dimly remembered as places of the dead and probably had not been visited for centuries. There is no evidence to show that Hawaiians ever reached French Frigate Shoals or beyond.

Nihoa and Necker were surely altered to some degree when Hawaiians lived on them. The archaeology of the two islands was recently summarized by Pacific prehistorian Patrick Kirch. Most of the work was done in 1923 by the eminent archaeologist Kenneth Emory on an expedition for the Bishop Museum.[14]

On Nihoa, the ruins include religious structures, dwelling sites, and prominent agricultural terraces. No irrigation was possible, so it is surmised that the main crop was the sweet potato; low rainfall made more common Polynesian staples such as taro and bananas impossible to grow. Emory calculated that the estimated twelve acres of terraces, which occupied every possible location on Nihoa's gentler slopes, could have produced about forty-eight tons of sweet potatoes annually. From this and the number of stone dwellings and shelters in evidence, it has been suggested that the island could have supported a human population of 100 to 200 persons, their existence always threatened by drought.

Although Nihoa has no reef, protein sources were available in the shallow surrounding sea, and were also readily at hand during much of the year in the huge seabird colony. The Nihoa finch and millerbird obviously survived the Hawaiian occupation, but one wonders if other land birds, perhaps a flightless rail, might have concentrated on Nihoa from a wider late-Pleistocene range and was clinging to existence until the Hawaiians arrived. One wonders too about the vegetation. No doubt the people used *Pritchardia* for thatching, but they didn't destroy it. *Pandanus* is not known to have existed on Nihoa. If it was introduced, it did not—surprisingly—survive into historical times. It is uncertain how long people stayed on Nihoa. Although they seem to have occupied it to the maximum extent, they left what Wayne Gagné calls the most intact native shoreline ecosystem in modern Hawaii.

If Nihoa was a difficult place to inhabit, even for an oceanic people, Necker would seem to have been impossible. The island has an area of only forty-five acres, mostly steep rocky ridges, peaking at 276 feet above the sea. Nevertheless, some sixty archaeological sites have been found, mainly of a religious nature, but with a few dubious agricultural terraces on very shallow soil. Perhaps the people who endured on Necker for an uncertain span of time, which, as on Nihoa, was probably fairly early in the Hawaiian period,* were castaways. Still, they were quite industrious in their stone-age fashion—for example, carrying up to several tons of wave-rounded cobbles to the top of the island to pave a large marae (temple platform). Their fate may have been as imagined by the naturalist Sherwin Carlquist:

> I would guess that they were marooned, unable to sail for another island (there are no really woody plants on Necker, so even a raft could not be constructed). They might have survived for a while on birds and eggs and the small seeps of water, but perhaps they eventually died, building their maraes as a sort of desperate symbol of hope.[15]

On both Nihoa and Necker, fresh water is extremely scarce. Except during actual rainstorms, the only terrestrial sources are tiny seeps. Researchers have found three seeps on Nihoa, two on Necker. The water is badly tainted with bird dung; possibly at times it is even toxic with nitrogen compounds and unsuitable for long-term human consumption. The problem of water availability on the two islands has always been

---

*Kirch (1985) suggests around 1000 A.D.

viewed by archaeologists as the greatest constraint on sustained human occupation there, but perhaps more water is available in such midocean desert spots than can be collected on the surface. Clusters of vertical dikes, especially on Nihoa, may create storage compartments for fresh water, and lava channels may lead water out under the seabed. That Hawaiians were adept at locating and exploiting such undersea springs, which sometimes form room-size upwellings off waterless coasts on the main islands, is known from the observations of such explorers as William Ellis and Titus Coan. But the location of any potential hidden water resources around Nihoa and Necker is a secret lost long ago. Perhaps it died on the utterly lonely ridges of Nihoa, where traces of human skeletal remains have been found. At one site were four adults with petrels nesting among their bones. At another, an adult and two children shared an open ledge facing the sea.[16]

Much later, in November 1786, the discovery of the outer leeward chain began when the great French navigator, La Pérouse, nearly ran aground on French Frigate Shoals in the middle of the night. The two vessels under his command were fresh from the rediscovery two days earlier of Necker Island, named by La Pérouse for the French minister of finance under King Louis XVI. La Pérouse had missed Nihoa, which was restored to the seafarer's ken in 1789 by British Captain William Douglas commanding HMS *Iphigenia*. Apart from Kaula Rock, first fixed on Western charts by James Cook, the rest of the NWHI were found helter-skelter by whalers, traders, and naval expeditions. Englishmen, Americans, and Russians are credited with the discoveries. Midway was the last to be charted, in 1859, by which time nearby Kure Atoll (then called Ocean Island) had been known for at least two decades. But these two islands, only fifty-six nautical miles apart, are at nearly the same latitude and are so similar in geography that early mariners, whose errors in longitude were often large, may have frequently confused them.

The fate of these low, sandy scraps of land, with their evolutionary curiosities, breaks into many tales—of desperate castaways and failing entrepreneurs subsisting on the islands' meager resources, and of industrial and military turmoil on fragile terrain. Many of the stories deserve telling by a Louis Becke or a Stevenson. In fact, late-nineteenth-century Midway is a setting in one of the latter's novels.* The following pages summarize the major surges of environmental change that swept over the NWHI.

In all the NWHI, the island most famous for human disturbance is Laysan. In 1890, a permanent settlement was established there by the North Pacific Phosphate and Fertilizer Company, based in Honolulu. The company's objective was to mine the island's guano deposits, which

---

The Wrecker (London: Cassell, 1893).

had been known at least since Captain John Paty's visit in 1857.[17] Also in 1890, the company was granted mining rights to Lisiansky, and a few years later to Kure, Midway, Pearl and Hermes Reef, and French Frigate Shoals. Traces of phosphate (guano) occurred on all those islands, but only Laysan proved to have commercially exploitable quantities.

With pickaxes, gangs of contract laborers who were predominantly Japanese hacked out the loosely consolidated guano—a mixture of limy sandstone and petrified bird dung. It was loaded in small hopper cars and hauled by mules over a narrow-gauge railway to storage sheds at the settlement near the boat landing on Laysan's western shore.

Max Schlemmer came to the island in 1894. Two years later he became superintendent of the guano operation. His early years with the mining firm, which changed its name in 1894 to the Pacific Guano and Fertilizer Company, marked the heyday of guano extraction on the island. In 1904, with its phosphate reserves and profits from Laysan largely depleted, the company sold its mining rights and equipment on the island to Schlemmer. He was just beginning a meteoric antienvironmental career that would impact on Laysan with irresistible force.

There was something of the western pioneer in Max Schlemmer; he settled on a difficult frontier, and he treated the resources of his land in classic pioneer fashion. Perhaps he was deceived by his limitless horizon, wider even than that on the Great Plains. The essence of Schlemmer's story is pathetic rather than sinister. Both he and the island he obviously loved were all but ruined by 1915, when he quit the NWHI for good. In a pellucid, windswept world festooned with albatrosses, Captain Schlemmer doggedly pursued various unsound economic schemes that failed at every turn—first the declining guano reserves, then a coconut plantation in a less-than-tropical climate, then the feather trade, which quickly became illegal.

Schlemmer created a homestead on Laysan and brought his family there. Several of his children were born on the island, although after 1910 the family spent most of its time in Honolulu. But in those earlier years, Schlemmer planted flowers and vegetables around his living quarters and brought in a few livestock and pets—guinea pigs and rabbits—for his children. In some of the old photographs, the Laysan community resembles a ramshackle frontier town. Loitering amid the dusty wooden buildings, big albatrosses look like bewildered aboriginals, absurdly out of place. Shortly thereafter the seabird massacres began, and not long after that the survivors' nesting habitat, and indeed Laysan's entire terrestrial ecosystem, was reduced to a sandy wasteland.

The crucial element was the rabbits, specifically the European hare *(Ortylagus cuniculus)*. Schlemmer let them go on Laysan in about 1903, as did he or someone else shortly later on Lisiansky.[18] They were a handy local source of protein and were intended eventually to support a com-

mercial meat cannery—yet another ill-conceived Schlemmer scheme—
and so Laysan and Lisiansky became rabbit ranches. By 1911, visiting
naturalists reported a noticable decline in Laysan's vegetation. Among
the low shrubs and grasses there were "so many ears protruding that
they resemble a vegetable garden."[19]

In 1912–1913, a four-man biological expedition visited Laysan and
attempted to deal with the rabbits. During a three-month stay, they killed
more than 5,000, accounting for an estimated two-thirds of the population.[20] Apparently, the remainder became somewhat gun-shy; at any
rate, as mentioned by several observers, they readily escaped into the
myriad seabird burrows that augmented holes of their own making. The
rabbits remained virtually unmolested for the next ten years and Laysan
became a metaphor for the classic Malthusian reckoning.

A major research effort in 1923, dubbed the Tanager Expedition for
the ship that carried it, focused on the NWHI. When the scientists landed
on Laysan, they found a desert. Most of the native plants were entirely
gone. Others, like the once-common Laysan sandalwood, were down
to a few leafless stumps on the southwestern side of the island and they
did not survive. Of the native flora, only a few scattered mats of the
succulent, salt-loving *Sesuvium* appeared to be holding out against the
rabbits, of which the expedition found a few hundred.[21] The only plants
that were actually untouched were a couple of stunted coconut palms
and ironwood trees along with domestic tobacco, which the rabbits
wouldn't eat. Introduced in the guano era, the tobacco flourished on
Laysan in healthy green patches and it persists to the present day. Fortunately, the rabbits did not. Some were killed by the 1923 expedition's
shore parties; the rest evidently soon starved.

The saddest stories told by the Tanager scientists were about the birds.
The expedition actually recorded the day that the Laysan honeycreeper
became extinct. For many years, visitors had been charmed by these
sprightly little birds. In 1891, one naturalist had written, "A most touching thing occurred: I caught a little red Honeyeater in the net, and when
I took it out the little thing began to sing in my hand."[22] On a 1902
visit, the ornithologist Walter Fisher had studied the species in its favorite
haunts near the central lagoon where, he related, "Their bright scarlet
plumage renders them especially conspicuous as they flit about amid
the soft green of the chenopodium bushes. . . ."[23]

In 1912, several of these little singers had greeted scientists as they
set up their quarters at the old settlement amid the rapidly disappearing vegetation. They were remembered as "confiding birds, bouncing
in and out of windows and doorways, searching for small insects and
millers."[24] The last of them were found when the USS *Tanager* reached
Laysan in April 1923. The birds had probably subsisted around the remaining patches of *Sesuvium,* mentioned by early observers as a pre-

ferred foraging habitat. The final recorded images of the living species are frames from a film made by the expedition. They show a male singing vigorously from a perch on a naked lump of coral. A few days later the birds were gone forever. According to Alexander Wetmore, leader of the expedition,

> Three individuals alone of the little Honey-Eater remained on our arrival; these perished during a three-day gale that enveloped everything in a cloud of swirling sand.[25]

The millerbird was already extinct, possibly having disappeared before 1920. When the Tanager Expedition left Laysan, two rails were known to be still alive on the island, but they were never seen again. The Laysan finch and duck survived, probably because of their omnivory, which allowed them to partake substantially of marine-derived foods. As might be imagined, the loss of shading vegetation in nesting areas adversely affected a number of seabird species just as they were beginning to recover from the feather hunts that had ended barely a decade earlier.

Lisiansky's plague of rabbits was just as severe as that of Laysan, but on the former island nature's course went more swiftly, and the rabbits along with the vegetation had disappeared by early 1916.

One early visitor to Lisiansky may have seen flightless rails there. Herr C. Isenbeck, surgeon aboard the Russian exploring ship *Moller,* landed on the island in April 1828 and reported, "A kind of fowl . . . running on the ground, singly, but at the same time rather numerous . . . very rapid and rather shy."[26] Some modern skeptics think Isenbeck may have been describing a migratory shorebird. Forty-five Laysan rails were brought to Lisiansky and released in 1913. Two were seen on the island's barren sandy wastes in 1916, and after that no more were seen.[27] The Lisiansky ducks noted in the first half of the nineteenth century had long since disappeared.

Both Laysan and Lisiansky recovered much of their flora, but the process was gradual. For example, the dominant grass, *Eragrostris variabilis,* which had been extirpated from Laysan by 1923, had only begun to recover in 1936.[28] On both islands, much of the vegetation had to be restarted artificially from seeds, rhizomes, and rootstocks brought from other islands in the NWHI.

Apparently, only one other island in the group suffered the introduction of rabbits. These animals were first reported on tiny Southeast Island at Pearl and Hermes Reef in 1916. The conjecture was that they had been left by fishermen. When the *Tanager* arrived in 1923, parties from it saw an estimated 120 rabbits and shot 90. Later visitors kept after them, and by 1928 the rabbits were gone. None ever turned up on other islets of the atoll.[29]

During their recorded history, the sandspit islands of Pearl and Hermes Reef have varied in number between six and twelve. Although long-sustained exploitation has not occurred here, the islets have been heavily trammeled. Shipwrecked sailors, fishermen, pearl-oystermen, seal, turtle, and bird hunters, scientists, and military personnel have all occupied this lonely atoll for up to two years at a time, and they probably managed to exterminate a species or two.

Although Laysan takes the prize for sheer intensity of environmental destruction, several other islands have experienced long-term institutional disturbance. They are Midway, Kure, French Frigate Shoals, and Kaula Rock. Midway is the island with the longest and most variegated history of ecological upheaval. This atoll, with its two sandy islets, was the site of several well-publicized shipwrecks in the late nineteenth and early twentieth centuries. The ill-fated dredging project funded by the U.S. government in 1870 was mentioned in chapter 6, and Midway's invasion by Japanese plumage hunters in chapter 9. Institutional disturbance on Midway settled down to business in 1902–1903, when a permanent relay station was established by the Commercial Pacific Cable Company for its new submarine communications link between Asia and North America. On Sand Island, the larger of Midway's two islets, the company erected docks, windmills, water towers and catchments, and steel and concrete buildings, and it also effected a massive landscaping, with thousands of tons of imported topsoil (which reportedly contained ants and other alien anthropods) and introduced grasses and trees. Soon the company planted vegetables and brought ducks, chickens, pigs, turkeys, and cows.[30]

In 1935, Pan American Airways joined the cable company on Sand Island to set up a base for the support of its trans-Pacific flying boats. The airline built a hotel and other facilities for its passengers and staff, and

[T]hus a modern little town was set up . . . with electricity, running hot and cold water (sun heaters), modern plumbing, and nearly all the comforts of home.[31]

During this time, Midway's Eastern Island had remained relatively undisturbed. It was a fine sanctuary for two of Laysan Island's birds: the flightless rail, which had been brought to Midway as early as 1891, and the finch, introduced shortly after the turn of the century.[32] Large populations built up, and both species were common until World War II. For most of this period, both birds were also present on Sand Island, where the rail was lauded by Cable Company and Pan Am gardeners for its insectivory while the finch was despised. "This fearless little rascal [the finch] does more damage to plants on the island than all other pests combined. It should be outlawed and destroyed at every opportunity."[33]

Shortly after that sentiment was expressed by F. C. Hadden, an entomologist employed on Midway by the Hawaii Sugar Planters Association to decontaminate Pan Am's aircraft and cargoes bound for Honolulu from the Far East, both the finch and the rail were destroyed on Midway—by rats that went ashore from naval vessels in the early 1940s. The last Laysan rails were seen on Eastern Island in 1944.[34] The finch fortunately recovered on Laysan, where rats never became established.

Midway was perhaps foredoomed. It had been nominally under U.S. Navy jurisdiction since 1903—hence its exclusion from Theodore Roosevelt's 1909 Hawaiian Islands Bird Reservation. However, all of the NWHI from FFS to Kure Atoll saw some military disturbance related to World War II. Midway, of course, was heavily garrisoned and its remaining natural environment virtually obliterated under bulldozers and even enemy bombardment. At present, Sand Island—with its modern naval base, port terminal, airfield, suburban landscapes of introduced trees and other plants, canaries and myna birds, rats and mosquitoes—is the most thoroughly transformed of the NWHI. Nearby Eastern Island is a weedy junkyard of military refuse.

The lightest such impact seems to have been on Lisiansky, where apparently the only wartime operation was the demolition of a mine that had washed ashore. French Frigate Shoals served as an amphibious training area during the 1930s and an emergency airbase during the war. Its largest islet was reshaped entirely into a rectangular airfield. This was accomplished by covering the existing land with hundreds of acres of dredge spoils from the lagoon. Kaula Rock, which possesses some unique vegetation and a major seabird colony, has been used for many years as a naval bombing and strafing target.

After the war, the navy stayed on Midway, and the U.S. Coast Guard got FFS and Kure Atoll. Both of the latter rank only slightly behind Midway as the most disturbed land ecosystems of the NWHI. The coast guard finally left FFS in 1979, but the advanced navigational and communications station at Kure continues in service and, with its airstrip, dominates mile-long Green Island. Gracefully shaped like an arching seal, that islet is presently Kure's only vegetated land mass.

Kure is infamous for its rats *(R. exulans,* the Polynesian species). They were introduced well back in the nineteenth century, and were described as abundant as early as 1870.[35] Their predation on Kure's seabirds was mentioned in chapter 9. Next to the historic rabbits of Laysan and Lisiansky, the rats of Kure and Midway are the worst of the introduced animals in the NWHI. Mosquitoes carrying avian diseases (so far only on Midway) and introduced ants that may have extinguished native land invertebrates (snails, insects, spiders, and the like) on various of the NWHI also rank as formidable ecological threats. It may be to Max Schlemmer's credit that rats never became established on Laysan despite twenty years of potential opportunity. In addition, he apparently disallowed dogs and cats on that island.

Cats and dogs have turned up at various times on several of the NWHI. On the more remote islands, they have sometimes lived for years in a feral state after shipwrecks. Even pigs have gone wild in unlikely places. In 1872, the crew of a wrecker searching the NWHI discovered "two large hogs" on a sandspit at FFS. The animals had been there since the loss of a ship five years earlier, and they readily swam to another islet to evade capture.[36]

Introduced plants in the NWHI are less dramatic than the animals, but they may be just as damaging if left to spread unchecked. According to a 1981 study,[37] of 312 species of vascular plants in the NWHI, 263 are nonnative. Among the latter are common coastal weeds that have spread through the main islands—for example, *Cenchrus echinatus,* the prickly sandspur grass, and the aggressive shrubby *Pluchea indica* and *P. odorata.* One of the worst, *Verbesina enceloides,* was introduced on Green Island at Kure Atoll in the 1950s or 1960s. It crowds out native plants with its dense stands up to four feet high. Birds such as masked boobies are said to have great difficulty penetrating it in order to nest.[38]

Attempts have been made since the midnineteenth century to start trees on various of the untenanted NWHI. Only a few trees seem likely to survive in the wild state on the low islands. Among them are ironwood *(Casuarina equisetifolia)* and tree heliotrope *(Messerschmidia = Tournefortia argentea).* At present, they are few and scattered and besieged by birds, but in a few places such as Laysan and Lisiansky and perhaps on undeveloped acreage at Kure they may spread. And, especially in the case of *Casuarina,* which inhibits the growth of most other plants beneath it, they may change the character of the ecosystem.

In the Northwestern Hawaiian Islands, there is still a resource more valuable than guano or shipwrecked cargo. Current scientific thinking is that the NWHI still harbor parts of an ecosystem that has disappeared on the dry coasts of the main Hawaiian Islands. In a sense, the NWHI are an evolutionary library whose records, like ancient tablets inscribed with information, have been scuffed and chipped by careless past treatment. Still there is much to discover, read, and interpret in the contents. Basic, vital understanding about the living earth comes from progressively fewer places such as the NWHI, where the information has not been completely erased. One need not go there to benefit from the realization that a Nihoa or a Lisiansky lives with much of its Hawaiianness intact. Assuring the preservation of those deliciously lonely islands should be a matter of pride to all with a love of *Hawaii-nei.*

11

Coasts of Change

Hawaii's coasts are wonderfully varied. Geologically, they include a small continent of coastal landforms. On the island of Hawaii from time to time they feature new lava, black and steaming on shores that, depending on location, range from desert to rain forest. Elsewhere, the older landscapes abutting the ocean vary from broad coastal plains near sea level to dramatic cliffs and sudden valleys with relief that may measure in the thousands of feet.

In the biologist's view, however, these island coasts have been nearly completely transformed by human beings. Even most of the remote coastal places, which to a casual observer look undisturbed—whether lush with jungle, parklike with open space under big trees, or arid with desert-type plants—have become dominated by exotic vegetation. It consists of a handful of Polynesian-introduced species together with a vast array of plants brought to Hawaii after European contact. Hawaii's coasts were once largely forested with wondrous suites of plants, marvelously evolved on varied terrain and adapted to climates ranging from wet to very dry. But everywhere that planters (including the ancient Hawaiians), and later ranchers (with their free-roaming grazing stock), went, the native vegetation was razed. Recent human activities and new patterns of settlement have all but completed the transformation and wasted a great biological treasure.

In exploring the coastal flora of the main Hawaiian Islands and tracing its changing character from prehuman times to the present, this chapter considers three general areas: the immediate shoreline, the dry lowlands, and the relatively wet coasts, typically where windward slopes or cliffs rise straight out of the sea. However, it should be remembered that intergradations of vegetation have always existed among these zones.

ON THE SHORELINE

Except in a few rugged, out-of-the-way places, the native trees are gone from the coastal zone. Some are already extinct, a few still grow in remote valleys or uplands, but most have become exceedingly rare. Other native coastal plants have fared only a little better than the trees. Some of these smaller plants can still be found in scattered patches near

11.1 Coastal dunes and native flora. In the foreground (left to right): the Hawaiian cotton shrub (*mao*), *Gossypium sandvicense;* coast sandalwood (*iliahi*), *Santalum ellipticum;* and *ilima, Sida fallax.*

the shore, where they are threatened by aggressive weeds, introduced diseases and insects, and off-road vehicles. Perhaps surprisingly, the best survivors among these plants are those that grow closest to the sea; they constitute a distinctive vegetation of the uppermost beach zone and adjoining sand dunes and rock fields just behind the shoreline.

In most cases these plants are the same as or very closely related to species that constitute the native flora of the NWHI. A number of native beach and dune plants are still found even on Oahu. Some of them are endemic, but perhaps a majority are indigenous species of strandline vegetation that range widely in the Indo-Pacific region. Whether carried by birds or as ocean flotsam, the seeds of these plants tend to be good travelers. Unlike plants in the interiors of the islands, most of this beach vegetation would have been instantly recognized by the Polynesians when they first came ashore in Hawaii.

They found *naupaka (Scaevola sericea),* the bright green shrub of the foreshore with its peculiar white demiflowers. It is still abundant on all of the Hawaiian Islands. They found the spindly, spreading *alena*

(Boerhavia), with its fleshy, drought-resistant root, said to have medicinal value in old Hawaii. Other plants that are still fairly common include several native morning glories, notably *koali* and *pohuehue (Ipomoea indica* and *pes-caprae* respectively) that form long, trailing vines across dunes and fields of surf-rounded boulders. Also found in the seaside community is the *ilima (Sida fallax)*, whose small, yellow-orange, wafer-thin flowers make a favored lei. The beach *ilima* is a low, spreading plant that grades into taller, shrubby inland varieties in dry, leeward habitat. Historically, the broad Ewa Plains west of Pearl Harbor on Oahu were largely covered with *ilima* until the late nineteenth century. The fate of this plant there was summarized by a visitor to the Honouliuli Ranch near Ewa in 1881. "The ilima which grows in endless quantities on the plains of this ranch is considered excellent for feeding cattle."[1] Certainly, *ilima* is scarcer now than in times before the proliferation of livestock.

The same is true of *nanea (Vigna marina)*, the indigenous, yellow-flowered beach pea, and especially the *ohai (Sesbania tomentosa)*, a beautiful endemic legume shrub with red flowers. Draping its long, delicate compound foliage over harsh, dry coastal ground, the *ohai* has a milky green look from a distance; the light tint in its leaves probably helps reflect intense solar radiation. Sadly, the *ohai* is now found only in a few remote shore locations. Although grazing animals are no longer a threat on most Hawaiian beaches, this lovely plant is *in extremis* due to uncontrolled motorcycle and off-road vehicle use—for example, near Kaena Point, its last retreat on Oahu.

A few other native shrubs were once common near the beach. Declining fast but still to be found here and there is the coast sandalwood *(Santalum ellipticum)*, a spindly shrub and smallest of the six or seven endemic Hawaiian sandalwood species. Growing in the same habitat, the so-called false sandalwood, or *naio (Myoporum sandwicense)*, is also a shrub or very small tree, differing from *S. ellipticum* in its light-colored berries and long, narrow leaves arranged alternately (instead of opposite each other) on branches. But the latter species also ranges high into the mountains (to at least 7,000 feet), where it grows to the stature of a sizable tree. Improbably, a tiny grove of coastal *naio* still survives with other native plants only a stone's throw from the sea on the arid shoreline near bustling Hawaii Kai.

Once too, the *mao*, or Hawaiian cotton *(Gossypium sandvicense)* was abundant behind the beach and across dry island coastal plains. Quite probably, these attractive shrubs, four or five feet high with maple-shaped leaves and large, sulfur-yellow flowers, fringed a primeval dry coastal forest that covered all but perhaps the driest shore regions. Away from the newest lava flows, only a few such places—Kawaihae on Hawaii, the northern coast of Lanai, and westernmost Kahoolawe—

which receive less than ten inches of rain per year, might have constituted Hawaii's original coastal deserts with no significant forest cover.

LOWLAND DRY FORESTS

Hawaii's ancient coastal forests must have been especially impressive on the broad lowlands of the older islands that often appear so barren today. These were (and are) dry regions. Even in windward areas, such lowlands seldom receive more than thirty or forty inches of rain annually, most of it coming during the winter and spring. Leeward coasts are drier still, and today often look like desert country, but nearly everywhere they were once forested with native trees. Two of the survivors, holding their ground in a few scattered patches on various islands, are *alahee (Canthium odoratum)* and *lama (Diospyros ferrea)*. The former, a small indigenous tree with shiny green foliage resembling that of mock orange, produces clusters of fragrant white flowers during the heat of summer. The *lama* is a native Hawaiian persimmon that produces small, edible orange fruits; this tree is densely foliated with small, leathery leaves arranged alternately on the branch and khaki-green in color (except for new growth, which is often tinted light red or almost pink). It is the most common native tree left in the dry lowland community, although one may have to look for it well inland, for example in the northern Koolau foothills of Oahu, where, with the *alahee,* it struggles to reach the light amid dense guava scrub.

Another common species of Hawaii's ancient dry coastal forest was the *wiliwili (Erythrina sandvicensis).* * This tree is unusual for a Hawaiian endemic in having (like its Indo-Pacific congeners) thorny branches. Even the trunks of most *wiliwili* specimens are armed with stout, claw-shaped thorns. Striking clusters of large, curving leguminous flowers appear amid the tree's sparse foliage in the spring. *Wiliwili's* flowers can be white or greenish, but in most trees they are blood red. Ancient Hawaiians had a legend that when these trees bloomed along the coast, sharks were especially prone to bite. Native *wiliwili* can still be seen in the taluses and weed-ridden hills behind the coastal shelf of northwestern Oahu. You can also hike to a mature grove in Koko Crater near Hawaii Kai. Scattered trees can still be found in similar settings on other islands, but the species has sadly declined in the decades since the turn-of-the-century botanical authority, Joseph Rock, termed *wiliwili* a "feature of the lowland vegetation up to 1,500 feet in the hottest and

---

*Introduced species, *Erythrina variegata* and others, commonly called coral trees, tiger's claw, or *wiliwili haole,* resemble the Hawaiian species and now greatly outnumber it in the islands.

driest districts of all the islands." Around 1910, he and fellow botanist
C. N. Forbes found it still growing on goat-ravaged Kahoolawe.[2]

Together with *alahee, lama,* and *wiliwili,* other native trees—*ohe-
makai (Reynoldsia sandwicensis), hao, (Rauwolfia degneri),* and *maua
(Xylosma hillebrandii)*—once grew abundantly on or near many dry
Hawaiian coasts. *Maua,* which also ranges into wet forest, is a tree of
rich green foliage recognized by its serrate-edged leaves. It has vanished
from the coastal zone. In 1912, Joseph Rock referred to the last pitiful
specimens of dryland *maua* on arid western Molokai as "the remnant
of what was once a beautiful forest."[3] Additional trees characteristic
of dry leeward slopes, such as the *aulu (Sapindus oahuensis),* the
vanishing dryland *mehame (Antidesma pulvinatum),* and the *aiea
(Nothocestrum latifolium),* an outlandish endemic tree nightshade, may
have intergraded with the ancient coastal-plain forests. Some of the
native dry-forest trees, notably *wiliwili* and *ohe-makai,* exhibit a decidu-
ous habit. They lose their leaves in late summer or fall, the hottest, driest
time of year, and apparently store water through the winter and spring.
Then flowers appear briefly along with new leaves, which only remain
for a few months.

Plant fossils are rare in Hawaii, but near Salt Lake on the coastal plain
west of Honolulu, 40,000-year-old specimens attributable to the genera
Pteralyxia and *Pritchardia*[4] enrich our image of the once flourishing
native coastal forests. The former has stiff, erect leaves and large-seeded,
plum-sized fruits. It is now found in leeward mountains on Kauai and
in Oahu's Waianae Range. The latter, called *loulu,* is Hawaii's only native
genus of palm and is indigenous, with several endemic species. In the
main islands, its several species are now found primarily in wet forests
and on rainy seaside cliffs and ledges such as those of Northeast Molokai.
Dry-adapted *Pritchardia* are extremely rare, although they still survive
on tiny Nihoa Island in the NWHI and perhaps on Niihau, but the Salt
Lake finding proves that their broad, fan-shaped fronds once rustled
on the xeric, leeward plains of Oahu.

On the leeward coast of Kauai, another sandy plain was probably
once covered with dryland forest that long ago was obliterated by native
Hawaiian agriculture followed by grazing and plantation development.
Although the earliest Western visitors characterized this region west of
Waimea, Kauai, as barren, it is unclear how completely they explored
the area. Even in midnineteenth century, it still may have featured one
of Hawaii's most beautiful native trees, the now extremely rare "tree
cotton" of the endemic genus *Kokia.*

Around June 1853, George Washington Bates, a tourist with an eye
for natural history, traveled on horseback across the dry plain from
Waimea to Barking Sands, at the western end of the island. About
halfway, at a place called Waiawa, he visited some early "flourishing"

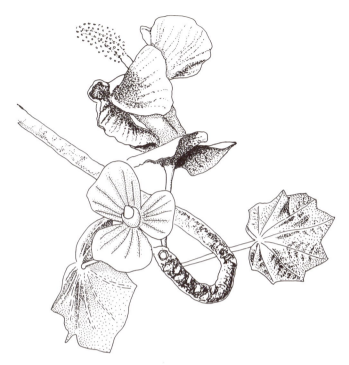

11.2   *Kokia kauaiensis,* the cotton tree of Kauai. After Sohmer and Gustafson.

tobacco farms (they may have been irrigated even at this time by a
forerunner of the Kekaha Ditch System, a large water project that later
served giant sugar plantations in the region). At Waiawa he observed
that "on these plains the wild cotton tree, *Gossypium vitifolium,* is
found in abundance. . . . In this region, vegetation luxuriates in a manner surpassed by few places even in the tropics."[5]

It is tempting to believe that the wild cotton tree here was *Kokia*
(originally classified as a species of *Gossypium)* rather than the shrubby
mao, Gossypium sandvicense, and that the luxuriance of the scene was
not due to the tobacco but to the spectacular abundance of *Kokia*'s
showy, six-to nine-inch-wide red flowers, 2,000 of which may appear
on a mature tree at the peak of the blooming season in May or June.[6]
It is possible that at Waiawa a resurgence of the original Hawaiian flora
was stimulated by excess runoff from an early irrigation works.

If the remnants of a *Kokia* forest were present on southwest Kauai
in 1853, they had surely disappeared by the 1880s, when sugar cane
blanketed the region. Hillebrand's great compendium of the Hawaiian
flora,[7] published in 1888, places the tree cotton, then known as *Gossypium drynaroides,* only on Oahu (near Makapuu Point and Koko

Head) and on extreme western Molokai, where it shared the coastal country with *maua* trees and the fragrant *alahee.* By then, however, tree cotton was exceedingly rare on both of those islands. Later, another *Kokia* species was rediscovered on the Big Island.

Presently, of four named species on four islands, only two survive in the wild as scattered individuals: *Kokia drynarioides* on the island of Hawaii and, surprisingly, *Kokia kauaiensis,* probably the former glory of the Waiawa Plains. Now on Kauai, only an estimated thirty wild trees still grow—in Waimea Canyon and in roadless Kalalau and Milolii valleys on the western Na Pali Coast. A few of these are giants of their genus, forty or fifty feet tall. Molokai's *Kokia* survives only as tissue cultures and a few grafts on *K. drynarioides* rootstock. Oahu's cotton tree is extinct.

The island of Hawaii is the best place to see patchy remnants of the primeval dry-lowland forest. It persists in two marginal localities. In North Kona, most of the trees mentioned above can still be found along a several-mile stretch of the highway between Kailua and Waimea, on and just north of the 1800–1801 lava flows from Mount Hualalai. *Lama* and *wiliwili* are dominant trees in this area. However, many of them, along with much rarer trees, were lost in a September 1986 fire that consumed thousands of acres here. A rapid growth of the thick, tussocky alien grasses that have invaded the region may prevent return of the native trees, most of which grow very slowly on this semidesert terrain. The elevation here approximates 2,000 feet, seemingly an upper limit for many coastal plants in the islands. And, indeed, this flora intergrades here with species such as *mamane (Sophora chrysophylla)* and the increasingly rare *kauila (Colubrina oppositifolia),* which are characteristic of leeward mountain slopes. Even *koa (Acacia koa),* and *ohia lehua (Metrosideros polymorpha),* typically moisture lovers, grow in the vicinity and become abundant slightly higher in the region where rainfall is greater.

The second such area of ancient native dry forest is in western Puna under the lee of the high eastern flank of Kilauea Volcano. About two miles west of Kalapana on the coast, the country rapidly becomes more arid, and here within sound of the surf are relict stands of *lama, alahee, hao,* and *ohe-makai,* among others. Some of these grow as small trees around the coastal Wahaula Visitor Center of Hawaii Volcanoes National Park. Groves of larger specimens up to twenty-five feet high still survive nearby in undeveloped areas of the Royal Gardens residential subdivision. In both Kona and Puna, these forest remnants grow on very rough old *aa* lava; it is land unsuitable to farming or grazing, and probably marginal even for the growth of native forest. The earlier field surveys by Rock and others revealed much larger specimens of most of these trees on land with better developed soils.

West of the park boundary in Puna, the land is sere and very dry, crossed by ever more recent lava flows. As the highway swings inland and starts up toward the cool, moist Kilauea summit area, one can see a surprising sight that is easily overlooked along this splendid, sea-bitten desert coast. It is the presence of *ohia lehua* trees right down at thirty feet above sea level, virtually within range of windblown salt spray. The trees are widely spaced and scruffy looking but reach fifteen or twenty feet in height on this botanically inimical-looking ground. *Ohia,* with its blooming sprays of scarlet, is Pele's favorite tree. Even here it is the vanguard that grows on land too new and raw for others to succeed. Probably on such arid coastal ground, however, barring artificial developments and fresh lava flows, it will later disappear in long-term ecological competition with *lama* and company.

The ancient dry forests of the Hawaiian lowlands were more comprehensively destroyed than any other natural community in the islands, and mounting archaeological evidence, coupled with the early historical record, indicates that most of the deforestation of the leeward lowlands was accomplished late in the prehistoric period by the Hawaiians themselves (see chapter 19). Agricultural transformation of the land for miles around major population centers such as Waimea on Kauai, Honolulu on Oahu, Lahaina on Maui, and Kailua, Kona, on the Big Island, was virtually complete. On January 19, 1778, Captain Cook's first detailed views of the land were along the south shore of Kauai between Poipu and Waimea. He reported, ''We saw no wood but what was up in the interior of the island and a few trees about the villages.''[8] It is doubtful that by Cook's time any of the trees found commonly around coastal settlements were native to Hawaii.

It has long been suggested that *Pandanus* (what the tourists call the pineapple tree) reached Hawaii unaided by man, its fibrous, floating fruits (the simple, wedge-shaped fruits, or keys, not the big pineapple-shaped compound structures) having drifted thousands of miles from the southwest. But *Pandanus,* unlike the *kamaaina* (Pritchardia),* was not reported by early surveyors on any of the NWHI. *Pandanus (hala),* with its numerous species scattered around the tropical Pacific, has a long history of use by island peoples. It yields an edible starch and sometimes shows evidence of selection for its food value, especially on islands with marginal growing conditions for more favored crops such as taro and bananas. Its leaves were also widely used for weaving mats. But in Hawaii this plant needs no cultivation; it propagates itself extremely well in most lowland areas.

It is reasonable to speculate that Hawaiian *hala* is not a native plant but was brought in the first canoes. In a land of exceptional fertility,

---

*Native, or long-term islander; literally, ''child of the land.''

it was simply abandoned as a food crop. Thriving in the wild, *hala* was still available as a weaving and thatching material, but no selection was exerted for food quality, which deteriorated over the centuries. "Wild-type" features in Hawaiian *Pandanus,* among them a relatively low starch content and excessively fibrous fruits, might have arisen in that long lapse of intensive cultivation. Only further research in archaeology and palynology (fossil pollen identification) will resolve these questions.

All of the other trees that were common on the shore near Hawaiian settlements were apparently brought by the Polynesians. They include *kou, milo, hau, noni, kamani, kukui, ulu, wauke, ohia-ai,* and of course *niu,* the coconut palm.* Nearly everywhere in the Pacific the distribution of this group coincides with that of the Polynesian people.

Kou trees *(tou* in some early spellings), *Cordia subcordata,* were especially common on dry leeward coasts. They reminded the early New England missionary C. S. Stewart of "large and flourishing, full, round-topped apple trees."[9] Large groves of them stood in the early post-contact period in and near such places as Lahaina and Honolulu. *Kou* wood was light and strong. Prized by the Hawaiians for its beautiful wavy grain streaked with light and dark brown, it was carved into calabashes, bowls, and temple idols. And the tree provided welcome shade on some of the sunniest Hawaiian shorelines. A famous old *kou* grove covered an acre or more at Lahaina. From the 1820s to the 1840s, it was used for prayer meetings and other community events such as outdoor banquets attended by missionary families, whaling captains and their wives, and civil officials.[10]

By about 1850, these big trees had all been felled in Lahaina by order of "the king" and converted into "bowls, spittoons, and pounding boards for kalo [taro]."[11] This was a late stage in the degreening of the region; it had happened with startling swiftness. When William Ellis, a visiting London missionary, walked Lahaina's coastline in the spring of 1823, he observed not only that the shoreline was "adorned with shady clumps of *kou* trees," but also that "the level land of the whole district, for about three miles, is one continued garden." He saw large

---

Kou, Cordia subcordata, family Boraginaceae
Milo, Thespesia populnea, family Malvaceae
Hau, Hibiscus tiliaceus, family Malvaceae
Noni, Morinda citrifolia, family Rubiaceae
Kamani, Calophyllum inophyllum, family Guttiferae; another tree, *Terminalia catappa,* the so-called false *kamani,* introduced in the Western era, has largely replaced true *kamani* on Hawaiian shorelines
Kukui, Aleurites moluccana, family Euphorbiaceae (the candlenut tree)
Ulu, Artocarpus incisa, family Moraceae (breadfruit)
Wauke, Broussonetia papyrifera, family Moraceae (paper mulberry)
Ohia-ai, Eugenia malaccensis, family Myrtaceae (the mountain apple)
Niu, Cocos nucifera, family Palmae

11.3 Polynesian imports to Hawaii: *Pandanus* (*hala* tree) and *ti, Cordyline terminalis.* Both are still common as cultivated ornamentals and grow wild in undeveloped lowlands.

crops of bananas and taro, coconut and breadfruit groves, and large ponds stocked with fish, and he noted the "sloping hills immediately behind and the lofty mountains in the interior clothed with verdure. . . ."[12]

Compare Ellis's perceptions with those of H. T. Cheever, another visiting clergyman, who arrived in 1850. "Lahaina is one of those places you like much better as you approach or recede from it than when you are actually in it." He goes on to recite a dismal litany of dust, dirt, fleas, mosquitoes, and heat.[13] Dust and heat had been the norm in Lahaina for years, according to accounts by resident missionaries. The verdure had disappeared through neglect of the Hawaiian irrigation systems that tapped nearby springs and inland streams. Depredations by livestock and other side effects of imported agricultural practices had also denuded the area at a time when Hawaiians were succumbing to Western diseases.

In the decades following 1850, a wide variety of exotic trees gradually restored greenery to Lahaina's coastline while sugar cane eventually came to cover dozens of square miles of the rising ground toward the mountains. But even today, the earth here and there across this region continues to be bared and wounded; red dust is lifted by strong, down-valley winds and is carried down by torrential winter storms and flash floods. The substance that gives life to the land bleeds in billows and plumes toward the sea, and you can even find it underwater as a reddish mud that settles everywhere in crannies of the beautiful coral reefs of Olowalu and elsewhere.

Like Lahaina, Honolulu has a dry leeward setting. Reportedly, an earlier name for the site, at least the harbor area opposite a major natural passage through the coral reef, was Ke Awa o Kou, or Kou Landing.[14] However, Honolulu's *kou* trees seem to have been cut down very early. Quite possibly, they were sold as firewood, always in demand by visiting ships. Early visitors such as Archibald Campbell in 1809–1810 trekked over the Oahu Plain as far west as Pearl Harbor and commented on its treelessness and the intensity of the cultivation there.[15] The village of Honolulu in April 1822, as seen by touring English missionaries Daniel Tyerman and George Bennet, encompassed some 500 to 600 mostly native houses along and near the shore. Behind the settlement, "the plain . . . bears grasses of different kinds and wears the appearance of a beautiful flat meadow."[16] William Ellis, who first saw Hawaii in 1822 in the company of Tyerman and Bennet, climbed Punchbowl Hill to sketch the surroundings and noted that "not a tree overshadowed the town."[17]

Andrew Bloxam, a twenty-three-year-old naturalist aboard HMS *Blonde,* saw Honolulu in May 1825. He noted the absence of trees at least as far west as "Pearl Lochs," and compared Honolulu proper with the early village of Waikiki, three miles to the east. Walking toward the latter, Bloxam encountered "innumerable artificial fishponds extending a mile inland from the shore." Most of these ponds (Bloxam estimated several hundred) were fresh water and "are the resort of wild ducks and other water fowl." And abundantly watered Waikiki was situated amid "numerous groves of coconut and other trees."[18]

A modern visitor may have difficulty imagining the former abundance of wetlands along Oahu's south coast (see chapter 13), let alone the primeval forests that were converted to aboriginal cultivation. By the 1830s, visitors were referring to the beautiful meadows of a decade earlier as a wasteland. A U.S. naval attaché in 1832 characterized Honolulu as barren, with two or three coconut groves and "a great many horses."[19] The scientifically inclined missionary Titus Coan, before he went on to his permanent station at Hilo, remarked of Honolulu in 1835,

Along the shore in sandy and marshy places the cocoa palm flourished with rushes, hibiscus, and pandanus growths, but over the extended plain some three miles in length and about one mile in breadth, there was little but an arid desert of burning coral sand and detritus from the rocky hills. . . . [20]

The plain of Honolulu, trampled and eroded by herds of cattle, goats, and horses, persisted in this state for at least two more decades. Some early introduced plants found uncontested niches and, in the absence of natural controls, flourished to a startling degree. A visitor in 1839 on an excursion to nearby Salt Lake commented on "immense clusters of the prickly pear overtopping in their luxuriant growth the head of horse and rider."* [21]

During this period, more and more exotic seeds and seedlings were being brought to Hawaii by ships' captains and botany-minded visitors and immigrants. After a mere horticultural ripple of Hawaiian-introduced species on the coastal zones, Cook and Vancouver, followed by such early agriculturalists as the "master planter" Don Francisco De Paula Marin (see chapter 20), had started a tidal wave of plant introductions. By midnineteenth century, the world's tropics and temperate zones were being scoured for all manner of plants—food, fiber, timber, medicinal, and ornamental—that would grow in the islands, and an eclectic reforestation of the plain of Honolulu was under way.

As late as 1856, an editorial in *The Friend* urged the people of Honolulu to convert "our sandy plain to a beautiful grove of shade trees."[22] In this 1856 article, the algeroba *(Prosopis pallida),* called *kiawe* in Hawaiian, was especially recommended for its ability to thrive in hot, dry conditions. This tree, which grows to a height of fifty feet, is a mesquite native to arid western South America; it had been introduced to Hawaii in 1828 by a French priest, Father Bachelot. It was abundantly planted on leeward coasts of the main islands and became economically valuable for rough lumber, charcoal, and honey production, and its sugary seed pods were used as fodder for pigs and cattle. The piercing thorns on its twigs, which often littered the ground underneath, made it something of a nuisance, but its ferny foliage provided a delightful dappled shade.

Algeroba was only a start. Many kinds of trees were planted in Honolulu and grew along with rapid improvements in the town's water works. Soon, streams were tapped in the valleys and piped down to the plain. Of Honolulu, the adventuress Isabella Bird on her arrival in 1873 was able to rhapsodize

> we drove through the town . . . along roads with overarching trees, through whose dense leafage the noon sunshine only trickled in dancing broken lights; umbrella trees, caoutchouc, bamboo, mango, orange, breadfruit, candlenut, monkey pod, date and coco palms, alligator pears, "prides" of Barbary, India, and Peru, and huge-leaved, wide-spreading trees, exotics from the South Seas, many of them rich in parasitic ferns, and others blazing with bright, fantastic blossoms.[23]

*The cactus *Opuntia,* introduced from Mexico.

The subsequent history of the Honolulu area is generally familiar. By the late nineteenth century, its wetlands were used extensively for rice farming. Later they were filled, and finally their feeder streams were channelized in concrete as the whole region of residential, commercial, industrial, and military developments congealed in a megalopolis that now sprawls along more than twenty-five miles of Oahu's south coast.

THE WET COASTS

On the wetter, windward coasts of the islands, the native forests were decimated nearly everywhere as thoroughly as they were in the dry, leeward lowlands. Only one windward coastal region has retained a significant piece of its ancient vegetational heritage into modern times. It is on the Big Island east of Kalapana, near the much smaller patches of native dryland forest mentioned earlier; with the sharp increase in rainfall to the east, this region is rain forest. Apparently, the exceptionally rough terrain here has largely denied entry to the cattle and goats that have proved so destructive to forests elsewhere in the islands.

This remaining native lowland forest of the Big Island's Puna District is dominated by the endemic tree *ohia lehua;* a rich understory of smaller native trees, shrubs, vines, and ferns accompanies it. Occasional *kukui* trees are unblatant intruders in the primeval ambience. The rocky ground and trunks of trees are covered with epiphytes. *Ohia lehua* spread their canopy up to 100 feet overhead, and beneath one can sometimes smell the sea in the humid air. The forest is filled with deep shades of green and the sounds of the last lowland populations of endemic Hawaiian forest birds. At least five species still inhabit and may breed in this significant pocket of native wilderness.[24]

Ironically, the remnants of coastal forest in Puna, located below the active East Rift of Kilauea Volcano, have always been threatened with natural destruction. There is terrain here representing every stage of recovery from the utter sterility of volcanic inundation. The area is a natural laboratory prized by ecologists worldwide who seek to understand the process of recolonization and regrowth of a natural landscape.

The human modification of the Puna region began with the first Hawaiians. However, while they used the interior forests lightly for construction materials and made medicines, dyes, and other products from various plants, their real impacts in Puna remained very close to the immediate shoreline. William Ellis and his American companions, on their celebrated walking tour of the Big Island in 1823, passed through village after populous village as they followed the coast from Kealakomo, a site now within the national park boundary, eastward around Cape Kumukahi to Hilo. For miles they passed through a virtually continuous strip of "well-cultivated" country that featured groves of coconut palms, shady *kou* trees, *ti (Cordyline terminalis),* breadfruit, bananas, and taro. Common, too, were the conspicuous *kukui* trees, with their milky green, maple-shaped leaves, and groves of *ohia* (here, Ellis is probably refer-ring to the introduced mountain apple, *Eugenia malaccensis,* called *ohia-ai,* rather than the native *ohia lehua,* by the Hawaiians).

Thus, virtually the entire immediate coastal strip of Puna was a land-scape remade by the Hawaiians with plants introduced from the South Pacific. Even fifty years later, when the vigorous villages visited by Ellis had been largely depopulated and abandoned after decades of disease and migration of survivors to Hilo and elsewhere, this shoreline bore living witness to the magnitude of the original transformation. Isabella Bird, who explored the region on horseback in 1873, provided this vivid testament:

> For thirty miles the track passes under the deep shade of coco palms of which Puna is the true home; and from under their feathery shadow, and from amidst the dark leafage of the breadfruit, gleamed the rose-crimson apples of the *Eugenia* and the golden balls of the guava.[25]

The guava was a latecomer, introduced after European contact along with others such as the ironwood *(Casuarina equisetifolia),* which now forms groves of big trees that resemble ragged pines overhanging the sea along eastern Puna's jagged coastal bluffs.

In the mid-1980s, only fragments of the lowland rain forest remain here, beginning slightly inland of the immediate shoreline. Believed to have been once continuous with rain forest along the entire windward coast of the Big Island, these coastal woodlands, in many ways different from mountain rain forests, are the last of their kind, and they acquire even greater significance when viewed as the only remaining example of the lowland tropical rain forest ecosystem in the United States. (Similar forests in American Samoa, Micronesia, and Puerto Rico have been destroyed and were never strictly under U.S. jurisdiction.) Hence, it seems astonishing and unconscionable that while American voices, official and unofficial, have been raised in the 1980s against the destruc-tion of rain forests worldwide, thousands of acres of this ecosystem were being clearcut in Puna. The rarest flora in the United States was being chipped for burning in a power plant. The effects could extend beyond the logged-out areas themselves. Removing so much of the remaining native forest in lowland Puna may have jeopardized the naturally slow vegetative restoration of the region's recent lava flows, and a landscape replete with scientific, aesthetic, and historical values may now be lost.[26]

The older wet shorelines of the islands were also greatly modified in prehistoric times, but patches of native coastal forest remained on some of them well into the nineteenth century. Many of these coastal forests, as in Puna, were dominated by *ohia lehua* and, with a rich accompaniment of other trees and understory species, spread from near the edge of the sea to merge imperceptibly with the mountain rain forest.

Windward lowlands on the Big Island from Hilo northward must have been deforested extensively by the early Hawaiians. In the 1820s, Hilo visitors such as Andrew Bloxam and C. S. Stewart described the environs as a lush garden of food plants and ornamentals. In 1823, William Ellis sailed by native canoe from Hilo to Lapahoehoe in the Hamakua District, where he and his party continued their journey on foot. They passed through numerous villages along this low-cliffed, ravine-wrinkled coast. The country was "extremely fertile and well cultivated" with taro, bananas, native sugar cane, and other crops, along with "rich fields of potatoes" (recently introduced) in plots of up to five acres. What trees they saw were described as small in stature; uncultivated areas between villages were typically covered with grass and ferns. Well inland and upland from the coast, at a distance that Ellis estimated as five or six miles, the dense forest began and swept upward thousands of feet toward the heights of Mauna Kea.[27] Ellis's report of the cleared zone along the Hamakua coast may have been an overestimate. In the mid-1830s, to the eye of the American missionary-explorer Titus Coan, the coastal inhabited belt of Hamakua was one to three miles wide. At its inner edge, the forest formed a much wider band around the windward contours of the tremendous mountain.[28]

Still later, in 1855, after the decline of the Hamakua villages and just before the first big surge of sugar planting here, these coastal lands— viewed from sailing vessels bound into Hilo—were described as great grassy slopes with only widely scattered trees.[29] These may have been the last of the native forest giants: *ohia lehua* or *koa*. Almost certainly they were not *Eucalyptus* species, or *Malaleuca* (paperbark), or *Casuarina*. These imports, which are the main big trees seen here today, seem not to have reached the islands in force for another decade or so. Today, the coastal Hamakua slopes are still mostly grassy (with sugar cane and introduced pasturage). The sweeping views along the main highway to Hilo are much the same as those that captivated Ellis, although most of the villages he visited are missing from modern maps. But long ago these well-watered slopes were surely part of a great continuous forest, many of whose species might have been specialized for low elevations and have become extinct, while others have retreated to final refugia high on the flanks of Mauna Kea.

Maui's fertile eastern region around Hana and Kipahulu was also heavily settled in Hawaiian times. The French navigator La Pérouse was the first Westerner to closely view this area. Coasting just offshore on May 20, 1786, he remarked on "the habitations of the natives, which are so numerous that a space of three or four leagues may be taken for a single village."[30] Wrote H. T. Cheever, who toured East Maui in 1850 before significant incursions by foreigners and found the gentle slopes near Hana to be (as today) largely open grassy country, "you can ride on horseback quite up to the clouds." There were scattered "copses and woody dells," and everywhere were Polynesian introductions—sugar cane, *ti, wauke* (the *tapa* bark tree), *noni,* and *hala.* At that time all were approaching a wild state but they still suggested long occupation and remaking of the landscape.[31] *Hala (Pandanus)* was and still is especially abundant here. In 1913, Joseph Rock noted that along the rugged coastline from Keanae through Nahiku to Hana "it forms a thick forest exclusive of everything else."[32]

The list of Polynesian plants in this wet coastal region of eastern Maui is now eclipsed by the latecomers—guava, mango, ironwood, java plum, and eucalypts dominate the trees—but there are hundreds of others of every possible stature. Most of the gentle slopes where native forest undoubtedly reached all the way down to the sea were probably first cleared by the fires of prehistoric Hawaiians. Then, after Cook and Vancouver, they would have been kept open by goats and wild cattle. Later, coffee and sugar farms and cattle ranches were established in the region. As late as 1859 or 1860, according to W. P. Alexander, the Wailuku missionary and land surveyor, easternmost Maui was still in a fairly natural condition, but changes were on the way. After leaving Hana, Alexander noted,

> We went on to Nahiku through a most romantic and wild country, abounding in fierce mountain torrents that taxed our skill and hardihood to cross with our mules. I was pleased to find in this wild region such marks of civilization as spendid dahlias and other beautiful flowers and a fine field of coffee.[33]

Toward the west, around the northern curve of Haleakala, the rainfall diminishes gradually, and this seems to favor the growth of *koa* trees in the lowlands. In 1850, Cheever saw remnants of a mesic (moderate rainfall) coastal forest of this species. "In returning from Makawao to Wailuku you may take a romantic path down to the sea by way of Haiku through dells and groves of kukui and the deep-green, moon-leaved koa with its beautiful mimosa-like blossoms."[34] *Koa* trees still grow on these slopes of small farms and new residential subdivisions, but perhaps not as far down as when Cheever rode through the region.

A similar forest featuring lowland *koa* once grew on the windward coast of Kauai. Reportedly, around 1850, as massive land clearing was beginning for the debut of Big Sugar, "the greater part" of the new Lihue Plantation between Nawiliwili and the Hanamaulu River was covered with native forest trees, especially *koa* and *ahakea* (genus *Bobea),* among other species.[35]

Koloa Marsh (now Koloa Reservoir), near Kauai's southeastern shore, was drained in the early 1850s in preparation for agricultural use of its bottomland. Drainage canals dug in the area revealed the subfossil remains of "a buried forest . . . huge trees of ohiaha, lehua, and loulu palms above them," according to a commentary by George Dole in 1875.[36] These endemic trees, apparently *Eugenia sandwichensis, Metrosideros polymorpha,* and an unknown *Pritchardia* species, might have been felled by ancient Hawaiians, but possibly died of some natural cause—perhaps a sudden land subsidence or shift in the water table. Along this coast today, failing sugar plantations stand next to expanding resort and retirement developments, with their exotic plantings of hundreds of alien species.

A BURGEONING OF WEEDS

Such cultivated areas are now no different from the rest of Hawaii's coastal zone in one sense: nearly everywhere the native plant assemblages have been erased. The only significant exceptions are tiny Nihoa Island (see chapter 10) and the last lowland forest vestiges in North Kona and Puna on the island of Hawaii. Here and there a few beaches retain scraps of their original vegetational character. But today what one expects to find along any untended Hawaiian shore is a landscape largely taken over by the weeds of the world's tropics.

A few of the weeds came with the ancient Hawaiians. *Zingiber zerumbet,* now known as shampoo ginger, with its bulbous red and green flower head and inconspicuous blossoms, has spread widely in the moist Hawaiian lowlands. The taller culinary, flowering, and fragrant kinds of ginger were brought to the islands after Western contact and have followed the Polynesian species into the wet forest understory. *Ti, hala,* and *hau* might also qualify as weeds in areas where their invasions have been so extensive as to form dense, monotypic jungles, sometimes covering acres of ground, as, for example, in windward Oahu's Kahana Valley State Park.

Except perhaps for the prolific shampoo ginger, Polynesian-introduced plants all but fade into the background when one considers incursions of weeds brought by later immigrants. Some of these plants arrived accidentally with various cargoes. Many were introduced purposefully as ornamental or commercial cultivars. From time to time, one species or another has broken out of normal ecological bounds and grown like a green plague over miles of altered land. One of the first spectacular

11.4 Nineteenth-century Honolulu coastal scene. State Archive Photo.

examples involved indigo *(Indigofera),* a tough, shrubby legume of which at least one species was introduced as early as 1836 in an attempt to start a dye industry.[37] The plant spread rapidly. By 1853, it was being said that indigo "continues to overrun some of the most valuable lands on the islands . . . making fearful ravages at Koloa, Kauai."[38] In 1856, when W. P. Alexander arrived at his new station at Wailuku, Maui, in the mission house yard, "the wild growth of indigo reached over the smaller childrens' heads."[39] Two years later in the same area, it was still reported that, "farmers at Wailuku succumb to the indigo."[40]

The infestation of indigo eventually subsided, to be replaced during later decades by other exotic outbreaks—sumach, spiny amaranth, *haole koa,* and many others, all indicators of the drastic ecological destabilization that befell the Hawaiian lowlands. *Haole koa (Leucana leucocephala)* is one of the most prominent coastal-zone and low-elevation weeds today. A spindly, scruffy distant relative of the majestic Hawaiian *koa,* it was introduced to Hawaii as livestock fodder.* On fairly dry coasts, *haole koa* is often found with *klu (Acacia farnesiana),* the foliage

*Fast-growing *Leucana* species are now being selected for reforestation projects in parts of the Third World tropics, where the demand for firewood is decimating the native forests.

of which appears similar. This similarity is dispelled by close contact, however; *klu* possesses sharp thorns and intensely fragrant yellow blooms (the species was brought to Hawaii to serve a perfume industry that never really flowered). Both *haole koa* and *klu* somewhat resemble a third legume, algeroba *(kiawe),* which, however, grows into a much more robust tree. All three of these introduced woody weeds now share some large dry-coastal tracts such as in the vicinity of Mokuleia on Oahu.

In coastal country ranging from dry to wet, *haole koa* is often accompanied by Christmas berry, or Brazilian holly *(Schinus terebinthifolius),* a small spreading tree whose clusters of small, red, fall-ripening berries are sown widely by birds. When these two aggressive species grow together, they often form a practically impenetrable scrub. *Lantana camara,* simply called lantana, is another ubiquitous invader of disturbed terrain in the islands. The lovely colors of its small, clustered flowers belie the prickly, tenacious nature of this weedy shrub. *Pluchea odorata* is a more recent arrival, but has spread very fast in the main islands and has reached the NWHI. Known by its flannel-textured leaves and strong scent reminiscent of oregano, it is tolerant of an extreme range of environmental conditions. This weed is a low shrub on arid shores, but reaches the stature of a small tree in rainy windward valleys. Both lantana and *P. odorata* now range from the coast to at least 4,000 feet in elevation.

On the rainier Hawaiian coasts, even large trees may be called weeds. One of the most abundant is the java plum, *Eugenia cuminii.* Reaching to heights between sixty and eighty feet, it spatters the ground beneath it with small, astringent purple fruits, making for messy walking. This is a tree of waste places and disturbed valleys near sea level, especially on windward Oahu, but it also occurs on other islands and in much more remote settings. On Oahu java plum frequently shares its vacant lots and hillsides with other weed trees, especially yellow guava *(Psidium guajava)* and octopus tree *(Schefflera actinophylla),* a well-liked ornamental of Australian origin that recently seems to have escaped from cultivation in large and growing numbers.

Perhaps the most remote and least accessible shores in the main islands are the awesome cliffs and valleys of Northeast Molokai, but even here the vegetation is predominantly exotic. Many of the native plants on this coast have probably been extinguished by large flocks of goats that are still common today; these animals dot the high, steep, grassy defiles and peer over the edges of hanging valleys a thousand feet above the sea. Only a few places here seem to have remained beyond the reach of these "hooved locusts," whose appetites seem to favor native plants far more than exotics. Only on the rugged seaward cliffs in a few impossible-to-reach spots, often within range of pelting storm spray, can one still find such plants as the outlandish endemic lobelioid *Brig-*

hamia. This rare living treasure of the ancient coastal flora has been likened to a "big cabbage head stuck on a naked pole." It has tubular yellow blossoms with a fragrance like that of violets. According to Hillebrand, this five- to twelve-foot-high plant once grew abundantly near the coast on the flanks of East Molokai's Halawa Valley, but it disappeared there long ago.[41] Now its place has been taken by the introduced century plant, *Agave.* Scattered on the hillsides, rising out of big rosettes of bayonetlike, goat-proof leaves, the tall flower stalks of *Agave* rear above stunted *haole koa* and provide a crude reminder of the eccentric forest of *Brighamia.*

Halawa is the easternmost valley on the high Molokai seacoast. It is at the end of the road that comes from the south shore. West of Halawa on the north coast is a little-known place of superlatives, one of the wonders of the world. It is difficult of access. The other valleys here are hemmed in by ragged mountain walls rising 2,000 to 3,000 feet out of the sea. In winter the sea route is closed by surf that sometimes reaches heights of twenty to thirty feet. Nevertheless, these valleys have had a long history of human occupation. Even tiny, steep Papalaua, with its pounding, three-tiered cataract falling from around 1,700 feet, was extensively terraced for agriculture, probably several centuries ago. Along the valley's rushing, boulder-filled stream, virtually the whole present forest community was introduced by Hawaiians. *Pandanus,* mountain apple, *kukui,* and *hau* dominate overwhelmingly, with taro and shampoo ginger in the understory. Only a fern species or two seems to be native here. It looks, however, as if no one has tried to make a living in this difficult valley since traditional Hawaiian times.

The other well-watered valleys of this coast farther west—Wailau, Pelekunu, and Waikolu—are huge in comparison to Papalaua, and at low elevations they have been used and abused by human beings from early Hawaiian times to the present. They contain the same jumble of Polynesian and *haole*-imported plants that one can see in similar situations on Oahu. For two miles inland from its bouldery beach, Wailau is dominated by big java plum, guava, and octopus trees. Occasional giant mangoes grow along the stream in the company of *kukui* and mountain apple. *Cannabis* is a patchy but common understory plant here, of recent introduction, and tended more or less by transient agriculturists who have built bamboo and plastic-sheet shacks close to the beach. In Pelekunu, the lower reaches of the beautiful stream are choked by a dense thicket of *Pluchea odorata,* some almost qualifying as trees. Copper plant *(Acalypha wilkesiana),* an exotic ornamental shrub, also thrives here in brushy copses amid a sea of coarse, tall grass that has overgrown a huge, irrigated former Hawaiian taro plantation near the coast. At the seacoast in Pelekunu Valley, goats have no fear of humans and approach in plain sight within thirty yards, a sign that they are not hunted here, and that *Brighamia* and other native plants are unlikely to reestablish in any accessible place nearby.

Hawaii's shores of many moods range from raw, new lava to urban waterfronts, from hot, arid beaches to enormous, rainy seacliffs, and on nearly all of them the native wildness has gone. It has been destroyed with a finality that no volcano could match. Once replete with beautiful native plants, many of which were wholly unique on these far shores, Hawaii's remaining unsettled and uncultivated coastal zone has come to resemble botanically the scruffier vacant lots of the world's lowland tropics. Sad to say, with the vanishing lowland forest of Puna, the coasts of the main islands will no longer have any truly native plant communities.

What must the ancient Hawaiian shoreline have looked like after a winter and spring of abundant rain, with whole forests of *wiliwili* and cotton trees flaring into bloom? What lost fragrances were carried on the trade winds to the nostrils of canoe paddlers approaching from leeward? What vanished birds lived in those coastal forests and sang above the rush of wind and crash of surf? These were true Hawaiian things, and the islands are much the poorer for their passing.

Green Crags and Canyons

12

Rain Forests in Transition

The wet mountain forests, although greatly diminished in the last two centuries, are the least disturbed of Hawaii's major terrestrial ecosystems. They contain most of the remaining native plants and animals, some of them relics, refugees from the islands' lowland biota that was decimated by the prehistoric Hawaiians and all but destroyed in the time since Captain Cook.

Wet-forest habitat occurs in Hawaii where prevailing moisture-laden winds are forced to rise along mountain slopes. Hence, it is most characteristic of windward sides of the islands, but extends to where some of the moist airflow is able to reach leeward sectors. On Kauai, Oahu, and Molokai, native rain forest, dominated by the ubiquitous *ohia lehua* tree *(Metrosideros polymorpha)*, is now restricted to upper elevations and extends over the summits of those islands. West Maui's native forest is similar. However, on the much higher slopes of Haleakala (East Maui) and Hawaii above approximately 5,500 feet, the rain forest grades into drier habitat featuring *koa (Acacia koa)* and *mamane (Sophora chryso-phylla)*, among others. Still higher and drier, the forest is succeeded by alpine scrub, and finally, on Mauna Loa and Mauna Kea, by mountain tundra and stone desert.

To be sure, *koa* along with associated types such as *iliahi*, Hawaii's famous fragrant sandalwood trees *(Santalum)*, are also found at lower elevations, but they thrive best outside the very high rainfall zones (more than 150 inches per year), where the dense *ohia* rain forest is in its element. In this chapter, we will explore both types of forest, wet and mesic, and what befell them on the mountain slopes of the islands.

Hawaiian rain forest vegetation is typified by several dozen trees and conspicuous understory species (shrubs and ferns), but the total plant diversity here is in the hundreds of species, many of which are endemic to single islands in the chain. It is likely that a few new species of smaller plants still remain to be discovered. Of the moisture-loving trees, few match the *ohia lehua* at its greatest stature—shag-barked giants more than 100 feet high and five or six feet thick near the base. But the species' name, *polymorpha*, is an apt one, reflecting as it does the great variety of genetically distinct races, or subspecies, of *ohia* adapted to an exceptionally broad range of island environments.

Polymorphism in the mountain flora is by no means restricted to *ohia lehua*. However, many of the other highly variable types of plants are classified as suites of species rather than races within a single species. They often feature striking differences in flowers, seeds, and foliage. Common examples include the *hoawa (Pittosporum)*, among whose thirty-odd Hawaiian species are many shrubs and some respectable trees thirty to forty feet high. A similar range of stature characterizes *kolea (Myrsine)*, some of whose species stand out in the dark forest understory by virtue of their new foliage, tinted pastel pink. An especially variable group constitutes the genus *Pelea* (called *alani* in Hawaiian). These citrus-family plants range from shrubs to slender rain-forest trees, and one species, the licorice-scented *Pelea anisata*, or *mokihana*, has become vinelike in its pattern of growth.[1]

Yet another genus, *Platydesma*, related to *Pelea*, illustrates several common adaptations to the deeply shaded understory of the island rain forest. Species of *Platydesma* have the large seeds typical of many wet-forest trees. Large seeds probably help them to shoot up quickly into tall whips, which can bend to extra lengths and perhaps track any available and consistent patch of midday light through the seasons. Even when mature, these plants have a tall, stalky appearance with few branches and with clusters of leaves at their tips. One species, *P. cornuta*, has enormous leaves up to three feet long and arranged palmlike in a terminal rosette atop a tall, flexible pole of a trunk. This evolutionary approach to gathering light in dim surroundings parallels that embodied in tree ferns and certain lobelioids that share the same habitat beneath the *ohia* canopy.

Resembling everyone's dream of jungle foliage, the huge indigenous Hawaiian tree ferns, called *hapuu (Cibotium splendens* and *C. chamissoi)*, rear up on trunks fifteen to twenty-five feet high in the mountain forests. Their big, rugged fronds reach ten feet in length and have a "prehistoric" look. Indeed, the ancestors of these plants may have come very early to the Hawaiian Archipelago, their tiny spores wafted on ancient winds from their continental homeland. Another robust group of ferns forms the endemic genus *Sadleria*. Named *amau*, these ferns do not grow as large as the *hapuu*. A five-foot trunk and spreading crown of fronds represents a prime specimen of *S. cyathoides*, the largest and most common species. Sadlerias range from wet areas to quite dry locations, such as the northwestern walls of Haleakala Crater on Maui. Here these ferns are common along the spectacular cliff trail leading to the National Park Service cabin at Holua. *Amau* is also abundant around the Kilauea summit region in Hawaii Volcanoes National Park, where it is one of the conspicuous plants appearing on new lava. The growth of the fern bears a certain resemblance to a familiar sequence of events here. First, the often dull-red, upthrusting new frond mimics the form of an aerial plume of erupting lava. Then, unfolding fully and extending horizontally, it models the glowing, branching lava streams spreading

12.1   Hawaiian *koa (Acacia koa)* left—top and bottom, and *ohia lehua (Metrosideros polymorpha)* right.

across the mountainside. Finally, the frond turns green like the older landscapes in this lush region.

In general, plant colonization of new lava proceeds faster in the cloudy, more continuously moist upper rain-forest belt than down closer to the coast. While *amau* ferns and small flowering plants quickly appear in the cracks and crannies of *pahoehoe* lava, a silver-gray lichen (*Stereocaulon vulcani*), called Hawaiian snow or volcano moss, is often the first noticeable growth to cover *aa*, sometimes to the exclusion of virtually every other form of vegetation at an early stage of plant succession, or recovery.

The lobelioids constitute yet another group of plants for which Hawaiian rain forests are justly famous. Represented in Hawaii by an array of seven genera,* all but one of which are endemic, these plants present striking examples of adaptive radiation and coevolution with birds and perhaps Hawaiian moths. Although many lobelioids grow in the dim wet-forest understory, some have become adapted to mountain bogs and others to treeless, windswept ridgelines; a few are still found in relatively dry mountain forests. Probably a majority of the recently extinct lobelioids were from this last-named habitat, reached by the livestock that consume such plants with gusto.

The genus *Cyanea* includes the largest as well as some of the smallest Hawaiian lobelioid species. Colonization of new habitats accompanied by natural selection in the islands has produced cyaneas ranging from modest herbs to slender palmlike trees that rise halfway to an *ohia* or *koa* canopy. Leaf forms in *Cyanea* are typically elongate; different species vary in having smooth or slightly ripply edges, oaklike margins, or, in species where maximum leaf surface is required to capitalize on the stingy and scattered stippling of sunlight in the forest depths, fernlike shapes.

Clermontia includes plants with a bushy or shrublike form. Unlike most of the cyaneas, they often tend to grow in fairly open patches of the forest, along trails, and beside jeep roads. They exhibit an extreme variation in flower color, size, and curvature. The curvature in some species exactly matches that of the beaks of certain long-billed, nectar-feeding Hawaiian forest birds observed foraging at these "host" plants. It has long been suggested that *Clermontia*'s flower forms, along with those of some other Hawaiian rain-forest plants, evolved in concert with

---

* *Lobelia (oha, ohawai)*; the only nonendemic genus
Trematolobelia (Kolii); contains only one species in several varieties
Delissea; mainly known from upper dry forests; most species now extinct
Cyanea (aku); numerous species, many rare or extinct
Rollandia; related to *Cyanea*; mostly found on Oahu
Clermontia (oha kepau); numerous species
Brighamia (puaala, aluli, ohaha); inhabits remote coastlines (Molokai and Kauai); see chapter 11

the native birds. With the lack of appropriate insects such as bees in the wet forests, the chief pollinators of these plants were birds. The tragic loss of most of the Hawaiian avifauna probably sealed the fate of many lobelioids. Or maybe it happened the other way around. A majority of both are now extinct or nearly so.

Several other kinds of plants of the mountain forests have evolved tubular flowers of the sort that seem to favor the foraging of nectar-sipping birds and long-tongued moths. Among these plants are the several exceedingly rare species of *Hibiscadelphus*, endemic Hawaiian trees related to the familiar hibiscus, but in the former, flowers never actually open. Their cross-fertilization was dependent on avian visitors intent on probing with delicate, curved bills. Another example involves several kinds of *naupaka (Scaevola). Naupakas* have evolved in more than one direction. Their story is partly a sea saga and partly a tale of adaptation and diversification in the rain forests, where a number of species have long-throated flowers—some straight that are visited by moths, and some curved and probed by birds such as the *apapane*.[2] These forest *naupakas* have evolved other features as well that make them quite different from their close relative, the common beach shrub *Scaevola sericea.*

A variety of native plants was sought in the mountain forests by the Hawaiians for medicines, dye and cosmetological substances, construction materials, ornamentation, and so on. Two of the most prized species, still extant, are a vinelike shrub called *maile (Alyxia oliviformis)* and a tall, robust shrub with large, attractive red-veined leaves called *olona (Touchardia latifolia). Maile* grows best in areas with moderate rainfall. It looks equally graceful whether draped among tree branches or over the shoulders of a favored person wearing it as one of the classic types of Hawaiian leis. *Maile* leis are always open and worn as ornamental chains. The flexible viney stem and smooth, dark green leaves have a fresh, vanillalike fragrance, especially when lightly crushed, and are the essence of the lei. *Maile's* yellow flowers are small and appear to have little ethnobotanical significance.

Olona was one of very few native plants to be cultivated by the Hawaiians. It was planted in clearings in wet valleys and its bark harvested in strips, dried, and manufactured into cordage. *Olona* fiber is one of the strongest natural fibers; it is flexible, and resistant to rot. In old Hawaii it was made into general-purpose twine for lashings as well as many other products ranging from fishing nets to the mesh matrix of elaborate feather capes and ceremonial helmets.[3] Reportedly, *olona* was in great demand during the classic whaling era, when it was made into harpoon line, and as late as the 1930s (before the invention of nylon) it was exported to Switzerland for the manufacture of climbing rope.[4] Another fiber plant was *mamaki (Pipterus albidus)*, in the same family as *olona. Mamaki* sometimes grows into a small tree and, unlike *olona*, is still common in well-watered regions from near sea level to as high as 5,000 feet.

Yet another rain-forest classic in Hawaii is *ieie, Freycinetia arborea*, a vining relative of *Pandanus*. Typically, *ieie* spirals up around tree trunks and limbs, branching as it goes, airing its terminal tufts of narrow pointed leaves out in the understory midlevels to which it lends a very jungly look. Happily, *ieie* is still abundant, even in many disturbed valleys on Oahu. It sometimes grows amid grasses and low shrubs on deforested windward slopes where it snakes over the ground, questing upward here and there to compete for sunlight.

Some of the flora appealed to artistic sensibilities in old Hawaii. Two of the most distinctive rain-forest associates of *ohia* are species of *Cheirodendron (trigynum* and *platyphyllum)*. The Hawaiians called these species *olapa* and *lapalapa*, respectively. The main peculiarity of these moderate-size trees is in their petioles, which are so delicate that the leaves are almost constantly in motion, even when the air seems still. To the Hawaiians, the slow fluttering and twisting foliage of these trees suggested the motions of the hula.

At high, rainy elevations, most notably in the summit regions of Kauai and West Maui, are the other-worldly habitats of Hawaiian bogs. These are often cold and fogbound places where clouds touch the earth for days at a time. The soil is highly acidic and peaty with partially decomposed vegetation. A dwarf flora is the norm here; even the *ohia* trees mature and flower at a few inches high. One that reaches two feet may be as old as a forest giant in kinder surroundings a mile away. Certain lobelioids love the bogs; their tufted heads loom over the low spongy turf; each has a mysterious presence in the mist. A few Maui bogs are graced by extremely rare greenswords and a small, wet-adapted silversword, relatives of the famous silverswords of the Hawaiian alpine regions (see chapter 16).

On rare sunny days, the bogs emerge from the nether world into an entirely different light but remain just as magical. One of the most evocative descriptions of a Hawaiian bog in its sunlit glory was written in 1884 by the mountaineering clergyman J. M. Alexander after he had climbed to the summit of the West Maui mountains:

> Everywhere is swamp covered with a sedge of strange stunted plants, rare ferns and exquisite mosses. The ohia tree dwindles from a monarch of the forest to a shrub a few inches in height, still bearing its scarlet plumes. On all sides are pools of standing water, and in every hollow, rushing streams. This is the paradise of mosses . . . they carpet the whole earth and every rock and decaying log with their feathery beauty. . . . Rare plants abound here . . . dwarf silverswords plants and lobelias rising with long red and yellow blossoms like candelabra of a cathedral.[5]

12.2 Rain-forest understory. Tree ferns—species of *Sadleria* (lower left) and *Cybotium*. Also *olapa* (*Cheirodendron trigynum*); large-leaved sapling *kolea* (Genus *Myrsine*); and (mid-level left) a palmlike lobelioid (Genus *Cyanea*). After Sohmer and Gustafson in part.

Hawaiian bogs are islands of unique vegetation within the rain forest. Wholly different kinds of insular habitat exist on the island of Hawaii in zones of recent lava flows. These islands within an island, called *kipukas*, are pieces of the original landscape that were spared from the volcanic desolation that overran their surroundings. Scattered and isolated from each other on terrain ranging from sea level to the alpine zone, they are varied remnants of forest with dependent communities of insects and birds—diminutive ecosystems evolving in risky symbiosis with living volcanoes. Few visitors to Hawaii ever explore a *kipuka* and experience its oasislike ambience. For those who don't want to miss such an exquisite fragment of Hawaiian natural history, Kipuka Puaulu on the Mauna Loa Road in Hawaii Volcanoes National Park is readily accessible. A loop trail winds for nearly a mile through a forest of giant *ohia, koa,* and other native trees. The nearly mile-high air is cool and its scents and wind sounds are those the old Hawaiians knew.

A kind of antithesis of a *kipuka* in the Hawaiian forests is an area denuded of vegetation by a landslide. The long vertical scars—typically brown, yellow, or red, colors of bare earth against a background of green vegetation—are common on the steep slopes and valley walls of the older islands. Such freshly bared ground is the natural habitat of *uluhe (Dicranopteris)*, a native genus of fern called staghorn owing to its dichotomously branching growth. The spores of *uluhe* disseminate widely on the wind and, on the older islands before the coming of livestock, its existence must have depended on colonizing the openings left by landslides, for *uluhe* is intolerant of shade. Under an open sky, however, this fern must be one of the world's fastest growing ground covers. It rapidly greens over the bare earth to form a tough meshlike mat that can be several feet thick.

Many more unique plants, products of long-ago chance arrival and adaptive radiation in the mountain forests, deserve mention in extolling the Hawaiian Islands as our planet's greatest living laboratory of evolution. There are so many stories here: Hawaiian euphorbias *(akoko)*, whose species range from small, succulent coastal mats to big-leaved trees of the rain forest; amaranth trees *(Charpentaria)* and woody violets *(Viola)* up to eight feet tall. Excellent descriptions of these and many other Hawaiian evolutionary wonders are provided by Sherwin Carlquist in his book *Hawaii, A Natural History*, whose major theme is the evolution of the terrestrial biota.

One of the most dramatic and interesting stories in Hawaiian natural history is that of the *ohia lehua* itself. Recent scientific studies by Lani Stemmerman and others have shown that the Hawaiian *ohia (M. polymorpha)*, is a species consisting of numerous races with genetically controlled differences in morphology and physiology.[6] Natural selection and adaptation have produced *ohia* types from the bog dwarfs, to

100-foot-high forest monarchs, to sun-desiccated shrubs high on desert shingle. Recent research indicates not only that different races of *ohia* trees evolved at different altitudes over the species' extraordinary range, from sea level to about 10,000 feet, but that suites of *ohia* with consistent racial differences can be found within a given altitude/climate belt. Such races appear to be especially adapted to different soil types, beginning with freshly cooled lava.

The potpourri of island soils results from the greatly variable mix of age, temperature, texture, moisture content and drainage, acidity, nutrient availability, and other chemical effects. One or another form of *ohia* is found to grow on nearly every natural island soil type, and *ohia* forests even cover the soils poorest in nutrients and those with aluminum and other metals in concentrations toxic to many kinds of plants. In fact, it is often in areas with poor quality soils that native forests are best preserved, since alien species generally do not thrive on such substrates.[7]

Research by Stemmerman strongly suggests that races of *ohia lehua* replace each other in a succession related to the age of the terrain. Thus, there appear to be identifiable pioneering and seral varieties of *M. polymorpha*. This phenomenon parallels the well-established ecological model for continental forests in which wholly different species succeed each other in the long-term development of forest ecosystems. Note, however, that *M. polymorpha* would not be a long-term dominant in most continental forests. It is small-seeded and intolerant of shade, and should be overtopped eventually by massive, slow-growing canopy species. But this does not happen on the wetter terrain and poorer volcanic soils of Hawaii, because no native tree in the islands can grow as well and as large as *ohia* in those conditions.

Superimposed on the simplified successional pattern involving *ohia* varieties, which may take millennia on slowly maturing ground, is a shorter-term phenomenon called *ohia* dieback. This refers to the mass senescence and death of *ohia lehua* canopy trees without any obvious extrinsic causes such as disease, insect infestations, drought, or flooding. All of the dying trees, sometimes in stands up to many square miles in extent, are of similar stature and probably close to the same age. While the actual dying takes place over only a decade or two, the trees within the stand may be 300 or 400 years old. In such stands there are almost never any saplings, but waiting to grow under the dying canopy is the latest crop of *ohia* seedlings. As pointed out by University of Hawaii botanist Dieter Mueller-Dombois, they replace their parents with a new uniform stand in the manner of a high-yield, commercially managed forest, albeit with self-thinning and an absence of neat rows and blocks of trees.

Thus, the Hawaiian rain forest seems to feature a peculiar mosaic of *ohia* cohorts, each a group of trees of uniform stature and age that dominates the canopy for a time and then gives way altogether to the next generation. For this pattern to operate in the manner suggested by modern research,[8] severe disturbance must be relatively infrequent within fairly large tracts of forest. If lava flows, volcanic ashfalls, hurricanes, and so on clear away parts of any *ohia* forest more often than once in a few tree generations, the uniformity of a large stand will eventually disappear in a hodgepodge of regenerating patches of different ages. The existence of what appear to be large cohort stands of *ohia*, now restricted mainly to the Big Island, implies that, away from the most active volcanic regions, Hawaii represents a kind of Eden for forest development. Presumably, after some initial setting of the forest clock by lava or ash or millennial storm, vast mountainsides of *ohia* can grow old and pass away, to be replaced generation after generation by a single wave of offspring.

In Hawaii, with its simple forest community and benign environment, orderly cohort replacement might be a true end point, or climax, to forest succession. Hawaii may be one of few places on earth where this ecological process has evolved to such precision, and now perhaps it is the last place where the result can be observed. This stately natural climax *cum* transition may well have been the norm for eons in rain forests on the major high Hawaiian islands before the arrival of man. Then, the pace of ecological disturbance increased dramatically with the Polynesian expansion in the lowlands and, after 1778, accelerated all over the archipelago.

THE FATE OF HAWAIIAN FORESTS

Early Hawaiians clearly destroyed vast tracts of coastal forest, apparently with the use of fire to clear land for agriculture (see chapter 19). However, in the mountains at elevations exceeding about 2,000 feet, plant communities probably remained little changed until the nineteenth century. Although some impacts may have accompanied the Polynesian introductions of rats and pigs, direct exploitation of the mountain forests by Hawaiians would have been light and patchy, with sustained use of only perhaps a few dozen species of plants. Hawaiian woodworkers learned to use native trees to supplement in terms of hardness, durability, and flexibility the South Pacific species introduced by their ancestors. *Ohia lehua* was one of the trees in modest demand in aboriginal times. Reportedly, Hawaiians used this wood for carving idols, and they also shaped it into mallets and spears.[9] And *ohia* had a strong spiritual standing. The tree was celebrated in poetry for the beauty of its radiant scarlet blossoms, which were sacred to Pele, the volcano goddess.

Perhaps the most prized native tree in ancient Hawaii was the *koa*; it was certainly one of the most famous, judging from the surviving lore and mystique regarding its use for the hulls of the largest sailing canoes. By the time of Western contact, the Hawaiians expended great effort to procure giant, straight-trunked *koa* trees in the high forests. As late as 1833, the missionary W. P. Alexander, on a trek across the Big Island from Waimea to Kilauea Caldera, came upon a Hawaiian encampment on the eastern slope of Mauna Loa several miles above "Luapele" (Kilauea), and at least twelve miles from the sea. He observed "many large trunks of the koa, partly hewn into canoes, beside which were erected little huts, the temporary abodes of the carpenters."[10]

The first large-scale, destructive exploitation of Hawaii's mountain forests was the historic harvest of sandalwoods *(Santalum)*. In Hawaii, these trees are known to be root parasites, obtaining some essential nutrition by penetrating with networks of tiny hairlike structures the roots of *koa* and other species. Hawaiian upland sandalwoods tend to be distributed through their range in small discontinuous groves, most often associated with *koa* in mesic forest, including zones above and below the true rain forest belt on Hawaii and Maui. In the mountains of Molokai, Oahu, and Kauai, these trees grow in regions between the wet windward and dry leeward extremes. On Lanai, an endemic sandalwood barely survives in remnants of the former native dry forest. Both *koa* and sandalwoods have been largely displaced from their former lower range, which has become weed-ridden with such trees as guava *(Psidium)* and java plum *(Eugenia cuminii)*, taken over by sugar cane and pasturage, or planted with the likes of Cook Pine *(Araucaria columnaris)*. eucalypts, and others.

Santalum is a genus of many species. They are scattered widely in the Indo-Pacific region, and demand for the fragrant heartwood of certain of these trees had existed in China since antiquity. There, such wood was made into coffers and coffins as well as incense. By 1791, some of the Hawaiian sandalwoods were suspected of being valuable (six endemic Hawaiian species are now recognized, although others may have been eradicated by Polynesian settlers, for example on Kahoolawe; see chapter 19). In that year, a Captain John Kendrick left three of his crew on Kauai to prospect for the trees. Kendrick, a Yankee trader who had made profits in furs on the Oregon-to-China route, went home to Boston to attend to business. When he returned to Kauai in 1794, his men had indeed found sandalwood, but Kendrick was killed almost immediately in a cannonading accident at Honolulu.[11]

Although others began to carry sandalwood to China, the trade did not qualify as big business until after 1810. Then, in little more than two decades of frantic commerce that all but destroyed a renewable resource, traders "came loaded with brandy, arms, and trinkets . . . requesting as compensation only those good-for-nothing trees of the forest."[12] As the ruling *alii* quickly acquired tastes for imported goods, the sandalwood business brought some hefty trinkets to the islands.

Sandalwood trader James Hunnewell (later a founding partner in the company that became C. Brewer, now a Honolulu-based multinational corporation) recorded that the big-ticket items were ships. Schooners and brigs, which cost several thousand piculs of sandalwood apiece, were sold like used cars to Hawaiian royalty (the picul, a measure used in China, was about 133 pounds).[13] In 1822, the visiting missionaries Tyerman and Bennet examined a 170-ton brig that had just been sold to King Kamehameha II (Lihiliho) for about $90,000 worth of sandalwood. "Her principal timbers were found to be rotten. She can last but a short time longer."[14] Even in perfect condition, they opined, the ship would have been worth about a tenth of the purchase price.

Sometime before 1820, the early kingdom's largest cannon, already a Prussian antique, was installed in the fort at Honolulu. Reportedly, the big gun had cost 1,000 piculs of sandalwood, worth about $10,000 at the time.[15]

British naval captain F. W. Beechey, at Honolulu in 1827, described the incongruity of finding luxurious silks and velvet sofas, fancy services of plate, and expensive cut glass from London in the low, dark, dirt-floored, and thatch-roofed houses of the high chiefs. All of these things were purchased for sandalwood through a mail-order business dominated by Americans.[16]

By 1827, the price per picul had declined to about eight dollars, assuming that the Spanish dollar, then standard coinage in the Pacific, had remained stable. An agreement in that year between the Hawaiian Kingdom and the United States resulted in a decree that every able-bodied man deliver one-half picul of sandalwood to the governing chief of his district. This was a tax levied to retire a $500,000 debt of the late Kamehameha II, who had reigned only four years. The money was owed to U.S. merchants, and Hawaiian subjects had the option of paying in cash (four Spanish dollars) or property of equal value (pigs were acceptable).[17] For most however, the "good-for-nothing trees" were the choice of necessity.

Like provincial pharaohs, the *alii* set in motion spectacles of slave labor. Tyerman and Bennet in 1822 reported seeing (apparently in Oahu) "nearly two thousand persons laden with fagots of sandalwood coming down from the mountains to deposit their burthens in the royal store houses."[18] William Ellis encountered intensive sandalwood gathering on the Big Island. In 1823, at Kawaihae, he witnessed an incredible procession of 2,000 to 3,000 men carrying sandalwood down from the Kohala Mountains, reportedly for the powerful chief Kalanimoku.[19] Ellis had earlier seen lava caves near the coast in South Kona used to store sandalwood cut in that region,[20] and on another occasion noted a human

12.3 Oahu sandalwood tree, *Santalum freycinetianum.*

sandalwood train of 300 to 400 in the Hilo District. They carried pieces ranging from logs of heartwood more than a foot in diameter—the sap-wood was typically hacked away at the gathering site—down to bundles of sticks.[21] The larger roots also had value and were grubbed up with greater diligence as the aboveground resource became scarcer.

Yet another early account gives an impression of the magnitude of the exploitation on Kauai. Tersely describing the lightering of sandal-wood out to waiting ships at Waimea in March 1818, a seaman wrote, "About 500 canoes were employed in bringing it off." [22] Such a flotilla seems astounding, but at the time the south coast of Kauai was densely settled for miles around Waimea, and a regional chief might easily have assembled it.

By about 1830, Kauai, Oahu, Molokai, and Hawaii were all largely stripped of mountain sandalwoods in accessible areas. In the frenetic years of the trade, near many harbors and landings, pits were dug to specifications representing ships' holds; they were filled with sandal-wood as fast as it could be brought down from the hills and sold by the cargo load. Some of these pits, called *lua moku iliahi*, can still be found, for example near Waikolu Lookout on Molokai.

In retrospect, the price of sandalwood was highest in human terms.

In 1827, the official royal sandalwood tax of one-half picul must have seemed a model of reform. In earlier years, such levees could be imposed at whim by local or regional chiefs. Reportedly, men, women, and children were all assessed a whole picul. But the burden fell mainly on the men and resulted in such anguish and desperation among the commoners in Hawaiian feudal society that families were split and rates of abortion, infanticide, and suicide soared.[23] In the search for sandalwood, whole villages were driven away from their subsistence activities. Even as late as 1830, the missionaries in some quarters could still be blasé about it all: "Our people continue to give pleasing attention to the means of grace . . . most of them are now in the mountains cutting sandalwood."[24] There is little doubt that the sandalwood trade was partly responsible for the terrible demoralization and decimation of the Hawaiian population in the first half of the nineteenth century.

As sandalwood gathering was winding down in the 1830s, far more systematic efforts toward deforestation of the islands were gathering steam. The demand for firewood was rising steadily as port towns grew, whaling ships were calling by the hundreds, and, by midcentury, the steam engine was coming to dominate the islands' development, especially in sugar production and shipping. On Kauai, the cutting of firewood was said to have largely denuded the lower slopes above the early port of Koloa. There, during the 1840s and 1850s, a retired sea captain named George Charman became a kind of cordwood magnate; he provisioned ships, then plantations, and finally even exported wood to Honolulu.[25] The cordwood business greatly expanded from a cottage industry with the growth of steam power, but soon the sheer appetite for cleared land on the part of sugar planters and cattle ranchers outstripped all other resource concerns. An irresistible, industrial-scale deforestation began in upland regions that had been virtually untouched by the Polynesian people. By the 1850s, massive clearcutting was under way on the slopes of all the forested islands.

Only a few Hawaiian trees were valued by Westerners. Foremost among them was *koa*, whose beautiful, heavy, straight-grained wood became known as Hawaiian mahogany (although the tree is a legume and not at all related to mahogany). The second most abundant canopy tree in the native island forests, *koa* can grow to a majestic 150 feet in height. In regions of moderate rainfall, it typically dominates over *ohia*. On the island of Hawaii, the first major logging operations were in such prime *koa* forest above Waimea, between Makahalau at 4,000 feet and Hanaipoe at 5,200 feet. This land on the western slopes of Mauna Kea belonged to the nascent and growing Parker Ranch. When the inquisitive sightseer George Washington Bates toured the region in 1853, he already found in the high, cool environs of Hanaipoe "several sawmills employed in cutting lumber, an abundance of which was supplied by the extensive forests of *Acacia* that flourish in this region.''[26]

This site quickly became famous, for as the mountain slopes far and wide were shorn of trees, the *koa* lumber was stacked in huge, lattice-like piles on low hills and ridges. The area took on such an unusual appearance that local Hawaiians gave it its own name—Palihooukapapa (cliffs of piled lumber).[27] As the Parker Ranch and others expanded beyond the major forested zones, they treated *kipukas* in the same fashion. These small, insular ecosystems in the midst of sere lava lands were clearcut, fenced, and then used for grazing.[28]

Ohia lehua was mostly for burning. The wood's tendency to warp made it unsuitable for many construction purposes, although it saw some use as flooring, and around the turn of the twentieth century large cargoes of *ohia* railroad ties were shipped to the mainland for the Santa Fe Railroad.[29]

Ohia forests on the island of Hawaii were first razed in the midnineteenth century as big sugar plantations began to expand into the uplands of the North Hilo District. In 1868, Samuel Damon, publisher, editor, and reporter for *The Friend*, enthusiastically described how the forests were being cleared with the aid of the recently introduced technique of fluming:

> The flumes now extend up into the forests and immense quantities of wood are brought down. . . . The flume on the Onomea Plantation, we were informed, answered to bring down seventy-five cords of wood in a single day. . . . The Hitchcock brothers have a flume on their ranch which is used alone for the transportation of wood and lumber. Their flume is three and a half miles long.[30]

The flumes—big wooden troughs into which a mountain stream was diverted—also carried bundles of cane down to storage and processing areas. At the end of the working day, Damon and other visitors were amused by the Hawaiian field workers' sport of riding the flumes; the more daring individuals stood on rough-sawn planks as they surfed down the slopes of Mauna Kea.

Throughout the islands, the clearing of the mountain forests received its main impetus from the Great Mahele of the late 1840s. This was a series of land-law revisions in which the Hawaiian Kingdom first permitted land ownership by commoners, including white men, who quickly garnered the best and biggest acreages. On Maui, the missionary W. P. Alexander was a trained land surveyor, and he spent the summer of 1850 camping out and plying his secular trade on the slopes of Haleakala near Kula. His young sons, Sam and James, accompanied him that summer and wrote letters home. Sam wrote, ''Father is cutting roads through the forests so as to divide the land among the natives.'' James wrote,

"They have finished three lines through the woods which are two miles wide. . . . The woods are quite dense and contain much valuable timber. . . . "[31]

Along with the Alexander boys' references to nearby potato fields, these observations suggest that clearcutting and probably burning in the area had been in progress for some time, resulting in an already patchy landscape. The "woods" here were part of the primeval, *koa*-dominated forest in the vicinity of the switchbacking road that now leads up through miles of pasture to Haleakala National Park. This native forest was completely erased. Most of the trees one sees here now are eucalypts planted in scattered stands in the late nineteenth or early twentieth century. Beautiful, big trees with a resinous fragrance that evokes Australian byways, they nevertheless lack the associated biotic diversity, along with the spiritual standing and pride-in-place of the ancient *koas*, which would have matched them in stature.

Patchwork clearcutting, which left the land a crazy quilt of forest remnants, increasingly exposed the vulnerable Hawaiian biota to its unnatural enemies. Livestock, foreign insects, and diseases could now infiltrate and spread with unprecedented impact. The relentless foraging of cattle and goats must have spread year after year like a slow fire through the retreating forests, especially those on dry and mesic slopes. This was surely a time of multiple extinctions, when many lobelioids and other understory species were lost along with birds and insects that had special, highly evolved relationships with the doomed plants.

Another intensive occupation in the rain forests at this time, especially in the Hilo region, was the wild harvest of *pulu*, a soft, golden wool that grows as a dense covering at the bases of the fronds (leafstalks) of the giant *hapuu* ferns *(Cibotium)*. In the early 1850s, "when pulu was king" in Hilo's trade, whole cargoes of the stuff were shipped on schooners, such as the famous *Liholiho*.[32] For many years, California was a regular importer of *pulu*. Renowned for its softness, it was used as stuffing for mattresses and pillows, but its serviceability was limited to a few years at best. *Pulu* deteriorated to dust; the pillows and mattresses went flat, and eventually so did the markets for *pulu*.

According to Hillebrand (1888), writing of the 1850s or 1860s, extensive areas of tree-fern understory on Hawaii "have been nearly cleared away by the *pulu* gatherers who ruthlessly sacrifice the whole tree in order to get easily at the wool."[33] Certainly, native forests were damaged in the quest for *pulu*, and the industry probably opened up virgin areas to greater penetration by feral livestock.

For some time, beginning in the midnineteenth century, residents and travelers in the islands had reported finding areas of apparently intact native forest that were dying. Between the 1850s and 1870s, a dieoff of *koa* was conspicuous, especially on Maui.[34] Also at this time on the Big Island, native palms *(Pritchardia)* in the Mauna Loa rain forest were being attacked by a borer that killed the trees.[35] Such observations led to discussions among the cognoscenti of the islands regarding what was referred to as "the decadence of Hawaiian forests."[36] There were even references to a similar state of affairs in New Zealand and other parts of Oceania. Viewing Hawaiian forests from a new perspective, one Honolulu writer in 1875 declared,

> We believe the literary and scientific world is under obligation to Darwin for this intensely significant and pregnant expression, "Survival of the Fittest." Everywhere around us may be witnessed an intense struggle for existence . . . on the Hawaiian Islands, native grasses, shrubs, plants, and trees are gradually giving place to those of foreign origin.[37]

Unfortunately, this misapplication of Darwinism vis-à-vis a misunderstood and grossly disturbed flora was to bolster value judgments in Hawaiian forestry for decades.

Large-scale reforestation had been called for as early as 1870, when an editorial in *The Friend* entitled "Plant Trees" advised that "the time has come for refurbishing the islands with forests."[38] Foreign trees were heavily recommended, especially the rain tree, or monkeypod *(Samanea saman)*, and for the driest zones, algeroba, or *kiawe (Prosopis pallida)*. Pride of India *(Melia azederach)* and eucalypts were also early favorites on logged-over mesic slopes. Both of those last-named types were dominants in the massive reforestation executed by James Makee in the denuded uplands of his giant Ulupalakua Plantation on the southwestern slopes of Haleakala. A report in 1867 stated that Makee had planted 15,800 exotic trees on his land in a two-year period, and that pace seems to have continued into the early 1870s.[39]

About this time on Kauai, sugar planters G. N. Wilcox and latecomer Paul Isenberg were becoming concerned about watershed protection amid the "ever receding forests."[40] The first ironwoods *(Casuarina equisitifolia)* on the island were planted by Wilcox in 1874 on the Grove Farm Plantation. Beginning about 1880, Isenberg made the first systematic effort at reforestation on Kauai. He experimented with ironwood, monkeypod, and pride of India. The last-named species failed after a few years, and Isenberg, perhaps acquiring a kind of *kamaaina* pride, replaced it with thousands of *koa* seedlings, which grew into a large, dense forest.

Isenberg's example, or at least his success, was rare, and vastly more acres of *koa* died than were replanted. But then the dieoff, or dieback, changed its character and began to gain notoriety in major *ohia* forests of Maui and Oahu. Part of this great forest decline now appears to be traceable to a natural dieback of *ohia* cohorts. This interpretation was recently applied to what was termed the "Maui forest trouble,"[41] which was at its height in the first decade of the twentieth century.

Feral livestock must have continued to exacerbate the natural mortality of dieback episodes. The livestock problem was universally recognized in the islands; epithets such as *ravaging* and *all-devouring* were used by nearly every observer who described these animals' activities in the Hawaiian forests. For a century or more, sustained populations of hundreds of thousands or more goats and cattle ran wild on the major Hawaiian Islands (see chapter 20 for documentation). In all but the densest forest, they destroyed understory, promoted erosion, and spread weeds. By disturbing soil, damaging shallow roots, and consuming tree seedlings, they certainly would have prevented or delayed the normal regrowth of any areas undergoing natural dieback. Concerted efforts to control feral animals on public lands in Hawaii were not made until the twentieth century, and even today, in the two national parks, wild goats and pigs continue to pose serious ecological problems.

By 1900, the dying of the forests had spread over the mountain slopes like a colossal vegetative mange and had brought mounting concern over erosion and the loss of water resources for the sugar industry. This concern led directly to Hawaii's most grandiose and misguided reforestation scheme. The localized, largely private reforestation efforts since the 1860s on various islands were only sideshows to the eventual main attraction, whose peak performances were on Oahu but also involved various regions on other islands. The ringmaster was Harold Lloyd Lyon, a mainland botanist hired in 1970 by the Hawaii Sugar Planters Association (HSPA). Lyon arrived in the islands in that year as a young Ph.D., and with great energy and productivity planted his fifty-year career in Hawaii. He eventually embraced several diverse fields of tropical botany and horticulture. And very early he must have become imbued with the notion of the decadence of Hawaiian forests, which in the first decade of the twentieth century was still being discussed in learned media such as the *Proceedings of the HSPA.*[42]

Within weeks of his arrival, Lyon went to Maui to view the dying forests there and to discuss remedies with sugar baron H. P. Baldwin and other planters worried about their irrigation sources. After studies ruled out insect attack or disease as causes of the forest collapse, Lyon came to believe firmly in decadence.[43] His view was that *ohia* and most of the other Hawaiian plants were suceptible to toxic conditions that developed in aging volcanic soils. In other words, the Hawaiian flora, by nature, was an early successional type only. It was destined to wither away on older terrain, and, as his later activities bear witness, Lyon felt it was his destiny to replace it.

First, however, years went by while Lyon busied himself with sugar cane pathology and numerous biological problems of the fledgling pineapple industry. Meanwhile, the new Territorial Board of Agriculture and Forestry made some feeble—and vain—attempts at reestablishing *ohia* and *koa* on the denuded mountainsides. On the other hand, at Lyon's recommendation, introduced trees such as eucalyptus, ironwoods, and the Australian silver oak *(Grevillea robusta)* were planted and began to thrive from low to medium elevations at numerous sites in the islands, but they were judged to be less than effective in holding back water runoff.[44] Experimental plots at higher elevations were planted with temperate-zone species. Ralph Hosmer, Hawaii's first territorial forester (1904–1914), imported Douglas firs, redwoods, pines, and junipers, among other trees. One of the early test plantings of these species is a delightful spot, now called Hosmer's Grove, situated close to the 7,000-foot level near the headquarters of Haleakala National Park on Maui. The air is eternally October and redolent with continental woodsy fragrances under big trees, but this whole mountainside was once covered with a mixed forest of *koa, ohia, mamane, naio*, sandalwood, and others with rare endemic fragrances that permeated an exquisitely unique and vanishing ecosystem.

Harold Lyon traveled widely in the Indo-Pacific region, and he and his assistants also went to the Caribbean area. Their main priority was to study cane and pineapple diseases and to collect samples for breeding to improve the Hawaiian crops, but they also gathered seeds of trees that might be suitable for remaking the mountain forests of Hawaii. The HSPA joined forces with the territorial board, and by 1920 Lyon had added a forester's hat to his collection as he experimented with hundreds of exotic tree species. Almost immediately he became convinced that the salvation of Hawaii's watersheds lay in planting banyans and related species of *Ficus* (fig trees). Lyon's early experiments showed that various figs grew well in a wide range of soils and climates. Once established, the trees would readily spread by means of birds, which ate the fruit and dropped the undigested seeds. The seeds had the capacity to sprout almost anywhere, including the crotches of other trees, on deadfalls, and so on. From such perched seedlings, aerial roots—the trademark of the banyans—would find their way down to the soil, eventually to form multiple trunks. This would even permit these trees to take over wide areas covered by the smothering *uluhe* fern. Such areas were typically spotted with dead snags and massive fallen trunks of former forest giants, from which the banyans could easily get started. Most important of all, the banyans, with their inverted Medusa's tangle of adventitious roots, had excellent soil- and water-holding properties, and the interlocking banyans would also form a barrier to the penetration of livestock into watershed areas. It was meant to be a simple solution to the problem of irresponsible ranching practices that fit the primitive ecological concepts of the time.

On behalf of the sugar industry, Lyon planned to vastly simplify the flora of Oahu's Koolau and Wainae ranges. By 1923, thousands of young banyan trees had been planted along the lower mountain slopes. In addition, Lyon reported:

> Large quantities of fig seed have also been sown from army airplanes and we are justified in expecting favorable results from this operation. . . . This is carrying out our general plan which contemplates the construction of a continuous barrier forest below the remaining native forest. When the trees in this barrier forest reach a fruiting stage, the seeds will be carried by natural agencies into the dead and dying forest above. At the same time, the trees will sprout down the mountain slopes onto the waste lands below.[45]

During the 1920s and 1930s, this impending ecological debacle was virtually unopposed. Today, although such outrages against natural history and genetic diversity continue without publicity in hundreds of small, scattered places in the islands, Lyon's mammoth project would undoubtedly draw the fire of every professional botanist who heard of it. One of the few who opposed the great fig fiasco at the time was the late Otto Degener, an eminent plant taxonomist and long an ardent defender of Hawaii's priceless floral heritage.

> He [Lyon] never fully sensed the sacredness of our endemic plants that had taken nature millions of years to evolve. It was of course his duty as an employee of the Sugar Planters' Experiment Station to increase the fog drip and the water holding capacity of our soils. . . . It was his rash aim, consequently, to introduce and scatter banyan and other *Ficus* species throughout our islands. When I remonstrated he answered that his choice of *Ficus* species was prompted by the plants' commercial worthlessness. Were our jungles planted to timber trees, these would be harvested in due time, necessitating reforestation, while worthless forests of sinuous banyans, on the contrary, would be left alone forever."[46]

Lyon was stubborn, misguided, touched perhaps with a horticultural megalomania, but he was a mainstream conservationist of his time, saving the resources of the land for what he considered the highest and best use: sugar production. In the thirties, he employed the Civilian Conservation Corps. They started reforestation projects on several islands and, especially on Oahu, they planted thousands more fig trees. Most of the banyans standing today along Oahu's back roads and trails are Lyon's legacy. In the end, however, the scheme failed; the great barrier forest never materialized. The reason seems to have been that, despite repeated attempts to introduce them, the several species of tiny fig wasps that are exclusive pollinators for these trees have never become well established in Hawaii. However, this may be changing, according to entomologist Wayne Gagné of Bishop Museum.

Then World War II intervened, and forestry research was cut back for the war effort. In the same period, it became clear that the *ohia* forests were beginning to regenerate, as feral grazers had finally been significantly reduced in most of Hawaii's forest reserves. A combination of factors, especially the fencing of ranchlands (which had been slowly gaining ground since the late nineteenth century) along with organized drives and hunts, finally broke the back of the feral livestock problem. Today, however, wild pigs, goats, and sheep are again in the ascendancy and, in the twisted logic of state natural resource agencies besieged by a powerful hunters' lobby, promoted for their wilderness value.

As in the lowlands, disturbance on the mountainsides opened up niches for invasion by foreign weeds. Among the most aggressive are passion flower vines *(Passiflora)*. Numerous species and varieties have been introduced to Hawaii from the tropical American region. The worst of these tough, wiry climbers is *P. mollissima*, called banana *poka*. This species generally favors mesic conditions, where it grows rapidly up to canopy levels, covering even giant *koa* trees with a thick mesh of vines. The rapid growth of these vines is a serious threat to stands of native forest in some areas, such as the uplands of Kauai, near Kokee, where they hang down from the tall trees like giant, leafy chains and smother and kill understory species as well as canopy trees. Like other members of its family, the banana *poka* produces fabulous flowers and edible fruits; the latter, unfortunately, are avidly consumed by wild pigs, which help to spread the seeds.

Another favorite of pigs in the mountain forests is the guava—actually fruits of trees in the genus *Psidium*. Since the midnineteenth century, these Caribbean-area imports to Hawaii have crowded out native species in broad forest belts on most of the islands in climates from wet to moderately dry. In 1873, Isabella Bird found many places "where the hill slopes are now only a wilderness of guava scrub . . . ,"[47] and this description applies at least as widely today.

Other major weeds of the mountain forests range from the familiar—bamboo—to the obscure—*Clidemia hirta*. The latter, another native of South America, apparently came to Hawaii from Fiji shortly after World War II. It was cultivated for some time at Harold Lyon's experimental nursery in Wahiawa, leeward of Oahu's Koolau Range. Otto Degener recalled in a 1986 conversation that it was being planted out from pots in the Koolau foothills sometime before 1950. Now it has become devastatingly aggressive in the wet-forest understory and threatens to displace many native plants. With small seeds (in purple berries), readily dispersed by birds and in mud shed from hikers' boots, *Clidemia* has infested Oahu and has begun to spread on Molokai, Maui, Kauai, and Hawaii.

The list of aggressive mountain weeds goes on: blackberry, gorse, fire tree, *Tibouchina*, and more. Some were introduced as hopeful cultivars, others by accident, but now all are part of the pattern of decline of Hawaii's remaining mountain forests. Much of that decline, however, has been consciously pursued and in recent times is inexcusable. Hawaii conservationists toll a sad litany of public and private callousness:

- In the 1950s, burning and bulldozing by government agencies of large tracts of *ohia* and planting of exotic pines for an ill-conceived timber industry that never developed

- In the 1960s, military testing of defoliants, including the infamous Agent Orange, over wide stands of Kauai's native rain forest

- In the 1970s, bulldozing by the state of Hawaii of large areas of native dry *(mamane)* forest to "improve" the terrain for introduced game birds

- In the 1980s, clearcutting and chipping over hundreds of acres of private land containing the last native lowland forest in Hawaii

Although this chapter began by implying that some largely intact Hawaiian mountain forests still exist, that statement must be qualified by the observation that the decline of those forests is a lingering process that continues today. Some of the present decline began long ago and may be inexorable. A loss of coevolved pollinators may explain what is happening to trees such as the mountain *ohe (Tetraplasandra hawaiiensis)* on the moist slopes above Keauhou-Kona on the Big Island. Here, groves of this species—big handsome trees sixty to ninety feet high and probably well over a century old—flower year after year, but no seedlings appear around them.[48] Unlike *koa*, they do not sprout vegetatively from outlying roots. Barring some technological rescue, these *kamaaina* trees may be in their final generation.

It is quite possible that except for the two national parks and a few small privately protected parcels, the Hawaiian forests with their exquisite and priceless surviving flora will disappear within the next human generation. It is possible that a continuing resurgence of interest in Hawaiian culture will leave us with at least some arboreal ghosts—perhaps a memorial chant filled with *"iliahi, kauila, halapepe, olapa"*—the melodious names of the islands' trees—and a hula to evoke their styles of growth and their leafage and movements in the mountain winds.

13

Fresh Waters

The old Hawaiians had dozens of descriptions, often single rippling words, for the rain as it came to various parts of the islands. Even in translation, the descriptions are poetic and richly sensual. At Hilo there was the rain that "makes the *lehua* blossom quiver," and at Hana, Maui, the "rain of the low-lying heavens." Also on Maui (at Waiehu) came the "rain that pricks the skin" and "the fine mist of Waihee"; and at Kaupo there was "the rain that drives one to the rocks for shelter."[1]

Rain falling on the main Hawaiian Islands comes mainly from the northeast trade winds that originate under the large high-pressure zone that often prevails near 30 degrees north latitude. These low-altitude winds absorb moisture from the ocean as they blow from northeast to southwest, back toward the equatorial region of low pressure with its rising masses of air. Flung across the trades, the islands intercept some of this immense airflow and wring water out of it. Where it meets Hawaiian mountain slopes, the humid air near sea level is forced to rise. As it rises, the air cools and is unable to hold all of its moisture, which falls as precipitation. Most of the time, island rainfall is heaviest on windward slopes between about 2,000 and 5,500 feet elevation. Near the upper end of this vertical range on Hawaiian mountains, especially in the summit regions of Kauai and West Maui, annual rainfall may be higher than anywhere else on earth. On Kauai's Mount Waialeale, more than fifty feet of rain has been recorded in a single year.

At higher elevations and on leeward flanks of the islands, conditions are relatively dry. Even whole islands—Lanai, Kahoolawe, and Niihau—lie in the rain shadows of their larger neighbors, and some leeward terrain in Hawaii is truly desert country.

Less common weather patterns, mainly in the winter months, bring wind and rain from the south or southwest as low-pressure systems approach the islands from the north. At such times, the meeting of moisture-laden tropical air and an advancing cold front can trigger torrential rains, even on the usually dry southern and western slopes. During these episodes, which at their most intense are called *kona* storms, as much as ten to twenty inches of rain may fall in less than twenty-four hours. Flash floods race down typically tranquil watersheds and carry trees, boulders, tons of soil, and sometimes bridges, automobiles, and even houses.

About 360 streams are represented on modern maps of the main

Hawaiian Islands. Most of them have their primary sources in the upper montane forest, the belt of high rain fall; however, a large number of Hawaiian streams exhibit intermittent flow, and on leeward exposures many remain dry for months at a time. All Hawaiian streams are flashy, rising in minutes and diminishing within hours of heavy rainfall in their watersheds. Along their courses many streams gradually lose water owing to the extremely high porosity of the ground; yet at lower elevations rejuvenation may occur where a stream intersects springs gushing from vertical dike fields that have been exposed by erosion.

On the young volcanic terrain of Kilauea, Hualalai, and Mauna Loa, surface streams are virtually nonexistent. The land is an enormous rocky sponge. Even in the rainy region of Puna, the drainage is far below the surface until the flows reach the seacoast. There, in a few places the hidden streams well out into view. Even at the coast, however, most of the region's tremendous freshwater drainage remains underground. Early explorers such as Titus Coan reported discovering these "Stygian realms" with a sense of wonder and delight:

> Some of these waters are very cold, some tepid, and some at blood heat, furnishing excellent warm baths. There are large caves near the sea where we enter by dark and crooked passages and bathe by torchlight far underground in deep and limpid water.[2]

Today, these flooded caverns, along with smaller hot springs and natural saunas, are not on the tourist maps, but can be located by respectful inquiries of local residents.

PREDOMINANT FRESHWATER COMMUNITIES

Of the freshwater ecosystems in Hawaii, streams, along with coastal marshes (a few of which grade into brackish estuaries), are overwhelmingly dominant. The only other habitats we will explore briefly in this chapter are lacustrine: a handful of isolated, crater-bound ponds and the unique brackish anchialine pools formed on recent coastal lava flows. Throughout the islands, few fresh or brackish habitats remain even close to pristine, and very few are now being protected and have the chance of maintaining an essentially natural character.

Much of the current knowledge of the Hawaiian fresh- and brackish water faunas has been elucidated by limnobiologist John Maciolek of the U.S. Fish and Wildlife Service, along with others, mainly based at the University of Hawaii. The following accounts of Hawaiian stream animals are based on recent general works by these specialists.[3]

The conspicous native inhabitants of Hawaiian streams—fishes, shrimps, and a large species of snail—have diadromous life cycles. That is, they migrate between fresh waters and the sea. Their young, or larvae, develop in the sea, and long before they attain adulthood, the creatures return to make their way up the streams, sometimes high into mountain valleys. All of these species have clearly evolved from marine ancestors, and all are closely related to forms that have colonized island streams in many archipelagoes across the vast Indo-Pacific region (see chapter 3).

Five species of fish can be regarded as true freshwater forms,* as opposed to inshore marine fishes such as mullets and jacks, which commonly enter Hawaiian estuaries and lower reaches of streams. Four of the true stream fishes are gobies, distinct members of a large, primarily marine family with common representatives around coral reefs and in rocky tidepools on the coast. The gobies have a striking adaptation for life in turbulent water, including rushing island streams that are often punctuated by high waterfalls. These fishes' pelvic fins have fused together and become modified into a suction disk that enables the fish to cling to smooth, rocky surfaces and even wriggle up the faces of the waterfalls.

Hawaiians called these freshwater fishes by the general name *oopu wai* to distinguish them from marine relatives, classified as *oopu kai*. Females of all of the *oopu wai* are prolific spawners, some producing more than 100,000 eggs in a single season (summer to fall). The eggs, no larger than pinheads, are deposited on clean, rocky stretches of streambed, where they adhere to the bottom. At least one species *(Awaous stamineus)* seems to make a partial spawning migration downstream to leave its eggs relatively close to the ocean. The eggs hatch quickly, in some cases within a day or two, and the nearly microscopic larvae are carried down to the sea.

The ocean phase of existence of the *oopu wai* is all but unknown. Typically, the larvae seem to remain members of the marine plankton for months. Their slow growth must be related to their extremely small size at hatching. Finally, they return to the mouths of Hawaiian streams as one-inch fry, called *hinana* by the Hawaiians. Even at this stage the gobies can climb waterfalls, and some do—straight out of the ocean to reach hanging streams that plunge over seacliffs—for example, along Kauai's Na Pali Coast.

One of the smaller stream gobies, *Lentipes concolor* (about five inches long) is reputedly the best climber, and it often lives thousands of feet

---

Stenogobius (or *Chonophorus*) *genivittatus (oopu naniha)*, indigenous
Awaous stamineus (oopu nakea), endemic
Sicyopterus stimpsoni (oopu nopili), endemic
Lentipes concolor (oopu hiu-kole), endemic
Eleotris sandwicensis (oopu okuhe), endemic

above the sea in the highest reaches of streams that traverse spectacular cliff and jungle terrain. Somehow this fish struggles up valley headwalls whose wetness can vary from moss-slick rock to awesome cataracts, pounding down from hundreds of feet above. *Lentipes* is now the rarest of the *oopu wai*. A predator on small invertebrates, it is unusual in being almost without scales. It has a translucent appearance and exhibits striking differences in color and other anatomical features between the sexes. Males are orange to red in the tail region; females are mottled in shades of gray. This species is the only Hawaiian stream fish endemic at the generic level.

Sicyopterus stimpsoni, called *oopu nopili,* or clinging *oopu,* was a food resource in old Hawaii. It was also a good-luck omen, used in weaning ceremonies and house warmings in the hope that fortune would cling to the child or house as tenaciously as the fish to a rock.[4] This species reachs about cight inches in length. It feeds primarily by scraping algae from stones, and it reportedly prefers the swifter parts of streams.

Awaous stamineus is the largest of the Hawaiian stream gobies. According to Maciolek, this fish can grow to fourteen inches in length. It was greatly esteemed by Hawaiians for food. *Awaous* generally inhabits the middle reaches of major island streams. It is thought to be an omnivorous feeder on drift material. This species is able to burrow in gravel in the streambed, apparently to hide itself. One wonders if this adaptation has spread in the population during the last 1,500 years that humans have been predators on these fish. Before this time, adult fish may have been virtually free of predation.

Unlike the three species described above, *Stenogobius genivittatus,* an indigenous species also found on South Pacific islands, is still locally common on several islands in Hawaii. Reportedly, this small *oopu* (up to six inches long) prefers quieter waters in lower reaches of streams and may be found in brackish conditions near the sea. This fish is identifiable by a conspicuous black band under the eye, and its overall skin pigmentation, typically a fairly uniform gray or tan, can be altered rapidly to feature dark vertical stripes. Like the closely related *Awaous,* this goby has been observed hiding in sand or gravel.

The fifth *oopu wai, Eleotris,* is not a true goby. Although this fish belongs to a related family (Eleotridae), it lacks the pelvic modification and is confined to lower elevations. It shares the estuarine zone and coastal creeks with *Stenogobius* but reaches a larger size (up to a foot in length). *Eleotris* had many different Hawaiian names in different locations. It is a predator and still fairly common, surprisingly even on Oahu in relatively undisturbed places such as the estuary of Kahana Stream at Kahana Valley State Park.

Diadromous life cycles also characterize two Hawaiian species of

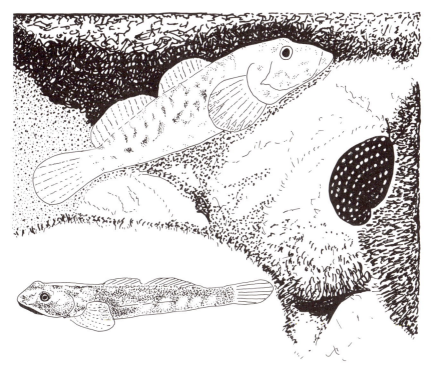

13.1   Native Hawaiian stream animals. Gobies: *Lentipes concolor (oopu hiu-kole)* and the larger *Awaous stamineus (oopu nakea)*; freshwater snail, *hihiwai (Neritina granosa)*. After Ford, Kinzie, and Mendez.

stream shrimp, *opae (Atyoida bisulcata* and *Macrobrachium grandimanus)*, and a large snail, *hihiwai (Neritina granosa)*. Like the fishes, these invertebrates return from the sea as tiny postlarval forms. They too work their way through the lowland creeks, up rushing brooks and waterfalls, and into the mountain watersheds. The shrimp presumably climb the mossy rock faces with the aid of their claws and pin-tipped feet; the snails follow with their slow, splay-footed crawl.

One of the shrimp *(Atyoida)*, called *opae-kala-ole*, meaning "spine-less," is also known as the mountain *opae*. It favors fast water in upland streams. Large populations of these small (two-inch long) crustaceans used to frequent streams on all of the large islands. The other *(Macrobrachium)*, known as *opae-oehaa* (crooked legs) is a larger species reaching three and a half inches in length, with the males featuring an especially gangly first pair of legs that bear prominent claws. Its primary habitat is the lower streams and estuaries.

It is impossible to know how long these creatures of island fresh waters have existed in Hawaii. Their sparse habitat has been recreated again and again by volcanic upheaval and the endless midocean rains, and it is probable that the origins of species such as *oopu-hiu-kole* antedate their present haunts. Quite possibly, they squirmed up slick headwalls and rested in sun-dappled brooks amid green crags that towered thousands of feet above places now called Nihoa and Necker, Laysan, Lisiansky, and others at a time when *Homo sapiens* was only a glint in a faraway anthropoid's eye.

A variety of less conspicuous and less well-studied animals inhabit Hawaiian streams in various zones from their spring-fed seeps to the estuaries. They include several other species of snails and an indigenous sponge, which resembles a greenish felt on rocks of upper elevation streams. Oligochaetes, and a freshwater polychaete, *Namalycastis abiuma,* represent the segmented worms in Hawaiian streams. Polychaetes are nearly exclusively marine animals, and *Namalycastis* lives in the lowland zone not far from the sea. By far the greatest diversity among native stream dwellers belongs to the insects, whose origins and life histories in the islands are, of course, independent of the ocean. Although some typical insects of continental waters—mayflies, stoneflies, caddisflies, and alderflies—are missing from Hawaii, a variety of insect orders are members of the native fauna. They include wholly aquatic forms as well as those that emerge from a watery larval existence to become flying adults. Many of the Hawaiian insects, such as damselflies, are evolutionary prodigies (see chapter 15).

Most conspicuous of all habitués of Hawaiian fresh waters are birds. Several native species and a variety of winter migrants are frequently seen in the lowlands. However, few venture into the mountain valleys. One native that can be encountered almost anywhere in an island watershed is the black-crowned night heron *(Nycticorax nycticorax),* apparently a race of the common North American species. Known to Hawaiians as *aukuu* for its sharp croak, the night heron typically announces itself as it flushes ahead of hikers on streamside trails on all of the larger islands. It is a top predator in the freshwater ecosystem, but its foraging is not restricted to that habitat. Although the daytime range of the night heron extends from cool, shaded valleys to lowland marshes, many of these birds appear along the seacoast at dusk. Some take up their patient hunting stations along the reef flats and estuarine sloughs, while others continue to fly offshore to seabird nesting islands, where, in the nesting season, they are known to prey on hatchling sooty terns.[5] The *aukuu* is also learning to take advantage of coastal aquaculture ponds, where it finds unprecedented concentrations of shrimp in range of its rapierlike bill.

The night heron is thought to be a fairly recent arrival in Hawaii, although it probably predates man. In its exploitation of a variety of uncontested feeding opportunities in several ecological settings from mountain streams to coral reefs and offshore islets, we may be seeing the earliest stages of an adaptive radiation.

A few migrants such as the wandering tattler, or *ulili (Heteroscelus incanus),* are occasionally seen along interior Hawaiian streams, and the remaining wild populatons of the native Hawaiian duck called *koloa (Anas wyvilliana)* have been significantly displaced to remote upland watersheds. But the main story of Hawaii's freshwater birds is set in the coastal marshes.

Mere vestiges remain of the islands' coastal wetlands, which, pre-historically, were probably best developed on Oahu. Hawaiian fresh- and saltwater marshes are less clearly defined by vegetational types than their counterpart continental habitats. Island marshlands often tend to grade almost imperceptibly from saline to freshwater forms, although the latter are usually dominant owing to the small tidal range. All marshes, however, are ephemeral. They alter their boundaries season-ally, especially on leeward, drier shores, even as they migrate, landward or seaward, at a much slower pace through millenia of changing sea level. In recent time, Oahu's major coastal wetlands included areas of the northern coastal plain near Kahuku; the lowlands of Kahana and other large windward valleys; several sites around Kaneohe Bay; Kawainui and Kaelepulu (Enchanted Lake, near Kailua); parts of the Waimanalo coastal plain; the Hawaii Kai lowlands; and numerous outwash plains from Waikiki to beyond Pearl Harbor.

On neighbor islands, important wetland locations included the Big Island's Waipio Valley, parts of Maui's central isthmus, numerous sites on the south shore of Molokai, and, on Kauai, big lowland valleys, such as Hanalei and Waimea, and the coastal plain district of Mana.

The native vegetation of Hawaii's wetlands represents a partial com-plement of a widely distributed Pacific island flora.[6] Characteristic plants in areas of relatively high salinity include the indigenous (and pan-tropical) grass *Sporobolus virginicus* and the succulent *Sesuvium por-tulacastrum*—not to be confused with the introduced *Batis maritima,* now a feature on many Hawaiian tidelands. A number of sedges also make an appearance in seaward tidal locations, but reach their greatest diversity and luxuriance farther inland in weakly brackish to freshwater zones. Here the modest, one-foot-high *Sporobolus* gives way to dense stands of the larger sedges—*Cladium, Cyperus,* and *Scirpus.* All of these genera have indigenous or endemic species in Hawaii. Some, such as the giant *Cladium leptostachyum,* grow up to ten feet high.

Many of the plants now common in Hawaiian wetlands have been introduced by humans. They range from *Batis* on the open salt pans and mangrove trees in shallow tidewater, to pond weeds such as *Pistia,* the water lettuce, and *Eichornia,* the water hyacinth—plants any Florid-ian would recognize. One can often find *Typha,* the cattail reed, bordering the ponds. And back just above normal floodwaters the aggressive *Pluchea (indica* and *odorata,* which sometimes hybridize here) may dominate the fringe of the marsh. Very little is known about the ecological effects of such invading plants, especially regarding competition with the native vegetation for limited wetland habitat. Reportedly, however, some of the introduced plants—for example, the giant bullrush *(Scirpus californicus)*—are providing food for wetland birds.

It is the birds that give Hawaii's marshes much of their appeal and provide a remembrance of a wildlife tableau that has nearly vanished. Four native species inhabit the coastal wetlands: *koloa,* the Hawaiian duck, which also ranges into mountain streams to above 3,000 feet; *alae-ula,* a gallinule; *alae-keokeo,* a coot; and *aeo,* the Hawaiian stilt. These four share the marshes, shoreside ponds and estuaries, and drainage ditches with a more diverse but spotty and mainly seasonal contingent of migratory species.

By the midtwentieth century, the wild *koloa (Anas wyvilliana)* was practically extinct everywhere but on Kauai. Captive breeding programs and releases have made small strides toward reestablishing these small, mottled brownish ducks in remnants of their natural habitat on the main high islands. The mallard, *Anas platyrynchos,* appears to be the closest continental relative of the *koloa,* and it also must share a fairly recent common ancestor with its NWHI cousin *Anas laysanensis,* endemic to Laysan Island (see chapter 10).

The Hawaiian gallinule and coot *(Gallinula chloropus sandvicensis* and *Fulica americana alai,* respectively), known colloquially as mudhens, are both considered subspecies, or races, of widely distributed continental species. The former, whose name means "red browed," has a Promethean role in Hawaiian mythology. The legendary *alae-ula,* responding to the needs of a fireless people, stole a burning ember from the abode of the gods and brought it back to earth. However, during this escapade, the bird's beak and forehead were scorched, and they have been red ever since. The coot's forehead and beak are white.

Both mudhens are much reduced in numbers from former times (see the historical section later in this chapter). The coot seems to be the better survivor, perhaps because of its more fully aquatic lifestyle. Coots build large floating nests and keep more to open water than gallinules, which prefer the densely vegetated pond margins. Thus, predators such as feral dogs and the mongoose may take a larger toll of the latter.

The *aeo (Himantopus mexicanus knudseni)* is a race of the black-necked stilt of the Americas. The species' range also includes the Galápagos Islands. These striking black and white birds with their long red legs most often frequent mud flats along the edges of shallow ponds, where they probe for worms and other small invertebrates. According to Berger, these birds make no real nest but lay their clutches of, typically, four eggs in a poorly defined spot on open ground, sometimes with a sparse assemblage of twigs, pebbles, or other debris pulled together around and under them.[7] Stilts do not give the impression of being doughty fliers, but they are known to cross the ocean channels separating the main islands.

CRYPTIC WATERS

There is another kind of coastal wetland in Hawaii, radically different from the typical marsh and pond (or channel) systems described above, where waterbirds are the most conspicuous faunal element. This other wetland is a rock-bound (lava or limestone) habitat of pools and hidden interconnecting channels called the anchialine ecosystem. In Hawaii, this type of habitat develops mainly on young volcanic coasts, such as those of North Kona on the Big Island and Cape Kinau on Maui, before erosion and alluvial distribution can produce significant stream courses and the classic sort of open estuarine development near the shore. However, limestone coasts, such as near Oahu's Barbers Point, develop similar underground drainage systems by virtue of the dissolving power of rain fall and runoff, with its natural slight acidity. On such porous ground, most of the freshwater drainage meets the seawater table a little below the surface of the land. The resulting estuarine labyrinths are thus largely hidden from view.

Where the land features depressions of ten or twenty feet, sometimes just cave-ins of old, thinly roofed lava tubes, there are windows into the subterranean estuaries. These irregular pools in rough rock are called anchialine. The word refers to their typically brackish water and tidal character and lack of surface connection to the sea. While one of the pools on the Kona coast is a "great lake" of its kind, with a surface encompassing nearly fifteen acres (an area larger than six football fields), most of them are smaller in area than a suburban backyard swimming pool and reach eight to ten feet deep. In and around and under the pools, a strange ecosystem has evolved dominated by a variety of small shrimps of mysterious provenance and often brilliant red color.

They are known as anchialine shrimp, or, just as appropriately, hypogeal shrimp, for the pools themselves are continuous with the underground estuarine networks that permeate suitable rocky coastal regions such as North Kona. Much of the known biological information concerning these animals has been summarized by John Maciolek, who has studied them in their natural rock pools and also as aquarium specimens.[8]

In Hawaii, six species of true anchialine shrimp (found only in this habitat), along with a few others that also occur elsewhere in coastal waters or streams, inhabit the pools and adjoining subterranean channels.* Anchialine species are relatively small (most are about one inch long) and share some striking characteristics, including red pigmentation and poorly developed eyes. Most are also tolerant of wide changes in the salinity of the water in which they swim. Such a combination of features sets this group apart from continental cave shrimp, which are typically pale or albino, restricted to fresh water, and completely blind. Anchialine shrimp are mainly omnivorous, and, based on aquarium studies, some species seem to be unusually long-lived; five- and six-year-old specimens have been recorded. Reproduction has been little studied, although females of one species seem to require temporary residence in darkness while their eggs are developing.

Perhaps the most intriguing thing about the anchialine shrimp is their distribution. On the local scale, biologists have been as yet unable to trace their movements in the subterranean water table. At what stages the shrimp migrate in the hidden estuaries and how far they travel is uncertain. However, it is known that various species have colonized new artificial coastal wells and even a bomb crater. A larger-scale mystery is encompassed in the geographically disjunct distributions of some of these shrimp. One of the Hawaiian species, *Calliasmata pholidota,* has also been recorded from the Ellice Islands and the Sinai Peninsula and, as yet, from nowhere in between. The genus *Procaris* is another farflung marvel of a crustacean. This little shrimp was first discovered in an anchialine pool on Ascension Island in the tropical Atlantic Ocean in 1971. Its discovery excited crustacean experts, for the animal seemed to be an evolutionary throwback; it lacked claws on any of its feet and exhibited certain other primitive features, arguably placing it in a whole new order of crustaceans.[9] In 1972, *Procaris* turned up in anchialine habitat on Maui and Hawaii, and very recently it has been found in Bermuda. Specimens from the three locations each have been labeled different species, but from whence came the founders of such scattered populations in such apparently restricted habitat is a significant biogeographical mystery.

Perhaps the habitat is actually more extensive than we think. Maciolek comments on the anatomical uniformity of specimens from widely

---

Antecaridina lauensis (family Atyidae); adults less than one inch long
Calliasmata pholidota (family Hippolytidae); adults reach two inches in length
Halocaridina rubra (family Atyidae); adults less than one inch long
Parhippolyte uvea (family Hippolytidae); largest of the group with adults up to four and
    a half inches long
Metabetaeus lohena (family Alpheidae); adults slightly more than an inch long
Procaris hawaiana (family Procarididae); adults slightly more than an inch long

Note: At this writing, two new species, *Vetericaris chaceorum* and *Halocaridina palahemo,* have been found near South Point on the Big Island.

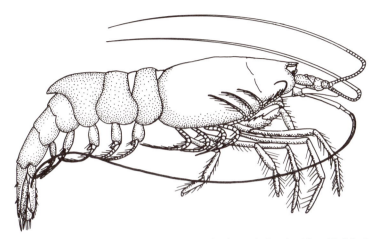

13.2   Procaris hawaiiana (endemic anchialine shrimp). After Holthuis.

separated populations, and speculates that gene flow between anchialine outposts must be significant.[10] He suggests that actual islands are not required by these shrimps, but that they probably occupy nooks and cracks in the rocky layers of seamounts, old submerged atolls, and the like. Their larval forms might colonize such completely hidden habitats much more often than they do emergent islands. Founders of some of these little aquatic cavernicoles might even colonize submarine volcanoes before they reach the surface. Away from actively erupting zones, a growing undersea volcano would have ample suitable habitat for small crevice dwellers. However, to live there these crustaceans might have to be resistant to toxic concentrations of various minerals, such as sulfur. How deep in the rocky recesses they live probably depends on the availability of food, but it would be interesting to see if any anchialine shrimp would feed on the sulfur bacteria that are commonly associated with volcanic activity both above and below sea level.

The possible founding of coastal anchialine shrimp populations by upward mobility in live volcanic terrain is still in the realm of rank speculation. But it would fit right in with the general pattern of astonishing phenomena in the nature of Hawaii. Serious exploration of the anchialine ecosystem in the islands only began around 1970, and more surprises may yet be encountered in the cryptic estuaries. This habitat, in its emergent form along island coasts, is extremely rare worldwide. In our geological era, it has been represented at its greatest state of development in North Kona on the Big Island—until very recently, when the richest concentration of anchialine pools in the world was destroyed by the erection of a gargantuan tourist complex.

In 1985 and 1986 this construction at Waikaloa on the North Kona

coast destroyed more than 150 of the approximately 500 known anchialine pools in Hawaii. This belied the tourist industry's benign image vis-à-vis the environment. The rarity of this ecosystem worldwide
makes Hawaii a truly special place. The loss to Hawaiian nature on the
Kona coast brings to mind the insensitive adage, "You see one redwood
tree, you've seen them all." But suppose we were down to the last 500
redwood trees in the United States. Would any reasonable jurisdiction
allow the destruction of a third of them to make space for a new hotel?

HAWAIIAN LAKES

A few tiny perennial lakes constitute the last general category of natural
aquatic habitat in the Hawaiian Islands. Again, the scarcity of lacustrine
waters is due to the great porosity of the overall volcanic terrain. By
strictly defining a lake in terms of minimum size (0.1 hectare [one-quarter
acre] in area and 2 meters [6.6 feet] in depth) and a closed basin, Maciolek
recognizes only five such natural bodies of water on the main islands.[11]
Three of the lakes—Nomilu on Kauai, Kauhako on Molokai, and Green
Lake in Poamoho Crater on Hawaii—are at sea level, intersect the marine
water table, and have suffered considerable human disturbance. Lake
Waieleele on Maui's Haleakala and Lake Waiau on the Big Island's Mauna
Kea are high montane ponds. The latter, at just over the 13,000-foot
elevation, is one of the highest lakes in the United States. A sixth lake
of saline water occupies the central part of limestone-formed Laysan
Island in the NWHI (chapter 10).

Maciolek's classification distinguishes "true" Hawaiian lakes (above)
from several other types of inland waters—namely, temporary, rainfall-
controlled lakes, or playas; those with direct, natural tidal connections
to the sea; those formed or altered by artificial impoundments (reservoirs); and small bog pools in mountain rain forests.

The native biota of Hawaiian lakes and lakelike waters lacks large
and showy life forms. There are no endemic or indigenous lacustrine
fishes. However, invertebrates can be numerous and fairly diverse,
especially in sea-level lakes. One of the denizens of Molokai's brackish
Lake Kauhako is the anchialine shrimp *Halocaridina rubra*. How it and
other organisms with marine affinities became established in such non-
tidal waters is uncertain. By contrast, the mountain lakes harbor very
few kinds of aquatic animals, predominantly larvae or nymphs of insects. Lake Waiau is cold and windswept and without vegetation on
its shoreline (see chapter 17). Its meager fauna, including a midge and
a beetle, differs wholly from that of Maui's Waieleele. At 6,700 feet on
windward Haleakala, Waieleele's waters are more temperate but harshly

acidic from decomposing vegetation that enters the little lake all around its lush, wet shoreline. Dragonfly and damselfly nymphs are conspicuous in the small community of aquatic animals here.

FLOODS OF CHANGE

When the first Polynesians came exploring up into Hawaiian watersheds, the streams ran clear and fast in their upland valleys of undisturbed native vegetation. Many streams that descended to significant expanses of lowlands served wide, productive wetlands and estuarine bays. From high to low elevation, the Hawaiian forests served to maintain their watersheds in various ways. Forest vegetation represents a hugely expanded surface for condensation of water vapor from the air and actually provides its own drip irrigation. Thus, humidity and soil moisture were conserved, even in many leeward and low-elevation locations. Naturally composted soils, permeated by a complex community of roots, resisted erosion and retarded runoff from torrential rains, delivering water to the streams in timed-release fashion. During most years, the extremes of flood and drought were probably moderated, and it is likely that even streams of the drier districts frequently ran all the way to the sea.

Ultimately, the prehistoric Hawaiians produced major changes in freshwater ecosystems throughout the main islands. Most of those modifications, however, were confined to lower elevations—from sea level up to about 2,000 feet. In the millenium or so before the arrival of Captain Cook, there was a progression of human-related changes in Hawaiian watersheds that began in moist windward locations and, after an interval of several centuries, shifted to large leeward valleys and coastal plains. Kawainui, near Kailua on Oahu, was an early site of intensive agricultural development, and recent archaeological investigations indicate that massive soil erosion was triggered there some time after 1,500 years ago by destruction of primeval forest on the surrounding hillsides.[12] The erosion apparently filled a large shallow marine embayment that in historic times has been known as Kawainui Marsh (see also chapter 19).

After about 1100 A.D., Hawaiian activities that focused on vital aquatic resources became more constructive, although they still produced vast changes in the valleys and on coastal wetlands. Streams were tapped by well-engineered irrigation ditches *(auwai);* the water was led laterally along the sides of the valley, and at intervals directed to flow via numerous sluiceways down over a giant's staircase of agricultural terraces lining the valley slopes and finally back to the parent stream. The scale of these works impressed early Western observers. One remarked, "I have seen whole mountains covered with such fields, through which

the water gradually flowed; each sluice formed a small cascade. . . . "[13]
Massive losses of soil were inevitable, even in such terraced systems.
Lower-valley streams could never have retained their pristine clarity
beneath Hawaiian agricultural terraces. Additionally, thin deltas of topsoil probably formed periodically on valley outwash plains only to disappear seaward during major storms. Among the first major watersheds
modified in this way were Hanalei on Kauai and Halawa on Molokai;
later, in the leeward progression of Hawaiian community development,
Oahu's Makaha Valley and giant Waimea Valley on Kauai, among others,
were scenes of immense and sophisticated neolithic engineering projects devoted to irrigating crops under relatively arid conditions.

The Hawaiians always considered the *oopu wai* and the *opae* of the
streams delectable foods, and these organisms do not seem to have been
greatly affected by human activities in their habitat prior to Western,
industrial-strength developments. Some *oopu,* it appears, are tolerant
of high seasonal silt concentrations in the lower reaches of streams, although they seek the clearest water available. The Hawaiians exploited
this behavior to catch these fish during the rainy season. At favorable
places they built platforms reaching nearly to the surface of the water
when a stream was running in flood stage. The top of the platform,
with its relatively clear water a few inches deep, would soon be populated by clinging *oopu,* which had materialized out of deeper waters
with the color and opacity of chocolate milk.[14]

Increased siltation from watersheds that had been developed for
Hawaiian agriculture may have attracted even greater than usual numbers
of juvenile *oopu (hinana)* returning from the sea. Sediment plumes extending far offshore might have served to guide the fish. The Waimea
River Valley (lower Waimea Canyon) in leeward Kauai was massively
developed in *auwai* and terraces, yet even well into the twentieth century it remained famous for its immense returns of *hinana.*[15] However,
overfishing of some streams may have occurred by late prehistoric times.
The tiny *hinana* were fanatically sought and in some localities came
to be known as "fish stingily regarded." One description of a procedure
for catching them indicated that fine-meshed nets were stretched across
entire streams as the little fish began their landward migration. Other
circumstantial evidence suggesting scarcity comes from Hawaiian legends
indicating that fishermen were sent on quests to distant streams for such
highly esteemed species as the *oopu nopili.*[16] Do these stories hint of
depletion? Unlike the case for lowland deforestation and destruction
of land faunas, we cannot know for sure about early losses of the stream
biota. There is no reliable evidence from archaeology, and the first
Western naturalists all but ignored Hawaiian streams. Assuming depletion did occur, it seems reasonable that during the historic period, with
far fewer Hawaiians to catch them, some of the stream species could

have reestablished the large populations noted in a few watersheds such as at Waimea, Kauai.

On low-lying coasts, wherever water was readily accessible from surface streams or high-volume springs, paddies of *taro,* the staple starch-and-greens crop, merged into artificial, stone-walled fishponds that ranged from fresh water to full-salinity seawater. Most of the marine ponds could be diluted when sluice gates to an adjoining freshwater stream or *auwai* were opened. This option was especially important in long dry seasons when excess evaporation could drive the salinity of the shallow ponds well above that of normal seawater.[17]

By the end of the prehistoric era, nearly every major marsh and estuarine system in the main islands had been transformed into networks of fishponds. One of the greatest concentrations of these waterworks was at Waikiki on Oahu, where hundreds of Hawaiian-built ponds persisted into the nineteenth century. Aboriginal aquaculture was an endemic cultural development in Hawaii; there was nothing to match it elsewhere in Oceania. The species raised in the ponds were few—mostly the euryhaline fishes: mullet, milkfish, and the perchlike *Kuhlia,* or *aholehole.* The latter species readily adjusts to fresh water and, along with *oopu wai,* was sometimes raised in ditches that watered the taro fields. Certain freshwater ponds were stocked exclusively with *oopu wai.* The imperious chiefess, Kaahumanu, favorite wife of King Kamehameha I, owned such a pond in Waipio Valley on the Big Island.[18]

That the ponds were productive is seen not only from descriptions by early Western explorers of huge captive populations of fish in them, but also from reports of the abundance of wild waterfowl around them.[19] Apparently, the *koloa* duck, the coot and gallinule, and the stilt were little disturbed by the native Hawaiians. These birds were permitted to flourish in tended lowland watering places coincident with some of the highest human population densities in old Hawaii.

The Hawaiians seem to have had little if any impact on the anchialine ecosystem. Difficult access to most of these pools on harsh, lava coasts probably precluded their development for aquaculture. Elsewhere, some of the coastal lakes and lakelike bodies were stocked with fish. On Niihau, where in human experience there may never have been all-season streams running to the sea, *oopu* and *opae* were apparently imported and stocked in spring-fed freshwater pools. This may have happened in historic time, however.[20]

For several decades after Captain Cook, foreign settlers in the islands largely adapted themselves to the water resource as they found it. Some use was made of Hawaiian irrigation systems for early, small-scale rice production, but agriculture largely developed in zones of appropriate rainfall. In some districts, the supply was more than ample, even for sugar cane, which requires between six and nine feet of water annually.

This acquiescence in the sufficiency of water, as distributed by God and the old Hawaiian waterworks, lasted until the midnineteenth century. Then water projects began to precipitate at numerous locations; freshets of activity rose steadily until they burst into a flood of industrial irrigation beginning on Maui in the late 1870s. Unlike Hawaiian modifications, which rerouted water merely within a given valley, eventually returning it to the mainstream, water was now taken irretrievably from streams and carried to remote places far from the watersheds of origin. Moreover, the scale of diversion went far beyond that engineered by the Hawaiians; many of the "fierce torrents" crossed at risk by the likes of Titus Coan, W. P. Alexander, and Isabella Bird were not only tamed but virtually drained during the dry season of the year.

William H. Rice, a pioneer sugar planter on Kauai, built the first significant irrigation system of the postcontact era.[21] Completed in 1857 at a cost of approximately $7,000, the project was basically a shallow trench slightly more than ten miles long that carried water from the mountains to the new Lihue Plantation. It was a primitive example of what was to come. Around this time as well, other simple forerunners of later huge and elaborate water diversions were built. These were the flumes used for the transport of cordwood and cane. On the Big Island, some of these early wooden water chutes were more than three miles long (see also chapter 12). Such projects were only child's play in comparison to the almost incredible hydroengineering works that ensued as, within a generation, sugar cultivation became vastly profitable, thanks primarily to favorable economic treatment of Hawaii by the United States.*

The new surge of water diversion in Hawaii reached unprecedented heights in 1878 with the completion of a project on Maui called the Hamakua-Haiku Ditch, or, in many accounts of the time, simply the Big Ditch, denoting its scale. The Big Ditch established patterns and principles for subsequent massive relocations of surface water on several of the main islands. Built for about $80,000 by rising sugar moguls H. P. Baldwin and Samuel T. (Sam) Alexander, the Big Ditch was seventeen miles long. It tapped six major streams on the northern slope of Haleakala and carried their waters on a course that included sections of excavated channels, tunnels, flumes, and valley-crossing siphons made of huge, jointed pipes, all leading to a distant debouchment on the lower slopes and plains of Makawao and Haiku, at the edge of Maui's dry central isthmus. An article in *Thrum's Hawaiian Annual and Almanac*

---

*A treaty of reciprocity between the Hawaiian Kingdom and the United States went into effect in 1876. It admitted unrefined grades of Hawaiian sugar into the United States duty free, an economic privilege that prevailed until the 1890s and greatly stimulated sugar production in the islands.

for 1878[22] celebrates the completion of the project and describes the tremendous travail encountered in the work. The article mentions the numerous access roads and clearings hacked into the wilderness and notes in passing that the ditch traversed "a rich botanical region" at its upper end.

In the late nineteenth century, pristine Hawaiian streams were ironically termed "waste waters" by the economic community and the media.[23] The success of the Big Ditch began a rush by Hawaii's sugar planters, who now enjoyed a very favorable trading climate with the United States, to put such waters to use, wherever possible, in the service of agriculture. On Maui, the shrewd San Francisco sugar refiner Claus Spreckels, acquired immense acreages in the central isthmus, and by 1880 he was harvesting his first irrigated crops. His waterworks extended a total of thirty miles and tapped streams from both Haleakala and the West Maui mountains. System after water system followed, each progressively more sophisticated than the last, with miles of rock tunnels cutting through mountain ridges between valleys. The volumes of water diverted rose steadily. The Lowrie and Koolau Ditches, completed just after the turn of the century, tapped sixty to eighty million gallons per day (mgd) from windward Haleakala. Maui's ultimate water project was the Wailoa Ditch, completed in 1924. It reached all the way to the high Nahiku watershed in the Hana District and carried 145 mgd for thirty miles across the northern face of Haleakala to a point of release at the 1,100-foot elevation above the central Maui plains.[24]

Irrigation developments on Kauai, Oahu, and Hawaii paralleled those on Maui. The first-named island eventually developed the most concentrated irrigation patterns in the archipelago. One part of southeastern Kauai featured more than sixty miles of ditches, tunnels, and valley-crossing water trestles serving four giant plantations.[25] In 1913, entrepreneurs on Oahu began the most spectacular irrigation project of them all—a water tunnel clear through the central Koolau massif. Completed in 1916, this system, which encompassed thirty-seven stream intakes, collected water from four windward valleys and shunted it through the mountain to the island's dry central plains. This immense relocation of water was expanded even further in subsequent decades.[26] The Big Island, too, has seen mighty diversions of water. Perhaps the greatest was the Kohala Ditch, which went into service in 1906 with 46,000 feet of rock tunnels interspersed with 23,000 feet of open trench and 20 flumes.[27]

Besides dewatering the streams at middle to upper elevations, the ditch and tunnel projects opened many of the last pure wilderness areas in the islands to easy penetration by feral grazers, especially pigs, which thrive in the rain forest but follow paths of least resistance. Pig tracks and wallows abound on the access roads and trails to and along the remote aqueducts. Thus abetted by human beings for nearly a century, they have destroyed native vegetation, spread weeds, and promoted erosion and stream siltation in many watersheds that had probably been untouched by alien influences until the coming of the *haole* water seekers. Native Hawaiians had never developed those high valleys and wild pigs were not noted in the chronicles that described the making of the Big Ditch.

The industrial catheterization of the islands' surface freshwater arteries was so extensive that by 1923, according to an enthusiastic summary published by the Hawaiian Sugar Planters' Association, almost every available permanent stream was being bled to nourish Big Sugar.[28] In streams where the average flow was already interdicted, "freshet rights" began to be sold.[29] This allowed additional intakes to be built just above the average flow level so that flood-stage waters could be led off to fill reservoirs. In many cases, whole streams were captured for much of the year.

Today, most of the great aqueducts are still flowing at full capacity. For decades, the dewatered streams have been taken for granted. You can see many of them as you drive island roads such as Maui's Hana Highway. Except after major storms, the former brawling torrents are typically trickles. If you hike a short way upstream, you will find rock ramparts that once framed pounding waterfalls; most often now they are all but dry with just a central dribble of water over algae and mosses. Along the borders of these once perennially vibrant streams are stagnant pools breeding myriad mosquitoes. In many cases, the only reason the streams flow at all in their lower reaches is that they receive some water from small tributaries or dike-fed springs at points below the irrigation intakes.

Surface streams were not the only sources sought for irrigation. Those hidden watersheds in the porous volcanic strata of the islands could be efficiently developed in various places. On coastal plains near sea level, the giant subterranean flows in some areas became trapped and backed up beneath overlying caps of thick clay or finely cemented old reef rock. This so-called artesian water was first tapped near Barbers Point, Oahu, in 1879. A second rich source was discovered in the mountains, where the water was contained in enormous vertical sections of porous lava surrounded by dense, impervious volcanic dikes. Both situations would yield pure fresh water under pressure. It would flow in seemingly inexhaustible volumes when released from its confines by drilling or tunneling into the aqueous lode.

Artesian wells were drilled in great numbers during the late nineteenth century, especially on Oahu's Ewa Plains west of Pearl Harbor. One plantation there eventually linked sixty-one wells in a system that delivered more than 80 mgd to its sugar fields.[30] Blind-ended tunnels blasted several hundred feet into dike fields at places such as Waianae Valley on Oahu and behind Lahaina on Maui, among numerous other locations, brought in minor gushers of several mgd each.[31] However, the exploitation of these natural reservoirs—both artesian and dike fields—was so intense, and, by many accounts, so wasteful, that depletion was inevitable. Within thirty years, artesian fountains that had initially arched up to forty feet high were down to seeps. By one account, Oahu's Ewa water table had been drained to a third of its former level.[32] Moreover, many natural springs, located in a zone from behind Pearl Harbor east to Punahou in back of Honolulu proper, diminished in flow or dried up. These springs on the inner coastal plain had been known and used since Hawaiian antiquity. Obviously, they depended on outflows near the top of the huge artesian water lens and were left high and dry as it was drawn down. The water tunnels bored into dike fields were also seen to greatly diminish streamflow in nearby valleys.[33]

Water relocations also affected wetlands and estuaries near the coasts. While artesian runoff created new freshwater wetlands in a few areas, many natural expanses of such habitat contracted owing to diminished streamflow. Most of the old Hawaiian taro paddies and fish ponds had been abandoned and were returning to weedy marshlands on the coastal plains and in the valley bottoms when, in a tremendous surge of agricultural enterprise between the 1870s and 1890s, they were reclaimed by rice farmers. For several decades, that crop was grown nearly everywhere on the main islands where wet flatlands existed (including new ones created by artesian runoff), and it became a major export as well as the staple food for the great influx of Oriental plantation labor on the islands at this time. Oahu's wetlands were nearly entirely covered by rice. From the Pearl Harbor plains to Hawaii Kai and in windward valleys from Kailua and Kaneohe to Kahana, Punaluu, and beyond, the sight of watery expanses with slender, grassy clusters in precise green rows was commonplace.[34] Often this Oriental tableau was complete with conical-hatted planters and an Asian water buffalo—that species was imported and bred during this period, but has by now virtually died out.

Rice farmers were blamed for a precipitous decline in the abundance of waterfowl in the lowlands. The blame came from hunters—those who considered themselves gentlemen sportsmen. They had access to the prominent media and expressed themselves on the scarcity of gamebirds, especially the favored *koloa*, as in the following 1881 lament:

The wild duck is being driven away from its former habitat by rice plantation development . . . in the marshlands. This is evident in Waikiki, Manoa flats, Kalihi, and Ewa near town. The sportsman may now look in vain for a brace where a few years ago he might have found them by the dozen.[35]

Rice farmers at this time were nearly all Chinese and the sportsmen all *haole*. Perhaps the scarcity of ducks added a small element of tension in the racist society of the time.

Duck hunting in Hawaii was a nonsport for decades before killing dozens at a time somehow became a gentlemanly pursuit. Market hunters went after ducks by the hundreds in the 1840s and delivered them by the sackful to provision whaleships. On Kauai, whole stream valleys of *koloa* were cleaned out in late summer when the birds were molting and, unable to fly, had retreated to the inland watersheds. Firearms were not even necessary during this season. Hunters stunned birds on the water with stones and chased them on foot through the valley underbrush.[36]

For some time after agricultural development accelerated during the 1850s, Kauai remained famous for its waterfowl. However, the birds were progressively driven from open wetlands such as the crater marsh at Koloa (named by the Hawaiians for its spectacular population of the ducks). Such places were drained and put into agricultural service, and the waterbirds retreated permanently into the mountain-stream valleys. Seeking the wonderful concentrations of them there, sportsmen began coming from other islands. Young Sam Alexander, over from Maui, enthused with a hunter's hyperbole, "Kauai abounds in thousands of ducks and millions of mud hens," and with his colleagues he shot hundreds of both kinds of birds.[37]

A number of chronicles of the time have it that mud hens (the Hawaiian coot and gallinule) were esteemed neither as food nor for sport. It is probable that the sheer spectacle of massed birds often triggered a weasel-like instinct for slaughter. Perhaps more than changes in the character of wetlands, which these birds had weathered before, hunting was responsible for the decimation of native waterbirds, and despite token modern attempts to restore and protect their habitat, they have yet to recover healthy populations anywhere in the islands. Of the Hawaiian stilt it was said in 1879 that it "often troubles the sportsman . . . by keeping just out of shooting range."[38]

Dewatered and/or biotically decimated, many of Hawaii's freshwater ecosystems were in ruins by about the 1920s. In the modern era, most of the rest, including the anchialine pools untouched by earlier developments, have been damaged or destroyed by a variety of new impacts.

Hydroelectric power generation is a many-headed industrial creature that threatens to gobble up those few Hawaiian streams that still maintain significant flow. Actually, a few small hydroelectric plants were built more than a half-century ago in places such as Kauai's Wainiha Valley and at scattered sites on other islands. Mainly, they served individual plantations. Now much bigger systems are in the offing—valley-spanning dams on Maui, Molokai, and Kauai with access roads up into the last sensitive regions of rain forest. Is somewhat cheaper electricity worth the permanent destruction of these rare Hawaiian places?

Dams have been built in other places for irrigation, flood control, and aquaculture, and some of the reservoirs are now replete with alien freshwater organisms (this topic is discussed below). A major environmental threat related to the reservoirs concerns human health. These warm, shallow, semistagnant waters are ideal incubatoria for the causative agents of diseases such as schistosomiasis, ameobic meningitis, and leptospirosis. The last-named horror, a swift-acting bacterium that infects through cuts or abrasions on the skin, seems particularly prevalent in aquafarm ponds. In Hawaii, it has killed several people in recent years. New waterborne diseases are not limited to humans. In the Wailuku River above Hilo on the Big Island, a recent mass mortality of native *opae-kala-ole* was traced to a never-before-seen bacterial pathogen. Comparative studies in this stream correlate the fatal shrimp disease with stagnation that develops in isolated stream pools when stream flow is at a minimum.[39]

Artificial stream channelization in the lowlands has accompanied modern urban and suburban expansion, especially on Oahu. Most of Oahu's streams are now huge concrete flumes for their last lowland miles. With the cloudbursts of Kona storms, they run full and wild with filthy water and floating trash. Such flows are now injected straight into the sea to settle on the reefs and in the nearshore bays. This runoff contains high concentrations of fertilizers that stimulate the growth of unsavory marine life and of poisons that kill the sensitive forms. How has this happened? It is called flood control. The developers have built on the old stream deltas, marshes, and outwash plains that once absorbed, filtered, and purified the flood waters. Oahu's hardening of coastal arteries is already starting to spread to the neighbor islands.

During most of the year, however, the dewatered streams are only trickles in the lowlands, and, wherever they have been concretized, the thin veneer of water over merciless, unshaded pavement heats up in the noonday sun, and this is thought by stream ecologists to effectively bar the native diadromous species—the *oopu-wai, opae,* and *hihiwai*—from making their gradual way upstream to more suitable environs.

The introduction of alien freshwater life has come mainly in the twentieth century and has been intensifying for decades. Certainly the very early arrivals, such as mosquitoes, were inadvertent, but most freshwater creatures required the conscious effort and care of human beings to reach the islands. Sometimes the effort was quickly recognized as a mistake, as when North American crayfish threatened rice production by their incessant burrowing in the earthen dikes that maintained the fields. Dozens of fishes—game species including American black bass; numerous ornamentals and aquarium species; aquaculture mainstays such as several species of tilapia; and utilitarians such as the mosquitofish *(Gambusia)*—now, in eclectic mixtures, dominate the majority of low-land freshwater habitats.[40] Other aquatic vertebrates that are now part of the nature of Hawaii include several species of frog, the Caribbean toad *(Bufo marinus),* newts, and freshwater turtles. Frogs and toads came to Hawaii as hopeful agents of insect control. Newts and turtles are popular in the pet trade; however, more and more of them are being released by well-meaning owners in island fresh waters where they compete with and probably consume the remaining native stream fauna. Oddball vertebrates turn up here and there, such as an alligator in an Oahu reservoir (apparently a former pet that outgrew its bathtub); somehow, the infamous "walking catfish" *(Clarias)* became established in Green Lake on the Big Island. This pestiferous fish is also now being promoted as an aquaculture crop in the islands. Invertebrates such as the alien prawns *Macrobrachium lar* and *M. rosenbergii,* introduced for aquaculture, have escaped into freshwater ecosystems on all of the major islands. They are bigger than their native Hawaiian congener, *opae-oehaa,* and may be driving it toward extinction.

It is one thing to introduce predatory game fish to individual closed reservoirs, as has been done on several of the islands, especially Oahu, and it is quite another to seed them into fresh waters that still retain significant ecological endemicity. In recent decades, Kauai seems to have suffered most from such avoidable destruction of its native stream fauna. On Kauai, rainbow trout from hatcheries in Oregon have long been stocked in some of the cold, clear upland streams bordering the pristine Alakai Swamp region. The practice, however, has been to keep some of these waters in the eastern part of this high, rugged plateau closed to trout, which represent top predators here. But lately, some closed streams have been illegally stocked, reportedly at the behest of fly fishermen staking out private preserves. For the fisherman, the way into the remote streams is difficult, making for a hardy brand of poaching, but trout fry are now routinely dropped from a low, hovering helicopter, making for easy destruction of an ecosystem. The Oregon trout have not yet become self-sustaining breeders on Kauai, where they may be close to their upper temperature limit; some fishermen would like to see perhaps Mexican races of trout introduced to correct this deficiency.

The same streams that are losing native life forms, especially aquatic insects, to trout at higher elevations on Kauai are beset by different alien predators in the lowlands. North American freshwater bass (largemouth and smallmouth) have been unconscionably seeded into the major streams of the Lihue Basin, which receives its drainage from the erstwhile pristine eastern Alakai. And these formidable predators have been very successful breeders. The bass barrier from the ocean to the first upland waterfalls probably accounts for the fact that *oopu-wai* no longer run in these suitable streams.

Extremely few Hawaiian freshwater ecosystems are left in fairly natural condition. They have been nearly as comprehensively destroyed as the lowland forests. The handful of remaining unaltered Hawaiian streams and the anchialine pools are rare treasures that deserve unquestioned protection. Even some of the watery places that have been disturbed but not destroyed are worth saving, and perhaps restoring as far as possible. Examples include the large Kahana watershed on Oahu, with its lowland marsh and estuary, and Molokai's Wailau Stream, which, despite great changes in its flanking lowland vegetation, runs clear and cool to the sea with large populations of *oopu wai* still thriving in its lower reaches. A sudden movement by a human explorer along the bank sends them skittering across the Wailau's riffles, several at a time. These are scenes the old Hawaiians saw. They link us to the past in the same way ancient art does. These relics, like the entire native Hawaiian biota, are a living heritage and of inestimable value for what they may yet inspire.

14

Dying Songs: Hawaii's Forest Birds

One of the most significant and, to conservationists, compelling elements in the Hawaiian biota is the small suite of forest birds. They have intrigued ornithologists for two centuries and more recently have become world famous as evolutionary phenomena. Although less well publicized than those other famous island birds, the Galápagos finches, Hawaii's preeminent (and endemic) avian family Drepanididae* (commonly called honeycreepers or, perhaps more correctly, Hawaiian finches) provides an even more spectacular example of adaptive radiation.

When the first Polynesians appeared in Hawaii, endemic bird sounds were heard nearly everywhere, except perhaps on the frigid summits of the two highest volcanoes. The greatest diversity of birds probably occurred in the leeward lowlands, whose dry forests also may have contained the richest plant assemblages in the islands. Gradually, those calls and songs, unique in all the world, diminished and retreated; many were

---

*Recently, arguably demoted to a subfamily, Drepanidinae, or even to the next lower rung, the tribe Drepanini within the widespread finch family, Fringillidae.

stilled forever. By the time Captain Cook's expedition touched these shores, as many as two-thirds of the species of aboriginal birds were extinct (see chapter 18).

We now recognize that eleven families of native (nonmigratory) land birds remained in Hawaii when the early Western naturalists and collectors began to take stock of them. Six are families in the largest order of birds, Passeriformes, or passerines (also called perching birds and songbirds). This order contains all but one family, Rallidae, of the forest birds described in this chapter. Table 14.1 summarizes the historically known native Hawaiian land birds.

Although this chapter, like some others, departs from the habitat approach taken in much of the book, the birds that form the primary focus here are (or were) inhabitants of the remaining wet to mesic native forests, and their fates are irrevocably linked to the survival of these habitats. Other native land birds, including waterfowl, a hawk, an owl, and a few extremely restricted passerines (in the Northwestern Hawaiian Islands and in high, subalpine retreats) are discussed elsewhere in this book. Hawaii's stunning, recently discovered fossil avifauna is the subject of chapter 18.

This chapter, then, is the story of the small forest species that were alive at Western contact and, with few exceptions, are gone or barely survive today. Anyone not dead to the meaning of nature regrets the loss of these creatures, who enlivened the wilderness of old Hawaii and might still communicate a *kamaaina* brand of enjoyment and enchantment, inspiration, and freedom as Hawaii and the world approach a climax of artificial amusements and plastic satisfactions.

This account of Hawaii's forest birds is based largely on recent comprehensive summaries, in particular Andrew J. Berger's *Hawaiian Birdlife,* published in 1972 and updated in 1981, and results of the monumental Hawaii Forest Bird Survey (HFBS), conducted between 1977 and 1983 by J. M. Scott and co-workers and published in 1986.[1] Much of the historical information on the fate of Hawaii's birds comes from the equally heroic fieldwork of R. C. L. Perkins (published mainly in 1903),[2] and also from the succinct summary by George C. Munro (1941) of a half-century of Hawaiian birding.[3] Quotes and specifics from these sources are numerically referenced along with material drawn from other sources.

Unique among the Hawaiian birds at European contact were flightless rails (family Rallidae). One species inhabited tiny Laysan Island far to the northwest of the main islands (see chapter 10). Flightlessness may well have evolved several times in rails after founders reached Hawaii and the forces of evolution changed them from (presumably) species of continental marshes to small upland ground birds. When HMS *Dis-*

TABLE 14.1: NATIVE HAWAIIAN LAND BIRDS AT WESTERN CONTACT

INDIGENOUS BIRDS

Fam. Ardeidae	*Nycticorax nycticorax,* Black-crowned night heron (chapter 13)
Fam. Rallidae	*Fulica americana alai,* Hawaiian coot, or *alae,* (chapter 13) *Gallinula chloropus sandwicensis,* Hawaiian gallinule, or *alae-ula* (chapter 13)
Fam. Recurvirostridae	*Himantopus mexicanus knudseni,* Hawaiian stilt (chapter 13)
Fam. Strigidae	*Asio flammeus sandwichensis,* Hawaiian owl, or *pueo* (chapter 16)

ENDEMIC BIRDS

Fam. Anatidae	*Nesochen sandvicensis,* Hawaiian goose, or nene (chapter 16) *Anas laysanensis,* Laysan duck (chapter 10) *A. wyvilliana,* Hawaiian duck, or *koloa* (chapter 13)
Fam. Accipitridae	*Buteo solitarius,* Hawaiian hawk, or *Io* (chapter 16)
Fam. Corvidae	*Corvus tropicus,* Hawaiian crow, or *alala* (rare; chapter 16)
Fam. Sylviidae	*Acrocephalus familiaris kingi,* Nihoa millerbird (chapter 10) *A. f. familiaris,* Laysan millerbird (extinct; chapter 10)

ENDEMIC FOREST
BIRDS DISCUSSED IN
THIS CHAPTER

Fam. Turdidae	*Phaeornis obscurus,* Hawaiian thrush, or *omao* *Phaeornis palmeri,* small Kauai thrush, or *puaiohi* (rare)
Fam. Muscicapidae	*Chasiempis sandwichensis,* elepaio
Fam. Meliphagidae	*Moho braccatus,* Kauai oo (rare) *M. apicalis,* Oahu oo (extinct) *M. bishopi,* Bishop's oo (believed extinct) *M. nobilis,* Hawaii oo (extinct) *Chaetoptila angustipluma,* kioea (extinct)
Fam. Drepanididae (or Fringillidae)	*Note:* Controversy over the classification of these birds is rife at all levels. The following list is a conservative accounting of genera (italics) as discussed in this book. A recent (1979) proposal to split the honeycreepers into many more genera has been accepted by some researchers but opposed by others. The

Fam. Drepanididae
(or Fringillidae)
continued

result is a confusing tangle of names, some of which have been retrieved from the primeval forests of honeycreeper classification. Hence, certain of the italicized genera listed are followed by other names now in use for birds which by any classification are closely related near the generic level.

Loxops, also *Hemignathus*, *Oreomystis*, and *Paroreomyza*

L. coccineus, *akepa*, several races (rare)

L. (or H.) virens, common *amakihi*, several races

L. (or H.) parvus, *anianiau*, or lesser *amakihi* (Kauai only)

L. (or H.) sagittirostris, greater *amakihi* (believed extinct)

L. (or O., or P.), Hawaiian creepers, several species

Hemignathus (also see *Loxops*)

H. obscurus, Hawaiian *akialoa* (believed extinct)

H. procerus, Kauai *akialoa* (believed extinct)

H. munroi, *akiapolaau* (rare, Hawaii only)

H. lucidus, *nukupuu* (rare)

Psittirostra, also *Loxioides*, *Rhodacanthus*, *Chloridops*, and *Telespyza*

P. psittacea, *ou* (rare)

P. (or L.) bailleui, *palila* (rare, Big Island only)

P. (or R.) palmeri and *flaviceps*, *koa* finches (extinct)

P. (or C.) kona, Kona grosbeak (extinct)

P. (or T.) cantans (Nihoa and Laysan Islands; chapter 10)

Pseudonestor xanthophrys, Maui parrotbill (rare, Maui only)

Himatione sanguinea, *apapane*

Palmeria dolei, crested honeycreeper (rare, Maui only)

Vestiaria coccinea, *liwi*

Ciridops anna, *ula-ai-hawane* (extinct)

Drepanis

D. pacifica, Hawaii *mamo* (extinct)

D. funerea, Black *mamo* (extinct)

Melamprosops phaeosoma, *poo uli* (rare, Maui only). Some ornithologists suggest this recently discovered species is not a honeycreeper.

covery and HMS *Resolution* anchored at Kealakekua Bay, the expedition's collectors in the Kona forests secured the first scientific specimens of Hawaiian flightless rails, which were later named *Pennula sandwichensis*. This species must have had an island-wide distribution at that time. It diminished over the decades until the last Big Island rails were found in fairly open, seral lava country above Hilo and around Kilauea Caldera. They became extinct in the second half of the nineteenth century.

Hawaiians called these little (about 5.5 inches long) fast-running, brownish birds by the name *moho*. This was presumably confused in records of Captain Cook's third voyage with specimens of Hawaiian honeyeaters (family Meliphagidae), which were christened *Moho* in scientific Latin by European taxonomists.

It is possible that two species of flightless rail were alive on the Big Island, perhaps another one on Molokai, and one on Maui for some time into the historic period. The records are hearsay, unconfirmed by professional naturalists of the times.[4] Even if all of them were valid species, they were a pitiful remnant of the magnificent fauna of flightless birds that greeted the first Hawaiians (see chapter 18).

Of the six families of passerine birds with endemic Hawaiian forms, three are currently represented by a single species. These are the families Corvidae (Hawaiian crow); Sylviidae (Nihoa millerbird); and Muscicapidae (a Hawaiian flycatcher called the *elepaio).* Because of their very restricted and special habitats, the crow and the millerbird are described respectively in chapters 16 and 10, which deal with those habitats. The *elepaio,* on the other hand, is at home in a variety of forest types and is still widely distributed on Kauai, Oahu, and Hawaii.

The little insectivorous *elepaio, Chasiempis sandwichensis,* endemic to Hawaii at the generic level, had its ultimate ancestry in the Indo-Pacific region. Classically, ornithologists divided the species into three races, or subspecies, one on each of the islands named in the paragraph above. It is a minor biogeographical mystery that these adaptable birds do not seem to have inhabited Maui, Lanai, or Molokai. So far they are missing even in fossil collections from those islands.

Races of the *elepaio* vary mainly in color patterns. They are feisty, active little birds; perching or on the ground, they often carry the tail cocked at a high angle in a manner reminiscent of wrens. They forage on the wing in typical flycatcher fashion, but also in trees and on the ground, where they poke and rustle energetically amid the forest leaf litter. The most common song is a cheery phrase that seems to enunciate the Hawaiian name: *e-le-pa-i-o.*

Ancient Hawaiian folklore featured the *elepaio* as a guide to canoe builders prospecting in the mountains for tall, old *koa* trees, from whose trunks they would hew out the hulls of their great sailing craft. These men closely watched the behavior of the *elepaio*. If a bird showed much interest in a particular tree, pecking at its bark, this was taken as a sign that the wood was unsuitable—perhaps already insect ridden and beginning to decompose. If the bird merely sat on the tree and sang its name (or in some tellings, prophesied *o-na-ka-ia,* meaning "sweet the fish") the work would proceed with confidence.[5]

Berger calls the *elepaio* the most adaptable native land bird with respect to human-made environmental change. On Oahu this species can be found in numerous locations—for instance, in valleys and ridges behind Honolulu at elevations less than 1,000 feet, where introduced vegetation such as guava and java plum prevails. From that extreme, it ranges throughout much of the Koolau and Waianae mountains, from very wet to fairly dry habitat. The Kauai race is also widely distributed and tolerant of some disturbance. On the island of Hawaii, the species' environmental tolerance is exhibited in its great altitudinal range, from near sea level to the subalpine zone, where it is abundant in the highest remaining Hawaiian forests (see chapter 16). Recent studies suggest that the *elepaio* is divisible into more than the classic three subspecies.[6] On the Big Island alone, this taxonomic rank may apply to several widely separated breeding populations, including two on Mauna Kea and one in Kona. In addition, Scott and his co-workers report hopeful indications that some populations of *elepaio* have become resistant to the introduced diseases—mosquito-borne avian pox and avian malaria—that seem to have devastated the Hawaiian forest birds as a group.

Two of the Hawaiian forest birds belong to the family Turdidae, which includes the thrushes and the familiar continental robins and bluebirds. The *omao* (called *kamao* on Kauai), or Hawaiian thrush *(Phaeornis obscurus),* evolved into several races, arguably different species, inhabiting the major islands. As adults these birds are brown to olive-brown with lighter, grayish undersides; juveniles have sparsely mottled or spotted plumage. *Omao* are omnivorous, feeding on insects, native fruits, flowers, and berries, which they find in the upper montane rain forest that forms their virtually exclusive habitat. Like continental thrushes, these birds sing loudly and melodiously from the concealment of dense thickets, but also from high perches in trees, and they have what Berger calls a flight song, delivered during a quick trajectory above the forest canopy. The song stops abruptly as the bird lands. Several simpler calls are included in this thrush's vocal repertory; one is said to sound like a harsh *meow.*

The second thrush is *Phaeornis palmeri,* called *puaiohi,* or the small Kauai thrush, and historically it is known only from that island. It is slightly smaller than the *kamao (omao),* averaging about seven inches long. Its bill is also longer and narrower than the *kamao*'s. And these birds have long been much scarcer. In the 1890s, after a three-week survey in Kauai's wet mountain forests, the astute British field biologist

R. C. L. Perkins concluded that in the areas he had traversed there were at least a hundred times more *kamao* than *puaiohi*. Scattered observations indicate that the diet of the *puaiohi* in general resembles that of the *kamao*. The song of the former, however, was reported by Perkins to consist of merely a simple trill.

Both of the native thrushes are now nearly extinct on Kauai. Estimates of the recent Hawaii Forest Bird Survey indicate that between twenty and thirty individuals of each species survive there, all of them, it appears, in a few square miles of the extremely wet Alakai Swamp, high on the island's central mountain plateau. The *kamao* was said by Munro to be the most common native forest bird on Kauai in the 1890s. By the 1920s, it had become much reduced. By the early 1970s, surveys could account for only a few hundred *kamao*. Since that time, both thrushes on Kauai have declined drastically and have retreated from former haunts in the area of Kokee State Park west of the Alakai.

On other islands, the *omao's (kamao's)* story is similarly sad: Oahu—extinct in the early nineteenth century; Lanai—extinct by the 1930s; Maui—unknown historically, but possibly an early extinction; Molokai—current population estimate, nineteen birds in high, remote rain forest. Only on Hawaii does this species still thrive, although, according to Scott and his co-workers, its range is only 30 percent of that formerly occupied. Nevertheless, the *omao* still sings in populations scattered in the high *ohia-koa* forests from Hamakua through Puna in the windward region, and around to Kau on the southern slopes of Mauna Loa. And, on a hopeful note, the HFBS found a small number of populations living within zones of mosquito infestation, which suggests that the *omao* may be starting to build resistance to the diseases now blamed for much of the species' decline.

Birds of the family Meliphagidae are known as honeyeaters, nectarivores (although they also eat insects) with evolutionary origins in the Australo-Indonesian region. At least two different genera of these birds evolved in Hawaii. Historically, the better known is *Moho,* the name bestowed in the late eighteenth century on specimens collected in Kona on Captain Cook's last Pacific voyage. The Hawaiians called these birds by the general name *oo,* thought to derive from the birds' bisyllabic call, which to some ornithologists sounded like *beep beep.* Given a musical intonation, the Hawaiian transcription is more accurate, at least in the case of the last surviving species on Kauai, whose recorded notes are deep, bell-like, and haunting.

They were elegant birds, plumed in black, dark brown, or midnight blue, with long, sometimes forking and curving tails. The species on different islands were trimmed variably with vivid yellow and white on the head, tail, legs, throat, and/or beneath the bases of the wings. The Big Island's *oo, M. nobilis,* was the largest, with males 12 to 13

14.1 Native forest birds. Upper: *Elepaio, Chasiempis sandwichensis;* center: *Kioea, Chaetoptila angustipluma* (extinct); lower: Bishop's *Oo, Moho bishopi* (believed extinct). From Rothschild.

inches long (females 9 to 9.5 inches), and one of the most strikingly patterned. Its rich glossy blackness was set off by large golden feather tufts projecting from under the wings, forming fluffy shoulder patches. Another large patch of yellow bordered by white was centered beneath the base of the tail.

These striking colors were used by the birds in mating displays and were also, according to some observers, flourished aggressively in competition with other species over choice feeding sites. Because of them, *oo* were avidly sought by feather collectors from ancient Hawaiian times until at least the late nineteenth century, and this was probably a major factor in *Moho's* extinction on Hawaii and perhaps other islands.

There have been recurrent rumors of *oo* sightings on several islands—including some recent tantalizing reports from Maui, where the bird is not known historically. Nevertheless, ornithologists consider it only remotely possible that a small refugee population of the Molokai, or Bishop's, *oo (M. bishopi)* is holed up in a patch of the practically inaccessible high rain forest on northeastern Haleakala. The last living *oo* seem(s) to be on Kauai (as the story below suggests, there may be only one left).

The Kauai species, *M. braccatus* is (or was?) the smallest (7.5 to 8.5 inches long) and least colorful *oo,* a quirk of evolution that may have helped it avoid an earlier extinction at the hands of feather hunters. *Ooaa,* as these birds were originally called on Kauai, were common in the late nineteenth century, even down to sea level in some untrammeled spots, and recently discovered fossils show that in pre-Polynesian times they occurred in dry lowland forest near the south coast. The birds suffered a drastic decline after 1900, probably caused by mosquito-borne diseases to which they are highly susceptible; they could not be found in naturalists' surveys in the 1920s and 1930s and were thought extinct, but were rediscovered in the sixties by then Bishop Museum ornithologists Richardson and Bowles[7] and federal biologist John Sincock. A dozen or so individuals were found—most of them heard, not seen—along the high canyons bordering the Alakai Swamp. In 1981, spotters with the HFBS found only two. The same pair of birds was seen six times, carrying nesting material, and uttering the loud, eager "oo" call that seems to be especially prevalent during breeding.[8] In a postscript to this vision of last hope for the species, mid-1980s sightings were of a lone bird, each time probably the same male individual, near a known nesting site in a large *ohia* tree at the edge of a cliff. It was calling over and over without response.[9]

Least known of the Hawaiian honeyeaters was the *kioea, Chaetoptila augustipluma,* historically found only in dry, forested uplands on the island of Hawaii. Slightly larger than the Hawaii *oo,* this bird's appearance was very different, being largely streaked in brown and white like a giant immature thrush, but with olive tinges on the wings and tail. The bill was large and moderately curved, and the face masked with black. This bird was reported as rare at the time of its discovery in 1840. Only four specimens were ever documented in ornithological collections,[10] the last of them taken about 1859. Reportedly, the bird was an active and musical singer that frequented various native trees in flower.

Honeycreepers, not to be confused with the honeyeaters described above, are Hawaii's premier birds. One of their important anatomical features is the possession of nine primary flight feathers on the wings. In this they are allied to a minority of mainly New World families of passerine birds. Most passerines have ten functional primaries. The weight of ornithological evidence now overwhelmingly supports a founder closely related to the American cardueline finches as the ancestor of the Hawaiian honeycreepers that may have reached the Hawaiian Archipelago as long as 15 million years ago.[11] Whether they should be classified as a family, subfamily, or tribe, in their sheer virtuosity of evolutionary diversification they eclipse all other birds at comparable taxonomic levels.

The most amazing anatomical structure of these birds is the beak. As with the famous Galápagos, or Darwin's, finches, speciation coincided with changes in the shape of the beak that correlated closely with the development of specialized feeding habits. This naturally would have involved the birds in broader ecological specializations for different plant communities, and hence different climates, elevations, and so on. However, while the beaks of the Galápagos birds are revealing, those of the Hawaiians are spectacular. The potential plasticity that underlies birds' deceptively simple feeding apparatus is huge. In honeycreepers the beak, along with its hidden skeletal and muscular features, was ultimately forged by natural selection into a variety of organic tools that ranged in approximate proportion and function from heavy pliers to long, curving pipettes and entomologist's forceps. In a variety of the species, the tongue assumed a tubular shape and the function of a straw to sip nectar from deep within long-throated native flowers such as lobelioids.

Perhaps surprisingly, beaks and feeding behavior have tended to shape ornithological discriminations on the interrelatedness of the honeycreepers less at the uppermost taxonomic levels than below, in the understory of detail. Although there is now more disagreement than ever on the classification of these birds,[12] the classic scheme, which dates back to Perkins's recognition in the 1890s of two major subdivisions of honeycreepers, green and black, may be as valid as any other. Now called the psittirostrines and drepaninines respectively, the two groups are distinguished by such characters as degree of sexual dimorphism, detailed feather morphology, thickness of skin, and coloration of (especially) immature and female birds—the green and the black. The middle-of-the-road classification followed here is based on that two-part separation, with a conservative accounting of genera that largely follows Berger's 1972 compilation.

Psittirostrines (the old green subdivision) include the majority of species and subspecies, classically divided among four genera: *Loxops, Hemignathus, Psittirostris,* and *Pseudonestor.* These birds, whose plumage also ranges to olive and yellow hues (and even orange in adult males of a few species), embody the widest variations in beak morphology, although now, owing to extinctions, it is far less wide than formerly.

Genus *Loxops:* Generally less specialized than other honeycreepers, *Loxops* are primarily insect eaters, secondarily nectarivores, with short, narrow, and fairly straight beaks. The birds known as *amakihi, anianiau, akikiki,* and *akepa* are conservatively assigned to this genus. Several are called Hawaiian creepers, foragers in trees whose bark-walking behavior resembles that of the continental birds known as creepers. The *akepa, L. coccinea,* with living races on Hawaii, Maui, and Kauai, is unusual in having the tips of the bill askew. They bend to opposite sides, but so slightly that the bird must be literally at arm's length for this oddity to be noticed. Pratt (1979) has removed all birds except the *akepa* from *Loxops* (which means twisted face) and installed them in other genera.

Genus *Hemignathus:* These are small birds, like the creepers and their relatives above, and with similar postures and movements in trees. The most striking difference is in the bill, which in species of *Hemignathus* is highly elongated and curved. In some species and subspecies, nectar may be (or may have been) as important as insects in the diet, and the former sipped from curving tubular flowers as well as from the ubiquitous *ohia* trees. In pursuing insects, these birds have developed the woodpecker's habit of rapping audibly on bark and dead wood. Such sounds were often heard, according to Perkins, in open woodlands of large *koa* trees, although these birds—*akialoa, nukupuu,* and *akiapolaau*—also frequented denser wet forest. The most spectacular of them was the Kauai *akialoa, H. procerus.* Its fantastic, delicate sickle of a bill exceeded 2.5 inches in length, half as long as the body proper of the little bird. The *nukupuu, H. lucidus,* with separate races historically inhabiting Maui, Oahu, and Kauai, was largely an insect eater. Its lower mandible, while sharply curved like the upper, was only half as long. *H. munroi,* the *akiapolaau,* found only on the island of Hawaii, is distinctive by virtue of having the upper mandible sickle-shaped and the lower short and straight.

Genus *Psittirostra:* These are the thick-billed honeycreepers that most resemble finches. Arguably, they are the most primitive of the group as a whole. The *ou, P. psittacea,* with a less massive bill structure than its congeners, is a feeder on insects, leaves, flowers, and fruits, including the introduced guavas; it is sometimes called the least specialized of the genus. Races of the *ou*—attractive greenish birds with yellow heads—until fairly recently inhabited all of the main islands except Kahoolawe but are now gone except for vestigal populations on Kauai and Hawaii. On the former island, as late as 1900, the birds were common in lowland valleys at elevations less than 300 feet.[13] According to Amadon, the *ou* strongly resembles the *akiapolaau* in many respects, and these two birds "show how the transition from a thin decurved bill to a finch-like bill (or vice versa) could have occurred."[14] Also conservatively included in this genus are the now isolated Laysan and Nihoa finches, each a subspecies of *P. cantans.* However, birds identical in every skeletal detail to *P. cantans* were common in the lowlands of the main islands in pre-

Polynesian times. The *palila, P. bailleui,* (see also chapter 16) is known historically only on the Big Island in dry upper-montane forests, but again, fossils have been found on Oahu that seem to place this species in primeval coastal habitat near Barbers Point. The extant palila, however, which is physiologically stressed by temperatures near 30 degrees Celsius (about 85 degrees Fahrenheit),[15] probably could not thrive on this hot leeward coast, so the Oahu *"palila"* may have been a different race or species. Three finch-billed species discovered in the mountain forests of Kona in West Hawaii only at the end of the nineteenth century were probably extinct by early in the twentieth. Two were the *koa* finches, *P. palmeri* and *P. flaviceps.* The former was the largest of the historically known honeycreepers, with the lovely red-orange, yellow, and black males reaching a length of about nine inches. The third was the Kona grosbeak finch, whose immense beak and commensurate skull and head musculature made it the most highly specialized of the heavy-billed honeycreepers. This bird seems to have been mainly a seed eater. According to Perkins, the sound of it cracking the extremely hard seeds of *naio,* the false sandalwood tree *(Myoporum),* could be heard for a considerable distance.

Genus *Pseudonestor:* A single species, *P. xanthophrys,* is known historically. Called the Maui parrotbill, its upper mandible is thick and strongly hooked, the sharp tip extending well beyond the short, straight lower mandible. These birds are insect eaters; like many other honeycreepers, they excavate bark and wood to find their prey and appear to extract it with the tongue. Relatively rare even by the late nineteenth century, the species was notably associated with Maui's former *koa* forests. The few tattered remnants of that habitat are now mosquito ridden and apparently uninhabitable by the disease-sensitive parrotbill. Its last-ditch population survives in high, cold *ohia* rain forest on northeastern Haleakala.

The drepaninine subgroup of honeycreepers features typically dark-colored plumage in immature birds. Also, adult males and females are generally alike in coloration, and the skin is thicker than in psittirostrines. Perkins, who observed most of the historically known honeycreepers in the field, reported that drepaninines invariably flew heavily and noisily. The sound of their wingbeats could be heard over a surprisingly long distance. Five genera have been classically recognized: *Himatione, Vestiaria, Palmeria, Drepanis,* and *Ciridops.* For all except *Drepanis* only a single species was recorded in the time since Captain Cook. Amazingly, a new genus, *Melamprosops,* was discovered only in 1973. Some ornithologists place it with the psittirostrines; others have deferred conclusions until more information becomes available concerning the exceedingly rare birds.

Genus *Himatione:* In the genus *Himatione* is the sprightly little red and black *apapane, H. sanguinea.* Two races, or subspecies, have been recognized. One was the Laysan honeycreeper, extinct in 1923 (see chapter 10). The other is still abundant and now the most common of all honeycreepers, inhabiting all the main islands except Niihau and Kahoolawe. The population on Lanai is the only one in jeopardy. According to Scott and his co-workers, about 540 birds survived there in the early 1980s. Elsewhere, thousands to tens of thousands of these birds still flock in their favored *ohia lehua* forests, where their crimson plumage is a close match for the sprays of color from blossoms of those trees' prevailing varieties. The recent HFBS found that the Big Island still hosts an estimated 2 million *apapane* in a virtually continuous band from Hamakua through Puna and Kau to Kona. Here they have been found from near sea level up to 9,500 feet on Mauna Kea. At least 20,000 more are believed to inhabit the Kohala Mountains on Hawaii's northwestern end, a thoroughly mosquito-infested region where most native birds were decimated in historic time. Resistance to deadly, mosquito-vectored disease is likely in the *apapane* elsewhere, too—for example, on northeastern Molokai, where the species has been found down to about the 300-foot elevation in the wet, remote Pelekunu Valley.

The *apapane* is a nectar feeder, especially in *ohia,* but also in *mamane,* and even in various introduced plants, reportedly including coconut blossoms on the seacoast. *Apapane* might have been the common birds observed by Hiram Bingham in 1824 around the landing at Waimea, Kauai, "flitting, chirping, and singing" among the *kou* trees and coconut palms.[16] Insects and spiders are also important in the bird's diet. Naturally, the *apapane* is the honeycreeper most likely to be seen by visitors to the islands. It still frequents places such as Kokee State Park on Kauai, Hosmer's Grove near the Haleakala National Park headquarters on Maui, and easily accessible environs of Hawaii Volcanoes National Park.

Genus *Vestiaria:* Slightly larger than the *apapane, V. coccinea,* or *iiwi,* is even more striking. Adults are bright reddish orange overall with a largely black tail and wings. The latter also feature some white trim. The bill is long and strongly curved, tapering to a needle point; it is flesh colored, while that of the *apapane* is dark, shorter, and much less curved. Young birds are yellowish, more nearly resembling the general run of immature psittirostrine birds than most of the *iiwi's* closer relatives. The voice of the *iiwi* is loud and sometimes harsh; one of its calls has been likened to the creaking of a wheelbarrow or a rusty-hinged gate.

Although its diet includes insects, this bird is a noted nectar feeder, and lobelioids have been confirmed as a major source for its nectarivory. One of Titian Peale's observations of *iiwi* in 1840 during the U.S. Exploring Expedition epitomizes an island's loss of a wonderful natural tableau: "at Oahu, we found them generally about the gigantic lobelias

which characterize the botany of that interesting island . . ."[17] The bird's
actual feeding on lobelioids has been described in detail by Spieth. He
describes what they do after perching on the cluster of blooms:

> The bird then quickly swings into an upside-down position . . . with the
> bill pointing upwards. It then easily and with precision slips its slender
> decurved beak into the corolla. The nicety of fit between the bird's head
> and bill and the fleshy corolla of the flower is indeed striking. . . . The
> entire bill and fore part of the head are thrust deeply into the corolla,
> reminding one of a finger slipping into a well-fitting glove.[18]

A wide variety of other flowers, including *ohia* and introductions such
as banana and passion flowers, provide nectar for *iiwi*. In many cases,
the bird pierces the base of a flower whose shape does not readily admit
the curving probe of the beak.

In the 1890s, the *iiwi* was one of the most widespread and abundant
of the honeycreepers. Once seen in coastal valleys at elevations as low
as 120 feet,[19] it is now extinct on Lanai, and nearly so on Oahu, Molokai,
and West Maui. On Kauai, the HFBS accounted for an estimated 5,400
in its study area (Alakai Swamp). East Maui (Haleakala) still has approximately 19,000 birds, and Hawaii perhaps somewhat more than 340,000,
most of them (an estimated 88 percent) on the Hamakua slopes between
about 4,200 and 6,200 feet. The *iiwi* prefers somewhat drier forest than
the *apapane.* Its distribution shows a strong negative correlation with
that of mosquitoes, except in lower Puna and the Kohala Mountains;
both areas on the Big Island have small, apparently isolated populations
of *iiwi,* a hopeful sign that some disease resistance is developing in the
species.

Genus *Palmeria:* Again a single species, *P. dolei,* represents its genus.
The species is now restricted to East Maui, having been once common
on Molokai as well as West Maui. Known as *akohekohe* to the Hawaiians,
it was later called the crested honeycreeper for its unique tuft of light-
colored feathers projecting up from the forehead. Orange-tipped feathers
form a bright collar around the neck and are also scattered over the
rest of the body; they contrast beautifully with the otherwise black, gray,
and white hues of this species. In feeding habits, *akohekohe* is said to
resemble the *apapane,* with which it is often seen. According to Perkins,
its common call was an unmistakable "loud, clear, and rather shrill whistle" that resembled that of the bobwhite quail. Perkins also indicated
that the species noticeably retreated from woods that were opened up
by the grazing of cattle. In such situations *akohekohe* could be heard
calling from deep gulches that retained their dense native flora owing
to their relative inaccessibility to the grazers, while in the surrounding
damaged country the birds could not be found. As a bird collector,

14.2 Hawaiian honeycreepers. Upper left: Maui *nukupuu,* rare; upper right: crested honeycreeper (*akohekohe*), rare; center: Hawaii *mamo,* (the "great hook-billed creeper"), extinct; lower left: Maui parrotbill, rare; lower right: Kona grosbeak, extinct (see Table 14.1 for scientific names). From Rothschild.

Perkins also provided a poignant glimpse of this bird's tameness, common to many of the native species. By imitating its whistle, he related, "the bird can always be easily called in numbers in a good locality. . . . a pair of adults and several young were quite an ordinary gathering. Even when fired at and obviously touched by the shot I have been able to call this bird back into range and secure it at the second attempt."[20]

The crested honeycreeper was thought extinct in the 1930s and 1940s, but was recently rediscovered in the high, rugged rain forests of northeastern Haleakala and in nearby upper Kipahulu Valley. The HFBS estimates a total population of 3,800 birds.

Genus *Drepanis:* Specimen collectors from Captain Cook's ships were the first Westerners to kill the Big Island species *D. pacifica,* which the Hawaiians called *mamo,* a name also applied to the prized feather cloaks made from the plumage of this avidly sought bird. In English, the species was first dubbed "the great hook-billed creeper,"[21] no doubt a name to conjure with two centuries ago in the dusty halls of European museums. These were stunning birds, among the largest honeycreepers, vividly plumed in black and yellow. The latter feathers, which covered the rump and base of the tail, were believed to have been the choicest of all, at Western contact, for Hawaiian featherwork, and the birds continued to be hunted to feed cruder versions of that craft during the nineteenth century.

The beak was long, black, and dramatically curved. Abundant hearsay indicates that the *mamo* fed extensively in lobelioid flowers, but the bird's behavior was never very well observed by naturalists. Its call, described as a long, plaintive note, was not heard after about 1900. The last known Hawaii *mamo* was shot by an ornithologist in July 1898. The bird was badly wounded but escaped into the dense Mauna Loa rain forest.[22]

A second species, the black *mamo, D. funerea,* was not discovered until 1893. R. C. L. Perkins found it in a terrain of bogs and soaked, moss-covered trees near the 5,000-foot elevation on East Molokai. It was nearly pure black, with only traces of white along the outer edges of the wings. Perkins described its behavior as pugnacious toward smaller species. As he watched, one chased several *apapane* out of a tree but the *mamo* itself gave way to a Molokai *oo.* Perkins also noted telltale smears of lobelioid pollen sticking to the heads of black *mamo* after the birds had visited the large tubular flowers. Among the vocalizations of this species was "a loud cry of extraordinary clearness, repeated at short intervals, such as I have never heard imitated by the old natives. . . ."[23] Perkins seems to have believed the nineteenth-century Hawaiians had lost their former knowledge of this bird. No one had much time to become acquainted with it. It could not be found after 1907.

Genus *Ciridops: Ula-ai-hawane,* scientifically named *C. anna,* was the least known of the honeycreepers. According to Berger, five specimens, collected between the 1850s and 1890s, represent the entire scientific data base for this species, which was known only from the Big Island—although apparent congeneric fossils have been discovered recently on Kauai, Molokai, and Oahu. *C. anna* was a small, attractive bird, with black, red, buff, and brown plumage. The Hawaiian name means a red bird that feeds on the *hawane* (a type of *loulu,* or *Pritchardia* palm). The bird reportedly utilized both blossoms and green fruits of the palm. In 1903, Perkins wrote, without seeing this bird, that it had been widespread on Hawaii. A decade earlier, the last-known specimen had been caught by local hunters in the Kohala forests and traded to ornithologists.

Genus *Melamprosops:* In the summer of 1973, two University of Hawaii undergraduate students, Tonnie Casey and James Jacobi, who were part of a research group studying rain forest ecology high on the outer northeastern slopes of Haleakala, discovered a honeycreeper unknown to science.[24] Confirmed by experts as a new genus and species, it was named *M. phaeosoma,* descriptive of its coloration: black face, brown body. The Hawaiian name bestowed on the five-inch-long bird, *poo uli,* means dark-headed. With a short, unspecialized bill, this species appears to feed primarily on insects and snails, finding them on foliage and in bark. According to Scott and his co-workers, its presence is strongly correlated with wet *ohia* forest and a well-developed endemic understory. Limited to the general vicinity in which it was originally found, *poo uli* is now considered extremely rare, probably even more so than a decade ago. In scant addition to recent incidental sightings, the HFBS confirmed only two. However, in the spring of 1986, biologists with the U.S. Fish and Wildlife Service discovered the first known *poo uli* nest and observed an active breeding pair. The initial nesting attempt of this pair failed in severe weather, and two eggs were lost; then, two more were produced, but only one survived to successfully fledge.[25]

Poo uli came as a lovely surprise to naturalists concerned with the fate of Hawaii's forest birds. Nowadays, this kind of zoological find is truly remarkable; the discovery of a brand new animal of such size and generic uniqueness is usually limited to remote and poorly known regions such as the deep sea. The find is one more phenomenon in the environmental history of Hawaii that makes the islands' nature so special and its decline so tragic. It is possible that the *poo uli* and most of the other remaining native birds will become extinct in the next decade or two, for they are on the very edge of oblivion. Well-focused environmental stewardship offers the only chance to save them, but many of the forces that have decimated them in the past are still in evidence.

DECLINE OF AN AVIFAUNA

What happened to the honeycreepers and other native birds can be surmised, in part, by anyone familiar with the fate of Hawaiian land ecosystems in general. Massive changes in the Polynesian era (see chapter
19) have now been clearly linked to the extinction of many birds and
the retreat and decline of others, setting the stage for the more variegated
assault on the birds that followed Western contact. The indirect effects
on birds of land clearing and grazing may well have been the most
deleterious overall. Not only were birds displaced over vast tracts of
land, but the destruction of specific plants and plant communities resulted in the collapse of food chains, affecting not only herbivorous birds
but also feeders on insects and snails. Even the climate changed after
deforestation, especially in the drier parts of the islands. Now, from
caches of fossils along with detailed observations of ornithologists have
come new insights that a majority of Hawaii's forest birds, both living
and extinct, were certainly abundant and perhaps most at home at
relatively low elevations and in once-forested dry country. According
to Bishop Museum's Wayne Gagné and other naturalists, this may mean
that many of the remaining species are actually in suboptimal habitat—
for example, on northeastern Haleakala and in Alakai Swamp—near the
limits of their tolerance for cold and wetness.

While gross changes in the land presumably caused extinctions in
the Polynesian era and certainly forced an archipelago-wide retreat of
the native land birds that continued into the twentieth century, other
destructive factors have been more acute. These include hunting by
humans and other predataors, introduced avian diseases, and possibly
competition with introduced birds.

From the start of their occupation of the islands, the old Hawaiians
probably hunted small forest birds. Bright, colored feathers were a
medium of exchange elsewhere in Polynesia, and the custom may have
traveled in early times. At European contact, no other Pacific islanders
surpassed the Hawaiians in the beauty and lavishness of manufactured
feather products. In part, this was due to the skill of the craftsmen,
preeminently male chiefs;[26] in part, it was due to the exquisite natural
resource.

Feathers were a form of tribute or taxes paid by commoners to their
ruling *alii*. By Captain Cook's time, the most valuable birds in the
islands may have been the Hawaii *mamo* and the flashier species of *oo*,
especially those on Hawaii and Oahu. Historical accounts indicate that
the yellow feathers from those birds were the most prized. Kamehameha
the Great's famous yellow cape was estimated to have consumed about
80,000 *mamo*.[27] Glossy black feathers from both *mamo* and *oo* were
also used, along with the red to deep orange of the *iiwi*, and less com-

14.3   Hawaiian feather capes, or cloaks. State Archive Photo.

monly, green plumage from the *ou*. Feathers from seabirds, the Hawaiian owl and crow, and even domestic roosters were also in use but reportedly were considered inferior to those of the small endemic forest birds.

A special guild of bird hunters existed in at least some villages. These men apparently attracted their quarry by playing on the birds' curiosity. They were said to plant strange trees in clearings in the forest. In the trees were wedged special sticks smeared with a sticky compound that Westerners called bird lime. In Hawaii it was a gum made from the sap of the *papala kepau (Pisonia)* or the *aulu (Planchonella),* both small trees; similar material was also derived from the breadfruit tree.[28] The wild birds became trapped by the feet as they alighted. Reportedly, special tame decoys were also used. In addition, some bird catchers used fine-mesh nets of *olona* thread that may have been thrown or dropped over the birds. One of the persistent myths about the traditional plumage hunters was that they merely plucked a few of the choicest feathers and released the birds. Given the high valuation of plumage from the forest birds mentioned, the only species thus treated might have been the Hawaii *oo*—if, on exceptional occasions, only the small yellow axial tufts were taken. Certainly most of the birds caught were killed. Large numbers of *iiwi* skins tied together in bunches were shown to Lieutenant King and others accompanying Cook on Kauai in 1778.[29] Many forest birds, including the prime plumage species, were also eaten by the Hawaiians.[30]

Foremost among the feather fashions were full-length capes, or cloaks, that often reached below the knees. They were prized possessions of chiefs, and according to most explorers' accounts were items with the highest value in trade, or were gifts to signify exceptional esteem. The designs were often intricate and beautifully executed; the handiwork, incorporating in the larger pieces an estimated half-million small feathers, was meticulous. That a number of these deceptively fragile garments, having been acquired in used condition, transported by primitive means, and stored in private and public museum collections around the world, are still in fine condition after more than two centuries attests to the quality of their manufacture. Then as now the wonderful colors delighted the eyes. One early reference was to a late-eighteenth-century parade in Boston in which the most exotic marcher must have been a Kauai chief who had sailed home with a Yankee captain. Wearing his endemic avian finery, the Hawaiian dazzled onlookers as he "moved up State Street like a living flame."[31]

Other featherwares included ceremonial helmets, many of them strangely similar to military styles of the Homeric Greeks, and *kahilis,* symbols of chiefly rank that the explorers' journals termed oversized "fly flaps." These were often made of fairly coarse seabird feathers. Feather leis made from a variety of species were worn by women. Carved images of Hawaiian gods were sometimes dressed with feathers.

Few cloaks, helmets, or *kahilis* were made after the eighteenth century, and the fine arts of featherwork were certainly extinct before 1850. Only leis remained popular, and the most sought-after species were the same as before, especially the Big Island's *mamo* and *oo.* Now there was no question of releasing the birds after plucking a few feathers, for shotguns had replaced bird lime as the tool of the trade. By 1898, the Hawaii *mamo* was all but extinct, and the once-abundant *oo* had disappeared from most of its Big Island haunts. Nevertheless, in that year lei hunters reportedly shot more than 1,000 of the latter species in its last retreat in the dense rain forests north of the Wailuku River above Hilo.[32] According to one estimate, two hundred *oo* were killed to make a small feather lei that sold for fifty dollars in the 1890s.[33]

Pursuit of the birds probably intensified in a cash economy, but a wholly new demand also arose with the coming of the *haole:* the urge to collect specimens. Insidiously, it focused more intensively on species as they became rare. The lack of restraint extended to scientists such as W. A. Bryan. Describing his ornithological excursion in the Waianae Mountains in 1901, he confided,

> The iiwi is by far the rarest of the five species of mountain birds yet to be found on Oahu. It is to be regretted that hours of patient search in the deep, quiet, shady valleys where the few specimens met with seemed to prefer to be, only resulted in our securing six specimens.[34]

By the late nineteenth century, the mania for collecting Hawaiian specimens—birds and other organisms as well—was evinced not only by resident and expedition scientists, who were few, but by a variety of local aficionados and at a distance by museum curators, gentlemen-scholars, and aristocratic dabblers from many parts of Europe and America. On most of the main islands elite families and amateur naturalists maintained private collections of stuffed birds and bird skins that were often traded abroad. Thus, for example, the Knudsen-Sinclairs and Robinson-Gays of Kauai and the Meyer family on Molokai had large and noted collections of Hawaii's showcase birds.[35] It was an intellectual pastime for gentlemen, for some no doubt an excuse to prowl the receding forests with their fowling pieces, and when a species became really scarce, native hunters were offered rewards to secure the birds. Writing in 1889 to Alexander Agassiz, director of Harvard University's Museum of Comparative Zoology, Judge (and later president of the fledgling Hawaiian Republic) Sanford Dole held out hope that the Big Island's flightless rail could still be found. "It is probable that the offer of say a hundred dollars for a skin would procure it. I think it necessary to offer a substantial inducement as the extreme scarcity of the birds would render it difficult to find them." Agassiz readily agreed to the price, but never got his rail.[36] Such collector's fever was also implicated on Molokai as being responsible for the annihilation of the black *mamo* within fifteen years of its discovery in 1893.[37]

Predators other than humans surely had some impact on the birds. Native predators once included several species of owls and hawks (all but one species of each now extinct). There was a Hawaiian eagle too, and at least two other species of crow that might have preyed on smaller birds. But of course there was no mammalian threat to the birds until the first Polynesians arrived. A subtle confirmation of this is seen in an instinct observed in the young of the *apapane*.[38] Especially in cases where the nest is disturbed (as confirmed by an ornitholgist climbing the tree), the fledglings jump out even before they can fly. In prehuman times, beneath a well-developed understory the ground could have served as a sanctuary for them, perhaps to escape windstorms and prowling owls.

That changed when the Polynesians brought pigs, dogs, and rats to the islands. Then, after Western contact, more aggressive varieties and species of those animals arrived and, along with cats, took up a feral existence in island forests. In the 1880s they were joined by the small Indian mongoose, *Herpestes auropunctatus.* Despite the destructive lore associated with the last-named animal, and its known depredations on ground-nesting birds including seabirds, the mongoose is only rarely found in trees. Its role in the drastic decline of Hawaii's songbirds is probably not a major one. The most serious predator of those birds seems to be a largely arboreal rat, *R. rattus,* the so-called roof rat, which may not have reached the islands until the 1870s. Historical research by Atkinson suggests that this species colonized Oahu first and then spread haphazardly to the other main islands, reaching Kauai and Lanai only after the turn of the century.[39] Now ranging from urban areas into pristine native forest, the roof rat is thought to prey heavily on birds' eggs and nestlings.

Pigs will eat birds they encounter on the ground, but most of their impact on the native island avifauna is indirect through destruction of habitat—specifically forest understory. Especially in the wetter regions, pigs rooting, wallowing, and hollowing out the trunks of tree ferns to consume the starchy core create pools of standing water, enhancing the spread of mosquitoes that carry diseases of birds.

Quite possibly the most potent of all the introduced impacts on Hawaii's forest birds have been diseases for which this long-isolated avifauna had little or no immunity.[40] Two types of avian disease are cited as extremely deleterious, if not deadly, to native species. The first, a form of malaria in birds, is caused by protozoan parasites similar to ones responsible for human malaria, and the second, avian pox, is caused by a virus. Both diseases are transmitted to the birds by mosquitoes, especially *Culex quinquefasciatus,* which is the only resident vector for malaria and one of the several species thought to transmit avian pox in Hawaii.

Although mosquitoes are believed to have arrived in Hawaii by the mid-1820s and were abundant on some islands by the 1830s (see chapter 15), no one is precisely sure when native bird populations began to feel the effects of the diseases. The grotesque swellings on the feet, legs, and faces of birds that characterize avian pox were first reported in the 1890s on Oahu and in Kona by Perkins and other field naturalists, and in those areas these "grievous afflictions" correlated with an astounding rate of diminishment of the native birds—from abundance to near-extinction for most in a decade or so, and, it appears, true extinction in that interval for some. Avian malaria was not confirmed until 1938, when it was diagnosed in pigeons in Honolulu,[41] although owing to its presence in migratory waterfowl, it might have always been waiting in the wings, needing only the mosquito carrier to be visited on Hawaiian forest birds.

Avian pox has its main reservoir in barnyard fowl, and occasionally pigeons. Its time of arrival in the islands is uncertain. A search of late-nineteenth-century agricultural records or even newspapers from Kona and Oahu, where the first signs of pox seem to have turned up in the wild, might be revealing of a pox connection to the mass destruction of native birds. On out-of-the-way Lanai, the precipitous dieoff came three decades later than in Kona, and the pox connection is supported by the meticulous observer George Munro, who lived on the island for many years. His bird censuses show that by 1920 several species, including a Lanai *iiwi,* an *ou,* and a race of the Hawaiian thrush, were increasing nicely with a gradual regrowth of native forest after earlier overgrazing. The birds' decline began in 1923, when the pineapple industry took over the island and almost overnight built Lanai City. Within a decade, the native birds were extinct or vanishingly rare on the island, and Munro related, "The people brought bird diseases with their poultry and these, evidently carried by mosquitoes, were fatal to the native bird populations."[42]

One other category of damaging impact on the native birds has been widely cited—namely, competition with introduced species. Approximately sixty species of nonnative birds are now listed as having established breeding populations in the Hawaiian Islands. Some were deliberately released; others were imported as cage birds and escaped from captivity. Many have remained at low elevations and occur most commonly in the vicinity of human habitation. Only a small minority have successfully invaded the typically remote tracts of native forest that sustain the remaining honeycreepers and other natives, and even in those cases clear competition to the disadvantage of endemic species appears to range from uncommon to nonexistent. Several of the new Hawaiian forest birds are thrushes (Turdidae) and laughing or babbling thrushes (Timaliidae). The *shama,* a true thrush native to Southeast Asia, was first brought to Hawaii in the 1930s. It has become widespread, especially on Oahu, where its cheery whistles and lovely varied melodies can be heard from coastal residential areas to the wettest mountain forests. The melodious laughing thrush, and the red-billed leiothrix, introduced earlier, are at least as common as the *shama* in both native and exotic forests of the islands. These birds prefer dense, shrubby cover close to the ground, where they typically feed and so are unlikely competitors with the tree-loving honeycreepers. It is possible that they have had some negative effect on the native thrushes, although big declines of those birds were noted on several islands before any significant competition could have developed.

The common mynah, *Acridotheres tristis,* released in the islands in the 1860s as part of an insect-control program, was long suspected of crowding out smaller native birds. Only a fragment of evidence for this appears in a remark that Laysan honeycreepers, which had been brought to Honolulu as pets and then escaped or were released, "have considerable trouble with the mynahs."[43] By the turn of the century, however, most naturalists were discounting the mynah as a major factor in the disappearance of native species. At present, this swaggering, aggressive bird is widespread up to elevations of 6,000 to 7,000 feet, although its presence usually coincides with human habitation. Large populations are only found in the urban and suburban lowlands, and the mynah does not seem to do well in the wetter parts of the islands.[44]

One exotic species that has succeeded in all kinds of habitat on the main islands and whose habits closely resemble those of many honeycreepers is the *mejiro,* or Japanese white-eye *(Zosterops japonica).* The HFBS recently found it to be "the most abundant, widespread, and omnivorous forest passerine" in the islands. First imported in 1929, these constantly active little birds are extremely adaptable, ranging from the driest to wettest habitats from Kauai to the Big Island, and from city streets through all manner of terrain, exotic and native, from sea level to the treelines of Maui and Hawaii.

The white-eye presents the most convincing case for competition with native birds. Negative correlations with established white-eye populations were found by the HFBS for *iiwi,* common *amakihi,* Kauai creeper, and even the *elepaio.* These birds may retreat from suitable habitat as the white-eye develops a taste for their foods or takes over the better nesting sites. Yet the white-eye's ecological role in native forests may be beneficial in another way. It seems to have become a major pollinator for the *ieie* (native climbing pandanus). This plant's sexual life was believed to be languishing on at least some islands because of the loss of the services of native birds, and a recent identification of *ieie* pollen adhering to head feathers of extinct honeycreepers in museum collections confirms the theory and puts the white-eye's expansion in a new light.[45]

A detailed, causal explanation of the decimation of Hawaiian forest birds has been considered irretrievable, although a comprehensive analysis and history of native bird observations being prepared by Winston Banko and Paul Banko[46] may help to resolve many of the questions of timing and severity of the destructive forces that impacted Hawaii's birds. All of the possible forces mentioned above probably played a role. Existing research supports a three-part historical decline in the birds (that is, the remaining avifauna when Captain Cook appeared in Hawaii):

1. A group of relictual species such as *kioea* and *ula-ai-hawane* still survived, but just barely, having been driven into upland, and perhaps nonoptimal, refugia by the Hawaiian transformation of lowland ecosystems. These birds were extinct by the midnineteenth century.

2. A majority of the remaining species (58 percent), most of them common to abundant, became extinct or extremely reduced between about 1890 and 1930. The rate of decline on individual islands was much more rapid. The few remaining populations of these birds are now dying in such places as Alakai Swamp and Northeast Haleakala.

3. An adaptable few such as *apapane,* common *amakihi,* and *elepaio* still survive in fairly large numbers but in greatly restricted habitat.

Hopeful voices have long been raised for Hawaii's birds. In 1864, before any significant importation of exotic birds, *The Friend* editorialized:

It is well known that in Europe the wanton destruction of small birds has seriously interfered with the harvests; that whole forests have been destroyed by the ravages of some small wood-boring beetle which only the woodpecker can keep in order . . . but a wiser spirit is growing up and efforts have been made in our own Legislature to check the wanton destruction of useful birds. . . . [47]

But not until very recently was conservation of Hawaii's birds taken at all seriously, chiefly on the part of the U.S. Fish and Wildlife Service and the National Park Service, aided by private individuals and groups such as the Sierra Club, Hawaii Audubon Society, and the Nature Conservancy. And it may be too late.

The worst problems still facing the endangered birds are probably mosquito-borne diseases and the forest-ruining activities of feral pigs. These two threats are now known to be linked, because the pigs create new breeding sites for mosquitoes. Eradication of wild pigs is now a major effort of the National Park Service, especially in the Kipahulu Valley section of Haleakala National Park, a critical habitat for the *ou, nukupuu, poo-uli,* Maui parrotbill, and possibly Bishop's *oo.*

The first mosquitoes were found in Alakai Swamp in 1881. In the last few decades, mosquitoes capable of transmitting avian pox have extended their range upward from an earlier average ceiling of about 2,000 feet. The islands of Kauai, Oahu, Molokai, and Lanai now have no significant mosquito-free areas. On Maui and Hawaii, the HFBS found the insects commonly up to nearly 5,000 feet, with populations in some areas reaching elevations of 6,000 to 7,000 feet. Such high country may be dry for much of the year, but the mosquitoes take advantage of human carelessness—for example, breeding in runoff from a state park campground. Much worse conditions were found at private ranches where livestock watering-troughs were often found swarming with the larval wigglers.

The tragedy of Hawaii's birds is nearly played out. A few species may be developing resistance to their microbiological afflictions. From those few perhaps eventual repatriations can be made to islands where suitable habitats remain, but most native songs of the forest will have been stilled. The few can be a living memorial to the many, which have taken with them so much of the liveliness and charm of Hawaii's nature.

Long ago, a thoughtful zoologist wrote an epitaph on extinction. It applies to Hawaii's birds and much more that is truly Hawaiian:

The beauty and genius of a work of art may be reconceived, though its first material expression be destroyed; a vanished harmony may yet again inspire the composer, but when the last individual of a race of living things breathes no more, another heaven and another earth must pass before such a one can be again.[48]

15

Insects and Snails: Evolutionary Tales

Among the biological treasures of Hawaii, inhabiting the remaining native forests and wildlands along with unique plants and celebrated birds, are other creatures whose evolutionary histories have been no less marvelous. There are two major groups of such animals: the arthropods (dominated by insects) and the land snails. Their adaptive radiations and sweeping patterns of speciation are sometimes even more striking than those of better known Hawaiian evolutionary "classics" such as the honeycreepers.

The insects are perhaps the best kept secret in the nature of Hawaii— despite extraordinary revelations about them by nineteenth-century naturalists such as R. C. L. Perkins,[1] the authors of a multivolume compendium on their systematics begun in 1948 and still not complete,[2] and reams of more recent specialized research on their evolutionary biology. Not surprising, given Hawaii's great oceanic isolation, is the fact that the known native insects represent only about 15 percent of the world's hundreds of insect families.[3] By one calculation, the recorded endemic Hawaiian insect fauna of approximately 6,500 species was generated by only about 250 successful founders.[4]

One of the less likely founders was a small fly in the family Drosophilidae. Common species in this family are familiar to most people as fruit flies, or more properly, pomace flies.* The garden variety worldwide are attracted to decomposing fruit, such as overripe bananas, on which they feed and lay their eggs. The Hawaiian Islands have proved to be a veritable paradise for drosophilid flies. Their adaptive radiation in the archipelago represents one of the contemporary evolutionary wonders of the world.

Since the arrival of one or perhaps two founding females, the drosophilid flies have multiplied through the island-hopping speciation process to form an incredible dynasty. Between one-fourth and one-third of the world's Drosophilidae are species endemic to Hawaii. In terms of biogeographic density, there seem to be more drosophilid species in Hawaii than in all of North America.[5] Nearly 500 of the Hawaiian species have been expertly studied and classified; about 200 other new

---

*Unlike drosophilids, true fruit flies (family Tephritidae) commonly oviposit in developing fruit that is still attached to the plant. Several species of the latter, including the infamous Med fly, are introduced agricultural pests in Hawaii.

262

species in existing collections await formal classification. And there may well be numerous species as yet undiscovered in poorly accessible regions, such as the high, chilly rain forests on Maui and Hawaii. Some entomologists suggest that the final tally of endemic species of these flies in the islands will exceed 800.

Two major groups of endemic drosophilids inhabit the islands.[6] One group is typified by the genus *Scaptomyza*; the second group, by the genus *Drosophila*. Major differences between the two are revealed at times of mating. Species in the *Scaptomyza* group perform little in the way of courtship behavior; in fact, the approach of a male to a potential mate has been characterized as an "assault."[7] However, *Scaptomyza* species generally possess well-differentiated genitalia, thus erecting physical barriers against hybridization. By contrast, *Drosophila* species exhibit widespread similarity in genital structure, but have evolved elaborate male courtship rituals that vary from species to species. The female's receptivity typically depends on a precise performance by the male. Here, then, the main mechanism maintaining the reproductive integrity of the species is behavioral.

Species totals for both groups number in the hundreds. However, the basic dichotomy of the Hawaiian drosophilids suggests to some scientists that two separate founding events took place. Others argue that an ancient common ancestor of both *Scaptomyza* and *Drosophila* was the sole founder. Recent studies of an inferred molecular clock in these flies—here, a certain type of protein, whose structure changes by mutation at a steady rate through evolutionary time—may provide evidence that a single founder reached the archipelago some 40 million years ago.[8] Of course, the current high-island homes of the flies had not yet appeared at that time. Geological correlates indicate that such a founder could have landed on an island in the vicinity of what is now Koko Seamount in today's Emperor Seamount Chain. Speciating as they went, the flies later would have island hopped along the entire ensuing chain of nominal Hawaiian Islands.

The sheer number of drosophilid species in Hawaii is astonishing enough, but the range of their adaptations comes as a surprise even to evolutionary biologists. Organisms evolving on islands often seem to develop eccentric food preferences; Hawaiian drosophilids are paragons of this principle. Here, the feeding of the flies' larvae, actually small maggots, is the main focus. Implicit in a larval adaptation, of course, is an additional behavioral adaptation of the species—namely, the female's choice of a site to deposit her eggs. Now, while some Hawaiian drosophilids do indeed utilize decomposing fruit, many others depend wholly on foods that are almost unheard of on continental fruit fly menus—rotting leaves and bark, various fungi, dead flowers, sap or gum bleeding from trees, and, perhaps strangest of all, the eggs of spiders.

Hawaiian drosophilids are often highly specialized with regard to such foods, and larval nutrition of a given species is commonly restricted to a single type of native tree or shrub. In one extreme case, two closely related species depend on sap that exudes from the *naio* tree *(Myoporum sandwicense)*, but it seems that one species oviposits, and its larvae develop, in fermenting gobs of sap adhering to the tree itself, while the other species relies on sap that has dripped on the ground beneath the tree. Perhaps the latter has come to require some extra ingredients of decomposition that derive from the soil.[9]

Some of the Hawaiian pomace flies are giants of their kind. With two-centimeter wingspans, they are thought to be the largest species of *Drosophila* in the world.[10] These large flies are members of a distinctive Hawaiian subgroup, the picture-winged flies, named for the graceful, pigmented patterns on their wings. The extremely elaborate courtship behavior of this group has been well studied in recent years and has wonderfully exemplified in insects Darwin's insight on sexual selection: "a struggle between individuals of one sex, generally the males, for the possession of the other sex." Darwin saw this mechanism, one concomitant with natural selection, as a driving force in evolution. "The result," he concluded of the former, "is not death to the unsuccessful competitor, but few or no offspring."[11]

Unlike congeners elsewhere in the world, Hawaiian *Drosophila* usually mate in locations away from active feeding sites. Picture-winged males seem especially choosy about a proper location for mating. This may be on a prominent leaf, frond of a fern, or peeling piece of tree bark. The male treats such a site as a breeding territory, or lek, and events that occur in this little reproductive arena resemble those associated with the breeding of certain birds, such as the North American sage grouse, and a few mammals, such as some antelope species.[12] The lek is defended vigorously against wandering males of the same species and sometimes individuals of other species. With rapidly fluttering wings, a territorial male charges unwelcome intruders and attempts to evict them. Some species engage in head-butting contests during these male-to-male encounters, while others have been seen to wrestle with the tips of outstretched wings. Sometimes the challenger manages to take over the lek. However, when a potentially receptive female appears, a territorial male launches into a very different and complex display that appears to involve visual, auditory, tactile, and olfactory components.[13]

The male courtship ritual has some broad elements common to many species. For example, the male often dances around the female in a stereotypic fashion, beginning and ending with his head under her wing. While he dances, one or the other of the male's fluttering wings is extended (less often both are extended). Here, however, definitive pigment patterns and perhaps buzzing frequencies of the wings at these

15.1 Picture-winged *Drosophila.*

close quarters seem to entice a female of his species, while other females that might be courted initially will ignore or even repel his advances. The stroking of a female's abdomen by the male's forelegs and the proffering to her of droplets of sexual attractant, or pheromone, from the tip of his abdomen are also parts of the specific ritual. Some of the Hawaiian flies exhibit the ultimate in olfactory seduction. A sense of wonder pervades a Hawaii entomologist's description of the mating dance of an endemic male *Drosophila,* "which has evolved huge scent-dispersing brushes at the end of his tail which he curls over his head and shakes at his ladylove to overwhelm her with a shower of aphrodisiac perfume."[14]

The female seems to control the situation. She may heighten the male's ardor through so-called evocative behavior, beginning with specific postures as a kind of drosophilid coquettishness, continuing with foreplay that includes tasting the tongue of her suitor, and ending in copulation. All this depends on the male's communicating to her the right signals in her species' choreography of love. If the performance is imprecise or the signals are garbled, she does not respond and usually flies away after a short time, although occasional courtship episodes have been seen to continue for hours without consummation.

Detailed analysis of drosophilid mating rituals has provided evidence to suggest the direction of evolution among Hawaiian species—that is, which species of a closely related group are ancestral and which are derived. Reasoning that in many cases a relatively new species resulting from an island-hopping founder might lose some of the complexity of its ancestral mating dance, University of Hawaii entomologist Kenneth Kaneshiro staged singles encounters between closely related picture-winged species. As expected, results showed strong asymmetries in mating preferences among species thought to have diverged recently in evolutionary time.[15] Males from apparent derived populations were rarely able to satisfy ancestral females, which demanded the full, traditional precoital panoply. However, females from the derived population nearly always accepted ancestral males, which seemed to provide more than enough detail in the courtship ritual. By such behavioral tests it may be possible to distinguish ancestors and descendants among a good many species that are related by fairly recent interisland founding events. Older, settled species on a given island, however, presumably evolve new steps to their dances, new pheromone perfumes, and other complexities in their courtship.

Drosophilid flies constitute only part of the marvelous native insectary in the Hawaiian Islands. Other groups, while not such prolific generators of species (although several have evolved hundreds from a single founder), more than match the drosophilids for sheer adaptive *chutzpah*. For example, larvae of a number of species in the moth genus *Eupithecia* have become "ambush predators."[16] The caterpillar lies in wait for small prey such as a fly or a spider, snatches it with a lightning-quick lunge, and feeds on its body fluids. Among the myriad Lepidoptera in the world, this predatory habit is seen only in these Hawaiian moths.

Crane flies (family Tipulidae), sometimes mistaken for extra-large, gangly mosquitoes, have evolved in unusual ways in Hawaii. In general, their larvae live in moist leaf litter or are aquatic, but at least one Hawaiian species has invaded lava-tube caves (that unique ecosystem is covered later in this chapter). Still other endemic crane flies have become leaf miners. Their larvae form meandering tracks and tunnels as they feed and grow within the narrow confines of a living leaf before finally emerging to pupate and metamorphose into the adult. Other insect types such as moths and beetles include leaf-mining species, but crane flies with this way of life are unique to Hawaii.

During their evolution on oceanic islands, typically flying animals, both insects and birds, often lose the power of flight. Eleven orders of flying insects are represented in the Hawaiian native fauna, and in ten of them flightless species have evolved. Some may have simply divested themselves of an unneeded adaptation in a nonthreatening environment. Oahu's flightless fly may have fit that category. Unfortunately, by about 1900 that delightfully contradictory dipteran had vanished from its only known habitat on the slopes of Diamond Head; introduced ants are blamed for its extinction.[17] Hawaii's flightless lacewings, however, did not simply lose their wings. Those appendages evolved into hard, case-like body coverings as the normally delicate flying forms took up the appearance and habits of ground beetles in Hawaiian forests.

Hawaiian damselflies in the genus *Megalagrion* have achieved radical evolutionary changes in their ecology and physiology. Damselfly larvae, or naiads, typically grow to maturity in quiet streams or ponds, and some of the Hawaiian species find their ecological niche in such places. These insects do not leave the water until they are ready to transform into the winged adult. Certain species in the islands, however, have evolved larvae specialized for living on wet stream banks, the rocky edges of waterfalls, moist cavities formed by the leaf axils of rain forest shrubs and trees, and even in the leaf litter of the forest floor. Is there a progressive trend here? Are we witnessing a rare evolutionary event, a new example of the colonization of land? Entomologist Elwood Zimmerman suggests that these arboreal and turf-crawling damselfly larvae might eventually form a whole new group of terrestrial organisms.[18] Thus, the extraordinary becomes expected on oceanic islands, although we can never predict the artful changes nature will work in the living clay.

The mosaiclike nature of the Hawaiian Islands with regard to habitat— that is, the sharp boundaries between environmental extremes of climate and physical terrain—must have been an important factor in speciation of insects with fairly feeble powers of locomotion. The Big Island in particular has been recognized to contain numerous islands-within-an-island, where the physical isolation of a small breeding population from its parental stock could set the stage for evolution of a new species.

Kipukas, those small patches of forest spared when molten lava overran their surroundings, may be settings for what biologists call evolution by genetic drift. The key to this process is the isolation of a small breeding population that by chance possesses, or acquires by mutation, some feature that is outside the norm for its species. This becomes characteristic of the *kipuka* population but is not mingled with the greater gene pool of the species (which after an eruption may have been wiped out for miles around). Further genetic change of the small population, coupled with new adaptations in an environment of ecological opportunity, can bring additional shifts in anatomical, physiological, and behavioral norms for the population that constitutes the basic phenomenon of evolution. Beginning passively with *kipuka* formation, such events parallel those that ensue after a founder actively establishes a new population on an island.

The most surprising recently discovered evolutionary treasure hidden in islands-within-islands in the archipelago has come from lava-tube caves. Most of those still containing a highly evolved native ecosystem are on the Big Island, but a few have also been discovered on Maui and Kauai. Hawaiian caves had always been ignored by biologists. They were considered too young—all are thought to have formed less than half a million years ago—to have fostered the evolution of a native cave-adapted fauna. Such animals (cavernicoles) in continental regions were considered to be products of a long, slow adaptive process that began in truly ancient times. And virtually without exception, mainland cave species were so specialized that their chances of becoming founders of Hawaiian populations were absolutely zero. Exploration of Hawaiian caves over the last decade has substantiated the last judgment but uncovered a spectacular array of endemic cavernicoles dominated by insects and other arthropods with often bizarre adaptations. These animals have evolved in situ from surface-dwelling ancestors, and their discovery has radically changed scientific thinking on rates of evolution in the cave habitat everywhere.

Lava-tube caves are formed rapidly in the paroxysm of a thick *pahoehoe* flow on a mountain slope. In places, the flow may break into streams running along depressions or channels in the underlying landscape. Frequently, a crust begins to cool along the edges of such a flow and arches over the hot, fluid core. If something diverts the stream from above, or if the flow happens to stop around this time, the liquid core of an enclosed channel may drain downhill before freezing. The resulting cave is often highly irregular in form, now constricted to a crawl space, now expanded to a tunnel forty or fifty feet wide and almost as high. Some lava tubes branch extensively where original feeder channels nourished a central flow or a lava stream broke into distributaries. The largest Hawaiian lava tube explored to date has more than six miles of passages.

On the Big Island, lava tubes occur at elevations from sea level to about 13,000 feet. Correspondingly, cave temperatures vary from about 25 degrees Celsius (77 degrees Fahrenheit) in the lowlands to less than 5 degrees Celsius (41 degrees Fahrenheit) in the highest caves explored. High humidity and, away from entrances and eroded skylights, extensive zones of total darkness are consistent features of the cave environment. Above the immediate seacoast, with its sometimes elevated water table, Hawaiian caves never contain streams or lasting pools of water; the lava rock is too porous. In areas of high rainfall, trickles and seeps of water do carry small amounts of organic matter into lava tubes. But this source of food for cave animals, so important in mainland caves with significant streamflow, is minimal in Hawaii. Most of the food energy for the Hawaiian cave community is derived from the roots of a variety of trees, grasses, and ferns that penetrate the cave ceiling. Roots serve as fodder in both the fresh and decomposing states. Colloidal matter derived from overlying soil produces deposits of organic slime that are another nutritional resource for many Hawaiian cavernicoles. In turn, those animals that subsist on roots, slimes, and products of their decomposition are preyed upon by a variety of other creatures.

Here, then, is a unique Hawaiian community of insects and other small animals whose biology has only just begun to be investigated by researchers (it is from their recently published work that this much abbreviated summary is drawn[19]).

In keeping with nomenclature developed for continental cave ecosystems, resident life forms are classified in four categories. Troglobites are animals restricted entirely to caves. They are commonly blind, lack skin pigmentation, and feature other adaptations, especially enhanced tactile, acoustic, and olfactory senses. Troglophiles—for example, cockroaches—can show clear adaptations to life in caves, but may not be fully committed in an evolutionary sense to life in the perpetually dark, damp depths of a cave. Trogloxenes habitually utilize caves to roost or shelter, but always forage outside. Bats are classic examples in much of the world, but the small, insectivorous native bat of Hawaii, *Lasiurus cinereus*, roosts in trees and apparently never enters lava-tube caves. No true trogloxenes have been identified in Hawaiian caves. Finally, a wide variety of animals recorded from caves are termed accidentals. They enter and leave haphazardly or may consistently frequent the cave entrance but cannot survive in the dark zones. Introduced species such as the roof rat *(Rattus rattus)* and the barn owl *(Tyto alba)* are the largest of the accidental group found in Hawaiian caves.

About 100 species (all arthropods) are now considered true cave species in Hawaii. A large majority are conservatively classified as troglophiles, and many in this category are nonnative species that are more abundant in habitats outside of the caves. About thirty kinds of the deep-cave dwellers, however, are troglobites; all of them are endemic to individual islands—Hawaii, Maui, and Kauai—and have evolved from surface-living ancestors into remarkable new forms of their kind. They include the following:

- Crickets descended from species characteristically living in trees. They are unrelated to mainland cave crickets.

- An unusual blind species of earwig that nestles in cracks and rarely crawls out into the open.

- Pale cave moths and plant hoppers. Long-ago and much-changed immigrants from the forests above, they subsist respectively on fresh tissues and juices of exposed roots in lieu of the greener stuff consumed by their ancestors.

- Outlandish predators such as thread-legged bugs and a blind water treader turned rock walker in the humid darkness.

Native noninsects in Hawaiian caves include unusual terrestrial amphiphods (evolved from better known seacoast relatives called beach hoppers or beach fleas); a white, blind millipede and a small, pale centipede (unrelated to the big introduced centipede that invades both caves and

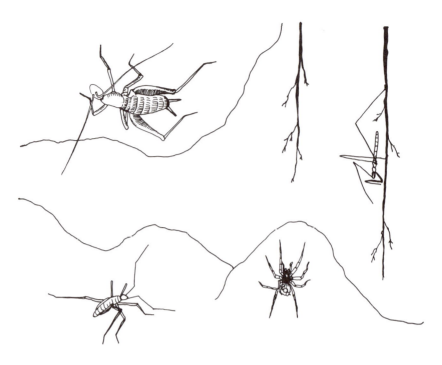

15.2 Hawaiian endemic cave arthropods. Cave cricket, Genus *Thaumatogryllus;* water treader, *Speovelia aaa* (lower left); thread-legged bug, *Nesidiolestes ana* (upper right); cave spider, *Adelocosa anops* (female carries young on her back). Drawings based on material from F. Howarth.

suburban homes in lowland areas of the islands); and spiders. The most impressive of the last-named group are two species of wolf spiders (family Lycosidae). One on the Big Island and one on Kauai, they are top predators in Hawaiian caves. Wolf spiders do not build webs; they are large, long-legged runners that catch prey on open ground, and all aboveground species have prominent eyes, but in Hawaiian caves they have become blind. Laboratory studies by speleobiologist Francis Howarth suggest they use sound waves to locate and track their prey in utter darkness.[20] The Kauai species *Adelocosa anops* in particular seems highly specialized for acoustic hunting. It appears to listen through its first pair of legs, which it holds high in the air like the tines of a tuning fork and, according to Howarth, it zeroes in on its prey with "uncanny accuracy."

Francis Howarth believes that many Hawaiian caves are initially inoculated with animal life from *kipukas.* Caves in the young lava surrounding a *kipuka* offer greatly expanded living space for arthropods that can make the transition to life underground. Even in the early period of vegetative recolonization, the labyrinths beneath the sere, shrubby lava fields are cool and humid and richly invested with roots. The caves themselves are new involuted islands awaiting founders to evolve in strange new directions.

ALIEN INVASIONS AND INFESTATIONS

Throughout the islands, native habitats such as *kipukas*, lava tubes, freshwater streams, even whole forests have been damaged and destroyed by human beings, and the loss of endemic Hawaiian species in some of the less conspicuous categories such as insects has been incalculable. Aside from gross habitat destruction, far more subtle human actions have taken a huge toll of native insect life. One such continuing action has been the introduction of myriad foreign insects. Travelers have brought them to Hawaii both intentionally and unintentionally. In the former case, for example, various species of small parasitic wasps, imported to control introduced agricultural pests, have all but destroyed many endemic moth populations.[21] Among the worst of the unintentional introductions were ants, all post-Cook imports. Wherever scattered populations of native insects had survived the gross deforestation of the Hawaiian lowlands, they were eaten alive by ants, especially *Pheidole megacephala*, the "house ant of Madeira," which, judging from an 1882 report of its widespread abundance,[22] must have reached Hawaii by the midnineteenth century or earlier. Another extremely aggressive species, the Argentine ant *(Iridomyrmex humilis)*, was inadvertently introduced in the 1940s. Unlike *Pheidole*, it thrives at high elevations—ranging nearly to the summit of Haleakala on Maui and above the 9,000-foot level on Hawaii's Mauna Kea.[23]

Lacking pestiferous species, Hawaii was originally a true paradise. Crop plants were virtually untouched by native insects. There were no ants. Nor were there mosquitoes, cockroaches, scorpions, or large venomous centipedes. In their careless introduction of such creatures along with hundreds of agricultural pests, humans spoiled the islands for themselves. Selected gleanings from historical accounts illustrate the creeping invasions of Hawaii by noxious arthropods.

Among the early commentators on the unnatural fauna of the islands, Adelbert von Chamisso, a naturalist accompanying the Russian expedition captained by Otto von Kotzebue, noted on Oahu in 1816 an abundance of fleas and "some species of blatta" (cockroaches).[24]

"There are no mosquitoes here."[25] It is hard not to read enthusiasm into that observation by the touring London missionaries Tyerman and Bennet when they reached the Hawaiian Islands in 1822 after previous tropical landfalls. Such exultation was short-lived, however. Later nineteenth-century writers—for example, E. M. Bailey[26]—date the initial appearance of mosquitoes at Lahaina in 1826. Reportedly, mosquitoes were introduced when sailors from the British ship *Wellington*, newly arrived from Mexico, went ashore to replenish their freshwater supply. According to the story, the men emptied the dregs of their water casks containing mosquito larvae into local springs before refilling the casks. By the mid-1830s mosquitoes were described as "numerous and very annoying" on Oahu[27] and were also abundant (along with roaches, rats, and mice) at Hanalei, Kauai.[28] Four bloodsucking species of mosquitoes are now established in Hawaii, mainly at low elevations. Some of them carry diseases that have devastated native birds (see chapter 14).

One of the most spectacular early surges of an agricultural pest in the islands was an outbreak of army worms, most likely larvae of the moth *Spodoptera exempta*. It seems to have begun around the late 1840s in the vicinity of Makawao, Maui, an early center for diversified agriculture that supplied whaling fleets and population centers as far away as Honolulu. By 1850, the army worm, locally called *pelula* or *pelua*, was so numerous around Makawao it was appearing in large numbers above the surface of the ground, or at grassroots level, where it typically feeds.[29] In 1853, the worm was reported to be a wide-spectrum threat to Maui's crops and pastures,[30] and soon it began to spread to other islands. The unchecked plague of *Spodoptera* was directly responsible for the 1865 importation to the islands of the common mynah bird from India. But even against that predatory force, the army worms were slow to retreat; they besieged Hawaiian agribusiness at least until the 1890s and have not yet surrendered unconditionally.

The introduced scorpion and centipede (one species each) were said by a visitor to Oahu in 1836 to have had arrived "recently."[31] These nasty creatures became abundant nearly everywhere in the settled Hawaiian lowlands by the late nineteenth century. One chronicler of those times reported that scorpions were numerous at Waikiki Beach around the 1890s, and that they were especially prone to hide in swimsuits that had been hung up to dry.[32]

Historical correlates abroad helped to make some species' introductions memorable. In November 1870, a short article in *The Friend* ruefully noted the appearance in Honolulu of bookworms (small, paper-consuming beetle larvae), concluding that "they are as persistent as the Prussians upon the French."[33]

Today, insect introductions in Hawaii continue, probably at a more rapid pace than ever before. New predatory species are still deliberately released to control new agricultural pests that reach the islands by accident or through human carelessness. Recent estimates are that every year more than two dozen species of foreign insects are inadvertently introduced and become established.[34] Hawaii entomologists have discovered that entry of arthropod aliens can often be traced to certain hot spots. More than anywhere else, new insects turn up in traps placed near military bases on Oahu. Air transport of the U.S. armed services is not subject to state of Hawaii agricultural inspection. It would appear that the military could do a better job of fumigating its planes and cargoes arriving in the islands. This should even be done with flights direct from the U.S. mainland. Certain damaging introductions are still in the offing. For example, temperate-zone mosquitoes might well be adaptable to Hawaii's cool montane environments and carry deadly diseases into the last refuges of the islands' native birds.

HAWAIIAN LAND SNAILS

Like Hawaii's native insects, the land snails of the islands have a history of drastic decline. And like the insects, these endemic snails were never a threat to agriculture, but they too were in the way of progress; they were defenseless against new predators, and some of them were extremely attractive to human collectors.

Nine families of snails,* a majority of them widespread in the Indo-Pacific region, have native representatives in Hawaii's land ecosystems. The total number of recognized endemic and indigenous Hawaiian species, many of them now extinct, approximates 1,000.[35] Although the classification of many of these snails has been in flux for more than a century, and new revisions may yet appear, malacologists are in general agreement that a whole family (Amastridae) and several subfamilies, such as the Achatinellinae, have evolved in Hawaii. They agree too that a majority of Hawaiian land-snail genera are endemic; some genera are highly restricted within the archipelago—for example, *Carelia* to Kauai and Niihau and the famous *Achatinella* to Oahu. Such *kamaaina* mollusks must have been in the islands for eons. However, the scientists think they can recognize some rank newcomers, too—for example,

---

*Fam. Achatinellidae: predominantly tree snails of several subfamilies including the Achatinellinae, which is endemic to the Hawaiian Islands except Kauai-Niihau. Genera include *Partulina, Perdicella, Newcombia*, and *Achatinella*.

Fam. Amastridae: mainly ground snails; produced major radiations of species, especially on Kauai. Genera include *Carelia, Amastra, Laminella*.

Fam. Endodontidae: small ground and tree snails formerly of tremendous diversity in the Hawaiian lowlands. Most apparently became extinct during the prehistoric expansion of Hawaiian agriculture.

Fam. Succineidae: small tree and shrub dwellers with fragile shells resembling slightly twisted scoops. Still relatively common.

Fam. Limnaeidae: typically inhabit fresh water, but some Hawaiian forms reportedly emerge on wet terrain.

Fam. Helicarionidae; Fam. Helicinidae; Fam. Pupillidae; Fam. Zonitidae: less well-studied than the families above. Their Hawaiian forms are generally small and inconspicuous, although some have diversified extensively in the islands

several species in the family Zonitidae. These appear very similar to congeners found in northwestern North America. Zonitid snails are confirmed passengers on bird feathers.[36] One of the species in this family is restricted to high elevation on the Big Island, which makes possible an educated guess about which air carrier brought it to Hawaii—the golden plover, about the only migratory bird frequenting high country and low on its Hawaiian winter sojourns.[37]

All of the endemic Hawaiian land snails probably evolved from small founders that originally hitchhiked on birds to reach the islands from very remote land masses. Once in the archipelago, species that remained small must have found continuing opportunities for interisland migration. However, in some families adaptation and natural selection led to great increases in size. The giants among native Hawaiian land snails were *Carelia* and *Amastra* species from Kauai; shells of some of the former reached nearly three inches long. All of the twenty or so recognized species of the elongate, high-spired *Carelia* are now very rare or extinct.

Great plasticity in the shape of the shell characterized the evolution of the smaller *Amastra* or their progenitors as they spread and speciated on various islands, including Kauai, Oahu, Lanai, and Maui. Some shells are elongate, nearly grading into *Carelia*, while others are stubbier, and some have become considerably flattened with the spiraling growth of the animal extending the shell's girth in nearly one plane like neatly coiled rope on a ship's deck. These shells grade into a sister genus, appropriately named *Planamastra*, in which the flattening trend becomes essentially complete. Sadly, of more than 150 species of *Amastra* and several of *Planamastra*, most are now extinct or extremely rare and threatened with extinction.

Hawaii's most famous native mollusks belong to the genus *Achatinella*. To briefly clarify a somewhat confusing taxonomic wilderness, their namesake family, Achatinellidae (formerly Tornatellinidae), includes hundreds of species and numerous genera in several subfamilies widely distributed on islands throughout the tropical Pacific. As mentioned, one of the subfamilies, Achatinellinae, is endemic to the Hawaiian Islands, though none have been discovered on Kauai or Niihau. Finally, the genus *Achatinella* is considered by most experts to be endemic to the island of Oahu, although sister genera with similar tree-dwelling lifestyles, especially *Partulina*, are represented by species on other islands, including Molokai, Lanai, Maui, and Hawaii.

Achatinella and its sister genera are tree snails. Most of them subsist chiefly on so-called black fungi, or sooty molds, that form thin, plaquelike deposits on the leaves and stems of plants.[38] A variety of native Hawaiian trees and shrubs are hosts to especially luxuriant growths of the fungi, and the snails literally live on top of their food supply. Such

15.3   Endemic Oahu tree snail (*Achatinella mustelina*).

fungi are not toxic to a host plant but may somewhat reduce its photo-synthesis. Hence, grazing actions of the snail may be beneficial to the native forest cover.

These tree snails are viviparous; an individual* bears a single living young, which in the achatinellas (meaning the genus) has a shell about one-fifth of an inch long at birth. Recent research by zoologist Michael Hadfield and his students at the University of Hawaii indicates a patheti-cally slow reproductive rate. To produce such large young, achatinellas must grow to a relatively large size—the shells of adults are typically between one-half and one inch long. The onset of reproduction begins at about six or seven years of age and continues for perhaps another five or six years, with females bearing as few as one offspring per year.[39] Creatures with such a slow rate of increase had surely found a secure and nurturing ecological niche in the Hawaiian forests.

Achatinella species have a simple conical shape, but a clean, crisp surface texture defines their coiling, making them quite attractive even when dead-white. However, most are colorful, with lovely and highly varied patterns of bands in yellow, russet, and brown ringing the shell, and this made them irresistible to collectors.

Modern experts recognize the existence of about thirty-five to forty species of *Achatinella* from shell collections deposited in museums, mainly since the midnineteenth century.[40] Earlier estimates of the diver-sity of the genus based on the great range of banding patterns on the

*These snails are hermaphroditic, so an individual is both male and female.

shells ran to hundreds of species, subspecies, and varieties. The evolution of this great diversity derives from the habits of snails and the geography of a volcanic island. Achatinellas are homebodies in the extreme. Numerous field observations suggest that populations remain isolated on a single tree or bush for many years despite similar suitable and unoccupied habitat nearby. As a number of evolutionary biologists have noted, on a rugged island such as Oahu it must have been easy for an initial founding population to gradually become subdivided into numerous segments, or demes, with gene flow greatly restricted among them. In particular, speciation seems to have been rife along the linear trend of the Koolau Range, with its many valleys and intervening ridges. Distributions of a majority of *Achatinella* species are local in extent here, typically clustering in a few adjoining valleys.

Early Hawaiian impacts on the land snail fauna of the forests above the agricultural belt cannot be ascertained. However, in prehuman times achatinellas were living, presumably in trees, right down to the seacoast. Shells of one of them (a species never seen alive by Western eyes) have been found in the sand dunes at Kahuku in northwestern Oahu; reportedly some of the shells were no more than 100 feet from the ocean.[41] Many other low-elevation populations were surely wiped out during the original lowland deforestation by the Hawaiians. Any scattered populations remaining on the coastal plains were then buried by the wave of nineteenth-century agricultural development. The malacologist Pilsbry, writing around 1912, observed, "Once forests with Achatinellidae and Endodontidae shaded the plains far seaward from the lovely peak of Kaneohe, where now dead shells may be picked up in ploughed fields, or gathered out of pockets in the rocks."[42]

Hawaiians sometimes made leis from the land shells. This was the provenance of the first achatinella recorded by science, collected in 1786 by the expedition of Portlock and Dixon, the first British captains after Cook to reach Hawaii.[43] Later naturalists reported on the abundance of the snails on Oahu. F. J. F. Meyen, who arrived in 1831 with a Prussian expedition, commented after exploring the Koolau Mountains behind Honolulu, "Here . . . nature has placed countless land snails instead of insects on the leaves of the trees."[44] Surely in 1831 there were lots of insects too, but the colorful dominance of the achatinellas must have dazzled Meyen and his assistants.

There is something about overwhelming abundance and easy pickings that may trigger an insatiable gluttony—the coyote amid sheep, and the weasel in the henhouse. In Hawaii, a unique predatory interest in achatinellas developed by 1850. Visitors and residents (in the European and American community), scientists and amateurs alike, evolved a manic interest in land shells, especially the larger and brightly colored ones. Students at Punahou School were demon shell collectors. For decades, school outings were devoted to hunting achatinellas. Valley after valley on Oahu was scoured for the bright-banded shells, whose powers of replacement were so feeble. Off Oahu, the collecting rage was just as intense. At Lahaina, the missionary W. P. Alexander wrote of his sons and their numerous summer-vacation guests from Punahou in the early 1850s: "They are all infected with a conchological fever and daily traverse the ravines in quest of land shells."[45] He also mentions a boat trip to nearby Lanai, and the collection in one swoop of several thousand land shells by the boys. The Lanai snails and those sought on Maui were probably *Partulina* species.

Some collectors made money. There was a brisk trade in these gemlike shells in faraway places such as New York City, where college-bound John T. Gulick "sold a few shells for $100" around 1854 or 1855.[46] A second-generation missionary who left Hawaii to serve in Japan and China, Gulick had a keen scientific interest in the shells. He later was to write a major work in support of Darwinian evolution in which he concluded, "These achatinellinae never came from Noah's Ark."[47] The number of shells he amassed was astonishing for the period, an estimated 44,500 from 1851 through 1853.[48]

Scientists and scientifically devoted amateurs were among the greediest collectors, even after the turn of the twentieth century, when the snails were fast disappearing. The same unholy attitude that drove ornithologists of the time to fire on the last-known specimens of various Hawaiian birds prompted the conchologists. In the earlier decades some of them rode into valleys, filling saddlebags with the shells they could pluck without dismounting. Then they paid natives to scour areas that were harder to reach. They built their collections by the tens of thousands and stored thousands of shells unsorted in drawers, boxes, and kegs. They bragged about their prowess—for example, "the writer's own collection is one of the most extensive in the islands, containing over 30,000 examples."[49] He may not have known about one estimated at 116,000.[50]

As over-collected regions became depleted, professionals enthused over any new largesse, such as a population of *Partulina* discovered in the late 1880s in the Kohala Mountains of the Big Island. "During a recent visit to the locality, in a few minutes I collected several hundred specimens, picking them from trees and low bushes as rapidly as one would gather huckleberries from a prolific field."[51] That species is now believed extinct.

Fifty years of intensive shell collecting was surely a major cause for the decline of most and extinction of many of those of the larger Hawaiian land snails, which had survived the centuries of Polynesian changes on the land. However, a number of other impacts have certainly also destroyed vast numbers of snails. The list includes montane deforestation (especially by cattle and goats), confirmed predation by rats, possible predation by ants and the big terrestrial flatworm *Geoplana septemlineata*, and possible introduced diseases. Hadfield's 1986 paper in the journal *Malacologia* (cited earlier) provides a thorough review of all of these impacts, including shell collecting, and interprets the snails' vulnerability to extinction in light of reproductive potential and motility.

Today, the worst threat to the few remaining scattered and decimated populations of achatinellas and their sister genera is a deliberately introduced predator. It is a carnivorous land snail, *Euglandina rosea*, brought to the Hawaiian Islands from Florida in 1955. *Euglandina*, called the "killer snail," feeds only on other snails, and its release in Hawaii was an attempt to control the earlier-introduced African snail, *Achatina fulica*, a voracious plant eater and agricultural pest. The only problem is that the killer seems to prefer the harmless native species to the African. *Euglandina* has now spread far beyond the agricultural lowlands and at least on Oahu has penetrated the entire range of the surviving *Achatinella* species. The killer snail readily climbs trees, and according to Michael Hadfield, wherever it turns up, the achatinellas are doomed. Hadfield and colleagues actually observed *Euglandina* invade a small isolated population of *Achatinella mustelina* in the Waianae Mountains. In 1974, the killers were first seen more than 1,000 feet below the small copse of trees containing the achatinellas. By 1977, *Euglandina* were found on the outskirts of the study site, and in 1979, the native snails were gone, except for dead shells on the ground.[52]

With a modern understanding of the history of Hawaiian land environments in general, it becomes possible to speculate reasonably regarding the overall fate of *Achatinella* and its relatives. This tragedy would seem to have had three acts:

Act One. Before the arrival of the Hawaiians, the snail populations were probably held in balance by predation by a variety of birds. Thrushes are well known as snail eaters, and the Hawaiian fossil avifauna appears to include additional subspecies of the larger of the two existing native thrushes. The rare Maui *poo-uli*, a bird only discovered in 1973, feeds on snails from the foliage and bark of trees. Fossil remains of this bird indicate that it was far more widespread in prehistoric times than today. Other potential snail predators were a small extinct hawk, several crows, and numerous honeycreepers, including some unlike any known historically. All of these birds appear to have been thriving at the time of Polynesian discovery (see chapter 18).

Act Two. Extensive clearing of the lowlands by the prehistoric Hawaiians eliminated many populations of snails and endemic predators alike. Among the snails, endodontids and amastrids were decimated at this time, perhaps even more thoroughly than the achatinellids. At this time, snails were faced with an efficient new predator, the Polynesian rat, *R. exulans*. And the larger ground-dwelling types such as amastrids would have been eaten by pigs.

Act Three. Little mention is made of the snails in the earliest post-Cook decades. Surely achatinellids were abundant in the mountain forests, but perhaps they were well dispersed in the more or less continuous canopy. At any rate, they did not garner much attention from the earliest explorers, naturalists, and missionary trekkers. After about the 1820s, progressive deforestation by livestock and loggers in the mountains and interior valleys probably concentrated remnant tree-snail populations into the dazzling displays found through the midnineteenth century. Isolated in small groves, with (at first) no significant predation, they would have multiplied to the maximum. Such overabundance then became conspicuous. The rest of the story is pretty well documented.

Now an epilogue seems to be in the offing, and it may become an epitaph for *Achatinella* if *Euglandina* finds the few scattered fugitive populations that remain on Oahu. *Euglandina* has been introduced to many other Pacific Islands far from Hawaii. For example, in 1977, it was released on the small island of Moorea, near Tahiti, and in six years had spread over most of the island, extinguishing as it went most native species of *Partula*, a relative of *Achatinella*.[53] Despite such destruction of natural heritage and little evidence that *Euglandina* does the intended job, research and development agencies such as the South Pacific Commission were still recommending the killer snail in the mid-1980s as a control agent against the African snail, which has now spread widely in the Pacific.

Today, all surviving *Achatinella*—probably fewer than half of the historically known species—are officially recognized as endangered under federal law. How long their besieged, scattered populations will last, along with those of related genera on islands other than Oahu, is only hopeful guesswork. Most of the amastrids are gone; ditto for the endodontids. The last healthy Hawaiian species populations of the latter seem to be on tiny Nihoa Island, 160 miles northwest of Kauai (see chapter 10). On the main islands, the native snails that still seem to be thriving are those characterized by small size and relatively high reproductive capacity. These are presumably the types that make the best founders of new island populations. So, in a sense, with the elimination of the large and highly-evolved forms, we have a regression back to an early stage in the saga of land snails in the Hawaiian Islands. It will be a very long time before any new forms such as the large, colorful achatinellas assume roles in the evolutionary drama.

In the Hawaiian era and throughout the nineteenth century, a legend told of singing snails in the trees. According to the original story, a young Hawaiian couple traversing the mountain forests at night was protected from malevolent spirits by the incessant and mysterious singing of the snails. The legend was investigated by a number of Western naturalists, and the eventual conclusion was that tree crickets, not snails, were the singers. Today, like Hawaiian birdsong, this other music endemic to the islands' forests is more and more muted and must serve as a fading dirge for all the unique insects and land snails that came so far on oceanic and adaptive journeys and now are dying so quickly.

PART FIVE

Volcanoes in the Sky

16

Cloudlands and Drylands

On the islands of Maui and Hawaii, vast expanses of open dry forest, broken by lava flows and lines of recent cinder-cone hills, used to extend from near sea level up gently rising leeward terrain—through belts of typically sparse clouds touching the ground at middle levels on these slopes—to elevations of 10,000 feet and higher. This type of forest has been nearly eliminated at lower elevations. Only in the higher zones do major remnants still survive. In these high cloudlands, volcanic rock, rugged trees, and gnarled shrubs assume mysterious qualities. In a minute or an hour, softness and vagueness evanesce with the mist to reveal a world of pure light and desert air that grows increasingly rarified toward the remote summits.

On windward slopes the dry forest lies at upper elevations, where it is part of a continuum above mesic, *koa*-dominated woodland. This itself emerges out of upper rain forest at around 6,000 feet. Progressively drier and cooler conditions at higher elevations together with the historical stress of grazing by feral livestock now limit tree growth to near 9,000 feet, although in a few places desiccated *kamaaina* types, with far more limb than leaf, may still straggle higher. Above the tree line, windward or leeward or in between, is a belt of variable width called the alpine heath zone.

The biota of these Hawaiian cloudlands and drylands is controlled by the age of the terrain as well as the climate, since it takes a very long time for vegetation to regenerate here on new lava or ash. Many of the life forms and natural communities of the Hawaiian high country are wonderfully unique. Unfortunately, a majority of species here are now endangered, and experts believe that some world-class marvels of evolutionary biology have been lost.

CLOUDLANDS PLANT LIFE

Hawaii's dry-adapted mountain flora evolved into its greatest diversity on the leeward sides of the highest islands in such places as Kona and South Haleakala. Some of the trees here, such as the *naio, Myoporum sandwicense* (also discussed in chapter 11) are found on leeward exposures through virtually the whole altitudinal range of the forest. *Naio* reach their prime as forty- to fifty-foot trees at elevations of 6,000 to

7,000 feet above the sea. The heartwood of *naio* has a sharp, spicy scent. Known as the false or bastard sandalwood—because it failed to gain acceptance as a substitute for the fragrant species of *Santalum*—the *naio* is presently far more abundant.

Another tree, the *mamane (Sophora chrysophylla)*, with its beautiful sprays of yellow blossoms and its twisted, winged bean pods, is a true mainstay of the upper dry forest, although, like the *naio*, it used to be common down to low elevations. *Mamane* wood is extremely tough and flexible; the best of it was used by *haoles* for making the spokes, axles, and frames of wagons, and it was cut to provide posts for thousands of miles of ranchland fences.[1] *Sophora* and *Myoporum* trees are so often found together in the high xeric forests on Hawaii and Maui that this habitat is sometimes characterized as the *mamane-naio* vegetational zone. However, *ohia lehua* is also well represented in the dryforest community with races that grow variably from near sea level to the treeline. On relatively recent lavas, *ohia* dominates the uppermost sparse forest on Mauna Loa—for example, on the trail to that mountain's summit in Hawaii Volcanoes National Park. But around and under these conspicuous trees and in the harsher, colder, nonforested places above treeline on Hawaiian Island slopes there is much more in the way of exquisitely evolved biota. The necessarily abbreviated account of the dry-adapted Hawaiian montane flora that continues here is based on several sources.[2]

Besides the dominants, *mamane, naio*, and *ohia*, with their great elevational range, other prominent trees found on the dry slopes at lower to middle levels include the *uhi-uhi (Mezoneurum kauaiense)*, a legume with dense, blacker-than-ebony heartwood; *kauila*, (a name given to both *Colubrina oppositifolia* and *Alphitonia ponderosa)*. Woods of the *kauila* and *uhi-uhi* trees are extraordinarily hard. The Hawaiians used them for spears and mallets. Women reportedly fashioned rounded, polished hairpins from long, durable splinters of *kauila*.[3] An unusual fishing lure was made from *uhi-uhi*, which sinks like a stone in sea water.[4] Yet another striking tree of the dry mountain forest is the *koaia (Acacia koaia)*, a dwarf relative of the *koa* monarch of the mesic forests. *Hibiscadelphus*, a peculiar small tree of the hibiscus (mallow) family, was also a Hawaiian evolutionary product in this habitat. Its large, curving, yellow-to-magenta flowers never open. Their color and shape are thought to reflect coevolution with now vanished, long-billed, dryland honeycreepers, which were probably the chief pollinators of the several species of *Hibiscadelphus*. Except for the dominants *(ohia, mamane*, and *naio)*, all of the trees named above are now rare. However, native dry forest featuring most of them once grew on the deeply dissected leeward slopes of the older islands—even on Oahu, where some of the world's rarest woods were early consumed for fenceposts and firewood.

On Maui and the Big Island are found large expanses of suitable habitat for this forest type, but most of it has been infested with livestock, grazed to stubble, and replanted with exotics for nearly two centuries. Thus, to speak of the Hawaiian dry forest in the present tense is to belie its near devastation at lower and middle elevations on all the islands and its continuing demise in the upper montane zone.

In addition to the trees, a rich dry-adapted flora of smaller plants once spread over the high cloudlands and drylands. Two of the native shrubs (sometimes almost trees) that are still locally common are *puki-awe (Styphelia tameimeiae)* and *aalii (Dodonea viscosa)*. The former includes species or varieties that range into mesic forests where the plants are much larger (fifteen feet or more in height) than on near-desert terrain—for example, in Haleakala Crater. Densely branched and foliated *pukiawe* is readily distinguished by its tiny, light green leaves and often abundant clusters of bright red or red and white berries. In Hawaiian times, chiefs who wished to mingle with commoners were supposed to first remove their aura of sacredness by fumigating themselves beside a smoky fire of *pukiawe*. *Dodonea* is easily recognized in the fruiting stage. It produces fingertip-sized seed capsules that have from two to four wings. The capsules are mainly red or reddish brown when mature. Hawaiians used them to make a red dye for *kapa* cloth.

One of the rarest plants of the cloudlands is the endemic legume *Vicia menziesii*, named after its discoverer, the Scottish naturalist Archibald Menzies. In February 1794, he found this large, red-and-white-flowered vining broadbean near the 6,500-foot elevation on the southern slope of Mauna Loa. Other early collectors found it near the upper limits of forest growth on windward Mauna Kea, but once grazing livestock began to multiply throughout this plant's range, it all but disappeared. In the twentieth century, it has been pronounced extinct three times. Redis-covered in 1974, sixty years after its last confirmed sighting, this plant appears restricted to an area of less than one square mile straddling private and state of Hawaii lands at 5,500 feet near the site where Men-zies first found it. Reduced in the wild to a few scattered, struggling patches, *V. menziesii* in 1978 was the first Hawaiian plant to be placed on the federal endangered species list by the U.S. Department of the Interior.[5]

Also among the rarest of the smaller plants in the dry mountains are Hawaiian mints in the genera *Haplostachys* and *Stenogyne*. Endangered by browsing livestock—because they have lost most or all of their minty essence, which serves as a herbivore repellant in continental mints—these plants, whose species feature delicate white, yellow, or red flow-ers, are making their last stand on the high lava plains of Hawaii bet-ween Mauna Kea and Mauna Loa. Some of the mints had not been seen since the nineteenth century and were thought extinct but have been

16.1 Hawaiian alpine plants. In foreground, left to right: ohelo, *Vaccinium reticulatum; kupaoa, Dubautia menziesii;* and the rare mint, *Haplostachys haplostachya.* Behind: the *mamane* tree, *Sophora chrysophylla.*

recently rediscovered in the wild by University of Hawaii botanists.[6]

Native geraniums are another feature of the Hawaiian uplands. Various species inhabit the cloud-forest zone, and some range far up the slopes above treeline. These alpine plants, along with others, exhibit several adaptations to the intense wind, cold, dryness, and sunlight.

This vegetation of the high Hawaiian heathland typically features small or narrow leaves, and in areas exposed to wind the plants usually grow close to the ground. Several types including the geraniums, the mints, and the famous silverswords (see below) have leaves densely covered with tiny hairs. The hairs may have several functions. Frost, which frequently occurs at night above about 7,000 feet, tends to form on the hairs and is held away from the vital cell surfaces of the leaf itself. The wind is also intercepted by the hairs, and its drying effect on the leaf as a whole thereby lessened. In addition, the hairs seem to enhance fog drip, a condensation of liquid water from the thin, ground-hugging clouds that for much of the year are the main source of moisture in this high country. Away from windward exposures, only infrequently do such clouds produce general rain or snow, but beneath the vegetation itself there is often a very light and slow precipitation.

In several kinds of the high-altitude plants, the hairs coating the leaves are silvery and form a reflecting surface. This adaptation provides relief from punishing levels of solar radiation. One prominent example is seen in the silvery Haleakala geranium *Geranium tridens*, found between about 7,000 and 10,000 feet. Many of the Hawaiian alpine plants also possess relatively thick, leathery leaves with waxy surfaces and other water-conserving features.

The most famous plant of the Hawaiian alpine region is the silversword, genus *Argyroxiphium*, known as *ahinahina* to the Hawaiians, a name which can mean "gray," "white," or "shining." In the Polynesian pantheon, Hina was a goddess associated with the moon. The most common silversword species, *A. sandwicense*, grows on East Maui (Haleakala) at elevations above about 7,000 feet. On the island of Hawaii is a close relative, the Mauna Kea silversword; its range extends up to 12,000 feet. Once vast populations of these silverswords have been decimated, and most of the remaining plants are in Haleakala National Park, where a few natural concentrations, augmented by plantings, are afforded partial protection from browsing goats.

On the Big Island is another silversword, *A. kauense*, whose distribution is restricted to Mauna Loa's leeward slopes and the saddle region facing Mauna Kea. Until recently this species was thought to be nearly extinct, but it has now been found growing on remote, nearly inaccessible lava slopes, and its total population may still number in the thousands.[7] However, most of these plants are close to the 6,000-foot contour flanking Mauna Loa's huge active southwest rift zone and are thus naturally at risk. They are also browsed by goats and sheep wherever these animals can reach them on this rugged terrain. The Kau silversword differs from the better known *A. sandwicense* in having fleshier, more angular leaves (the leaf cross-section is triangular in the former, more nearly flat in the latter). The Kau form also has a smaller flowering stalk, or spike.

The flowering of the silverswords is a spectacular event. The dryland species grow very slowly as spherical rosettes. The long, narrow, densely clustered leaves protect the plant's meristem—its growing heart, which lies deep within the silvery globe and whose diameter may reach more than two feet. Then, at an age ranging from seven to thirty years, the plant flowers in a single season (May to October).[8] With a startling sexual exuberance, a massive single stalk rears out of the heart of the plant and grows, in *A. sandwicense*, up to nine feet high. As many as 500 yellow to red-brown flowers (the colors vary from species to species and plant to plant) crowd the stalk. They resemble little sunflowers and reveal that this Hawaiian evolutionary marvel belongs to the family Com-

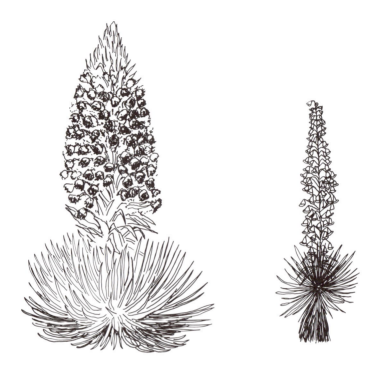

16.2 Silverswords: *Argyroxiphium sandwicense* (found on Haleakala and Mauna Kea) and (on right) *A. kauense* (found only on Mauna Loa).

positae. Within weeks the seeds mature, the big stalk withers and falls, and the leafy base of the plant begins to decompose. After a few winter rains and with the return of dry weather, *A. sandwicense* resembles nothing more than a small pile of silvery ash on the ground.

The third silversword species, *A. caliginis*, grows in very different surroundings. It is a bog species found only in the cool summit region (around Puu Kukui) of West Maui. Its growth form is quite different from the dryland silverswords. *A. caliginis* branches at the base to form prostrate, creeping stems from which sprout small silversword rosettes. Newly formed rosettes then root in the bog, becoming individual plants that begin a new cycle of branchings as the original base eventually dies. Drenched by more than 350 inches of rain per year, this species is thought by some botanists to reproduce more by such vegetative means than by flowering. Carlquist suggests that during typically lengthy periods of cold drizzle, insect pollinators may be ineffective in the high-bog habitat.[9]

Two further species *(A. grayanum* and *A. virescens)* have been assigned to the Hawaiian endemic genus *Argyroxiphium*. (However, a recent study suggests they are very closely related.)[10] These plants are called greenswords. They have lost their silvery tint, and both are plants of wet mountain habitat. *A. grayanum* grows on West Maui with the bog silversword. It too is a branching species, but differs from the latter in growing as a spindly shrub with terminal rosettes occasionally topped by small flowering stalks. Thus, as in the bog silversword, death after flowering only accrues to a given branch and not the whole genetic entity of the plant. This greensword's flowers are light yellow or yellow-green, while the bog silversword's are described as more nearly brown. The variety classically known as *A. virescens*, the Haleakala greensword, grows at the upper edge of East Maui's windward rain forest. It is a spectacular plant that resembles the dry-adapted alpine silverswords by flowering in a single, giant upthrusting stalk.

The silverswords and greenswords occupy a remote and spectacular position on a Hawaiian evolutionary trail that has branched in surprising directions for millions of years. Most botanists believe that the trail began with the arrival in the islands of seeds from a small coastal composite plant called a tarweed. The most likely place of origin of this founder is arid southern California and northwestern Mexico. Even today there are tarweeds in that region that resemble the simplest and least specialized silversword relatives in Hawaii—small, spreading shrubs called *kupaoa*, found on dry, semibarren hillsides and lava flows. These unlikely silversword relatives, which grow in medium to very high elevations, are members of the genus *Dubautia*.* Nor are they restricted to dry habitats. Some of the *Dubautia* species grow in the wettest rain forests and bogs. And they are not all shrubby forms; several grow to the stature of small trees (generally known as *naenae*) reaching twenty feet or more in height, with trunks of proportionate diameter. One species has evolved into a woody vine. Yet another odd silversword relative, the *iliau* (genus *Wilkesia*), grows only on relatively dry mountain slopes of Kauai. Visitors can easily see these small, tufted trees sprouting from cliffsides near highway lookouts along the rim of Waimea Canyon. The offshoots of this remarkable evolutionary burgeoning— species of *Argyroxiphium, Dubautia,* and *Wilkesia*—have collectively been termed the silversword alliance, and Carlquist suggests that this group is the most profound of all Hawaiian examples, both plant and animal, of adaptive radiation.

In the alpine region of Hawaii, until the early twentieth century, there were *Dubautia,* or *Raillardia,* trees—gnarled, ancient, *kamaaina* specimens up to twenty feet high with foot-thick trunks, ecological analogs to the bristlecone pines of California's high-desert mountains. These desiccated naenae were probably the highest actual trees on Mauna Kea.

---

*Another genus, *Raillardia*, has recently been subsumed into the genus *Dubautia*.

Shortly after the turn of the century, Joseph Rock could still find a few of them there between 10,000- and 11,000-foot elevations, and young or perhaps livestock-damaged ones reportedly straggled another 500 feet higher. These naenae were resistant to almost nightly freezing and were sometimes seen covered with snow. Trees of the silversword alliance were also once common on Maui. *Dubautia reticulata* (or *Raillardia menziesii*) grew to twenty feet high in dry gulches at the 6,000- to 7,000-foot level on Haleakala. Today this species is still fairly common, but only as a shrub (one of the *kupaoa*) at higher elevations on the mountain.[11]

It should not be surprising to find native plants high in the Hawaiian mountains that have evolved from cool-temperate ancestors. Three examples are familiar to North American foragers after wild berries. The *ohelo*, which consists of several species in the genus *Vaccinium*, is the Hawaiian blueberry—not quite as recognizable as it sounds, because the ripe fruit is typically red. Still, the flavor is pure blueberry, although berries from the driest terrain are apt to be mealy. *Ohelo* is often abundant from elevations of 3,000 feet up to well above the treeline. It frequently dominates the alpine heath on young volcanic ground and even occurs on Oahu along the highest ridge crests. In forested zones it commonly appears as an early successional plant. This fruit, in legend, was a favorite of Pele, and in volcano country failure to toss a handful of the best berries into one of the goddess's portals was to risk her wrath.

Another familiar is the wild strawberry, *Fragaria chiloensis*, a species also found from California to Chile. Migratory birds must have sown the first strawberry seeds in the Hawaiian mountains, perhaps not very long ago in evolutionary time. The red fruit of the native strawberry distinguishes this plant from an introduced white-fruited variety that has gone wild in comparable habitats ranging from clearings in dry or mesic mountain forests to the alpine zone. Early explorers of the Hawaiian highlands such as the botanist David Douglas characterized the alpine heath of Mauna Kea as carpeted with wild strawberry plants.[12]

The Hawaiian raspberry, called *akala (Rubus hawaiiensis)* is remarkable for its virtual lack of thorns—only rarely is a plant found with thorny canes—and for the size of its fruit. Berries nearly two inches long can be found; in the nineteenth century they were sometimes described as the size of a hen's egg (perhaps that variety has vanished). Despite their luscious look and juiciness, these raspberries have a flavor that ranges from flat to bitter.

Of the three berry plants, the *ohelo* is the most widespread, and the *akala* perhaps the most endangered, in particular by the rooting activities of mountain pigs. An indication of the past vegetational glory of Hawaii's alpine heathlands was recorded by George Washington Bates in June 1853, when he hiked to the summit of Mauna Kea. High on sunny slopes above the Hamakua forests, he found "immense beds of strawberries" and "immensely tall raspberry bushes with fruit of incredible size." All around were native birds, including many Hawaiian mountain geese (nene), eagerly feeding on this summer bounty. At night, Bates made his campfire with piles of withered silverswords.[13]

CLOUDLANDS FAUNA

Birds are certainly the most conspicuous of the native fauna of the dry mountain slopes. The Hawaiian goose, or nene *(Branta [Nesochen] sandwicensis)*, is a surprise in this habitat. Ornithologists generally agree that it evolved from the same stock as the Canada goose *(B. canadensis)*. The nene is smaller than most subspecies of its continental cousin and is also distinguishable by its prominent creamy yellow to brown pigmentation and peculiar furrowed feather tracts around the neck and head. Its calls in the thin mountain air have a higher pitch than those of its congener, heard every spring and fall on North American flyways. In adapting to life on the rough, lava-floored heath, far from marshes and ponds, the nene's feet have lost some of their webbing.

Now the state bird of Hawaii, the nene's wild populations add up to a few hundred birds on the Big Island, mostly in and around Hawaii Volcanoes National Park, and in Haleakala National Park on Maui. It is the last of several Hawaiian geese and gooselike birds that became extinct within the last 1,500 years. A majority of those other species, distributed variably on the main islands, were flightless or nearly so (see chapter 18). The nene, apparently a more recent evolutionary product and still a strong flier, survived the Polynesian transformation of the islands, but populations that must have numbered in the tens of thousands at the start of the nineteenth century were eventually reduced nearly to extinction.

Several other native birds typically inhabit the drier mountain slopes. Three of them are familiar to continental birders in the same sense that the nene is clearly identifiable as a goose. They are all endemic species: a crow *(Corvus tropicus)*, a hawk *(Buteo solitarius)*, and an owl *(Asio flammeus)*. The Hawaiians called them *alala, io*, and *pueo*, respectively. The *alala* is the most endangered. In fact, it is close to extinction in the wild. Found only on the leeward side of the Big Island, its habitat is the low to midelevation native forest, which itself is almost gone in this vast expanse of "cattle country." The Hawaiian crow is about the same size as North American crows. It differs in having a slight brownish cast to the wings, and some discriminating observers have claimed it otherwise lacks the glossy blackness of its American congeners. Its call is said to be softer and more musical than the raucous *"caw"* associated with the common crow *(C. brachyrynchos)* in the United States. One listener likened the sound to a blending of tones from a pair of reed pipes.[14] When the first Polynesians arrived, native crows existed on several of the main islands, including Oahu (see chapter 18). By European contact, these birds seem to have been extirpated everywhere but in West Hawaii. There, the *alala* was progressively displaced by the loss of its habitat and shot as a pest by ranchers and farmers who "made war on it" in the late nineteenth century.[15] Now the species is known to be susceptible to introduced avian malaria. There may be fewer than ten birds left in the wild. Captive breeding programs, begun in the 1970s, have met with difficulties, and now there may not be enough birds left alive to recoup.[16]

The Hawaiian hawk is a small buteo with a total length of fifteen to eighteen inches. Females average slightly larger than males. There are two color phases. Dark birds are mottled brown overall; the light phase exhibits brown above and a light gray underbody often streaked with brown. Although considered rare and restricted in its breeding to the Big Island, the hawk has been a better survivor than the crow. The *io* seems to prefer the drier mountain forests for nesting, which occurs to at least 6,000 feet,[17] but its foraging range covers virtually the entire island of Hawaii below treeline. Along the windward coast, from vantage points such as the Pololu Valley overlook, it can sometimes be seen hovering on the trades like a seabird. Occasionally it is seen as a straggler on other main islands of the chain. Perhaps it is this bird's wide acceptance of introduced prey species that has staved off extinction while its native ecosystem collapsed. Since at least the 1890s, ornithologists have reported finding remains of mice, rats, large spiders, praying mantises, mynahs and other birds, and even a crayfish—all introduced animals—along with various native prey in the stomachs of *io* specimens.[18]

The native owl has been far more successful in adapting to the human presence in the islands than either the crow or the hawk. *Pueo* breeds on all the main islands and is occasionally sighted in the NWHI, even on Kure Atoll,[19] where it must be an accidental visitor. *Pueo* ranges from garbage dumps to pristine native ecosystems, from sea level to at least 8,000 feet, and from rain forest to dry scrub and pastureland. It is a medium-sized owl, thirteen to seventeen inches in length, with buff- and brown-streaked or spotted plumage. Unlike most owls, it frequently forages in the daytime—a habit that probably lessens competition with the introduced barn owl *(Tyto alba)*, although at least some *pueo* also hunt at night. The barn owl can be instantly distinguished by its light-colored, heart-shaped face. Both owls are primarily rodent eaters; however this prey was not available to the *pueo* until the Polynesians arrived. The Hawaiian owl nests on the ground (judging from the few nests that have been discovered), and this suggests that a brooding bird holds its own against a prowling mongoose or feral cat. *Pueo* is sometimes seen in high, soaring flight, uncommon in owls, and on the Big Island this can make it difficult to distinguish from the Hawaiian hawk, which often flies in the same manner.

The remaining native birds of the dry cloudlands are not as conspicuous as those described above. Nor are they as familiar to visitors, for they lack close continental relatives. Four are honeycreepers (also now called Hawaiian finches), members of the endemic Drepanididae (or Drepanidinae). Although they are now primarily associated with wetforest habitat, these birds' greatest diversity, until Polynesian times, may well have been in much drier country (see chapter 18). Now, in the high remnants of the *mamane-naio* woodlands, several of these species are clinging to dying branches of an evolutionary tree millions of years old.

The *palila, Psittirostra* (or *Loxioides) bailleui*, is finchlike in general appearance, with a big bill and large yellow head and throat, brighter in males than females. Both sexes have grayish backs and lighter undersides. *Palila* feed largely on the seeds (beans) and flowers of the *mamane* tree; occasionally the birds have been seen consuming *naio* berries as well as fruits and seeds of a few other plants of the high cloudland forest. Although once common as low as 4,000 feet, this species has retreated upward with its unique and threatened habitat. Both bird and habitat are now restricted to a few areas on the slopes of Mauna Kea from about 7,000 feet to the treeline.

The *akepa (Loxops coccineus)*, historically common on most of the main islands, is probably extinct on Oahu and rare everywhere else. This small, colorful bird—the Big Island race features bright red-orange males and green and yellow females—once ranged over nearly the whole island of Hawaii from about 2,000 to 7,500 feet in elevation. Now it appears to be rare and confined to the upper part of this range in mesic to dry forest on Mauna Loa. This species has an unusual bill, short and tapering toward a point but with the tips twisted slightly in opposite directions. Several ornithologists have suggested that this is a feeding adaptation, for the *akepa* is a forager for insects in trees, where it appears to probe and twist apart bark, dried seeds, leaf buds, and leaves that have been curled or woven together by spiders and caterpillars. Occasionally the *akepa* has been observed sipping nectar from *ohia* and other flowers.

Another of the rarest of honeycreepers now is the curving-billed *akiapolaau (Hemignathus munroi)*, endemic to the Big Island. Actually only the upper mandible is curved, as well as elongated, while the lower is straight, stout, and only about half as long. This small, yellow-green bird is also primarily an insect eater, and treads in sure-footed style up and down tree trunks probing the bark for its hidden prey. Some eyewitness accounts make the long, curving upper mandible sound as flexible and strong as spring steel.[20] It is used sometimes as a twisting probe, sometimes as a hook to yank away pieces of loose bark. The lower mandible functions as an improbable axe. The bird has been seen, beak agape, delivering raps to trees that may be as audible as a woodpecker's. Grubs and other insect forms, disturbed by the vibration, may emerge to be snapped up, or the bird may extract them from their loosened woody refugia by using its long, thin, brushlike tongue. In the early twentieth century, the *akiapolaau* was still common and widely distributed from wet forests near Hilo to the dry *mamane-naio* zone around the island's great volcanic summits. Now this species is critically endangered in two tiny cloudland populations: one on Mauna Loa and one that overlaps the limited sheep-bitten range of the *palila* high on Mauna Kea.

Another species, the *amakihi (Loxops* [or *Hemignathus*] *virens),* is also found in this habitat. Similar in size and plumage to the *akiapolaau,* its beak is much shorter and nearly straight. Happily, the *amakihi* still ranges widely, from the wettest rain forests up to high, open slopes 9,000 or 10,000 feet above the sea. There are also races of *amakihi* on all the other main islands except Kahoolawe and Niihau. This is the second most abundant living honeycreeper (after the *apapane;* see chapter 14). The *amakihi* is primarily a nectar feeder, especially in *ohia* and *mamane* flowers. However, it also eats insects and spiders, and forages for flower nectar and even fruit juices of numerous introduced plants including bananas, passion fruit, and Jerusalem cherry *(Solanum pseudo-capsicum).* [21]

One other small native bird is frequently encountered in the high cloudland forest. It is the *elepaio (Chasiempis sandwichensis),* not a honeycreeper but a member of the family Muscicapidae, the old-world flycatchers. This species' russet coloration, trimmed with black and white, distinguishes it at a glance from its honeycreeper neighbors. Found on Kauai, Oahu, and Hawaii (and curiously not known on the other main islands), inhabiting wet environments and dry, the *elepaio* has been more tolerant of human-caused changes in its Hawaiian habitats than any other native forest bird. Although the *elepaio* nests as high as the *mamane-naio* zone, most of the present understanding of its natural history comes from observations in the wet to mesic forests at lower elevations (see chapter 14).

A few other native birds, such as the *omao, apapane,* and *iiwi,* reach the high country near treeline but are more characteristic of mideleva-tion forests of *koa* and *ohia* (see chapter 14). Perhaps the least expected denizen of these high, remote slopes is a seabird, the dark-rumped petrel, or *uau,* which nests in burrows above treeline on Maui and Hawaii (see chapter 9).

More secretive than the birds, and apparently a better survivor, is the Hawaiian native bat, *Lasiurus cinereus semotus,* a race of the American hoary bat. About the size of a mouse, with a 10- to 13-inch wingspan, the Hawaiian bat is an insect eater that roosts in trees. Observations of Hawaiian bats have come from sea level to over 13,000 feet, although

16.3 Cloudland birds: *Nene* (*Branta sandwicensis*) and *Palila* (*Psittirostra bailleui*).

this species seems to be most abundant below about 4,000 feet in dry to mesic environments. *L. cinereus* is found in areas of long-term human habitation as well as in wild country. The largest bat populations are on the Big Island, where they can almost always be seen during feeding flights at dusk in certain preferred locations, such as around Hilo Bay and in Waipio Valley. Native bats also occur on most of the other main islands, but there they are seen primarily between August and December, suggesting a possible migratory habit. The Hawaiian bat occupies a distinguished position as the only native land mammal in the archipelago. So far, at least on the Big Island, it seems to have adapted to changes wrought by humans in its surroundings.[22]

CHANGE COMES TO THE CLOUDLANDS

Prehistoric human impacts in these environs were generally slight. There were no permanent settlements above about 2,500 feet. On leeward slopes and in the high cloudlands, the climate was inimical to most Polynesian food crops. Surface water for irrigation was practically nonexistent. Aboriginal visits to these regions were primarily for religious or ceremonial purposes. For example, a large *heiau*, or temple, was built on the inland slope of Hualalai Volcano, under the vast shadows of both Mauna Kea and Mauna Loa. Its construction may have marked an early unification of the Big Island.[23] In Haleakala Crater on Maui, existing hiking trails follow traditional Hawaiian routes. One of them passes a deep fissure that reportedly was used for the ceremonial disposal of umbilical cords of noble-born Hawaiian infants.

Dryland vegetation, including most of the trees, saw moderate use by the Hawaiians. Above about 2,000 feet, however, the dry forests of *mamane, naio*, and the others must have been little disturbed by seekers after resources. The incidence of wildfire probably increased during the human tenure. Almost certainly, fire was a primary tool used by the Hawaiians to clear island lowlands for agriculture (see chapter 19), and at times conflagrations probably spread for miles into the uplands. It is possible that dry montane ecosystems on the Big Island, with its nearly continuous volcanic pyrotechnics, are better adapted to fire than counterparts on other islands, whose biotas are long past intense natural selection by fire. It would be interesting to look for differences in sensitivity to fire in the remaining native vegetation of Hawaii itself, vis-à-vis the other main islands.

One special natural resource that drew the Hawaiians to a site high on Mauna Kea was an extremely hard basalt, which archaeologists believe was probably the best source of rock for adz tools in the islands. Hawaiians apparently quarried this site since at least the fifteenth century. It extended over some nineteen square miles around the 11,000-foot level on the mountain and featured various excavation zones—where selected blocks were broken loose and rendered into manageable fragments—as well as workshops, shrines, and many living shelters.[24] Such intensive and prolonged human endeavor here may well have destroyed a fragile biota on the upper leeward part of the mountain. In particular, the highest Hawaiian forests of primeval *Dubautia* would have been cut for firewood for miles around the work zones. As the trees disappeared, so would have most of the associated plants and animals, such as two species of rail whose subfossil remains were discovered here recently.[25] Perhaps dozens of other species also became extinct before the first Western collectors reached the region. Even the climate on this barren rock shingle of today might have been less harsh if the region had been originally graced with trees and perhaps associated grasses and shrubs.

Birds constitute another resource that might have been exploited by the Hawaiians in upland zones. Special feathers for ceremonial garments and paraphernalia might have been the main focus of hunting expeditions here, rather than food, which was plentiful in lower zones. An exception to that speculation might have been upland hunting for flight-less species in their last retreats before prehistoric extinction. For ex-ample, as related by nineteenth-century Hawaiians, Haleakala Crater was a last-remembered habitat for a second *moho* (flightless rail), said to be slightly smaller than a chicken (and thus larger than the historically known species).[26] However, prehistoric hunting in the cloudlands did not greatly affect other less vulnerable species there, such as the nene and the delectable *uau*, the dark-rumped petrel. Both were found at modest elevations until after Western contact, when hunting began to take its toll of the nene, and feral dogs and the mongoose pushed the mountain-nesting seabird to its extreme altitudinal limits on Maui and Hawaii (see chapter 9).

In the dry montane ecosystem, human impacts intensified with the coming of the Westerners, and the nene goose was among the first wild resources exploited in this new age. Nene, which do not seem to have been greatly esteemed as food by the Hawaiians, were commonly traded as provender to the early explorers and later to whalers. Manifests of the British expeditions of Portlock and Dixon in 1786 and of Captain Douglas in 1789 list "mountain geese" among supplies taken aboard at Kohala and Kailua, Kona.[27]

Scientific interest in the nene had developed in England by the 1830s. The explorer and botanist David Douglas (reportedly in 1833 but prob-bly in 1834) sent a living pair of the birds to the Earl of Derby (Lord Stanley), a prominent zoological collector. Around this time, Mr. John Reeve of Honolulu sent another pair to Lord Stanley, who successfully bred the nene in England and read a paper on his observations of the captive birds to the Zoological Society of London.[28]

After midcentury, the numbers of nene declined precipitously. By 1920 there may have been as few as fifty birds on Hawaii, and perhaps none on Maui. New intensive efforts to propagate nene in captivity began in 1949. Since then, successful rearing programs in Hawaii, on the U.S. mainland, and once again in England have rescued the nene from ex-tinction. However, attempts since the 1960s to reestablish self-sustaining wild populations in Hawaii Volcanoes and Haleakala National Parks have met with little success. The big, handsome birds seen by visitors to both parks were most likely raised in pens; wildlife scientists who have studied the problem agree that only continued stocking of artificially reared birds is maintaining the wild populations—a few hundred on Hawaii and perhaps only a hundred or so on Maui.[29]

The main problems seem to be predation, especially by the mongoose, and, even more critically, a loss of native vegetation providing vital dietary requirements for the birds. Although adult birds are nesting in the wild, gosling mortality is terribly high. According to ornithologist Paul Banko and others who have studied the problem at Hawaii Volcanoes National Park, losses of young birds commonly reach 90 to 95 percent in the Kilauea area of the park, where nene bred abundantly in the nineteenth century. Hatchlings are primarily grass grazers, and park service researchers at Kilauea believe that most alien grasses now dominating the region do not properly nourish the birds. Moreover, nene nest mainly in the winter, and the cool, wet subalpine climate seems deleterious to the goslings. Virtually without exception, they lose weight steadily after hatching. If this continues for more than four days, they die.[30]

For some time, most Hawaii naturalists have doubted that the nene was primarily a bird of the highlands at least in the nesting season. Fossils with skeletal features identical to the living species have turned up at low elevations on Kauai and Molokai, where the nene was apparently extirpated before Captain Cook's time (see chapter 18). Most likely the species survived on Hawaii Island by virtue of the huge area of its habitat but became artificially concentrated at higher elevations by historic hunting pressure, introduced predators, and loss of lowland habitat, and is now largely unable to recolonize favorable low- to mid-slope breeding sites. It is possible that frequent fires in such zones during Hawaiian times actually enhanced nene habitat by encouraging native grasses where today alien vegetation often utterly chokes the seral landscapes and dry-forest understory.

The story of grasses in Hawaii is an important part of the overall saga of ecological change, especially in the cloudlands and drylands. Recent general references are available to provide an entry to the literature for those wishing to explore this topic beyond the brief summary here.[31] Native Hawaiians used grasses they found in the islands, especially *pili (Heteropogon contortus)*, for thatching and mats. They encouraged the growth of this bluish-green bunchgrass near their settlements, but after Western contact, introduced grass species began to spread—at first haphazardly, then with the purposeful assistance of ranchers. Native grasses were deemed poor pasturage for livestock, and so by about 1900 foreign grasses from all over the world were being seeded across vast leeward Hawaiian slopes, which already had been so drastically deforested. Parker Ranch was a leader in this remaking of an entire vegetational zone. After a period of lethargy, the ranch was spurred into the twentieth century by an energetic new manager, Alfred Carter, who expanded its holdings, modernized its operations, and imported new superior strains of livestock and forage plants. Carter introduced grasses and clovers from Africa, North America, Australia, and Britain.[32]

The alien grasses broadcast by the ranchers across their immense acreages had a head start that few introduced plants could match, and it is no wonder that species brought to Hawaii for their dense, pasture-forming habit of growth would come to dominate widely over native understory and heath plants. Among the worst of this competition in the drylands and cloudlands comes from fountain grass *(Pennisetum setaceum)*, Kikuyu grass *(P. clandestinum)*, guinea grass *(Panicum maximum)*, molasses grass *(Melinis minutiflora)*—all four from Africa— and European velvet grass *(Holcus lanatus).* Not only do these aggressive species form tall, thick tussocks and mats, shading and crowding out native plants, but they are also thought to inhibit adjacent vegetation by allelopathy, the underground release of chemical secretions that poison the roots of other plants.[33] Part of the legacy of Alfred Carter now constitutes an irony. He was a staunch defender of the nene; he drafted a bill in the 1907 territorial legislature to protect the birds even as he unwittingly introduced alien vegetation that would largely destroy their wild habitat.[34]

All the grasses named above are fire-adapted species. They quickly regenerate in the wake of a fire by sprouting from underground rhizomes. Except for Kikuyu grass, they burn fiercely, and molasses grass reportedly produces fires of exceptional heat. In a 1987 wildfire near Kipuka Nene in Hawaii Volcanoes National Park, where this grass crowded the understory at up to eleven tons per acre, tree trunks were completely burned through at the base while branches above were only singed.[35] In former times this burned-over area probably would have suffered little long-term damage to its trees, because the typically loosely clumped native understory would not have been able to support very intense fires.

As the ranchers expanded operations, along with their economically motivated introductions came others by choice and by chance, plants that became noxious weeds. Ranch-fostered disturbance of the land favored the spread of foreign scourges such as gorse, thistles, lantana, cactus, guava, and thimbleberry. The last named weed, a thorny vining shrub with insipid, raspberrylike fruit, became so threatening by 1912 that Alfred Carter was spending $2,000 per month to fight its spread in the Waimea region.[36] He won some local skirmishes with the plant, but today thimbleberry (with its hosts of foreign allies) is winning the war. It is now common on all major islands from sea level to as high as 4,000 feet.

Weeds such as thimbleberry, lantana, and guava took over largely on lower and middle slopes formerly occupied by native mesic forest. The drier regions to leeward from low to high elevations were invaded heavily by the new grasses. Livestock had prepared the ground for the alien plants by decades of eating and trampling the native vegetation. As detailed elsewhere in this book, cattle, goats, and pigs have been comprehensively destructive in various Hawaiian ecosystems. In the leeward cloudlands and drylands, sheep have proven to be an especially damaging force.

Sheep *(Ovis aries)* seem to have had a qualitatively different history from the other grazing species named above. Unlike the others, sheep were never very numerous in Hawaiian hinterlands until after large-scale ranching began in the latter half of the nineteenth century. In 1873, Isabella Bird visited a remote sheep station at Kalaieha on the southern flank of Mauna Kea, overlooking Hawaii's central saddle region. About 9,000 sheep were then being herded in the vicinity.[37] Around this time, too, large sheep ranches had begun operating on other islands including Lanai, Molokai, and Niihau. For a few decades, wool and mutton were in the ascendancy. Alfred Carter intensified sheep production on the Parker Ranch, where a flock of 18,000 was grazing by 1908. He acquired an additional 23,000 sheep in 1914.[38]

Sheep are especially noted for their turf-gnawing style of feeding. At ground level only stubble of the toughest introduced grasses would have been left in their wake. After the tender low growth was gone, sheep would have turned their attention to shrubs and trees. On Mauna Kea they became especially fond of the tender shoots and soft compound foliage of *mamane.*

Never as popular as the cattle business on the Big Island, sheep herding declined there in the decades after 1920. But sheep did not. Tens of thousands of feral sheep continued to roam the high saddle region and concentrated in the last great sweep of upper dryland forest on southwest Mauna Kea. By 1950, fencing and eradication programs had finally reduced their numbers to an estimated few hundred.[39] However, much of the native woodland of *mamane-naio,* rare mints, and honeycreepers had already been devastated by the large, uncontrolled flocks.

Then, in a significant change of perspective regarding natural resources, the feral sheep were accorded governmental protection as a big game animal. Sport hunting, which had all but wiped out native game such as the nene and *koloa* duck, was again in the ascendancy. For five years beginning in 1950, a closed hunting season applied to the wild Mauna Kea sheep, and they responded by a rapid increase in numbers to several thousand.[40]

As if to add insult to injury, in 1954, the first mouflon *(Ovis musimon),* wild bighorn mountain sheep native to Sardinia and Corsica, were brought to Hawaii by the territorial fish and game department. Some were released on Lanai, where they became established on dry, rocky western slopes; others were taken to the Big Island for captive interbreeding with domestic sheep. According to Hawaii mammalogist Quentin Tomich, the aim was to produce a robust trophy animal for big game hunting,[41] but there was a twinge of conscience concerning habitat degradation. It was hoped that hybrids of mouflon and domestic sheep would inherit the former's tendency to segregate widely in small bands. Ultimately, both hybrids and pure mouflon were released on Mauna Kea;

hybridization was seen to occur in the wild, but hybrids most often joined the large feral flocks, whose grazing razed the vegetation in wide, ragged swaths.

Despite alarming deterioration of the *mamane-naio* forests and mounting opposition from conservationists, the hunting lobby held sway into the 1980s. Ironically, the state of Hawaii represented the hunters in a series of lawsuits, defending first the wild sheep in general and finally the mouflon alone against the Sierra Club and others who were trying to save the Hawaiian montane ecosystem. The suits were entitled *Palila* v. *State of Hawaii*, since the contention was that the endangered bird *Loxioides bailleui*, which depends wholly on the *mamane-naio* woodland, was besieged by the sheep. After a century of relentless grazing, this habitat and the *palila's* range had receded by hundreds of square miles to their upper limits on Mauna Kea.[42]

Recreational hunting has been directly and indirectly detrimental to the nature of the cloudlands and drylands in many other instances. Perhaps better labeled as misguided than recreational, the shooting of Hawaiian crows, hawks, and owls when these birds were routinely classified as varmints decimated their populations. The importation of recognized game birds began in the midnineteenth century with two varieties of California quail *(Lophortyx californicus)*, followed by the ring-necked pheasant *(Phasianus colchicus)*. These birds ultimately became established on most of the main islands. Many of the early introductions seem to have been by upper-class landowners for stocking their private preserves. For example, the Robinson-Gays treated their 1890s guests to wild turkey shooting on their Koulu Valley lands on Kauai.[43]

Dozens of game bird species from all over the world—quails, partridges, francolins, chukars, pheasants, peacocks, turkeys, doves—were ultimately released in Hawaii, although only a few became established. By far the majority of these successful imports came in the 1950s and 1960s in a modern spate of enthusiasm for hunting. The enthusiasts, now led by bureaucrats in public agencies with responsibility for natural resources, focused on the *mamane-naio* zone as one of the most suitable habitats for many of these birds. However, in the neolithic ecological thinking of the time, the habitat needed "improvement." Recommended techniques included opening up the forest by bulldozing alleys and clearings among the trees to stimulate the weedy undergrowth that provides much of the forage for the alien game species. Even the active planting of foreign vegetation to replace native understory and heath plants was suggested in order to benefit the imported birds. These advisements came from Hawaii agencies such as the Territorial Board of Agriculture and Forestry,[44] and there was federal aid to assist implementation. It was still a formative period in the evolution of conservation in the islands. To be sure, soil, water, and wildlife were of great concern both in Hawaii and on the mainland. But the ethos of protecting resources and enhancing nature stopped short of valuing endemism, and the same basic thinking on reforestation, reclamation, and outdoor recreation applied from Appalachia to Mauna Kea.

On public lands—so-called Hawaiian forest reserves—the archaic, bulldozer-led school of outdoor recreation held sway until very recently. On some private ranches, the same insensitive treatment of rare and shrinking patches of endemic nature continues to be standard practice. The more remote Hawaiian cloudlands and drylands are no longer profitable places in which to raise livestock, but landowners today, who scrape away *kamaaina* species so that a few pheasants or partridges can scratch out a living, risk the condemnation of history. Because of such attitudes, the modern pace of destruction in the cloudlands and drylands has been even faster than that accomplished merely by the hordes of wild sheep, thus making for the maximum overall destruction of the native ecosystem.

The flight of an upland honeycreeper amid showers of yellow *mamane* blossoms, the wild call of an *alala*, the scents and colors and textures of native heath against vast slopes of rock—these have a standing in Hawaii no pheasant or mouflon or spray of alien grass will ever match. All the native plants and animals of the high Hawaiian mountains are diminishing in numbers, retreating upward toward the cold, bare summits and extinction. Halted tenuously only in the national parks and a few smaller refuges and preserves, this final retreat might be stopped and perhaps reversed in many other places by public and private concern.

Alpine Fire and Ice

The high ground of Hawaii is magnificently crowned by two volcanic summits nearly 14,000 feet above the sea. Both mountains are on the Big Island; they were named by the first Hawaiians some 1,500 years ago: Mauna Kea and Mauna Loa.

Mauna Kea means "white mountain." Presumably the name referred to the snow that sporadically mantles the peak from its 13,796-foot summit down sometimes for thousands of feet. Snow is possible at any time of year on the mountain but appears most often from late fall to early spring. During the last ice age, Mauna Kea was ice capped year round. At its greatest extent, this permanent snow and ice covered twenty-eight square miles and had an estimated maximum thickness of 350 feet. Glacial lobes extended the edges of the ice cap below the 11,000-foot level in several areas. Terminal moraines, those piles of fractured rock transported by the flowing ice and accumulated wherever glaciers pause for lengthy periods, are in evidence around much of the mountain.[1]

Mauna Kea is classified as volcanically dormant. The chemistry of its most recent lavas indicates a volcano of advancing age with a much diminished eruptive frequency but with considerable potential vigor. In fact, Mauna Kea has probably entered a phase in which eruptions are more explosive than those of younger Hawaiian-type volcanoes. The time of Mauna Kea's last eruption is uncertain, but was probably only a few thousand years ago. The volcano is almost certain to erupt again.

Mauna Loa was named for its shape. *Loa* means "long," "broad," or "great in size." Indeed, Mauna Loa is the most massive single mountain on earth, with an estimated volume of 10,000 cubic miles.[2] From a distance it looks like a huge, smooth dome, but to picture it all a viewer must, in the mind's eye, carry its long, gentle slopes outward and downward to some 16,000 feet below sea level. The shape of Mauna Loa derives from its frequent voluminous outpourings of lava. Two active rift zones and a huge summit caldera (Mokuaweoweo) are the foci of historic eruptions, averaging about once every four years; the most recent was in 1984. This pace of vulcanism is exceeded in Hawaii only by Kilauea, the smaller, separate shield volcano building on Mauna Loa's southern flank. Both are among the world's most active volcanoes.

Mauna Loa is 119 feet lower than Mauna Kea, but measured from their true bases on the deep seafloor, both are higher than Mount Everest. The summit of Mauna Loa lies in a partial precipitation shadow, to the southwest, or leeward of its giant older neighbor, and rarely receives as much snow. There is no indication of former glacial action on Mauna Loa. Frequent eruptions may have prevented the buildup of permanent snowfields even in the Pleistocene.

Today's climate on both summits is harsh. Subfreezing temperatures occur nightly. Permafrost is commonly found a few inches below the surface of porous rock or volcanic ash. However, despite sporadic snow and icy rain, the total annual precipitation on top of Mauna Kea and Mauna Loa averages less than twenty inches (in terms of rainfall).[3] These two great summits most often receive air that has been dehumidified by the tremendous discharges of moisture on lower windward slopes. Surprisingly, at the 13,100-foot elevation on Mauna Kea is a tiny permanent pond, Lake Waiau[4] (see also chapter 13).

In general, the weather in the highest Hawaiian regions may be less variable than that of the leeward cloudlands. The overall climate, biotic potential, and superficial appearance of the terrain are succinctly summed up in the lexicon of mountain environments. Around their summits, Mauna Kea and Mauna Loa are classified as alpine stone deserts.[*][5]

Despite minimal precipitation on the summits, statistics are misleading. Ferocious storms, actually blizzards of arctic intensity, do occur from time to time. High winds accompany such storms and also arrive less predictably out of clear air. On Mauna Kea, winds can exceed 100 mph, and gale-strength blows are common. Mauna Loa generally has somewhat less violent wind conditions. Recently, wind has been recognized as a vital ecological force here. The alpine stone desert of Hawaii has a small but unique suite of life forms with a food chain that depends on the wind.

The resident plants and animals here are easily overlooked. The plant life includes *Rhacomitrium lanuginosum,* a native moss, whose white, densely clustered branch tips make the plant resemble a tiny patch of snow. There are also native lichens of the genus *Lecanora,* which form small crusts clinging to rocks. Both kinds of plants grow only sparsely in sheltered places, such as shallow lava cracks, that trap small amounts of moisture. *Rhacomitrium* and *Lecanora* seem to be the most common plants of the summit regions of Mauna Kea and Mauna Loa. Recently, however, others have been discovered by University of Hawaii botanists.

Native animal life adapted to this difficult environment seems to be represented solely by arthropods: several insects and spiders and a tiny centipede. Most of these creatures range to the very mountaintops. Most of the time they shelter beneath boulders or in shallow layers of cinders above the permafrost. Such locations provide a modestly elevated humidity that is critical to life in this cold desert. The most unusual feature of this ecosystem, however, is the food chain, which has been drastically truncated. Nearly all the resident animals discovered here to date are predatory scavengers. They depend mainly on small insects, grounded and numb from the cold, having been blown by the wind upslope from richer life zones below.

This type of ecosystem has been called aeolian, in recognition of the wind's role as conveyor of its food resources. It is known on various high mountains around the world. In its classic form it occurs above the zones in which resident vegetation supports the food chain. At modest elevations in Hawaii, early successional biotas developing on recent lava flows amid older vegetated terrain were already known to be partially sustained by windborne fallout. The classic alpine aeolian system

---

[*]The term *alpine tundra* is also used, but is a poor descriptor owing to the paucity of plants.

was discovered only in the late 1970s on the summit of Mauna Kea.[6]

The Wekiu bug, named for Puu Wekiu, a cinder cone that forms the very summit of Mauna Kea, is perhaps the most unusual creature in this community. It is a small, flightless species named *Nysius* weikiucola. *Nysius* is a genus found worldwide. A number of other endemic *Nysius* species are known from lower elevations in Hawaii, where they all appear to be seed eaters. However, the Wekiu bug has evolved into a little carnivore. It roams the frigid rocky wastes seeking benumbed insects precipitated out of the wind. Such an adaptive shift may represent a rapid pace of evolution on this geologically youthful ground.

Sharing these environs and the imported food supply are two small, secretive spiders (family Linyphiidae), which build sheetlike webs beneath boulders, and a larger wolf spider (family Lycosidae). A favored microhabitat for both the spiders and the Wekiu bug seems to be the vicinity of large rocks, which by forming windbreaks appear to concentrate the fallout of airborne debris, including moribund insects.

Recent discoveries have added to the roster of native summit-area arthropods. A lichen-feeding moth in the genus *Agrotis,* a half-inch centipede in the genus *Lithobius,* and several mites are now known as denizens of the highest Hawaiian ecosystem. At this writing, most of these creatures are so new to science that they have not yet been assigned species names.

Perhaps the most unusual and astonishing life form discovered on the summit of Mauna Kea is not even classifiable in one of the major modern categories of life. Nevertheless, it has been assigned a scientific name at the generic and specific levels—*Kakabeckia barghoorniana*—and it appears to be the earth's oldest known living fossil. It was first observed in Wales in 1964. Then, during the late 1960s, soil samples from Mauna Kea were included in a search for organisms adapted to harsh environments. In those samples, and others from Alaska, Iceland, Japan, and a few additional locations, researchers found more living *Kakabeckia.* The only other traces of this life form had been discovered a few years before—as microfossils in the two-billion-year-old Gunflint formation of Ontario, Canada.[7]

The living form of *Kakabeckia* is a close stand-in for its ancient cousin, *K. umbellata.* The living organisms, which resemble cells, range between about 10 and 25 micrometers in diameter (a micrometer is one-thousandth of a millimeter). This is larger than most bacteria. In most views, *Kakabeckia* "cells" resemble tiny umbrellas with prominent spokes. In some there is a projecting stipe, or filament, possibly for attachment to a soil particle.

According to Sanford and Barbara Siegel of the University of Hawaii, who have closely observed living *Kakabeckia,* the umbrellalike forms do not appear to be present as such in the initial soil samples. The definitive

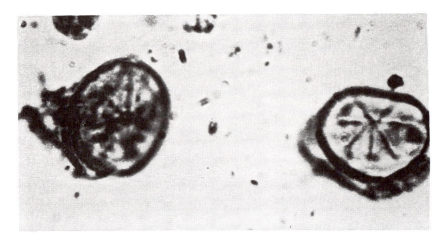

17.1   World's oldest living fossil, *Kakabeckia barghoorniana,* from soils on
Mauna Kea. Photomicrographs courtesy of Sanford Siegal.

organisms seem to grow or to appear by metamorphosis during incubation in the laboratory. They respond favorably to chemicals such as
ammonia and glucose, but have never developed the high population
densities characteristic of cultures of bacteria and algae. Most samples
have also proved thermally sensitive, generally requiring cool to subfreezing temperatures as found in soils of earth's midtemperate to arctic
regions. However, one type, or strain, isolated from Mauna Kea appeared
to be unique in tolerating a sultry 30 degrees Centigrade (86 degrees
Fahrenheit).[8]

The aeolian ecosystem has been better studied on Mauna Kea and
may be more developed there than on Mauna Loa. So far *Kakabeckia*
has not been found and fewer kinds of animals have been observed on
the latter's summit, although the Wekiu bug and a wolf spider species
are there. How long this system has persisted in alpine Hawaii, and how
it has changed over geological time, cannot be known. Presumably, the
spider, the Wekiu bug, and the others were displaced to somewhat lower
elevations during the ice ages and then recolonized upward. However,
so far it seems unlikely that many extinctions have occurred here as
a result of human actions.

A DEVELOPING FRONTIER

In prehistoric times, both the high summits must have remained virtually undisturbed, although Hawaiians probably explored all the way to
the mountaintops. High on Mauna Kea, in an area reaching beyond
12,000 feet, they found a hard, fine-grained basalt. For four centuries

they quarried this raw material as a source for superior stone tools (see chapter 16). It would be surprising if exploring parties had never reached the nearby summit in quests for additional resources. On Mauna Loa, visits to the summit might have been undertaken to appease the goddess Pele, whose wrath could bring fiery rivers down her mightiest mountain to destroy settlements on the east, south, and west coasts of the Big Island. By the time Westerners began to explore the islands, however, Hawaiian visits to the great summits must have been few and far between.

On Mauna Loa, the first European to reach the top was Archibald Menzies, naturalist with the expeditions of Captain George Vancouver. Menzies climbed Mauna Loa from Kau (the mountain's southern flank) in February 1794. Above the treeline, the Hawaiian guides leading his party became disoriented and largely disabled by the cold and altitude, and Menzies had to scout his own route to the summit.[9]

During more than a century and a half of scientific visitations, the aeolian ecosystem remained undiscovered. Above the alpine heath zone (at its highest on windward Mauna Kea, where silverswords were reported up to 12,000 feet by Western naturalists), both summits have always appeared barren. David Douglas in 1834 summarized this view. Atop Mauna Kea he noted "a death-like stillness . . . not an animal or insect to be seen . . . not a blade of grass." Douglas subsequently also climbed Mauna Loa, where, near the top, he found a dead hawk and a small bird so tame he was able to catch it in his hand. They were clearly out of place, for the explorer noted that "no other living creature met my view above the wooded region."[10]

George Washington Bates, who hiked up Mauna Kea in 1853, described the remains of other displaced animals near the summit. Around Lake Waiau, he observed "the bones of many a wild bullock were bleaching in the cold air."[11] Some of the animals obviously had died after becoming mired along the muddy lakeshore. Other bones were strewn on the "desolate plain." A number of later explorers also found remains of cattle, goats, and sheep in this region and speculated that these animals might have ascended the mountain to escape wild dogs or to find water during a prolonged drought. Whatever drove these animals to perish in the stony wilderness at the top of Hawaii, this improbable boneyard hinted at the huge numbers of the feral grazers that had built up in the vegetated belts below. One wonders about the polluting effect of giant carcasses in tiny Lake Waiau, which today harbors only two kinds of insects and some microscopic algae (see chapter 13).

Although they overlooked the native life forms and might well have failed to be inspired by them, the early explorers who struggled under primitive conditions to reach the high summits were invariably mightily impressed by the geology of Mauna Kea and Mauna Loa. Often, too, they remarked on the extreme purity of the air there and the outstanding views of the heavens at night. Today, these three aspects of science dominate human activity on the two mountaintops.

Geology is pursued on both Mauna Kea and Mauna Loa, but far more intensively on the latter. Since 1912, the U.S. Geological Survey has maintained its Hawaiian Volcano Observatory on the rim of Kilauea Caldera, but has since planted Mauna Loa to the very summit with seismometers, strain gauges, tiltmeters, and laser systems to measure crustal swelling and distortion, and the like. During eruptions, small swarms of geologists shuttle continuously from the observatory to the sites of blooming lava on the mountain, rummage and forage with technological appendages, and then return laden with samples.

Pure air is also pursued on Mauna Loa. For three decades, the high-altitude Mauna Loa Weather Observatory at 11,200 feet on the northern slope, has monitored the atmosphere, which is virtually untainted by local influences and thus represents widespread trends. In particular, the annual change in carbon dioxide content has been of interest, for this air far out in the central Pacific has shown a steadily increasing CO_2 concentration since the first measurements were made in 1958.[12] Atmospheric scientists generally interpret the Mauna Loa record as a harbinger of a developing worldwide greenhouse effect, the climatic warming caused by a buildup of gases that trap heat near the earth's surface.

The latest and fastest growing scientific activity in Hawaii is astronomy, and its major focus of development is on the summit of Mauna Kea. Haleakala, on Maui, has also been topped by facilities devoted to the space sciences, including some with military applications. Mauna Loa so far has only its weather station, located well below the summit. Unlike Mauna Loa, whose summit area is part of Hawaii Volcanoes National Park and remains a virtual wilderness, Mauna Kea now has an all-weather road to its peak. Observatories built by the United States, Canada, Great Britain, and France now stud the mountaintop, and several more are planned. The attraction of Mauna Kea is, in the astronomer's phrase, "the quality of the seeing." This attraction of clear, high-altitude, midocean air will persist. Lately, atmospheric clarity has diminished alarmingly on many continental mountains that have traditionally served as sites for astronomical observatories.

The University of Hawaii, a leader in the international astronomy community, has been given authority by the state to maintain and promote the summit region of Mauna Kea as a "science reserve." Besides astronomy, geology has been given some emphasis in this plan and there is a proposal to establish a natural area reserve around Lake Waiau. But so far very little interest or concern has accrued to the aeolian ecosystem.[13] This is unfortunate and narrow minded in a scientific sense. The aeolian ecosystem is a tiny fragment of Hawaii's living heritage, but its uniqueness is unquestioned. The adaptations of its creatures may even offer insights to space scientists who style themselves exobiologists, those interested in the possibilities of life beyond the earth. In a number of major ways,* the environment atop Mauna Kea represents an intermediate between more salubrious zones of the earth and the surface of Mars. Does the DNA of the Wekiu bug already contain genetic programs that are part of the way along the road to exoadaptations?

Conservationists cite overdevelopment of the summit area and the use of off-road vehicles as the greatest threats to the aeolian ecosystem. One recent proposal suggested that a total of thirteen large observatories could be crowded onto the summit by the end of the century.[14] There are now four, with one more under construction. According to entomologists Francis Howarth and Steve Montgomery, two of the discoverers of Mauna Kea's aeolian ecosystem, habitat disturbance is already eliminating the Wekiu bug and other summit arthropods. The inexcusable driving of trucks and jeeps off the roads of the "science reserve" is judged to be a prime cause in the disappearance of these creatures from apparently suitable habitat.[15] Recreational skiers now flock in growing numbers to the summit, and their vehicles may be causing most of the environmental damage. The University of Hawaii, however, must be responsible for controlling activities that threaten scientific values on the mountaintop.

There is a kind of symmetry between extremes in Hawaiian ecology represented by the highest summits and the twilight deeps, where the islands lose their identity and merge with the world's ocean floor. The life of both places is greatly thinned, and must adapt to extraordinary conditions and a food supply that originates in another realm. Both places are frontiers and so far have been less disturbed by humans than the zones in between. From the top of Hawaii to the bottom, the unique living edifice of these remote midocean environs is still threatened—in some places more than ever before. Ending this threat, even reversing some of the damage, is possible—again, more now than ever before. Saving what is left of the nature of Hawaii would be an act of responsible stewardship, of a mature resolve to care for the remaining diversity of life on earth, as human beings probe the deepest realms of the sea and the far reaches of space.

---

*Including reduced atmospheric pressure, strong ultraviolet irradiation, dry atmosphere with subsoil permafrost, high winds, and so on.

The Fate of the Living Land

18

Hawaii Before Man

Like a poorly charted landfall looming out of morning mists, a picture of primeval Hawaii is emerging from modern research in paleontology and other branches of geology along with archaeology and contemporary ecology. We now know that the familiar islands of the present were once very different places. This is certainly true of their shapes and structures, which have changed owing to local forces such as subsidence and erosion. Wholly extrinsic forces, too, such as the ebb and flow of faraway ice sheets, have drastically altered the sizes and shapes of the islands in the geological past. Maui Nui, with its sweeping lowlands, and the greatly expanded land areas in the NWHI were among the most recent examples of configurational differences in the archipelago. Even climate patterns were probably somewhat different on the main islands in ancient times. In particular, the once-forested leeward zones would have been less arid than today.

As related earlier in this book, most Hawaiian ecosystems have been greatly altered by human beings, and a loss of evidence has long hampered scientific elucidation of the earlier nature of the islands. Our understanding will never be complete, but very recent findings and insights have given us some striking and unanticipated images of Hawaii before people arrived in the islands.

In a very general way, we can imagine the pristine lowland habitats that have vanished—the varied forests occupying coastal plains, valleys, and ridges near the sea; the wetlands; and the estuaries where major streams came to the coast. On a gross topographic level, those places are still discernible, at least on maps. But in such areas we can now visibly detect only fragments of the former life of the land—for example, the scraps of native beach vegetation that have been missed by the bulldozers and off-road vehicles, and a few Hawaiian coastal trees smothered by alien species and nearing extinction in their last inland refugia (see chapter 11).

Few plant fossils have been discovered in the islands. This is especially true of macroscopic remains such as tree trunks and traces of foliage. A potential exception of great importance may lie with deposits of pollen and fern spores in Hawaiian bogs. Pollen grains and many kinds of spores are extremely resistant to decomposition; they form microfossils whose shapes and textures are recognizably different in virtually every kind of plant that produces them. As they accumulate layer by layer in lake bottoms and bogs, their relative abundance provides a

313

detailed record of the regional vegetation over thousands of years. From studies of core samples that penetrate down through the sediment and back in time, inferences can be made regarding climate change, forest succession, and plant extinctions and arrivals. Hawaiian bogs do hold such records. Samples taken forty years ago from Molokai contain abundant pollen along with fern spores and are being reinterpreted with the aid of modern dating techniques. One record may extend back 10,000 years.[1]

Significant findings of extinct insects, spiders, and similar land creatures are virtually nil. Ditto for freshwater animals such as fish and shrimp. So far, except for the promising pollen, preserved remains of only two kinds of Hawaiian land organisms—birds and snails—have been discovered in abundance. It is mainly through these guiding spirits that we may conjure images of the vanished Hawaiian ecosystems and the landscapes they occupied.

Of snails, deposits of centuries-old shells indicate that hundreds of species found suitable habitat in the coastal zones of the islands (see chapter 15). Ecological theory suggests that they must have been supported by a prodigious vegetational diversity. But it is the birds that open windows on more vivid scenes. Powerfully evoking our sensibilities of nature, they allow us to imagine the "benign Eden" that once prevailed along Hawaiian shores. Only in the 1970s did scientists begin to uncover massive evidence of a rich and unexpected fossil avifauna in the islands. This story is still unfolding, and more surprises are likely before the master Holocene bird list for the Hawaiian Islands is complete.

The first shock that triggered an avalanche of recent fossil discoveries was a chance finding on Molokai. In 1971, an amateur naturalist named Joan Aidem noticed a cluster of bones partly exposed in the face of a sand dune near Moomomi Beach on the northwestern side of the island. The bones constituted the remarkably intact skeleton of a large, unknown, flightless goose,[2] a fact confirmed after the bones had been forwarded via Honolulu's Bernice Bishop Museum to the Smithsonian Institution in Washington, D.C. This extinct bird, with its tiny wing structure and massive pelvis and leg bones, was named *Thambetochen chauliodous* (the generic name means "astonishing goose"). The excitement this find generated in a small group of professional and amateur paleontologists resulted in the discovery on several islands of tens of thousands of fossils belonging to more than three dozen species of Hawaiian birds new to science. They are summarized in table 18.1, based mainly on Olson and James.[3]

The remains of all of these birds have been found at low elevation (below about 2,500 feet); many of them ranged virtually to sea level. They filled the Hawaiian coastal forests with unknown calls and colors. Their relationships with their vanished ecosystems can only be dimly surmised. The big, landroving *Thambetochen* species and their relatives were probably grazers and browsers in fairly dry habitat; this ecological niche in continental situations is typically occupied by mammals, but in Hawaii it was for the birds and they have been less destructive of the vegetation than mammals. A hint supporting the latter speculation is that very few Hawaiian plants, including those of the drylands, possess thorns or other defenses against browsers.

The great geese would have had no significant predators except for the Hawaiian eagle, and must have dominated the wide lowland forests. The security of these birds before human domination of the islands is suggested by the finding of a huge egg on Molokai.[4] Probably attributable to *Thambetochen,* the egg indicates to Smithsonian avian expert Storrs Olson that, unlike typical geese and ducks, the ponderous Hawaiian birds produced only one chick at a time.

Among the strangest of the birds were the flightless ibises. Two species have become apparent from fossil discoveries to date. Both were restricted to the islands that constituted Maui Nui, and, given the geological ages of those islands, these species of *Apteribis* must have evolved in less than 2 million years. In skeletal anatomy they diverged remarkably from their tall, slender-legged ancestors. As their wings became diminutive and useless, the Hawaiian birds assumed a stocky stature, their stout leg bones having roughly the same proportions as those of New Zealand kiwis.[5] The discoverers of *Apteribis* speculate that these birds may have closely resembled kiwis in basic habits, feeding on insects obtained by fossicking and probing with their long bills in the leaf litter of the ancient island forests. Judging from where these birds' remains have been found, they ranged from relatively dry country on West Molokai to the lower wet forests of East Maui. Roaming this span in our mind's eye and ear, we may imagine a once-vast island alive with strange birds of unknown plumage and an unknowable dawn chorus that promulgated their undisputed rule of their sea-girt realm.

These birds, it would appear, were all restricted to the lowlands. If any did retreat upland ahead of the Polynesian agricultural transformation, they were poor survivors in the montane forests and became extinct or vanishingly rare by the time of Western contact. Memories of some of them, however, still may have been alive in 1823, when a Hawaiian informant told William Ellis that there had been an original *moa* in the islands.[6] *Moa* was a Polynesian word widely used for chickens, but it also referred to other large ground birds such as the various species of *Dinornis* in New Zealand. Those *moa* met the same fate as *Thambetochen* and the rest in Hawaii.

Side by side in the deposits with previously unknown Hawaiian birds have been found bones and beaks of many historically known species. Birds such as the *oo (Moho)* and *poo-uli (Melamprosops,* the rare new forest bird), which had been considered high-rain-forest species, were

TABLE 18.1: PREHISTORIC HAWAIIAN BIRDS
(believed extinct at European contact)

Classification	Site of Find	Remarks
Fam. Plataleidae (ibises)		
Apteribis glenos	Molokai	Both species of this endemic
Apteribis sp.	Maui	genus flightless.
Fam. Anatidae		
(ducks and geese)		
Branta sp.	Oahu	Related to existing nene.
Geochen rhuax	Hawaii	Another goose larger than the nene (flying ability uncertain).
Thambetochen chauliodous	Molokai	Large flightless goose.
Thambetochen sp.	Oahu	Apparently a second species of *Thambetochen*.
Other Anatidae		
Medium Kauai goose	Kauai	Apparently four distinct
Large Kauai goose	Kauai	species.
Supernumerary Oahu goose	Oahu	
Large Hawaii goose	Hawaii	
Fam. Accipitridae		
(hawks and eagles)		
Haliaeetus sp.	Oahu, Molokai	An endemic species of Hawaiian eagle.
Small Oahu hawk	Oahu	Distinct from surviving Hawaiian hawk (*Io*).
Fam. Rallidae (rails)		
Medium Kauai rail		All appear to be distinct
Medium-large Oahu rail		species; all were flightless.
Small Oahu rail		Two additional species of
Very small Molokai rail		flightless rails survived into
Larger Maui rail		the historic period, one on
Small Maui rail		Hawaii and one on Laysan
Large Hawaii rail		Island in the NWHI.
Fam. Strigidae (owls)		
Long-legged Kauai owl		Three related species of a
Long-legged Oahu owl		new endemic Hawaiian genus.
Long-legged Molokai owl		Not closely related to the existing *pueo*.
Fam. Corvidae (crows)		
Slender-billed *Corvus*	Oahu, Molokai	Both endemic species much larger than the existing
Deep-billed *Corvus*	Oahu	Hawaiian crow (*alala*).

Classification	Site of Find	Remarks
Fam. Meliphagidae (honeyeaters)		
Chaetoptila sp.	Oahu	This large *kioea* may have been distinct from *C. angustipluma,* known historically on the Big Island.
Fam. Drepanididae or Fringillidae—Drepanidinae, etc. (honeycreepers)		
Psittirostra sp. (small)	Molokai	Both finch-billed birds
Psittirostra sp. (medium)	Oahu, Kauai	resembling the Nihoa finch, *P. cantans.*
Psittirostra spp. Grosbeaks: Kauai species, Lesser Oahu species, Giant Oahu species		All three related to *P. kona,* recorded historically on the Big Island.
Other Prehistoric *Psittirostra*		
Ridge-billed finch	Oahu, Molokai	Unique variations in beak morphology set these fossil
Cone-billed finch	Kauai	species apart from all other
Additional Kauai finch		known finchlike
Additional Oahu finch		honeycreepers.
Additional Prehistoric honeycreepers		
Himatione sp.	Kauai, Molokai	May be identical to the *apapane.*
Ciridops sp.	Kauai	Three relatives of *C. anna,*
Ciridops sp.	Oahu	the Big Island's *ula- ai-hawane,*
Ciridops sp.	Molokai	which became extinct in the late nineteenth century.
Hoopoelike sickle bill	Kauai, Oahu	Nothing resembling these
Sickle-billed gaper	Oahu	birds is known from
Oahu icteridlike gaper		historical times.
Molokai icteridlike gaper		

Note: The interisland distribution of these birds still reflects more or less fortuitous fossil finds. In particular, the Big Island is thought to be greatly underrepresented in its primeval avifauna, and better focused searches of promising sites will almost certainly bring to light more species on that island.

18.1 Artist's reconstruction of pre-human scene on the Ewa Plain of Oahu, near Peal Harbor: *wiliwili* and *loulu* trees with associated shrubs. *Thambetochen* (flightless goose) in foreground. After Pratt and James and Olson.

once common in dry habitats not far above sea level. Such survivors of the former splendid lowland Hawaiian avifauna have progressively retreated into the cold, wet uplands that now retain the least disturbed native land ecosystems in the islands. But lately, ornithologists are becoming convinced that most of these remaining birds are in markedly suboptimal habitat, at the very edge of their survivable range. For most, there can be no return to the old avian Eden of the lower slopes, whose unsung forests have vanished, tempered climate has gone harsh, and songs now include those of deadly-disease-bearing mosquitoes.

Hawaii before human habitation also featured many more seabirds breeding in the main islands. Their fossils have been found in numerous coastal sites recently probed by paleontologists. One of the rarest species today—the dark-rumped petrel (see chapter 9)—was found abundantly at elevations near sea level on Oahu where this bird has not been recorded historically. Today the species is in extremis high on the dry slopes of Maui and Hawaii. Remains of the tiny Harcourt's storm petrel *(Oceanodroma castro),* whose Hawaiian breeding grounds are currently a mystery, were discovered in coastal sinkholes on Oahu. Adults and nestlings of the Bonin petrel *(Pterodroma hypoleuca)*, today an un-common breeder restricted to the NWHI, were common in one of the deposits on Molokai. At least one of the prehistoric seabird fossils of Hawaii appears to be a new species in the genus *Pterodroma*. Its remains were discovered in a flooded cavern near Barbers Point, Oahu.[7]

Fossils of the birds listed in this chapter are very recent; paleontologists commonly call them subfossils to indicate their lack of antiquity. Quite possibly, all these species greeted the first Polynesians to come ashore in the islands. An epidemic of extinctions followed, and before the arrival of Captain Cook a majority of the Hawaiian avifauna was gone. Many of the bird fossils were actually found in what archaeologists call cultural contexts—piles of bones in inhabited cave shelters and even left in place in ancient Hawaiian cooking hearths. Other sites clearly revealed native bird remains associated with the introduced Polynesian rat *(R. exulans)* and a small South Pacific land snail *(Lamellaxis)* that also accompanied the first human migrants.

Among the islands, Oahu has provided the richest assemblage of fossil birds to date, as well as some of the most telling evidence of their destruction by the Polynesians. By far, most of the discoveries on Oahu have come from the coastal plain near Barbers Point. This flat limestone land a few feet above sea level was a vast coral reef complex in bygone eons. Then, for tens of millennia up to the present, it became a relatively dry, Florida-like terrain, pockmarked here and there by channels and sinkholes created by the dissolving power of the natural slight acidity of rain and groundwater. Into the karst pits and holes, some of them as big as houses and some filled with fresh or brackish water, birds wandered and fell and died. In part, the remains of smaller birds may have been initially concentrated in owl pellets (found intact elsewhere, such as the Molokai sand dune sites). Later, Hawaiians found the more spacious pits with partial sheltering roofs useful for dwellings or storage bins for crops. Diverse middens of bird bones accumulated in some of those sites. One of the most productive of the Barbers Point sinkholes was found by accident when a bulldozer broke through a rocky domelike roof and almost tumbled into a natural cistern of clear brackish water. This cave was some thirty to forty feet in diameter and on the bottom, under about fifteen feet of water, were found several spectacular intact skeletons of an extinct deep-billed crow the size of a raven as well as the large Oahu *kioea*. Other specimens in the flooded cavern included dark-rumped petrels, an extinct owl, a flightless rail, and a thrush. Scientists who studied the cavern reasoned that water must have flooded it after the demise of those birds, leaving intact skeletons. Otherwise, the birds would have floated initially, and their bones would have reached the bottom in a scattered state; however, the exact manner in which the birds became entombed here is still a mystery.

Other locations on Oahu that have yielded fossil bird specimens in conjunction with prehistoric human occupation are coastal cave shelters near Hawaii Kai—the Kuliouou Shelter and an overhanging cliff at Hanauma Bay. In both, remains of now-rare seabirds are abundant in the middens among fish bones and marine mollusk shells. There is some circumstantial confirmation here that culinary selection was directed toward the dark-rumped petrel, Newell's shearwater, and the Bonin petrel. But also in the Kuliouou Shelter, among other land bird fossils, was a humerus of *Thambetochen,* indicating that only a geological yesterday has passed since these big, dodolike birds roamed the Hawaii Kai region.

Few radiocarbon dates (also called absolute dates by paleontologists) are available for the Hawaiian discoveries. The earliest date obtained so far places a *Thambetochen* specimen in the northwestern Molokai dunes some 25,000 years ago. The range of the dates associated with avian fossils on various islands, however, suggests that Hawaii's panoply of extinct and historically known birds lived through the changes in sea level and perhaps climate that accompanied the millennia of continental deglaciation.[8] However, when the rising sea inundated great expanses of the Hawaiian lowlands—resulting, for example, in the fragmentation of Maui Nui—many birds would have experienced sharpened competition for resources, and their populations would have declined. Perhaps this made them vulnerable, leaving them with a poor potential to survive in the face of any powerful new disturbance. The ultimate cataclysm for many species came with the establishment and expansion of Polynesians in the islands. Emerging scientific evidence confirms mass extinctions of birds in the centuries of that expansion. One radiocarbon date of 770 years before the present comes from charcoal in a hearth uncovered in a large Barbers Point sinkhole (labeled site 50-Oa-B6-22), which also contained bones of *Thambetochen* (although not in the hearth) and those of numerous other vanished birds. Some species found here may have been just missed by the early Western naturalists. Right at the surface, next to a Hawaiian wall, was an intact mandible of the giant Oahu grosbeak *(Psittirostra [Chloridops]).*[9] Another carbon date places human occupation of the Kuliouou Shelter, with its pickings of rare and extinct bird bones, at roughly 1,000 years ago.[10]

The fate of Hawaii's birds is only one index, albeit a conspicuous one, to the swift and massive degradation that overtook the islands' ecosystems in just a few centuries. Perhaps with refinements in research and the discovery of new repositories of fine-grained fossil material, such as pollen and insect parts preserved in the depths of Hawaiian bogs, new chapters in the prehuman natural history of Hawaii can be added. Today, only in a few places—on submerged flanks of the islands away from industrial coastal development, in high rain forests on rugged slopes, in remote lava-tube caves, in certain sections of Hawaii's national parks—can one have an essentially holistic encounter with primeval Hawaii. The rest, as we have seen in this and earlier chapters, has changed. Most of the change is permanent, and much of it represents a loss to Hawaii and the outside world that interacts with Hawaii. This loss can be measured partly in economic terms related to lost resources: soil fertility, fisheries, rare hardwoods, and so on. Partly it is a loss of endemism and distinctiveness—the erosion of Hawaiian essence. Before the arrival of the human species, Hawaii had a unique and magnificent living edifice composed of its birds, insects, plants, and other forms of life welded into irreproducible ecosystems. But the value of such things is a very modern perception. The first Polynesians to reach Hawaii may well have viewed the archipelago, whose land area far exceeded any territory their ancestors had inhabited for many centuries (New Zealand was a later discovery), with reverence and awe. However, they were far from being prehistoric conservationists and natural stewards of the land. This was an image of the Hawaiians that had been almost universally accepted by ecologists and anthropologists until the revelations in the 1970s on avian extinctions.[11] More recently, archaeological studies have focused intensively on the Hawaiian relationship to land and natural resources. Those findings, summarized in the next chapter, are proving that the Hawaiians were no different from any other people who began as determined pioneers and expanded their culture onto a yielding landscape.

19

Aina and Ahupuaa

If, as seems assured from modern Pacific archaeology, the first human colonizers of Hawaii were from the Marquesas Archipelago, some 2,500 miles to the southeast, their most probable route of discovery took them into Hawaiian latitudes east of the Big Island.[1] Anthropological and historical information regarding the Polynesians' mystical associations of prominent stars and islands leads us to believe they would have turned to sail down the trades to search for land under *Hokulea* (Arcturus), bright zenith star of Hawaii.

The time was between 200 and 500 AD.; that span represents the uncertainty and possible range of error in archaeological dates for the earliest known Hawaiian settlements. We may imagine a bright day and blue sea, boisterous with wind-tossed spray; one or more big double-hulled canoes with ponderous sails—*Pandanus* leaves woven in huge curving triangles mounted point downward—riding ahead of the easterly swell. After weeks on the empty ocean, the travelers must have been unspeakably awed by the sight of these immense unknown islands. Surely by such experience is a culture's sense of destiny confirmed.

Where they first landed is not known. Early sites of habitation have been found not only on the island of Hawaii, but also on Oahu and Molokai. The most attractive areas at first seem to have been big wind-ward valleys and coastal plains near the sea with ample fresh water— streams and marshes—close at hand. Remember that there were no mosquitoes—there was nothing at all that was noxious and a great deal that was supportive in the ecology of the land. The travelers had found a wilderness that was truly a paradise.

Initially, in small numbers they camped lightly on the land. Together with the sea, it provided a larder of great diversity. There were seafoods of every variety, never before fished by humans. The terrestrial counter-part to this rich and easy fishery was a largesse of tame lowland birds ranging in size up to the lumbering *Thambetochen,* which had never seen humans and must have stood like trees for the felling. Seabirds, too, would have nested underfoot and on well-stocked rocky shelves along the coast, requiring only a shopper's reach to secure enough for supper. Vegetable foods were definitely less diverse, although these Polynesians would have recognized most and probably consumed many of the pan-Pacific seaweeds that grow in Hawaii. While for a time the settlers must have missed their favorite sources of starch in taro, bananas, breadfruit, and sweet potato, they may well have eaten modest quan-tities of *Boerhavia (alena)* tubers, then probably abundant on sandy shores. Large stands of coastal *Pritchardia* may have supplied edible palm hearts. In the forests and uplands, there were at least a few edible plants (some may have become extinct before Captain Cook). Among those still extant are several kinds of hibiscus; large straplike sedges called *uki (Machaerina)* that have crisp bases like young celery; tree ferns with their abundant starchy pith; and the berry fruits: *ohelo, akala,* and Hawaiian strawberry.

As they were discovered by the early colonists, the aboriginal Hawai-ian forests were apparently poor in food plants, but did hold a wealth of materials for construction, cordage, and tools. Gradually more subtle uses of native plants and animals—for medicines, dyes, cosmetics, and so on—were found. And underlying it all was wonderfully fertile ground— lowlands of deep alluvium and untouched humus—and strongly, peren-nially flowing streams regulated by the runoff-retarding forest cover on the steep ridges. At first, the people must have become part of the nature of Hawaii, wedged into its ecosystems. For a short time their excess energies and wastes were undoubtedly absorbed, dissipated, and composted in the forests, marshlands, and coastal waters near their modest habitations.

The crop plants that the settlers brought from the South Pacific thrived in Hawaii. Starting with a few corms of taro and a handful of seedling sweet potatoes, a canoeload of settlers would have been self-sufficient in those crops in two or three years; with bananas, perhaps four or five years. Coconuts and breadfruit required more patience; a generation or more passed before they were available to the entire community. Mountain apples, started from seed, must have been eagerly awaited and relished first by the chiefs, as was the *awa,* the classic Polynesian narcotic and ceremonial beverage. Gradually, but at an accelerating pace, the transformation of settled areas proceeded. Much of the following account is based on recent studies summarized by Pacific archaeologist Patrick Kirch, who is responsible for a wealth of new information on the major environmental changes wrought by the early Hawaiians.[2]

Kirch has helped to develop a concept of transported landscapes that applies generally to high islands of the Pacific settled by Polynesians.[3] Wherever they went, these people brought the same suite of plants and animals, and altered and managed the land in much the same way. To early European explorers, the lowland terrain around native settlements on many of the islands they visited had an almost generic Polynesian appearance. Like other regional peoples, the islanders maintained a fairly fixed cultural image of efficient or proper or ideal physical surroundings, but they carried their concepts over an immense portion of the earth's surface.

As elsewhere in Polynesia, land in Hawaii was controlled in feudal fashion by a hierarchy of chiefs. Two general terms, *honua* and *aina,* applied to the land in general. *Honua* usually referred merely to the solid earth, as distinct from the ocean. *Aina* carried a connotation of human relationship to the land, and from it derived words such as *makaainana,* the commoner-farmer who was closest to the land, and *kamaaina* (literally, "child of the land"), meaning a native person of a given island or region.

The major political and economic divisions of land reflected the ranks of the Hawaiian chiefs. The largest jurisdiction was a whole island *(moku);* owing to its size, the Big Island was split into several *moku,* each governed by a chief of the highest rank called an *alii-ai-moku* ("chief who eats the island"). Each *moku* was divided into a large number of roughly wedge-shaped land sections called *ahupuaa,* which extended from the mountains out over the coastal bays and reefs to the deepening blue of the sea. On a perfectly circular volcanic island, these would have represented pie-shaped parcels that met at a point on the summit of the island. Each *ahupuaa* thus contained a variety of needed resources and was governed by a major chief who appointed overseers, tax collectors, and resource managers called *konohiki*. Lesser holdings within an *ahupuaa* apparently became common as island populations increased and society became more complex. Under this system, the Hawaiian commoners were akin to serfs.[4] In the last purely Hawaiian centuries before Captain Cook, they must have labored mightily to support proliferating social pyramids of chiefs and their retainers.

The results of their labor were everywhere noted, often with amazement, by the early explorers. Many of the changes in the land effected by this advanced Stone Age society are just being uncovered today, and with just as much amazement. Applying yardsticks of social and political complexity, Kirch argues that the term *civilization* is appropriate for the level of human development reached by the prehistoric Hawaiians. To this one could add, with a naturalist's regret, a crasser manifestation: the sheer magnitude of the transformation of land and destruction of native ecosystems by the Hawaiians made them the equal of any of their civilized contemporaries.

Certainly the greatest ecological impacts of the Polynesian era in the islands were related to deforestation. It began on windward shores, in particular in the well-watered valleys, such as Kahana and Maunawili on Oahu, Halawa on Molokai, and Waipio on Hawaii, which, according to recent archaeological evidence, were places that saw early bursts of population growth. In such initially fertile settings, after only two or three centuries, human fecundity could have produced thousands to crowd a major valley enclosing several square miles. Most of the common stresses, such as disease and climate, that retard population increase would not have had significant effects in Hawaii. More subtle ecological limits to population growth would then have come into play and might have finally matched the severity of a plague or glacial winter. Recent correlations of archaeological and geological findings on Oahu at Kahana Valley and near Kailua in the area of Kawainui Marsh suggest that spectacular erosion on surrounding steep terrain was the result of clearcutting or burning of forests for hillside agriculture very early in the Hawaiian period.[5]

Test corings through peaty soils at both sites reached a marine layer of coral and shell sediments just a few feet below the surface. Dates from these strata indicate that approximately 1,500 years ago, when the first Hawaiians arrived along this coast, Kahana Bay extended nearly a mile inland from its present shoreline, and Kawainui was an immense shallow lagoon that reached three or four miles back into the land from today's Kailua Beach. These great sheltered expanses of water, ranging from marine to brackish, probably teemed with inshore life. Fish populations from *nehu* to huge hunting jacks would have seemed limitless and child's play to catch.

Then, in what seems to have been a massive ecological reflex, the inshore bays were filled. Possible alternative explanations for the fate of Kahana and Kawainui and probably other bays on various islands—a several-foot drop in sea level, or a comparable unheaval of the land—cannot be sustained on the evidence. Sea level in general has not changed for several thousand years, and the buried seabed at both Oahu sites appears undisrupted except by its cover of alluvium, eroded from the surrounding hills.

If, as appears likely, the early Hawaiians were responsible for these catastrophic changes in local environments, with their accompanying losses of native ecosystems, one must wonder about the outcomes with respect to human ecology. Losses were twofold: marine resources of the bays were diminished and topsoil was lost from the hillsides. Hawaiian aquaculture, which was still being practiced during historical times in a few small pools and canals in Kawainui, may have partly made up for the loss of the inshore fishery. One archaeologist has suggested that the topsoil having slumped into the bay constituted an enhancement of the local environment's human-carrying capacity, creating more favorable ground for the growing of taro.[6] Still, the intermediate phases (over decades to centuries) of such unplanned resource shifts might have involved a severe combination of lost cultivable soil with a mud-polluted lagoon. We are far from having answers to such questions, but ongoing research may bring us closer to understanding what the Hawaiians did to the shallow bays of Kahana and Kawainui and how these actions affected their quality of life.

Most Hawaiians apparently stayed in the major windward valleys for centuries. Only a few of these wet locations, mainly on Oahu, have been studied by archaeologists. And while some of those sites provide evidence of nearly continous habitation, the populations seem to have grown extremely slowly, if at all,[7] during what may turn out to be a kind of Dark Age. Kirch terms this time, from 600 to 1100 A.D., the development period of Hawaiian prehistory. The dearth of archaeological information and scarcity of dated artifacts from most of these wet locations, however, permit speculation that a booming early population—resulting in the energies that could generate the evident massive erosion in the environs of Kawainui and Kahana—actually might have collapsed and remained suppressed for a time owing to a destruction of soil fertility and the siltation of nearshore reefs.

Resurgence and expansion came about via an agricultural renaissance. One of its most prominent features was the construction of massive irrigation projects in valleys, windward and leeward, that possessed permanent streams. Early Western visitors such as Vancouver marveled at

19.1 A landscape made over by Polynesians. Taro (*Colocasia esculenta*) paddies. State Archive Photo.

high-walled stone aqueducts carrying water along sheer canyon walls above Waimea, Kauai. Such sophisticated Hawaiian waterworks, whose remains are abundant in island valleys, were late developments. So far, none of these great Stone Age engineering projects have been dated from earlier than the fifteenth century. They were still being expanded at the time of Western contact, and remnants of them are kept in operation today in places such as Hanalei on Kauai, Keanae on Maui, and Waipio on the Big Island.

   The main crop grown in these systems of valley-bottom pondfields and tiers of flooded terraces extending up the sloping valley sides was the Polynesian staple, taro, most varieties of which grow best in very wet or paddy conditions. The general plan of construction for an irrigated taro farm began with stone-lined and -reinforced ditches that intercepted water upstream and led it along the sides of the valley well above the natural stream to sites where agricultural terraces were constructed. Extending downslope like enormous, ragged stone-faced stairsteps, the terraces were flooded by slow, controlled cascades of water from the ditches above. Closer to the coast, where valley floors widened, pondfields many acres in size were created by channeling streamflow into wide grids of parallel ditches.

   Among the greatest waterworks were those that served dry leeward coastal plains in the vicinity of Waimea on Kauai, Lahaina on Maui, and especially Honolulu. In those places, tremendous complexes of wet taro fields were combined with fish ponds that graded from fresh to marine as one approached the sea. Sources of fresh water were initially tapped far inland to serve upper-valley terrace systems, then partially reused again and again closer to the coast. Aided by the technology of irrigation, the expansion of Hawaiian populations into leeward valleys might have been expected to unleash new bouts of deforestation and consequent catastrophe. Evidence of this comes from Makaha Valley in western Oahu where archaeological investigation has implicated the removal of native forest above a system of terraces as a probable cause of disastrous avalanches that buried most of the agricultural complex.[8]

To what extent Hawaiian water projects altered the stream fauna itself will probably never be clearly understood. Whole streams do not appear to have been interdicted, as they were later, in postcontact times. At least during fairly high water, most of them probably remained coherent enough to permit the downstream flushing of spawn and upstream return of *oopu, opae,* and *hihiwai* to pristine habitat. If not, populations of those animals were obviously able to recolonize many much-used streams after the decline of Hawaiian rural populations in the early nineteenth century. Fishing pressure in certain streams may have been a much greater threat. Another question is whether any aboriginal stream life became extinct in the Hawaiian era. Careful examination of early valley middens might be revealing, but evidence would surely be scant.

The late prehistoric remaking of valleys all across the main archipelago (except for Niihau, Lanai, and Kahoolawe, which may have never had permanent streams) were arguably the most intensive ecological transformations wrought by the Hawaiians. After the start of what Kirch calls the expansion period (1100–1650 A.D.), for perhaps a century or two, population increase may have approached some maximum human potential. A doubling time of twenty or twenty-five years might have been easily achieved, although such estimates are still mere speculation. However, the fact that almost impossible-to-live-in places, such as tiny, boulder-filled Papalaua Valley (yet to be touched by an archaeologist) on Molokai's northeast coast, were once filled with Hawaiian gardens is mute testimony to the irresistible human forces that overwhelmed most of Hawaii's lowland ecosystems before the end of the prehistoric era.

Far more archaeological fieldwork has been done on drier leeward sides of the islands than in the wet windward valleys, and the ecological context of the research indicates that the lowland leeward ecosytems may have been destroyed faster and more comprehensively than any other in the Hawaiian era. This destruction came well after the initial windward phase of Hawaiian development, and nearly contemporaneously with the start of major works of valley irrigation. The leeward expansion of Hawaiian society that began to gain momentum during about the fourteenth century ultimately led to the wholesale deforestation of dry coastal plains and foothills noted in the early Western explorers' descriptions.

It is thought that the Hawaiians commonly relied on the use of fire to clear major tracts of land. Evidence comes from early eyewitnesses such as Vancouver, who reported the burning of lowland slopes near Waimea, Kauai.[9] Numerous later historical sources indicate that this was a common technique used to stimulate the growth of *pili* grass *(Heteropogon contortus)*, an endemic species widely used for thatching houses. For the earliest settlers, burning Hawaii's primeval forests was probably merely the most obvious and simplest way to convert land to agricultural use.

Regarding the fate of the coastal plains and lower slopes of southeastern Kauai and Niihau, as mentioned in chapter 11, the journals of Captain Cook and his officers are succinct: "We saw no wood. . . ." On Oahu, the barrenness of the leeward plains was taken for granted by the first naturalists to visit them, but archaeological evidence now reveals that even the driest areas near Barbers Point west of Pearl Harbor were forested when the Hawaiians arrived. Although they did not settle there in large numbers, they evidently destroyed a very productive ecosystem, most likely a vast, parklike dry forest. The best evidence for this is the diverse assemblage of fossil birds and snails (see chapter 18) that have been found in limestone sinkholes near the coast. By historic times, these dry plains were apparently still in a stage of slow successional recovery. They had become a seral shrubland dominated by *ilima* among a few other plants until ranching and industrially irrigated sugar cane took over in the late nineteenth century.

Of the major Hawaiian Islands, Maui has been the least explored by archaeologists. Yet aboriginal clearing of at least parts of the leeward slopes of Haleakala extended up to about 2,300 feet. Here, large villages and agricultural complexes within two traditional *ahupuaa* called Kipapa and Nakaohu have been explored. They were occupied beginning about 1300 A.D. According to Kirch, this area, with its thirty inches of annual rainfall, was probably a center for growing sweet potatoes[10]; apparently, irrigation was not feasible, which ruled out significant taro and banana production. Based on surficial evidence, which has yet to be thoroughly studied, by the middle of the second millennium there was widespread Hawaiian settlement of the South Haleakala region, and a wave of rapid ecological destruction is indicated by the discovery of fossils of several species of forest birds that once inhabited the region.[11] Most of these are extinct; a few, such as the *Poo-uli,* have retreated to a last stand high in the remote, cold rain forests to the east.

Maui's satellite island of Kahoolawe is now thought to have suffered the total destruction of its forests during an intensive phase of occupation from about 1400 to 1550 A.D. Plant remains traced to that era include *aiea,* sandalwood, and *alahee* trees, along with *Chenopodium* and *Nototrichium.*[12] The latter two are now usually seen as shrubs, but grow into small trees in remnants of climax-stage dry forest on the Big Island.[13] This Kahoolawe forest covered at least the high ground of the island, and the archaeologists believe the Hawaiians cleared these woodlands for sweet potato farming. Loss of the trees would have drastically altered Kahoolawe's climate and dried out the soils, and intensive cropping would have destroyed the land's fertility. A few decades after the last stands of trees were felled, the settlers were driven out by a desert of their own making. The island became a fishing outpost; European explorers viewing it two centuries later saw only barren, treeless terrain; they merely noted a few campfires along the shore at night.[14]

The island of Lanai and the southern shores and slopes of Molokai were in nearly the same shape by the time of Western contact. As HMS *Discovery* coasted along those shores in February 1779, just after the death of Captain Cook, the ship's surgeon, David Samwell, recorded that no trees were visible across entire leeward landscapes.[15] Dry-forest ecosystems, along with their fragile microclimates, had been all but destroyed, and massive runoff of silt may have adversely affected the great reefs that lie along major portions of both islands. Later, perhaps after partial recovery by the midnineteenth century, the drylands were found suitable for grazing (advancing erosion another notch), and finally, with a great focus of energy and importation of water and fertilizers, the much-abused land was made to grow crops again—sugar, pineapple, and others.

Even the vast island of Hawaii was noticeably transformed by the Polynesian agriculturalists. Again, a paucity of archaeological information is available about the wetter side of the island, although historical accounts from Captain Cook up to the descriptions of Isabella Bird indicate that large populations inhabited and transformed much of the coastal zone of the Big Island's windward districts. A prehistoric clearing of forest from the lower Hamakua slopes is also suggested by the observations of William Ellis and Titus Coan. But from recent studies, including numerous ground surveys and site excavations together with aerial mapping programs, the leeward districts of Kohala, Kona, and perhaps Kau have emerged as the most grandiose examples of prehistoric agricultural modification in the archipelago.[16]

Three major areas of West Hawaii were developed into intensively managed croplands (others are apparent in the southerly region of Kau, but have not been studied in any depth). These sprawling farms, made up of thousands of small, roughly rectangular fields bounded by stone walls, were all situated inland on the gently rising slopes. Overall, they ranged between about 500 and 2,500 feet in elevation. The largest such area of continous cropland is now called the Kona Field System. Extending along the slopes from approximately above Kailua to Honaunau (City of Refuge), it covered about fifty-five square miles. The crops were not irrigated, but supplementing the typical sweet potato staple of the drylands were bananas and taro. These flourished at the upper levels of the Kona Field System, because of the unique leeward climate regime of the Big Island, which brings more than 100 inches of annual rainfall to the central slopes of Hualalai Volcano. Other crops grown here included yams, gourds, breadfruit, mountain apple, and *wauke*—the paper mulberry tree. Sugar cane was also abundantly cultivated, and was especially planted along individual plot boundaries. As late as 1823, when William Ellis toured the Kona Field System, all of those crops still "flourished luxuriantly in every direction." He described a vast garden filling the countryside above Kailua-Kona, and he estimated he walked three or four miles inland before reaching the "thick woods" of the upper mountain slopes.[17]

The leeward slopes of Kohala on the northwestern end of the island were also developed as a huge agricultural continuum. The climate is drier than in Kona, and sweet potato was probably the main crop on the Kohala Field System, which covered an estimated twenty-two square miles. Inexplicably, the stone walls that delineate the Kohala System were built along the slopes parallel to its contours, while those in Kona ran up and down.

The third regional field system that has been investigated by archaeologists is smaller than the other two. It was constructed on the saddle plain near Waimea, headquarters of the historic Parker Ranch. The prehistoric Hawaiians in this region were able to partially irrigate the fields by diverting two local streams. Thus, certain varieties of taro, and even some bananas, which ethnobotanists have found in scattered wild patches, were cultivable here.[18] Still, at elevations approaching 3,000 feet, with exposure to mountain winds accompanied by prolonged chilly and cloudy spells of winter weather, yields of these tropical crops must have been small. Despite these developments, remnants of the forest cover on the Waimea Plain survived into the nineteenth century, although some of it may have been secondary growth of indeterminate age.

A sense of the *aina* near its peak of development in the last centuries before Western discovery can still be felt in West Hawaii. One of the best places for this is in the old *ahupuaa* of Lapakahi on Kohala's west side. Here, a coastal fishing village of the same name has been carefully restored. It is now a state monument open to visitors and provides a good illustration of the basic leeward pattern of settlement. All along this coast, from the ruins of numerous fishing communities, trails of water-worn stepping stones (which can still be found) led inland and upland to the even more populous habitations of the agricultural zones. In Kohala, the land between coastal and mountain villages, a strip some two miles wide, became an uninhabitable desert when its probably sparse trees were felled by the Hawaiians. Today, only a few desiccated *kiawe,* the desert mesquite from South America, and some hardy grasses survive on these heat-shimmering slopes.

From the coast at Lapakahi, in Hawaiian times, one probably could have seen workers in the vast field system, tiny figures far up against the cloudline. Today, their ancient handiwork is far more readily apparent than that in Kona, where several towns and numerous ranches, coffee farms, and residential subdivisions have disrupted the continuity. From the air above western Kohala, one perceives, especially with the lengthening of shadows near sunset, an incredible filigree on the naked land. It is those hundreds of miles of low walls, forming gridworks covering most of a mountainside, that convey so impressively the land-transforming energies of the prehistoric Hawaiians. Before there were walls there were primeval forests here, but they were obliterated before anyone could measure the loss.

Although deforestation was the paramount ecological impact during Polynesian tenure in Hawaii, serious supplementary effects probably came from the introduction of several new kinds of vertebrate animals and from *Homo sapiens'* role as a hunter in the islands. The animals purposefully transported in the big canoes of colonization were pigs, dogs, and chickens. Probably as stowaways amid the cargo, the tropical Pacific rat, *R. exulans,* and two kinds of small lizard also made the voyage to Hawaii.

Hawaiian pigs, with their ancestry in the South Pacific and Southeast Asia, were quite different from European and American stocks, which arrived much later. The original pigs in the islands were smaller, and, it seems, more docile and less prone to taking up a feral existence than those introduced in historic times. Captain Cook recorded that of the pigs received in trade in Hawaii in 1779, "we could seldom get any above fifty or sixty pounds weight."[19] A year earlier, he had presented a pair of English pigs to the inhabitants of Niihau. This was the first of many porcine introductions, and foreign breeds are thought to have replaced or genetically swamped the Polynesian strain.[20] Anecdotal accounts of the early Western explorers suggest that Hawaiian pigs were highly domesticated; they were not reported as frequenting remote or forested terrain. Feral pigs appear to have been very scarce until well into the nineteenth century. William Ellis in 1823 was one of the first to mention them, and said that, along with wild cattle, they were considered dangerous.[21] This description is hard to apply to the little pigs found by Cook, but it certainly fits the introduced feral boars that in Hawaii can weigh more than 500 pounds and closely resemble Eurasian strains, also introduced in North America. It may be permissible to speculate that away from lowland agricultural zones serious ecological damage by pigs did not begin in Hawaii until the appearance of large, aggressive, Western breeds.

Dogs brought by the early Hawaiians were also limited to a single breed that had accompanied the Polynesians on most of their successful colonizations of Pacific islands. This was described as short-legged and long-bodied, resembling a chubby dachshund except for its erect ears. By all accounts it was sluggish, kept not for hunting or protection, but for food. Like pigs, the so-called *poi* dogs were fattened primarily on vegetable foods. Unlike pigs, which were usually reserved for males of higher classes, dogs provided meat for commoners and women.[22] Feral dogs do not appear to have existed in Hawaii until the nineteenth century. Before that time, the Polynesian dog was perhaps a modest threat to flightless and ground-nesting birds close to Hawaiian settlements.

Rats of the Pacific area species, *Rattus exulans,* may have been far more damaging in Hawaiian ecosystems than the other animals brought by the Polynesians. Rat bones appear in early Hawaiian archaeological deposits and become more numerous with time. Judging from the known adaptability of these animals, they must have spread rapidly into the Hawaiian forests, and, like humans, probably found in these new ecosystems a paradise. As omnivores, rats would have found many new foods to their liking among Hawaii's endemic plants, insects, birds and their eggs, and perhaps land snails. The ability of mobs of *R. exulans* to kill large seabirds, including albatrosses (see chapter 9), suggests that predation by rats may have been a factor in the extinction of *Thambetochen* and other flightless terrestrial species in the islands. As fires set by the Polynesian settlers steadily consumed the lowland forests, many endemic species of plants and animals in their shrinking habitats may well have been finished off by rats.

Almost nothing is known of the ecological effects of the few other animal introductions of the Polynesians; chickens, two small lizards, and one or two small land snails round out the list. Of these, the first chickens in the islands, related to the jungle fowl of Southeast Asia, may have had some impact. They have occasionally gone wild and built up local populations, some of which have inhabited mid-level mountain forests for indefinite periods. Such a population has been thriving around Kokee State Park on Kauai for some time.

Major Polynesian plant introductions were detailed in chapter 11. Only one or two became noxious weeds of any standing in Hawaii. The most prominent example is shampoo ginger, but its invasion of native plant communities, restricted to moist lowlands, has been feeble compared to many of the *haole* imports.

The islands must have loomed immense and infinitely fruitful to the

Polynesian discoverers. But after a dozen centuries, limits to growth within a tropical Neolithic subsistence economy were probably approaching. Kirch cites evidence that major centers such as West Hawaii were losing population in the last century before the arrival of Captain Cook.[23] Part of the cause may well have been environmental degradation, soil desiccation, and erosion with loss of agricultural productivity—the apparent nemesis of the short-lived Kahoolawe community that peaked around 1550 A.D. and then went into precipitous decline. Archaeological evidence of warfare increases dramatically in the late Hawaiian period, but even that social illness may have been exacerbated by the diminishment of cultivable lands.

The Polynesians' crops generally were not adaptable to upland climates in Hawaii, so the Hawaiians made little or no attempt to establish farms or settlements above about 2,500 feet. Perhaps from their sweet potato stocks they could have selected varieties to grow at cooler elevations, and perhaps with such a staple and their skills at irrigation and landscape engineering they might have expanded their cultivated realm, but nothing of the sort happened. They could have been deterred by the upland climate and the dense mountain forests. And by the time they would have been served by such expansion, they had little time left. Outsiders were about to arrive who were expansionists with far greater engineering and agricultural powers in their service and who would not be deterred by cool climates and dense forests. In a century, they were to make over the Hawaiian Islands into a microcosm of the domesticated earth.

The Remaking of Eden

When the first Western explorers, naturalists, and clergy reached Hawaii, they noted the large, vigorous populations of Polynesians and were often amazed at the extent and intensity of the prehistoric transformation of the landscape. But from the start they recognized that a huge reservoir of fertility and potential for development remained untapped. A few of them were prophets. La Pérouse, at his anchorage off arid southwestern Haleakala in March 1786, mused that an engineered redistribution of Maui's water supply would greatly improve productivity in the leeward zones.[1] He had not seen Hawaiian irrigation projects but imagined operations on a much grander scale.

George Vancouver brought various livestock and crop plants to the islands between 1792 and 1794. Initially, he compared Hawaii's natural resources unfavorably to those of Tahiti. But his views soon changed, and he envisioned a future in which Hawaii would "render those abundant and excellent supplies . . . to maintain the commerce of north-west America" (at the time he was thinking of the fur trade). In particular, he was hopeful that "the breeds of black cattle, sheep, and goats already introduced, when established under such happy circumstances, would soon greatly increase."[2]

Urey Lisiansky, commander of the Russian expeditionary vessel *Neva*, anchored his ship for a few days at Kealakekua Bay in June 1804. Lisiansky was especially taken with the potential for wealth in the cultivation of the sugar cane he saw growing in scattered patches in Hawaiian field systems. However, he envisioned that the Hawaiians themselves would reap the profits from the fertility of their islands.[3]

The rising swell of Western ideas and technology was irresistible. First came new ways of warfare and weaponry, which led to a unified archipelago under the Kamehameha dynasty. This influx was closely followed by new economic imperatives that developed with the markets for sandalwood and whale products. The shifting political and economic climate was confirmed by the powerful nimbus of Christianity, and a tempest of change battered the islands. The new religion certainly helped to accelerate changes on the land, beginning with missionary acquiescence in the sandalwood slavery instituted by important chiefs. The Christian establishment also encouraged Americans and Europeans to settle permanently in the islands. Eventually, a number of church leaders or their scions, turned agriculturalists, proved more powerful than any of the earlier *alii* in transforming the Hawaiian environment. However, a certain irony can sometimes be glimpsed here. On first impression, the influential Pacific missionary William Ellis, among others, thought of Hawaii literally as an Eden: "We have often had occasion to notice with admiration the merciful and abundant provision which the God of nature has made for the comfort of these insulated people. . . . "[4] But right away, most newcomers, including the missionaries, saw ways to improve upon the Lord's as well as the Hawaiians' handiwork.

Thus appeared the two major, ground-level forces that devastated the endemic Hawaiian landscapes and biota in the historic period. One was an extension of the Polynesian planters' activities, which, as the stone adz gave way to the steel axe, began to reach ever higher into the mountain forest. Soon, industrial-scale deforestation was rampant;

whole mountainsides of *koa* were consumed by sawmills, and other areas clearcut for firewood as waves of sugar cane began to lap up over the mesic slopes. The second major land-transforming force was at least as powerful, even more widespread, and for a long time essentially uncontrollable: the grazing of millions of feral mammals. Except for the uncertain but perhaps light impact of the Polynesian pig, it was unprecedented in the islands. This chapter reviews and summarizes the development of these two forces, whose effects in a variety of ecosystems were alluded to in earlier chapters.

LIVESTOCK IN PARADISE

The feral animal problem developed first. An early voyager arriving at Kealakekua Bay in July 1796 described goats, cattle, sheep, and domestic ducks in abundance, especially goats and cattle, which would subsequently become the two most catholic consumers of the Hawaiian flora.[5] Goats had been the first ashore; two females and a male were left by Captain Cook on Niihau in early 1778. Those animals were killed by the Hawaiians in a dispute over ownership, but it has been suggested that others may have been landed on the Big Island by Cook's expedition shortly before the great navigator met his death a year later. Beginning with his 1792 voyage, Captain Vancouver presented goats to various Hawaiian chiefs, although at the time he noted that some were already being raised in West Hawaii. Vancouver also introduced cattle and sheep on his 1793 and 1794 voyages, but sheep had already reached Kauai in 1791, delivered by a Captain Colnett. The first horses arrived later—in 1803 on Maui and Hawaii, brought by a Captain Shaler (sometimes reported as Captain Cleveland).[6]

In the early nineteenth century, some livestock owners such as Anthony Allen of Oahu apparently maintained their animals in controlled herds, but this practice became the exception on the Hawaiian frontier. Allen must have been schooled in tidy Yankee farming methods. Improbably, he was a former black slave from Schenectady, New York. His Waikiki farm in the early 1820s was described as a model of efficiency, and already included a herd of several hundred goats, which he traded to whaleships and sandalwood freighters. A brisk business in goats was being conducted in 1822, when Allen was visited by the London missionaries Tyerman and Bennet. They reported that he had lately sold half his flock to ships' captains and was down to about 200 animals.[7]

Early controlled husbandry such as that practiced by Anthony Allen may actually have exacerbated the feral grazing problem by retarding the buildup of hunting pressure on wild livestock populations. Also, chiefs could declare a *kapu*, or ban, on hunting on lands they controlled. Following Vancouver's importation of several cattle on Hawaii in 1794, Kamehameha I released them on the slopes of Hualalai above Kailua Kona and placed such a *kapu* on them. Vancouver had demanded that the *kapu* last ten years; other sources suggest it lasted longer in some localities.[8] The beasts got a big head start and soon spread through most of the Big Island's forested uplands; a few were taken to other main islands. Then, for decades hooved hordes multiplied in an ungulate's paradise of fodder without thorns, toxins, distasteful substances, or other vegetative defenses that help prevent extinction in continental plants that have coevolved with grazers. For a long time there was little to slow the animals' relentless increase—no endemic disease, and only token predation by humans and wild dogs. At least until the turn of the next century, wild and semiwild livestock outnumbered humans in the islands by orders of magnitude.

Feral goats probably outpaced the cattle in their early rate of increase. In 1816, an expeditionary naturalist on Oahu observed modest herds of cattle near Honolulu, but noted that "goats seem to be more generally spread."[9] It appears well within the capacity of a population of goats, which commonly produce twins and sometimes triplets, to double every two years under benign environmental conditions. Thus, even allowing for modest general mortality from falling off cliffs, flash floods, eruptions, and the like, it is possible that after their first few decades of increase, the goat populations on several of the islands numbered in the millions.

Goats could also reach places inaccessible to cattle and humans, and this may have aided their early spread. The American missionary Hiram Bingham, on a visit to Kauai in 1824, saw them near Waimea. He reported, "goats grazing and bleating, and their kids frisking on the rocky cliff."[10] During the 1840s on Kauai, schoolteachers' salaries were paid with goats, and it may be an indication of the animals' abundance that the teachers were reportedly required to catch them.[11]

On Oahu, numerous herds of unconfined goats along with cattle continued to be seen on the Honolulu Plain and surrounding hills such as Punchbowl Crater for most of the nineteenth century.[12] The unseen goat population in the wilds of the Koolau and Waianae Ranges was probably astronomical. Goatskins became a significant export of the Hawaiian Kingdom. Available custom house statistics reveal that from the port of Honolulu between the 1840s and 1880s, an average of more than 50,000 goatskins were shipped yearly. This harvest built up quickly, reached high levels in the 1850s (1855 was a banner year with 103,700 skins reportedly shipped), and was then sustained for most of the period.[13] Undoubtedly, many more goats were killed than were recorded in the shipping manifests, and islands other than Oahu were probably just as heavily infested with goats, although records of their exploitation are not as complete as those from Honolulu. The numbers certainly suggest that Oahu suffered the presence of an enormous goat population unaffected by huge losses year after year. Reduced exports after the early 1880s may well have been due to diminished demand rather than supply. On several islands, two or three more decades of uncontrolled grazing by wild goats and cattle reduced whole mountainsides of native forests to a kind of tropical tundra.

By most accounts, wild cattle eventually outstripped goats in destructive force and perhaps even numbers. Hunting feral cattle in the mountains was a common occupation in the first half of the nineteenth century. Salted Hawaiian beef was an early staple on whaleships long before any semblance of organized ranching existed. It was gathered and traded by bullock hunters—Hawaiian mountain men who secured their meat either by shooting the wild steers outright or by trapping them in pitfalls, such as the one that claimed the life of the botanist David Douglas in 1834. John Palmer Parker, founder of the family dynasty from which emerged the huge Parker Ranch on the Big Island, got his start as "a genuine nimrod and a mighty hunter before the Lord."[14] The old man in midcentury was proud to show visitors such as George Washington Bates the rifle with which he had slain hundreds of wild bullocks. They were a trifling few out of the irresistible slow stampede that grazed away nearly every Hawaiian plant community in its path.

During these decades, residents and travelers in Hawaii commented increasingly on the abundance of wild cattle and on their damage to the mountain forests. In the 1850s, on the high slopes of Maui's Haleakala above Makawao were "endless bullock paths" amid groves of huge dead *koa* trees "rotting and bleaching like forsaken skeletons in the rain and sunbeams."[15] Great expanses of the Big Island were also browsed and trampled into grassland. In 1856, an anonymous observer wrote of the country surrounding Waimea,

> It is in the memory of many foreigners now living there, when the whole of those plains were covered with a thick wood, to the very edge of the slope. The clearing of the land has been almost entirely effected by cattle. At this moment they swarm in the thick jungle that covers the windward or eastern slope toward Hamakua. They are now gradually destroying this . . . for whilst the old trees die of age, no young ones are seen taking their places, as during the last thirty or forty years, the cattle have eaten or trodden them down.[16]

In the same article, the writer pointed to increasing desertification of the climate downslope from Waimea as a consequence of deforestation and laid primary blame on the cattle.

20.1   Logging operation in late nineteenth century, Kona forest. State Archive Photo.

Nearly twenty years later, Isabella Bird, exploring the Hamakua District, reported in her vivid prose the worsening onslaught of the herbivores:

> There are herds of wild goats, cattle, and pigs on the island, and they roam throughout this region, trampling, grubbing, and rending, grinding the bark of the old trees and eating up the young ones. This ravaging is threatening at no distant date to destroy the beauty and alter the climate of the mountainous region of Hawaii. The cattle are a hideous breed—all bones, hide, and horns.[17]

In her account, penned in 1873, Bird also described the slapdash cattle ranching evolving on Hawaii—breakneck droves of forty or fifty animals on precipitous country trails attended by "vaccheros," who seemed as wild and crazed as the steers they followed.

On West Molokai, according to the memoirs of *kamaaina* rancher George P. Cooke, cattle had destroyed the forests before the turn of the century and, until major fencing efforts were begun in 1898, were encroaching on the higher watersheds of the eastern half of the island.[18]

Photographs taken from the summit areas of central and western Molokai around this time show vistas utterly devoid of trees. One such photo captures the incredible barrenness of the southwest view from "Phallic Rock," an old basalt formation (now a tourist stop) near the summit cliff overlooking Kaulapapa Peninsula.[19] The place where the photographer stood is currently in a dense pinelike forest of introduced ironwood *(Casuarina)*, which, by producing toxic soil conditions for most other kinds of plants, confers another sort of barrenness.

On Molokai, too, local estimates of climate change correlate with the intensification of grazing during the second half of the nineteenth century. With warming and desiccation of the denuded slopes, the average elevation of the cloudline over upper portions of the island may have retreated hundreds of feet.[20] Gradually the cattle came under increasing control on rangelands, most of which had been created by the animals themselves. The magnitude of the losses of Hawaiian native flora and fauna resulting from ecosystem destruction by cattle is uncertain but probably immense. Although wide-area fencing of ranchlands brought former wild herds under nominal control, most accounts of the feral-grazing era attribute its denouement to organized drives and hunts in the 1920s and 1930s.[21] The reported roundup statistics of those times, however, seem to represent only fractions of the feral-livestock abundance of several decades earlier. Witness the huge, midnineteenth-century harvests of goats (see note 13), most of which were probably not managed on controlled pasture and were doubtless coextensive with wild populations in the mountain forests. It seems probable that by 1920 the populations of feral grazers were already in severe decline. In many areas their populations, like those of the Laysan and Lisiansky rabbits toward the end, may have been collapsing from drastic overgrazing of the most readily exploited habitat—namely, the former areas of dry and mesic forest. Certainly, the dust-bowl conditions that developed on several islands by the late nineteenth century, when in windy weather "the red flag flew" off leeward uplands, testifies to a near terminal state of devegetation.

Today, feral cattle are still seen occasionally on nominally protected wildlands. However, they are not considered as much of a threat as goats, which still roam ecologically sensitive areas in large numbers. Only a few years ago, before effective new fencing was erected, goats were rapidly consuming the rare silversword plants in Haleakala Crater. The problem is that Hawaii's native ecosystems have diminished so greatly in land area that a minor, local resurgence of goats has greater significance than ever before. Now, it is the wild landscapes that are found inside the fences.

While goats and cattle were surely the most damaging of the alien vertebrates loosed on Hawaiian ecosystems, a variety of others escaped or were released into the wild on various islands. Some of them founded large and often destructive populations that have persisted to the present. Others were only partially successful in adapting to the wild regions of the islands, or else were eventually brought under human control. Major examples include several mammals whose history in Hawaii has been ably summarized in separate reviews by Tomich and Kramer.[22] Their books and a handful of other sources provided the details for the following summaries.

European Pig (Sus scrofa). Various breeds of European pig were introduced on numerous occasions beginning with Captain Cook. Tomich suggests they may have genetically overwhelmed the smaller Polynesian strain through generations of hybridization, or else simply replaced it. Today, all Hawaiian pigs have predominantly European characteristics. Feral animals typically resemble a cosmopolitan strain of wild boar that has developed from introductions in a number of localities around the world, including the southeastern United States and California. These large (up to 500 pounds) omnivores are extremely destructive of Hawaiian native forests, including some of the wettest rain forests, where goats and cattle were never a serious threat. Wild pigs are said to rototill the landscape. In particular, they devastate understory; one of their favorite foods is the starchy pith of the giant *Cybotium* tree ferns. The pigs gnaw out the big fern trunks leaving cavities that fill with rainwater and often nurture thousands of mosquito larvae. Piggish activities in the understory can eventually change the whole character of the rain forest, for these animals introduce and spread aggressive alien plants such as guava and *Passiflora*, which can stifle even the dominant native canopy trees, *koa* and *ohia lehua*.

Domestic Sheep and Mouflon (Ovis aries and O. musimon). Unlike goats and cattle, domestic sheep apparently did not multiply greatly in the wild until well after the development of large-scale husbandry. Sheep ranching became important in the latter half of the nineteenth century on several islands. On Lanai, sheep constituted the first major industry. In 1864, a letter to Samuel Damon from Walter Murray Gibson, leader of the Mormon colony on Lanai and later a notorious figure in Hawaiian politics, spoke of the spring shearing of 2,300 sheep and the packing of some thousands of skins.[23] Later estimates of up to 50,000 sheep on Lanai are cited by Kramer. Lanai's sheep ranching era was the shortest-lived; it was over by about 1920.

The Sinclair family, emigrés from New Zealand who bought the island of Niihau from King Kamehameha V in 1864, brought a few sheep with them for breeding. By the early 1870s, there were 15,000 to 20,000 head on Niihua together with a rapidly growing cattle population.[24] Sheep ranching has continued on Niihau to the present. Herds of up to 30,000 animals have clearly exceeded the carrying capacity of the island and triggered recent disastrous incidents of overgrazing and stock reductions as years of drought have exacerbated the naturally dry climate.

Various breeds of domestic sheep have taken up a feral existence in dry Hawaiian uplands. Tomich suggests that their success in the wild is correlated with an absence of predators. During the nineteenth century, feral dogs (see below) on most of the main islands would have had a powerful controlling influence on the sheep. The vast expanse of suitable grazing habitat on the Big Island may have partially insulated sheep from such predation, but in the century after Captain Cook none of the islands saw wild sheep populations expand to match the numbers and impact of goats and cattle. In confrontations with packs of dogs, presumably, goats were more agile in escape and cattle were more formidable antagonists than sheep. Pigs may simply have been less accessible. Sheep were probably the prey of choice.

By about the 1920s, on the Big Island, feral sheep began to thrive on leeward Mauna Kea perhaps better than ever before as wild dog packs were significantly reduced by hunting and poisoning efforts on the sprawling ranches.[25] Then in 1954 came the wild European mouflon, foisted on tattered dryland landscapes by the Hawaii Division of Fish and Game in league with powerful hunting advocates. Some of these bighorn sheep were released on Lanai, where they became established on the rocky western slopes; others were taken to the Big Island, where they exacerbated the ecological damage being done by their feral congeners in the high central cloudlands inhabited by some of Hawaii's rarest native plants and birds. The presence of the sheep on Mauna Kea has been challenged under the law by environmental groups representing Hawaii's endemic wildlife. Two-time losers in the courts to the *palila* et al., the sheep, the hunters, and, inexcusably in an age of ecological enlightenment, the state of Hawaii have barely retreated and remain a threat to all that is truly Hawaiian on the slopes of Mauna Kea (see also chapter 16).

Horse (Equus caballus). Although horses were present on the islands in great abundance for most of the nineteenth century and into the twentieth, and although they were most often domiciled in the most casual manner, only occasional mention is made of horses having taken up a truly feral existence in Hawaiian hinterlands. Their impact as a herbivore in native ecosystems never seems to have approached that of cattle, goats, or pigs. However, their fondness for guava fruits may have aided the early spread of those weedy trees. Chemical erosion from passage through the digestive tract greatly enhances the germination potential of the hard-shelled guava seeds.

Around the 1820s, some two decades after the first horses arrived, donkeys *(E. asinus)* and mules (horse-donkey hybrids) began to appear in Hawaii. In our own time, they both have been seen in small numbers in the wild, primarily on the Big Island. A few of them, along with some uncontrolled horses, persist in the mountain lands of the larger Hawaiian ranches.

Axis Deer (Axis axis) and Mule Deer (Odocoileus hemionus). Brought to the islands from India as a gift to Kamehameha V, eight axis deer—five males and three females—were released on Molokai in 1868. They multiplied so abundantly and their herds were so destructive of vegetation by the turn of the century that professional hunters were hired in an attempt to bring them under control. Reportedly, hunters killed between three and four thousand deer on Molokai in a single year (1900 or 1901), but the deer population quickly recouped its losses.

Despite clear indications of their destructiveness to island ecosystems and watersheds, axis deer were introduced to Lanai in 1920 and eventually, with the backing of the hunters' lobby, to Maui in 1960. This species is now ranked by environmentalists as a major threat to the remaining native forests on all three of the islands named above. The growing population on Maui is spreading on the southwestern slopes of Haleakala, and is of special concern.[26] Ironically, the individual responsible for the initial importation of axis deer seems to have been Dr. William Hillebrand, the conservation-minded, botanizing physician who so eloquently lamented the destruction of Hawaiian forests by the likes of cattle and *pulu* gatherers.

Mule deer from Oregon were released on public lands of western Kauai in 1961 and again in 1962 and 1966. From the total importation of nine males and twenty-six females, a thriving population has established itself in a region of dry to mesic forest with highly significant stands of the rarest remaining native vegetation on the island. The insensitive mentality that fostered this herbivore's invasion of sensitive habitat is sure to be condemned in the future as awareness spreads regarding the value of the threatened Hawaiian life forms.

Pronghorn (Antilocapra americana). A pathetic story is told about this misguided introduction.[27] Thirty-eight pronghorns arrived on Lanai in December 1959, having been trapped in the wild and shipped from Montana. Twelve animals had died en route. Upon being released, the panicked survivors bolted all the way to the seashore where, apparently severely dehydrated and with no prior experience of the ocean, they drank seawater, probably worsening their dehydration. Some died on the beach. Some tried to swim out to sea. Stupefied and bewildered, many wandered into dense brush along the coast, where they became trapped—not surprisingly, given this species' dependence on completely open country. A number of them died in a tortured state, some with their eyes pierced by *kiawe* thorns. Within a month over half of the released animals were dead.

Subsequently, the surviving antelope established a small population that subsists marginally on the meager, eroded grasslands of northern Lanai. Like the mule deer on Kauai, a toy of state wildlife officials, the antelope population is occasionally sanctioned for brief bouts of hunting, which, on a few square miles of open range laced with jeep roads, can hardly be termed challenging.

Feral Dogs (Canis familiaris). From the absence of observations in the writings of the earliest Western explorers of Hawaii's wildlands, it appears that dogs did not form significant feral populations until the introduction of European breeds. However, during much of the nineteenth century, they seem to have roamed like wolves in the rugged mountain country of various of the main islands. For example, in the 1840s, they were common on the densely wooded flanks of Mauna Loa above Hilo. Titus Coan encountered them on a hiking expedition to an eruption site high on the volcano. Camped at night, Coan and his companions listened to wild dogs barking through the deep forest.[28] At this early date (1843), the Mauna Loa rain forest would have been an unlikely place for feral sheep, and one wonders what could have sustained these large predators here—wild pigs, perhaps. Flightless rails inhabited this region, and dogs might have greatly reduced the populations of those small ground birds, but one wonders if there also could have been larger flightless birds, their populations contracted into a last significant refugium in this difficult terrain. They would have been defenseless against dogs and could have disappeared in a decade or two without ever having been discovered by the few scientifically inclined Westerners on the island.

Wild dogs could be a threat to wilderness travelers, as revealed in heroic Victorian prose by George Washington Bates. In 1853, he was attacked on Maui by a pack of a dozen animals, "like so many hungry devils ready to pounce on my horse, or myself, or both of us together, casting at us their fiery glances and sending forth their Cereberean yells."[29] He finally managed to drive them away by throwing rocks.

Dogs in wild and semiwild packs now seem much less abundant than formerly. Control measures—poisoning and hunting—instituted primarily on private ranches early in this century have helped, but these animals are still a threat on public lands, especially to ground-nesting birds such as the Hawaiian owl, nene goose, and various seabirds.

Feral Cats (Felis catus). In warm climates, domestic cats seem to have a strong tendency to revert to the wild and have probably been significant feral predators on all the main islands for a long time. Tomich imagines that early in the postcontact period, ships' cats would have made novel gifts and items-in-trade. It is not clear whether cats were eaten by Hawaiians, as they apparently were by New Zealand's Maoris,[30] but they were acceptable as pets. Isabella Bird visited a family in remote

Waimanu Valley on Hawaii, which maintained "a whole tribe of amicable cats."[31] Feral cats are now known to range up to 7,000 feet in elevation on Maui and Hawaii. According to records cited by Tomich, they occur most often in fairly dry habitat, and have even been common at times on the island of Kahoolawe.

Confirmed as predators of birds, Hawaiian feral cats also subsist on mice, lizards, insects, centipedes, and scorpions. Native birds must be far less common in the diet of cats now than a century ago. Cats might have been a significant factor in exterminating various species, especially in the drier zones of the islands, but, because of the solitary, secretive habits of this predator, there are few historic records of its depredations.

Other Vertebrate Introductions. By design or accident, a few other foreign mammals have invaded the wild regions of various of the islands. As mentioned in earlier chapters, rats are suspected of having been among the worst despoilers of an arthropodan and avian Eden. The mongoose *(Herpestes auropunctatus),* introduced to control rats in sugar cane fields, has had a bad press almost from its arrival. These deceptively shy little predators were first released on windward Mauna Kea plantations in 1883; they were soon distributed to the other sugar-growing islands except for Kauai. As early as 1890, one account referred to the proliferation of the mongoose as a "plague."[32] Most of the conservation concern has focused on bird predation, and ground-nesting species—both native birds such as the nene and dark-rumped petrel and aliens such as the ring-necked pheasant—have been hard hit by the mongoose in some areas. However, current thinking is that forest birds nesting in trees have been little affected. Yet again, as a wide-spectrum carnivore, the mongoose may have been a significant force in the extermination of some of the native land snails and ground-dwelling insects.

Perhaps the least well-known mammalian introduction has been a kangaroo, the rock wallaby *(Petrogale penicillata).* A pair of these animals escaped on Oahu in 1916 and established a population that still persists in the mountains behind Honolulu.

Besides the mammals, many other vertebrate animals—marine and freshwater fishes; frogs and toads; freshwater turtles; lizards ranging from tiny skinks to a five-foot-long species of iguana; a small, secretive snake; and numerous birds—were brought to various of the islands and established wild populations (specific examples are noted in earlier chapters). Even today, laws governing the importation of live vertebrates are very uneven, and enforcement is often lax. "Bird pollution"[33] is highly evident and casually accepted by many people in Hawaii, while pandemonium breaks out over the escape of an occasional small boa constrictor smuggled into Honolulu, where it might thrive happily at the expense of the rat population. Foreign birds are certainly the most conspicuous of the vertebrate invaders. Released purposely or escaped from cages, they have spread widely. They have adapted primarily to the Hawaiian lowlands, thus replacing the vanished native birds there with an eclectic mix of temperate and tropical species. Alien birds in alien vegetation—in the flash of a century, they have swept in from all points like some wildly improbable founding event in which the components of a whole community arrive virtually at once. If evolution is able to continue in Hawaii, what will it sift and shape from this radical remaking of the islands' biota?

THE ASCENDANCE OF AGRICULTURE

The changes wrought by alien organisms entering the wild is one major part in this story of the remaking of many of the islands' landscapes and ecosystems that greeted Captain Cook. A second and often overlapping consumption of Hawaii's land and biotic heritage came with the development of large-scale agriculture, including livestock ranching.

Organized Hawaiian ranching was underway by the mid-1800s. The Mexican *vaqueros* observed by Isabella Bird had been brought to the islands to assist in small-scale roundups of feral cattle as early as the 1830s. They taught their skills to Hawaiians, many of whom became expert cowboys and today, after several generations, still call themselves *paniolos* (the term is a transliteration of *español*).

The Big Island is traditionally associated with ranching, and the cattle business is still important there in several locations. Molokai and Niihau, too, still maintain a semblance of ranching amid problems of overgrazing and epidemics of livestock disease. The heyday of the era, however, came between the late nineteenth and early twentieth centuries, when all the main Hawaiian Islands saw relatively large-scale efforts devoted to livestock production, chiefly on dry, leeward terrain. In xeric and mesic ecosystems, of course, it made no difference whether the grazers were fenced in or free to roam; after a couple of decades, the living Hawaiian essence of the land was utterly destroyed wherever the herds grazed in any numbers. The ranchers of that pioneering time intensified the destruction by clearcutting *kipukas* and seeding aggressive, smothering alien grasses (see chapter 16). Today, with the conservation of one of the world's rarest biotic assemblages at stake, some island ranchers still seem to be stuck in time—developmentally, not historically. No longer pioneers, they act like juvenile yahoos in their attitudes toward the land when, for example, they bulldoze native forest into miles of crude barriers that serve as cattle fencing.

In the modern era, more than half the land controlled by the state of Hawaii has been made available for grazing, mainly by cattle. Most of these lands are on the Big Island. Numerous complaints, controversies, and court battles brought by environmentalists concerning abuses by lessees on these lands suggest that stewardship by the state of its public land trust is uncaring and irresponsible. History may record that another breed of goat ranged widely in another kind of Hawaiian wilderness—the state and county bureaucrats dealing with public lands and natural resources.

On the islands of Maui, Oahu, and Kauai, large tracts of land that were initially managed (more or less) as ranches were eventually converted into sugar plantations. That transition began around the 1880s, when a surge of dry-land irrigation by massive stream diversions and artesian water projects led the way to an immensely profitable regreening of badly overgrazed Hawaiian hinterlands. The high-water mark of agricultural irrigation in the islands would not be reached for a few decades, but, just as irrigation technology seems to have led the Hawaiian expansion into the great leeward valleys on several islands in the late prehistoric period, so has this technological fix been a key factor in rejuvenating economic and population growth in modern Hawaii.

Sugar has been king of Hawaii's agriculture only since the mid-1800s, although crudely refined sugar products were produced in the first decade of that century. Early Chinese immigrants on several islands are generally credited with introducing sugar refining to Hawaii; the first of them reportedly operated a backyard sugar mill on Lanai in 1802.[34] A variety of sugar cane introduced by the Polynesians grew widely in the islands up to elevations of nearly 3,000 feet, and for much of the nineteenth century this was the industry's convenient choice, although eventually it gave way to other varieties imported from the Indo-Pacific region.

Don Francisco de Paula Marin, a pioneer horticulturist in the islands—as well as a commercial agent, translator, and minister of state for the early unified Hawaiian government—had begun producing small quantities of sugar in Honolulu by 1819.[35] Marin was a self-made individual from Spanish California who sailed with Captain John Kendrick, the fur trader and early sandalwood prospector. Marin became a resident of Hawaii in the mid-1790s.

Called Manini* by the Hawaiians, he built up major herds of various livestock on Oahu and introduced dozens of new plants to the islands. He also imported doves from California—these may have been the first introduced birds in Hawaii. Among his successes was the establishment of several kinds of fruit trees. He experimented with many crops, such as coffee and pineapples, that had been imported by others, and developed an experimental rice plantation more than a half-century before that crop became significant in Hawaiian agriculture. Marin is known

---

*This word is apparently the Hawaiian pronunciation of *Marin*. *Manini* also means stingy and may refer to Marin's style in business dealings.

above all for his elegant vineyard, reportedly a Honolulu showcase for Western visitors by 1815, the year he first made wine and drew off thirty-eight gallons.[36] Until his death in 1837, Marin's vintage was generally esteemed by his European and American guests.[37] His grapes were grown on ground that now lies beneath one of the busiest parts of downtown Honolulu, but the site is traceable from its namesake, Vineyard Boulevard, which runs along the approximate upland *(mauka)* border of Marin's old fruitful fields.

Marin was a leading figure in what amounted to the first Western-style agricultural community in Hawaii. This was a group of small farmers scattered through the area extending approximately from Pearl Harbor to Waikiki. The community included notables such as Anthony Allen. In 1825, another entrepreneur, John Wilkinson, established a small sugar and coffee plantation in Manoa Valley, where the University of Hawaii now stands.[38] There were still other farmers in the region whose names went unrecorded—perhaps they were withheld, since some of them were said to be escaped convicts from Botany Bay, Australia. The varied crops they grew and the livestock they raised were sold to whalers and sandalwood traders, exploring expeditions, and the growing Western establishment in Honolulu. These agricultural developments occurred on lands whose ecology was already grossly altered by previous Hawaiian use. Except, perhaps, for siltation in the Pearl Harbor area—an impact that may also have accrued to sandalwood cutting in the region—little environmental damage was probably felt. However, by the 1830s and 1840s, new theaters of agricultural development appeared, and Hawaiian nature became an antagonist easily mastered as the immigrant planters rapidly expanded their activities up into the native forests.

Kauai and Maui were first to feel the major thrusts of the new Hawaiian agriculture. Large-scale commercial production of sugar had its debut at Koloa near Kauai's southeast coast. The plantation there was begun in 1835 on land leased from local chiefs by Ladd and Company, a venturesome trio of young "solid men of Boston." Although by 1838, sugar production at Koloa reportedly reached 5,039 pounds, plus 400 gallons of molasses,[39] the operation went bankrupt a few years later. Koloa was the most ambitious agribusiness venture of its time. However, by 1840 there were more than twenty commercial sugar operations in the islands. Most of them raised cane on very small acreages; their milling facilities were crude and primarily powered by animals—oxen and mules driving turnstiles—and the sugar was coarse and impure. Given these drawbacks, and with periods of prolonged drought and poor market penetration, by 1857 the number of sugar plantations archipelago-wide had contracted to a competitive five.*

---

*One of them was Koloa Plantation, resurrected under new management.

However, during this time a considerable variety of crops competed with sugar for commercial prominence on various of the islands. Maui and Kauai were leaders in mixed agriculture as well as sugar, and some of the less well known crops held considerable sway in the economy even after sugar came indisputably to the fore in the 1860s.

Wheat. By 1861, 25,000 bushels were being produced annually at Makawao on Maui,[40] a temperate locality on Haleakala's western slope that has been a center of "truck farming" for nearly 150 years. Wheat soon faded, however, as a serious competitor for Hawaiian agricultural lands.

Potatoes. While the sweet potato, a Polynesian staple, continued to be a backyard cultivar throughout the islands, commercial concentrations of introduced Irish, or white, potatoes were established at a few sites, including Makawao. In 1856, Kawaihae on the Big Island was called the Irish potato capital of the islands.[41] The crops were grown in the cool mesic uplands in the old Hawaiian field systems, not down on the desiccated Kohala coast. The big market for potatoes was the whaling fleet.

Coffee. In midcentury, lush Hanalei Valley on Kauai was the coffee-growing center of the archipelago, although production was also advancing on Oahu, Maui, and Hawaii. At Hanalei, one ambitious planter named Titcomb had reportedly started 100,000 coffee trees by 1853. This came after the man had failed in an 1840s bid to start a large-scale production center for silk in the valley, complete with imported mulberry trees and silkworms from China. A number of sources around this time described Hanalei as a tropical garden of pineapples, peaches, oranges, and bananas, albeit dominated by coffee. Sugar and rice were also growing there in substantial acreages flanking the remaining taro patches of the dwindling native population.[42]

Cotton. The cotton industry in Hawaii, with small plantations on several islands, peaked around the time of the American Civil War. The district of Kau on the Big Island was touted for its cotton in 1862.[43] In 1864, an observer on Oahu recommended the northern coastal plains of that island as a good region for cotton farming,[44] but proposed expansions in the cotton crop never materialized. Today the Hawaiian native cotton, called *mao,* which was never used for commercial production, has been found to possess a useful genetic trait: it lacks so-called nectar glands on its leaves and, hence, is unattractive to many insects that plague the trade varieties of cotton. Modern cross-breeding techniques have begun to meld those useful Hawaiian genes into the world's commercial cotton crops, thereby reducing the use of expensive and environmentally damaging insecticides.

Tobacco. Introduced by early Western visitors, tobacco was a common Hawaiian commercial crop on modest acreages through much of the nineteenth century. Marin was perhaps the first commercial grower.

He raised tobacco near Honolulu, and the quality of his leaf was praised by the captain of a Russian warship in 1819.[45]

Rice. Cultivation of rice apparently began soon after 1800. A few immigrant Chinese raised it for their own use. Marin experimented with it, but significant commercial production was not evident until midcentury. In the 1860s, rice cultivation proliferated, and great expanses of old taro fields were put into production. In the 1880s, artesian wells and stream diversion allowed rice growers to utilize otherwise marginal areas. For a decade or two between centuries, rice was second only to sugar in importance as a Hawaiian crop, and its cultivation brought major ecological changes in wetlands and lowland streams (see chapter 13).

Pineapple. The pineapple, too, was a very early introduction. It was grown by Marin and others of his generation. However, even in the late nineteenth century pineapple fields were rarely more than two or three acres in size. The first irrigated pineapples were reportedly grown in Waiawa Valley on Oahu in 1893.[46] After 1903, some of the first twenty-acre homesteads deeded by the territory of Hawaii were put into pineapples; then a rapid rise in production, which quickly became overproduction, occurred during World War I. Advances in canning technology boosted the prospects of the pineapple industry in the 1920s. Production rose again, and the island of Lanai was dedicated to the spiky fruit at this time by the Dole Company. Production spluttered through the Depression, and then exploded in the late 1930s.[47]

THE END OF THE GROWING SEASON

There was a time in midcentury when, after land-law reforms (The Great *Mahele*) provided the impetus for rampant clearing of upland forests, the potential for Hawaiian agriculture seemed ordained by Providence. Like unmade gardens in a perpetual spring, the islands awaited intensive cultivation. Virtually no caveats had yet accrued to erosion and loss of watersheds; agricultural pests were only just beginning to be noticed. Western visitors were dazzled by the near-perfect climate, rich soils, and rapidly developing capabilities for business operations and transportation. In an era of pioneers taming difficult terrain in North America and elsewhere, Hawaii was seen as an uncommonly benign frontier, where

> With the right kind of men—thorough go-ahead Yankees, and a little capital, together with the right kind of governmental protection, the agricultural portions of the group could be rendered a terrestrial paradise.[48]

That perfectly modern statement was made in 1853, just as the first great industrial eruptions in agriculture were about to spring up and roll over the major islands.

20.2 Waves of sugar cane lapped the slopes. State Archive Photo.

There followed the scattering of seeds that would grow into a mighty wastage of resources and abuse of nature, for the environmentally ruinous development of modern-era Hawaii really got its start at this time (see especially the chapters on rain forests and fresh waters for details). After the midnineteenth century, it was a measure of Hawaii's natural fragility that destruction so rapidly became visible and a conservation movement, albeit skewed to the concerns of the era, appeared so soon. Crop pests such as the army worm and the awful "coffee blight" had become impossible to ignore by 1860. The latter was a scale insect or aphid, apparently introduced from Ceylon. Its outbreaks first devastated Kauai (Hanalei was particularly hard-hit) and later spread as far as Kona. It destroyed entire valleys of plantings, especially trees—and not only coffee but also citrus, guava, fig, *kukui,* and even native *koa,* among others.[49] One factor in the dominance of sugar, which dates from this time, may have been that it was largely unscathed by these early scourges.

Some of the strongest conservation sentiments of the era were expressed over losses of forest cover with consequent drastic soil erosion. Writing in 1884, the clergyman-naturalist J. M. Lydgate declared that the fate of Hawaii's forests was a perpetual shame to the tropics, a shame to the ranches and plantations that have sapped the vitality and beauty of the land for short-sighted and mercenary purposes, a shame to the shiftless councils of the nation that have dallied or bartered away the welfare of the country.[50]

Then, on the larger islands, came the vast influx of industrial irrigation, which, as noted above, provided a "fix." It allowed the wealthy agriculturalists to exploit remote water sources after uncontrolled grazing and other poor land-management practices had damaged the soils of formerly suitable growing areas.[51] The ultimate response to Lydgate's lament was a second kind of fix, the misguided forestry project engineered by Harold Lyon and his cohorts. Fortunately, Lyon's grand scheme to remake the mountain forests of the islands—that is, what remained of them in the 1920s—with alien weedy species did not reach full fruition.

The modern plantation era that began in the 1880s covered hundreds of square miles of the main islands with sugar cane, later joined by pineapple. Production of these mainstays in Hawaii's agricultural economy peaked around the 1960s.* Recent severe and steady decline has been experienced by both the sugar and pineapple industries in the islands. Hawaiian plantations have been going bankrupt, unable to compete with cheaply produced crops in the Third World tropics. A variety of lesser crops such as bananas, papaya, and macadamia nuts have become economically important only fairly recently, although all of them go back a long way. Bananas, of course, came with the Polynesians. Macadamias, a comparative latecomer, were being grown in Oahu's Makiki Valley behind Honolulu in the 1920s and may even have been planted by Marin a century earlier.[52]

Today, the lesser crops, too, are subject to intense competition in overseas markets. And they cannot take up the vast acreages formerly commanded by sugar and "pine." Big agriculture seems to be dying in Hawaii. It has gone over crests and troughs before, but this time may truly have reached doldrums where rescue and return are impossible. What new waves of change will appear to break over the coastal plains and low-elevation slopes, and how far will the run-up reach into the remaining endemic nature of Hawaii?

---

*The 1960s peak for all Hawaiian growing regions was about 300,000 acres in sugar and pineapples, or about 470 square miles.

21

The Wave of the Future

From the ocean to the mountaintops, Hawaii's less-disturbed environments and remaining native flora and fauna are national and, in many cases, world treasures. Only in the last few decades has there been a gradually growing awareness of Hawaii as a living museum of ecology containing many holdings of priceless evolutionary art. Today, despite such enlightenment, powerful developers and industrialists, with countless smaller commerical enterprises in their wake, are threatening Hawaiian nature in most of its last retreats. Outside of a few places in the islands—those under the protection of the federal government and a handful of private conservation organizations—this latest great surge of change is poised to sweep away or radically alter remaining Hawaiian ecosystems and extinguish much of their life.

Thus, the story of environmental destruction in Hawaii, detailed in earlier chapters, continues today and, in the quest for endless economic growth on finite islands, old themes repeat. The clearcutters and hydroelectricians continue to covet the native forests and wild valleys. But now they threaten last-of-a-kind places of natural heritage. New themes, too, are beginning to play. They may prove dirges for Hawaiian nearshore marine environments and the last undisturbed coastlines in the main islands as overfishing and massive resort development accelerate. Even the summit of Mauna Kea, with its fragile, other-worldly ecosystem, is being degraded, perhaps at a faster rate than any other habitat in the archipelago. Behind the scenes, the controlling forces remain unchanged. Despite a plethora of modern paper protections, the same attitudes govern in the "shiftless councils" lamented by Lydgate a century ago. Nearly everywhere in Hawaii, the dominant shade of green is the color of money, and environmental abuse in this mid-Pacific Eden continues apace.

With the potential to destroy Hawaiian nature under water as well as on land, the wave of the future has already appeared all along the main islands. From its immensely powerful and largely obscure base, formed of economic energies converging from around the Pacific, this wave is looming higher and higher and already spilling from parts of the crest. An exceptional area of turbulence represents the tourist industry together with a growing influx of affluent retirees from around the world. Other widening and agitated sectors of activity that may have major effects on the Hawaiian environment include proposed alternative-energy programs and potential new heavy industries. Future military activities in the islands may also prove inimical to Hawaiian nature in the sea and on the land.

Oahu has lost much of its nature already. Parts of the island have become as crowded and polluted as some of the most environmentally degraded regions of the continental United States. With more than 80 percent of the population of the state of Hawaii, Oahu's native land environments and biota are almost gone, and much of the island is in a rapid state of development and redevelopment. A so-called second city is slated to rise from now defunct sugar cane lands west of Pearl Harbor. Huge new resorts and condominium projects are planned for the last major undeveloped coasts such as Mokuleia and Queen's Beach near Makapuu Point. Future water supplies are uncertain; some current sources have already been poisoned with agricultural chemicals.[1] So far, all the official state and county* action to alleviate what promises to be a very stressful future for Oahu has only hastened the paving over of the island. Ever more housing developments are being built—which could help address an already critical shortage for low- and middle-income residents, but the projects are overwhelmingly designed for the affluent market. More highways and superhighways are appearing; one such is the controversial "interstate," known as H-3, which will pass through a wild valley with a swatch of endemic forest left in its uppermost reaches. More shopping centers, artificial tourist attractions, office buildings, parking garages, and the like invade the land—growth breeding growth in the classic pattern of terminal cancer.

Now the degradation has greatly accelerated in the shallow seas surrounding Oahu and on the reefs. Brand new threats to the reefs have surfaced—for example, the aquarium-trade fishery, which serves a seemingly insatiable demand in North America and Europe for the small, gemlike species of the coral rim. Regulations are slow to catch up with such innovations as the aquarium trade and commercial shell hunting, both especially intense around Oahu. Defenders of a laissez-faire policy toward these newest fisheries claim that their activities are less destructive to the reefs than a single hurricane would be.[2] The reasoning is flawed, however, because of the continuing, relentless activity of the fishermen—and also, of course, their obsession with certain species. If the price is right, extinction can result.

Perhaps the crucial question to ask those who call such impacts insignificant as compared to a hurricane is this: When will the combination of pressures from coastal dredging, legal and illegal fishing, and the massive removal of shells, aquarium specimens, algae, and so on become equivalent to a hurricane every year, every month, or every

*Local government on Oahu is administered by the City and County of Honolulu.

week? Hurricanes are rare in Hawaii. Those other forces are growing irresistibly. What will be their effects on the reefs next year or a decade from now?

Also largely concentrated on Oahu is the U.S. military, which has come under fire for alleged environmental damage. Most recently, the U.S. Navy has been implicated as a polluter of coastal waters with a variety of noxious materials, ranging from floating trash disposed of at sea southwest of the islands to leachates from antifouling hull paint, especially the new, wide-spectrum toxin and carcinogen called TBT (tri-butyl tin).[3] The navy's plastic wastes and other flotables return to Hawaiian shores with Kona weather conditions, and TBT is feared as a potential deadly contaminant of nearshore fisheries in and around such places as Kaneohe Bay and Pearl Harbor.

On several of the other major islands, growth is now even more rapid than on Oahu, although the population bases are much smaller on them. The pace and level of destruction of the remaining nature of Hawaii on the so-called neighor islands promise to be disproportionately high. This is partly because those islands harbor most of what is left of native ecosystems and biota and most of the quiet and least disturbed places, and partly because the scale of the projects in those little-visited places is often so large. What follows is a summary of the major kinds of environmental disturbance to watch on the neighbor islands.

HAWAII

The Big Island has the most variegated potential for development in the archipelago. In the middle and late 1980s, the fastest growing region has been the west coast of the Big Island. "Boom Days in Kona"[4] have dawned here with a feverish and rising spate of land speculation. This is where new massive resorts on the dry, rugged volcanic coastline north of the Keahole Airport have recently destroyed so many anchialine pools. Their golf links have been built with soil from mountain forests and tremendous infusions of fresh water for irrigation. Water is at a premium in this region; there are no surface streams. Tapping of hidden aquifers or a basal lens tends to remove pure water from the systems that serve anchialine pools. Bringing water in from more remote regions such as Waimea or the Hualalai highlands may deplete overall supplies for those regions owing to the city-sized volumes needed by the resorts. Then, having passed through the resorts, the water will lose its purity as it carries a polluting load of chemical excrescence from the golf courses, parking lots, and sewage treatment plants back into the water table and ultimately the nearshore sea. More and more of this is going to happen in the developing regions.

Development in Kona is rapidly spilling over into the neighboring district of Kohala to the north. More behemoth resorts are slated for the dry leeward coast here, and in the uplands, sprawling dude ranches are for sale. The latter subdivide hundreds of thousands of acres of the old Hawaiian field systems, so the losses to posterity there are not endemic animals and plants but something as precious to many—the roots of native Hawaiian culture.

High up in the central saddle region of the Big Island, between Mauna Kea and Mauna Loa, military use of the rough dryland country around Pohakuloa for infantry and artillery training has been blamed recently for ecological disturbance. Tanks rolling over the landscape here, explosions of ordnance, and bivouac activities by large numbers of soldiers cause obvious damage. In 1986, a state facility in this area for captive propagation of the critically endangered Hawaiian crow, the *alala,* was moved to Haleakala on Maui. Reportedly, the relocation was partly prompted by the crows' adverse reactions to the frequent noise of artillery. Ironically, however, it is also possible that this same noise and other disturbances may be helping to preserve the native vegetation in the region—rare mints and the Kau silversword, among others—by frightening off feral goats and sheep. Then again, on the Big Island and elsewhere, the military has been suspected of spreading alien weeds in remote zones and starting brush and forest fires.

So far, except for partially mechanized agriculture, the state of Hawaii has little that could be termed heavy industry. Small-scale tank farms and petroleum-handling facilities cluster around Honolulu International Airport and major military installations on Oahu. Public utilities are still of modest stature, even on Oahu. Since the late 1970s, however, proposals for one kind of large-scale "smokestack industry" have been taken very seriously by promoters, including private business interests and local, state, and federal government agencies. And the proposals have largely focused on the Big Island. The new industry would involve processing deep-sea manganese ores (mainly for their cobalt and nickel, two metals vital to the manufacture of high-strength steel). Prospects for the industry—both the mining itself, which would occur far from the islands on the flanks of Hawaiian seamounts and beyond (see chapter 4), and the processing, or refining, on land in Hawaii—have been envisioned in volumes of feasibility and environmental impact studies.[5]

Conservationists have begun to strongly oppose the siting of a cobalt-nickel refinery in the islands. Sites touted in the most recent studies are in the Puna or Kohala districts on the Big Island or at Barbers Point on Oahu. Processing plants designed to handle the deep-sea ores are huge. Based on currently favored designs, one such facility would cover hundreds of acres, with the majority of the land area devoted to leaching and tailings, or waste-treatment, ponds. This is especially worrisome on the earthquake-prone Big Island. If the sealing layers in the pond bottoms are ruptured, potentially toxic liquids would rapidly penetrate the porous terrain to the water table and then flow off in the hidden drainage toward the sea. Because the refineries would be built close to shore, where aquifers remain close to the surface, contaminants such as heavy metals and processing reagents could be taken up by plants' roots—perhaps leaving a swath of yellowing vegetation tracing the unseen drainage—and toxins also might emerge in shallow undersea springs, especially in the Puna region, where they are common.

Geothermal energy, wind energy, biomass conversion, solar (direct) conversion, and ocean-thermal energy are all subjects of intense research in Hawaii. Geothermal development is foremost among these proposed alternative methods for electrical generation. Its potential in the southeastern sector of the Big Island is believed vast and inexhaustible. Pilot programs on Kilauea's East Rift in the Puna District have demonstrated the ease of producing electricity from superheated steam released by drilling shallow wells into Pele's plumbing. Many other areas throughout the region could also be tapped by going deeper. Geothermal resources weigh heavily in the thinking of those who envision major industrial facilities, such as metallurgical refineries, on the Big Island.

Of course, building power plants right on top of the eruptive zone of the world's most active volcano is risky, and in the future any electricity put into service by such a system will require a large redundancy, or reserve, capacity. This might have to be in the form of a complete, standard backup capability to be maintained in constant readiness by the power utility. If, as planned, huge cables will carry geothermal electricity from Puna overland and undersea as far as Oahu, all the islands served may still have to hold onto their old, oil-fired power plants, with all the upkeep and expertise it takes to make them run. Risks associated with undersea power cables in Hawaii are probably high owing to the frequency of offshore earthquakes and landslides on the islands' underwater slopes. A bad break could take weeks to locate and repair. Ratepayers in Hawaii will find geothermal electricity no bargain.

Geothermal development has already threatened the nature of Hawaii. In 1981, the Campbell Estate proposed unrestricted drilling in pristine native rain forest located on Kilauea's East Rift adjacent to the national park boundary. The estate, a major Hawaiian landholder, manages its assets for the descendants of James Campbell, a nineteenth-century Scottish emigré and entrepreneur who made his fortune in the islands. Although owned by the estate, these East Rift lands, known as Kahaualea, had been designated as a conservation district in the 1960s. However, the powerful estate was able to persuade the Hawaii Board of Land and Natural Resources that conservation included the full use of the area's geothermal resources. In an opposing lawsuit, conservationists pointed to the massive abuse the project—with its five drilling sites, hundreds of wells, and more than twenty-nine miles of roads—would visit on this lovely *ohia*-canopied wilderness borderd by stark new lavas. Among other native species here was found a rare endemic fern, *Adenophorus periens,* perhaps now restricted as a breeding population to the Kahaualea site.[6] In addition, this area is one of the last habitats on the Big Island for the endangered honeycreeper called the *ou (Psittirostra psittacea).* The value of the whole native ecosystem here was strenuously defended by scientists studying the interactions between vulcanism and a naturally evolved landscape.

Late in 1982, the case was decided in favor of the developers, who were permitted to start test drilling and opening up the area. Their experts had even pooh-poohed the volcanic hazard to the project, estimating that a century would pass before any disturbance was likely to reach the sites planned for the actual power stations.[7] Then, within weeks, in January 1983, a massive series of eruptions began on the East Rift that have continued into the late 1980s, and within a year one of the projected power plant sites was buried under sixty feet of fresh lava. The conservationists and some native Hawaiians, the latter citing offense to their spiritual values, threatened to appeal the case, but Madame Pele's warning may have finally convinced the developers to retreat. In late 1985, the Campbell Estate traded its interest in Kahaualea to the state of Hawaii for state land downslope with a history of less frequent vulcanism and far less endemic biotic value. Then, in April 1987, Hawaii governor John Waihee officially designated the disputed 16,726 acres of rain forest at Kahaualea a natural area reserve, according it the state's highest status of protection from development. Further plans involve the state trading an especially lush parcel of 5,650 acres at Kahaualea (known as Tract 22) to the National Park Service—this area, directly adjoining the park boundary, is considered to have the highest endemic value.[8]

Campbell estate is free to develop the geothermal resources on its new piece of land closer to Hilo. Other groups are already drilling on the lower rift and have brought in several successful test wells. If ways are found to produce geothermal electricity with conventional backup or well-dispersed overproduction more cheaply than now seems possible, local threats to small rain-forest tracts in the 1980s may seem quaint indeed. Geothermal power production could become the key factor leading to virtually unlimited development—the ultimate conversion of Hawaii to an insular Los Angeles.

MAUI, LANAI, AND MOLOKAI

On the island of Maui, rampant development associated with tourism is proceeding in two major concentrations: one on the westernmost

21.1   New Hawaiian landform—the "world-class destination."

coast around the major resort centers of Lahaina and Kaanapali, and
one along the southwestern shore of Haleakala from Kihei to Makena.
In both areas, beautiful leeward coral reef ecosystems are threatened
with pollution and trampling by growing hordes of snorkelers and
divers. The area near Makena is especially sensitive. Resort construction
there is edging its way into a formerly rural coastal region featuring a
large and pristine state reef preserve and Maui's sole concentration of
anchialine pools. How pristine will these nominally protected places
remain as the new ease of access to the area opens it up to further com-
mercialism and vastly increased numbers of people, cars, and boats? The
fate of these coastal regions, with their fine, dry climate and once-quiet,
uncrowded beaches, is probably to resemble Waikiki on Oahu—another
great wall of resorts, no more Hawaiian than if they were in Mexico
or Singapore. Maui's natural heritage will recede in such places until
it is unrecognizable.

Elsewhere on the island, new threats have surfaced to tap the handful
of remaining undisturbed or little-disturbed streams for hydroelectric
power. In the eastern region around Hana and Kipahulu, there are still
numerous endemic values at upper elevations on the flank of Haleakala.

They include pristine native forests with rare birds and invertebrates, and streams rich in native life. Fossils of the outlandish Hawaiian flightless ibis have been found here in a lava-tube cave at an elevation of 1,400 feet. Furthermore, at lower elevations, there is a rich assemblage of Hawaiian prehistoric remains throughout this region awaiting the archaeologists.[9] No doubt much will be learned here, now that we know more about the aboriginal setting, regarding the early Hawaiians' interactions with nature and how they altered it. However, the Hana region is extremely attractive to developers. Old ranches and plantations in the area have been converting their acreages to home lots. So far, sales have been mainly to rich retirees and speculators, but all that is lacking is efficient transportation. The old, narrow, winding Hana Road, notorious in Hawaii for slow rural traffic, is now jammed by tourists' rental cars. But if the present tiny airport were enlarged, or if rapid, efficient ocean transit appeared on the scene, perhaps in the form of a new generation of hydrofoil or hovercraft, Hana could turn into a boom town overnight, and another rare part of the islands where glimpses of truly Hawaiian things still exist would be paved over.

Even on Lanai and Molokai, never historically prominent as tourist destinations, huge, upscale resorts are rising like new improbable landforms. Retirement and second-home communities are also planned, especially on Molokai. Both islands have major limitations in their freshwater resources, and during periods of natural drought, acute shortages may be felt. If the new, city-sized demands on water by major resorts merely tap the surplus that is no longer needed for irrigation for the dwindling agriculture on Lanai and Molokai, crises seem unlikely. But development of new water supplies may precipitate environmental problems. On Molokai, for example, a major aqueduct has long been proposed to carry water from the high, lush eastern half of the island to the low, arid western region. Previously, the main motivation was irrigated agriculture; now several new resorts have staked out the sunny western shoreline as prime tourist country. The danger is that drilling for water in East Molokai and siphoning away the vast volumes required could well deplete sources for major north-coast streams such as Wailau and Pelekunu, which retain some of the highest endemic riparian value in the islands.

KAUAI

The lush "Garden Isle" has major remnants of endemism in its wonderful, wet mountain forests and along its last roadless coast, the spectacular Na Pali. New proposals for hydropower loom as a formidable threat to the watersheds, directly to the streams and indirectly to the forests by allowing access roads into remote upper windward valleys. The threat to the Na Pali Coast is simply that it is being loved to death. Too many people by far camp in the valleys and pollute the streams that come down from high, pristine realms. The worst of the traffic now comes by motorboat—whole flotillas of inflatables in such numbers that they now sometimes produce a choking smog of engine exhaust in the great sea arches that are a feature of this coast. The arches are becoming as unsuitable for nesting noddies as an underpass on an urban freeway. This is an intolerable example of overtourism spoiling the remote areas that everyone treasures, that make the islands so special. Off road vehicles running over *ohai* and *mao* on the coastal shingle are abhorrent in proportion to one's education regarding Hawaiian nature, but a smog-filled sea arch on the Na Pali should bring groans even in the halls of the Hawaii Visitor's Bureau.

Of course, the appalling motorized exploitation of untrammeled places is not restricted to Kauai. Helicopter tours are invading all the formerly quiet places, spreading their infernal racket for miles, and the machines are often flown at dangerously low elevations. Fortunately, the National Park Service, prompted by a spate of crashes, which in the mid-1980s involved a number of fatalities, has begun to impose strict minimum-altitude regulations on overflights of the parks, and the state of Hawaii may follow the federal lead. However, the noise has not receded; in places such as Kauai's Na Pali Coast it is a nearly constant intrusive nuisance for people on the ground seeking experience of the real Hawaii. Tourist magazines are now filled with advertisements for both helicopter rides to view the Hawaiian wilderness and motorized trips into the back country by land and sea. Some of these ads feature photos of jeeps and ORVs being driven in valley streams and on remote beaches. One tour company clearly implies that the stream shown is used as the road into the interior.[10] This kind of abuse should border on criminal behavior in today's Hawaii.

DECADENCE AND DECLINE

The state of Hawaii and its separate counties* have seldom shown any real concern about protecting the living treasures of the islands. Although scientists and field managers in state agencies such as the Department of Land and Natural Resources typically deplore the tragic, near-terminal decline of Hawaii's nature, the attitudes of their high-echelon supervisors (at least until very recently) have often seemed to be rooted in

*Kauai County; Honolulu City and County (includes all of Oahu and the NWHI); Maui County (includes Maui, Molokai, Lanai, and Kahoolawe); and Hawaii County (the Big Island).

the nineteenth century. While renowned environmental planner Ian McHarg, on a visit to the islands in January 1987, praised Hawaii's current land-use laws as the most progressive in the nation,[11] it is clear that priceless endemism has been accorded little standing in the controlling legislation. For example, massive subdivisions have been allowed in last-of-a-kind ecosystems such as dry coastal forest in the Big Island's Puna District. Even given specifications in the law to recognize such tracts, it is unlikely they would be spared if a powerful, politically connected individual owned the land.

In their exhaustively researched recent book *Land and Power in Hawaii,*[12] George Cooper and Gavan Daws point out the massive corruption that has been the norm in Hawaiian land deals in the decades since statehood was achieved. An overwhelming majority of the state's recent political leaders have been enriched by land sales, which often exuded more than a whiff of conflict of interest. A peculiar irony has come out of a number of these deals worked by the state's politicians and their pals.[13] Lots in remote subdivisions such as Royal Gardens in Puna, with typically poor-quality roads and often without basic utilities, were bought on speculation, but few people actually built houses and settled them. Those who did frequently had illegal reasons for seeking the isolation and remoteness and camping-style privations. They were planting and harvesting marijuana by the ton—world-renowned as Puna Butter, Kona Gold, and Maui Wowee—grown on lands lately bereft of its venerable Hawaiian flora. The guerrilla agriculturists were getting as rich as the people who had sold them the land, while the latter were continually voting large sums from state and county treasuries for "Green Harvest" operations to cut down the groves of illicit crops for which they had cleared the way.

Throughout the main islands, the threat of overdevelopment is now most closely associated with tourism. New resort construction is at an all-time high, and the scale of individual projects is unprecedented. Some of the new pleasure palaces in the late 1980s will resemble small cities in their use of resources such as water and electricity. They will sprawl over hundreds to thousands of acres. A majority of them are planned for (or already built on) remote or rural coastlines, the places with the least disturbed coral reefs, significant stands of native coastal plants, and rare ecosystems such as anchialine pools.

The crassness of developers in our time is exemplified by the fact that the same individual who caused the destruction of nearly a third of Hawaii's anchialine pools, which were in the way of a new hotel on the Kona coast, imports monkeys, flamingos, swans, and other displaced creatures to roam the contrived settings of his similar projects on several of the islands. By themselves, such actions are really no different from trends that have prevailed since the first Polynesian settlers came ashore. But now, the rarity of Hawaiian habitats and biota and the emerging, educated sensitivity to endemism and natural diversity throw into high barren relief the anachronistic standards of the latest despoilers of Hawaiian nature.

In the formerly quiet rural and remote settings where the gargantuan resorts and condominium complexes are rising, an environmental alienation accompanies development, and all the Hawaiianess is ebbing. The destruction inevitably extends beyond the actual boundaries of the construction. Once a remote site becomes easily accessible by road, there follows a thrashing and trashing of the general area for miles around, as the four-wheeled drives and ORVs mingle in their destructive herds and frenziedly stampede over the landscape. Then, too, like industrial accidents, the huge projects under construction and the finished resorts alike spread debris and pollution well beyond their property boundaries—especially out into coastal waters, where plastic litter and oily runoff from vast parking facilities silently kill marine life.[14]

Perhaps the main reason developers and conservationists cannot understand each other's point of view is that the developers believe they are really making improvements on the land, and that eventually the dominant landform on earth will be (and perhaps should be) a cityscape inspired by Disney. Beaverlike, and with a paranoia that traces to "the Tragedy of the Commons,"[15] they hurry to build their masterworks before another can usurp their space. Disguised by layers of industrial makeup, the unpaved places in such projects are cleverly molded facades that can resemble natural environments. But with captive flamingos posturing next to chlorinated waterfalls, these facades are tricked out to offer cheap and unnatural thrills without the depth of understanding and personal commitment that is necessary for really exploring nature.

The untended vacant lands between the contrived megalithic projects lose their remoteness and any remnant of natural character. Grazed by ORVs, they become mere waste places—desert dumping grounds or weed-infested hinterlands—awaiting new developments, perhaps modern industrial parks. Farther away, greener parks that retain some endemic values and a few other protected natural areas will, in the end, be tiny islands of nature in oceans of concrete. The pressure on them from eventual multitudes of people seeking relief from the cloying and inimical aspects of overdevelopment will be immense. Eventually, the parks themselves may require Disneyland techniques for crowd management and throughput of people and may have to be hardened to withstand the traffic.

We tend to view such developments as possible only far in the future, nearly in the realm of science fiction. Yet islands that have become world-class tourist destinations are much closer to an inescapable denouement of developmental mania than most other places. A case in point is Bermuda. In 1981, a comprehensive environmental assessment was made of this small, subtropical island in the western North Atlantic Ocean.[16] Bermuda's environmental history has many parallels with that of the Hawaiian Archipelago. Both have suffered comprehensive deforestation, devastation of native vegetation by feral livestock, ravages by introduced weeds and predators, decline of seabirds and land birds to extinction or endangered status, and great losses to the coral reef ecosystem by siltation, pollution, and, in modern decades, overfishing. In both Bermuda and Hawaii, tourism began in about the midnineteenth century. Now Bermuda has a permanent population density of approximately 3,000 persons (and nearly 2,000 automobiles) per square mile, making it one of the most crowded countries in the world. In addition, about 600,000 tourists visit Bermuda annually. Once an exporter of seafood and agricultural crops, Bermuda now imports nearly all its food, including two-thirds of its fish. Severe problems with solid wastes and sewage, loss of open space to urbanization, transportation nightmares on highways and in harbors, and a perenially acute freshwater shortage all now contribute to a declining quality of life on the island.

In Hawaii, so far, only the island of Oahu begins to approach the status of Bermuda. The latter is a much smaller island, but Oahu, with its permanent population approaching one million and climbing rapidly, has already reached half of Bermuda's residential population density. As in Bermuda, the great engine fueling growth on Oahu today is tourism. The hard question now facing Oahu is how to avoid doubling its population in as little as thirty years (according to recent projections of increase)[17] and bringing the acknowlegedly acute environmental woes of Bermuda to Hawaii.

Bermuda and now Hawaii appear to be excellent examples of an early reckoning with the folly of open-ended development, as identified by prominent environmental scientist George Woodwell. He asks, "Do we still believe that environment is infinitely divisible by compromise each time a new claim appears?"[18] This approach—divide and conquer by compromise—which has been so commonly applied in the main islands, has even surfaced down in the Northwestern Hawaiian Islands in arguments over commercial fishing rights around French Frigate Shoals, unique for its beds of immigrant corals and butterflyfishes, and presently indispensable for survival of the Hawaiian turtle and seal.

Stanford University ecologist Paul Ehrlich, noted for his analyses of the limits to growth and affluence, on a 1986 visit to Hawaii, lamented, "It's the edge of history here, watching biological destruction. . . . The extinction crisis facing the world has progressed much further here."[19] Indeed, Hawaii is providing an early warning of what the prospects for the natural heritage of our global island are likely to be in the next century.

HOPE AND CONTENTION

Of course, in nature and human nature deepening crises stimulate efforts at relief and amelioration. Mere lamentation and rhetoric over Hawaii's declining nature are being replaced with positive action. The federal government, primarily through two agencies—the National Park Service and the Fish and Wildlife Service—have come to the forefront of efforts to preserve the endemic biota and ecosystems of the islands. A third, the National Marine Fisheries Service (NMFS), navigates a fine line between fostering commercial fishery development and preserving necessary marine ecological balances to assure sustainable yields for human consumption. In Hawaii, the NMFS, through the work of its able scientists and enforcement officers, has recently performed yeoman service in the protection of whales, turtles, and monk seals, together with their critical habitats, especially in the NWHI. The strong federal commitment to endemic values has evolved significantly in recent decades. As late as the 1950s and 1960s, the Fish and Wildlife Service, for one, devoted much of its energies to what are now recognized as environmentally damaging pursuits—for example, the promotion through federal aid of introduced species for sport hunting—and the same agency once carried out large-scale lethal seabird control for the navy on Midway Island.

The greatest strides in preserving Hawaiian endemism today are being taken by private organizations. The Nature Conservancy, the Hawaii Audubon Society, the Sierra Club, and the Conservation Council of Hawaii, among numerous others on the state and local level on most of the main islands, are highly active and generally work cooperatively, sharing expertise and the labor needed to identify critical habitat and biota, document threats and abuses to Hawaiian nature, publicize endemic values, lobby for protection of sites, and so on. The Nature Conservancy has been especially successful in its "Islands of Life" campaign. With its strategy of identifying the most pristine ecosystems left and then raising money to buy those tracts, the conservancy has acquired tens of thousands of acres, including whole watersheds such as the exquisite Pelekunu Valley on Northeast Molokai. The conservancy does not take sides on conservation battlegrounds; it merely concludes its deals quietly with the aim of preserving unique wilderness places for perpetuity. In Hawaii, as elsewhere, it has turned over newly acquired lands to federal protection; for example, the large Hakalau tract of high mesic *koa* forest on Mauna Kea, acquired by the conservancy in 1986, will become a national wildlife refuge under the jurisdiction of the U.S. Fish and Wildlife Service.

Hawaii Audubon and numerous other conservation groups in the islands take on causes the Nature Conservancy does not join. Many of these involve publicity, education, and even litigation. They also involve efforts to preserve and protect places with great natural value in which the conservancy does not take action. A case in point is the wonderful seabird rookery, with its precarious albatross colony, on Kauai at Kilauea Point (see chapter 9). The area is certainly no pristine wilderness, but the tiny wildlife refuge clearly needed to be expanded to include an adjacent ridge and cliffside with important concentrations of birds. Some criticism was aimed at conservancy purists for refusing to help in the acquisition, but, with leadership by Hawaii Audubon and perseverence by local conservationists, federal funding for the expansion was secured, and this vantage, with its incomparable denizens on the edge of the marine wilderness, will inspire many future generations.

Others are at least sensing the urgency for protecting what is left of Hawaiian nature. Even the great landed estates are paying lip service to the concept of holistic value in endemic ecosystems. At a 1986 conference on the current status of native *koa* forests, Richard Lyman, chairman of the board of trustees of the giant Bishop Estate, criticized the bulldozing of natural forest lands.[20] But actions are often at odds with rhetoric. The Bishop Estate itself had recently destroyed tracts of old *koa* ecosystem on its Keahou Ranch lands on the Big Island for a silviculture project—ironically, not the usual eucalypt plantation, but instead a native *koa* tree farm. But all that is tall and green and even endemic is not a Hawaiian forest. These tree plantations are no different from any crop. Weed control is vigorously pursued so that no native understory can develop. Native birds and insects will not find the resources to maintain breeding populations here. Clearcut harvests will repeatedly denude the land—as frequently as possible through the technological forcing of the trees' growth by artificial fertilization at maximum tolerable levels and artificial selection of the fastest growing individuals. Moreover, the estate, which used to have constructive relationships with the scientific establishments of the University of Hawaii, Bishop Museum, and U.S. Fish and Wildlife Service, has blacklisted a number of top Hawaii botanists, entomologists, ornithologists, ecologists, and naturalists from those institutions and forbidden them to enter its lands. This move seems to stem from discoveries of threatened or endangered species on Bishop Estate holdings—findings that would impede development. Some individuals also seem to have evoked ire by publicly criticizing the estate's positions on conservation issues.

In recent years, proposals have been made by international conservation organizations for another sort of silviculture in Hawaii. The islands, with their great range of climates, have been viewed as a potential sanctuary for the endangered flora of the world's tropical and subtropical regions. Botanical gardens might be established at different elevations and in windward and leeward locations in an attempt to forestall the extinction of selected species in rapidly developing countries of the Third World. Although this seems a laudable use for perhaps tens of thousands of acres of abandoned canelands and marginally productive ranches, critics point out that such a new wave of introductions to Hawaii might include new noxious weeds. Precedents are everywhere in the islands. The likes of the fire tree *(Myrica faya)* from the Azores have eminent standing in their places of origin, but in Hawaii have become serious invaders of native ecosystems.[21]

Most proposals for the last-chance tropical botanical collections in Hawaii all but ignore the native flora. Why not start with efforts to bring back *kauila, kokio, iliahi, aiea, koaia, uhiuhi,* and many others from the brink of extinction on their home ground?

THE APPRECIATION OF ISLANDS

As the onrushing new wave of biotic destruction affects reefs, shorelines, mountain forests, streams, and perhaps a variety of specialized ecosystems such as lava tubes and anchialine pools, the loss of life forms, we may imagine, will be strongly skewed toward the obviously sensitive native Hawaiian organisms. However, if the overdevelopment cum industrialization of Hawaii reaches a Los Angeles level of intensity, even various kinds of introduced plants and animals—the kinds susceptible to chronic air and aquatic pollution, retreat and contamination of underground freshwater lenses, and other excesses of civilization—may begin to disappear. Ironically, certain manifestations of air pollution—in particular, the accumulation of sulfurous gases that promote acid rain—might actually favor some of the native Hawaiian plants. For example, some races of *ohia lehua* are known to be well adapted to such conditions on the Big Island in the lee of Kilauea and Mauna Loa, which cause plenty of acid rain. But, overall, there will be a great loss of natural diversity if the footprint of continental-style development presses much more heavily on the islands.

Perhaps Hawaii should seek to be only a testing ground for hopeful change, a place where small-scale projects, new ideas with promise for harmonious human coexistence with nature, including our own kind, can be tried. The "small is beautiful" concept seems especially apt for islands that all but disappear in the vastness of their oceanic setting. Overdevelopment and excess growth has always brought out the worst in Hawaii, including strife among the early Polynesians. First detected in archaeological deposits several centuries after colonization, traces of warfare in old Hawaii correlate with rapidly rising population and large-scale agricultural development.[22] In our own time, big agriculture, pushed beyond its limits, finally led to a serious poisoning of groundwater and even milk with carcinogenic pesticides.[23] The historical lesson seems to be that the fragility of islands demands a lighter tread.

Such a lesson would suggest that geothermal conversion be tested, that ocean-thermal energy be demonstrated, that pilot-scale windfarms be perfected, that aquaculture research be fostered, perhaps even that a small-scale spaceport be built (taking advantage of Hawaii's proximity to the equator, where rockets launched in the direction of the earth's rotation receive the greatest boost in velocity). All these forward-looking ideas are being discussed with great interest in Hawaii and are being evaluated by thoughtful leaders such as U.S. Senator Spark Matsunaga. It seems, however, that in the best of futures Hawaii would become the world's teacher in such things and not build them on a scale to overwhelm and overdevelop the natural peace and harmony and grandeur that still linger in parts of the islands.

Hawaii is still very much a venue in which we can sense the human place in nature, to become conscious of the roots that connect us with the essences of earth and life. Those values of a place that communicate to the peaceful atavism in the human spirit are going to become very precious indeed in the world that lies ahead.

Of all the epiphanies of nature, few can match Mauna Loa in summit eruption. We are fortunate that Isabella Bird trekked to this realm of fire and ice in 1873 (she was the first woman known to do so) and wrote a magnificent evocation of her encounter with Hawaii's ultimate spectacle.[24] On a high ledge at midnight, overlooking the immense Mokuaweoweo Caldera, she was transfixed by

the indescribable glories of the fire fountain . . . its surges beating and the ebb and flow of its thunder-music . . . while the earth trembled and the moon and stars withdrew abashed into far-off space.

There, in the contrast of the freezing, fiery night, she perceived the essence of the reward in human experience of nature:

How far it was from all the world, uplifted above love, hate, and storms of passion, and war and wreck of thrones, and dissonant clash of human thought, serene in the eternal solitudes.

Isabella Bird's sense of wonder and spiritual refreshment at Mauna Loa's summit might as well apply to the composite endemism of the Hawaiian Archipelago. The nature of Hawaii—not only the volcanic eruptions, but all that is truly of the islands, from remote summits to misty jungles, great cliffs rearing from the sea, and quiet beaches and valleys—still has the capacity to inspire. The more subtle evocations of the islands are the native plants and animals. Their tiny living fires are like no other.

The programs in their genes, having evolved in unique isolation, may hold secrets of future value to mankind—medicines, agricultural aids, and so on. Even without practical value, the native life of Hawaii has great intrinsic worth for its rarity and precarious status in the earth's biota and the universe at large. The Hawaiian Archipelago is indeed a place apart, but, despite uniqueness and geographical isolation, these islands, which display so much of our planet's dynamism and hospitality to life, have come to represent common ground and environmental hope worldwide. How well we protect the remaining native essences of Hawaii and learn to live there within our ecological means will foreshadow our success in preserving the vital natural systems of our ultimate island, the earth.

Notes

CHAPTER 1

1. G. A. Macdonald, A. T. Abbott, and F. L. Peterson, 1983. *Volcanoes in the Sea: The Geology of Hawaii* (2nd ed.). Univ. of Hawaii Press, Honolulu. Also, G. A. Macdonald and A. T. Abbott, 1970. *Volcanoes in the Sea* (1st ed.). Univ. of Hawaii Press, Honolulu.
2. See, for example, A. Malahoff, 1987. Geology of the summit of Loihi submarine volcano. Chap. 6, pp. 133–44, in R. W. Decker, T. L. Wright, and P. H. Stauffer (Eds.). *Volcanism in Hawaii*, Vol 1. U.S.G.S. Prof. Paper 1350, Wash., D.C. Also, W. R. Normark, D. A. Clague, and J. G. Moore, 1982. The next island. *Natural History 91*(12): 68–71.
3. M. W. Beckwith, 1970. *Hawaiian Mythology*. Univ. of Hawaii Press, Honolulu. See pp. 169–71, on legends of Pele wandering from Kauai southeastward.
4. See, for example, R. S. Detrick, and S. T. Crough, 1978. Island subsidence, hot spots, and lithospheric thinning. *J. Geophysical Res. 83* (83): 1236–44. Also, J. G. Moore, 1987. Subsidence of the Hawaiian Ridge. Chap. 2, pp. 85–100, in Decker.
5. H. T. Stearns, 1938. Ancient shore lines on the island of Lanai, Hawaii. *Geol. Soc. Amer. Bull. 49*: 616–28.
6. The giant *tsunami* scenario is based on recent research on the instability of volcanic slopes. See J. G. Moore, and G. W. Moore, 1984. Deposit from a giant wave on the island of Lanai, Hawaii. *Science 226*: 1312–15. Also R. A. Kerr, 1984. Landslides from volcanoes seen as common. *Science 224*: 275–76.
7. Macdonald and Abbott, 1970. See the photo and caption on p. 337; the caption has been changed in the second edition of this book, leaving no explanation for the surface demarcation at the 800-foot level.
8. C. Darwin, 1842. *On the Structure and Distribution of Coral Reefs*. Smith Elder and Co., London.
9. H. S. Ladd, J. Tracey, Jr., and M. G. Gross, 1967. Drilling on Midway Atoll, Hawaii. *Science 156*: 1088–95.
10. Macdonald, Abbott, and Peterson, p. 303.
11. Ibid., pp. 256–59.
12. B. L. Oostdam, 1965. Age of lava flows on Haleakala, Maui, Hawaii. *Geol. Soc. Amer. Bull. 76*: 393–94.
13. Macdonald and Abbott, pp. 211–12.
14. Macdonald, Abbott, and Peterson, p. 414.
15. Macdonald and Abbott, pp. 209 and 356.
16. J. G. Moore, 1964. Giant submarine landslides on the Hawaiian Ridge. U.S.G.S. Prof. Paper 501-D, Wash., DC, pp. 95–98. Also, R. K. Mark and J. G. Moore, 1987. Slopes of the Hawaiian Ridge. Chap. 3, pp. 101–08, in Decker. See pp. 102–03.
17. Macdonald and Abbott, pp. 376–80.
18. Macdonald, Abbott, and Peterson, p. 461.
19. D. J. Fornari and J. F. Campbell, 1987. Submarine topography around the Hawaiian Islands. Chap. 4, pp. 109–24, in Decker. See p. 113.

CHAPTER 2

1. G. E. Hutchinson, 1965. *The Ecological Theater and the Evolutionary Play*. Yale Univ. Press, New Haven, CT.
2. E. C. Zimmerman, 1970. Adaptive radiation in Hawaii with special reference to insects. Reprinted. Pp. 528–34, in E. A. Kay (Ed.). *A Natural History of the Hawaiian Islands: Selected Readings*. Univ. of Hawaii Press, Honolulu (1972). See p. 534.

3. D. Lack, 1947. *Darwin's Finches.* Cambridge Univ. Press, Cambridge, U.K.
4. K. Y. Kaneshiro, 1983. Sexual selection and direction of evolution in the biosystematics of the Hawaiian Drosophilidae. *Ann. Rev. Entomology 28:* 161–78. Also, K. Y. Kaneshiro and A. Ohta, 1982. The flies fan out. *Natural History 91*(12): 54–59.
5. W. L. Brown, Jr., and E. Wilson, 1956. Character displacement. *Systematic Zool.* 7: 49–64.
6. D. G. Howell, 1985. Terranes. *Scientific American 253*(5): 116–25. Also, D. L. Jones, A. Cox, P. Coney, and M. Beck, 1982. The growth of western North America. *Scientific American 247*(5): 70–84.

CHAPTER 3

1. See, for example, R. S. Scheltema, 1968. Dispersal of larvae by equatorial ocean currents and its importance to the zoogeography of shoal water tropical species. *Nature 217:* 1159–62.
2. W. A. Gosline and V. E. Brock, 1960. *Handbook of Hawaiian Fishes.* Univ. of Hawaii Press, Honolulu. See pp. 20–27.
3. J. E. Randall, P. S. Lobel, and E. H. Chave, 1985. Annotated checklist of the fishes of Johnston Island. *Pacific Science 39*(1): 24–80. See page 77.
4. E. A. Kay and S. R. Palumbi, 1987. Endemism and evolution in Hawaiian marine invertebrates. *Trends in Ecol. and Evol. 2*(7): 183–86. Also, T. F. Hourigan and E. S. Reese, 1987. Mid-ocean isolation and the evolution of Hawaii reef fishes. *Trends in Ecol. and Evol. 2*(7): 187–91.
5. D. Mueller-Dombois, 1981. Some bioenvironmental conditions and the general design of IBP research in Hawaii. Pp. 3–32, in D. Mueller-Dombois, K. W. Bridges, and H. L. Carson (Eds.). *Island Ecosystems: Biological Organization in Selected Hawaiian Communities.* U.S. IBP Synthesis Series, No. 15. Hutchinson Ross Pub. Co., Stroudsburg, PA. See pp. 15–16.
6. S. Carlquist, 1980. *Hawaii: A Natural History* (2nd ed.). Pacific Tropical Botanical Garden, Lawai, Kauai, Hawaii. See Chapter 8, pp. 163–73.
7. S. Carlquist, 1982. The first arrivals. *Natural History 91*(12): 20–30.
8. R. H. MacArthur and E. O. Wilson, 1967. *The Theory of Island Biogeography.* Princeton Univ. Press, Princeton, NJ.
9. See, for example, D. Simberloff, 1983. When is an island community in equilibrium? *Science 220:* 1275–77.
10. J. Juvik, 1979. The Hawaiian avifauna: Biogeographic theory in evolutionary time. *Jour. of Biogeography 6:* 205–24.
11. S. L. Olson and H. F. James, 1982. Prodromus of the fossil avifauna of the Hawaiian Islands. *Smithsonian Contrib. Zool.* No. 365. See p. 53.

CHAPTER 4

1. V. E. Brock and T. C. Chamberlain, 1968. Geological and ecological reconnaissance off western Oahu, Hawaii, principally by means of the research submersible *Asherah.* Reprinted 1972. Pp. 283–304, in E. A. Kay (Ed.). *A Natural History of the Hawaiian Islands: Selected Readings.* Univ. of Hawaii Press, Honolulu. See pp. 298–99.
2. P. Struhsaker and D. C. Aasted, 1974. Deepwater shrimp trapping in the Hawaiian Islands. *Mar. Fisheries Rev. 36*(10): 24–30.
3. Brock and Chamberlain, pp. 297–302.
4. J. J. Magnuson, 1978. Introduction, in G. D. Sharp and A. E. Dizon (Eds.). *The Physiological Ecology of Tunas.* Academic Press, New York. See p. XI.
5. A. E. Dizon and R. W. Brill, 1979. Thermoregulation in tunas. *American Zoologist 19:* 249–65. Also, A. E. Dizon and R. W. Brill, 1979. Thermoregulation in yellowfin tuna, *Thunnus albacares. Physiological Zoology 52*(4): 581–93.
6. M. M. Walker, J. L. Kirschvink, S. R. Chang, and A. E. Dizon, 1984. A candidate

magnetic sense organ in the yellowfin tuna, *Thunnus albacares*. *Science 224*: 751–53. Also, M. M. Walker, 1984. Learned magnetic field discrimination in yellowfin tuna, *Thunnus albacares*. *Jour. of Comp. Physiology A 155*: 673–79.

7. H. S. H. Yuen, 1970. Behavior of skipjack tuna, *Katsuwonis pelamis* as determined by tracking with ultrasonic devices. *Jour. Fisheries Research Board of Canada 27*(11): 2071–79. Also, R. W. Brill, K. N. Holland, and R. K. C. Chang, 1987. Horizontal and vertical movement patterns of yellowfin tuna associated with fish aggregating devices. (Abstract.) Fourth Intl. Conf. on Artificial Habitats for Fisheries (Miami, FL, Nov. 1987).

8. P. S. Lobel, 1978. Diel, lunar, and seasonal periodicity in the reproductive behavior of the pomacentrid fish, *Centropyge potteri*, and some other reef fishes in Hawaii. *Pacific Science 32*(2): 193–207. Also, W. Watson and J. M. Leis, 1974. Ichthyoplankton of Kaneohe Bay, Hawaii. Univ. of Hawaii, Sea Grant, Report 75–101.

9. M. Titcomb, 1977. *Native Use of Fish in Hawaii* (2nd ed., paperback). Univ. of Hawaii Press, Honolulu. See p. 119.

10. S. I. Fefer, C. S. Harrison, M. B. Naughton, and R. J. Shallenberger, 1984. Synopsis of results of recent seabird research conducted in the Northwestern Hawaiian Islands. Pp. 9–76, in R. W. Grigg and K. Y. Tanoue. *Proc. 2nd Symp. on Resource Investig. in the NWHI*. Vol. 1. UNIHI-SG, MR 84–01. See p. 55 and Table 9, p. 56.

11. P. S. Lobel and A. R. Robinson, 1986. Transport and entrapment of fish larvae by ocean mesoscale eddies and currents in Hawaiian waters. *Deep-Sea Research 33*(4): 483–500. Also, J. M. Leis, 1982. Nearshore distribution gradients of larval fish (15 taxa) and planktonic crustaceans (6 taxa) in Hawaii. *Mar. Biol. 72*: 89–97. Also, P. F. Sale, 1970. Distribution of larval Acanthuridae off Hawaii. *Copeia* 1970: 765–66.

12. B. P. Boden and E. M. Kampa, 1953. Winter cascading from an oceanic island and its biological implications. *Nature 171*: 426.

13. Brock and Chamberlain, p. 299.

14. E. C. Jones, 1971. *Isistius brasiliensis*, a squaloid shark, the probable cause of crater wounds on fishes and cetaceans. *Fishery Bull. (NMFS) 69*(4): 791–98.

15. L. R. Taylor, L. J. V. Campagno, and P. J. Struhsaker, 1983. Megamouth—A new species, genus, and family of lamnoid shark (*Megachasma pelagios*, family Megachasmidae) from the Hawaiian Islands. *Proc. Calif. Acad. Sciences 43*(8): 87–110.

16. V. E. Brock, 1962. The experimental introduction of certain marine fishes from the Society Islands to the Hawaiian Islands. *Final Rept. to Hawaii Div. of Fish and Game*, p. 9.

17. H. Okamoto and B. Kanenaka, 1984. Preliminary report on the nearshore fishery resource assessment of the Northwestern Hawaiian Islands 1977–1982. Pp. 123–143, in Grigg and Tanoue. In volume 1, see Table 2, p. 135. Also, D. K. Oda and J. D. Parrish, 1981. Ecology of commercial snappers and groupers introduced to Hawaiian reefs. *Proc. 4th Intl. Coral Reef Symp. 1*: 59–67.

18. R. L. Humphreys, Jr., D. T. Tagami, and M. P. Seki, 1984. Seamount fishery resources within the southern Emperor-northern Hawaiian Ridge area. Pp. 283–327, in Grigg and Tanoue, vol. 1.

19. R. W. Grigg, 1984. Resource management of precious corals: A review and application to shallow water reef building corals. *Mar. Ecol. 5*(1): 57–74.

20. State of Hawaii Marine Mining Program, 1987. Mining development scenario for cobalt-rich manganese crusts in the exclusive economic zones of the Hawaiian Archipelago and Johnston Island. DPED (State of Hawaii) and Minerals Management Service (U.S. Dept. of Interior), Honolulu. Also, P. B. Humphrey (Ed.), 1982. *Marine Mining: A New Beginning*. (Conf. Proc.). State of Hawaii Marine Mining Program, DPED, Honolulu.

21. Remarks attributed to Robert G. Paul of the U.S. Dept. of Interior, Office of Strategic and International Minerals. Editorial page, *Sunday Star Bulletin and Advertiser* (July 7, 1985), Honolulu.

22. State of Hawaii Marine Mining Program, pp. 80–84.

23. U.S. Dept. of Interior, 1987. Proposed marine mineral lease sale in the Hawaiian Archipelago and Johnston Island exclusive economic zones. Draft Environmental Impact Statement. Minerals Mgmt. Service (U.S. Dept. of Interior) and DPED (State of Hawaii), Honolulu.

24. J. C. Wiltshire, 1982. The potential of the Puna Submarine Canyon for slurry disposal of manganese nodule tailings. *Oceans 82*, Conf. Record. Mar. Technol. Soc., Wash., DC. See pp. 1069–73. Also, J. Borg, 1984. Undersea oddity: Puna Canyon called ideal mining dump ground. *Honolulu Advertiser* (Nov. 26, 1984): A3.

CHAPTER 5

1. S. Leatherwood and R. R. Reeves, 1983. *The Sierra Club Handbook of Whales and Dolphins*. Sierra Club Books, San Francisco. See p. 242.
2. E. C. Jones, 1971. *Isistius brasiliensis*, a squaloid shark, the probable cause of crater wounds on fishes and cetaceans. *Fishery Bull. (NMFS)* 69(4): 791–98.
3. See, for example, K. S. Norris and T. P. Dohl, 1980. Behavior of the Hawaiian spinner dolphin, *Stenella longirostris*. *Fishery Bull. (NMFS)* 77: 821–49.
4. K. S. Norris, 1974. *The Porpoise Watcher*. W. W. Norton, New York.
5. K. Pryor, 1975. *Lads Before the Wind*. Harper & Row, New York. See pp. 151–52.
6. G. Bateson, cited as pers. comm. in P. Q. Tomich, 1969. *Mammals in Hawaii*. B. P. Bishop Museum Spec. Pub. 57. Bishop Museum Press, Honolulu. See pp. 43–44.
7. T. R. Peale, 1848. U.S. Exploring Expedition Vol. VIII. *Mammalia and Ornithology*. Lee and Blanchard, Philadelphia, PA. See p. 32. Also, J. Cassin, 1858. U.S. Exploring Exped. Vol. VIII. *Mammalogy and Ornithology*. Sherman and Sons, Philadelphia, PA. See p. 28.
8. Leatherwood and Reeves, p. 156.
9. National Marine Fisheries Service, 1981. Final environmental impact statement on the incidental take of Dall's Porpoise in the Japanese salmon fishery. U.S. Dept. of Commerce, Wash., D.C. Also, G. H. Balazs, 1982. Driftnets catch leatherback turtles. *Oryx XVI*(5): 428–30.
10. D. E. Gaskin, 1972. *Whales, Dolphins, and Seals*. Heinemann, London. Also, R. Payne (Ed.), 1983. Communication and behavior of whales. Selected Symposia Series. AAAS and Westview Press, Inc., Boulder, CO. Also, P. Tyack, 1981. Interactions between singing humpback whales and conspecifics nearby. *Behav. Ecol. Sociobiol. 8*: 105–116. Also, C. S. Baker and L. M. Herman, 1984. Aggressive behavior between humpback whales *(Megaptera novangliae)* wintering in Hawaiian waters. *Canad. J. Zool. 62*: 1922–37.
11. R. G. Chittleborough, 1953. Aerial observations on the humpback whale, *Megaptera nodosa* (Bonnaterre), with notes on other species. *Austral. J. Mar. and Freshwater Research 5*: 35–63.
12. J. D. Darling and C. M. Jurasz, 1983. Migratory destinations of North Pacific humpback whales *(Megaptera novangliae)*. Pp. 359–70, in Payne.
13. J. D. Darling, K. M. Gibson, and G. K. Silber, 1983. Observations on the abundance and behavior of humpback whales *(Megaptera novangliae)* off West Maui, Hawaii, 1977–79. Pp. 201–22, in Payne. Also, Payne, p. 4.
14. For recent population history, see A. A. Wolman and C. M. Jurasz, 1977. Humpback whales in Hawaii: Vessel census 1976. *Mar. Fish. Rev. 39*: 1–5. Also, L. M. Herman and R. C. Antinoja, 1977. Humpback whales in the Hawaiian breeding waters: Population and pod characteristics. Sci. Rep. Whales Res. Inst.(29): 59–85. Also, Darling, Gibson, and Silber.
15. L. M. Herman, 1979. Humpback whales in Hawaiian waters: A study in historical ecology. *Pacific Science 33*(1): 1–15.
16. M. Titcomb, 1977 (2nd ed.). *Native Use of Fish in Hawaii*. Univ. of Hawaii Press, Honolulu. See p. 90.
17. J. Montgomery (Ed.), 1832. Journal of voyages and travels by the Rev. Daniel Tyerman and George Bennet Esq., deputed from the London Missionary Society to visit their various stations in the South Sea Islands, China, India &c. between the years 1821 and 1829 (3 vols.). Crocker and Brewster, Boston. See Vol II, pp. 15 and 26.
18. Anon. *The Polynesian* (May 20, 1848), p. 3.
19. Anon. *The Pacific Commercial Advertiser* (May 1, 1869), p. 3.
20. C. K. Ai, 1960. My seventy-nine years in Hawaii. Cosmorama Pictorial Publisher, Hong Kong. See p. 71.

21. Gaskin, p. 82.
22. U.S. Dept. of Commerce, 1982 (April). Proposed Hawaii Humpback Whale National Marine Sanctuary. Issue Paper. Sanct. Programs Office, CZM, NOAA. Also, U.S. Dept. of Commerce, 1983 (Dec.). Proposed Hawaii Humpback Whale National Marine Sanctuary. Draft Management Plan and Environmental Impact Statement. Sanctuary Prog. Div., Office of Ocean and Coastal Resource Management. National Ocean Service, NOAA.
23. I. McT. Cowan, 1980 (June). Letter reprinted in *Report of the Humpback Whale Sanctuary Workshop*, Maui Committee Report (from files of Greenpeace Hawaii).

CHAPTER 6

1. See, for example, T. F. Goreau, N. I. Goreau, and T. J. Goreau, 1979. Corals and coral reefs. *Scientific American* (August): 124–36. Also, S. V. Smith and D. W. Kinsey, 1976. Calcium carbonate production, coral reef growth, and sea level change. *Science 194*: 937–39.
2. D. M. Devaney and L. G. Eldredge (Eds.), 1977. *Reef and Shore Fauna of Hawaii* (rev. ed.). Section 1: Protozoa through Ctenophora. B. P. Bishop Museum Spec. Pub. 64(1). Bishop Museum Press, Honolulu. Also, R. W. Grigg, 1983. Community structure, succession and development of coral reefs in Hawaii. *Marine Ecology—Progress Series II*: 1–14. Also, S. J. Dollar, 1982. Wave stress and coral community in Hawaii. *Coral Reefs 1*: 71–81.
3. J. E. Maragos, 1977. Order Scleractinia, in Devaney and Eldredge, p. 161.
4. T. Coan, 1882. *Life in Hawaii*. A.D.F. Randolph and Co., New York. See p. 40.
5. J. F. Campbell and D. L. Erlandson, 1981. Geology of the Kohala Submarine Terrace, Hawaii. *Marine Geology 41*: 63–72.
6. W. H. Magruder and J. W. Hunt, 1979. *Seaweeds of Hawaii*. Oriental Pub. Co., Honolulu.
7. C. H. Edmondson, 1946, in D. M. Devaney and L. G. Eldredge (Eds.), Sect. 1, 1977. *Reef and Shore Fauna of Hawaii*. B. P. Bishop Museum Spec. Pub. 22. Bishop Museum Press, Honolulu. Also, E. A. Kay, 1972. The composition and relationships of marine molluscan fauna of the Hawaiian Islands. Pp. 446–55, in E. A. Kay (Ed.). *A Natural History of the Hawaiian Islands*. Univ. of Hawaii Press, Honolulu. Also, E. A. Kay, 1979. *Hawaiian Marine Shells (Reef and Shore Fauna of Hawaii*, rev. ed. Section 4: Mollusca). B. P. Bishop Museum Spec. Pub. 64(4). Bishop Museum Press, Honolulu. Also, E. S. Hobson and E. H. Chave, 1972. *Hawaiian Reef Animals*. Univ. of Hawaii Press, Honolulu. Also, A. Fielding, 1979. *Hawaiian Reefs and Tidepools*. Oriental Pub. Co., Honolulu.
8. H. Bertsch and S. Johnson, 1981. *Hawaiian Nudibranchs*. Oriental Pub. Co., Honolulu.
9. R. L. Caldwell and H. Dingle, 1976. Stomatopods. *Scientific American 234*(1): 80–89.
10. W. A. Gosline and V. E. Brock, 1960. *Handbook of Hawaiian Fishes*. Univ. of Hawaii Press, Honolulu. Also, S. W. Tinker, 1978. *Fishes of Hawaii*. Hawaiian Service Inc., Honolulu. Also, J. E. Randall, 1981. *Underwater Guide to Hawaiian Reef Fishes*. Harrowood Books, Newtown Square, PA. Also, J. E. Randall, 1985. *Guide to Hawaiian Reef Fishes*. Harrowood Books, Newton Square, PA.
11. J. L. Meyer, E. T. Schultz, and G. S. Helfman, 1983. Fish schools: An asset to corals. *Science 220*: 1047–49. Also, R. N. Bray, A. C. Miller, and G. G. Geesey, 1981. The fish connection: A trophic link between planktonic and rocky reef communities? *Science 214*: 204–05.
12. M. A. DeCrosta, L. R. Taylor, Jr., and J. D. Parrish, 1984. Age determination, growth, and energetics of three species of carcharinid sharks in Hawaii. *Proc. 2nd Symp. on Resource Investig. in the NWHI*, Vol. 2. UNIHI-SG-MR-84-01, pp. 75–95.
13. E. S. Hobson, 1984. The structure of reef fish communities in the Hawaiian Archipelago, *Proc. 2nd Symp. on Resource Investig. in the NWHI*, Vol. 1. UNIHI-SG-MR-84-01. Pp. 101–22.

14. R. W. Grigg, J. W. Wells, and C. Wallace, 1981. *Acropora* in Hawaii. Part 1. History of the scientific record, systematics, and ecology. *Pacific Science 35*(1): 1–14. Also, R. W. Grigg, 1981. *Acropora* in Hawaii. Part 2. Zoogeography. *Pacific Science 35*(1): 15–24. Also, P. L. Jokiel, 1987. Ecology, biogeography, and evolution of corals in Hawaii. *Trends in Ecol. and Evol. 2*(7): 179–82.
15. Hobson, pp. 115–16.
16. Grigg, *Acropora*, Part 2, or see Abstract (1984) in *Proc. 2nd Symp. on Resource Investig. in the NWHI*, Vol. 2. UNIHI-SG-MR-84-01, p. 326.
17. R. W. Grigg, 1981. Coral reef development at high latitudes in Hawaii. *Proc. Fourth Intl. Coral Reef Symp.* (Manila). See Vol. 1, pp. 687–93.
18. M. Titcomb, 1977 (paperback ed.). *Native Use of Fish in Hawaii.* Univ. of Hawaii Press, Honolulu. See pp. 110–11.
19. Titcomb, *Native Use of Fish.* This work provides a summary of the *kapu* system as it applied to fisheries. See pp. 13–18.
20. Department of Geography, Univ. of Hawaii, 1983. *Atlas of Hawaii* (2nd ed.). Univ. of Hawaii Press, Honolulu. See p. 113.
21. S. M. Kamakau, 1961. *Ruling Chiefs of Hawaii.* (trans. from Hawaiian) Kamehameha Schools Press, Honolulu. See p. 301.
22. Anon., 1858. Article in *The Friend 8*(7): 50. Also, G. W. Bates, 1854. *Sandwich Island Notes.* Harper and Bros., New York. See p. 34.
23. J. D. Dana, 1872. *Corals and Coral Islands.* Dodd and Mead, New York. See p. 146.
24. Bates, p. 34.
25. J. N. Reynolds, 1835. *Voyage of the United States Frigate* Potomac *under the Command of Commodore John Downes During the Circumnavigation of the Globe in the Years 1831, 1832, 1833, and 1834.* Harper and Bros., New York. See p. 418.
26. Anon., 1859. *The Friend 8*(1): 4.
27. Anon., 1871. *The Friend 21*(2): 12.
28. A. B. Amerson, Jr., 1971. The natural history of French Frigate Shoals, Northwestern Hawaiian Islands. *Atoll Research Bull.* (150). Smithsonian Inst., Wash., D.C. See p. 49.
29. See, for example, A. Campbell, 1816. *A Voyage Round the World from 1806 to 1812.* Reprinted 1969. N. Israel/DaCapo Press, New York. See p. 160. R. H. Gast, 1973. *Don Francisco de Paula Marin.* Univ. of Hawaii Press, Honolulu. See p. 33. In the same volume, A. C. Conrad. *The Letters and Journal of Francisco de Paula Marin.* See p. 203ff. (Oahu's pearl fishery was apparently thriving in 1812.) Also, Otto von Kotzebue, 1821. *A Voyage of Discovery into the South Sea and Bering's Straits . . . in the Years 1815–1818, etc.* Reprinted 1967. N. Israel/Da Capo Press, New York. See Vol. 1, p. 338, and Vol. 3, p. 238. (Kotzebue indicates that by 1816 the pearls from Pearl Harbor were scarce and inferior.)
30. Gast, pp. 37–38. Extensive sandalwood cutting was done before 1820 in the area of Waimalu in the drainage of a major stream flowing to Pearl Harbor.
31. A. B. Amerson, Jr., R. B. Clapp, and W. O. Wirtz, 1974. The natural history of Pearl and Hermes Reef, Northwestern Hawaiian Islands. *Atoll Research Bull.* (174). Smithsonian Inst., Wash., DC. See pp. 29–31.
32. C. K. Ai, 1960. *My Seventy-Nine Years in Hawaii.* Cosmorama Pictorial Publisher, Hong Kong. See pp. 165–66.
33. C. A. Ely and R. B. Clapp, 1973. The natural history of Laysan Island, Northwestern Hawaiian Islands. *Atoll Research Bull.* (171). Smithsonian Inst., Wash., DC. See p. 39.

CHAPTER 7

1. W. H. Easton and E. A. Olson, 1976. Radiocarbon profile of Hanauma Reef, Oahu, Hawaii. *Geol. Soc. Amer. Bull. 87*: 711–19. Also, W. H. Adey, 1978. Coral reef morphogenesis: A multidimensional model. *Science 202*: 831–37.
2. D. M. Devaney, M. Kelly, P. J. Lee, and L. S. Motteler, 1982. *Kaneohe: A History of Change.* The Bess Press, Honolulu. See pp. 6–8.
3. W. K. Kikuchi, 1976. Prehistoric Hawaiian fishponds. *Science 193*: 295–99. Also,

R. A. Apple and W. K. Kikuchi, 1975. *Ancient Hawaii Shore Zone Fishponds: An Evaluation of Survivors for Historical Preservation.* Rept. for the State Director, National Park Service, U.S. Dept. of Interior, Honolulu.
4. Devaney *et al.*, pp. 114, 118, and 140.
5. Ibid., p. 51.
6. S. M. Kamakau, 1976. *The Works of the People of Old.* Bishop Museum Press, Honolulu. See p. 70.
7. Devaney *et al.*, p. 130.
8. Ibid., p. 116.
9. Ibid., p. 75.
10. P. Helfrich, 1973. A review of the ecology and biota, in D. C. Cox *et al. Estuarine Pollution in the State of Hawaii: Kaneohe Bay Study, Vol. 2.* Water Resource Research Center Tech. Rept. 31, University of Hawaii, Honolulu. Also, S. V. Smith, K. E. Chave, and D. T. O. Kam, 1973. *Atlas of Kaneohe Bay: A Reef Ecosystem under Stress.* University of Hawaii, Sea Grant Prog., TR-72-01, Honolulu. Also, R. E. Johannes, 1976. Life and death of the reef. *Audubon 78*(5): 36–55. (This article contains dramatic photographs of damaging impacts on Kaneohe Bay reefs.)
11. Devaney, *et al.*, p. 104, citing Judd.
12. D. J. Russell, 1983. Ecology of the imported red seaweed *Eucheuma striatum* on Coconut Island, Oahu, Hawaii. *Pacific Science 37*(2): 87–107.
13. E. A. Kay, 1979. *Hawaiian Marine Shells: Reef and Shore Fauna of Hawaii,* (rev. ed., Sect. 4, Mollusca). B. P. Bishop Museum Spec. Pub. 64(4). Bishop Museum Press, Honolulu. See p. 19.

CHAPTER 8

1. C. A. Repenning and C. E. Ray, 1977. The origin of the Hawaiian monk seal. *Proc. Biol. Soc. Wash. 89*(58): 667–88. Also C. E. Ray, 1976. Geography of phocid evolution. *Systematic Zool. 25*(4): 391–406.
2. J. Cousteau, 1953. *The Silent World.* Harper & Row, New York. See Chap. 10.
3. P. Matthiessen, 1959. *Wildlife in America.* Viking Compass Ed. (1964). Viking Press, New York. See p. 39.
4. K. W. Kenyon, 1977. Caribbean monk seal extinct. *Jour. Mammalogy 58*(1): 97–98.
5. J. W. Bickham, 1981. Two-hundred-million-year-old chromosomes: Deceleration of the rate of karyotype evolution in turtles. *Science 212*: 1291–93.
6. A. Carr and P. J. Coleman, 1974. Sea floor spreading theory and the odyssey of the green turtle. *Nature 249*: 128–30.
7. A. Carr, 1967. *So Excellent a Fishe.* Anchor Books Ed. (1973). Anchor Press/Doubleday, Garden City, NY. Also, see 1986 ed., *The Sea Turtle.* Univ. of Texas Press, Austin.
8. G. H. Balazs, 1980. Synopsis of biological data on the green turtle in the Hawaiian Islands. NOAA Tech. Memorandum, NMFS SWFC-7.
9. S. J. Morreale, G. J. Ruiz, J. R. Spotila, and E. A. Standora, 1982. Temperature-dependent sex determination: Current practices threaten sea turtles. *Science 216*: 1245–47.
10. A. Carr, 1986. Rips, FADS, and little Loggerheads. *Bioscience 36*(2): 92–100.
11. G. H. Balazs and G. C. Whittow, 1979. Revised bibliography of the Hawaiian monk seal, *Monachus schauinslandi* Matschie, 1905. Univ. of Hawaii Sea Grant Prog. UNIHI SG MR-79-03.
12. F. V. Schlexer, 1984. Diving patterns of the Hawaiian monk seal, Lisiansky Island, 1982. NOAA-TM-NMFS-SWFC-41.
13. D. J. Alcorn, 1984. The Hawaiian monk seal on Laysan Island: 1982. NOAA-TM-NMFS-SWFC-42. See pp. 18 and 21–22.
14. W. Gilmartin *et al.*, 1980. An investigation into unusual mortality in the Hawaiian monk seal, *Monachus schauinslandi.* Pp. 32–41, in R. W. Grigg and R. T. Pfund (Eds.). *Proc. Symp. on Status of Resource Investig. in the NWHI.* Univ. of Hawaii Sea Grant. UNIHI SG MR-80-04.
15. Ibid., pp. 38–40.

16. B. Morrell, Jr., 1832. *A Narrative of Four Voyages to the South Sea, North and South Pacific Ocean, Chinese Sea, Ethiopic and Southern Atlantic Ocean, Indian and Antarctic Ocean from the Year 1822 to 1831.* J. and J. Harper, New York. See pp. 215–19.
17. J. Paty, 1857. Report of the exploring voyage of the schooner *Manuokawai. The Friend* 6: (6): 42–43.
18. J. H. Kemble, 1966. *To California and the South Seas: The Diary of Albert G. Osbun, 1849–1851.* The Huntington Library, San Marino, CA. See pp. 154–55.
19. A. M. Bailey, 1918. The monk seal of the southern Pacific. *Nat. History 18*: 396–98.
20. T. Gerrodette, 1985. Estimating the 1983 population of Hawaiian monk seals from beach counts. Admin. Rept. H-85-5. NMFS (NOAA), Honolulu. See p. 12.
21. G. H. Balazs, 1982. Driftnets catch leatherback turtles. *Oryx 16*: 428–30.
22. A. Carr, 1987. Impact of nondegradable marine debris on the ecology and survival outlook of sea turtles. *Marine Pollution Bull. 18*(6B): 352–56.
23. U.S. Dept. of Commerce, NOAA, NMFS, 1985. Supplemental Environmental Impact Statement: Proposed designation of critical habitat for the Hawaiian monk seal in the Northwestern Hawaiian Islands. Also, G. H. Balazs, 1983. Status-review document for Pacific sea turtles. Admin. Rept. H-83-15. NMFS (NOAA), Honolulu.

CHAPTER 9

1. S. I. Fefer, C. S. Harrison, M. B. Naughton, and R. J. Shallenberger, 1984. Synopsis of results of recent seabird research conducted in the Northwestern Hawaiian Islands. Pp. 9–76, in R. W. Grigg and K. Tanoue (Eds.), *Proc. 2nd Symp. on Resource Investig. in the NWHI,* Vol. 1. Univ. of Hawaii Sea Grant Report MR 84-01. See p. 13.
2. E. L. Caum, 1933. The exotic birds of Hawaii. *Occ. Papers, B. P. Bishop Museum 10*: 1–55.
3. C. G. Sibley and J. E. Alquist, 1983. Phylogeny and classification of birds based on the data of DNA-DNA hybridization. Chap. 9, pp. 245–292, in R. F. Johnston (Ed.). *Current Ornithology,* Vol. 1. Plenum, New York.
4. J. Alquist, pers. comm., June 1985.
5. Fefer *et al.,* p. 13.
6. K. Schmidt-Nielsen, 1979. *Animal Physiology: Adaptation and Environment* (2nd ed.). Cambridge Univ. Press, New York. See pp. 328–30.
7. Fefer *et al.,* pp. 34–36.
8. W. B. King (Ed.), 1974. Pelagic studies of seabirds in the central and eastern Pacific Ocean. *Smithsonian Contrib. Zoology 158.* Smithsonian Inst. Press, Wash., DC. See p. 9. Also, Fefer, p. 39.
9. A. J. Berger, 1972. *Hawaiian Birdlife.* Univ. of Hawaii Press, Honolulu. See p. 48.
10. Ibid., p. 48.
11. Ibid., p. 47.
12. L. T. Hirai, 1978. Possible dark-rumped petrel colony on Lanai, Hawaii. *Elepaio 38*(7): 71–72.
13. C. B. Kepler, J. Jeffrey, and J. M. Scott, 1979. Possible breeding colonies of Manx Shearwater on the Island of Hawaii. *Elepaio 39*(10): 115–16. Also, S. Conant, 1980. Recent records of the *uau* (dark-rumped petrel) and the *ao* (Newell's Shearwater) in Hawaii. *Elepaio 41*(2): 11–13.
14. Berger, p. 55.
15. Ibid., p. 50.
16. R. P. Shulmeister, 1980. Short-eared owl preys on white terns. *Elepaio 41*(5): 41.
17. J. D. Parrish, M. W. Callahan, J. M. Kurz, J. E. Norris, *et al.,* 1984. Trophic relationships of nearshore fishes in the Northwestern Hawaiian Islands, pp. 221–25, in Grigg and Tanoue. Vol. 1, see p. 224.
18. E. S. C. Handy and E. G. Handy, 1972. Native planters in old Hawaii: Their life, lore, and environment. *B. P. Bishop Museum Bull. 233.* Bishop Museum Press, Honolulu. See pp. 258–59.

19. Berger, p. 48. Also, G. C. Munro, 1944. *Birds of Hawaii.* Tongg Publishing Company, Honolulu. See p. 26.
20. Handy and Handy, p. 256.
21. C. Nordoff, 1874. *Northern California, Oregon, and the Sandwich Islands.* Centennial Reprint (1974). Ten Speed Press, Berkeley, CA. See Appendix, p. 246.
22. Munro, p. 26.
23. E. M. Damon, 1931. *Koamalu.* Vol. 1. Priv. printed, Honolulu. See p. 393.
24. Schmidt-Nielsen, p. 49.
25. W. T. Brigham, 1899. Hawaiian feather work. *Mem. B. P. Bishop Museum 1*(1): 11.
26. S. B. Dole, 1879. List of birds of the Hawaiian Islands (2nd ed.). *Thrum's Hawaiian Annual for 1879.* Honolulu. See p. 58.
27. Brigham, p. 11.
28. Handy and Handy, p. 258.
29. Brigham, p. 2 (citing the journal of Captain King, 1784).
30. G. V. Byrd and T. C. Telfer, 1980. Barn owls prey on birds in Hawaii. *Elepaio 41*(5): 35–36.
31. G. V. Byrd, 1979. Common myna predation on wedge-tailed shearwater eggs. *Elepaio 39*(7): 69–70. Also, G. S. Grant, 1982. Common mynas attack black noddies and white terns on Midway Atoll. *Elepaio 42*(11): 97–98.
32. Fefer *et al.*, p. 63.
33. Berger, pp. 32–33.
34. For a discussion, see P. Matthiessen, 1964. *Wildlife in America.* Viking (Compass ed.). See Chap. 8.
35. F. C. Hadden, 1941. Midway Islands. *The Hawaiian Planters' Record. XLV*(3): 179–221. Haw'n Sugar Planters' Association. See p. 17.
36. E. H. Bryan, Jr., 1942. *American Polynesia and the Hawaiian Chain.* Tongg Publishing Company, Honolulu. See p. 194. Also, F. C. Hadden, 1941, p. 17.
37. C. A. Ely and R. B. Clapp, 1973. The natural history of Laysan Island, Northwestern Hawaiian Islands. *Atoll Res. Bull.* 171. Smithsonian Inst., Wash., DC. See pp. 37–41. Also, R. A. Apple, 1973. Prehistoric and historic sites and structures in the Hawaiian Islands National Wildlife Refuge. U.S. Dept. of Interior. Honolulu. See p. 6. Also, Hadden, p. 17.
38. Ely and Clapp, p. 38.
39. Ibid., p. 39.
40. J. L. Eliot, 1978. Hawaii's far-flung wildlife paradise. *Natl. Geographic Mag.* (May 1978): 672.
41. C. K. Ai, 1960. *My Seventy-Nine Years in Hawaii.* Cosmorama Pictorial Publisher, Hong Kong. See p. 254.
42. Bryan, p. 187.
43. T. N. Pettit and Anon., 1980. Rifle-range impacts on red-footed boobies. *Elepaio 41*(3): 22–23.
44. Berger, p. 89. Also, P. W. Woodward, 1972. The natural history of Kure Atoll, Northwestern Hawaiian Islands. *Atoll Research Bull.* 164. Smithsonian Inst., Wash., DC. See p. 77.
45. G. V. Byrd and C. F. Zeillemaker, 1981. Seabirds of Kilauea Point, Kauai Island, Hawaii. *Elepaio 41*(8): 67–70. G. V. Byrd and T. C. Telfer, 1980. The Laysan Albatross on Kauai. *Elepaio 41*(1): 1–3. F. Richardson and J. Bowles, 1964. A survey of the birds of Kauai. *B. P. Bishop Museum Bull. 227:* 19.
46. W. B. King, R. G. B. Brown, and G. A. Sanger, 1979. Mortality to marine birds through commercial fishing. Pp. 195–97, in J. C. Bartonek and D. N. Nettleship (Eds.). *Conservation of Marine Birds of Northern North America.* U.S. Fish and Wildlife Service Wildlife Research Rept. 11. Wash., DC.
47. See, for example, D. H. S. Wehle and F. C. Coleman, 1983. Plastics at sea. *Natural History 92*(2): 20–26.
48. Fefer *et al.,* pp. 57–58.
49. Ibid., p. 68.
50. D. W. Anderson, *et al.*, 1975. Brown pelicans: Improved reproduction off the southern California coast. *Science 190:* 806–08.
51. Fefer *et al.*

CHAPTER 10

1. W. H. Adey, 1978. Coral reef morphogenesis: A multidimensional model. *Science* 202(4370): 831–37.
2. G. A. Macdonald and A. T. Abbott, 1974. *Volcanoes in the Sea* (1st. ed.). Univ. of Hawaii Press, Honolulu. See p. 268.
3. A. B. Amerson, Jr., 1971. The natural history of French Frigate Shoals, Northwestern Hawaiian Islands. *Atoll Research Bull. 150.* Smithsonian Inst., Wash., DC. See pp. 37–38 and 57.
4. C. A. Ely and R. B. Clapp, 1973. The natural history of Laysan Island, Northwestern Hawaiian Islands. *Atoll Res. Bull. 171:* 71.
5. C. Lamoreaux, 1963. The flora and vegetation of Laysan Island. *Atoll Res. Bull. 97:* 8. Also, Ely and Clapp, p. 65.
6. S. Carlquist, 1980. *Hawaii: A Natural History* (2nd ed.). Pacific Tropical Botanical Garden. Lawai, Kauai. See pp. 409 and 417.
7. S. Conant *et al.*, 1984. The unique terrestrial biota of the Northwestern Hawaiian Islands. *Proc. 2nd Symp. on Resource Investig. in the NWHI.* Univ. of Hawaii Sea Grant. MR 84-01. Vol. 1, pp. 77–94. See p. 83.
8. D. Amadon, 1986. The Hawaiian Honeycreepers revisited. *Elepaio* 46(8): 83–84.
9. F. C. Hadden, 1941. *Midway Islands.* Advertiser Publishing Company, Honolulu. (Reprinted from *The Hawaiian Planters' Record* 45[3].) See p. 41.
10. A. J. Berger, 1972. *Hawaiian Birdlife* (1st ed.). Univ. of Hawaii Press, Honolulu. See p. 86 (citing Palmer).
11. Berger, pp. 86–87.
12. Ibid., p. 80.
13. Ibid., p. 81.
14. K. P. Emory, 1928. Archaeology of Nihoa and Necker Islands. *B. P. Bishop Museum Bull. 53.* Also, P. V. Kirch, 1985. *Feathered Gods and Fishhooks.* Univ. of Hawaii Press, Honolulu. See pp. 89–98.
15. Carlquist, p. 387.
16. R. B. Clapp, E. Kridler, and R. R. Fleet, 1977. The natural history of Nihoa Island, Northwestern Hawaiian Islands. *Atoll Research Bull. 207:* 14.
17. Ely and Clapp, p. 21.
18. Ibid., p. 263.
19. H. R. Dill and W. A. Bryan, 1912, p. 10 (cited by Ely and Capp, p. 264).
20. A. M. Bailey, 1918. The monk seal of the southern Pacific. *Natural History 18:* 396–98. See p. 396. Also, Ely and Clapp, p. 264.
21. Ely and Clapp, pp. 72 and 265.
22. Berger, p. 177 (quoting Palmer, 1891).
23. Ibid., p. 177 (citing Fisher, 1906).
24. Ibid., p. 178 (citing Bailey, 1956).
25. Ibid., p. 178 (quoting Wetmore, 1925).
26. R. B. Clapp and W. O. Wirtz, 1975. The natural history of Lisiansky Island, Northwestern Hawaiian Islands. *Atoll Research Bull. 186:* 115.
27. Ibid., p. 115.
28. Ely and Clapp, p. 68.
29. A. B. Amerson, Jr., R. B. Clapp, and W. O. Wirtz, 1974. The natural history of Pearl and Hermes Reef, Northwestern Hawaiian Islands. *Atoll Research Bull. 174:* 252–53.
30. Hadden, pp. 6–7.
31. *Ibid.,* p. 8.
32. Berger, p. 12.
33. Hadden, p. 16.
34. Berger, pp. 12 and 89.
35. P. W. Woodward, 1972. The natural history of Kure Atoll, Northwestern Hawaiian Islands. *Atoll Research Bull. 164:* 26.
36. *The Friend 21*(Oct. 10, 1872): 81. See Memoranda, Capt. E. Wood, correspondent.
37. Conant *et al.*, p. 79.
38. Woodward, p. 77.

CHAPTER 11

1. L. V. Briggs, 1926. *Experiences of a Medical Student in Honolulu and on the Island of Oahu, 1881*. David D. Nickerson, Boston. See p. 62.
2. J. F. Rock, 1974. *The Indigenous Trees of the Hawaiian Islands*. Pac. Trop. Botanical Garden, Lawai, Kauai, and C. E. Tuttle Co., Rutland, VT. See p. 191. Also, C. N. Forbes, 1913. Notes on the flora of Kahoolawe and Molokini. An enumeration of Niihau plants. *Occ. Papers B. P. Bishop Museum* 5(3): 1–26, plus plates and maps.
3. Rock, p. 315.
4. S. Carlquist, 1980. *Hawaii, A Natural History* (2nd. ed.). Pac. Trop. Botanical Garden, Lawai, Kauai. See p. 61.
5. G. W. Bates, ("A Haole"), 1854. *Sandwich Island Notes*. Harper and Brothers, New York. See p. 245.
6. J. TenBruggencate, 1985. Kokia trees: Rare, beautiful, and fighting for survival. *Sunday Star Bulletin and Advertiser* (Feb. 24, 1985). Honolulu. See p. A-14.
7. W. F. Hillebrand, 1965 (Facsimile of 1888 ed.). *Flora of the Hawaiian Islands: A Description of the Phanerogams and Vascular Cryptogams*. Hafner Pub. Co., New York and London. See p. 51.
8. James Cook, 1778. (Remarks on the discovery of Kauai.) P. 216, in A. G. Price (Ed.). *The Explorations of Captain James Cook in the Pacific, as Told by Selections of His Own Journals, 1768–1779*. (1971). Dover, New York.
9. C. S. Stewart, 1970 (Facsimile of 1830 ed.). *Journal of a Residence in the Sandwich Islands during the Years 1823, 1824, and 1825 . . .* Univ. of Hawaii Press, Honolulu. See p. 176.
10. J. Montgomery (Ed.), 1832. *Journal of Voyages and Travels by the Reverend Daniel Tyerman and George Bennet, Esq. . . . Between the Years 1821 and 1829*. Crocker and Brewster, Boston. See Vol. II, p. 91.
11. H. T. Cheever, 1851. *Life in the Sandwich Islands, or the Heart of the Pacific as It Was and Is*. A. S. Barnes and Co., New York. See p. 69.
12. W. Ellis, 1833. *Polynesian Researches during a Residence of Nearly Eight Years in the Society and Sandwich Islands*. J. and J. Harper, New York. See Vol. IV, pp. 63 and 69.
13. Cheever, pp. 69–72.
14. E. M. Damon, 1931. *Koamalu*. Priv. printed, Honolulu. See Vol. 1, p. 389.
15. A. Campbell, 1816. *A Voyage Round the World from 1806 to 1812*. Reprinted 1969. Da Capo Press, New York. See p. 145.
16. Montgomery, Vol. II, p. 47.
17. W. Ellis, 1872. (Reprinted remarks about Honolulu.) *The Friend* 21(8): 68 (Supplement, August 1872).
18. A. Bloxam, 1925. Diary of Andrew Bloxam, naturalist of the *Blonde* on her trip from England to the Hawaiian Islands, 1824–25. *B. P. Bishop Museum Spec. Pub. 10*. Bishop Museum Press, Honolulu. See pp. 33–36.
19. J. N. Reynolds, 1835. *Voyage of the United States Frigate* Potomac *Under the Command of Commodore John Downes During the Circumnavigation of the Globe in the Years 1831, 1832, 1833, and 1834*. Harper and Brothers, New York. See p. 399.
20. T. Coan, 1882. *Life in Hawaii*. A. D. F. Randolph and Co., New York. See p. 240.
21. F. W. Taylor, 1842. *A Voyage Around the World in the United States Frigate* Columbia, *Attended by Her Consort the Sloop of War* John Adams *and Commanded by Commodore George C. Read* (2nd Ed.). H. Mansfield, New Haven. See Vol. II, pp. 248–49.
22. Anon., 1856. *The Friend* 5(8): 62 (new series).
23. I. L. Bird, 1974. *Six Months in the Sandwich Islands* (7th ed., paperbound). Tut Books, C. E. Tuttle Co., Rutland, VT. See p. 17.
24. R. Warshauer, 1984. Cash in Your Chips, or Where Have All the Forests Gone. *Elepaio* 45(6): 49.
25. Bird, p. 243.
26. Warshauer. Also, D. Mueller-Dombois, 1985. The biological resource value of native

forests on Hawaii with special reference to the tropical lowland rainforest at Kalapana. *Elepaio* 45(10): 95–101.
27. Ellis, *Polynesian Researchers*, pp. 250–57.
28. Coan, p. 29.
29. S. Damon, 1855. Quick trip to Kilauea. *The Friend* 4(9): 70.
30. J. F. G. La Pérouse, 1799. *A Voyage Round the World Performed in the Years 1785, 1786, 1787, and 1788, etc.* Reprinted 1968 by Da Capo Press, New York. (Bibliotheca Australiana No. 27.) See p. 340.
31. Cheever, 1851, pp. 146–47.
32. Rock, p. 97.
33. M. C. Alexander (Ed.), 1934. *William Patterson Alexander in Kentucky, the Marquesas, Hawaii.* Priv. printed, Honolulu. See p. 451.
34. Cheever, p. 122.
35. Damon, Vol. 1, p. 415.
36. Damon, Vol. 1, p. 216.
37. Hillebrand, p. 94.
38. Bates, p. 174.
39. Alexander, p. 386.
40. Anon., 1858. *The Friend* 8(7): 49.
41. Hillebrand, p. 235.

CHAPTER 12

1. S. Carlquist, 1980. *Hawaii: A Natural History* (2nd ed.). Pacific Tropical Botanical Garden, Lawai, Kauai. See p. 132.
2. Ibid., p. 135.
3. E. S. C. Handy and E. G. Handy, 1972. Native planters in old Hawaii: Their life, lore, and environment. *B. P. Bishop Museum Bull.* 233. Bishop Museum Press, Honolulu. See pp. 225–26.
4. C. Lamoureux, 1985. Pers. Comm. Dept. of Botany, Univ. of Hawaii.
5. J. M. Alexander, 1884. Mountain climbing on West Maui. *Thrum's Hawaiian Almanac and Annual for 1884.* See p. 33.
6. L. Stemmermann, 1983. Ecological studies of Hawaiian *Metrosideros* in a successional context. *Pac. Science* 37(4): 361–73. Also, C. A. Corn and W. M. Hiesey, 1973. Altitudinal variation in Hawaiian *Metrosideros. Amer. Jour. Botany* 60(10): 991–1002.
7. D. Mueller-Dombois, 1985. Ohia dieback in Hawaii: 1984 synthesis and evaluation. *Pac. Science* 39(2): 150–70. See p. 165. Also, D. Mueller-Dombois, 1985. The biological resource value of native forest in Hawaii with special reference to the tropical lowland rainforest at Kalapana. *Elepaio* 45(10): 95–101. See p. 97.
8. For a comprehensive summary of *ohia* dieback, see Mueller-Dombois, Ohia dieback.
9. J. F. Rock, 1974. *The Indigenous Trees of the Hawaiian Islands* (rev. ed.). Pac. Tropical Botanical Garden, Lawai, Kauai, and C. E. Tuttle Co., Rutland, VT. See p. 333.
10. M. C. Alexander (Ed.), 1934. *William Patterson Alexander in Kentucky, the Marquesas, Hawaii.* Priv. printed, Honolulu. See p. 129.
11. W. D. Alexander, 1890. Early visitors to the Hawaiian Islands. *Thrum's Hawaiian Annual for 1890.* See pp. 37–53.
12. Excerpt from "Admiral Bille's report on the voyage of the Danish Korvette, *Galathea*, round the world in the years 1845, '46, and '47." Reprinted in *The Friend* 12(5): 35. (1863).
13. Anon., 1867. *The Friend* 18(1): 6.
14. J. Montgomery (Ed.), 1832. *Journal of Tyerman and Bennet, etc.* Vol. II. Crocker and Brewster, Boston. See p. 78.
15. G. W. Bates (A Haole), 1854. *Sandwich Island Notes.* Harper and Brothers, New York. See p. 49.

16. F. W. Beechey, 1831. *Narrative of a Voyage to the Pacific and Bering's Strait, etc. in the Years 1825, '26, '27, '28.* Henry Colburn and Richard Bentley, London. See Vol. II, p. 97.
17. Anon., 1854. *The Friend* 3(3): 17–18. Also, J. Hobbs, 1935. *A Pageant of the Soil.* Stanford Univ. Press, Stanford, CA. See p. 24.
18. Montgomery, p. 43.
19. W. Ellis, 1833. *Polynesian Researches Etc.* Vol. IV. J. and J. Harper, New York. See p. 289.
20. Ibid., p. 131.
21. Ibid., p. 226.
22. E. M. Damon, 1931. *Koamalu.* Priv. printed, Honolulu. See Vol. 1, p. 241.
23. Ibid., pp. 250–51.
24. Ibid., p. 275.
25. Ibid., p. 202; also, Vol. II, p. 770.
26. Bates, pp. 367–68.
27. J. Brennan, 1974. *The Parker Ranch of Hawaii.* John Day Co., New York. See p. 82.
28. Ibid., p. 138.
29. J. M. Lydgate, 1883. Hawaiian woods and forest trees. *Thrum's Hawaiian Annual for 1883.* See pp. 33–34. Also, Rock, p. 333.
30. S. M. Damon, 1868. *The Friend* 18(9): 74–75 (Sept. 1868).
31. Alexander, pp. 307–08.
32. Anon., 1890. Hawaiian maritime history. *Thrum's Hawaiian Annual for 1890.* See p. 78.
33. W. F. Hillebrand, 1965. *Flora of the Hawaiian Islands: A Description of the Phanerogams and Vascular Cryptogams.* Hafner Publishing Company, New York and London. See p. 546.
34. Bates, p. 322. Also, E. M. Bailey, 1888. The flora and fauna of the Hawaiian Islands. *Thrum's Hawaiian Annual for 1888.* See p. 52.
35. Anon. ("F. L. C."), 1875. Decadence of Hawaiian forests. *Thrum's Hawaiian Annual for 1875.* See pp. 19–20. Also, C. R. Bishop and S. B. Dole, 1883. Report of the committee on forestry. *Planters' Monthly* 2: 241–44. Reprinted in *Elepaio* 46(15). See p. 164.
36. Anon. ("F. L. C.").
37. Anon., 1875. "Survival of the Fittest," or strongest. *The Friend* 24(2): 14.
38. Anon., 1870. Plant trees. *The Friend* 20(9): 85.
39. Anon., 1867. (Article on reforestation at Ulupalakua.) *The Friend* 18(9): 85. Also, I. L. Bird, 1974 (7th ed.). *Six months in the Sandwich Islands.* C. E. Tuttle Co. (Tut Books, paperback), Rutland, VT. See p. 228.
40. Damon, *Koamalu*, Vol. 1, p. 206; also, Vol. 2, pp. 770–72.
41. D. Mueller-Dombois, 1985. *Pac. Science* 39(2): 150–70 (citing a manuscript by R. A. Holt, 1983).
42. A. C. Manglesdorf, 1980. P. 32, in C. E. Hartt (Ed.). *Harold Lloyd Lyon: Hawaiian Sugar Botanist.* H. L. Lyon Arboretum, Univ. of Hawaii, Honolulu.
43. C. E. Hartt (Ed.), 1980, in Hartt, *Harold Lloyd Lyon*, p. 4. Also, H. L. Lyon, 1918. The forests of Hawaii. *Haw'n Sugar Planters' Record* 18: 276–80.
44. Hartt, p. 6.
45. H. L. Lyon, 1923. Letter to H. P. Agee, in Hartt, *Harold Lloyd Lyon*, p. 48.
46. O. Degener (Comments), in Hartt, *Harold Lloyd Lyon*, pp. 39–40.
47. Bird, p. 176.
48. N. J. Mitchell, 1980. Why are the *ohe* trees not reseeding? *Elepaio* 41(1): 5.

CHAPTER 13

1. C. M. Hyde, 1887. Hawaiians and nature. *Thrums Hawaiian Almanac and Annual for 1887.* Honolulu. See p. 81.
2. T. Coan, 1882. *Life in Hawaii.* A. D. F. Randolph and Co., New York. See p. 40.

3. For recent general references to Hawaiian stream faunas, see J. A. Maciolek, 1978. Insular aquatic ecosystems: Hawaii. Pp. 103–20, in *Classification, inventory, and analysis of fish and wildlife habitat, proceedings of a national symposium.* U.S. Fish and Wildlife Service, FWS/OBS-78/76. Also, A. S. Timbol, 1979. Freshwater macrofauna and habitats in the Hawaiian Archipelago and U.S. Oceania. Pp. 4–1 to 4–24, in J. E. Byrne (Ed.). *Literature review and synthesis of information on Pacific island ecosystems.* U.S. Fish and Wildlife Service, FWS/OBS-79/35. Also, J. I. Ford and R. A. Kinzie III, 1982. Life crawls upstream. *Natural History 91*(12): 61–66.

4. M. Titcomb, 1977. *Native Use of Fish in Hawaii* (2nd. ed., paperback). Univ. of Hawaii Press, Honolulu. See p. 128.

5. A. J. Berger, 1983. *Bird Life in Hawaii.* Island Heritage in association with Honolulu Publishing Co., Ltd., Honolulu. See p. 18.

6. For a compact reference to wetland vegetation in Hawaii and other Pacific islands, see L. Stemmermann, 1981. *A Guide of Pacific Wetland Plants.* U.S. Army Corps of Engineers, Honolulu District.

7. A. J. Berger, 1972. *Hawaiian Birdlife* (1st ed.), Univ. of Hawaii Press, Honolulu. See p. 92.

8. J. A. Maciolek, 1983. Distribution and biology of Indo-Pacific insular hypogeal shrimps. *Bull. Mar. Sci. 33*(3): 606–18. Also, J. A. Maciolek, 1986. Environmental features and biota of anchialine pools on Cape Kinau, Maui, Hawaii. *Stygologia 2*(1/2): 119–29.

9. F. R. Schram, 1986. *Crustacea.* Oxford Univ. Press, New York. See p. 254.

10. Maciolek, Distribution and biology, p. 615.

11. J. A. Maciolek, 1982. Lakes and lake-like waters of the Hawaiian archipelago. *Occ. Papers of the B. P. Bishop Museum,* Honolulu.

12. P. V. Kirch, 1985. *Feathered Gods and Fishhooks.* Univ. of Hawaii Press, Honolulu. See p. 74.

13. Otto von Kotzebue, 1821. *A Voyage of Discovery in the South Sea and Bering's Straits . . . in the years 1815–1818, etc.* Reprinted 1967. Da Capo Press, New York. See Vol. 1, p. 341.

14. Titcomb, p. 123 (citing Beckley).

15. *Ibid.,* pp. 122–123.

16. Ibid., pp. 32 and 123.

17. W. K. Kikuchi, 1976. Prehistoric Hawaiian fishponds. *Science 193*: 295–99.

18. Titcomb, p. 123.

19. Early comments on waterfowl abundance around Hawaiian fishponds—see, for example, A. Menzies, 1920. *Hawaii Nei 128 years ago* (reprint of Menzies' journal of 1792). Priv. printed, Honolulu. See p. 24. Also, A. Bloxam, 1925. *Diary of Andrew Bloxam, naturalist of the* Blonde . . . *1824–25.* B. P. Bishop Museum Spec. Pub. 10. Bishop Museum Press, Honolulu. See pp. 35–36.

20. Titcomb, p. 124.

21. H. A. Wadsworth, 1933. A historical summary of irrigation in Hawaii. *Haw'n Planters' Record 37*(3): 124–62. See pp. 141–42.

22. *Thrum's Hawaiian Almanac and Annual for 1878.* See pp. 18 and 39. Also, *The Friend 26*(11): 89 (1877).

23. *Thrum's,* 1878, p. 18. Also, *Thrum's Hawaiian Almanac and Annual for 1884.* See p. 44 (on "waste streams" and "waste waters").

24. Wadsworth, pp. 151–56.

25. W. P. Alexander, 1923. *The Irrigation of Sugar Cane in Hawaii.* Honolulu Experiment Sta., Haw'n Sugar Planters' Assoc. See p. 3 (on the density of irrigation systems on Kauai).

26. K. I. Takasaki, G. T. Hirashima, and E. R. Lubke, 1969. Water resources of windward Oahu. *U.S. Geol. Survey Water Supply Paper 1894:* 1–119. Wash., DC, U.S. Govt. Printing Office. See map, p. 15, and pp. 102–03.

27. M. M. O'Shaughnessey, 1906. Irrigation works in the Hawaiian Islands. *Jour. of Electricity, Power, and Gas 17*(22): 459–66. See p. 459.

28. W. P. Alexander, p. 3.

29. A. C. Alexander, 1937. *Koloa Plantation 1835–1935.* Printed by *Honolulu Star Bull.,* Honolulu. See p. 138.

30. W. P. Alexander, p. 6 (on linked artesian wells delivering 80 mgd).
31. O'Shaughnessey, p. 462.
32. T. Coffman, 1979. *Rediscovering Water.* Board of Water Supply, Honolulu. See p. 22.
33. D. M. Devaney *et al.*, 1982. *Kaneohe: A History of Change.* The Bess Press, Honolulu. See p. 81.
34. Anon., 1877. Capsule history of rice culture in Hawaii. *Thrum's Hawaiian Almanac and Annual for 1877.* See pp. 45–49.
35. Anon., 1881. Game laws and game of the Hawaiian Islands. *Thrum's Hawaiian Almanac and Annual for . . . 1881.* See pp. 39–40.
36. E. M. Damon, 1931. *Koamalu.* Priv. printed, Honolulu. See Vol. 1, p. 186.
37. M. C. Alexander (Ed.), 1934. *William Patterson Alexander in Kentucky, the Marquesas, Hawaii.* Priv. printed, Honolulu. See p. 398.
38. S. B. Dole, 1879. List of birds of the Hawaiian Islands (2nd ed. of Dole's list). *Thrum's Hawaiian Almanac and Annual for . . . 1879.* See p. 52.
39. J. G. Chan, 1986. Bacteria-caused mortality of freshwater shrimp *(opae-kala-ole, Atyoida bisulcata)* from the island of Hawaii. *Elepaio* 46(17): 191–92.
40. J. A. Maciolek, 1984. Exotic fishes in Hawaii and other islands of Oceania. Chap. 7, pp. 131–61, in W. R. Courtenay, Jr., and J. R. Stauffer, Jr. (Eds.). *Distribution, Biology, and Management of Exotic Fishes.* Johns Hopkins Univ. Press, Baltimore.

CHAPTER 14

1. A. J. Berger, 1972 and 1981. *Hawaiian Birdlife.* Univ. of Hawaii Press, Honolulu. Also, J. M. Scott, S. Mountainspring, F. L. Ramsay, and C. B. Kepler, 1986. Forest bird communities of the Hawaiian Islands: Their dynamics, ecology, and conservation. *Studies In Avian Biology 9:* 1–431.
2. R. C. L. Perkins, 1903. Vertebrata. Part 4 of Vol. 1, pp. 365–465, in D. Sharp (Ed.). *Fauna Hawaiiensis.* The University Press, Cambridge, England. Also, R. C. L. Perkins, 1901. An introduction to the study of the Drepanididae, a family of birds peculiar to the Hawaiian Islands. *Ibis* (1901): 562–85.
3. G. C. Munro, 1944. *Birds of Hawaii.* Tongg Publishing Company, Honolulu.
4. Various accounts of flightless rails are summarized by Berger (1972), p. 89.
5. R. C. L. Perkins, 1893. Notes on collecting in Kona, Hawaii. *Ibis* (1893): 101–14.
6. J. M. Scott *et al.*, p. 86
7. F. Richardson and J. Bowles, 1964. A survey of the birds of Kauai. *B. P. Bishop Museum Bull. 227:* 27–28.
8. J. M. Scott *et al.*, p. 103.
9. H. Ten Bruggencate, 1983. *Honolulu Advertiser* (June 14, 1983): A-3. Also, H. Ten Bruggencate, 1987. *Sunday Star Bulletin and Advertiser* (August 23, 1987): G-6.
10. W. E. Banko, 1979. History of endemic Hawaiian birds, specimens in museum collections. *CPSU/UH Avian History Rept.* No. 2. Univ. of Hawaii, Honolulu.
11. C. G. Sibley and J. E. Alquist, 1982. The relationships of the Hawaiian honeycreepers (Drepaninini) as indicated by DNA-DNA hybridization. *Auk 99:* 130–40.
12. Prevailing disagreements on honeycreeper classification are reflected in the following: D. Amadon, 1986. The Hawaiian honeycreepers revisited. *Elepaio* 46(8): 83–84. Also, A. J. Berger, 1981. Hawaiian Birdlife (2nd ed.). Univ. of Hawaii Press, Honolulu. Also, S. L. Olson and H. F. James, 1982. Prodromus of the fossil avifauna of the Hawaiian Islands. *Smithsonian Contrib. Zool.* No. 365. Smithsonian Inst. Press, Wash., DC. Also, H. D. Pratt, 1979. *A systematic analysis of the endemic avifauna of the Hawaiian Islands* (thesis). Univ. Microfilms CDM-79-21977, Ann Arbor, MI. Also, H. D. Pratt, P. L. Bruner, and D. G. Berrett, 1987. *A Field Guide to the Birds of Hawaii and the Tropical Pacific.* Princeton Univ. Press, Princeton, NJ. Also, Sibley and Alquist.
13. W. A. Bryan and A. Seale, 1901. Notes on the birds of Kauai. *Occ. Papers B. P. Bishop Museum 1*(3): 129–37. See p. 137.
14. Amadon, p. 83.

15. W. W. Weathers and C. Van Riper III, 1982. Temperature regulation in two endangered Hawaiian honeycreepers: the Palila *(Psittirostra bailleui)* and the Laysan Finch *(Psittirostra cantans)*. *Auk 99*: 667–74.
16. E. M. Damon, 1931. *Koamalu*. Priv. printed, Honolulu. See Vol. 1, pp. 257–58.
17. J. Cassin, 1858. Mammalia and ornithology. Vol. 8, in United States Exploring Exped. (1838–1842). C. Sherman and Son, Philadelphia. See p. 178.
18. H. T. Spieth, 1966. Hawaiian honeycreeper, *Vestiaria coccinea* (Forster), feeding on lobeliad flowers, *Clermontia arborescens* (Mann) Hillebr. *Amer. Naturalist 100*: 470–73.
19 W. T. Brigham, 1899. Hawaiian feather work. *Mem. B. P. Bishop Museum 1*(1): 1–79. See p. 9.
20. Perkins, 1903, p. 406.
21. D. Medway, 1979. Some ornithological results of Cook's third voyage. *Jour. Soc. Bibliogr. Nat. History 9*(3): 315–51. Also, D. Medway, 1981. The contribution of Cook's third voyage to the ornithology of the Hawaiian Islands. *Pac. Science 35*(2): 105–75. See p. 141.
22. Berger, p. 190 (citing Henshaw).
23. Perkins, 1903, pp. 401–02.
24. T. L. C. Casey and J. D. Jacobi, 1974. A new genus and species of bird from the island of Maui, Hawaii (Passeriformes: Drepanididae). *Occ. Papers B. P. Bishop Museum 24*(12): 216–26.
25. Anon., 1986. Nest discovered for the first time of endangered poo-uli. *Elepaio 47*(1): 4–5.
26. A. L. Kaeppler, 1970. Feather cloaks, ship captains, and lords. *Occ. Papers B. P. Bishop Museum 24*(6): 92–114. See p. 92.
27. Berger, 1972, p. 119.
28. Brigham, p. 2.
29. Ibid., p. 5 (quoting King).
30. E. S. C. Handy and E. G. Handy, 1972. Native planters in old Hawaii: Their life, lore, and environment. *B. P. Bishop Museum Bull. 233*. Bishop Museum Press, Honolulu. See p. 258.
31. Kaeppler, p. 111.
32. Berger, 1972, p. 121 (citing Henshaw).
33. Ibid., p. 119 (citing Wilson).
34. W. A. Bryan, 1904. Notes on the birds of the Waianae Mountains. *Occ. Papers B. P. Bishop Museum 2*(3): (Director's Annual Rept.). See p. 45.
35. Munro, pp. 77, 85, 116, and 128.
36. A. Manning, 1982. Hawaiian and Laysan rails: S.B. Dole corresponds with A. Agassiz. *Elepaio 42*(10): 87–88. See p. 87.
37. Munro, p. 93.
38. Berger, 1972, p. 177.
39. I. A. E. Atkinson, 1977. A reassessment of factors, particularly *Rattus rattus* L., that influenced the decline of endemic forest birds in the Hawaiian Islands. *Pac. Science 31*(2): 109–33.
40. S. G. van Riper and C. van Riper III, 1985. A summary of known parasites and diseases recorded from the avifauna of the Hawaiian Islands. Chap. 10, pp. 298–371, in C. P. Stone and J. M. Scott (Eds.). *Hawaii's Terrestrial Ecosystems: Preservation and Management*. Coop. Natl. Park Resources Studies Unit, Univ. of Hawaii, Honolulu.
41. Munro, p. 68.
42. Ibid., p. 74.
43. E. L. Caum, 1933. The exotic birds of Hawaii. *Occ. Papers B. P. Bishop Museum 10*(9): 1–55. See p. 44.
44. Berger, pp. 219–21.
45. P. A. Cox, 1983. Extinction of the Hawaiian avifauna resulted in a change of pollinators for the *ieie, Freycinetia arborea. Oikos 41*(2): 195–99.
46. P. C. Banko, pers. comm., Jan. 1988.
47. Anon., 1864. *The Friend 13*(6): 46.
48. Beebe, C. W. 1906. *The Bird, Its Form and Function*. H. Holt and Co., New York. See p. 18.

CHAPTER 15

1. D. Sharp (Ed.), 1899–1913. *Fauna Hawaiiensis . . .* (3 vols.). The University Press, Cambridge, England.
2. E. C. Zimmerman and D. E. Hardy, 1948–1981. *Insects of Hawaii* (14 vols.). Univ. of Hawaii Press, Honolulu.
3. C. M. Simon, W. C. Gagné, F. G. Howarth, and F. J. Radovsky, 1984. Hawaii: A natural entomological laboratory. *Bull. Entomol. Soc. Amer. 30*(3): 8–17.
4. C. E. Zimmerman, 1970. Adaptive radiation in Hawaii with special reference to insects. Reprinted 1972. Pp. 528–34, in E. A. Kay (Ed.). *A Natural History of the Hawaiian Islands.* Univ. of Hawaii Press, Honolulu. See p. 528.
5. Ibid., p. 529.
6. For overviews and history of modern research on Hawaiian drosophilid flies, see H. L. Carson, D. E. Hardy, H. T. Spieth, and W. S. Stone, 1970. The evolutionary biology of the Hawaiian Drosophilidae. Chap. 15, pp. 437–543, in M. K. Hecht and W. C. Steere (Eds.). *Essays in Evolution and Genetics in Honor of Theodosius Dobzhansky.* Appleton-Century-Crofts, New York. Also, H. L. Carson and J. S. Yoon, 1982. Genetics and evolution of Hawaiian *Drosophila.* Pp. 297–344, in M. Ashburner, H. L. Carson, and J. N. Thompson, Jr. (Eds.). *Genetics and Biology of Drosophila* (Vol. 3b). Academic Press, London. Also, K. Y. Kaneshiro and C. R. B. Boake, 1987. Sexual selection and speciation: Issues raised by Hawaiian *Drosophila. Trends in Ecol. and Evol. 2*(7): 207–12.
7. H. L. Carson *et al.*, p. 482.
8. R. Lewin, 1985. Hawaiian Drosophila: Young islands, old flies. *Science 229*: 1072–74.
9. Simon *et al.*, p. 12.
10. Carson *et al.*, 1970, p. 455.
11. C. Darwin, 1859. *The Origin of Species.* 1970. Reprinted excerpts, in P. Appleman (Ed.). *Darwin: A Norton Critical Edition.* Norton, New York. See p. 126.
12. For a vivid description of lek behavior in Hawaiian *Drosophila*, see K. Y. Kaneshiro and A. T. Ohta, 1982. The flies fan out. *Natural History 91*(12): 54–58.
13. J. E. Leonard and L. Ehrman, 1976. Recognition and sexual selection in *Drosophila*: Classification, quantification, and identification. *Science 193*: 693–95. Also, C. P. Kyriacou and J. C. Hall, 1986. Interspecific genetic control of courtship song production and reception in *Drosophila. Science 232*: 494–97.
14. Zimmerman, 1970, p. 528.
15. K. Y. Kaneshiro, 1983. Sexual selection and direction of evolution in the biosystematics of the Hawaiian Drosophilidae. *Annual Rev. Entomol. 28*: 161–78. Also, Kaneshiro and Boake.
16. S. L. Montgomery, 1982. Biogeography of the moth genus *Eupithecia* in Oceania and the evolution of ambush predation in Hawaiian caterpillars. *Entomol. Gen. 8*: 27–34.
17. Zimmerman, 1970, p. 530.
18. Ibid., p. 533.
19. Numerous studies now exist on the ecology of Hawaiian caves, beginning with F. G. Howarth, 1972. Cavernicoles in lava tubes on the island of Hawaii. *Science 175*: 325–26. See especially F. G. Howarth, 1981. Community structure and niche differentiation in Hawaiian lava tube caves. Chap. 7, pp. 318–36, in D. Mueller-Dombois, K. W. Bridges, and H. L. Carson (Eds.). *Island Ecosystems: Biological Organization in Selected Hawaiian Communities.* US/IBP Synthesis Series 15. Hutchinson Ross, Stroudsburg, PA. Also, ibid., pp. 222–29 (lava-tube ecosystem as a study site).
20. Howarth, pp. 334–35.
21. Zimmerman, 1970, p. 530.
22. T. Blackburn, 1882. (Article on Hawaiian entomology.) *Thrum's Hawaiian Almanac and Annual for 1882,* Honolulu, pp. 58–61.
23. L. L. Loope and D. Mueller-Dombois, 1986. The characteristics of invaded islands. (Oral conf. paper, Scope-international synthesis symposium on the ecology of biological invasions, Nov. 13, 1986, East-West Center, Honolulu.) To be published in J. Drake *et al* (Eds.). *Biological Invasions: A Global Perspective.* J. Wiley and Sons.

24. A. von Chamisso, 1821. Remarks and opinions of the naturalist of the expedition, in Otto von Kotzebue. *A Voyage of Discovery into the South Sea and Bering's Straits . . . in the Years 1815–1818 . . .* (Vols. 2 and 3). Reprinted 1967, Da Capo Press, New York. See Vol. 3, p. 237.
25. J. Montgomery (Ed.), 1832. *Journal of Voyages and Travels by the Reverend Daniel Tyerman and George Bennet, Esq. . . .* Vol. 2. Crocker and Brewster, Boston. See p. 56.
26. E. Bailey, 1888. The flora and fauna of the Hawaiian Islands. *Thrum's Hawaiian Almanac and Annual for 1888.* See p. 54.
27. S. Parker, 1967. *Parker's Exploring Tour beyond the Rocky Mountains.* Ross and Haines, Minneapolis, MN. See p. 353.
28. M. C. Alexander (Ed.), 1934. *William Patterson Alexander in Kentucky, the Marquesas, Hawaii.* Priv. printed, Honolulu. See p. 230.
29. Ibid., p. 308.
30. G. W. Bates (A Haole), 1854. *Sandwich Island Notes.* Harper and Brothers, New York. See p. 318.
31. Parker, p. 353.
32. E. Waldron, 1967. *Honolulu 100 Years Ago.* Fisher Printing Co., Honolulu. See p. 89.
33. Anon., 1870. *The Friend* 20(11): 100.
34. J. W. Beardsley, 1979. New immigrant insects in Hawaii: 1962 through 1976. *Proc. Haw'n Entomol. Soc. 13*(1): 35–44.
35. About one thousand species of snails, see D. Mueller-Dombois, K. W. Bridges, and H. L. Carson (Eds.), 1981. *Island Ecosystems . . .* Hutchinson Ross, Stroudsburg, PA. See p. 21.
36. W. J. Rees, 1965. The aerial dispersal of Mollusca. *Proc. Malacol. Soc. London 36*: 269–82.
37. Zimmerman and Hardy, Vol. 1, p. 103.
38. M. G. Hadfield, Dec. 1986. Pers. comm.
39. M. G. Hadfield, 1986. Extinction in Hawaiian achatinelline snails. *Malacologia 27*(1): 67–81. Also, M. G. Hadfield and B. S. Mountain, 1980. A field study of a vanishing species, *Achatinella mustelina* (Gastropoda, Pulmonata), in the Waianae Mountains of Oahu. *Pac. Science 34*: 345–58.
40. About 35 to 40 species of *Achatinella,* see Hadfield, p. 67 (citing Federal Register and Welch).
41. Hadfield, p. 72 (citing Pilsbry and Cooke).
42. Ibid.
43. G. Dixon, 1789. *A Voyage Round the World . . . in 1785, 1786, 1787, and 1788 . . .* Geo. Goulding, London. Reprinted 1968. Da Capo Press, New York. See Appendix 1, p. 354, and the plate facing p. 355.
44. F. J. F. Meyen, 1981. *A Botanist's Visit to Oahu in 1831.* Excerpted from the original. Press Pacifica, Kailua, Hawaii. See p. 45.
45. Alexander, p. 325.
46. Ibid., p. 330.
47. A. Gulick, 1932. *Evolutionist and Missionary: John T. Gulick.* Univ. of Chicago Press, Chicago. See p. 113.
48. Hadfield, p. 69 (citing Clench on J. T. Gulick's shell collection).
49. E. W. Thwing, 1907. Reprint of the original descriptions of the Genus *Achatinella. Occ. Papers B. P. Bishop Museum 3*(1): 1–190. See remarks in author's introduction.
50. Hadfield, p. 74 (citing Kondo on Meinecke collection).
51. D. D. Baldwin, 1888. The land shells of the Hawaiian Islands, *Thrum's Hawaiian Almanac and Annual for 1888*: 55–63. See p. 62.
52. Hadfield and Mountain, p. 357.
53. B. Clarke, J. Murray, and M. S. Johnson, 1984. The extinction of endemic species by a program of biological control. *Pac. Science 38*(12): 97–104.

CHAPTER 16

1. J. M. Lydgate, 1883. Hawaiian woods and forest trees. *Thrum's Hawaiian Almanac and Annual for 1883*: 33–35. See p. 34.

2. Some general references to the montane dryland flora include S. Carlquist, 1980. *Hawaii: A Natural History* (2nd ed.). Pacific Tropical Botanical Garden, Lawai, Kauai. Also, J. F. Rock, 1974. *The Indigenous Trees of the Hawaiian Islands* (rev. ed.). Pacific Tropical Botanical Garden, Lawai, Kauai, and C. E. Tuttle Co., Rutland, VT. Also, D. Mueller-Dombois, K. W. Bridges, and H. L. Carson, 1981. *Island Ecosystems: Biological Organization in Selected Hawaiian Communities*. Hutchinson Ross, Stroudsburg, PA. See especially Part II.

3. O. Degener, 1930. *Plants of Hawaii National Parks* . . . Reprinted 1975. Priv. printed. See p. 208.

4. Rock, p. 185.

5. F. R. Warshauer and J. D. Jacobi, 1982. Distribution and status of *Vicia menziesii* Spreng. (Leguminosae): Hawaii's first officially listed endangered plant species. *Biol. Conservation 23*: 111–126. Also, A. Menzies, 1920. *Hawaii Nei 128 Years Ago* (reprint of Menzies' journal, with an introduction by W. F. Wilson). Priv. printed, Honolulu. See pp. 190–91.

6. B. Y. Kimura and K. M. Nagata, 1980. *Hawaii's Vanishing Flora*. The Oriental Publishing Co., Honolulu. See pp. 46–49.

7. Ibid., pp. 20–21.

8. C. H. Lamoureux, 1976. *Trailside Plants of Hawaii's National Parks*. Hawaii Natural History Assoc., Hawaii Volcanoes National Park. See p. 73.

9. Carlquist, p. 264.

10. G. D. Carr, 1985. *Allertonia* 4(1), see pp. 50–59.

11. Rock, pp. 503–05.

12. D. Douglas, 1914. *Journal Kept by David Douglas During his Travels in North America* . . . W. Wesley and Son, London. See Appendix 2, p. 299.

13. G. W. Bates (A Haole), 1854. *Sandwich Island Notes*. Harper and Brothers, New York. See pp. 370–72.

14. A. J. Berger, 1972. *Hawaiian Birdlife* (1st ed.). Univ. of Hawaii Press, Honolulu. See p. 103 (citing Tomich).

15. Ibid., p. 103 (citing Munro).

16. J. M. Scott *et al*, 1986. Forest bird communities of the Hawaiian Islands: Their dynamics, ecology, and conservation. *Studies in Avian Biology 9*: 1–431. See p. 82. Also, J. G. Giffen, J. M. Scott, and S. Mountainspring, 1987 (in press). Habitat selection and management of the Hawaiian crow. *Jour. Wildlife Management*. Also, P. Stein, U.S. Fish and Wildlife Service, July 1986. Pers. comm.

17. R. L. Walker, 1969. Field notes 1958–1962: Hawaiian hawk. *Elepaio 30*(2): 17.

18. Berger, p. 84.

19. Ibid., p. 93.

20. R. C. L. Perkins, 1903. Vertebrata. Vol. 1, Part 4, pp. 365–465, in D. Sharp (Ed.). *Fauna Hawaiiensis*. The University Press, Cambridge, England. See p. 428.

21. Berger, p. 125 (citing Baldwin and others).

22. R. J. Kramer, 1971. *Hawaiian Land Mammals*. C. E. Tuttle, Rutland, VT. See pp. 55–69.

23. P. V. Kirch, 1985. *Feathered Gods and Fishhooks*. Univ. of Hawaii Press, Honolulu. See p. 179.

24. Ibid., pp. 179–80.

25. S. L. Olson and H. F. James, 1982. Prodromus of the fossil avifauna of the Hawaiian Islands. *Smithsonian Contrib. to Zoology* No. 365. Smithsonian Inst. Press, Wash., DC. See p. 30.

26. W. H. Pease, 1867. (Article on the nene goose and other Hawaiian bird lore.) *The Friend 18*(12): 106.

27. W. D. Alexander, 1890. Early visitors to the Hawaiian Islands. *Thrum's Hawaiian Almanac and Annual for 1890*: 37–53. See p. 39.

28. Anon., 1867. *The Friend 18*(10): 92. Also, Pease, p. 106. Also, Derby, The Right

Hon. the Earl of (Lord Stanley), 1834. Letter on the breeding of the Sandwich Island goose *(Bernicla Sandvicensis*, Vig.). *Proc. Zool. Soc. London*, Part 2. See pp. 41–43.
29. For recent population history and status of the nene, see P. H. Baldwin, 1945. The Hawaiian Goose, its distribution and reduction in numbers. *Condor 47*(1): 27–37. Also, C. P. Stone, R. L. Walker, J. M. Scott, and P. C. Banko, 1983. Hawaiian goose research and management—where do we go from here? *Elepaio 44*(2): 11–15.
30. C. P. Stone, H. M. Hoshide, and P. C. Banko, 1983. Productivity, mortality, and movement of Nene in the Kau Desert, Hawaii Volcanoes National Park, 1981–1982. *Pac. Science 37*(3): 301–11. Also, P. C. Banko, Jan. 1988. Pers. comm.
31. For general references about grasses in Hawaii, see P. P. Rotar, 1968. *Grasses of Hawaii*. Univ. of Hawaii Press, Honolulu. Also, C. W. Smith, 1985. Impact of alien plants on Hawaii's native biota. Chap. 8, pp. 180–243, in C. P. Stone and J. M. Scott (Eds.). *Hawaii's Terrestrial Ecosystems: Preservation and Management*. Cooperative Natl. Park Resources Studies Unit, Univ. of Hawaii, Honolulu. (Characterizes major weeds in Hawaii, including alien grasses; see also other papers in this volume.)
32. J. Brennan, 1979. *The Parker Ranch of Hawaii* (paperback ed.). Harper & Row, New York. See pp. 132 and 141.
33. C. W. Smith, 1985, in Stone and Scott (Eds.). See pp. 192–98; see also the summary chart in this paper.
34. Brennan, p. 168.
35. R. Thompson, 1987. Big Isle fire blamed on foreign grass. *Honolulu Star Bulletin.* March 14, 1987.
36. Brennan, p. 142.
37. I. L. Bird, 1974. *Six Months in the Sandwich Islands* (7th ed.). C. E. Tuttle Co. (Tut Books, paperback), Rutland, VT. See pp. 233–34.
38. Brennan, pp. 136–39.
39. J. O. Juvik and S. P. Juvik, 1984. Mauna Kea and the myth of multiple use: Endangered species and mountain management in Hawaii. *Mountain Research and Devel. 4*(3): 191–202. See p. 195 (citing Judd and Giffen).
40. Ibid., p. 195.
41. P. Q. Tomich, 1969. Mammals in Hawaii. B. P. *Bishop Museum Spec. Pub. 57.* Bishop Museum Press, Honolulu. See pp. 117–18.
42. Juvik and Juvik, pp. 198–201. Also, L. Catterall, 1986. Bighorn sheep must bow out on Mauna Kea. *Honolulu Star Bull.* Nov. 19, 1986. Also, Berger, p. 162 (on historical contraction of the palila's range).
43. A. D. Baldwin, 1915. *A Memoir of Henry Perrine Baldwin*. Priv. printed. See p. 65.
44. C. W. Schwartz and E. R. Schwartz, 1949. *The Game Birds in Hawaii.* Board of Commissioners of Agric. and Forestry, Territory of Hawaii. Pp. 1–168.

CHAPTER 17

1. G. A. Macdonald and A. T. Abbott, 1970. *Volcanoes in the Sea: The Geology of Hawaii.* Univ. of Hawaii Press, Honolulu. See pp. 235–37.
2. Ibid., p. 11.
3. Dept. of Geography, Univ. of Hawaii, 1983. *Atlas of Hawaii.* Univ. of Hawaii Press, Honolulu. See p. 63.
4. A. H. Woodcock, 1980. Hawaiian alpine lake level, rainfall trends, and spring flow. *Pac. Science 34*(2): 195–209.
5. D. Mueller-Dombois, K. W. Bridges, and H. L. Carson, 1981. *Island Ecosystems: Biological Organization in Selected Hawaiian Communities.* US/IBP Synthesis Series 15. Hutchinson Ross, Stroudsburg, PA. See p. 38.
6. For recent references on Hawaii's alpine aeolian ecosystem, see F. G. Howarth and S. L. Montgomery, 1980. Notes on the ecology of the high altitude aeolian zone on Mauna Kea. *Elepaio 41*(3): 21–22. Also, P. G. Ashlock and W. C. Gagné, 1983. *Internatl. Jour. Entomol. 25*: 47–55. Also, F. G. Howarth, 1987. Evolutionary ecology of aeolian and subterranean habitats in Hawaii. *Trends in Ecol. and Evol. 2*(7): 220–23.

7. B. Z. Siegal and S. M. Siegal, 1980. Biology of the Precambrian genus *Kakabeckia*: Geographic and microenvironmental determinations in the distribution of living *K. barghoorniana*. *Natl. Geogr. Soc. Research Repts.* 12: 639–46.
8. Ibid., Table 1, p. 642.
9. A. Menzies, 1920. *Hawaii Nei 128 years ago* (reprint of Menzies' journal). Priv. printed. See pp. 192–99.
10. D. Douglas, 1914. *Journal Kept by David Douglas During his Travels in North America . . .* W. Wesley and Son, London. See Appendix 2, pp. 299–302 and 315.
11. G. W. Bates (A Haole), 1854. *Sandwich Island Notes.* Harper and Brothers, New York. See p. 375.
12. See, for example, J. L. Richardson, 1977. *Dimensions of Ecology.* Williams and Wilkins, Baltimore. See p. 251.
13. M. Mull, 1982. *Elepaio 43*(2): 13.
14. M. Schmicker, 1982. The economy of astronomy. *Hawaii Business 28*(4): 22–31.
15. Howarth and Montgomery, pp. 21–22.

CHAPTER 18

1. D. Mueller-Dombois, 1985. Ohia dieback in Hawaii: 1984 synthesis and evaluation. *Pac. Science 39*(2): 150–70. See p. 158.
2. Some of the Hawaiian fossil birds initially identified as geese seem to be more closely related to ducks. See H. F. James and S. L. Olson, 1983. Flightless birds. *Natural History 92*(9): 30–40. See p. 34.
3. S. L. Olson and H. F. James, 1982. Prodromus of the fossil avifauna of the Hawaiian Islands. *Smithsonian Contrib. Zool.* No. 365. Smithsonian Inst., Wash., DC.
4. S. L. Olson, 1986. Prehistoric human impact on the avifauna of Hawaii (oral conference presentation). New Directions in Pacific and Hawaiian Archaeology. East-West Center, Univ. of Hawaii, Honolulu. March 22, 1986.
5. James and Olson, p. 40 (comparing *Apteribis* to New Zealand's kiwis).
6. W. Ellis, 1833. *Polynesian researches . . . etc.* Vol. IV. J. and J. Harper, New York. See p. 26.
7. Olson and James, Prodromus, pp. 32–33.
8. Ibid., pp. 29–30. Also, S. L. Olson and H. F. James, 1982. Fossil birds from the Hawaiian Islands: Evidence for wholesale extinction by man before western contact. *Science 217*: 633–35. Also, H. F. James *et al.*, 1987. Radiocarbon dates on bones of extinct birds from Hawaii. *Proc. Natl. Acad. Science USA 84*: 2350–54.
9. Olson and James, Prodromus, p. 31.
10. P. V. Kirch, 1985. *Feathered Gods and Fishhooks: An Introduction to Hawaiian Archaeology and Prehistory.* Univ. of Hawaii Press, Honolulu. See pp. 115–16.
11. See, for example, the discussion in Kirch, p. 290.

CHAPTER 19

1. B. R. Finney, 1977. Voyaging canoes and the settlement of Polynesia. *Science 196*: 1277–85.
2. P. V. Kirch, 1985. *Feathered Gods and Fishhooks: An Introduction to Hawaiian Archaeology and Prehistory.* Univ. of Hawaii Press, Honolulu.
3. P. V. Kirch, 1982. Transported landscapes. *Natural History 91*(12): 32–35.
4. Unlike serfs, the Hawaiian commoners could migrate to another *ahupuaa*. Good workers would be welcomed in the new jurisdiction. See, for example, E. S. C. Handy and E. G. Handy, 1972. Native planters in old Hawaii. *B. P. Bishop Museum Bull. 233*. Bishop Museum Press, Honolulu. See pp. 41–45. Also, Kirch, *Feathered Gods*, pp. 2–7.
5. Kirch, *Feathered Gods*, pp. 74–75 and 292.

6. M. Spriggs, 1986. Prehistoric human impact on the landscape of Oceania (oral conference presentation). New Directions in Pacific and Hawaiian Archaeology. East-West Center, Univ. of Hawaii. March 22, 1986.
7. Kirch, *Feathered Gods*, p. 300.
8. Ibid., pp. 217–18 (citing Green) and 222 (citing Yen).
9. G. Vancouver, 1798. *A Voyage of Discovery to the North Pacific Ocean and Round the World.* Reprinted 1967. Da Capo Press, New York. See Vol. 1, pp. 170 and 175.
10. Kirch, *Feathered Gods*, p. 138.
11. H. F. James *et al.*, 1987. Radiocarbon dates on bones of extinct birds from Hawaii. *Proc. Natl. Acad. Sci. USA 84*: 2350–54. See Table 1, p. 2353.
12. Kirch, *Feathered Gods*, p. 151 (citing Hommon).
13. S. Carlquist, 1980. *Hawaii: A Natural History* (2nd ed.). Pacific Trop. Botanical Garden, Lawai, Kauai. See p. 147.
14. See, for example, D. Samwell, 1967. Some account of a voyage to South Seas in 1776–1777–1778. Appendix II, pp. 989–1300, in J. C. Beaglehole (Ed.). *The voyage of the* Resolution *and* Discovery *1776–1780.* Part Two. See p. 1219. Also, Otto von Kotzebue, 1821. *A Voyage of Discovery in the South Sea and Bering's Straits . . . in the Years 1815–1818, etc.* Reprinted 1967. Da Capo Press, New York. See Vol. 1, p. 318.
15. Samwell, p. 1220.
16. Kirch, *Feathered Gods,* pp. 167 and 223–31.
17. W. Ellis, 1833. *Polynesian Researches During a Residence of Nearly Eight Years in the Society and Sandwich Islands.* Vol. IV. J. and J. Harper, New York. See pp. 51–52.
18. Handy and Handy, p. 162.
19. P. Q. Tomich, 1969. *Mammals in Hawaii. B. P. Bishop Museum Spec. Pub. 57.* Bishop Museum Press, Honolulu. See p. 79 (citing Cook).
20. Ibid., p. 80.
21. Ibid., p. 79 (citing Ellis).
22. Handy and Handy, pp. 242–43.
23. Kirch, *Feathered Gods*, pp. 288 and 307.

CHAPTER 20

1. J. F. G. La Pérouse, 1799. *A Voyage Round the World Performed in the Years 1785, 1786, 1787, and 1788 . . .* Reprinted 1968. Da Capo Press, New York. See Vol. 1, p. 345.
2. G. Vancouver, 1798. *A Voyage of Discovery to the North Pacific Ocean and Round the World.* Reprinted 1967. Da Capo Press, New York. See Vol. 2, p. 180.
3. D. D. Tumarkin, 1979. A Russian view of Hawaii in 1804. *Pacific Studies 2*(2): 109–31. See pp. 114–15.
4. W. Ellis, 1833. *Polynesian Researches . . .* Vol. IV. J. and J. Harper, New York. See p. 273.
5. W. R. Broughton, 1804. *A Voyage of Discovery to the North Pacific Ocean . . . in the Years 1795, 1796, 1797, 1798.* Reprinted 1967. Da Capo Press, New York. See p. 69.
6. P. Q. Tomich, 1969. *Mammals in Hawaii. B. P. Bishop Museum Spec. Pub. 57.* Bishop Museum Press, Honolulu. See pp. 69, 96, 106, and 111. Also, Anon., 1862 (article noting introduction of horses in Hawaii). *The Friend 11.*
7. J. Montgomery (Ed.), 1832. *Journal of Voyages and Travels by the Reverend Daniel Tyerman and George Bennet, Esq. . . . Between the Years 1821 and 1829.* Crocker and Brewster, Boston. See Vol. II., p. 50. Also, C. S. Stewart, 1970 (facsimile of 1830 ed.). *Journal of a Residence in the Sandwich Islands during the Years 1823, 1824, and 1825 . . .* Univ. of Hawaii Press, Honolulu. See p. 157.
8. Vancouver, Vol. 3, p. 53. Also, R. J. Kramer, 1971. Hawaiian Land Mammals. C. E. Tuttle, Rutland, VT. See pp. 272–73.
9. A. von Chamisso, 1821. Remarks and opinions of the naturalist of the expedition,

in O. von Kotzebue. *A Voyage of Discovery into the South Sea and Bering's Straits . . . in the Years 1815–1818, etc.* Reprinted 1967. Da Capo Press, New York. See Vol. 2, p. 237.

10. E. M. Damon, 1931. *Koamalu.* Priv. printed, Honolulu. See Vol. 1, pp. 257–58.
11. Ibid., p. 406.
12. A. Campbell, 1816. *A Voyage Round the World from 1806 to 1812.* Reprinted 1969. Da Capo Press. New York. See p. 164. Also, G. W. Bates, 1854. *Sandwich Island Notes.* Harper and Brothers, New York. See pp. 31 and 98.
13. Early published records of exported goatskins include H. T. Cheever, 1851. *Life in the Sandwich Islands . . .* A. S. Barnes and Co., New York. See pp. 307 and 314. Also, C. Nordoff, 1874. *Northern California, Oregon, and the Sandwich Islands.* Reprinted 1974. Ten Speed Press, Berkeley, CA. See p. 69. *The Friend* (Honolulu). "Custom House Statistics" (usually published in Feb. or March issues for the previous year). See, for example, issues of Feb. 1853; March 1855; March 1856; Feb. 1857; March 1867, etc.) Also, *Thrum's Hawaiian Almanac and Annual* (Honolulu). See, for example, the 1876 issue.
14. Bates, p. 367.
15. Ibid., p. 322.
16. Anon., 1856. The influence of the cattle on the climate of Waimea and Kawaihae. *Sandwich Islands Monthly Mag. 1:* 44–47. Reprinted in *Hawaiian Planters' Record 30:* 289–92.
17. I. Bird, 1974. *Six Months in the Sandwich Islands* (7th ed., paperback). Tut Books, C. E. Tuttle, Rutland, VT. See pp. 154–55.
18. G. P. Cooke, 1949. *Moolelo o Molokai.* Printed by *Honolulu Star Bull.*, Honolulu. See pp. 62–63.
19. Ibid., photograph from "Phallic Rock," p. 103.
20. Ibid., p. 64.
21. For accounts of organized feral livestock drives in the 1920s and 1930s, see, for example, R. K. LeBarron, 1970. The history of forestry in Hawaii—from the beginning through World War II. *Aloha Aina.* Dept. of Land and Natural Resources, State of Hawaii (April 1970). No pagination. Also, Cooke. Also, Tomich.
22. Tomich. Also, Kramer.
23. W. M. Gibson, 1864. Letter from Lanai. *The Friend 13*(10): 74–75.
24. Nordoff, pp. 68 and 94. Also, Bird, p. 202.
25. Tomich, p. 54.
26. C. P. Stone, 1984. The "10 most wanted" management actions for terrestrial Hawaiian ecosystems: A survey. *Elepaio 45*(6): 41–48.
27. Kramer, p. 249 (citing Nichols).
28. T. Coan, 1866. (Letter describing an expedition on Mauna Loa in 1843.) *The Friend 17*(2): 11.
29. Bates, p. 323.
30. J. R. H. Andrews, 1987. *The Southern Ark: Zoological Discovery in New Zealand 1769–1900.* Century Hutchinson Ltd., London. See p. 104.
31. Bird, p. 152.
32. J. La Farge, 1912. *Reminiscences of the South Seas.* Doubleday, Page and Co., New York. See p. 57.
33. O. Owre, 1974. Bird pollution. *Animal Kingdom* (Dec. 1974): 21–27. (This article concerns Florida, but numerous parallels may be drawn with Hawaii.)
34. J. Hobbs, 1935. *Hawaii, A Pageant of the Soil.* Stanford Univ. Press, Stanford, CA. See p. 49. Also, A. C. Alexander, 1937. *Koloa Plantation 1835–1935.* Printed by *Honolulu Star Bull.*, Honolulu. See pp. 1–2.
35. R. H. Gast, 1973. *Don Francisco de Paula Marin: A Biography.* Univ. of Hawaii Press/Hawaiian Historical Soc., Honolulu. See p. 70.
36. Ibid., p. 51.
37. Ibid., p. 51 (citing Tyerman and Bennet).
38. H. A. Wadsworth, 1933. A historical summary of irrigation in Hawaii. *Haw'n Planters' Record 37*(3): 124–62. See p. 137.
39. Ibid., p. 137. Also, compare Hobbs, p. 49.
40. Anon., 1862. (Article on a visit to Hawaii and Maui by Samuel Damon.) *The Friend 11*(8): 60.

41. Anon., 1856. *The Friend* 6(2): 13–14.
42. Bates, pp. 202–06. Also, Anon., 1860. *The Friend* 9(9): 65.
43. M. Hopkins, 1862. *Hawaii: The Past, Present, and Future of its Island Kingdom.* Longman, Green, Longman, and Roberts, London. See p. 406.
44. Anon., 1864. *The Friend* 13(12): 89.
45. Gast, p. 67.
46. Wadsworth, p. 148.
47. C. K. Ai, 1960. *My Seventy-Nine Years in Hawaii.* Cosmorama Pictorial Publisher, Hong Kong. See pp. 212–16.
48. Bates, p. 146.
49. Anon., 1860. Things on Kauai—seen, heard, and experienced. *The Friend* 9(9): 65, 68. Also, Anon., 1861. *The Friend* 10(1): 6. Also, Hopkins, p. 406.
50. J. M. Lydgate, 1884. Hawaiian woods and forest trees (concluded). *Thrum's Hawaiian Almanac and Annual for 1884:* 30–32. See p. 32.
51. Interestingly, per-acre yields from irrigated sugar cane around 1900 seem to have been little more than those from good nonirrigated fields around 1860. Compare Hopkins, p. 406, with production figures from the *Atlas of Hawaii* (2nd ed.), pp. 154–55.
52. Gast, p. 56, n. 15.

CHAPTER 21

1. D. Weir and T. Freeman, 1986. Hawaii: Tropic of cancer? *Mother Jones* 11(11): 16–19.
2. J. Sylvester, 1986. Isle tropical fish in high demand. *Honolulu Star Bull.* (Sept. 11, 1986), pp. E-1 and E-4.
3. S. Scott, 1988. Boat-paint input deadline near. *Honolulu Star Bull.* (Jan. 4, 1988), p. A-2.
4. Staff of the *Honolulu Advertiser*, 1986. Boom days in Kona. *Sunday Star Bull. and Advertiser* (March 16, 1986), p. D-4. Also, J. Tune, 1987. Big Island billions. *Sunday Star Bull. and Advertiser* (Feb. 22, 1987), p. D-1.
5. Major development documents and impact studies on ferromanganese ore processing in Hawaii include R. W. Jenkins *et al.*, 1981. *The Feasibility and Potential Impact of Manganese Nodule Processing in the Puna and Kohala Districts of Hawaii.* DPED (State of Hawaii) and NOAA (U.S. Dept. of Commerce), Honolulu. Also, P. B. Humphrey (Ed.), 1982. *Marine Mining: A New Beginning.* (Conf. Proceedings). State of Hawaii Marine Mining Program, DPED, Honolulu. Also, State of Hawaii Marine Mining Program, 1987. *Mining Development Scenario for Cobalt-Rich Manganese Crusts in the Exclusive Economic Zones of the Hawaiian Archipelago and Johnston Island.* DPED (State of Hawaii) and Minerals Management Service (U.S. Dept. of Interior), Honolulu. Also, U.S. Dept. of Interior, 1987. Proposed marine mineral lease sale in the Hawaiian Archipelago and Johnston Island exclusive economic zones. Minerals Mgmt. Service (U.S.) and DPED, Honolulu.
6. K. R. Kupchak, 1984. Aloha Kahaualea? *Sierra* 69(6): 53–56.
7. Ibid., p. 56.
8. Anon., 1987. Conservation news. *Elepaio* (see April and Aug. 1987 issues).
9. H. Altonn, 1987. Science plans a look at Hana. *Honolulu Star Bull.* (Sept. 4, 1987), pp. A-1 and A-4.
10. Advertisement, 1987. *Big Island Drive Guide* 11(3): 12. (June–Aug. 1987).
11. B. Siler, 1987. Planning consultant proposes ecological inventory for Isles. *Honolulu Star Bull.* (Jan. 8, 1987).
12. G. Cooper and G. Daws, 1985. *Land and Power in Hawaii: The Democratic Years.* Benchmark Books, Honolulu.
13. Ibid., pp. 275–77.
14. J. L. Culliney, 1976. *The Forests of the Sea.* Sierra Club Books, San Francisco.
15. G. Hardin, 1968. The tragedy of the commons. *Science* 162: 1243–48.

16. S. J. Hayward, V. H. Gomez, and W. Sterrer, 1981. *Bermuda's Delicate Balance: People and the Environment*. The Bermuda Natural Trust and Bermuda Biological Station for Research. Spec. Pub. 20. St Georges, Bermuda.
17. Dept. of Geography, Univ. of Hawaii, 1983. *Atlas of Hawaii*. Univ. of Hawaii Press, Honolulu. See p. 107.
18. G. M. Woodwell, 1985. Resources and compromise (letter). *Science 229*: 600.
19. S. Manuel, 1986. Paul Ehrlich: Views of Planet Earth. *Honolulu Star Bull.* (Nov. 13, 1986) p. F-1.
20. R. Thompson, 1986. Lyman chides Hilo conference on koa forests. *Honolulu Star Bull.*, Dec. 18, 1986, p. A-8.
21. P. M. Vitousek *et al.*, 1987. Biological invasion by *Myrica faya* alters ecosystem development in Hawaii. *Science 238*: 802–04.
22. P. V. Kirch, 1985. *Feathered Gods and Fishhooks*. Univ. of Hawaii Press, Honolulu. See pp. 301 and 306.
23. Weir and Freedman.
24. I. L. Bird, 1974. *Six months in the Sandwich Islands* (7th ed.). C. E. Tuttle Co. (Tut Books, paperback), Rutland, VT. See pp. 271–72.

Supplementary Sources for Illustrations

Because of budgetary limitations and structural constraints in this book, it was impossible to illustrate more than a fraction of the plants and animals described. Also, the book's approach is primarily evocative; it does not pretend to the systematic treatment one would find, for example, in an elementary college text. However, many readers may wish for visual representations of native and introduced species that were not illustrated here. The following sources contain pictures of most of the marine and terrestrial life of the islands mentioned in this book.

MARINE LIFE

Fielding, A. 1979. *Hawaiian Reefs and Tidepools*. Oriental Publ. Co., Honolulu.
Hobson, E. S. and E. H. Chave. 1972. *Hawaiian Reef Animals*. Univ. Press of Hawaii, Honolulu.
Kay, E. A. 1979. *Hawaiian Marine Shells (Reef and Shore Fauna of Hawaii, Rev. Ed., Sect. 4. Mollusca)*. B. P. Bishop Museum *Spec. Publ.* 64(4). Bishop Museum Press, Honolulu.
Magruder, W. H.. and J. W. Hunt. 1979. *Seaweeds of Hawaii*. Oriental Publ. Co., Honolulu.
Randall, J. E. 1985. *Guide to Hawaiian Reef Fishes*. Harrowood Books, Newtown Square, PA.
Tinker, S. W. 1978. *Fishes of Hawaii*. Hawaiian Service Inc., Honolulu.

TERRESTRIAL PLANTS AND ANIMALS

Carlquist, S. 1980. *Hawaii: A Natural History* (2nd ed.). Pacific Tropical Botanical Garden, Lawai, Kauai. (includes plants, land snails, some insects)

Degener, O. 1930. *Plants of Hawaii National Parks.* Privately published. (nomenclature somewhat outdated)

Hargreaves, D. and B. Hargreaves. 1964. *Tropical Trees of Hawaii.* Hargreaves Co., Kailua, Oahu. (mainly introduced species)

Haselwood, E. L. and G. G. Mottes (Eds.). 1983. *Handbook of Hawaiian Weeds.* (2nd. ed., revised by R. T. Hirano). Univ. of Hawaii Press, Honolulu.

Hawaii Audubon Society. 1986. *Hawaii's Birds.* Privately published, Honolulu. (includes seabirds).

Kimura, B. Y. and K. M. Nagata. 1980. *Hawaii's Vanishing Flora.* Oriental Publ. Co., Honolulu. (emphasizes rare and threatened species)

Lamb, S. H. 1981. *Native Trees and Shrubs of the Hawaiian Islands.* Sunstone Press, Santa Fe, N.M.

Lamoureux, C. H. 1976. *Trailside Plants of Hawaii's National Parks.* Hawaii Natural History Assoc., Hawaii Volcanoes National Park.

McKeown, S. 1978. *Hawaiian Reptiles and Amphibians.* Oriental Publ. Co., Honolulu.

Rock, J. F. 1913 and 1974. *The Indigenous Trees of the Hawaiian Islands.* C. E. Tuttle, Tokyo, Japan and Rutland, VT. (recently reprinted in paperback)

Sohmer, S. H. and R. Gustafson. 1987. *Plants and Flowers of Hawaii.* Univ. of Hawaii Press, Honolulu.

Tomich, P. Q. 1986. *Mammals in Hawaii.* (2nd. ed.). Bishop Museum Press, Honolulu.

Index

Abudefduf abdominalis, 102
Acacia: koa, 176, 193, *195; koaia,* 284
Acanthaster, 96
Acanthurus: sandvicensis, 100; *trio-
stegus, 101*
Achatinella genus, 273, 274–80
Achatinellidae family, 158, 274
Achatinellinae family, 273
Acid rain, 366
Acridotheres tristis, 145, 259
Acrocephalus familiaris, 159, 160
Acropora spp., 103–04
Actinopyga genus, 96–97
Adelocosa anops, 270
Adenophorus periens, 357
Aeo, 222–23
Aetobatus narinari, 61
Agassiz, Alexander, 257
Agriculture: as cause of water pollution,
107, 151, 235, 353, 366–67; com-
mercial, environmental destruction
from, 349–51; development of, 346–
47; effects of Polynesian, 324; mixed,
348–49
Agrotis genus, 305
Ahinahina, 287
Ahnfeltia, 92–93
Aholehole, 113, 117
Aidem, Joan, 314
Aiea, 174, 329
Akala, 290–91
Akepa, 247, 293
Akiapolaau, 247, 293–94
Akohekohe, 250, *251,* 252
Aku, 63, 65
Alae-keokeo, 222
Alahee, 173, 329
Alakai Swamp, 236, 243, 245, 250, 254
Alala, 291–92, 302, 355
Alani spp. 194
Albatrosses: avian pox on, 145; black-
footed, 135; feeding patterns of, 138;
hunting of, 147, 148, *148;* Laysan,
135, *140,* 145, 147, *148,* 149; move-
ment patterns of, 139; predators of,
149; royal, 150
Alena, 157, 171–72
Alexander, J. M., 198
Alexander, Sam, 234
Alexander, W. P., 185, 187, 203, 207–
08, 230, 277
Alfonsin, 70, 73
Algae: coral reefs and, 88, 89, 92–93;
disease, 128; growth of, from sew-
age effluent, 115–16; introduction
of, 117; on seals, 127; types of, 89
Algeroba, 181, 209
Allen, Anthony, 335, 347
Alphitonia ponderosa, 284
Alquist, Jon, 136
Alyxia oliviformis, 197
Ama-ama, 111–12, *112*
Amakihi, 247, 294
Amaranth trees, 200
Amastra genus, 273, 274
Amastridae family, 273
Amau, 194, 196
American Museum of Natural History,
130
Anae, 111–12, *112*
Anas: acuta, 44; laysanensis, 160–61,
222; *platyrynchos,* 222; *wyvilliana,*
160, 221, 222
Anchialine pools, 354, 358, 361
Anemones, 94
Angelfish, 100
Angiosperms, 43
Anianiau, 247
Anous: minutus, 135, 141; *stolidus,*
135
Antelopes, 342–43
Antidesma pulvinatum, 174
Antilocapra americana, 342–43
Antipathes, 70, 71
Ants, Argentine, 271; introduction of,
271; on NWHI, 168
Ao, 139, 141
Apapane, 197, 249, 257, 294

Cross Seamount: geologic description of, 26; undersea mining at, 73
Crows, 257, 291–92; feathers of, 255; Hawaiian, 241, 355; hunting of, 301
Crustaceans, 98
Culex quinquefasciatus, 145, 258
Cyanea genus, 196, *199*
Cybotium, 199, 340
Cypraea, 97–98; *ostergaardi,* 108

Damon, Samuel, 207, 340
Damselfish, 99, *101,* 102; sergeant major, 102, 117
Damselflies, 220, 227
Dana, James Dwight, 105
Darling, Gibson, and Silber, 79
Darwin, Charles, 15, 30–31
Dascyllus albisella, 101
Dasyatis hawaiiensis, 61
Daws, Gavan, 361
Deer: axis, 342; mule, 342
Degener, Otto, 212, 213
Department of Land and Natural Resources, 360
Dermochelys coriacea, 132
Development: in Bermuda compared, 363; environmental effects of, 352, 362–63, 366–67; land sales for, 361; of space sciences facilities, 308–09; tourism as cause of, 363–63
Dicranopteris, 200
Dictyospheria cavernosa, 115–16
Diomedea: immutabilis, 135, 148; *nigripes,* 135
Discovery, 238, 241
Diseases: effect on forest birds of, 258–59; effect on seabirds of, 142, 145; of forest birds, 242, 245; freshwater, 235
Dixon (expedition of), 297
Dodonea viscosa, 285
Dogs, feral, 343; as predator, 222, 297, 341
Dole, George, 186
Dole, Sanford, 144, 257
Dole Company, 349
Dolphins, spinner, 68, 75–77
Donkeys, 341–42
Douglas, Captain William, 163, 297
Douglas, David, 290, 307, 337
Dragonfish, 68
Dragonflies, 227
Dredging, 115, 167
Drepanis: funerea, 252; genus, 248, 252; *pacifica,* 252
Drosophila genus, 263, 264–66, *265*
Drosophilidae family, 262
Dubautia, 36, 289–90, 296; genus, 289; *menziesii, 286; reticulata,* 290

Ducks: Hawaiian, 221, 222; hunting, 233–34; *koloa,* 229, 300; Laysan, 160–61, 166; transport of seeds and land snails by, 44, 46

Eagle: Hawaiian, 143, 257; ray, 61
Earthquakes, 21
Eastern Island, 167–68
Ecosystem: aeolian, 304–05, 306, 307, 308–09; anchialine, 223–26, 229; biotic diversity of, 53–56; compared to Bermuda, 363; freshwater, 216, 227–33, 237; greenhouse effect in, 308; introduction of vertebrate, 331–32; *kipukas,* 207; layers of ocean's, 62–64; plant fossils of, 313–14; prehuman, 313–21; radiocarbon dating of prehuman, 320; remaking of valley, 327; role of hunter on, 331; tropical rain forest, 183
Ecosystem, destruction of: by alternative energy, 352–53; by cattle grazing, 339; by development, 352; by grazing, 335; by industry, 353; by plant introductions, 366; by Polynesian colonization, 324, 325; by rats, 332; forest, 324, 327, 328, 331, 335; freshwater, 234–35; garden, 327; *koa,* 365; lowland leeward, 327–28; prehuman, 320–21; stream, 327
Eels, moray, 99, 102
Ehrlich, Paul, 363
Eleotris sandwicensis, 217, 218
Elepaio, 241–42, *244,* 294
Ellis, William, 163, 178–79, 180, 182–83, 184, 204–05, 315, 329, 330, 331–32, 334
Emory, Kenneth, 161
Emperor Seamounts: bottom fish trawling at, 70; chain, 3, *5;* coral at, 70–71
Endemism, 42, 43
Endodontidae family, 158, 273
Epipelagic layer, 63, 64
Eragrostris variabilis, 166
Eretmochelys imbricata, 132–33
Erythrina sandvicensis, 173–74
Etelis: carbunculus, 62; *coruscans,* 62
Eucalyptus trees, 185, 203, 209, 211
Eugenia cuminii, 188, 203
Euglandina rosea, 278
Euphorbias, Hawaiian, 200
Euphotic zone, 62–63
Evolution: adaptive radiation in, 37–38; based on Theory of Island Biogeography, 47–48; character displacement in, 36; effect of island drift on, 38–39; effect of isolated gene pools on, 32–33; effect of reproduction on, 31–32; effect of reproductive isola-

tion on, 33–35; hybrids in, 35–36; importance of disjunctions in, 32, 33; natural selection in, 30–31, 36; opportunity for, through niches, 37; process of, 36–37; role of mutation in, 30, 31, 33, 35, 36, 37; species generation in, 34–35, 36; of vegetation from coastal to inland, 46. *See also* Genetics

Ewa Plains, 172, 232–33

Exclusive Economic Zone (EEZ), 72–73

Feather industry: European, 145; hunting birds for, 167; *mamo* hunting for, 252; Max Schlemmer's, 146–47; Polynesian, 144–45, 254–57, 296–97

Fefer, Stewart, 151

Felis catus, 343–44

Fern trees, 194, 196, 340

Ferns: endemic, 43, 357; *hapuu,* 208; introduction of, 43; staghorn, 200; tree, 194, 196, *199; uluhe,* 211

Ficus spp., 211–12

Fig trees, 211–12

Finches: Galapagos (Darwin's), 34, 237, 246; Hawaiian, 237, 245–53, 293; *See also* Honeycreepers; *koa,* 248; Kona grosbeak, 248; Laysan, 160, 166, 167–68, 247; Nihoa, 159, 162, 247; species generation in, 34

Fisher, Walter, 165

Fisheries: aquarium-trade, 108–09, 353–54; effect of, on seabirds, 150–51; for pearls, 107; pollution from, 354; squid, 150

Fishes: bottom, 69–70, 72; coral reef, 99–104; flying, 137–38; freshwater, 216–18; game, 235–36; inshore, 65–67; midwater, 67–69; Polynesian aquaculture for, 229

Fishing: commercial, 363; gillnet, 108, 132; illegal methods of, 108; regulated by *kapus,* 105

Flies: crane, 266; damsel, 267; drosophilid (fruit or pomace), 262–66; flightless, 266; Hawaiian fruit, 35; lacewing, 266; picture-winged, 264–66, *265;* salt-pan, 161

Flotsam, 41, 43–45

Flycatchers: Hawaiian, 241–42

Forbes, C. N., 174

Forest birds: conservation of, 260–61; effect of diseases on, 258–59, 261; effect of introduced species on, 259–60; effect of Polynesians on, 237–38, 254–56; extinct, 245, 248, 249, 250, *251,* 253; passerine species of, 238, *239–40,* 241–53, 241, *244, 251;* predators of, 257–58

Forests: aboriginal, 322–23; coastal, 182–86; decadence of, 208–09; hydropower threat to, 359–60; lowland dry, 173–82; *mamane-naio,* 284, 293, 300, 301; plan to remake, 351; rain, 182; reforestation of, 210–11; reforestation of rain, 209; reserves, 302

Forests, deforestation of, 214, 324, 327, 328, 329, 335; by agriculture, 350–51; by deer, 342; by goats and cattle, 337–38, 345; by pigs, 340; for firewood, 206; rain, 203–09; upland, 349

Fragaria chiloensis, 290

Fregata minor, 135, 136

French Frigate Shoals (FFS), 27; *Acropora* species at, 103–04; commercial fishing at, 363; coral reefs at, 91, 106–07; discovery of, 163; fish at, 103–104; guano mining on, 164; Max Schlemmer's lease of, 146; military on, 148, 168; population of, 161; seabirds on, 135; seals at, 122, 126; size of, 155; *tsunamis* at, 156; turtles at, 122, 123, 126, 131

Freshwater: alien life in, 235–36; anchialine ecosystem, 223–26; animals, 216–23; birds, 220–21, 222–23; ecosystems, 216, 227–33, 237; fishes, 216–18; flood control, 235; lakes, 226–27; plants, 221–222; rainfall, 215–16; streams, 215–16; wetlands, 221, 222, 233

Freycinetia arborea, 198

Friend, The, 181, 207, 209, 272

Frigatebirds, *140,* 141; classification of, 136; described, 136; feeding patterns of, 138; great, 135; hunting feathers of, 145; movement patterns of, 139; predators of, 143

Fruits, 43–44

Fulica americana alai, 222

Gagne, Wayne, 158–59, 162, 212, 254

Galeocerdo cuvieri, 103, 129, 143

Gallinula chloropus sandvicensis, 222

Gallinules, 222, 229, 234

Gambusia, 236

Gardner Pinnacles, 155; life on, 157; size of, 156

Geese, 44; flightless, 314–15; Hawaiian mountain, 291; nene, 291, *295,* 297, 299, 300, 343, 344

Genetics: breeding populations (demes) in, 32–33; dominant-recessive pairs in, 31–32; gene pool in, 32; hybridization in, 35–36; modes of reproduction in, 31; natural selection in, 31,

Ocean Island. *See* Kure Atoll
Oceanic birds, 44, 46, 65
Oceanodroma: castro, 135, 142, 318; *tristrami,* 135
Octopuses, 98, 113
Ocypode ceratopthalmus, 123
Odocoileus hemionus: feral, 342
Ohai, 157, 158, 172
Ohelo, 286, 290
Ohia, 293, 294; dieback of, 201, 209, 210; forest birds of, 248, 253; reforestation of, 210–11
Ohia lehua, 176, 177, 182–83, 184, *195,* 284, 340, 366; deforestation of, 207; effect of Polynesians on, 202; forest birds in, 249; history of, 200–01; in rain forests, 193
Ohia-koa, 243
Olapa, 198, *199*
Omao, 242–43, 294
Oo, 243–45, 315–16, 318; Bishop's, *244,* 245, 261; feathers of, 254, 256
Ooaa, 245
Oopu, 228; *-hiu-kole,* 220; *nakea,* 217, 218, *219; naniha,* 217–18, *219; nopili,* 217, 218, 228; *okuhe,* 217, 218
Oopu wai, 217–18, 228, 229, 235, 236, 237
Oostdam, B. L., 18
Opae, 219, 228, 235; *-kala-ole,* 219, 235; *-oehaa,* 219, 236
Opakapaka, 62, 69
Ophiocoma, 96
Ophiodesoma, 97
Opihi, 98
Ortylagus cuniculus, 164–65
Osbun, Albert, 130
Ou, 247, 255, 261, 357
Ovis: aries, 300, 340–41; *musimon,* 300, 340–41
Owls: barn, 145, 255, 292; feathers of, 255; Hawaiian, 143, 257, 291, 292–93, 343; hunting of, 301
Oysters, 98, 117; Chesapeake, 117; hatchet, 98; jewel box, 98; pearl, 98, 107

Pacific Guano and Fertilizer Company, 146, 164
Pacific Mail and Steamship Company, 106
Pali. See Cliffs
Palila, 248, 293, 294, 295; endangerment of, 301
Palm, Nihoa fan, *157,* 158
Palmeria: dolei, 250, 252; genus, 248, 250, 252
Palms: coconut, 28; Hawaiian, 174, 208; hearts of, 322; Nihoa fan, 158; *Pritchardia,* 253

Pan American Airways, 167–68
Pandanus, 162, 177–78, *179,* 185
Panicum maximum, 299
Panulirus, 99
Papio, 113
Parker, John Palmer, 337
Parker Ranch, 206, 207, 298, 300, 330
Parrotbills, Maui, 248, *251,* 261
Parrotfishes, 65, 100, *101,* 102, 117
Partulina genus, 273, 274, 277
Passiflora, 213; *mollissima,* 213
Paty, Captain John, 129–30, 131, 164
Payne, Roger, 79, 85, 86
Peale, Titian, 77, 249–50
Pearl Harbor: development of, 353; fish at, 113; fishery pollution at, 354; oysters at, 117; pearls at, 107; siltation in, 347
Pearl and Hermes Reef: guano mining at, 164; population of, 167; rabbits on, 166; seabirds on, 135; seals on, 129–30, 131; size of, 155; turtles on, 126; vegetation on, 158
Pelea: anisata, 194; genus, 194
Penguin Bank, 21–22, 60, 63
Pennisetum: clandestinum, 299; *setaceum,* 299
Perch, yellow Tahitian, 69–70
Perdicella genus, 273
Perkins, R.C.L., 238, 243, 246, 248, 252, 253, 258, 262
Pervagor spilosoma, 65
Petrels, 143; Bonin, 149, 318–19, 320; Bulwer's, 135, 145; dark-rumped, 135, 136, 139, 143–44, 294, 297, 318, 320, 344; Harcourt's storm, 135, 138, 142, 318; movement patterns of, 139; predators of, 149
Phaeornis: obscurus, 242; *palmeri,* 242–43
Phaeton: lepturus, 135, 136; *rubricauda,* 135, 136, 144–45
Phasianus colchicus, 301
Pheasant, ring-necked, 301, 344
Photosynthesis, 62–63
Pigs: effect on forest birds of, 258, 261; effect on plants of, 290; European, 340; Hawaiian, 331–32, 340; protection of, 213; in rain forests, 231–32
Pili, 298, 328
Pinctada, 98, 107
Pines, Cook, 203
Pintails, 44
Pipterus albidus, 197–98
Plankton: larvae, 65–67; nutrients for, 64; reappearance, 65–67
Platydesma: cornuta, 194; genus, 194
Plovers, golden, 45, 274
Pluchea: indica, 169, 222
Pluchea odorata, 169, 222

Plums: java, 185, 188, 203, 242
Pocillopora, 88; *damicornis*, 111; *ey-douxi*, 95
Polihali State Park, 26
Pollution. *See* Water pollution
Polydactylus sexfilis, 105
Polynesian: aquaculture, 229; basalt mining, 296; colonization, 321–33; coral reef exploitation by, 104–05; crop plants, 323, 326–27, 329–30, 333; deforestation, 324, 327, 328, 329; effect on birds of, 237–38, 254–56, 292, 319, 320; effect on cloud-lands of, 295–97; effect on rain forests of, 182–84, 202–03; effects of agriculture, 324, 329; feather hunting, 144–45, 296–97; field system, 330–31; impact on seabirds, 143–44; introduction of vertebrates, 331–32; irrigation, 227–28, 229–30, 325–26; land distribution, 323–24; politics, 323; population, 105, 111, 325, 327, 333; settlements, 321–22; transported landscapes, 323–24, 326
Pomacanthus imperator, 100
Poo-uli, 253, 261, 278, 315–16, 318, 329
Porites, 88; *compressa*, 111; *lobata*, 95
Porolithon, 89
Porpoise Watcher, The (Norris), 76
Portlock and Dixon expedition, 276, 297
Portuguese Man-of-War, 94
Portulaca lutea, 157
Porzanula palmeri, 147, 159–60, *160*
Pox disease, avian, 142, 145, 242, 258
Pride of India trees, 209
Pristipomoides filamentosus, 62
Pritchardia, 162, 208, 322; genus, 174; *remota*, *157*, 158
Procaris: genus, 224; *hawaiiana*, *225*
Procellariiform spp., 136
Pronghorns, 342–43
Prosopis pallida, 181, 209
Pryor, Karen, 76–77
Pseudonestor: genus, 246, 248; *xan-thophrys*, 248
Psidium, 203, 213; *guajava*, 188
Psittirostra: bailleui, 248, 293, 295, 301; *cantans*, 247; *flaviceps*, 248; *palmeri*, 248; *psittacea*, 247, 357
Psittirostris, genus, 246, 247–48, 320
Pterodroma: hypoleuca, 135, 149, 319; *phaeopygia sandvichensis*, 136
Pterois sphex, 103
Puaiohi, 242–43, 243
Pueo, 291, 292–93
Puffinus: nativitatis, 135; *pacificus*, 135, 142; *phaeopygia sandwichen-sis*, 135; *puffinus newelli*, 135, 136

Puki-awe, 285
Pulu, 208
Puna District: effect of humans on, 182–83; geothermal development on, 356; mining on, 74, 355; streams on, 216; vegetation on, 176
Punahou School, 277
Pupillidae family, 273
Puu Kukui, 288

Rabbits, 147–48, 164–65, 166
Raillardia, 289–90; *menziesii*, 290
Rails, Laysan flightless, 159–60, *160*, 166, 167–68, 238–39, 297; extinction of, 147, 166, 167–68, 257
Rain forests: bogs of, 198, 200; destruction of, 183; effect of Polynesians on, 202–03; *kipukas* and landslides of, 200; lobelioids in, 196–97; vegetation of, 193–202, *199*
Rallidae family, 238–39
Raspberries, Hawaiian, 290–91
Rats, 278, 279; introduced, 319; on NWHI, 168; Pacific, 331, 332, 344; Polynesian, 149; predation of birds by, 139, 142, 143, 149, 168; roof, 257–58, 269
Rattus: exulans, 142, 143, 149, 168, 279, 331, 332; *rattus*, 257–58, 269
Rauvolfia degneri, 174
Razor fishes, 60–61
Reef fishes, 64–65; decline, 108; reap-pearance, 65–67
Reefs: destruction of, 329, 358; marine life at, 61; threats to, 353–54
Reeve, John, 297
Resolution, 241
Reynoldsia sandwicensis, 174
Rhinecanthus rectangulus, *101*, 102
Rhizophora mangle, 116–17
Robinson-Gay family, 108, 257, 301
Rock, Joseph, 173, 174, 176, 185, 290
Roosevelt, Theodore, 130, 146, 168
Rubus hawaiensis, 290–91

Sadleria genus, 194, 196, *199*
Salt Lake, *174*
Samanea saman, 209
Samwell, David, 329
Sand Island, 167, 168
Sandalwood, 107, 193, 203–06, *205*, 329; coast, *171*, 172; effect of Poly-nesians on, 203; false, 172, 248, 283–84; Laysan, 158, 165, 347
Santalum, 193, 203–06; *cuneatum*, 158; *ellipticum*, 158, *171*, 172; *frey-cinetianum*, 205
Scaevola, *140*, 141, 197; *sericea*, 157, 171, 197
Scaptomyza genus, 263

Schistosomiasis, 235
Schlemmer, Max, 108, 146–47, 164–65, 168–69
Scirpus, 221; *californicus,* 222
Scorpionfish, 99, 102
Scorpions, 271, 272
Scott, J. M., 238, 242, 243, 249, 253
Sea cucumbers, 96–97
Sea Life Park, 76–77, 124
Sea squirts, 93–94
Sea urchins, 43, 94, *95,* 96, 98
Seabirds, 134–51, *137;* adaptations to seawater of, 137; breeding habits of, 139, 151; cloudlands, 294; collecting eggs of, 147, *148;* effect of fisheries on, 150–51; effect of pollution on, 151; feathers of, 255, 256; feeding patterns of, 137–138; fossils of, 318–19; gillnet fishing and, 132; human impact on, 143–51; impact of military on, 148–49; movement patterns of, 138–39; ornithological classifications of, 135–36; predation of, 142, 143, 147–48, 149–50, 297, 343; rookery, protection of, 365; species of, 134, *135*
Seals, 103, 118, 126–29; breeding biology of, 126–28; causes of death of, 128–29; endangered, 131–32; habitat for, 131–32, 133; monk, 107, 118–20, *121,* 122, 129–33, 364; wildlife management efforts for, 133
Seamounts: geologic description of, 26–27; underwater mining of, 355
Sesbania tomentosa, 157, 158, 172
Shaler, Captain, 335
Sharks, 68, 103, 128, 129; cookie-cutter, 68, 76; Galapagos, 103; gray reef, 103; megamouth, 68–69; tiger, 103, 143
Shearwaters: breeding habits of, 139; Christmas, 135; effect of pollution on, 151; feeding patterns of, 138; movement patterns of, 139; Newell's, 135, 136, 139, 145, 320; predators of, 145; wedge-tailed, 135, *140,* 142, 144, 145, 151
Sheep: bighorn mountain, 300; described, 340–41; history of, 300–01; introduction of, 335; predation of, 341; protection of, 213; silverswords browsed by, 287
Shells, 97–98; achatinella, 275–77; characteristics of, 274; collecting, 108; cone, 97
Shorebirds, 44, 46
Shrimps, 60; anchialine, 223–25, *225,* 226; bottom fishing of, 69; disease of, 235; freshwater, 217, 219
Sibley, Charles, 136

Sicyopterus stimpsoni, 217, 218
Sida fallax, 171, 172
Siegel, Barbara, 305–06
Siegel, Sanford, 305–06
Sierra Club, 364
Silent World, The (Cousteau), 120
Siltation, 105, 106, 107
Silverswords: alliance, 289, 290; alpine, 307; in bogs, 198; described, 286–89, *288;* destruction by goats of, 339; evolution of, 289; Hawaiian, 36; Kau, 287, 355; Mauna Kea, 287
Sinclair family, 340–41
Sincock, John, 245
Snails, 97–98; fossil remains of, 314; freshwater, 217, *219,* 220; ground, 273; introduced land, 46, 319; killer, 278; land, 158, 262, 273–74, 344; tree, 273, 274, 274–80, *275*
Snappers, 62; blue-lined, 69–70; introduced species of, 69–70
So Excellent a Fishe (Carr), 122
Sophora chrysophylla, 176, 193, 284, *286*
Southwest Fisheries Center, 126
Spiders: cave, *270;* methods of arrival of, 46–47; secretive, 305; wolf, 270, 305, 306
Sponges, 93–94, 220
Spreckels, Claus, 231
Squids, 68, 98, 132, 138, 150
Squirrelfish, 99, 102
Stanley, Lord, 297
Starfishes, *95,* 96; crown-of-thorns, 96
Stemmerman, Lani, 200, 201
Stenella longirostris, 68, 75–76
Stenogobius genivittatus, 217, 218
Stenogyne genus, 285–86
Stereocaulon vulcani, 196
Sterna: fuscata, 135, 136–137
Sterna lunata, 135, 149
Stewart, C. S., 178, 184
Stilts, Hawaiian, 222, 229, 234
Stolephorus, 150; *purpureus,* 112–13
Strawberries, wild, 290
Succineidae family, 273
Sugar cane: commercial production of, 347, 350, 351; early irrigation systems for, 229–30; industrial irrigation for, 230–31; plantations, 346; Polynesian, 346
Sugar Planters' Experiment Station, 212
Sula: dactylatra, 135; *leucogaster,* 135
Surgeonfishes, 65, 99, 100

Taape, 69–70
Taenianotus triacanthus, 102–103
Tanager, 165, 166
Tanager Expedition, 165

Tangs, 100, *101,* 117; convict, 100, *101;* lemon, 108; unicorn, *101*
Tarweeds, 289
Tattlers, 44; wandering, 221
Telospyza cantans: cantans, 160; *ultima,* 159
Terns, 143; described, 136–37; feeding patterns of, 138; gray-backed, 135; grey-backed, 149; hunting feathers of, 146; hunting of, 148; movement patterns of, 139; predators of, 145, 149; snow-white, 146; sooty, 135, 136–37, *140,* 141, 147, 149; white, 135, 141
Territorial Board of Agriculture and Forestry, 210, 301
Tetraplasandra hawaiiensis, 214
Thambetochen chauliodous, 314–15
Thaumatogryllus genus, 158–59, 270
Theory of Island Biogeography, 47–48
Thermocline, 64
Thrum's Hawaiian Annual and Almanac for 1878, 230–31
Thrushes: Hawaiian, 242–43, 259; Kauai, 242–43; laughing (babbling), 259; *shama,* 259
Tipulidae family, 266
Toads, Carribbean, 236
Tobacco, 348–49
Tomich, Quentin, 300, 341, 343, 344
Tomich and Kramer, 340
Touchardia latifolia, 197
Tourism: destruction of ecosystem by, 352; effect on humpback whales, 85; overdevelopment as cause of, 361–63
Tournefortia argentea, 169
Triggerfishes, 43, *101,* 102
Tropicbirds: classification of, 136; described, 136; hunting feathers of, 144–45; movement patterns of, 139; predators of, 149; red-tailed, 135, 136, 142, 144–45, 145, 149–50, 149; white-tailed, 135, 136, 141
Tsunamis, 15, 156
Tunas: yellow fin, 63
Tunicates, 93–94
Turkeyfishes, 103
Turtles, 103; consumption of plastics by, 132–33; efforts to protect, 364; freshwater, 236; hawksbill, 132–33; leatherback, 132; regulated by *kapus,* 105; wildlife management efforts for, 133
Turtle, green sea, 118, *121, 125;* breeding biology of, 122–26; endangered status of, 125–26, 131–32; evolutionary development of, 120–22, habitat for, 131–32, 133; human impact on, 129–33; shark killings of, 129
Tyerman, Daniel, 180, 204, 271, 335

Tyerman and Bennett, 81
Typha, 221–22
Tyto alba, 145, 269, 292

U.S. Coast Guard, 156, 168
U.S. Department of the Interior, 73, 285
U.S. Endangered Species Act, 125
U.S. Exploring Expedition, 77, 249
U.S. Fish and Wildlife Service, 216, 253, 364; studies of seabirds, 134, 151
U.S. Geological Survey, 308
U.S. National Marine Fisheries Service (Honolulu), 126
Uau, 139, 141, 143, 144, 294, 297; -*kani,* 144
Uhi-uhi, 284, 366
Ula-ai-hawane, 253
Uluhe, 200, 211
Ulupalakua Plantation, 209
Underwater: destruction of ecosystem, 352–53; features, 59–60
Unicorn fish, 100
University of California at Santa Cruz, 76
University of Hawaii, 216, 286, 305, 308
Urchins: burrowing, *95;* heart, 60

Vaccinium: genus, 290; *reticulatum, 286*
Vancouver, Captain George, 18, 307, 325–26, 328, 334, 335, 336
Vegetation: in cloudlands, 285–89, *286,* 290–91; colonization of, 53; destruction by deer, 342; effect of geologic change on, 51; effect of, on habitat development, 48–51; evolution of coastal to inland, 46; fossils of, 313–14; freshwater, 221–222; introduction of new, 365–66; loss by cattle grazing, 339; prehuman, 322; shoreline, 43–45, 170–73; weeds, 186–90. *See also* Habitat, biotic
Vestiaria: coccinea, 249–50; genus, 248, 249–50
Violets, woody, 200
Viperfish, 68
Volcanoes: eruptions of, 11–13, 14; hazards of building geothermal plants near, 356, 357; hot spots of, 4–5, 7, 12, 14; island evolution and, 7–27; lava of, 7–8, 11, 12–13; living, 3, 303

Waianae Range, 242, 278; goat population at, 336; vegetation on, 174
Waianae Shield, 22, 60
Waiau Lake, 226, 303, 307, 308
Waiawa Valley: pineapples on, 349; vegetation on, 174, 175, 176

Waieleele Lake, 226–27
Waihee, John: Gov., 357
Waikaloa, 225–26
Waikiki, 229, 272
Wailau Stream, 237
Wailoa Ditch, 231
Wailuku River, 235
Waimanalo, 23, 103, 142
Waimea, 205, 206, 221, 326, 327, 328;
    effects of cattle at, 337; field system
    at, 330; watershed on, 228, 229
Waimea Canyon, 176, 289; geologic
    description of, 24–25; tropicbirds
    on, 141
Wainae Range, 211
Wainiha Valley, 234
Waipio Valley, 221, 229, 295, 326
Wallabies, rock, 344
Warbler, old-world, 159
Wasps, 271
Waste disposal: by mining, 74, 355;
    sewage as, 115–16
Water pollution: by military, 354; of
    freshwater, 235; from agriculture,
    107, 151, 235, 353, 366–67; from
    development, 354, 362; from mining
    waste disposal, 356; from sewage,
    115–16
Water treaders, 269, *270*
Waterbirds: at aquaculture ponds, 229;
    hunting of, 233–34; on wetlands,
    234

Watersheds: artesian, 232–33; changes
    in, 227–33; hydropower threat to,
    359–60; protection of, 209; purchase
    of, 364
Weeds, 203, 299; foreign, 213, 213–
    14
Wetmore, Alexander, 166
Whales: commercial hunting of, 81–85;
    efforts to protect, 364; humpback,
    75, 77–80, 82–87; melon-headed,
    77; protection of, 86, 364
White-eyes, Japanese, 259–60
Wiliwili, 173–74, *174,* 176
Wilkesia, 36, 289
Wilkinson, John, 347
Witham, Gene, 87
Woodwell, George, 363
Worms: army, 272; book, 272; Christ-
    mas tree, 97; feather duster, 97; flat,
    278; marine, 97; segmented, 220;
    spaghetti, *95,* 97
Wrasses, 65, 99, 100, 102, 117

Zanclus cornutus, 41–42, *101*
Zebrasoma flavescens, 100, 108
Zimmerman, Elwood, 267
Zingiber zerumbet, 186
Zoanthids, 94
Zoanthus, 94
Zonitidae family, 273, 274
Zooxanthellae, 88–89
Zosterops japonica, 259–60